A
Business
Enterprise Value

Anthology

Second Edition

Readers of this text may be interested in the following publications from the Appraisal Institute:

- *The Appraisal of Nursing Facilities*
- *The Appraisal of Real Estate,* 13th edition
- *Convenience Stores and Retail Fuel Properties: Essential Appraisal Issues*
- *The Dictionary of Real Estate Appraisal,* 5th edition
- *Shopping Center Appraisal and Analysis,* 2nd edition
- *The Valuation of Billboards*

Professionals Providing
Real Estate Solutions

A
Business
Enterprise Value

Anthology

Second Edition

Edited by
David C. Lennhoff, MAI, SRA

Appraisal Institute • 550 West Van Buren • Chicago, IL 60607 • www.appraisalinstitute.org

The Appraisal Institute advances global standards, methodologies, and practices through the professional development of property economics worldwide.

Reviewers: Micheal Lohmeier, MAI, SRA
Maureen Mastroieni, MAI
Henry Wise, MAI

Chief Executive Officer: Frederick H. Grubbe
Director, Marketing & Member Resources: Hope Atuel
Senior Manager, Publications: Stephanie Shea-Joyce
Technical Book Editor: Emily Ruzich
Manager, Book Design/Production: Michael Landis

For Educational Purposes Only
The materials presented in this text represent the opinions and views of the authors. Although these materials may have been reviewed by members of the Appraisal Institute, the views and opinions expressed herein are not endorsed or approved by the Appraisal Institute as policy unless adopted by the Board of Directors pursuant to the Bylaws of the Appraisal Institute. While substantial care has been taken to provide accurate and current data and information, the Appraisal Institute does not warrant the accuracy or timeliness of the data and information contained herein. Further, any principles and conclusions presented in this publication are subject to court decisions and to local, state and federal laws and regulations and any revisions of such laws and regulations.

This book is sold for educational and informational purposes only with the understanding that the Appraisal Institute is not engaged in rendering legal, accounting or other professional advice or services. Nothing in these materials is to be construed as the offering of such advice or services. If expert advice or services are required, readers are responsible for obtaining such advice or services from appropriate professionals.

Nondiscrimination Policy
The Appraisal Institute advocates equal opportunity and nondiscrimination in the appraisal profession and conducts its activities in accordance with applicable federal, state, and local laws.

Library of Congress Cataloging-in-Publication Data
A business enterprise value anthology / edited by David C. Lennhoff. -- 2nd ed.
     p. cm.
   Includes bibliographical references and index.
   ISBN 978-1-935328-20-9 (alk. paper)
1. Real property--Valuation--United States. 2. Commercial buildings--Valuation--United States. 3. Business enterprises--Valuation--United States. I. Lennhoff, David C.
   HD1389.5.U6B87 2011
   658.15--dc23
                                                                          2011017442

Table of Contents

Part I.
General Issues

Part II.
Hotels and Motels

About the Editor

David C. Lennhoff, MAI, SRA, is president of PGH Consulting, LLC, which has its office in Rockville, Maryland. He has been closely involved with the topic of this book since serving as a member of the Appraisal Institute's Study Group on Business Enterprise Value in 1997-1998. He was a development team member, chief reviewer, and frequent instructor of the original Appraisal Institute Course 800, Separating Real and Personal Property from Intangible Business Assets, and editor of the first edition of *A Business Enterprise Value Anthology*. Mr. Lennhoff continues to teach regularly for the Appraisal Institute, both nationally and internationally, and has been a frequent contributor to *The Appraisal Journal* since 1982.

Acknowledgments

As I learned the last time I undertook this project, assembling the articles to include in this book is no easy task. Not only was the selection process difficult, but gaining the authorizations for publication was even more time consuming. I received a lot of help with this project. I especially want to thank Elizabeth R. Lennhoff and Kathy D. Smith for their assistance with the organization and assembling of the authorizations. Their persistence was crucial to obtaining the rights to include most of the articles we sought. Also, of course, the staff of the Appraisal Institute was instrumental in the production process. Stephanie Shea-Joyce was particularly helpful, cheerful, and professional in her contributions.

Foreword

The appraisal of real property with a business component is constantly evolving and the methods to be applied are a source of controversy. The debates surrounding this topic have progressed and much has changed in the 10 years since the publication of the first edition of *A Business Enterprise Value Anthology*. This new second edition will help bring appraisers up to date on this important issue.

The updated compilation contains 27 articles on the topic written since the first edition was published. Some are original, some are reprinted from various journals and periodicals. These articles are divided into three sections: Part I contains articles that address tangible real property, tangible personal property, and intangible personal property in general; Part II focuses on hotels and motels; and Part III deals with a variety of special-purpose properties, including nursing facilities, convenience stores, and shopping centers. The book concludes with a case law update summarizing recent court rulings related to these topics.

This second edition of *A Business Enterprise Value Anthology* has been compiled to assist real estate appraisers in valuing real property with business elements. This collection of articles from various authors with differing points of view presents all sides of this somewhat controversial topic and will help appraisers develop their own methods for addressing the separation of tangible and intangible assets in their professional work.

Joseph C. Magdziarz, MAI, SRA
2011 President
Appraisal Institute

Preface

Real estate appraisers are sometimes confronted with assignments that require valuing just the real estate component of a business enterprise. Good examples of properties that present this challenge include hotels, regional malls, restaurants, nightclubs, senior housing, and convenience stores. Situations in which the necessity for such an analysis might occur include real estate tax assessment, condemnation, and lending. The need to separate the real estate value from the other business assets in these situations and with these properties is not contested. How the separation is accomplished still divides some appraisers. The Appraisal Institute's educational offering on this topic is one of the few available to assist appraisers with this real estate valuation problem.

This second edition of *A Business Enterprise Value Anthology* presents articles on the evolving appraisal methodology related to the analysis of businesses with real property components. Some of the articles are new, most are reprints, and all were written or published after the production of the first edition of this anthology. This book is designed to be a companion text for the new Appraisal Institute educational program on the topic of separating the total assets of a going concern. The intention of this text is to offer assistance to real estate appraisers with these types of valuation assignments, not to be a guide to valuing businesses. This anthology begins with articles that generally address the various interests that make up a going concern: tangible real property, tangible personal property, and intangible personal property. This is followed by a section devoted to hotel valuation issues, and then a section covering a variety of property types. The final piece is a summary of court decisions dealing with business enterprise value (BEV) that have occurred since the first edition of this book was published in 2001.

Part I of this book begins, appropriately enough, with an article addressing the new terminology associated with BEV assignments. This piece is based on the Appraisal Institute's former Course 800 material, which recognized that there were misunderstandings relating to basic terminology that had to be cleared up before the discussion of the topic could be ad-

vanced. This piece is followed by several articles that deal with intangibles and how they might be valued–including the new Appraisal Foundation Working Group on Contributory Asset Charges monograph on contributory assets–and closes with an article by Robert W. Owens, PhD, entitled "Contemplating the Future of Business Enterprise Valuation." (Another of Dr. Owens' articles opened the first edition of this book.)

Part II deals with the topic of business enterprise value in the context of hotels. This is by far the longest section of the book, but not specifically because of the particular importance of this property type. This book is not strictly about hotels (neither is the Appraisal Institute's educational offering). Rather, the length of this section is due to the fact that most of the writing relating to this issue has been done in the context of a hotel assignment. The concepts and methods revealed by this group of articles, however, can be applied to almost all property types. Included here are various positions on separating the intangible and tangible personal property from the real property component. An important original article by Bernice T. Dowell dealing with hotel sale price allocations appears in this section. This application has not received the attention it demands, and I am hopeful this piece will fill that void. Also in this section are several articles that describe the Marriott v. Saddle Brook, New Jersey, tax appeal case, including one by Stephen Rushmore, MAI, CHA, who testified for the jurisdiction, and one by John Garippa, who represented Marriott. This case was decided in favor of the jurisdiction, but the clear undercurrent from the judge reflected a concern for the ramifications of the business enterprise concepts on the local economy. Another excellent original article by John W. O'Neill, PhD, MAI, appears in this section and tackles the issue of the effect of a hotel brand or franchise on the value of the hotel total assets.

Part III covers a variety of property types, including sand and gravel property, nursing homes, day spas, and billboards. It ends with another original manuscript, a major piece on shopping centers by the prominent academic James D. Vernor, PhD, MAI, and coauthored by me. Dr. Vernor was the primary writer of the Appraisal Institute's book on shopping center valuation, *Shopping Center Appraisal and Analysis*. Outside of this article, not very much has been written about intangible assets and shopping centers, and although the article is lengthy it moves the discussion well forward.

This book closes—as did the first edition—with a comprehensive review of court decisions dealing with the topic of intangibles. Researched and written by a leading Texas law firm specializing in tax appeals, the work allows the reader to trace the evolution of court opinion on the matter.

Much has transpired since the publication of the first volume, and this compilation will bring you up to date. If you work with these property types, you will find these articles helpful in researching the various methodologies available to solve your valuation problems. If you are new to the topic, it will guide you past the various pitfalls that await the uninitiated. By having all sides of the issues before you, you will be better equipped to develop an informed opinion as to how to proceed.

Note that none of these articles have been edited from their original versions. As such, some minor errors may be found. Also, although the first anthology included a bibliography, this one does not. The reason for this is that the Appraisal Institute's Lum Library offers a much better alternative. Its convenience and availability make a printed list of resources obsolete upon publication.

Part I
General Issues

Allocation of Business Assets Into Tangible and Intangible Components: A New Lexicon

Marvin L. Wolverton, PhD, MAI; David C. Lennhoff, MAI, SRA; James D. Vernor, PhD, MAI; and Richard Marchitelli, MAI, CRE

This article originally appeared in the January 2002 issue of *The Appraisal Journal*.

Allocation of total appraised value for certain operating properties between tangible and intangible components, if not required by investors, is mandated by USPAP and required for taxation, underwriting, and condemnation. Not well covered in the appraisal literature, the dialogue has been complicated by contradictions among the meanings of terms used by the various appraisal subgroups. Because the terms business enterprise, business enterprise value, going concern, going concern value, *and* goodwill *are so confounded, new terms were coined coincident with developing the Appraisal Institute's Course 800. This article defines these new terms and introduces a methodology for allocating tangible and intangible asset values.*

Allocating the assets of operating properties into tangible and intangible components is a timely topic for discussion and examination due to the frequency with which this topic is now being confronted in journal articles, case law, appraisal standards, and state statutes. Examples of the currency of this issue include:

- Senate Bill 5286, amending the Revised Code of Washington (RCW) to exempt intangible property from ad valorem taxation, enacted on July 27, 1997.[1]

---

1. See RCW 84.36.070, Intangible Personal Property–Appraisal, for a detailed list of assets considered to be intangible and exempt under this newly enacted legislation.

Marvin L. Wolverton, PhD, MAI, has been appraising real property since 1976. He is currently a visiting associate professor at the Department of Finance, University of Nevada-Las Vegas. He previously held the position of Alvin J. Wolff Distinguished Professor of Real Estate at Washington State University. He holds a PhD in Business Administration from Georgia State University in Atlanta, Georgia, and a MS in economics from Arizona State University. His bachelor's degree is from New Mexico Tech, Socorro, New Mexico, in mining engineering.

David C. Lennhoff, MAI, SRA, is president of PGH Consulting, LLC, which has its office in Rockville, Maryland. He has been closely involved with the topic of this book since serving as a member of the Appraisal Institute's Study Group on Business Enterprise Value in 1997-1998. He was a development team member, chief reviewer, and frequent instructor of the original Appraisal Institute Course 800, Separating Real and Personal Property from Intangible Business Assets, and editor of the first edition of A Business Enterprise Value Anthology. Mr. Lennhoff continues to teach regularly for the Appraisal Institute, both nationally and internationally, and has been a frequent contributor to The Appraisal Journal since 1982.

James D. Vernor, PhD, MAI, is the Chairman Emeritus and Associate Professor Emeritus of Real Estate at Georgia State University. Mr. Vernor received his PhD at the University of Wisconsin-Madison in real estate and urban land economics. He has published articles in numerous publications such as The Appraisal Journal, Assessment Journal, Valuation Insights & Perspectives, The Journal of Property Tax Management, Economic Development Review, The Quarterly Byte, Real Estate Review, Appraisal Review Journal, Real Estate Issues, and Real Estate Appraiser/Analyst.

Richard Marchitelli, MAI, CRE, is a director in the real estate valuation/consulting practice of Pricewaterhouse-Coopers LLP, where he counsels private and public sector clients on use, capital deployment, valuation, dispute resolution, litigation support, and strategic asset management issues. He is a former Editor-in-Chief of The Appraisal Journal (1989-1994) and is a past contributor. He has chaired various Appraisal Institute committees and has been a recipient of several awards of that organization including the Lum Award (1998), the Wagner Award (1995), and the George L. Schmutz Memorial Award (1984).

- California Revenue and Tax Code, °±110, specifically exempting intangible property from ad valorem taxation by stating in part, "[t]he value of intangible assets and rights to the going concern value of a business using taxable property shall not enhance or be reflected in the value of the taxable property."
- California Code of Civil Procedure, §1263.510, requiring that an "owner of a business conducted on the property taken, or on the remainder if such property is part of a larger parcel, shall be compensated for loss of goodwill if the owner proves...."[2]
- Courts awarding compensation for the "going concern value" of a business located on property condemned through the exercise of eminent domain.[3]
- Differences in depreciable lives for tangible and intangible business assets[4] requiring separate value estimates for numerous property classes and categories.
- USPAP SR 1-2(e) and 1-4 (g) requiring appraisers to "identify and consider the effect on value of any personal property, trade fixtures, or intangible items that are not real property but are included in the appraisal."
- Numerous journal articles published over the past decade debating "business enterprise value" issues for operating properties and retail malls in particular.[5]

Because most viable operating enterprises trade as going concerns and inasmuch as most investors are not interested in allocating the value among the components, issues of the existence and magnitude of the non-real estate components and how they are to be allocated pose problems to anyone analyzing such transactions. This dilemma notwithstanding, for reasons such as proper assessment valuations, condemnation and lending requirements, and tax issues, allocations must be made. Unfortunately, there has been little definitive direction in the appraisal body of knowledge as to composition of the intangibles or how the allocation of the components of the operating enterprise could be performed.

To a great extent, dialogue concerning these issues has been hampered by a lack of a common language among various disciplines such as accounting, business, and property valuation. In particular, participants in the ongoing debate have adopted differing terminologies and assigned disparate meanings to terms commonly used in a variety of contexts. What is meant by going concern, going concern value, going value, business enterprise, business value, business enterprise value, or goodwill depends on the root discipline of the user of the term, the authoritative source consulted, and/or the legal citation referenced. As the following will show, there is no consensus concerning which term to apply to a given situation nor the appropriate definition to assign to a given term.

Welcome to Babylon

Business Enterprise Value

A limited search of the literature reveals at least five different definitions of business enterprise and/or business enterprise value. Examples of varying perceptions of what these terms mean include:

- *The Appraisal of Real Estate*[6] refers to business enterprise value (BEV) as:

    a value enhancement that results from items of intangible personal property such as marketing and management skill, an assembled work force, working capital, trade names, franchises, patents, trademarks, non-realty related contracts or leases, and some operating agreements.

- The *Dictionary of Real Estate Appraisal*[7] provides the following definition of "business value":

    a value enhancement that results from items of intangible personal property such as mar-

---

2. The owner must satisfy four requirements (requisite proofs) in order to be eligible for compensation for goodwill. Interested readers are referred to the code for additional detail. The code defines goodwill as "the benefits that accrue to a business as a result of its location, reputation for dependability, skill or quality, and any other circumstances resulting in probable retention of old or acquisition of new patronage." For further clarification and interpretation of this statute, see *People v. George H. Muller, et al,* 36 Cal.3d 263 and P. M. Millar, "Understanding Goodwill Appraisals," *Right of Way* (May/June 2000): 14.

3. See *City of Detroit v. Michael's Prescriptions,* N.W.2d, 1985 Mich. App LEXIS 2772, July 1, 1985; which relied on *Grand Rapids and Indiana Railroad Company v. Weiden,* 38 NW 394 (1888).

4. See IRS publication 946, *How to Depreciate Property.*

5. See David C. Lennhoff, ed., *A Business Enterprise Value Anthology* (Chicago: Appraisal Institute, 2001).

6. Appraisal Institute, *The Appraisal of Real Estate,* 11th ed. (Chicago: Appraisal Institute, 1996), updated in the 12th edition.

7. Appraisal Institute, *The Dictionary of Real Estate Appraisal,* 3rd ed. (Chicago: Appraisal Institute, 1993).

keting and management skill, an assembled work force, working capital, trade names, franchises, patents, trademarks, contracts, leases, and operating agreements.

- The IAAO *Glossary for Property Appraisal and Assessment*[8] defines BEV as:

  a term applied to the concept of an intangible, nonrealty component of a property's value probably ascribable to supramarginal management competence. Different from goodwill and going concern value.

- In *Journal of Property Tax Management*, Fisher and Kinnard[9] describe BEV as:

  an intangible asset.... the measurable and transferable present worth of the business organization, management, assembled workforce, skills, working capital, and legal rights (trade names, business names, franchises, patents, trademarks, contracts, leases, and operating agreements) that have been assembled to make the business a viable and valuable entity in its competitive market.

- *International Valuation Standards 2000*[10] doesn't define BEV, per se. A definition of business enterprise, however, is offered:

  [a] commercial, industrial, service or investment entity pursuing an economic activity; generally a profit-making enterprise.

These five perspectives on business enterprise and business enterprise value differ in substantive ways. First, none specifically includes the value of entrepreneurship in the traditional sense of excess, economic, or entrepreneurial profit (a topic discussed in more detail later), although the International Valuation Standards may be construed to include this under the rubric of "generally a profit-making enterprise." It is unclear, however, whether the definition is referring to accounting profit or economic profit,[11] which is fundamental in determining the extent to which revenue should actually accrue to the entrepreneur. Second, the

IAAO definition fails to recognize that supramarginal management expertise must be paid a supranormal management fee. In a competitive market for management, the supranormal management fee would be sufficient to exhaust any revenue derived from the activities of a supranormal manager, leaving no revenue to ascribe to BEV. Third, the *Dictionary of Real Estate Appraisal* definition seems to include the value of all forms of leases. However, real property lease revenue has always been ascribed to the value of the realty, not the intangibles.

Going Concern

In addition to uncertainty regarding the definitions of "business enterprise" and "business enterprise value," confusion exists concerning the degree to which these terms are synonymous with "going concern" and "going concern value." Desmond and Kelley, writing from a business valuation perspective, hold that "going concern [value] is an intangible that attaches to the tangible assets of some businesses."[12] This position is echoed in *Northern Natural Gas Company, et al. v. United States of America*[13] and appears in Real Estate Appraisal Terminology[14]:

It (going concern value) is an excess of value over cost, which arises as a consequence of a complete and well-assembled operation production mechanism; it is the value of an efficient layout and operational control system resulting in the most desirable synchronization of the merchandising, production, or distribution activities of the enterprise.

Conversely, other authoritative sources hold that going concern includes all of the assets of a business, tangible or intangible, with the proviso that the value of the business in continuing operation exceeds the liquidation value of the business assets, less liquidation costs. As an example of mainstream thinking in financial accounting, Ingram and Baldwin[15] hold that a going concern is:

---

8. International Association of Assessing Officers, *Glossary for Property Appraisal and Assessment* (Chicago: International Association of Assessing Officers, 1997).

9. Jeffery D. Fisher and William N. Kinnard, "The Business Enterprise Value Component of Operating Properties," in *A Business Enterprise Value Anthology*, David C. Lennhoff, ed. (Chicago: Appraisal Institute, 2001).

10. *International Valuation Standards Committee, International Valuation Standards 2000* (London: International Valuation Standards Committee, 2000).

11. Accounting profit is computed in accordance with generally accepted accounting practices, whereas economic profit includes deductions for additional implicit business expenses and opportunity costs such as uncompensated or under-compensated owner work effort.

12. G. M. Desmond and R. E. Kelley, *Business Valuation Handbook* (Los Angeles: Valuation Press, 1980): 168.

13. 407 F2d 1107, 1973.

14. B. N. Boyce, *Real Estate Appraisal Terminology* (Cambridge, MA: Ballinger, 1975).

15. Robert W. Ingram and Bruce A. Baldwin, *Financial Accounting: A Bridge to Decision Making,* 3rd ed. (Cincinnati: South-Western College Publishing, 1998).

an organization with an indefinite life that is sufficiently long that, over time, all currently incomplete transformations [transforming resources from one form to a different, more valuable, form] will be completed.

The unencumbered value of the organization (corporation, partnership, or sole proprietorship) would presumably include the value of all of the organization's assets, which would likely include tangible and intangible property.

Goodwill

As with business enterprise, there are also many differing viewpoints concerning what goodwill is and how it is defined. Five examples follow:

- *The Business Valuation Handbook:*[16]

    those elements of a business or person which cause customers to return to that business or person and which usually enable a firm to generate profit in excess of that which is required for a reasonable return on all of the other assets of the business.

- *Financial Accounting,*[17] a financial accounting textbook:

    the value of all favorable attributes that relate to a business enterprise. These include exceptional management, desirable location, good customer relations, skilled employees, high-quality products, fair pricing policies, and harmonious relations with labor unions.

- Ingram and Baldwin provide a different financial accounting-based definition:

    the excess of the purchase price of a company over the fair market value of its net assets (assets-liabilities) . . . value that is not recognized on the balance sheet.

- The American Society of Appraisers:

    an intangible asset that arises as a result of name, reputation, customer patronage, location, products, and similar factors that have not been separately identified and/or valued but that generate economic benefits.[18]

- *International Valuation Standards 2000:*

    an intangible but marketable asset based on the probability that customers will continue to resort to the same premises where the business is carried on under a particular name, or where goods are sold or services provided under a trade name, with the result

that there is likely to be the continuing prospect of earning an acceptable profit.

    arises as a result of name, reputation, customer patronage, location, products and similar factors that have not been separately identified and/or valued but which generate economic benefits.

Critical examination uncovers several problems with these definitions. First, one of the financial accounting definitions includes assets common to some of the definitions of business enterprise such as exceptional management, an assembled work force, and business name. Second, the Desmond and Kelley definition refers to "those elements of a business, which cause customers to return." Couldn't such elements be tangible? If so, are they goodwill? Third, several of the definitions include "location." Location seems to imply that goodwill is an attribute of real property, since location is meaningless in any sense other than spatial. Is goodwill an element of realty? Finally, what is meant by an "acceptable profit" or "profit in excess of what is required for a reasonable return on all of the other assets of the business"? Are the definitions referring to accounting profit or economic profit? Is a "reasonable return" to be interpreted in an opportunity cost context? The definitions are imprecise and unclear.

A New Lexicon

Language is the means by which we communicate what we are doing and precisely what is being valued. Because the terms *business enterprise, business enterprise value, going concern, going concern value,* and *goodwill* are so confounded, new terms were coined coincident with developing an Appraisal Institute course dealing with tangible and intangible business assets. The new course, *Separating Real and Personal Property from Intangible Business Assets* (Course 800), covers the theory of the firm, entrepreneurship, an introduction to business valuation, measuring intangible asset capitalization rates, and provides procedural examples—all of which rely on the new lexicon. It introduces methodology for estimating the value of the total assets of the business (TAB); and, using a case study of a full-service hotel, illustrates how

---

16. Desmond and Kelley.

17. J.J. Weygandt, D. E. Kieso, and P. D. Kimmel, *Financial Accounting,* 2nd ed. (New York: John Wiley & Sons, 1998).

18. As cited in S.P. Pratt, *Business Valuation Body of Knowledge* (New York: John Wiley & Sons, 1998).

the tangible and intangible components of value can be allocated. The real property residual model illustrated in the course hotel example is summarized as follows:

+ Value of total assets of the business
– Furnishings, fixtures, and equipment value
– Cash and equivalents value
– Skilled workforce value
– Name/reputation/affiliation value
– Residual intangible assets value
= Real property value as a residual

Figure 1 shows some of the bases for development and discussion of the new terminology. It breaks down the asset side of a firm's balance sheet into underlying tangible and intangible property components. By ignoring the liability side of the balance sheet, it looks at a firm or business as if it has no accounts payable, no other short-term or long-term debt, and concentrates solely on business assets.

The following discussion begins by precisely defining the going concern, the entity owning all of the business assets. The new definition comes from a financial accounting perspective, enabling clearer dialogue with financial market professionals.

Definitions

Going Concern
A *going concern* is an established and operating business having an indefinite future life.

A going concern is a business that can own tangible and intangible assets. The definition's phrase "indefinite future life" distinguishes going concerns from businesses that have no future, requiring valuation under an alternative liquidation premise rather than the going concern premise applicable to businesses having an indefinite future life. The term "going concern value" should be abandoned for two reasons. First, there is little agreement as to the term's meaning; second, it is a sloppy construct. More often than not, when we say "going concern value" what we really mean to say is "market value of the going concern," but the imprecise going concern value phrase could just as easily be interpreted as "investment value of the going concern" or "insurable value of the going concern." In order to precisely identify what is being valued, Course 800 introduced the term "market value of the total assets of the business." This term is consistent with valuing all of the assets shown in Figure 1, and it is clearly different from "business value," used by business valuers when estimating business value net of short-term liabilities.

Market Value of the Total Assets of the Business (MVTAB)
Market value of the total assets of the business is the market value of all of the tangible and intangible assets of a business as if sold in aggregate as a going concern.[19]

As Figure 1 shows, total business (going concern) assets are divided into two primary categories–tangible property and intangible property. Tangible property consists of items

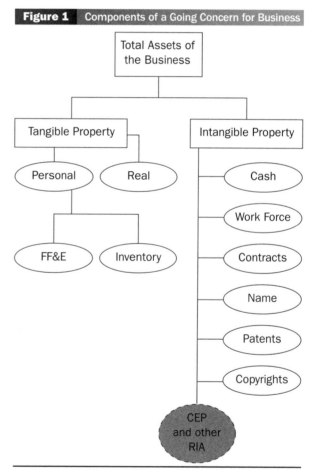

Figure 1 Components of a Going Concern for Business

Note: The term *CEP* stands for Capitalized Economic Profit and the term *RIA* stands for Residual Intangible Assets.

---

19. This means that the "going concern premise" applies, i.e., the business is expected to continue operating well into the future. A value estimate made under the going concern premise assumes that the entire business would change hands if it were sold at a price equal to the value estimate.

that can be seen, touched, and felt. Tangible business assets are further divided into real property and personal property, such as inventory, furnishings, fixtures, and equipment. No new terminology is needed to precisely describe the tangible business assets.

Intangible property includes numerous ethereal assets such as cash,[20] a workforce, contracts, business name, patents, copyrights, and potentially numerous other assets. Three new terms are being adopted to enable better appraisal-client communication: *total intangible assets, identified intangible assets,* and *residual intangible assets.*

Total Intangible Assets (TIA)

Total intangible assets are all of the intangible assets owned by a business (going concern), which can be further divided into two categories for valuation purposes: identified intangible assets and residual intangible assets.

Identified Intangible Assets (IIA)

Identified intangible assets are those intangible assets of a business (going concern) that have been separately identified and valued in an appraisal.

Residual Intangible Assets (RIA)

Residual intangible assets are those intangible assets of a business (going concern) that have not been separately identified and valued in an appraisal. The value of residual intangible assets equals the value of total intangible assets minus the value of identified intangible assets.

Figure 1 includes an item labeled CEP (an acronym for *capitalized economic profit*) as one possible intangible business asset. CEP is based on economic theory dating from Richard Cantillon (1680-1734) and contributed to over time by highly regarded scholars such as Joseph Schumpeter (*The Theory of Economic Development,* 1912) and Frank Knight (*Risk, Uncertainty and Profit,* 1921).[21] Briefly, economic profit is what remains after all productive agents (land, labor, and capital) have been paid

the full opportunity cost of their contribution to the firm's production process. Economic profit differs dramatically from accounting profit because opportunity cost is not considered in the computation of accounting profit. *Economic profit can be, and usually is, fleeting due to the effects of competition.* Thus, it is capitalized at a very high rate indicative of the uncertainty associated with its future continuation. Because economic profit is often temporary in nature, any value attributable to it is apt to exist for a finite period until it is fully eroded by market competition. Nevertheless, economic profits do occur, and expectations of continuing future economic profits are valuable intangible assets. Since economic profits are nearly impossible to isolate and value separately, CEP is included in the figure as an element of residual intangible assets for valuation purposes. The new definition for CEP follows.

Capitalized Economic Profit (CEP)

Capitalized economic profit is the present worth of an entrepreneur's economic (pure) profit expectation from being engaged in the activity of acquiring an asset, or collection of assets, at a known price and then selling, or being able to sell, the same asset or collection of assets at a future uncertain price. The amount of the entrepreneur's expected economic profit, and consequent CEP, is determined by the nature of the risks taken and/or the expected return to the entrepreneur's innovation. CEP is the value of a residual claim, which is subordinate to the opportunity cost claims of all agents of production employed by the business (e.g., land, labor, and/or capital).

Conclusions

Course 800 introduces five new terms and six new definitions to the valuation lexicon, dispensing with vague and confusing terminology including going concern value, business enterprise, business enterprise value, and goodwill

---

20. The concept of money being an intangible asset is sometimes difficult to grasp because money can be seen, touched, and felt. However, physical money is intrinsically worthless. According to P. A. Samuelson and W. D. Nordhaus, *Economics,* 13th ed. (New York: McGraw-Hill, 1989), money "is an artificial social convention." Since we abandoned our commodity money (gold) standard, money has been valued for what it can purchase and the degree to which society honors the statement that its paper money is "legal tender." Thus, cash and equivalents are classified as intangible assets. For in-depth reading on this topic see Samuelson and Nordhaus, "History of Money," 226–230; D. Foley, "Money in Economic Activity," *Money,* J. Eatwell, M. Millgate, and P. Newman, eds. (New York: W. W. Norton, 1989): 248–262; and B. T. McCallum, "Monetary Standards: Fiat Versus Commodity Money," *Monetary Economics: Theory and Policy* (New York: Macmillan, 1989): 22–24.

21. For a more complete discussion of this concept, see the essay on the theory of profit in M. Blaug, *Economic Theory in Retrospect* (Cambridge: Cambridge University Press, 1985): 458–465.

(which remains a valid, yet ill-defined, term in a financial accounting sense). Going concern is precisely defined, making it clear that the going concern is the business, which may own both tangible and intangible assets.

The five new terms introduced are *market value of the total assets of the business, total intangible assets, identified intangible assets, residual intangible assets,* and *capitalized economic profit.* This new lexicon will enable appraisers to precisely describe what is being included in the various asset categories when separating real and personal tangible business asset values and intangible business asset values. This will go a long way toward clearing up confusion resulting from the current multitude of meanings for commonly used and commonly misinterpreted business asset valuation terminology. The new definitions provide a linguistic foundation, applying the theory of the firm to the real world problem of separating the values of tangible and intangible business assets in a logical and systematic way.

The Identification of Contributory Assets and Calculation of Economic Rents

The Appraisal Foundation

Foreword

This document regarding best practices for *The Identification of Contributory Assets and Calculation of Economic Rents* was developed by a working group sponsored by The Appraisal Foundation.

With changing financial reporting requirements, there is increased interest in the effect of valuation conclusions on financial statements. Because of the need for financial statements to be both reliable and relevant, valuation practices must provide reasonably consistent and verifiable value conclusions. To this end, the valuation community believed that guidance regarding best practices surrounding certain specific valuation topics would be helpful. The topics are selected based on those in which the greatest diversity of practice has been observed.

The Appraisal Foundation sponsored this endeavor as an independent body interested in the advancement of professional valuation and whose stated goal is assuring public trust in the valuation profession. The Appraisal Foundation convened a series of working groups to

Working Group on Contributory Asset Charges

Anthony Aaron, Chair - *Ernst & Young, LLP - Los Angeles, CA*

Paul Barnes - *Duff & Phelps, LLC - Philadelphia, PA*

Jim Dondero - *Huron Consulting Group - Boston, MA*

Gregory Forsythe - *Deloitte Financial Advisory Services LLP - Pittsburgh, PA*

Mark Zyla, Vice Chair - *Acuitas, Inc. - Atlanta, GA*

Jay Fishman, Steering Committee Oversight & Facilitator *- Financial Research Associates – Philadelphia, PA*

Task Force (Steering Committee) on Best Practices for Valuations in Financial Reporting

Jay Fishman, Chair - Financial Research Associates

Anthony Aaron - Ernst & Young, LLP

Paul Barnes - Duff & Phelps, LLC

Carla Glass - Hill Schwartz Spilker Keller LLC

John Glynn - PricewaterhouseCoopers LLP

Lee Hackett - American Appraisal Associates

Steve Jones - Mesirow Financial

Gerald Mehm - American Appraisal Associates

Matt Pinson – PricewaterhouseCoopers LLP

Contributors & Special Thanks

Dayton Nordin, Ernst & Young, LLP

Gary Roland, Duff & Phelps, LLC

Shawn Suttmiller, Deloitte Financial Advisory Services LLP

Carla Glass, Hill Schwartz Spilker Keller LLC

Lee Hackett, American Appraisal Associates

The Appraisal Foundation Staff

David Bunton, President

John Brenan, Director of Research & Technical Issues

Paula Douglas Seidel, Executive Administrator

The Appraisal Foundation served as a sponsor and facilitator of this Working Group. The Foundation is a non-profit educational organization dedicated to the advancement of professional valuation and was established in 1987 by the appraisal profession in the United States. The Appraisal Foundation is not an individual membership organization, but rather, an organization that is made up of other organizations. Today, over 130 non-profit organizations, corporations and government agencies are affiliated with The Appraisal Foundation. The Appraisal Foundation is authorized by the U.S. Congress as the source of appraisal standards and appraiser qualifications.

develop guidance to assist in reducing diversity in practice in valuations performed for financial reporting purposes.

This document presents best practices for the first topic, *The Identification of Contributory Assets and Calculation of Economic Rents,* and was created by the first Working Group. This final document follows the issuance of a discussion draft on June 10, 2008 and an exposure draft on February 25, 2009, as well as a public hearing for oral comments on May 12, 2009, and reflects full consideration of all comments received.

This document includes a Comprehensive Example as well as a Practical Expedient as Appendices. While creating these Appendices, the first Working Group also created a "Toolkit," which is an expansion of the Comprehensive Example. The Toolkit contains additional sample spreadsheets that illustrate application of typical calculations in which contributory asset charges are used. It will be published under separate cover.

The Identification of Contributory Assets and Calculation of Economic Rents was developed by a Working Group comprising individuals from the valuation profession who regularly deal with this issue in the context of valuations performed for financial reporting purposes. Its conclusions reflect what the developers believe are best practices. This document has no official or authoritative standing for valuation or accounting.

This document was approved for publication by the Board of Trustees of The Appraisal Foundation on May 22, 2010. The reader is informed that the Board of Trustees defers to the members of the contributory asset Working Group for expertise concerning the technical content of the document.

Questions on the development of this document can be addressed as follows:

Paula Douglas Seidel
The Appraisal Foundation
1155 15th Street NW, Suite 1111
Washington, DC 20005
202.624.3048 (phone); 202.347.7727 (fax);
paula@appraisalfoundation.org (email)

1.0 Introduction

1.1 This document setting forth best practices for *The Identification of Contributory Assets and Calculation of Economic Rents* ("Monograph") is the result of deliberations by the Working Group on Contributory Asset Charges ("CACs") and input received from interested parties.

1.2 CACs (also known as capital charges or economic rents) are a requisite consideration in applying the Multi-Period Excess Earnings Method ("MPEEM")[1] to estimate the fair value of a subject intangible asset.

1.3 The MPEEM is a method under the income approach. In applying this form of analysis, the starting point is generally Prospective Financial Information ("PFI") for the entity that owns the subject intangible asset. From this, a stream of revenue and expenses are identified as those associated with a particular group of assets. This group of assets includes the subject intangible asset as well as other assets (contributory assets) that are necessary to support the earnings associated with the subject intangible asset. The prospective earnings of the single subject intangible asset are isolated from those of the group of assets by identifying and deducting portions of the total earnings that are attributable to the contributory assets to estimate the remaining or "excess earnings" attributable to the subject intangible asset. The identification of earnings attributable to the contributory assets is accomplished through the application of CACs in the form of returns *"on"* and, in some cases, *"of"* the contributory assets. These CACs represent an economic charge for the use of the contributory assets. The "excess" earnings (those that remain after subtraction of the CACs) are attributable to the subject intangible asset. These excess earnings are discounted to present value at an appropriate rate of return to estimate the fair value of the subject intangible asset. Thus, the MPEEM could be described as an attribution model under the income approach.

1.4 Expressed in a slightly different manner, when PFI is used to determine the fair value of a subject intangible asset it might include contributions from a number of different assets working together as a group. To arrive at the

---

1. This term was introduced and is used in the 2001 AICPA Practice Aid Series: "Assets Acquired in a Business Combination to Be Used in Research and Development Activities: A Focus on Software, Electronic Devices and Pharmaceutical Industries". (An update of this Practice Aid was underway as of the finalization of this Monograph.)

excess earnings solely attributable to the subject intangible asset, the valuation specialist needs to identify other assets that are contributing to the generation of the asset group's earnings. If the specific revenues and expenses of these other assets cannot be separated from the PFI for the group of assets, the subtraction of CACs is necessary to recognize the economic benefit provided by the contributory assets. If the contribution of these assets is separated from the group's aggregate PFI, then CACs are not necessary.

1.5 Whether CACs are theoretically viewed as an attribution of earnings to a contributory asset owned by the entity or as a payment for use assuming the contributory asset is owned by a third party, the fundamental premise is that a contributory asset must be assigned a portion of the economic earnings of the group of assets to derive the excess earnings attributable to the subject intangible asset.

1.6 A fundamental attribute of the MPEEM and of CAC calculations relates to a basic principle of financial theory known as Return on Investment ("ROI"). From the perspective of an investment in contributory assets, an owner of such assets would require an appropriate ROI. The ROI, in turn, consists of a pure investment return (what is referred to herein as *return on*) and a recoupment of the original investment amount (what is referred to herein as *return of*). Thus the most basic underpinning of CAC calculations is that contributory assets should earn a fair ROI.

1.7 The distinguishing characteristic of a contributory asset is that it is not the subject income-generating asset itself; rather it is an asset that is required to support the subject income-generating asset. The CAC represents the charge that is required to compensate for an investment in a contributory asset, giving consideration to rates of return required by market participants investing in such assets.

1.8 During the Working Group's discussions and the public hearing, it became apparent that it was necessary to define the specific scope of this Monograph. The discussion of CACs requires the understanding of many accounting and valuation requirements and methods. Discussion of these requirements and methods is beyond the scope of the CAC Monograph and the reader is assumed to already have this understanding. More specifically, this Monograph assumes the reader has sufficient understanding of the following issues:

A. The PFI used in the MPEEM is to reflect market participant assumptions. This Monograph does not address the identification of market participants or include a detailed discussion of all adjustments to the PFI potentially required to reflect such assumptions.

B. The application of a specific valuation approach, method, or technique to an asset is based on facts and circumstances from a market participant perspective, and the reader is assumed to have the ability to make this judgment. This Monograph does not discuss the variety of approaches, methods, and techniques or the judgment required to select one. Those applied to any of the assets identified herein are provided for demonstration purposes only.

C. The discussions in this Monograph as well as the Comprehensive Example and Practical Expedient included in Appendices A and B, respectively, make certain assumptions that might impact the valuation of the contributory assets. Assumptions used in the valuation of an asset are based on facts and circumstances and the reader is assumed to have the ability to make these judgments. The assumptions reflected in the discussions and examples contained in this Monograph are for demonstration purposes only. General principles have been provided for guidance to assist in the calculation of CACs in the application of the MPEEM.

D. The models used in the sample calculations are for demonstration purposes only and are not intended as the only form of model or calculation, or final report exhibit, that is acceptable. In some cases, these models include details to demonstrate a point made in this Monograph and would not be expected in a typical analysis.

1.9 In writing this document, the Working Group recognizes that professional judgment is critical to effectively planning, performing, and concluding a valuation. Professional judgment requires both competency (appropriate knowledge and experience) and ethical behavior (objectivity and independence). Questioning and skepticism are appropriate because of the nature of judgments. Knowledgeable, reasonable, objective individuals can reach different conclusions for a given set of facts and circumstances. Professional judgment reflects a process of fact-gathering, research, and analysis employed while reaching well-reasoned conclusions based on relevant facts and circumstances available at the time of the conclusion.

1.10 The following important clarifications regarding this document are also made:

A. These best practices have been developed with reference to US GAAP effective as of the date that this document was published. While the Working Group believes that the best practices described herein may have application outside of US GAAP the valuation specialist should not apply these best practices to valuations prepared under different applicable standards/statutory requirements without a thorough understanding of the differences between them and US GAAP guidance existing as of the date of this publication.

B. The Working Group has not used the terms "cash flow," "earnings" and "income" as commonly used in the accounting literature. When the terms "cash flow," "earnings" or "excess earnings" are used, they refer to an "economic earnings" concept associated with the netting of expense and other charges against revenue.

C. The Working Group recognizes that there is often a difference between the total amount of goodwill recorded as the result of an acquisition and the amount of goodwill (or "excess purchase price") that the valuation specialist is typically dealing with during the valuation. For example, an amount is typically recorded to deferred taxes and this amount is not defined until after the work of the valuation specialist is completed. However, the term goodwill is used in this document in both situations to mean the difference between the purchase price being used (either during the valuation process or the recording process) and the net value of all separately recognized assets and liabilities.

D. The terms "value," "valuation," "valuing," "fair value" and any other reference to value throughout this document are intended, for the purposes of this document, to be stated in accordance with "fair value" as defined in the Financial Accounting Literature, Financial Accounting Standards Board ("FASB") Accounting Standards Codification ("ASC") Topic 820 (formerly FASB Statement of Financial Accounting Standards No. 157 ("FASB Statement No. 157")).

E. Throughout this document the asset being valued is referred to as the "subject intangible asset" and other assets in the group of assets that also contribute to the group's earnings as "contributory assets."

F. From a historical perspective, the so called "formula approach" of the U.S. Internal Revenue Service's Revenue Ruling 68-609, 1968- 2 C.B. 327 and the earlier ARM 34 are often referred to as the Excess Earnings Method and are different from the MPEEM, although the MPEEM has its roots in this literature.

G. It should be noted that other methods (aside from the MPEEM) exist for the valuation of intangible assets, and this document does not purport to recommend the use of a specific method for a specific asset.

1.11 This document discusses the definition and identification of contributory assets, calculation of CACs, and considerations when selecting appropriate rates of *return on,* and, in some cases, *return of,* those contributory assets in the application of the MPEEM.

2.0 Identification of Contributory Assets

2.1 What Constitutes a Contributory Asset
2.1.01 Contributory assets are defined as assets that are used in conjunction with the subject intangible asset in the realization of prospective cash flows associated with the subject intangible asset. Assets that do not contribute to the prospective cash flows associated with the subject intangible asset are not contributory assets. For example, a certain amount of real property (land and buildings) may be necessary to support the cash flow attributable to a subject intangible

asset. Alternatively, land held by an entity for investment (a non-operating asset) would not be appropriate to include as a contributory asset if the land is not necessary for, or expected to contribute to, the generation of the prospective cash flows of the subject intangible asset.

2.1.02 The valuation of the subject intangible asset needs to reflect those assets that market participants would treat as contributory assets, regardless of whether an entity has acquired them in a transaction, already owns them, or would need to purchase them.

2.2 Contributory Assets

2.2.01 The types of asset categories required to support the cash flows associated with a subject intangible asset are based on the facts and circumstances of the entity and the subject intangible asset. The asset categories and examples of their components that might be considered as contributory assets are illustrated in the following table:

Asset Category	Illustrative Components
Working Capital[2]	Cash, Receivables, Inventory, Payables, Accruals
Fixed (Tangible) Assets	Real Property, Machinery and Equipment, Furniture and Fixtures
Intangible Assets	Trademarks and Trade Names, Technology, Software, Customer Relationships, Non-Compete Agreements, Assembled Workforce[3]

2.2.02 The assumptions used in arriving at the fair value of the subject intangible asset should reflect those assumptions that market participants would use in pricing the subject intangible asset or the group of assets that includes the subject intangible asset. Therefore, the PFI should consider market participant assumptions regarding levels of required contributory assets, either on an individual or grouped basis, as appropriate.

2.2.03 The PFI should include normalized[4] levels of required contributory assets reflective of the market participants' view of the entity's position in its life cycle. For example, a normalized level of fixed assets for an entity in its infancy may be different from the level required once the entity reaches a mature stage in its life cycle. To the extent the PFI reflects excess or deficient levels of contributory assets, it should be adjusted to reflect normalized levels.

2.2.04 *Working Capital*

2.2.05 Working capital is a necessary element of an entity required to support the operations. Working capital, including, for example, operating cash, receivables, inventory, payables, accruals, and other short-term assets and liabilities, is continually needed by the entity and is constantly turning over to maintain the required level without a loss in value due to economic depreciation. As such, it is assumed to be an asset that does not deteriorate in value.

2.2.06 The appropriate level of working capital to use as a contributory asset is a normalized level of working capital. A normalized level of working capital would represent only those working capital items and amounts necessary for market participants to support the operations of the entity, or in the case of valuing a subject intangible asset, those working capital items that would support the generation of cash flow associated with the subject intangible asset.

2.2.07 If an entity has deferred revenue, this liability may or may not be included as a component of the working capital that is then used as the basis for a CAC. Whether to include or

---

2. Working Capital for purposes of this document specifically excludes excess cash above normal operating levels and all interest bearing debt and is often referred to in practice as "Debt Free Net Working Capital" or "Net Working Capital."

3. This list is not all inclusive. FASB ASC paragraphs 805-20-55-2 through 805-20-55-45 (formerly Paragraphs A29 through A56 of the Financial Accounting Standards Board, Financial Accounting Series, *"Statement of Financial Accounting Standards No. 141 (Revised 2007) – Business Combinations"*) provide a more detailed list of potential intangible assets. Industry-specific assets also may exist in specialized circumstances.

4. Normalized, as used in this document, refers to assumptions that are consistent with the entity or subject intangible asset from a market participant perspective. For example, if it is observed that the PFI includes excess (or deficient) levels of an asset, a normalized level of the asset would include adjustments to reflect the level needed to operate, and would exclude the impact of the excess (or deficient) level from a market participant perspective. This use of the term "normalized" is different from the normalization adjustments that may be applied in a business valuation when adjusting financial data to remove the effect of nonrecurring or unusual items.

exclude the deferred revenue as a component of the working capital will depend on how the PFI was developed. If the revenue component of the PFI was developed on an accrual basis, then it likely would be appropriate to include the deferred revenue as a component of working capital. The Working Group believes that deferred revenue should be included in working capital on a normalized basis if deferred revenue is a part of an entity's ongoing operation. The Working Group also believes that, in such a circumstance, the level of accrued deferred revenue included in net working capital for purposes of calculating the CAC should reflect an entity's ongoing operations and be consistent with the PFI, as opposed to a level reflecting a "one-time" adjustment[5] to the fair value of any legal performance obligation that would arise in a business combination accounting setting.

2.2.08 *Fixed Assets*

2.2.09 Fixed assets are needed primarily to enable the productive capability of an entity. These assets may include land, land improvements, buildings, machinery, furniture, fixtures and equipment, leasehold improvements, and natural resources, for example. Fixed assets frequently are assets that deteriorate and require replenishment/replacement to sustain the productive capability of the entity.

2.2.10 The stage of an entity in its life cycle may influence the level of fixed assets necessary for operations at a given point in time. For example, the fixed asset levels of an early stage entity may not be representative of the fixed asset levels required for mass product commercialization. An estimate of a normalized level for market participants would be necessary when calculating the CAC. This normalized level should represent the amount that market participants would consider appropriate to support the subject intangible asset.

2.2.11 If the fixed assets in place for an acquired entity (or other subject entity) as of the valuation date do not represent the level of fixed assets necessary to generate the prospective cash flow stream, then it would be appropriate to use an estimated level of those necessary fixed assets based on market participant assumptions. This normalized level of fixed assets should be measured at fair value and should be reflected in the PFI.

2.2.12 *Intangible Assets*

2.2.13 Intangible assets that meet the recognition criteria under FASB ASC Topic 805 (formerly FASB Statement of Financial Accounting Standards No. 141 (Revised 2007) ("FASB Statement No. 141(R)"), as being either legal/contractual or separable represent contributory assets if their use contributes to an aggregate economic earnings stream associated with the subject intangible asset. FASB ASC paragraphs 805-20-55-2 through 805-20-55-45 (formerly paragraphs A29 through A56 of FASB Statement No. 141(R)) provide additional guidance regarding, and examples of, intangible assets that meet the criteria for recognition as an asset apart from goodwill. Intangible assets identified in FASB ASC Topic 805 include marketing-related intangible assets, customer-related intangible assets, artistic-related intangible assets, contract-based intangible assets, and technology-based intangible assets. Valuation specialists should first consider whether the revenue or profits can be split to allocate the economic earnings stream among intangible assets. The use of a royalty savings method is viewed as a form of profit split in the context of this document. Absent the ability to make such a division, the use of a CAC is the best method for compensating for the contributory asset's contribution to the aggregate economic earnings stream associated with the subject intangible asset.

2.2.14 Additionally, other reliably measureable intangible assets (or elements of an entity) that do not meet the criteria under FASB ASC Topic 805 for recognition separate from goodwill, such as an assembled workforce, would be considered as contributory assets if they contribute to the generation of the cash flow stream associated with the subject intangible asset. An assembled workforce is one example of an element of goodwill that generally is recognized as a contributory asset although it is not recognized on the balance sheet apart from goodwill under FASB ASC Topic 805.

2.2.15 The determination of whether a CAC for elements of goodwill is appropriate should be based on an assessment of the relevant facts and circumstances of the situation, and the valuation specialist should be cautioned to not mechanically apply CACs or alternative adjustments for elements of goodwill if the circum-

---

5. See, for instance, the discussion of "one-time" adjustments in paragraph 3.2.03.

stances do not warrant such a charge. The Working Group believes that assembled workforce is typically the only element of goodwill for which a CAC is taken. Accordingly, the burden of proof is higher to support taking CACs or making alternative adjustments for elements of goodwill other than assembled workforce.

2.2.16 If other elements of goodwill are significant contributors to the stream of economic earnings associated with the subject intangible asset, the Working Group believes that the valuation specialist should a) seek to identify and estimate the fair value of those elements (when reliably measurable) for use in calculating CACs, b) make an alternative adjustment to the economic earnings stream in order to compensate for the contribution of the other element or elements of goodwill, or c) consider another method (e.g. the Greenfield method) that more accurately isolates the economic earnings stream attributable solely to the subject intangible asset.

3.0 Valuation Methodologies and the Application of Contributory Asset Charges

3.1 Introduction and General Concepts

3.1.01 All valuation methodologies applied in the valuation of any asset may be broadly classified into the cost, market, or income approaches. In a valuation study, all three would be considered (for application), and the approach or approaches deemed most appropriate would then be selected as the proper approach(es) to use in the valuation of that asset. The valuation of intangible assets is most commonly conducted using an income approach in which there is an identifiable stream of cash flows associated with that intangible asset. Typical income approach methods used in the valuation of intangible assets include the relief from royalty method, the MPEEM, and a number of other methods. The MPEEM is commonly employed in the valuation of certain technology (existing or in development), customer relationships, and many other assets.

3.1.02 Prior to application of the MPEEM, the valuation specialist should ensure that the PFI estimates are representative of the views of market participants. Inclusion of the effects of entity-specific synergies should be avoided, while market participant synergies are appropriate for inclusion in the PFI.

3.1.03 The MPEEM requires PFI estimates of cash inflows and cash outflows, combined with charges for *returns on,* and where applicable, *returns of* tangible and intangible assets employed in the generation of cash flows associated with the subject intangible asset (including elements of goodwill such as the assembled workforce).

3.1.04 Cash inflows are primarily represented by revenue. It is important to note that, in the application of the income approach to value a subject intangible asset, the valuation specialist should properly identify the correct stream of revenue associated with the subject intangible asset. For some intangible assets, this stream of revenue may be the same as the revenue estimates for the entire entity, while for other intangible assets the valuation specialist may identify a portion of this total revenue.

3.1.05 Cash outflows associated with the subject intangible asset might include direct and indirect expenses for costs to complete (in the case of in-process research and development ("IPR&D")), manufacturing, sales, marketing, routine technical maintenance, general and administrative expense, and taxes, for example.

3.1.06 The contributory assets reflected in the MPEEM should include all assets required by market participants to realize the cash flows associated with the subject intangible asset. An acquired or acquiring entity may already have access to some of these assets, or the acquiring entity may need to gain access to them in some other way if they are necessary to generate the prospective cash flows in the aggregate. The CACs should be based on the fair value of the required market participant levels of contributory assets. These charges generally represent a *return on* and, in some cases, a *return of* these contributory assets based on the fair value of such contributory assets.

3.1.07 In practice, for certain classes of assets (for instance, working capital and fixed assets), book value is often used as a proxy for the fair value on which to calculate CACs. The Working Group believes that the use of book value as a practical expedient for measuring fair value can be appropriate based on facts and circumstances so long as the use of book value is consistent with the fair value measurement objective as it is applied to the subject intangible asset. Further, market participant views of the levels of contributory assets for the subject entity are often estimated in practice with reference to industry comparable data, which is often only available based on book value. The Working Group believes that valuation specialists should exercise caution, however, because the concept remains that the book value of contributory assets may only be utilized when they are not believed to be significantly different from fair values.

3.1.08 The Working Group believes that the fair value of an asset should not differ depending on the tax structure of a particular transaction.[6] Market prices of fixed assets reflect the tax benefit of depreciation. Similarly, if an intangible asset were to be sold (either as a single asset or as part of a group of assets, depending on highest and best use), the purchase price would reasonably reflect the benefit of amortizing the asset for tax purposes. For this reason, the fair value of an intangible asset includes the benefit of the tax amortization when applying an income approach. Therefore, CACs on contributory assets should be based on the fair value of these assets including their tax depreciation benefit or tax amortization benefit ("TAB"). (It is not within the scope of this document to address whether application of the cost approach to value intangible assets should be on a pre-tax or after-tax basis. For examples in this document, pre-tax costs are used because the Working Group has observed this to be the most prevalent method. If a pre-tax cost is used, the addition of a TAB is not commonly considered appropriate, whereas the addition of a TAB is commonly considered appropriate with an after-tax cost.[7] If an after-tax method with the TAB is used in an analysis, adjustments would be necessary for consistency of assumptions.)

3.1.09 Careful analysis is necessary to determine which assets or elements of an entity contribute to a subject intangible asset. In some cases, a determination can be made to exclude (as contributory) assets that are not required by the subject intangible asset. Many assets are contributory to all subject intangible assets. In this circumstance, the CAC earned by a contributory asset should be allocated to each subject intangible asset using a method that appropriately reflects its utilization. For example, a subject intangible asset that uses twice as much of a contributory asset as another subject intangible asset should incur twice the CAC. When objective information is available, it forms the basis of a CAC allocation. In the absence of reliable data, a reasonable assumption should be used. The most common method to allocate CACs to assets generally is based on the relative revenue generated by each subject intangible asset each year. There may be instances, however, when other methods such as relative amounts earned, relative units produced, relative square footage occupied, relative headcount used or relative costs expended by each subject intangible asset, each year, may represent a more appropriate allocation method. When a contributory asset is not expected to contribute to a particular subject intangible asset, its return is not charged against that subject intangible asset. (Its return is, however, charged against all of the future or current intangible assets to which it does make a contribution.)

3.1.10 Following identification of the cash inflows and outflows associated with the subject intangible asset and the reflection of CACs, the remaining net cash flows (or multi-period excess earnings) are attributed to the subject intangible asset and, when discounted to present value, provide an estimate of the subject intangible asset's value (prior to application of the tax amortization benefit). (See, for example, FASB ASC paragraphs 820-10-35-32 and 820-10-35-33 (formerly paragraph 18b of FASB Statement No. 157) and paragraph 2.1.10 of the 2001 AICPA Practice Aid Series: *"Assets Acquired in a Business Combination to Be Used in Research and Development Activities: A Focus on Software, Electronic Devices and Pharmaceutical Industries"* ("IPR&D Practice Aid").)

3.1.11 The Working Group believes that valuation specialists should take special care when application of the MPEEM results in an individual year's excess earnings being negative or indicates a negative value in the aggregate solely as a result of the application of CACs. The valuation specialist should perform additional review of the calculations to ensure the integrity of the inputs and the structure of the analysis. In some cases, a negative value in the aggregate may indicate that there is no economic basis for recognizing the asset (e.g., a negatively valued customer relationship). In other cases, a negative value for an asset within a portfolio of assets may need to be offset against positive val-

---

6.   The discussion here and elsewhere assumes the tax benefits of depreciation and intangible asset amortization are available to market participants.

7.   This parenthetical is addressing the cost approach, not a cost-savings method that is an income approach.

ues of the remaining assets within the portfolio or recognized as a distinct liability (e.g., a single contract within a group of contracts, if appropriate from an accounting perspective). Further, a negative excess earnings amount for a given year within a projection period associated with a subject intangible asset should not be disregarded in measuring the fair value of that asset.

3.1.12 The Working Group believes that issues such as those discussed in Section 3.1.01 through 3.1.11 demonstrate the complexity of applying the MPEEM and the care that should be taken by valuation specialists in estimating fair value utilizing this method. An important attribute of this method is that it provides the ability to reconcile to the entity value and demonstrates that the calculation of the CAC does not create or destroy aggregate asset value. The application of CACs is essentially an attribution of earnings to the contributory assets.

3.2 Working Capital

3.2.01 In considering the appropriate CAC for working capital, it should first be noted that increases or decreases in required working capital would not be included as a charge or benefit to the cash flow because growth investments (or "dis-investments") are accounted for through increases or decreases in the CAC. It should be noted that individual components of working capital (e.g., accounts receivable and inventories) may be subject to write-downs from time to time. Such decreases in value are charged through the income statement, and recurring expense assumptions would encompass future expectations regarding write-downs. Thus, it is appropriate to charge the subject intangible asset only with an appropriate *return on* working capital that is based on the required level of working capital for each period. In other words, the *return on* working capital represents the charge for utilization of working capital by the subject intangible asset. When the working capital is no longer required (e.g., at the end of the economic life of the subject intangible asset), it can be used by other assets. One common method of calculating the period-specific working capital CAC would be based on the required *return on* total working capital as a percentage of total revenue with that percentage then applied to the specific revenue associated with the subject intangible asset. See Exhibit A-4 in Appendix A for an illustrative example of how to calculate a CAC for working capital on an annual basis (the Comprehensive Example). See also Appendix B for an illustrative example of a practical expedient in the calculation of a working capital CAC (the Practical Expedient).

3.2.02 One issue that arises in certain industry sectors is the appropriate treatment of negative working capital. This does not refer to those circumstances where inadequate working capital has been acquired as part of a transaction. Instead this is the circumstance in certain industry sectors for which negative net working capital is the norm. It is the view of the Working Group that negative working capital that is generated in the normal course of business in certain industry sectors enhances overall entity value and should be considered in determining the appropriate level of working capital to serve as the basis for calculating CACs. This will, in effect, create "negative" CACs for working capital, the apportioned amount of which would enhance the value of the subject intangible asset. This treatment is appropriate because it reflects the economic realities in those industry sectors and is consistent with the cash flow benefit reflected in the PFI.

3.2.03 Another issue is the impact of one-time business combination accounting adjustments to working capital such as inventory step-ups. The Working Group believes that such one-time adjustments should be excluded from the initial and ongoing levels of working capital (based on market participant assumptions) used in the CAC calculation. This view is based on the belief that whether a subject intangible asset is being valued as part of a business combination or for other purposes it would be valued the same. The inclusion of one-time business combination accounting adjustments may cause the subject intangible asset to be valued differently for different purposes and, further, is not representative of the long term need for working capital. The Working Group believes that valuation specialists should not only exclude one-time adjustments from market participant levels of working capital used in the CAC calculation, but should also make sure to adjust for the effects of any one-time modifications of the PFI utilized in the valuation of the subject intangible asset to avoid double counting profit or expense. More specifically, the profit included in the inventory step-up (if applied) would need to be removed from the PFI of the subject intangible asset so that the profit is not recognized more than once.

3.3 Land

3.3.01 The CAC calculation associated with land is different from that associated with other fixed assets that deteriorate in value over time and exhibits similarities to the CAC calculation for working capital. Land is not assumed to deteriorate in value over time. Special consideration should be given to the appropriate market participant level of land and its associated fair value serving as the basis for the calculation of the CAC, as land values, over time, may move independently from the value of the entity or of the subject intangible asset. The CAC should be based on the fair value of land necessary to support the earnings associated with the subject intangible asset at any time.

3.4 Fixed Assets (Not Including Land)

3.4.01 The Working Group is aware of many techniques for calculating CACs for fixed assets that are currently in use. This Section 3.4 and the Comprehensive Example present the two techniques that are believed to be the most common in the profession (in a comprehensive application). The Working Group understands these detailed calculations often are not necessary and that more simplified versions are often appropriate (please see the Practical Expedient, Appendix B). Both techniques assume that fixed assets other than land deteriorate in value and, as a result, the associated CAC needs to incorporate aspects of both *returns of* and *returns on* these assets. In addition, the Working Group believes that each technique should yield approximately the same aggregate CAC as it relates to the subject intangible asset when applied consistently. Finally, the Working Group has set forth these calculations assuming CACs are applied on an after-tax basis. Pre-tax presentations of these techniques should be considered equally acceptable presuming the appropriate adjustments to a pre-tax basis of presentation have been made.

3.4.02 The intent of applying a CAC is to provide a charge for the use of the appropriate level of fixed assets required to generate the revenue and earnings necessary to support the subject intangible asset in each year of the subject intangible asset's projection period. Acquired (or initial/current) fixed assets and future capital expenditures represent investments and cash charges at specific points in time. These investments in fixed assets have utility beyond the period of the cash charge as reflected by the capitalization and depreciation of these investments. CACs capture this future utility by replacing the cash charges with a series of charges over the economic life of the fixed asset, as represented by the required *returns of* and *returns on* the fair value of the necessary level of fixed assets. The present value of the series of charges in the aggregate should be equivalent to the investment such that no value is created or destroyed in the context of the entity as a whole.

3.4.03 Tax or accounting depreciation can be used in these techniques. In this document and the Comprehensive Example, tax depreciation has been used. Use of accounting depreciation as an option is addressed in the Practical Expedient. Care should be taken to make sure that all assumptions are consistent, whichever approach is used. Tax depreciation is a non-cash expense that decreases taxable income. As tax depreciation is added back to after-tax income to arrive at free cash flow, the net effect is to reflect the benefit of tax depreciation embedded in the fixed assets. Tax-effecting EBITDA has the impact of increasing taxes and removing the benefit of tax depreciation of the fixed assets. Alternatively, tax-effecting EBIT and adding back tax depreciation retains the benefit of tax depreciation in the projections. Although the Working Group is aware of techniques that tax-effect EBITDA, the calculations shown in the Comprehensive Example in Appendix A use tax-effected EBIT. By doing so, the benefit of tax depreciation, which is already reflected in the fair value of the fixed assets, is not double counted.

3.4.04 It is important to note that both Technique A and Technique B below rely on future estimates of fixed asset fair value balances. The valuation specialist should be careful to consider whether growth in fixed assets is required to achieve the estimates of future cash flows for the subject intangible asset as well as the entity and whether this growth occurs at the same rate as revenue growth or at a different rate. This consideration can be magnified by changes in fixed asset turnover for the entity as a whole, and reduced requirements for fixed assets at an individual subject intangible asset level.

3.4.05 A general description of the detailed version of each of the two most common techniques currently in practice is presented below. For purposes of this Monograph, the term "economic depreciation" is used to indicate the aggregate decline in value that occurs over the economic life of the asset. This term is used here in order to differentiate this concept from tax or accounting depreciation.[8]

3.4.06 Technique A: *"Average Annual Balance"*

3.4.07 The CAC is calculated based on two separate charges for the *return of* and *return on* the fair value of the fixed assets in each year of the projection. The *return of* for each year is equivalent to the sum of: a) annual economic depreciation for the fair value of the acquired or current fixed assets (adjusted to market participant levels) *and* b) annual economic depreciation for the projected market participant levels of capital expenditures required to support the entity's operations and the subject intangible asset over that asset's remaining useful life. The *return on* is derived by applying an appropriate after-tax rate of return consistent with the risk of an investment in the fixed assets. The *returns on* are calculated for each year of the projection based on the average balance of the required future estimated fixed assets at market participant levels. Typically, CACs for both the *returns of* and *returns on* are first calculated in aggregate for the entity and are then allocated across assets to which they contribute (based on a method such as relative annual revenue, discussed above). CACs are deductions that exclude capital expenditures (because the capital expenditures are replaced by and incorporated in the CAC for the fixed assets). The CACs are incorporated in the MPEEM in any given year as follows:

EBITDA
Less: Tax depreciation
EBIT (amortization assumed to be zero)
Less: Taxes
Debt free net income
Add: Tax depreciation
Less: *Return of* the fixed assets (economic
    depreciation of fair value)
Less: *Return on* the average balance of the
    fixed assets (at fair value)
Less: Other CACs (as necessary)
Equals: Excess earnings or cash flow

3.4.08 See Exhibit A-5 in Appendix A for an illustrative example of how to calculate a CAC for fixed assets using the average annual balance technique.

3.4.09 Deducting tax depreciation expense in calculating EBIT does not necessarily represent the *return of* the fixed asset investment because tax depreciation is not necessarily equivalent to economic depreciation in a given year. The Working Group recognizes that the sum of tax depreciation charges over the life of the fixed asset will be equivalent to the sum of the economic depreciation charges over the life of the fixed asset, presuming the tax basis of the fixed asset resets to fair value as of the date of valuation. The only difference would be that of timing. In practice, the *return of* the fixed assets is often assumed to be equivalent to the annual tax or accounting depreciation and is netted against the add back of depreciation and the CACs presented are thus limited to the *return on* the fixed assets. The Working Group recognizes that such a simplification may have an insignificant effect on the calculation of the fair value of a subject intangible asset, particularly when fixed assets represent a relatively insignificant proportion of the economic balance sheet of the entity.

3.4.10 Technique B: *"Level Payment"*

3.4.11 CACs are combined into one charge that takes into account both *return of* and *return on* the fair value of fixed assets. The principle behind this technique is that, in the application of the MPEEM, the cash flows associated with the subject intangible asset would need to be assessed a series of level annual payments for the use of the fixed assets required to produce the cash flows associated with the subject intangible asset. The level payment CAC calculation is applied to both the fair value of the acquired or current fixed assets *and* projected capital expenditures (adjusted to market participant levels). Just as in Technique A, the concept is that the required current and future fair values of fixed assets at market participant levels should serve as the basis for each year's CAC. Similar to Technique A, a CAC representing both the *returns of* and *returns on* is first calculated in aggregate and then applied in a prorated manner (such as that based on a percentage of revenue) to the revenues of the subject intangible asset. In Technique B, the CAC typically is calculated as a series of level annual payments based on a constant after-tax rate of return consistent with the risk for an investment in the fixed assets. Such payments can be calculated discretely for the acquired or current fixed assets and each projected annual capital expenditure (referred to herein as a "waterfall payment")

---

8.   The Working Group realizes that this use of the term is contrary to its common use regarding the factors of depreciation of tangible assets, which are described as including physical, functional, and economic obsolescence factors.

or some variation thereof that incorporates the annual beginning balance of the fixed assets and a weighted remaining useful life of each respective balance. The most precise manner to determine the CAC is to calculate an amount for each equivalent remaining useful life ("RUL") asset group (waterfall payment) for the acquired or current fixed assets and capital expenditures. Preparing calculations at this level results in outcomes that are essentially equivalent to those from Technique A. The CACs are incorporated in the MPEEM, in any given year, as follows:

EBITDA
Less: Tax depreciation
EBIT (amortization assumed to be zero)
Less: Taxes
Debt free net income
Add: Tax depreciation
Less: Level Payment CAC (*return of* and *on* the fixed assets, at fair value)
Less: Other CACs (as necessary)
Equals: Excess earnings or cash flow

3.4.12 See Exhibit A-6 in Appendix A for an illustrative example of how to calculate a CAC for fixed assets using the level payment technique.

3.4.13 Both techniques allow for the alignment of the entity value analysis with the asset fair values and demonstrate that the calculation of the CAC does not create or destroy aggregate asset value. The application of CACs is essentially an allocation of earnings to the contributory assets and, as such, should result in approximately the same aggregate earnings and asset values.

3.4.14 The Working Group is aware that certain practical expedients to both Technique A and Technique B have been used in practice. For instance, techniques have been observed that incorporate "smoothing" the annual CAC for fixed assets (and often for other asset categories as well) to a fixed percentage of revenue, which combines both the calculation of the CAC and the allocation (on a relative revenue basis) of the CAC to subject intangible assets into a single factor. Another variant of such techniques aggregates fixed assets into a single pool, rather than treating them as discrete "vintages" based on year of acquisition as is the case in both Technique A and Technique B. The Working Group recognizes that the use of such techniques may have an insignificant effect on the calculation of the fair value of a subject intangible asset, particularly when fixed assets represent a relatively insignificant proportion of the economic balance sheet of the entity. See Appendix B (Practical Expedient) for an illustrative example of calculating a CAC for fixed assets using a "smoothing" technique.

3.4.15 The Working Group believes that valuation specialists should be cautious in deciding whether to apply such practical expedients when fixed assets represent a significant proportion of an entity's economic balance sheet. Also, such calculations are particularly sensitive to RUL assumptions when aggregating fixed assets into a single pool rather than treating them as discrete "vintages" based on year of acquisition. Conceptually, the remaining life of a pool of fixed assets in a given year should be calculated as the weighted average of the RUL's of each "vintage." This assumption will likely vary from year to year, as existing fixed assets age, and new fixed assets are acquired. Precise estimates of an aggregate RUL are best extracted from applying either Technique A or Technique B, which would tend to counteract the time saving benefit of applying a practical expedient of this kind. Nonetheless, estimates of an aggregate annual RUL for a pool of fixed assets may be sufficient when the fixed asset balance is a relatively insignificant portion of the entity's economic balance sheet.

3.4.16 While the Working Group has applied these techniques on an after-tax basis in the example calculations, some believe that pre-tax calculations would more closely emulate an actual circumstance of renting or leasing assets, as rental or lease payments are deductible on a pre-tax basis. It is the Working Group's view that it does not matter whether these calculations are performed on a pre-tax or after-tax basis (since they are essentially subsets of the same methodologies) as long as the appropriate adjustments are made such that resulting value estimates are consistent, and value is neither created nor destroyed as a result of the technique selected. Terms such as "gross lease" or "gross rent" have been used to describe such pre-tax calculations. A sample "gross lease" calculation has been included in the Toolkit associated with this Monograph (see Foreword for additional description of the Toolkit). The Working Group has observed that CAC calculations are more commonly applied in practice on an after-tax basis and as a result has chosen an after-tax presentation as part of this Monograph.

3.5 Identified Intangible Assets and Contributory Elements of Goodwill (Including Assembled Workforce)

3.5.01 In calculating the CAC associated with contributory intangible assets, it is often assumed that the costs to maintain the value of a particular contributory intangible asset are considered a period expense (e.g., recruiting and training to replace people that leave and thereby maintain workforce value, sales and marketing expense to maintain customer relationship value when customer relationships are valued by a method other than MPEEM), and therefore these costs serve as a proxy for *return of* the investment in existing and future assets. While it may be theoretically correct to add back all expenses related to the maintenance of the contributory intangible assets to pre-tax cash flow and then take a true *return of* for a particular contributory intangible asset, there may be difficulty in estimating supportable costs to be added back. Expenses in the nature of identifiable growth investments might be an exception. Significant identifiable growth investments are analogous to incremental working capital and capital expenditures in excess of depreciation and should not be deducted (see Section 3.7 regarding assembled workforce).

3.5.02 It is the view of the Working Group that the common practice of assuming that costs to maintain and enhance intangible assets are part of the expense structure of the entity's business is an appropriate simplifying assumption (subject to the potential exception discussed above). Attempts to separate out expenses associated with maintaining or enhancing intangible assets, coupled with calculating an appropriate *return of* for a particular contributory intangible asset might be difficult in practice, because of the inherent challenge in isolating expenses that accurately match an appropriate *return of*. This common practice, however, should be supplemented by market participant research into appropriate expense levels for the aggregate entity and for the subject intangible asset to further support the use of the expense structure of the entity/ asset as a proxy for *return of,* when practical. Also, for entities that have grown through acquisition, valuation specialists should remove any amortization expense related to contributory intangible assets that could, in effect, "double count" the proxy for *return of.* Valuation specialists should be cautioned that,

in instances where the fair value of a contributory intangible asset is significantly different from a stream of foregone expenses, the use of the expense structure of an entity may not match an appropriate *return of* the fair value of the contributory intangible asset. The Working Group believes that in such an instance, an add back of expenses together with an appropriate calculation of the *return of,* based on fair value, would more accurately reflect the CAC associated with the contributory intangible asset.

3.5.03 The Working Group believes that an alternative approach to CACs for contributory intangible assets should be used when the contributory asset has been valued using a relief from royalty method. The relief from royalty method involves the estimation of an amount of hypothetical royalty savings enjoyed by the entity that owns the intangible asset because that entity is relieved from having to license that intangible asset from another owner. This same royalty rate should be used as a pre-tax charge in the calculation of earnings of the subject intangible asset because the use of a royalty savings method is viewed by the Working Group as a form of profit split. (Alternatively, the royalty rate could be converted to an after-tax rate and shown as an after-tax charge in the calculation of cash flow of the subject intangible asset, which would be a mathematically equivalent treatment.) A royalty rate should be analyzed to determine whether it compensates the licensor for all functions (ownership rights and responsibilities) associated with the asset. Such an analysis would include consideration of expenses recognized by the licensee versus expenses otherwise considered to be the responsibility of the licensor. A royalty rate that is "gross" would consider all functions associated with ownership of a licensed asset to reside with the licensor while a royalty rate that is "net" would consider some or all functions associated with the licensed asset to reside with the licensee.

3.5.04 The Working Group recognizes that there has been diversity in practice as to whether multiple subject intangible assets (which share the same revenue/cash flows) should be valued using an MPEEM and, if so, whether such analyses should reflect simultaneous cross charges between subject intangible assets. For example, both customer-related assets and technology assets have been observed in practice as being valued using this method with such cross charges reflecting an attempt to adjust for overlapping revenues/cash flows.

3.5.05 The Working Group strongly believes that the use of simultaneous application of the MPEEM with either single or multiple cross charges to multiple intangible assets that share the same revenue/cash flow is not best practice and should be avoided.

3.5.06 One alternative, when possible and supportable, for avoiding overlapping revenues/cash flows would be to "revenue/cash flow split" the PFI related to the multiple subject intangible assets such that their analyses are mutually exclusive. In such a case no one subject intangible asset should be charged for any other which has been subject to the revenue/cash flow split. Valuation specialists should be cautioned, however, against the use of arbitrary means by which they split revenues or cash flows. Thus, in performing a revenue or cash flow split, the valuation specialist may give consideration to factors such as the following as support for the split (this list is not intended to be exhaustive):

- a clearly delineated revenue split between assets,
- a rate of return analysis on marketing expenses versus research and development expenses,
- a projected revenue pattern associated with different generations of a product,
- the migration of relative product contributions between assets, or
- the relative contribution of core or base technologies as compared to applied technologies.

3.5.07 Another alternative is to value only one subject intangible asset using the MPEEM while any other subject intangible asset would be valued using an alternate method. Examples of these alternate methods are relief from royalty, cost approach, "with and without," and techniques that indicate a "synthetic" or "hypothetical" royalty (in which a portion of the earnings are identified that essentially represent a royalty payment, but without the use of royalty rate market data[9]). In this case, the asset valued using the MPEEM would be charged a royalty

as described above for the other asset(s) to the extent that the other asset(s) is (are) contributory or to the extent that the other asset's (assets') value(s) is (are) derived from overlapping revenues/cash flows.

3.6 Contributory Asset Charges in Future Periods (or Over Time)

3.6.01 The MPEEM, as a form of the income approach, relies on the PFI associated with the subject intangible asset. It is important that the valuation specialist understand that the composition of assets that generate cash flow associated with the PFI will change over time. For instance, fixed assets, technology and customer relationships that existed as of the valuation date will contribute a lesser amount to the PFI over time as these assets decay economically and are replaced by future assets. Therefore, the rate of replacement is a key assumption for the valuation specialist to consider. Further, the relative importance of the various types of assets (e.g. marketing vs. technology intangibles) may change over time impacting their relative contribution of earnings to the asset group's PFI in future periods. Valuation specialists should consider the contributions to cash flow of the various contributory assets (on a market participant basis) and charges for these assets should be estimated for each year in the projection period, rather than, for instance, automatically fixing such levels to amounts estimated at the valuation date. The Working Group does note that estimating the appropriate market participant level of contributory assets is highly dependent on facts and circumstances.

3.6.02 In calculating a CAC, the valuation specialist should consider whether each of the contributory assets used in the previous period CAC calculation remains relevant in the next period. There is diversity in practice as to what period CACs should be calculated when considering current versus future levels of intangible asset investment. It is the Working Group's position that, generally, CACs for the contributory intangible assets should be applied throughout the life of the subject intangible asset. This view is based on the premise that while the specific contributory intangible asset on hand as of

---

9. These techniques might include, among others, what has been referred to as a "quadrant" or "separation" technique, as discussed in Horvath, James L. and David W. Chodikoff. 2008. *Taxation and Valuation of Technology: Theory, Practice, and the Law*, and the subject of a recent presentation by Squires, Renton C., "Dual Primary Asset Valuation," Presentation at the American Society of Appraisers' Advanced Business Valuation Conference, Boston, October 20, 2009.

the valuation date may diminish over time, it will be supported, maintained, enhanced and/or replaced and, therefore, future levels of the contributory intangible asset will be present to contribute to the generation of cash flows. If a contributory intangible asset would not be maintained or replaced upon expiration, for example, in the case of a non-compete agreement arising from a transaction between a buyer and seller, the CAC would only be applied through the economic life of the contributory asset. Key to determining whether it is appropriate to continue to take a CAC on a particular asset or asset category is whether that type of asset continues to be necessary to support the earnings associated with the subject intangible asset.

3.6.03 The migration of the utilization of a contributory asset should not be confused with the economic deterioration in value of a contributory asset that was in place as of the valuation date. It may be assumed that the economic contribution of a certain type of contributory asset is maintained over the life of the subject intangible asset through investments to create the next generation(s) of the contributory asset. For example, an MPEEM analysis valuing customer relationships that shows no CACs for technology (that has been valued using a cost approach, for example) beyond the economic life of the existing developed technology overlooks the circumstance that new technology will most likely be developed and would be necessary to support the ongoing customer relationships. Note that, in such cases, the investment in creating the new technology beyond replacement of the existing technology (a growth investment) may need to be adjusted out to avoid double counting. (See discussion regarding pre-tax growth investments in Section 3.7.)

3.6.04 The Working Group notes that many contributory assets are valued using the relief from royalty method of the income approach. It is the Working Group's belief that if this method has been used to value a contributory asset, the appropriate corresponding method would be to perform a profit split by deducting a royalty from the cash flows of the subject intangible asset that is consistent with the royalty that was utilized to value the contributory asset. The valuation specialist should also consider whether the royalty would vary over time. Additionally, the valuation specialist should consider whether the derived royalty rate is all-inclusive of the

benefits and costs associated with the asset (see paragraph 3.5.03). If not, further analysis and adjustments may be necessary to reflect an appropriate royalty rate and expense structure.

3.6.05 In cases of business combinations, there may also be instances in which certain assets of the target (acquired) entity are being abandoned by the acquiring entity (reflective of market participants), but a CAC for that type of asset is still required. For example, the acquiring entity may plan to abandon the trade name of the acquired entity. However, the trade name of the acquiring entity would then be substituted in its place. When the abandoned asset is replaced by another asset (such as the acquiring entity's trade name) and is necessary to support the asset group's PFI, a CAC should still be included for this required contributory asset.

3.6.06 It should be noted that, for those situations above, the valuation specialist should also consider whether the contributory asset to be used or replaced in the future would have an economic return that varies over time. For example, the contribution to the earnings associated with a subject intangible asset by a particular contributory asset may increase over time. A trademark of an acquired entity being replaced by a stronger trademark (reflective of market participants) is an example of this situation. In such case, the PFI would need to reflect the potentially higher earnings caused by the use of a stronger trademark. As another example of such variability, the contribution to earnings by technology assets may initially be higher for early-stage technologies, but as customer relationships evolve over time, the technology asset's contribution to the PFI may decline relative to the contribution by the customer relationship asset. These changes could be reflected as a change in the royalty rate over time (based on market participant data).

3.6.07 In some circumstances, required levels of contributory assets will scale with revenues. Common examples of these are working capital, assembled workforce, and fixed assets. In these situations, the valuation specialist should understand if the contributory asset would grow at a rate equal to the rate of revenue growth or at a rate different from this rate of growth. Reference to market participant metrics such as asset turnover rate (in the case of working capital and fixed assets) may be helpful to the valuation specialist when making the determination.

See Appendix B, the Practical Expedient, for an illustrative example.

3.6.08 The stage of an entity in its life cycle (as viewed by a market participant) is important as the valuation specialist considers future contributory asset requirements. In many cases early stage companies may be experiencing rapid growth, which allows them to leverage existing assets more efficiently over time, as such, the level of contributory assets may decline as a percentage of revenue (in some cases this declining percentage may be offset through allocation of the aggregate CAC to current and future assets thereby effectively "smoothing" the CAC allocated to the subject intangible asset over time). Further, mature companies would expect to see relatively stable levels of assets in comparison to revenue. Finally, companies in decline may have assets that are no longer contributing to the cash flows associated with the subject intangible asset.

3.7 Special Adjustments for Growth Investments in Contributory Intangible Assets Valued Using the Cost Approach[10]

3.7.01 In the PFI for an entity, growth investments in net working capital and fixed assets are shown as "below the line" (after-tax) expenditures. In the application of the MPEEM, such expenditures are replaced with CACs on the "grown" value of the net working capital or fixed assets existing in each year of the PFI. Conceptually, the present value of the increment of the CAC relating to the growth investment should equal the amount of the growth investment.

3.7.02 In contrast, growth investments in the assembled workforce (and in other assets, at times) are pre-tax expenditures. Assuming the assembled workforce was valued based on pre-tax costs, the CACs on those growth investments are calculated at amounts that assume the value of the assembled workforce has grown by the same amount as the pre-tax expenditure. When it has a significant effect on the analysis, the growth investment in the assembled workforce should be differentiated from the maintenance expense, because the maintenance expense provides for the *return of* the contributory asset. See Exhibit A-7 in Appendix A for an illustrative example of the calculation of the CAC on the assembled workforce.

3.7.03 The application of the MPEEM should not create or destroy value when compared to the entity value. In order to a) accomplish this correct application, b) be consistent with the treatment of net working capital and fixed assets, and c) not double count the "costs" of the contributory assets in the valuation of a subject intangible asset (such as a customer relationship), it is necessary (when significant) in the application of the MPEEM to remove (add back) the growth investment in assembled workforce because it is being replaced with a CAC. The amount added back should be the increase in fair value. Assuming the acquired or current assembled workforce was valued based on pre-tax cost, the amount added back for the growth investment would be the pre-tax amount.

3.7.04 Although this add-back of the growth investment in assembled workforce is uncommon in current practice, in order to be precise, it is an adjustment that is required for the fair value of the total assets (net of non interest-bearing current liabilities) to balance with the entity fair value. The Working Group believes that this adjustment is typically insignificant and therefore unnecessary, but the valuation specialist should be alert for instances in which it is significant.

3.7.05 A further discussion of why this add-back should be calculated on a pre-tax basis is included in Appendix C.

4.0 The Stratification of Rates of Return by Asset or Asset Category

4.1 Introduction
4.1.01 A basic issue in the application of the MPEEM is what rate of return should be earned by each asset category including contributory assets. The fundamental premise is that the required rate of return should be commensurate with the relative risk associated with investment in each particular asset. However, there is a paucity of authoritative data on asset-specific returns. Therefore, valuation specialists must rely on what market evidence is available combined with judgment and tests of reasonableness based on considerations such as likely financing options. This Section will describe what the Working Group believes to be best practice.

4.1.02 While no specific empirical research or data on asset-specific returns was identified,

---

10. This section also applies to contributory assets valued using any other approach when the expenditure is viewed as a period expense.

there is some literature that addresses the topic of asset returns. One of the earlier and most often cited sources is the Internal Revenue Service ("IRS") Revenue Ruling 68-609. In this ruling, the IRS proposed that there is a hierarchy of returns for classes of assets with returns rising as one moves from fixed assets to intangible assets. Following on this same historical construct, the IPR&D Practice Aid[11] noted the expectation that high risk intangible assets, such as IPR&D projects, would exhibit returns that approached those required by venture capital investors in start-up ventures with the risk declining as the project neared completion (presuming use of the Discount Rate Adjustment Technique, see paragraph 4.2.08). Other references exist that relate to this topic.[12]

4.1.03 One reasonable proxy for risk (and related return) levels for specific assets within an entity is the level of debt financing that could be secured for that asset. The debt capacity for various classes of assets can vary widely over time based on current economic conditions and the availability of capital in the credit markets. Valuation specialists should seek information regarding debt capacity that is relevant to the date of valuation. As an example, Plewa (1985) cites guidelines for general loan to value ratios.[13]

4.1.04 Using relevant market data, valuation specialists can estimate the market participant cost of equity and cost of debt related to financing a particular type of asset. From that the valuation specialist can use market-based debt capacity ratios to develop the required return on specific classes of assets.

4.2 Rate of Return Selection

4.2.01 The concept underlying stratification of rates of return is that the required rate of *return on* a contributory asset should be estimated from market derived data reflecting the relative risk of that asset. The intuitive notion is that the perceived relative riskiness of assets reflects their liquidity/ease of transferability, their ability to be financed by debt or equity, as well as the degree of certainty of realizing future cash flows from the asset. For certain categories of assets, there are sources of data that can be used as support for the appropriate rate of return, such as working capital and fixed (tangible) assets (see following paragraphs regarding these asset types).

4.2.02 The risk profile of each asset category should be considered when estimating the appropriate rates of return. While there are exceptions, the Working Group believes that the risk profile of an entity's assets generally increases as you move down the balance sheet and, accordingly, the type of financing available for the assets shifts from debt to equity as the risk profile increases. For example, low risk assets such as working capital can usually be financed largely with debt and, as such, a short-term borrowing rate such as the prime rate often can be used to estimate the cost of debt component of the return requirement for this asset. On the other hand, the risk profile of intangible assets is often much higher and, as such, these assets are typically financed largely with equity.

4.2.03 Selection of an overall rate of return for the entity (the weighted average cost of capital, or WACC) is a necessary starting point prior to consideration of the stratification of the rates of return. Although it is common that the risk and return associated with the intangible assets of an entity tend to reflect risk and return levels of the overall entity, valuation specialists should be cautioned that "generic" contributory assets may exhibit costs of debt and equity that are independent of the entities that own them and would be more specific to the assets themselves. For example, contributory real estate owned by a high technology entity might not exhibit risk

---

11. AICPA Practice Aid Series, *"Assets Acquired in a Business Combination to Be Used in Research and Development Activities: A Focus on Software, Electronic Devices and Pharmaceutical Industries"*, 2001, Paragraphs 5.3.87 through 5.3.90.

12. See for example the following articles:

    Gooch, Lawrence B., ASA, "Capital Charges and the Valuation of Intangibles" *Business Valuation Review* March 1992: 5-21.

    Asbra, Marc, CFA. "Contributory Asset Charges in the Excess Earnings Method" *Valuation Strategies* March/April 2007: 4-17.

    Stegink, Rudolf, Marc Schauten, and Gijs de Graaff. "The Discount Rate for Discounted Cash Flow Valuations of Intangible Assets" March 2007.

    Grabowski, Roger, ASA and Lawrence B. Gooch, ASA, "Advanced Valuation Methods in Mergers & Acquisitions" *Mergers & Acquisitions,* Summer 1976: 15-29.

    Vulpiani, Marco. "Cost of Capital Estimation for Intangibles Valuation in Purchase Price Allocation," *Business Valuation Review*, Volume 27, Number 1, Spring, 2008.

13. Plewa, Franklin, Professor of Accounting at Idaho State and George Friedlob, Professor Clemson University, *Understanding Cash Flow*. 1985.

characteristics specific to the high technology industry, but instead would require equity and debt rates of return specific to real estate investments. Conversely, if the subject working capital or fixed assets are very risky or very specific to the entity (which may limit the liquidity of the assets due to the lack of a secondary market), the required *return on* these asset categories may be higher than otherwise indicated and should be based on the required returns for these types of assets prevalent in the industry.

4.2.04 Once the rates of return for the assets or asset categories are determined, they have three uses in the application of the MPEEM: a) application of CACs, b) returns on asset categories in the calculation of the weighted average return on assets ("WARA") (see paragraph 4.3.07), and c) the discount rate used to derive the present value of the cash flows attributable to the subject intangible asset. Additionally, if a discount rate is used to value an intangible asset, the Working Group believes that same rate should be used as the rate of *return on* that asset for CAC purposes and for calculating the WARA. Valuation specialists should take care to ensure that pre-tax rates have been appropriately adjusted to after-tax levels for use in computing after-tax CACs. See Section 4.3 for discussion of WACC and WARA.

4.2.05 *Working Capital* – The required *return on* working capital is typically considered to be at the lower end of returns of most, if not all, other asset classes and is assumed to be equal to the after-tax rate that would be charged to finance working capital. One common approach is to use the bank prime lending rate, adjusted for risk as needed. Another approach is to use rates associated with commercial paper, as these represent financing rates for corporations financing items such as accounts receivable or inventory. Another approach is to use rates associated with 30 to 90 day U.S. Treasury bills with consideration of additional risk factors that might slightly increase the rate of return. As noted earlier, the Working Group believes that these approaches could understate the required return since very few companies are able to borrow 100% of the value of working capital assets. The Working Group believes that a best practice, if it creates a significant difference, would be to consider the level of debt and equity financing required to fund working capital. When inventory has a limited specific market or when receivables are in a high default industry it may be appropriate to

adjust the various reference rates noted in this paragraph to reflect that additional risk.

4.2.06 *Fixed (Tangible) Assets* – The required *return on* fixed (tangible) assets may be estimated through rates of return that market participants would experience to finance similar assets. The rate of return should reflect the relative risk of the specific asset. Examples of rates of *return on* these fixed assets are the calculated after-tax interest rate based on a) observed rates charged by vendor financing, or b) bank debt that would be used to finance the specific fixed asset. If the asset cannot be financed with all debt (which is often the case) then the Working Group believes that use of a blended debt and equity rate would be representative of a best practice. As fixed assets become more risky (such as special purpose assets), it may be appropriate to adjust the various debt rates found in the marketplace.

4.2.07 *Intangible Assets* – The required rate of *return on* identified intangible assets may be estimated through the relative risk of the intangible assets compared to the entity's overall WACC. Typically intangible assets necessitate a higher rate of return than the WACC, due to the riskier and less liquid nature of intangible assets relative to working capital and fixed assets. Identified intangible assets and goodwill, in aggregate, usually have the highest required return of all the asset classes of an entity. Facts and circumstances will dictate the degree to which specific intangible assets require returns that are different from this aggregate asset class return. Circumstances can arise where the required *return on* an intangible asset is at or below the WACC, depending on the relative asset mix in the entity and the specific nature of the intangible assets. Backlog and short lived intangible assets such as a soon to be replaced developed technology are examples of intangible assets for which a lower required return may be appropriate. Since intangible assets are not typically financed with debt but with equity, the required rate of return for intangible assets is often highly correlated with equity rates of return.

4.2.08 *IPR&D Assets* – There is separate guidance related to the valuation of IPR&D assets. As outlined in the IPR&D Practice Aid, asset returns need to be determined based on the stage of completion of the IPR&D project and, in certain industries, will approximate venture capital returns for early stage development companies (to the extent that a discount rate adjustment technique is being used). The valuation specialist should consider the riskiness of the project and the typical returns in the industry, as not all development projects would yield high venture capital-like returns. The IPR&D Practice Aid also discusses FASB Statement of Financial Accounting Concepts No. 7 *Using Cash Flow Information and Present Value in Accounting Measurements* ("CON 7") which provides guidance for using present value techniques in financial accounting. CON 7 describes two theoretical techniques for using present value to estimate fair value. The two theoretical techniques described in CON 7 (as clarified in FASB ASC Topic 820) can be summarized as:

1. Discount Rate Adjustment Technique: This technique uses a single, most likely set of cash flows discounted at a rate which reflects the risk of eventually receiving those cash flows. In this technique the risk is incorporated in the development of the discount rate.

2. Expected Present Value Technique: This technique uses a set of cash flows that represents the probability weighted average of discreet scenarios and probabilities that capture the array of possible cash flows. The risk of receiving the cash flows is reflected in the selection of the probability factors and the discount rate used should be reflective of the expected rate of return associated with the probability-weighted cash flows (which may include a "cash risk premium").[14]

The Working Group notes both techniques may be theoretically acceptable for use in a discounted cash flow ("DCF") calculation under the MPEEM. However, when the discount rate used for a specific technique is derived in a fashion different from that for the other assets or for the entity as a whole, then diagnostics such as WACC to WARA comparisons may be difficult to apply and interpret (see Section 4.3 for discussion of such diagnostics).

4.2.09 *Goodwill (Excess Purchase Price)[15] and Other Elements of the Entity Not Recognized Separately* – These assets or elements consist generally of those for which future cash flows are expected that are not associated with otherwise separately identified assets. The uncertain nature of these prospective cash flows is commonly viewed as having incrementally more risk than separately identified assets. Therefore, the rate of return appropriate for this class of assets is commonly thought to be greater than that of the separately identified intangible asset with the next highest rate of return. The WARA analysis can be used as a diagnostic by setting the WARA equal to the calculated WACC and solving for the implied rate of *return on* goodwill rather than as a diagnostic that compares the calculated WACC to the calculated WARA. In this fashion, the valuation specialist can gauge the appropriateness of the returns on other assets by comparing them to the implied rate of return on goodwill (see Section 4.3 for additional discussion of these diagnostics).

4.2.10 While it is often the case that the goodwill component would be expected to earn the highest return, the Working Group believes that there are circumstances where returns on elements of goodwill will approach the calculated WACC. For example, an assembled workforce asset, an element of goodwill, is often assumed to earn a rate of return commensurate with the calculated WACC. The Working Group believes that the rate of return on elements of goodwill, including residual goodwill, will range from being the highest rate of return of all the assets to a rate approaching the calculated WACC. The rate of return on goodwill depends on the relative values of the other (identified) assets, their respective rates of return, and the nature of the risk inherent in the goodwill itself.

4.3 Issues Pertaining to WACC, IRR and WARA

4.3.01 The WACC is calculated as the *return on* the investment in the subject entity required by market participants, including both debt and equity investments. The WACC, based on the market participant's views (based on an assessment of guideline companies), includes the cost of equity and the after-tax cost of debt weighted by their respective proportions in the market participant's long-term view of the capital structure for the subject entity. The WACC that

---

14. FASB ASC paragraphs 820-10-55-4 through 820-10-55-20.

15. The Working Group recognizes that there is often a difference between the total amount of goodwill recorded as the result of an acquisition and the amount of goodwill (or "excess purchase price") that the valuation specialist is typically dealing with during the valuation. See paragraph 1.10, item C regarding this issue.

is initially derived from reference to guideline companies might need to be adjusted for specific facts and circumstances surrounding the entity whose assets are to be valued, but only if those facts and circumstances are consistent with long-term market participant views. For example, the subject entity may be smaller or less diversified or have higher cash flow growth than the pool of available guideline companies referenced in developing a market-derived WACC. It is assumed that market participants would reflect these characteristics in their risk assessment and the WACC would need to be adjusted accordingly. As applied to equity returns, such risk premiums are often referred to as being "unsystematic" adjustments. The Working Group's view, however, is that such risk premiums primarily represent adjustments to systematic risk resulting from a lack of comparability. Either way, judgment must be used regarding adjustments to the WACC for such factors. The Working Group refers readers to existing financial and valuation literature regarding models for developing the appropriate rates of return for equity and debt.

4.3.02 A detailed discussion of the identification of market participants is contained in the text of FASB ASC Topic 820 and is not repeated here. It should be noted that market participants are not always the same as the guideline companies. The Working Group does caution that when performing an MPEEM the valuation specialist must not confuse a market participant's view of the risk of the subject entity with a market participant's own overall risk. Nor should it be assumed that the market participant view of the risk of the subject entity matches the risk of an investment in an identified group of guideline companies before determining that such a group represents a reasonable proxy for the market participant view.

4.3.03 At times, in a transaction, the actual price paid might differ from the fair value of the acquired entity. While the purchase price is often the best indication of fair value, the valuation specialist needs to be alert for circumstances when this is not the case and there is evidence of over payment (if detectable and quantifiable)[16] or under payment (bargain purchase). The following paragraphs elaborate on this issue. The actual price paid is referred to as the "purchase price," where necessary, to differentiate it from the fair value of the acquired entity.

4.3.04 An implied internal rate of return ("IRR"), simply stated, is the compounded rate of return indicated to be earned on an investment. It is the rate that equates the amount or value of an investment and the present value of the cash flows assumed to be earned on that investment. For the purposes of this document, the IRR in a transaction is the discount rate at which the present value of the PFI of the acquired entity (adjusted if necessary for market participant assumptions) is equal to the purchase price (adjusted if necessary as noted in paragraph 4.3.03). Because of potential adjustments to the purchase price and to the PFI, the valuation specialist's IRR may not be consistent with management's internal assumptions.

4.3.05 The IRR for an acquisition (based on an adjusted PFI and/or adjusted purchase price, when necessary) should be compared for consistency to the WACC which is derived based on views of market participants. Both the WACC and IRR should reasonably reflect the perceived risk of achieving the PFI (adjusted if necessary for market participant assumptions). An IRR that is significantly different from the WACC may require a reassessment of the purchase price (actual or adjusted), the PFI, and the WACC (see paragraph 4.3.11 for further discussion).

4.3.06 Calculation of an IRR is relatively straightforward in an acquisition scenario. In other types of valuations when there is no purchase price to serve as a starting point, if the fair value of the entity is determined using multiple valuation methods, an IRR may be calculated using the PFI and the concluded fair value of the entity based on reconciliation of the valuation methods.

4.3.07 With the reconciliation of the WACC and IRR complete and the stratification of rates of return for the assets established, the Working Group believes that best practice would indicate an analysis of the WARA. In essence, the comparison of the WACC to the WARA is a diagnostic that assists the valuation specialist in reconciling the rates of return required by providers of capital (the WACC) with rates of return earned by various classes of assets (the WARA). Thus, the WARA calculation assists in assessing

---

16. Note that the original text of FASB Statement No. 141(R), Paragraph B382 indicates that, due to problems of identifying and reliably measuring an overpayment at the acquisition date, overpayments are best addressed through subsequent impairment testing.

the reasonableness of the asset-specific returns for identified intangible assets and the implied (or calculated) *return on* goodwill.[17] The WARA is calculated as the sum of the required rates of return for normalized working capital, fixed assets, and intangible assets, weighted by each asset's proportionate share of the total value of the entity (where "total value of the entity" means the combined value of debt and equity investment required in the subject entity adjusted to reflect a taxable purchase – see paragraph 4.3.08). A WARA that remains significantly different from the WACC may require a reassessment of both the asset values (or levels of assets) and the assumed returns on those assets to determine if they represent market participant assumptions.

4.3.08 The Working Group also notes that many transactions are "non-taxable" and management's PFI may not reflect the tax benefit (of amortization or depreciation) implicit in the fair value of underlying assets. In a business combination structured as a taxable purchase, the PFI and purchase price are likely to reflect the tax benefits. However, in the case of a deal structured as a non-taxable purchase, the Working Group recommends temporarily adjusting the purchase price for use in the WARA analysis. Because the individual asset values include the tax benefit of amortization and increased depreciation, the entity value must also be increased for comparison purposes. The Working Group believes the most straightforward adjustment technique is to calculate the additional tax benefit as if the deal had been structured as a taxable purchase and add it to the purchase price (see Exhibit A-10 in the Comprehensive Example). This adjustment would be necessary to ensure consistency in the WARA analysis, since the fair values of depreciable/amortizable assets would incorporate a proportional share of the tax benefit regardless of the structure of the deal itself (see paragraph 3.1.08).

4.3.09 When performing the WARA calculation, it is important to remember that the asset values used to calculate the WARA need to represent normal operating levels required to sustain the value of the entity. In other words, all non-operating assets and liabilities are excluded from the WARA calculation (both from the individual assets included and from the purchase price

used in the calculation). For example, a non-operating asset such as excess cash is excluded, and the WARA calculation reflects only normal levels of working capital for the entity (based on market participant perspectives).

4.3.10 The WACC, WARA, and IRR (fully adjusted) all should be calculated and, when applicable, compared and contrasted when using the MPEEM as discussed previously. The Working Group believes that the starting point for an analysis would be the derived market-based WACC for the acquired (or subject) entity. As stated above, this WACC is based on market participant assumptions specific to the entity's cash flows. One diagnostic test would be to compare the WACC to the IRR and reconcile any differences. Another diagnostic test would be to compare the WACC/IRR to the WARA to assess the reasonableness of the stratification of rates of return (as discussed in Section 4.2).

4.3.11 When the WACC, WARA and IRR do not easily reconcile, the valuation specialist will need to review the assumptions in the PFI to determine if they reflect market participant assumptions or if they may have acquirer-specific synergies or other assumptions imbedded in the projections. If the PFI is determined to reflect market participant assumptions, and no acquirer-specific synergies are included, and the WACC, WARA and IRR still do not reconcile, the Working Group recommends that the valuation specialist undertake additional procedures. These would include, but are not limited to, the performance of sensitivity analyses, the rechecking of inputs to both PFI and to WACC calculations, and the undertaking of a search for qualitative factors that would support the existence of either over-payments or bargain purchase conditions.

5.0 Summary

5.1 Intangible assets are often valued using an income approach. Within the income approach, the MPEEM has arisen as a commonly applied methodology in the valuation of intangible assets.

5.2 The MPEEM is an attribution model in which a stream of revenue and expenses are associated with a particular group of assets that are all necessary to support earnings associated with a particular subject intangible asset. The

---

17. Refer to Toolkit for alternative reconciliation calculations.

assets in this group other than the subject intangible asset are considered contributory assets. Through application of the MPEEM, earnings attributable to the contributory assets (in the form of *returns on,* and sometimes *returns of,* those assets) are deducted from the earnings stream so that what remains are the excess earnings attributable to the subject intangible asset. The excess earnings are discounted to present value to derive the fair value of the subject intangible asset. All assumptions required in application of the MPEEM are to reflect market participant assumptions.

5.3 Contributory assets are defined as assets that are used in conjunction with the subject intangible asset in the realization of prospective cash flows associated with the subject intangible asset. Assets that do not contribute to the prospective cash flows associated with the subject intangible asset are not contributory assets.

5.4 The types of asset categories required to support the cash flows associated with a subject intangible asset are based on the facts and circumstances of the entity and the subject intangible asset (from a market participant perspective) and may be the components of working capital, fixed (tangible) assets, and/or intangible assets. Care must be taken in determining which assets are contributory assets, what level of those contributory assets would be considered necessary to support the earnings associated with the subject intangible asset, and how that level might change over time, all from the perspective of market participants.

5.5 Once the level of contributory assets is determined, charges for the use of those assets by the subject intangible asset, or *returns on* those contributory assets (CACs), must be determined. Rates of return on the various contributory assets (and the resulting CACs) generally reflect the relative riskiness of those assets. In the end, the WACC, IRR, and WARA must be reconciled.

5.6 The application of CACs is essentially an allocation of earnings to the contributory assets. As such, the methodology applied should result in approximately the same aggregate earnings and asset values. The application of CACs, as either an earnings allocation or an economic charge, should not create or destroy value.

5.7 Many implementation issues arise in identifying contributory assets, calculating CACs, and

associating rates of return with particular assets. This document seeks to highlight these issues and set forth the Working Group's view of best practices. The Working Group notes that professional judgment is necessary in the valuation of any asset and that the purpose of this document is to assist in reducing diversity of practice in the specific topics addressed by the Monograph. It is the goal of the Working Group that the guidance set forth in this Monograph, combined with the application of professional judgment, will result in measurements of fair value that represent the highest level of professional practice and that are consistent with the goals of fair value measurement for financial reporting.

6.0 List of Acronyms Used

CAC	Contributory Asset Charge
EBIT	Earnings Before Interest & Taxes
EBITDA	Earnings Before Interest, Taxes, Depreciation & Amortization
IPR&D	In-Process Research & Development
IRR	Implied Internal Rate of Return
IRS	Internal Revenue Service
MPEEM	Multi-Period Excess Earnings Method
PFI	Prospective Financial Information
ROI	Return on Investment
RUL	Remaining Useful Life
WACC	Weighted Average Cost of Capital
WARA	Weighted Average Rate of Return on Assets

7.0 References

AICPA Practice Aid Series, *"Assets Acquired in a Business Combination to Be Used in Research and Development Activities: A Focus on Software, Electronic Devices and Pharmaceutical Industries"*

AICPA, "Bibliography of Publications and Web Site Sources in Connection with FASB Statements No. 141 and No. 142"

Appeals and Review Memorandum Number 34 (ARM 34)

Asbra, Marc, CFA. "Contributory Asset Charges in the Excess Earnings Method" *Valuation Strategies* March/April 2007: 4-17

Financial Accounting Standards Board *Accounting Standards Codification Topic 805, Business Combinations* (Previously Financial Accounting Standards Board, Financial Accounting Series, *"Statement of Financial Accounting Standards No. 141 (Revised 2007) – Business Combinations"*)

Financial Accounting Standards Board *Accounting Standards Codification Topic 820, Fair Value Measurements* (Previously Financial Accounting Standards Board, Financial Accounting Series, *"Statement of Financial Accounting Standards No. 157 – Fair Value Measurements"*)

Gooch, Lawrence B., ASA, "Capital Charges and the Valuation of Intangibles" *Business Valuation Review* March 1992: 5-21

Grabowski, Roger, ASA and Lawrence B. Gooch, ASA, "Advanced Valuation Methods in Mergers & Acquisitions" *Mergers & Acquisitions,* Summer 1976: 15-29

Hitchner, J. R. 2006. *Financial Valuation.* 2nd ed. New Jersey: Wiley

Horvath, James L. and David W. Chodikoff. 2008. *Taxation and Valuation of Technology: Theory, Practice, and the Law.* Irwin Law (Canada)

Internal Revenue Service Revenue Ruling 68-609, 1968-2 C.B. 327

International Glossary of Business Valuation Terms as adopted by the following professional societies and organizations:

- American Institute of Certified Public Accountants
- American Society of Appraisers
- National Association of Certified Valuation Analysts
- The Canadian Institute of Chartered Business Valuators
- The Institute of Business Appraisers

King, A.M. 2006. *Fair Value for Financial Reporting.* New Jersey: Wiley, 115

Mard, M.J., J. R. Hitchner, and S.D. Hyden. 2007. *Valuation for Financial Reporting.* 2nd ed. (New Jersey: Wiley)

Plewa, Franklin, Professor of Accounting at Idaho State and George Friedlob, Professor Clemson University, *Understanding Cash Flow.* 1985

Pratt, Shannon P., and Roger J. Grabowski. 2008. *Cost of Capital.* 3rd ed. New Jersey: Wiley

Reilly, R.F., and R.P. Schweihs. 1998. *Valuing Intangible Assets.* USA: McGraw-Hill

Smith, R.H., and R.L. Parr. 2005. *Intellectual Property: Valuation, Exploitation and Infringement Damages.* New Jersey: Wiley

Squires, Renton C., "Dual Primary Asset Valuation," Presentation at the American Society of Appraisers' Advanced Business Valuation Conference, Boston, October 20, 2009

Steginx, Rudolf, Marc Schauten, and Gijs de Graaff. "The Discount Rate for Discounted Cash Flow Valuations of Intangible Assets" March 2007

Vulpiani, Marco. "Cost of Capital Estimation for Intangibles Valuation in Purchase Price Allocation," *Business Valuation Review,* Volume 27, Number 1, Spring, 2008

8.0 Glossary

8.1 Glossary of Terms

Business Enterprise

A commercial, industrial, service, or investment entity (or combination thereof) pursuing an economic activity.
[Source: International Glossary of Business Valuation Terms]

Capital Charge

A fair return on an entity's *contributory assets,* which are tangible and intangible assets used in the production of income or cash flow associated with an intangible asset being valued. In this context, *income or cash flow* refers to an applicable measure of income or cash flow, such as net income, or operating cash flow before taxes and capital expenditures. A capital charge may be expressed as a percentage return on [sic][18] an economic rent associated with, or a profit split related to, the contributory assets.
[Source: AICPA Statement on Standards for Valuation Services, Appendix C, Glossary of Additional Terms]

Contributory Asset Charge (CAC)

See Capital Charge.

Cost Approach

A general way of determining a value indication of an individual asset by quantifying the amount of money required to replace the future service capability of that asset.
[Source: International Glossary of Business Valuation Terms]

---

18. The word "or" would be more appropriate.

Discount Rate Adjustment Technique

The discount rate adjustment technique uses a single set of cash flows from the range of possible estimated amounts, whether contractual or promised (as is the case for a bond) or most likely cash flows. In all cases, those cash flows are conditional upon the occurrence of specified events (for example, contractual or promised cash flows for a bond are conditional on the event of no default by the debtor). The discount rate used in the discount rate adjustment technique is derived from observed rates of return for comparable assets or liabilities that are traded in the market. Accordingly, the contractual, promised, ore most likely cash flows are discounted at a rate that corresponds to an observed market rate associated with such conditional cash flows (market rate of return). [Source: FASB ASC paragraphs 820-10-55-4 through 820-10-55-20 (Formerly Statement of Financial Accounting Standards No. 157, Appendix B)]

Economic Life

The period of time over which property may generate economic benefits.
[Source: International Glossary of Business Valuation Terms]

Fair Value (FV)

Fair value is the price that would be received to sell an asset or paid to transfer a liability in an orderly transaction between market participants at the measurement date.
[Source: Financial Accounting Standards Board *Accounting Standards Codification Topic 820, Fair Value Measurements* (formerly Statement of Financial Accounting Standards No. 157)]

Fixed Asset

Assets with a physical manifestation. Examples include land and buildings, plant and machinery, fixtures and fittings, tools and equipment, and assets in the course of construction and development.
[Source: International Valuation Standards, 7th Ed]

Goodwill

An asset representing the future economic benefits arising from other assets acquired in a business combination that are not individually identified and separately recognized.
[Source: Financial Accounting Standards Board *Accounting Standards Codification Topic 805, Business Combinations* (formerly Statement of Financial Accounting Standards No. 141 (Revised 2007))]

Going Concern

An ongoing operating business enterprise.
[Source: International Glossary of Business Valuation Terms]

In-Process Research and Development (IPR&D)

Research and development project that has not yet been completed. Acquired IPR&D is a subset of an intangible asset to be used in R&D activities.
[Source: AICPA Practice Aid – *Assets Acquired in a Business Combination to Be Used in Research and Development Activities: A Focus on Software, Electronic Devices, and Pharmaceutical Industries*, 2001, Appendix A, Glossary of Terms]

Income (Income-Based) Approach

A general way of determining a value indication of a business, business ownership interest, security, or intangible asset using one or more methods that convert anticipated economic benefits into a present single amount.
[Source: International Glossary of Business Valuation Terms]

Intangible Assets

Nonphysical assets such as franchises, trademarks, patents, copyrights, goodwill, equities, mineral rights, securities and contracts (as distinguished from physical assets), that grant rights and privileges, and have value for the owner.
[Source: International Glossary of Business Valuation Terms]

Internal Rate of Return (IRR)

A discount rate at which the present value of the future cash flows of the investment equals the cost of the investment.
[Source: International Glossary of Business Valuation Terms]

Invested Capital

The sum of equity and debt in a Business Enterprise. Debt is typically a) all interest bearing debt or b) long-term interest-bearing debt. When the term is used, it should be supplemented by a specific definition in the given valuation context.
[Source: International Glossary of Business Valuation Terms]

Market Participant

Market participants are buyers and sellers in the principal (or most advantageous) market for the asset or liability that are:
a.   Independent of the reporting entity; that is, they are not related parties

b. Knowledgeable, having a reasonable understanding about the asset or liability and the transaction based on all available information, including information that might be obtained through due diligence efforts that are usual and customary

c. Able to transact for the asset or liability

d. Willing to transact for the asset or liability; that is, they are motivated but not forced or otherwise compelled to do so.

[Source: Financial Accounting Standards Board *Accounting Standards Codification Topic 820, Fair Value Measurements* (formerly Statement of Financial Accounting Standards No. 157)]

Market (Market-Based) Approach

A general way of determining a value indication of a business, business ownership interest, security, or intangible asset by using one or more methods that compare the subject to similar businesses, business ownership interests, securities, or intangible assets that have been sold.

[Source: International Glossary of Business Valuation Terms]

Multi-Period Excess Earnings Method (MPEEM)

A specific application of the discounted cash flow method, which is more broadly a form of the income approach. The most common method used to estimate the fair value of an intangible asset.

[Source: AICPA Practice Aid – *Assets Acquired in a Business Combination to Be Used in Research and Development Activities: A Focus on Software, Electronic Devices, and Pharmaceutical Industries,* 2001, Appendix A, Glossary of Terms]

Prospective Financial Information (PFI)

A forecast of expected future cash flows.

[Source: AICPA Practice Aid – *Assets Acquired in a Business Combination to Be Used in Research and Development Activities: A Focus on Software, Electronic Devices, and Pharmaceutical Industries,* 2001, paragraph 5.2.07]

Rate of Return

An amount of income (loss) and/or change in value realized or anticipated on an investment, expressed as a percentage of that investment

[Source: International Glossary of Business Valuation Terms]

Relief From Royalty Method

A valuation method used to value certain intangible assets (for example, trademarks and trade names) based on the premise that the only value that a purchaser of the assets receives is the exemption from paying a royalty for its use. Application of this method usually involves estimating the fair market value of an intangible asset by quantifying the present value of the stream of market-derived royalty payments that the owner of the intangible asset is exempted from or "relieved" from paying.

[Source: AICPA Statement on Standards for Valuation Services, Appendix C, Glossary of Additional Terms]

Weighted Average Cost of Capital (WACC)

The cost of capital (discount rate) determined by the weighted average, at market value, of the cost of all financing sources in the business enterprise's capital structure.

[Source: International Glossary of Business Valuation Terms]

8.2 Glossary of Entities Referred to in Document

American Institute of Certified Public Accountants (AICPA)

The national, professional organization for Certified Public Accountants in the US. Provides members with resources, information, certification, and licensing. Established in 1887.

[Source: Derived from the AICPA's website, www.aicpa.org]

Financial Accounting Standards Board (FASB)

The designated organization in the private sector for establishing standards of financial accounting and reporting. Those standards govern the preparation of financial reports and are officially recognized as authoritative by the SEC and AICPA.

[Source: Derived from the FASB's website, www.fasb.org]

Internal Revenue Service (IRS)

A bureau of the Department of the Treasury organized to carry out the responsibilities of the secretary of the Treasury to enforce the internal revenue laws.

[Source: Derived from the IRS's website, www.irs.gov]

Appendix A: Comprehensive Example

The Working Group prepared this comprehensive example to further illustrate the concepts and best practices introduced in the discussion document.

Comprehensive Example

IMPORTANT NOTE: These sample calculations are for demonstration purposes only and are not intended as the only form of model or calculation, or final report exhibit, that is acceptable. In some cases, these calculations include details to demonstrate a point made in the Monograph and would not be expected in a typical analysis.

This Comprehensive Example demonstrates the concepts put forth in this document and applies them in a comprehensive manner to derive the fair value of customer relationships (as a sample asset) based on the application of the MPEEM. The contributory assets included in this example are as follows:

- Working Capital
- Fixed Assets (Techniques A&B)
- Assembled Workforce
- Trade Name*
- Intellectual Property*

The required rate of return on each asset should be commensurate with the relative risk associated with investment in that particular asset. For additional discussion, refer to Section 4 of the Monograph.

Acronyms

The following acronyms are used in the Appendices:

AWF	Assembled Workforce
DFCF	Debt Free Cash Flow
EBIT	Earnings Before Interest and Taxes
EBITDA	Earnings Before Interest, Taxes, Depreciation, and Amortization
FV	Fair Value
IP	Intellectual Property
IRR	Implied Internal Rate of Return
IRS	Internal Revenue Service
PFI	Prospective Financial Information
PV	Present Value
R&D	Research and Development
TAB	Tax Amortization Benefit
WACC	Weighted Average Cost of Capital

---

* These assets contribute to the revenue stream used in valuation of the customer relationships. However, because they are valued by use of the relief from royalty method, this is considered a profit split and contributory asset charges are not applied.

This example assumes that all potential entity-specific synergies and related value have been extracted from the PFI and the purchase price. Based on the market participant PFI and purchase price of $4,746, the IRR of the transaction is calculated to be 10%. In addition, a market-based WACC of 10% is estimated, which reconciles to the IRR. This example reflects a non-taxable transaction.

		Year 1	Year 2	Year 3	Year 4	Year 5	Year 6	Year 7	Year 8	Year 9	Year 10	Residual
Revenue		$ 1,000	$ 1,050	$ 1,165	$ 1,306	$ 1,456	$ 1,596	$ 1,718	$ 1,823	$ 1,907	$ 1,976	$ 2,035
Gross Profit	90%	900	945	1,049	1,175	1,310	1,436	1,546	1,641	1,716	1,778	1,832
Operating Expenses:												
Maintenance R&D (2)	0.5%	5	5	6	7	7	8	9	9	10	10	10
R&D - Future IP (3)	2.5%	25	26	29	33	36	40	43	46	48	49	51
Trade name advertising (4)	0.5%	5	5	6	7	7	8	9	9	10	10	10
Current customer marketing (5)	3%	27	26	23	18	13	8	4	2	1	-	-
Future customer marketing (6)		18	22	29	40	53	64	73	80	84	89	92
Total marketing	5%	50	53	58	65	73	80	86	91	95	99	102
Total G&A	7%	70	74	82	91	102	112	120	128	133	138	142
Total Operating Expenses	15%	150	158	175	196	218	240	258	274	286	296	305
EBITDA		750	787	874	979	1,092	1,196	1,288	1,367	1,430	1,482	1,527
Depreciation (7)		286	302	337	377	412	451	478	513	540	562	581
Amortization (8)		-	-	-	-	-	-	-	-	-	-	-
EBIT		464	485	537	602	680	745	810	854	890	920	946
Taxes	40%	186	194	215	241	272	298	324	342	356	368	378
Debt Free Net Income		278	291	322	361	408	447	486	512	534	552	568
less: Incremental Working Capital (9)	30%	15	15	35	42	45	42	37	32	25	21	18
add: Depreciation (10)		286	302	337	377	412	451	478	513	540	562	581
less: Capital Expenditures		286	400	450	500	525	541	557	574	591	609	627
Debt Free Cash Flow		263	178	174	196	250	315	370	419	458	484	504
Residual Value (11)												7,200
PV Factor (12)	10%	0.9535	0.8668	0.7880	0.7164	0.6512	0.5920	0.5382	0.4893	0.4448	0.4044	0.4044
PV DFCF		251	154	137	140	163	186	199	205	204	196	2,911
Entity Value		4,746										

(1) Entity Value projections based on market participant assumptions. Excludes entity-specific synergies.
(2) Maintenance R&D applicable to both current and future IP.
(3) R&D expense for the development of future IP.
(4) Advertising expense related to the trade name.
(5) Maintenance marketing expenses specific to current recognizable customer relationships with following revenue (Exhibit A-8 footnote 1):

	Year 1	Year 2	Year 3	Year 4	Year 5	Year 6	Year 7	Year 8	Year 9	Year 10
Customer relationship revenue	900	855	770	616	431	259	130	65	33	-

(6) Marketing expenses related to creating and maintaining unrecognized and future customer relationships.
(7) 7-MACRS tax depreciation based on carry-over tax basis of $745 and projected capital expenditures. For a detailed calculation see Exhibit A-2 of the Toolkit.
(8) Tax basis of intangible assets is zero.
(9) Represents 30% of incremental revenue. A beginning working capital balance of $285 is based on Year 0 revenue of $950.
(10) The residual year difference in depreciation and capital expenditures recognizes the long term growth in the business and the depreciation lag relative to capital expenditures.
(11) Based on constant growth model assuming a 3% long-term growth rate.
(12) The market participant based IRR is equivalent to the WACC of 10%. The mid-period convention is applied.

This exhibit summarizes the tax depreciation calculations based on the $1,000 fair value of the fixed assets and 7-year MACRS depreciation. Because CACs related to fixed assets are based on their fair value (which includes the tax benefit of depreciation), the depreciation reflected in the PFI is restated to reflect the fair value of the fixed assets. These projected depreciation amounts are reflected in Exhibit A-3.

Depreciation Of:		Year 1	Year 2	Year 3	Year 4	Year 5	Year 6	Year 7	Year 8	Year 9	Year 10	Residual
FV of Acquired or Current Fixed Assets	$	143	$ 245	$ 175	$ 125	$ 89	$ 89	$ 89	$ 45			
Capital Expenditures		41	127	212	287	352	411	468	513	540	562	581
Total Tax Depreciation		184	372	387	412	441	500	557	558	540	562	581

(1) 7-Year MACRS applied to the fair value of the fixed assets and projected capital expenditures.

	Year 1	Year 2	Year 3	Year 4	Year 5	Year 6	Year 7	Year 8
MACRS Percentages	14.29%	24.49%	17.49%	12.49%	8.93%	8.92%	8.93%	4.46%

The PFI in this Exhibit is adjusted to reflect the tax benefits that would result from a restatement of the tax basis of certain of the assets to fair value. The tax benefit inherent in the fair value of an asset is not reflected in the PFI of a non-taxable transaction. For example, the step-up in fixed assets or the fair value of an assembled workforce are not reflected in the entity's tax basis and the PFI for the transaction excludes this benefit. In order to maintain consistency between the PFI to be used in valuing the customer relationships and the fair value of the assets to which a CAC will be applied, the PFI should be adjusted to include the cash flow benefits of the increase in the tax basis of the contributory assets. The Working Group believes that the fair value of an intangible asset should not differ depending on the tax structure of a particular transaction. For additional discussion on the applicability of TABs see paragraphs 3.1.08 and 4.3.08 in this Monograph and paragraphs 5.3.9 - 5.3.108 in the 2001 AICPA IPR&D Practice Aid.

When the PFI is adjusted to include the additional cash flow benefit embedded in the fair value of the contributory assets, this results in an Adjusted Entity Value that is greater than the Entity Value by an amount equal to the present value of the tax benefits related to the increase in tax basis. The Entity Value is recalculated at the WACC/IRR of 10% to arrive at the Adjusted Entity Value of $4,855. This increase of $109 is equivalent to the present value of the incremental tax benefit related to the step-up in the fixed assets and the assembled workforce. This Adjusted Entity Value is used only for reconciliation at this phase of the analysis.

The Working Group recognizes that these adjustments might not be significant to the analysis and may be excluded based on the judgment of the valuation specialist.

		Year 1	Year 2	Year 3	Year 4	Year 5	Year 6	Year 7	Year 8	Year 9	Year 10	Residual
Revenue		$ 1,000	$ 1,050	$ 1,165	$ 1,306	$ 1,456	$ 1,596	$ 1,718	$ 1,823	$ 1,907	$ 1,976	$ 2,035
Gross Profit	90%	900	945	1,049	1,175	1,310	1,436	1,546	1,641	1,716	1,778	1,832
Operating Expenses:												
Maintenance R&D	0.5%	5	5	6	7	7	8	9	9	10	10	10
R&D - Future IP	2.5%	25	26	29	33	36	40	43	46	48	49	51
Trade name advertising	0.5%	5	5	6	7	7	8	9	9	10	10	10
Current customer marketing	3%	27	26	23	18	13	8	4	2	1	-	-
Future customer marketing		18	22	29	40	53	64	73	80	84	89	92
Total marketing	5%	50	53	58	65	73	80	86	91	95	99	102
Total G&A	7%	70	74	82	91	102	112	120	128	133	138	142
Total Operating Expenses	15%	150	158	175	196	218	240	258	274	286	296	305
EBITDA		750	787	874	979	1,092	1,196	1,288	1,367	1,430	1,482	1,527
Depreciation (1)		184	372	387	412	441	500	557	558	540	562	581
Amortization - AWF (2)		20	20	20	20	20	20	20	20	20	20	-
EBIT		546	395	467	547	631	676	711	789	870	900	946
Taxes	40%	218	158	187	219	252	270	284	316	348	360	378
Debt Free Net Income		328	237	280	328	379	406	427	473	522	540	568
less: Incremental Working Capital	30%	15	15	35	42	45	42	37	32	25	21	18
add: Depreciation (1)		184	372	387	412	441	500	557	558	540	562	581
Amortization - AWF (2)		20	20	20	20	20	20	20	20	20	20	
less: Capital Expenditures		286	400	450	500	525	541	557	574	591	609	627
Debt Free Cash Flow		231	214	202	218	270	343	410	445	466	492	504
Residual Value												7,200
PV Factor (3)	10%	0.9535	0.8668	0.7880	0.7164	0.6512	0.5920	0.5382	0.4893	0.4448	0.4044	0.4044
PV DFCF		220	185	159	156	176	203	221	218	207	199	2,911
Adjusted Entity Value (4)		4,855										

(1) Tax depreciation pursuant to Exhibit A-2 to reflect the fair value of the fixed assets.

(2) Reflects the amortization of the AWF. For purposes of this example the amortization period for the AWF is assumed to be 10 years rather than 15 years as is required in the U.S. under IRS Code Section 197. 10 years is applied for demonstration purposes as the projections presented are 10 years in length. Tax benefits related to the future replacement of, or increase in, the AWF are reflected in the operating expenses and no adjustment is required other than for the initial fair value.

(3) The WACC remains at 10%.

(4) The Adjusted Entity Value increase over the Entity Value is due solely to the incremental tax benefits. This Adjusted Entity Value is used only for reconciliation purposes.

The Identification of Contributory Assets and Calculation of Economic Rents

A Business Enterprise Value Anthology

The annual average balance of working capital, consistent with assumptions reflected in Exhibits A-1 and A-3, is calculated and an assumed 3% rate of return on working capital is applied to arrive at the annual CAC (see Section 3 in the Monograph). Working capital used in this analysis excludes non-operating cash and all interest-bearing debt.

The Working Group recognizes that under circumstances where working capital correlates directly with revenue (as is the case below), discrete annual calculations may not be required (see the Practical Expedient). However, in those circumstances where the relationship between working capital and revenue is projected to change significantly (e.g., reduced days receivable), the discrete annual analysis would be considered a best practice. The need to calculate discrete annual working capital CAC assumptions would be based on the judgment of the valuation specialist.

		Year 1	Year 2	Year 3	Year 4	Year 5	Year 6	Year 7	Year 8	Year 9	Year 10	Residual
Revenue	$ 950	$ 1,000	$ 1,050	$ 1,165	$ 1,306	$ 1,456	$ 1,596	$ 1,718	$ 1,823	$ 1,907	$ 1,976	$ 2,035
Beginning Balance Working Capital		285	300	315	350	392	437	479	516	548	573	594
add: Incremental Working Capital	30%	15	15	35	42	45	42	37	32	25	21	18
Ending Balance Working Capital		300	315	350	392	437	479	516	548	573	594	612
Average Balance		293	308	333	371	415	458	498	532	561	584	603
Mid-period Adjustment Factor (1)		0.9535	0.9535	0.9535	0.9535	0.9535	0.9535	0.9535	0.9535	0.9535	0.9535	0.9535
Return On (2)	3%	8	9	10	11	12	13	14	15	16	17	17
Percent of Revenue		0.84%	0.84%	0.82%	0.81%	0.81%	0.82%	0.83%	0.83%	0.84%	0.84%	0.85%

(1) The mid-period adjustment is a simplifying adjustment applied to the *return on* to reflect the changing level of the contributory assets over the year. A further discussion of this adjustment is provided in the Toolkit. Note: This calculation does not affect the mid-period discounting convention applied to derive present value elsewhere. The Working Group recognizes that this adjustment is generally minor and its application is based on the judgment of the valuation specialist.

(2) The 3% after-tax return (CAC) is based on market participant assumptions.

The annual average balance of the fixed assets, consistent with the Adjusted Entity Value projections and the fair value of the fixed assets, is calculated and an assumed 5% after-tax rate of return on fixed assets is applied to arrive at the annual CAC (see paragraph 3.4.06, Technique A). The *return of* and *on* the acquired or current and future fixed assets is based on an 8-year straight-line remaining economic useful life in accordance with Technique A "Average Annual Balance."

The Working Group recognizes that under circumstances where the fixed asset CAC as a percent of revenue would remain relatively stable (as is the case below) discrete annual calculations may not be required. However, in those circumstances where the fixed asset CAC as a percent of revenue is projected to change (e.g., increasing asset utilization) then the discrete annual analysis would be considered a best practice. The significance of this assumption would be based on the judgment of the valuation specialist.

Return Of:		Year 1	Year 2	Year 3	Year 4	Year 5	Year 6	Year 7	Year 8	Year 9	Year 10	Residual
FV of Acquired or Current Fixed Assets (1)	$	250 $	214 $	179 $	143 $	107 $	71 $	36 $	- $	- $	-	
Capital Expenditures (2):												
Year 1		36	36	36	36	36	36	36	36	-	-	-
Year 2			50	50	50	50	50	50	50	50	-	-
Year 3				56	56	56	56	56	56	56	56	-
Year 4					63	63	63	63	63	63	63	63
Year 5						66	66	66	66	66	66	66
Year 6							68	68	68	68	68	68
Year 7								70	70	70	70	70
Year 8									72	72	72	72
Year 9										74	74	74
Year 10											76	76
Residual												78
Total Return Of		286	300	321	348	378	410	445	481	519	545	567
Percent of Revenue		28.6%	28.6%	27.6%	26.6%	26.0%	25.7%	25.9%	26.4%	27.2%	27.6%	27.9%
Return On:												
Beginning Balance		1,000	1,000	1,100	1,229	1,381	1,528	1,659	1,771	1,864	1,936	2,000
add: Capital Expenditures		286	400	450	500	525	541	557	574	591	609	627
less: Return Of		286	300	321	348	378	410	445	481	519	545	567
Ending Balance		1,000	1,100	1,229	1,381	1,528	1,659	1,771	1,864	1,936	2,000	2,060
Average Fixed Assets		1,000	1,050	1,165	1,305	1,455	1,594	1,715	1,818	1,900	1,968	2,030
Mid-period Adjustment Factor		0.9535	0.9535	0.9535	0.9535	0.9535	0.9535	0.9535	0.9535	0.9535	0.9535	0.9535
Return On	5%	48	50	56	62	69	76	82	87	91	94	97
Percent of Revenue		4.8%	4.8%	4.8%	4.7%	4.7%	4.8%	4.8%	4.8%	4.8%	4.8%	4.8%
Total Return Of & On as Percent of Revenue		33%	33%	32%	31%	31%	30%	31%	31%	32%	32%	33%

(1) The economic depreciation (*return of*) of the acquired or current fixed assets is based on the fair value of the fixed assets of $1,000 as follows:

Remaining Economic Life (Years)	FV	Year 1	Year 2	Year 3	Year 4	Year 5	Year 6	Year 7
1	35.7	35.7						
2	71.4	35.7	35.7					
3	107.1	35.7	35.7	35.7				
4	142.9	35.7	35.7	35.7	35.7			
5	178.6	35.7	35.7	35.7	35.7	35.7		
6	214.3	35.7	35.7	35.7	35.7	35.7	35.7	
7	250.0	35.7	35.7	35.7	35.7	35.7	35.7	35.7
Total (rounded)	1,000	250	214	179	143	107	71	36

(2) Based on an 8-year economic life with the first year's *return on* occurring in the year of purchase.

The Identification of Contributory Assets and Calculation of Economic Rents

A Business Enterprise Value Anthology

In Technique B, the CAC reflects both the *return of* and *on* and is calculated as a series of level annual payments based on an assumed 5% after-tax rate of return on fixed assets (see paragraph 3.4.10, Technique B). In this exhibit, the CAC is calculated as a "loan payment" at the after-tax rate of return, or interest rate (with the loan payment conceptually including both principle and interest). The calculation incorporates the fair value of the fixed assets and the remaining useful life for each asset group (waterfall payment) and assumes an 8-year remaining useful life for capital expenditures in each year, consistent with the Adjusted Entity Value projections and the fair value of the fixed assets.

The Working Group recognizes that under circumstances where the fixed asset CAC as a percent of revenue would remain relatively stable (as is the case below) discrete annual calculations may not be required. However, in those circumstances where the fixed asset CAC as a percent of revenue is projected to change (e.g., increasing asset utilization) then the discrete annual analysis would be considered a best practice. The significance of this assumption would be based on the judgment of the valuation specialist.

Return On and Of:	Year 1	Year 2	Year 3	Year 4	Year 5	Year 6	Year 7	Year 8	Year 9	Year 10	Residual
FV of Acquired or Current Fixed Assets (1)											
1-year	37										
2-years	38	38									
3-years	39	39	39								
4-years (2)	40	40	40	40							
5-years	41	41	41	41	41						
6-years	42	42	42	42	42	42					
7-years	43	43	43	43	43	43	43				
8-years	-	-	-	-	-	-	-	-			
Capital Expenditures (3):											
Year 1 (4)	42	42	42	42	42	42	42	42	-	-	-
Year 2		59	59	59	59	59	59	59	59	-	-
Year 3			66	66	66	66	66	66	66	66	-
Year 4				74	74	74	74	74	74	74	74
Year 5					77	77	77	77	77	77	77
Year 6						80	80	80	80	80	80
Year 7							82	82	82	82	82
Year 8								85	85	85	85
Year 9									87	87	87
Year 10										90	90
Residual											92
Total Return On & Of	**324**	**346**	**373**	**408**	**445**	**483**	**523**	**565**	**610**	**641**	**667**
% of Revenue	32%	33%	32%	31%	31%	30%	30%	31%	32%	32%	33%

(1) The level payment related to the acquired or current fixed assets is based on the fair value of the fixed assets of $1,000 with an equal distribution of original cost over the prior 8 years, similar to Exhibit A-5. This waterfall calculation reflects individual level payment calculations for each asset life group.

(2) Sample calculation of the level payment for the acquired fixed assets with a remaining useful life of 4 years is as follows:

    CAC = -PMT(After-Tax Rate of Return,RUL,Fair Value,Future Value,Type = beginning of period) x (1+Discount Rate)^.5
         = -PMT(5%,4,143,0,1) x (1 + 10%)^.5 =   40

(3) Individual level payment calculations for annual capital expenditures.

(4) Sample calculation of the level payment for the $286 of capital expenditures occurring in Year 1 with a remaining useful life of 8 years is as follows:

    CAC = -PMT(After-Tax Rate of Return,RUL,Fair Value,Future Value,Type = beginning of period)
         = -PMT(5%,8,286,0,1) =   42

This exhibit calculates the growth investment in AWF and the *return on* the AWF (the CAC). The fair value of the acquired or current AWF of $200 is estimated based on the pre-tax replacement cost.

Future operating expenses include the cost to both grow and maintain the AWF. The initial investment to increase the AWF should be excluded to avoid double counting the initial investment and the future maintenance expenses. In other words, the *return on* the AWF would increase due to its growth and future operating expenses provide for maintaining the increase in the AWF (see Section 3.7 of the Monograph). The Working Group recognizes that this adjustment is generally minor and may be excluded in practice. However, such an adjustment provides for a complete reconciliation of value in the context of a financial overlay as discussed in the Toolkit.

The Working Group recognizes that under circumstances where the relationship between AWF and revenue (e.g., the revenue per employee) remains relatively stable, discrete annual calculations may not be required (see the Practical Expedient). However, in those circumstances where the relationship is projected to significantly change (e.g., increasing revenue per employee), the discrete annual analysis would be considered a best practice. The need for discrete AWF calculations (and the resulting AWF CAC) would be based on the judgment of the valuation specialist.

		Year 1	Year 2	Year 3	Year 4	Year 5	Year 6	Year 7	Year 8	Year 9	Year 10	Residual
Revenue		$ 1,000	$ 1,050	$ 1,165	$ 1,306	$ 1,456	$ 1,596	$ 1,718	$ 1,823	$ 1,907	$ 1,976	$ 2,035
Growth		5%	5%	11%	12%	11%	10%	8%	6%	5%	4%	3%
Beginning Balance		200	211	222	246	276	308	338	364	386	404	419
add: Pre-Tax Investment in AWF Growth (1)	-	11	11	24	30	32	30	26	22	18	15	13
Ending Balance		211	222	246	276	308	338	364	386	404	419	432
Average Balance		206	217	234	261	292	323	351	375	395	412	426
Mid-period Adjustment Factor		0.9535	0.9535	0.9535	0.9535	0.9535	0.9535	0.9535	0.9535	0.9535	0.9535	0.9535
Return On (2)	10%	20	21	22	25	28	31	33	36	38	39	41
Percent of Revenue		2.0%	2.0%	1.9%	1.9%	1.9%	1.9%	1.9%	2.0%	2.0%	2.0%	2.0%

(1) Growth investment correlates to the annual increase in revenue. For example in Year 2 revenue increases by 5% and the AWF grows by $11 (5% x $211).

(2) The required rate of return on identified intangible assets such as the AWF may be estimated through the relative risk of the intangible assets compared to the entity's overall WACC.

The Identification of Contributory Assets and Calculation of Economic Rents

A Business Enterprise Value Anthology

Customer Relationships MPEEM: Fixed Asset Contributory Asset Charge Based on Technique A - Average Annual Balance Exhibit A-8

This exhibit uses the Average Annual Balance technique (Technique A) for the calculation of fixed asset CACs in the valuation of customer relationships using an MPEEM. Aggregate CACs were estimated in the prior exhibits. An analysis of the subject intangible asset should be performed to assess the required levels of contributory assets. The aggregate CACs on those assets are then allocated appropriately to the subject intangible asset. For the purposes of this example all contributory assets have been assumed to benefit all customers equally and the CACs are allocated in proportion to revenue. The allocation of CACs is based on facts and circumstances. For example, in other circumstances a disproportionate amount of the fixed assets may be used to manufacture the products sold to the identified customer relationships ($900 in revenue in Year 1) versus the unidentified customers ($100 in Year 1). In a similar manner, the IP may be disproportionately allocable to the identified customer relationships rather than the unidentified customers.

In addition to the CACs related to working capital, fixed assets and AWF, profit splits in the form of royalty rates were also applied for the use of the trade name and IP. This example assumes that certain expense items (e.g., advertising and R&D) are included in the royalty rate and have been eliminated from the excess earnings to avoid double counting the expense.

		Year 1	Year 2	Year 3	Year 4	Year 5	Year 6	Year 7	Year 8	Year 9	Year 10	Residual
Total Revenue		$ 1,000	$ 1,050	$ 1,165	$ 1,306	$ 1,456	$ 1,596	$ 1,718	$ 1,823	$ 1,907	$ 1,976	$ 2,035
Customer Relationship Revenue (1)		900	855	770	616	431	259	130	65	33	-	-
Gross Profit	90%	810	770	693	554	388	233	117	59	30	-	-
Operating Expenses:												
Maintenance R&D (2)	0.0%	-	-	-	-	-	-	-	-	-	-	-
R&D - Future IP (2)	0.0%	-	-	-	-	-	-	-	-	-	-	-
Trade name advertising (3)	0.0%	-	-	-	-	-	-	-	-	-	-	-
Current customer marketing (4)	3%	27	26	23	18	13	8	4	2	1	-	-
Future customer marketing (5)		-	-	-	-	-	-	-	-	-	-	-
Total marketing		27	26	23	18	13	8	4	2	1	-	-
Total G&A	7%	63	60	54	43	30	18	9	5	2	-	-
Total Operating Expenses		90	86	77	61	43	26	13	7	3	-	-
EBITDA		720	684	616	493	345	207	104	52	27	-	-
Depreciation (6)		166	303	256	194	131	81	42	20	9	-	-
Amortization - AWF (8)		18	16	13	9	6	3	2	1	-	-	-
EBIT		536	365	347	290	208	123	60	31	18	-	-
less: Trade Name Royalty (7)	5%	45	43	39	31	22	13	7	3	2	-	-
IP Royalty (7)	10%	90	86	77	62	43	26	13	7	3	-	-
Adjusted EBIT		401	236	231	197	143	84	40	21	13	-	-
Taxes	40%	160	94	92	79	57	34	16	8	5	-	-
Debt Free Net Income		241	142	139	118	86	50	24	13	8	-	-
add: Depreciation (6)		166	303	256	194	131	81	42	20	9	-	-
Amortization - AWF (8)		18	16	13	9	6	3	2	1	-	-	-
AWF Growth Investment (9)		10	9	16	14	9	5	2	1	-	-	-
less: Return On Working Capital (10)		8	7	6	5	4	2	1	1	-	-	-
Return Of Fixed Assets (11)		257	244	212	164	112	67	34	17	9	-	-
Return On Fixed Assets (11)		43	41	37	29	20	12	6	3	2	-	-
Return On AWF (9)		18	17	15	12	8	5	2	1	1	-	-
Excess Earnings		109	161	154	125	88	53	27	13	5	-	-
PV Factor (12)	10%	0.9535	0.8668	0.7880	0.7164	0.6512	0.5920	0.5382	0.4893	0.4448	0.4044	0.4044
PV Excess Earnings		104	140	121	90	57	31	15	6	2	-	-
Total PV Excess Earnings		566										
Tax Amortization Benefit (13)		153										
Fair Value - Customer Relationships		719										

Customer Relationships MPEEM: Fixed Asset Contributory Asset Charge Based on Technique A - Average Annual Balance (Continued) Exhibit A-8

(1) Assumed to decline over a 9 year period. Therefore, calculations only continue for those 9 years.

(2) Maintenance and future R&D is assumed to be included in the 10% IP royalty rate (licensor responsible for all R&D in the future) and is therefore removed in the excess earnings. The R&D expenses would be reflected as a reduction to the royalty in the valuation of the IP. Alternately, it might be determined that the royalty rate is stated net of the R&D expenses in which case the R&D expenses would remain in the excess earnings.

(3) Advertising expenses removed under the same assumptions provided in footnote 2.

(4) Maintenance marketing expenses specific to current recognizable customer relationships.

(5) Marketing expenses related to creating and maintaining unrecognized and future customer relationships are excluded.

(6) Exhibit A-2 amounts allocated in proportion to revenue.

(7) Royalty rates assumed to be gross (e.g., inclusive of advertising and R&D expenses). The same rates would be incorporated in the valuation of the trade name and IP. Note that the royalty charge is applicable to both current and future contributory assets (see paragraphs 3.6.02 - 3.6.04).

(8) Exhibit A-3 amounts allocated in proportion to revenue.

(9) Exhibit A-7 amounts allocated in proportion to revenue.

(10) Exhibit A-4 amounts allocated in proportion to revenue.

(11) Exhibit A-5 amounts allocated in proportion to revenue.

(12) Discount rate assumed to be equivalent to the IRR/WACC and a mid-period convention.

(13) Based on a 15 year straight-line amortization period, 40% tax rate and a 10% discount rate using a mid-period convention.

The Identification of Contributory Assets and Calculation of Economic Rents

43

A Business Enterprise Value Anthology

Applies the Level Payment methodology for fixed assets to the customer relationships. All other CACs and adjustments discussed in Exhibit A-8 remain the same.

		Year 1	Year 2	Year 3	Year 4	Year 5	Year 6	Year 7	Year 8	Year 9	Year 10	Residual
Total Revenue		$ 1,000	$ 1,050	$ 1,165	$ 1,306	$ 1,456	$ 1,596	$ 1,718	$ 1,823	$ 1,907	$ 1,976	$ 2,035
Customer Relationship Revenue		900	855	770	616	431	259	130	65	33	-	-
Gross Profit	90%	810	770	693	554	388	233	117	59	30	-	-
Operating Expenses:												
Maintenance R&D	0.0%	-	-	-	-	-	-	-	-	-	-	-
R&D - Future IP	0.0%	-	-	-	-	-	-	-	-	-	-	-
Trade name advertising	0.0%	-	-	-	-	-	-	-	-	-	-	-
Current customer marketing	3%	27	26	23	18	13	8	4	2	1	-	-
Future customer marketing		-	-	-	-	-	-	-	-	-	-	-
Total marketing		27	26	23	18	13	8	4	2	1	-	-
Total G&A	7%	63	60	54	43	30	18	9	5	2	-	-
Total Operating Expenses		90	86	77	61	43	26	13	7	3	-	-
EBITDA		720	684	616	493	345	207	104	52	27	-	-
Depreciation		166	303	256	194	131	81	42	20	9	-	-
Amortization - AWF		18	16	13	9	6	3	2	1	-	-	-
EBIT		536	365	347	290	208	123	60	31	18	-	-
less: Trade Name Royalty	5%	45	43	39	31	22	13	7	3	2	-	-
IP Royalty	10%	90	86	77	62	43	26	13	7	3	-	-
Adjusted EBIT		401	236	231	197	143	84	40	21	13	-	-
Taxes	40%	160	94	92	79	57	34	16	8	5	-	-
Debt Free Net Income		241	142	139	118	86	50	24	13	8	-	-
add: Depreciation		166	303	256	194	131	81	42	20	9	-	-
Amortization - AWF		18	16	13	9	6	3	2	1	-	-	-
AWF Growth Investment		10	9	16	14	9	5	2	1	-	-	-
less: Return On Working Capital		8	7	6	5	4	2	1	1	-	-	-
Return On & Of Fixed Assets (1)		292	281	247	192	132	78	40	20	11	-	-
Return On AWF		18	17	15	12	8	5	2	1	1	-	-
Excess Earnings		117	165	156	126	88	54	27	13	5	-	-
PV Factor	10%	0.9535	0.8668	0.7880	0.7164	0.6512	0.5920	0.5382	0.4893	0.4448	0.4044	0.4044
PV Excess Earnings		112	143	123	90	57	32	15	6	2	-	-
Total PV Excess Earnings		580										
Tax Amortization Benefit		157										
Fair Value - Customer Relationships		737										

(1) Exhibit A-6 amounts allocated in proportion to revenue.

The Identification of Contributory Assets and Calculation of Economic Rents

A Business Enterprise Value Anthology

The WARA analysis is applied to the fair value of the assets and the implied rate of return on goodwill (excess purchase price) is calculated. The purpose of the WARA is the assessment of the reasonableness of the asset-specific returns for identified intangibles and the implied (or calculated) return on the goodwill (excess purchase price). The WARA then should be compared to the derived market-based WACC (see paragraph 4.3.07).

	Average Annual Balance			Level Payment		
	Fair Value	Rate of Return	Weighted Return	Fair Value	Rate of Return	Weighted Return
Working Capital (1)	$ 285	3%	$ 8.6	$ 285	3%	$ 8.6
Fixed Assets (2)	1,000	5%	50.0	1,000	5%	50.0
Trade Name (3)	80	10%	8.0	80	10%	8.0
IP (3)	196	10%	19.6	196	10%	19.6
Customer Relationships (4)	719	10%	71.9	737	10%	73.7
AWF (5)	200	10%	20.0	200	10%	20.0
Excess Purchase Price (6)	3,145	12.2%	383.7	3,144	12.2%	383.6
Total (7)	5,625	10.0%	561.7	5,642	10.0%	563.4

(1) Exhibit A-4.

(2) Exhibit A-5.

(3) See Toolkit for the valuation of these assets.

(4) Exhibits A-8 and A-9. The Working Group believes that both of these values are within an acceptable range of results as the difference is the result of timing differences inherent in the CAC calculations.

(5) Exhibit A-7.

(6) Other than AWF. In a business combination, actual recorded goodwill will differ from this due to other purchase accounting adjustments.

(7) Includes the depreciation tax benefit from the increase in fixed asset value and the TAB on all intangible assets.

Appendix B: Practical Expedient

The Working Group prepared this example of practical expedients to better illustrate simplifying assumptions that are often appropriate.

Practical Expedient Example

IMPORTANT NOTE: These sample calculations are for demonstration purposes only and are not intended as the only form of model or calculation, or final report exhibit, that is acceptable. In some cases, these calculations include details to demonstrate a point made in the Monograph and would not be expected in a typical analysis. In this example, a practical expedient was not used for the AWF calculations related to its amortization and the add-back of growth investments. Because of the fact pattern in this example (AWF fair value is high relative to the fair value of the customer relationships), using a practical expedient for the AWF has a significant affect on the FV of the subject intangible asset.

This example demonstrates concepts put forth in this Monograph. It provides a practical expedient in circumstances when certain assumptions can be made with regard to the application of CACs. Whether or not these practical expedients are appropriate should be evaluated by the valuation specialist and, to the extent that they are applied, the assumptions should be clearly stated in the analysis. The contributory assets included in this example are as follows:

- Working Capital
- Fixed Assets
- Assembled Workforce
- Trade Name*
- Intellectual Property*

The simplifying assumptions include the following:

- The use of accounting depreciation in combination with an appropriate effective tax rate approximates the effect of tax depreciation;
- The projections of fixed asset depreciation reflected in the PFI approximate a detailed waterfall calculation of existing basis in the fixed assets with an adjustment for step up, if any, to the fixed asset fair value;
- Future levels of contributory assets (non-income based: working capital, fixed assets, and AWF) are closely correlated with revenue and can be approximately represented with a "percent of revenue" calculation.

Exhibit B-1:   Entity Value

Exhibit B-1a: Depreciation: $745 of Financial Reporting Basis with an 8-Year Straight-Line Depreciation

Exhibit B-2:   Adjusted PFI and Entity Value

Exhibit B-2a: Incremental Depreciation due to the $255 Fair Value Step-up with an 8-Year Straight-Line Depreciation

Exhibit B-3:   Contributory Asset Charges - Basis for Practical Expedients

Exhibit B-4:   Contributory Asset Charges

Exhibit B-5:   Customer Relationships MPEEM: Practical Expedients

---

*   These assets contribute to the revenue stream used in the valuation of the customer relationships. However, because they are valued by use of the relief from royalty method, this is considered a profit split and contributory asset charges are not applied.

The Entity Value in this Practical Expedient is based on 8-year straight-line depreciation (rather than tax depreciation) and an effective tax rate to equate to the Entity Value in the Comprehensive Example. Based on the market participant PFI and purchase price of $4,746, the IRR of the transaction is calculated to be 10%. In addition a market-based WACC of 10% is estimated, which reconciles to the IRR. This example reflects a non-taxable transaction.

		Year 1	Year 2	Year 3	Year 4	Year 5	Year 6	Year 7	Year 8	Year 9	Year 10	Residual
Revenue		$ 1,000	$ 1,050	$ 1,165	$ 1,306	$ 1,456	$ 1,596	$ 1,718	$ 1,823	$ 1,907	$ 1,976	$ 2,035
Gross Profit	90%	900	945	1,049	1,175	1,310	1,436	1,546	1,641	1,716	1,778	1,832
Operating Expenses:												
Maintenance R&D (2)	0.5%	5	5	6	7	7	8	9	9	10	10	10
R&D - Future IP (3)	2.5%	25	26	29	33	36	40	43	46	48	49	51
Trade name advertising (4)	0.5%	5	5	6	7	7	8	9	9	10	10	10
Current customer marketing (5)	3%	27	26	23	18	13	8	4	2	1	-	-
Future customer marketing (6)		18	22	29	40	53	64	73	80	84	89	92
Total marketing	5%	50	53	58	65	73	80	86	91	95	99	102
Total G&A	7%	70	74	82	91	102	112	120	128	133	138	142
Total Operating Expenses	15%	150	158	175	196	218	240	258	274	286	296	305
EBITDA		750	787	874	979	1,092	1,196	1,288	1,367	1,430	1,482	1,527
Depreciation (7)		222	246	275	311	351	392	436	481	519	545	567
Amortization (8)		-	-	-	-	-	-	-	-	-	-	-
EBIT		528	541	599	668	741	804	852	886	911	937	960
Taxes (9)	38.4%	203	208	230	256	284	308	327	340	350	359	368
Debt Free Net Income		325	333	369	412	457	496	525	546	561	578	592
less: Incremental Working Capital (10)	30%	15	15	35	42	45	42	37	32	25	21	18
add: Depreciation (11)		222	246	275	311	351	392	436	481	519	545	567
less: Capital Expenditures		286	400	450	500	525	541	557	574	591	609	627
Debt Free Cash Flow		246	164	159	181	238	305	367	421	464	493	514
Residual Value (12)												7,343
PV Factor (13)	10%	0.9535	0.8668	0.7880	0.7164	0.6512	0.5920	0.5382	0.4893	0.4448	0.4044	0.4044
PV DFCF		235	142	125	130	155	181	198	206	206	199	2,969
Entity Value		**4,746**										

(1) Entity Value projections based upon market participant assumptions. Excludes entity-specific synergies.

(2) Maintenance R&D applicable to both current and future IP.

(3) R&D expense for the development of future IP.

(4) Advertising expense related to the trade name.

(5) Maintenance marketing expenses specific to current recognizable customer relationships with following revenue (Exhibit B-5 footnote 1):

	Year 1	Year 2	Year 3	Year 4	Year 5	Year 6	Year 7	Year 8	Year 9	Year 10
Customer relationship revenue	900	855	770	616	431	259	130	65	33	-

(6) Marketing expenses related to creating and maintaining unrecognized and future customer relationships.

(7) From Exhibit B-1a.

(8) Tax basis of intangible assets is zero.

(9) The effective tax rate is calculated such that the Entity Value is equivalent to that provided in the Comprehensive Example. Tax rate is not rounded.

(10) Represents 30% of incremental revenue. A beginning working capital balance of $285 is based on Year 0 revenue of $950.

(11) The residual year difference in depreciation and capital expenditures recognizes the long term growth in the business and the depreciation lag relative to capital expenditures.

(12) Based on constant growth model assuming a 3% long-term growth rate.

(13) The market participant based IRR is equivalent to the WACC of 10%. The mid-period convention is applied.

Depreciation: $745 of Financial Reporting Basis with an 8-Year Straight-Line Depreciation (1)   Exhibit B-1a

This is a reference schedule for the projected depreciation reflected in the Entity Value. The valuation specialist should have an understanding of the assumptions reflected in, and the calculation of, the depreciation provided in the PFI. Such an understanding will allow for an assessment of the reasonableness of the simplifying assumption that the tax depreciation and statutory tax rate are reasonably approximated by accounting depreciation and the effective tax rate.

Straight-Line Depreciation Of:	Year 1	Year 2	Year 3	Year 4	Year 5	Year 6	Year 7	Year 8	Year 9	Year 10	Residual
Acquired or Current Fixed Assets (2)	$ 186	$ 160	$ 133	$ 106	$ 80	$ 53	$ 27	$ -	$ -	$ -	
Capital Expenditures (3):											
Year 1	36	36	36	36	36	36	36	36	-	-	-
Year 2		50	50	50	50	50	50	50	50	-	-
Year 3			56	56	56	56	56	56	56	56	-
Year 4				63	63	63	63	63	63	63	63
Year 5					66	66	66	66	66	66	66
Year 6						68	68	68	68	68	68
Year 7							70	70	70	70	70
Year 8								72	72	72	72
Year 9									74	74	74
Year 10										76	76
Residual											78
Total Depreciation (4)	222	246	275	311	351	392	436	481	519	545	567

Fixed Asset Turnover											
Beginning Balance	745	809	963	1,138	1,327	1,501	1,650	1,771	1,864	1,936	2,000
add: Capital Expenditures	286	400	450	500	525	541	557	574	591	609	627
less: Depreciation	222	246	275	311	351	392	436	481	519	545	567
Ending Balance	809	963	1,138	1,327	1,501	1,650	1,771	1,864	1,936	2,000	2,060
Average Fixed Assets	777	886	1,051	1,233	1,414	1,576	1,711	1,818	1,900	1,968	2,030
Fixed Asset Turnover	129%	119%	111%	106%	103%	101%	100%	100%	100%	100%	100%

(1) Assumes accounting depreciation in combination with an effective tax rate is a reasonable proxy for tax depreciation in combination with the statutory tax rate and is included in the PFI.
(2) The carrying value of the fixed assets is $745 and the annual depreciation is assumed.
(3) Straight-line over 8 years with the first year of depreciation recognized in the year of acquisition.
(4) As reflected in the PFI.

The PFI in this exhibit is adjusted to reflect the tax benefits that would result from a restatement of the tax basis of certain of the assets to fair value. The tax benefit inherent in the fair value of an asset is not reflected in the PFI of a non-taxable transaction. For example, the step-up in fixed assets or the fair value of an assembled workforce are not reflected in the entity's tax basis and the PFI for the transaction excludes this benefit. In order to maintain consistency between the PFI to be used in valuing the customer relationships and the fair value of the assets to which a CAC will be applied, the PFI should be adjusted to include the cash flow benefits of the increase in the tax basis of the contributory assets. The Working Group believes that the fair value of an intangible asset should not differ depending on the tax structure of a particular transaction. For additional discussion on the applicability of TABs see paragraphs 3.1.08 and 4.3.08 in this Monograph and paragraphs 5.3.9 - 5.3.108 in the 2001 AICPA IPR&D Practice Aid.

When the PFI is adjusted to include the additional cash flow benefit embedded in the fair value of the contributory assets, this results in an Adjusted Entity Value that is greater than the Entity Value by an amount equal to the present value of the tax benefits related to the increase in tax basis. The Entity Value is recalculated at the WACC/IRR of 10% to arrive at the Adjusted Entity Value of $4,872. This increase of $126 is equivalent to the present value of the incremental tax benefit related to the step-up in the fixed assets and the assembled workforce. This Adjusted Entity Value is used only for reconciliation at this phase of the analysis.

The Working Group recognizes that these adjustments might not be significant to the analysis and may be excluded based on the judgment of the valuation specialist.

		Year 1	Year 2	Year 3	Year 4	Year 5	Year 6	Year 7	Year 8	Year 9	Year 10	Residual
Revenue		$ 1,000	$ 1,050	$ 1,165	$ 1,306	$ 1,456	$ 1,596	$ 1,718	$ 1,823	$ 1,907	$ 1,976	$ 2,035
Gross Profit	90%	900	945	1,049	1,175	1,310	1,436	1,546	1,641	1,716	1,778	1,832
Operating Expenses:												
Maintenance R&D	0.5%	5	5	6	7	7	8	9	9	10	10	10
R&D - Future IP	2.5%	25	26	29	33	36	40	43	46	48	49	51
Trade name advertising	0.5%	5	5	6	7	7	8	9	9	10	10	10
Current customer marketing	3%	27	26	23	18	13	8	4	2	1	-	-
Future customer marketing		18	22	29	40	53	64	73	80	84	89	92
Total marketing	5%	50	53	58	65	73	80	86	91	95	99	102
Total G&A	7%	70	74	82	91	102	112	120	128	133	138	142
Total Operating Expenses	15%	150	158	175	196	218	240	258	274	286	296	305
EBITDA		750	787	874	979	1,092	1,196	1,288	1,367	1,430	1,482	1,527
Depreciation (1)		222	246	275	311	351	392	436	481	519	545	567
Depreciation of fixed asset step-up (2)		63	54	45	36	27	18	9	-	-	-	-
Adjusted Depreciation		285	300	320	347	378	410	445	481	519	545	567
Amortization - AWF (3)		20	20	20	20	20	20	20	20	20	20	-
EBIT		445	467	534	612	694	766	823	866	891	917	960
Taxes	38%	171	179	205	235	266	294	316	332	342	352	368
Debt Free Net Income		274	288	329	377	428	472	507	534	549	565	592
less: Incremental Working Capital	30%	15	15	35	42	45	42	37	32	25	21	18
add: Adjusted Depreciation		285	300	320	347	378	410	445	481	519	545	567
Amortization - AWF (3)		20	20	20	20	20	20	20	20	20	20	
less: Capital Expenditures		286	400	450	500	525	541	557	574	591	609	627
Debt Free Cash Flow		278	193	184	202	256	319	378	429	472	500	514
Residual Value												7,343
PV Factor (4)	10%	0.9535	0.8668	0.7880	0.7164	0.6512	0.5920	0.5382	0.4893	0.4448	0.4044	0.4044
PV DFCF		265	167	145	145	167	189	203	210	210	202	2,969
Adjusted Entity Value (5)		4,872										

(1) From Exhibit B-1.

(2) See sample calculation in Exhibit B-2a.

(3) Reflects the amortization of the AWF. For purposes of this example the amortization period for the AWF is assumed to be 10 years rather than 15 years as is required in the U.S. under IRS Code Section 197. 10 years is applied for demonstration purposes as the projections presented are 10 years in length. Tax benefits related to the future replacement of, or increase in, the AWF are reflected in the operating expenses and no adjustment is required other than for the initial fair value.

(4) The WACC is not adjusted for the inclusion of the incremental tax benefit and remains at 10%.

(5) The Adjusted Entity Value increase over the Entity Value is due solely to the incremental tax benefits. This Adjusted Entity Value is used only for reconciliation purposes.

This is a reference schedule for the projected depreciation reflected in the Adjusted Entity Value and also provides the fixed asset turnover based on the fair value of the fixed assets. The valuation specialist should have an understanding of the assumptions reflected in, and the calculation of, the depreciation provided in the PFI. Such an understanding will allow for an assessment of the reasonableness of the simplifying assumption that the tax depreciation and statutory tax rate are reasonably approximated by accounting depreciation and the effective tax rate.

RUL (Years)	Step-up	Year 1	Year 2	Year 3	Year 4	Year 5	Year 6	Year 7
1	9	9						
2	18	9	9					
3	27	9	9	9				
4	36	9	9	9	9			
5	45	9	9	9	9	9		
6	54	9	9	9	9	9	9	
7	63	9	9	9	9	9	9	9
Total (rounded) (2)	252	63	54	45	36	27	18	9

Fixed Asset Turnover (3)

Beginning Balance	1,000	1,001	1,101	1,231	1,384	1,531	1,662	1,774	1,867	1,939	2,003
add: Capital Expenditures	286	400	450	500	525	541	557	574	591	609	627
less: Depreciation from Exhibit B-1a	222	246	275	311	351	392	436	481	519	545	567
less: Incremental depreciation above	63	54	45	36	27	18	9	-	-	-	-
Ending Balance	1,001	1,101	1,231	1,384	1,531	1,662	1,774	1,867	1,939	2,003	2,063
Average Fixed Assets	1,001	1,051	1,166	1,308	1,458	1,597	1,718	1,821	1,903	1,971	2,033
Fixed Asset Turnover (4)	100%	100%	100%	100%	100%	100%	100%	100%	100%	100%	100%

(1) Calculates the incremental depreciation due to the recognition of the fair value of the fixed assets. This is applied as an incremental amount to the depreciation reflected in Exhibit B-1. This example assumes that 1 year of depreciation was recognized in the year of acquisition, therefore 7 years of depreciation remain for the assets acquired in the prior year. The $3 difference from $255 is due to rounding.

(2) Reflects the incremental depreciation due to the recognition of the fair value of the fixed assets.

(3) The fixed asset turnover is provided to assess the ongoing relationship between the fixed assets and revenue. To the extent that the fixed asset turnover remains relatively constant, the practical expedient assumption may be appropriate. If there is a period during the early years of the projection where the relationship between fixed assets and revenue is migrating towards a long-term normalized amount, then this assumption should be applied on a blended basis or for periods after which a normalized amount is achieved. If, however, the turnover rate continues to vary significantly over the forecast period, the practical expedient assumption might not be appropriate.

(4) Annual revenue / average fixed assets.

The Identification of Contributory Assets and Calculation of Economic Rents

A Business Enterprise Value Anthology

One of the fundamental premises of a CAC is that investments made at a point in time have economic benefits extending beyond the year the investment was made. A CAC essentially replaces the initial investment with an annual charge over the life of the investment such that the PV of the charge is equivalent to the initial investment. In other words the PV impact to the projections is zero. This applies to the initial fair value of the acquired or current contributory asset as well as future investments that increase the investment in the respective contributory assets.

Working Capital: The initial balance is replaced with a perpetual *return on*. The nature of working capital (see paragraph 3.2.01) removes the need to provide a *return of* the asset over its RUL. Further, each annual investment in incremental working capital is replaced with a perpetual *return on* the incremental investment so that *return on* the working capital during any period reflects an accumulation of the perpetual charge for the initial balance and for any subsequent investments in incremental amounts. There is no maintenance investment reflected in the PFI.

Practical Expedient (Working Capital): To the extent that working capital is assumed to maintain a constant relationship with revenue, the incremental investments in working capital will correlate with revenue growth. As the rate of return on each annual investment in working capital remains the same, the accumulation of the *return on* working capital would also maintain a constant relationship with revenue. Therefore, calculating the initial *return on* the average balance of working capital and applying this CAC as a percent of revenue in the future reasonably approximates the detailed calculation provided in the Comprehensive Example and Toolkit. Note that if there is a period during the early years of the projection where the relationship between working capital and revenue is migrating towards a long-term normalized amount then this assumption should be applied on a blended basis or for periods after which a normalized amount is achieved.

Fixed Assets: The CAC for fixed assets varies from that of working capital in that fixed assets (other than land) are assumed to deteriorate in value and a *return of* in addition to the *return on* should be applied. The same underlying premise does hold; that the present value of the *return on* and *return of* is equal to the initial investment. Therefore, the initial balance as well as future investments are replaced with a present value equivalent *return of* and *return on*. In the Comprehensive Example, the annual fixed asset investments, which include both the replacement of fixed assets as well as incremental investment, are replaced with a *return on* and *return of* for each annual investment. The maintenance investment is reflected in the PFI as a sub-set of the projected capital expenditures.

First Practical Expedient (Fixed Assets): If the simplifying assumptions stated in the introduction, regarding the effective tax rate and detailed waterfall approximation, are appropriate, then a recalculation of the depreciation in the PFI would not be required. In addition, the adjustment to depreciation to arrive at the Adjusted Entity Value resulting from any differences between the carrying value and the fair value of the fixed assets can be calculated directly. This is incorporated into the analysis by calculating the increased (or decreased) depreciation related to the step-up (or step-down) of the fixed assets and reflected as an adjustment to the depreciation in the Entity Value PFI.

Second Practical Expedient (Fixed Assets): As with working capital, if it is reasonable to assume that the future level of fixed assets maintains a constant relationship with revenue (that is, the fixed asset turnover remains relatively constant), then investments in fixed assets will provide for the maintenance of the prior year's balance as well as any growth and the annual amounts will correlate with revenue growth (see Exhibit B-2a). As the rate of return on each annual investment in fixed assets remains the same, the *return on* the average balance of fixed assets would also maintain a constant relationship with revenue. Therefore, calculating the initial *return on* the average balance of fixed assets and applying this CAC as a percent of revenue in the future reasonably approximates the detailed calculations provided in the Comprehensive Example and Toolkit. Note that if there is a period during the early years of the projection where the relationship between fixed assets and revenue is migrating towards a long-term normalized amount then this assumption should be applied on a blended basis or for periods after which a normalized amount is achieved.

Third Practical Expedient (Fixed Assets): If it is assumed that projected depreciation in the PFI reflects the economic use of the fixed assets and the differences between tax depreciation and accounting depreciation are captured in the effective tax rate, then the *return of* the fixed assets in the Average Annual Balance Technique would be equivalent to accounting depreciation. The annual investment in fixed assets is excluded in excess earnings (the investment has been replaced by the CAC). Since the depreciation cash flow adjustment equates to the *return of* the fixed assets these two adjustments to debt free net income offset each other. Therefore, a reasonable presentation would be to exclude the depreciation cash flow adjustment, capital expenditure investment and the *return of* the fixed assets in the presentation of the excess earnings for the subject intangible asset.

Assembled Workforce (or any intangible asset valued with the cost approach): These contributory assets are similar to fixed assets in that they provide economic benefit beyond the period of the initial investment. However, the means by which the asset is maintained and increased is reflected as an expense rather than cash flow adjustment in the income and cash flow statements. Fixed assets are capitalized and the tax benefit is realized through the deduction of depreciation expense in the future. AWF investments are treated as an immediate expense for financial reporting and tax purposes. To the extent that the fair value of an AWF is based upon the pre-tax cost to create the asset, any investment to increase the AWF would also be measured based on the pre-tax investment rather than an after tax investment. CACs are applied to the annual balance of the fair value of the AWF. Therefore, just as with fixed assets, the investment (in this case, pre-tax expense) should be added back. Unlike fixed assets, the CAC is limited to a *return on* the AWF because the *return of* the AWF is contained in the operating expenses to maintain the fair value.

First Practical Expedient (Assembled Workforce): As discussed in Section 3.7, the initial pre-tax investment to increase the AWF should be added back in the excess income projection to avoid double counting the initial investment and the CAC. This adjustment can be simply calculated by applying the revenue growth rate to the beginning balance of the AWF in any period. This adjustment is also consistent with the approach applied to incremental working capital where the annual investment in increased working capital is removed from the excess earnings projection and is replaced with a *return on* the average annual balance.

Second Practical Expedient (Assembled Workforce): To the extent that the AWF is assumed to maintain a constant relationship with revenue (e.g. the revenue per employee remains relatively constant) the incremental investments in the AWF will correlate with revenue growth. As the rate of return on each annual investment in the AWF remains the same, the accumulation of the *return on* the AWF would also maintain a constant relationship with revenue. Therefore, calculating the initial *return on* the average balance of the AWF and applying this CAC as a percent of revenue in the future reasonably approximates the detailed calculation provided in the Comprehensive Example and Toolkit. Note that if there is a period during the early years of the projection where the relationship between the AWF and revenue is migrating towards a long-term normalized amount then this assumption should be applied on a blended basis or for periods after which a normalized amount is achieved.

The assumptions underlying the Comprehensive Example are consistent with the practical expedients discussed in Exhibit B-3. Working capital, fixed assets and the AWF maintain a reasonably constant relationship to the revenue. Therefore the *return on* the aggregate of the contributory assets in the initial period can reasonably be carried forward as a percent of revenue to apply the CACs. The following demonstrates one approach to these practical expedients.

Year 1		Working Capital		Fixed Assets		Assembled Workforce
Revenue	$ 950	$ 1,000		$ 1,000		$ 1,000
Beginning Balance		285		1,000		200
add: Incremental Investment	30%	15		286 (1)		11 (3)
less: Return Of (depreciation)		n/a		285 (2)		- (4)
Ending Balance		300		1,001		211
Average Balance		293		1,001		206
Mid-period Adjustment Factor		0.9535		0.9535		0.9535
Return On (5)	3%	8	5%	48	10%	20
Percent of Revenue		0.84%		4.77%		1.96%
Total *Return On* applied as a CAC		7.57%				

(1) Exhibit B-1.

(2) Exhibit B-2 includes incremental depreciation due to the fixed asset step-up.

(3) The percent increase in revenue ($50/$950 or 5.3%) applied to the initial fair value of $200, rounded.

(4) The *return of* is reflected in operating expenses as discussed in Exhibit B-3.

(5) After tax rates of return.

Applies the practical expedients in the valuation of the customer relationships.

		Year 1	Year 2	Year 3	Year 4	Year 5	Year 6	Year 7	Year 8	Year 9	Year 10	Residual
Total Revenue		$ 1,000	$ 1,050	$ 1,165	$ 1,306	$ 1,456	$ 1,596	$ 1,718	$ 1,823	$ 1,907	$ 1,976	$ 2,035
Customer Relationship Revenue (1)		900	855	770	616	431	259	130	65	33	-	-
Gross Profit	90%	810	770	693	554	388	233	117	59	30	-	-
Operating Expenses:												
Maintenance R&D (2)	0.0%	-	-	-	-	-	-	-	-	-	-	-
R&D - Future IP (2)	0.0%	-	-	-	-	-	-	-	-	-	-	-
Trade name advertising (3)	0.0%	-	-	-	-	-	-	-	-	-	-	-
Current customer marketing (4)	3%	27	26	23	18	13	8	4	2	1	-	-
Future customer marketing (5)		-	-	-	-	-	-	-	-	-	-	-
Total marketing		27	26	23	18	13	8	4	2	1	-	-
Total G&A	7%	63	60	54	43	30	18	9	5	2	-	-
Total Operating Expenses		90	86	77	61	43	26	13	7	3	-	-
EBITDA		720	684	616	493	345	207	104	52	27	-	-
Adjusted Depreciation (6)		257	244	212	164	112	67	34	17	9	-	-
Amortization - AWF (7)		18	16	13	9	6	3	2	1	-	-	-
EBIT		445	424	391	320	227	137	68	34	18	-	-
less: Trade Name Royalty (8)	5%	45	43	39	31	22	13	7	3	2	-	-
IP Royalty (8)	10%	90	86	77	62	43	26	13	7	3	-	-
Adjusted EBIT		310	295	275	227	162	98	48	24	13	-	-
Taxes	38%	119	113	106	87	62	38	18	9	5	-	-
Debt Free Net Income		191	182	169	140	100	60	30	15	8	-	-
add: Amortization - AWF (8)		18	16	13	9	6	3	2	1	-	-	-
AWF Growth Investment (9)		10	9	16	14	9	5	2	1	-	-	-
less: Return On Contributory Assets (10)		68	65	58	47	33	20	10	5	2	-	-
Excess Earnings		151	142	140	116	82	48	24	12	6	-	-
PV Factor (11)	10%	0.9535	0.8668	0.7880	0.7164	0.6512	0.5920	0.5382	0.4893	0.4448	0.4044	0.4044
PV Excess Earnings		144	123	110	83	53	28	13	6	3	-	-
Total PV Excess Earnings		563										
Tax Amortization Benefit (12)		152										
Fair Value - Customer Relationships		715										
Fair Value - Comprehensive Example (13)		719										

(1) Assumed to decline over a 9 year period. Therefore, calculations only continue for those 9 years.

(2) Maintenance and future R&D is assumed to be included in the 10% IP royalty rate (licensor responsible for all R&D in the future) and is therefore removed in the excess earnings. The R&D expenses would be reflected as a reduction to the royalty in the valuation of the IP. Alternately, it might be determined that the royalty rate is stated net of the R&D expenses in which case the R&D expenses would remain in the excess earnings.

(3) Advertising expenses removed under the same assumptions provided in footnote 2.

(4) Maintenance marketing expenses specific to current recognizable customer relationships.

(5) Marketing expenses related to creating and maintaining unrecognized and future customer relationships are excluded.

(6) Exhibit B-2 amounts allocated in proportion to revenue.

(7) Exhibit B-2 amounts allocated in proportion to revenue. The amortization of the initial assembled workforce differs from the *return of* reflected in the operating expenses. This is due to the tax treatment of recapturing the amortizable tax basis that has been expensed historically that would occur in a taxable transaction.

(8) Royalty rates assumed to be gross (e.g., inclusive of advertising and R&D expenses). The same rates would be incorporated in the valuation of the trade name and IP. Note that the royalty charge is applicable to both current and future contributory assets (see paragraphs 3.6.02 - 3.6.04).

(9) Exhibit A-7 annual growth investment amounts allocated in proportion to revenue (from Comprehensive Example).

(10) Exhibit B-4 percentage applied to revenue.

(11) Discount rate assumed to be equivalent to the IRR/WACC and a mid-period convention.

(12) Based on a 15 year straight-line amortization period, 40% tax rate and a 10% discount rate using a mid-period convention.

(13) See Exhibit A-8. Comparison is made to the Average Annual Balance technique.

Appendix C: Pre-tax versus After-tax Adjustments for Growth Investments in Certain Intangible Assets

This Appendix relates only to the topic discussed in Section 3.7. It is intended to address why the add-back of the growth investment in assembled workforce (or other intangible assets valued using a cost approach or other approach when the expenditure is viewed as a period expense) should be equal to the pretax growth investment and not an after-tax amount (assuming the acquired or current assembled workforce was valued using pre-tax cost).

The overall PFI includes future investment to maintain as well as increase the assembled workforce, reflected in the projected cost structure of the business and in the entity value. In the context of an MPEEM used to value a subject intangible asset (such as customer relationships), a CAC or *return on* the assembled workforce will be introduced into the analysis. As indicated elsewhere in this document, investments in assets have utility beyond the period of the cash charge. CACs capture this future utility by replacing the cash charges with a series of charges over the economic life of the asset, as represented by the required *return of* and *return on* the fair value of the necessary level of contributory asset. The following paragraphs address only the *return on* portion of the CAC because the *return of* portion is present in the operating expenses of the entity and is not the subject of this Appendix.

If the acquired or current assembled workforce has a fair value of $100 and the *return on* is 10%, then the annual CAC would be $10. This *return on* carries on into perpetuity (the acquired or current assembled workforce balance is maintained in the expenses). The present value of the *return on* is $100 ($10/10%) so the cash flow available to other intangible assets (including goodwill) is reduced by $10 annually in the form of a CAC, or $100 in present value terms.

Similarly, in the MPEEM used to value a subject intangible asset, CACs related to future assembled workforce investments equate to replacing a growth investment with a perpetual *return on* (the growth investment is replaced

with the CAC on that growth). In calculating the CAC, the fair value of the assembled workforce is reflected as having increased by the pre-tax growth investment (see Exhibit A-7 of Appendix A). Therefore, to ensure that the cash flow attributable to the subject intangible asset is not "over-charged" for the contribution of the assembled workforce, the add-back to the analysis has to be on a pre-tax basis.

Following is an example that looks at year one of the cash flows used in an MPEEM to value customer relationships. The example assumes a $20 growth investment in assembled workforce in year one. For purposes of this example, assume there are no other assets. This simple example shows that value is neither created nor destroyed by equating the MPEEM cash flow attributable to customer relationships to the cash flow used in the entity discounted cash flow.

Effect of assembled workforce (AWF) growth investment on the cash flow used in the entity value discounted cash flow:	
Year One Pre-tax growth investment in AWF	$(20)
Tax at 40%	8
After-tax investment*	(12)

* Appears in Entity Value discounted cash flow

Effect of assembled workforce (AWF) growth investment on the cash flow used in the customer relationship MPEEM:	
In MPEEM, the above after-tax investment effect still appears:	
After-tax investment	(12)
And the growth investment is replaced with the CAC:	
CAC on $20 increased "value", at 10% = $2 annually	
Year One PV of perpetual $2 CAC at 10% = $20	(20)
Add back growth investment at $20 pre-tax amount	20
Net reduction in cash flow available for customer relationships	$(12)

These calculations simply demonstrate that the cash flow effect in the entity value ($12) equals the cash flow effect on customer relationship value in the MPEEM ($12). No value created or destroyed.

Valuation of the Customer/Client Relationships Intangible Asset for Property Tax Purposes

Robert F. Reilly

This article originally appeared in the Spring 2002 issue of the *Journal of Property Valuation and Taxation,* © 2010 CCH, a Wolters Kluwer Law and Business. All rights reserved. Reprinted with permission from the *Journal of Property Valuation and Taxation.*

The Financial Accounting Standards Board (FASB) recently issued two new statements that materially change the financial accounting for merger and acquisition (M&A) transactions. FASB Statement No. 141 is titled "Business Combinations." Statement 142 is titled "Goodwill and Other Intangible Assets."

Statement 141 was issued to improve the generally accepted accounting principles ("GAAP") financial reporting for business combinations. Under Statement 141, the pooling-of-interests method of accounting for acquisitions is no longer acceptable. All corporate M&A business combinations will now have to be accounted for under the purchase method of accounting. Statement 141 is effective for business combinations initiated after June 30, 2001.

Statement 142 requires that goodwill acquired in a business combination can no longer be periodically amortized to earnings; rather, the value of acquired goodwill must be periodically reviewed for possible impairment charges. The FASB believes that this GAAP change will allow investors to better understand the true economics of a company's acquired goodwill. The amortization of acquired goodwill will no longer be allowed after a company's adoption of this Statement. Statement 142 must be adopted for fiscal years beginning after December 31, 2001. However, Statement 142 does allow for the periodic amortization of a significant number of discrete intangible assets acquired in an M&A business combination. Discrete intangible assets are those that may be (1) identified separately and (2) valued separately from acquired general goodwill. While Statement 142 identifies many categories of discrete intangible assets, one cat-egory of such a discrete intangible is acquired customer lists and customer relationships.

Customer/client relationships represent a valuable intangible asset to many industrial and commercial companies. Customer/client relationships may represent the most valuable asset–tangible or intangible–to many service-oriented companies. The expectation of periodic business from recurring customers/clients can be a substantial component of the value of service organizations, such as communications, transportation, pipeline, utilities, and cable TV companies. Accordingly, under the provisions of Statement 141, customer-related intangible assets will now be recorded on the GAAP balance sheets of acquisitive companies. However, there are numerous other reasons–including property taxation reasons–to value a company's customer relationship's intangible assets. For example, many taxing jurisdictions specifically exclude the value of such intangible personal property as customer/client relationships from ad valorem taxation.

This article will discuss the approaches and methods with respect to the identification, valuation, and remaining useful life analysis of customer relationship intangible assets for ad valorem property tax assessment or appeal purposes. In particular, we will discuss the importance of–and analytical methods related to–the remaining useful life of customer relationships.

Robert F. Reilly, ASA, CPA, CFA, CMA, is a Managing Director of Willamette Management Associates in Chicago, Illinois.

Finally, we will also present a simple illustrative example of the valuation of customer/client relationships within a property taxation context.

Identification of Discrete Intangible Assets

There are various definitions of the term "intangible asset." In a property tax valuation, the analyst may have to perform research to determine if a particular definition is appropriate to the subject analysis, given the purpose and objective of the valuation. Obviously, relevant judicial precedent and statutory authority should be consulted in this research. For purposes of this discussion, we will focus on the economic (and not the legal) questions that are relevant to the valuation of discrete intangible assets. From this economic perspective, there are two fundamental questions that the analyst should consider:

1. What economic phenomena qualify as discrete intangible assets?

2. What economic phenomena manifest–or are indicative of–value in discrete intangible assets?

For a discrete intangible asset to exist from an economic perspective, it should typically possess certain attributes. The following are some of the more common attributes:

1. It should be subject to specific identification and recognizable description.

2. It should be subject to legal existence and protection.

3. It should be subject to the right of private ownership, and this private ownership should be legally transferable.

4. There should be some tangible evidence or manifestation of the existence of the intangible asset (e.g., a contract, a license, a set of patient files, a set of client workpapers, a listing of customers, a set of financial statements).

5. It should have been created or have come into existence at an identifiable time or as the result of an identifiable event.

6. It should be subject to being destroyed or to a termination of existence at an identifiable time or as the result of an identifiable event.

In other words, there should be a specific bundle of legal rights associated with the existence of discrete intangible assets.

For a discrete intangible asset to have economic value, it should possess certain additional attributes. Some of these additional attributes include the following:

1. It should generate some measurable amount of economic benefit to its owner; this economic benefit could be in the form of an income increment or of a cost decrement; this economic benefit is sometimes measured by comparison to the amount of income otherwise available to the intangible asset owner (e.g., the company) if the subject intangible did not exist.

2. This economic benefit may be measured in any of several ways, including net income, net operating income, or net cash flow.

3. It should be able to enhance the value of the other assets with which it is associated; the other assets may encompass all other assets of the company such as: tangible personal property, real estate, or other intangible assets.

Economic phenomena that do not demonstrate these attributes typically do not qualify as discrete intangible assets. Some economic phenomena are merely descriptive or expository in nature. They may describe conditions that contribute to the existence of–and value of–identified, discrete intangible assets. But, these phenomena do not themselves possess the requisite elements to qualify as discrete intangible assets.

Examples of such "descriptive" economic phenomena–that do not qualify as identifiable intangible assets–include the following:

1. high market share of the firm,

2. high profitability of the firm,

3. general positive reputation of the firm,

4. monopoly position of the firm,

5. market potential of the firm, and

6. other economic phenomena.

However, while these "descriptive" conditions do not qualify as discrete intangible assets themselves, they may indicate that the actual intangible assets do have substantial economic value. For example, while these "descriptive" conditions do not qualify as discrete intangible assets, they may indicate the existence of–and greatly contribute to the value of–recurring customer/client relationships.

Valuation of Customer-Related Intangible Assets

There are several procedures and techniques that may be appropriately used in the valuation of discrete intangible assets, such as customer/client relationships. However, all of these methods logically group into the three general categories of analyses: the cost approach, the market approach, and the income approach. Each of these three approaches (or groups of related methods) has the same objective: to arrive at a reasonable indication of a defined value for the customer-related intangible asset. Accordingly, methods that are premised on the same fundamental economic principles are grouped together into general approaches. Collectively, the three intangible asset valuation approaches encompass a broad spectrum of economic theory and of property investment concepts.

The cost approach is based on the economic principle of substitution. This economic principle asserts that an investor will pay no more for an asset than the cost to obtain–by either purchasing or constructing–an asset of equal utility. For purposes of this economic principle, utility can be measured in many ways, including functionality, desirability, and so on. The availability of–and the cost of–substitute assets are directly affected by shifts in supply and demand within the universe of substitute assets. Unlike fungible tangible assets, there may be no reasonable substitutes for discrete intangible assets. Accordingly, the cost approach often has limited application in the valuation of customer/client relationships.

The market approach is based on the related economic principles of competition and equilibrium. These economic principles conclude that, in a free and unrestricted market, supply and demand factors will drive the price of an asset to a point of equilibrium. The principle of substitution also directly influences the market approach. This is because the identification and analysis of equilibrium prices for substitute assets will provide market-derived evidence with regard to the value of the subject discrete intangible asset. Due to a paucity of transactional data, the market approach often has limited application in the valuation of customer/client relationships.

The income approach is based on the economic principle of anticipation (sometimes called the principle of expectation). In this approach, the value of the discrete intangible asset is the present value of the expected economic income to be earned from the ownership of that intangible. As the name of this principle implies, the investor anticipates the expected economic income to be earned from the intangible. This expectation of prospective economic income is converted to a present worth–that is, the indicated value of the discrete intangible asset. The income approach is commonly used in the valuation of the customer/client relationships.

There are numerous alternative definitions of economic income that may be used in the valuation of customer/client relationships. Using this valuation approach, the analyst estimates the intangible asset owner's required rate of return on the investment that generates the prospective economic income. This required rate of return is a function of many economic variables, including the risk–or uncertainty–of the expected economic income.

Identification of Customer-Related Intangible Assets

The first step in any valuation process is to identify the subject property. In order for customer/client relationships to have economic value, there should be an active recurring relationship between the company and the customer (or patient, client, etc.). First, analysts exclude any "one time" customers. Such customers may be merely shopping around for the lowest price or friendliest practitioner. In any event, they have not established a recurring relationship with the company.

Second, analysts exclude any "retired" customer. "Retired" customers no longer have a recurring relationship with the company. And, the company would not expect to generate future income from such customers. There is no specific definition as to when a customer has "retired." The practical definition relates to the type of company (i.e., banking, insurance, publishing). In some cases, a customer has "retired" (and the customer relationship has no intangible value) if the customer has not done business with the company in a year or two. In some cases, it may be a much longer period of customer inactivity before the customer is considered to be "retired."

Third, there should be some form of personal relationship between the customer and the company. While this factor is difficult to quantitatively measure, analysts expect the customer to identify with the company. Because of the recurring relationship, we would expect the customer, if asked, to be able to specifically identify "his" or "her" service provider.

Fourth, and likewise, there should be some form of personal relationship between the service provider and the customer. Just as the customer should be able to identify the provider, the provider should be able to identify the customer. In other words, the provider should know something about the customer, such as his/her name, address, telephone number, customer account number, purchase history, or payment history.

To illustrate this point, a McDonald's restaurant and a Kmart store have customers. And, they probably have recurring (i.e., repeat) customers. But, they don't have customer relationships, because they don't collect data regarding individual customers. Without such a relationship, general retailers cannot directly influence a customer the way a service organization can. For example, McDonalds generally cannot send a card to an individual customer to remind him that it is time for his next Big Mac. However, a data processing firm or a commercial bank can send marketing notices to their individual customers.

Fifth, the company should possess or create some form of a file or other tangible documentation regarding the relationship with the customer. Typically, this file documents the services provided by the company for the customer. For example, these documents may include purchase records, service records, or credit/payment files. This factor is important because the customer is more likely to continue a professional relationship with the company that has his or her records.

Sixth, customer relationships generally may be sold or otherwise transferred. This does not mean that the actual customers themselves are sold from one company to another. Rather, the expectation of continued customer loyalty—and recurring customer income—may be sold from one company to another. Of course, the sale or other transfer of customer relationships is not an everyday occurrence. Clearly, most companies would rather maintain their customer relationships than sell their customer relationships. Nonetheless, customer relationships are bought and sold on occasion—and they may be bought and sold separately from any other tangible or intangible assets of the company.

Remaining Useful Life Analysis for Customer-Related Intangible Assets

The next step in the customer relationships valuation is an analysis of remaining useful life ("RUL"). As explained below, the estimation of RUL is an integral part of each valuation approach.

- **Income Approach**–RUL analysis should be performed to estimate the projection period for economic income subject to either yield capitalization or direct capitalization.
- **Cost Approach**–RUL analysis should be performed to estimate the total amount of obsolescence, if any, from the estimated measure of "cost."
- **Market Approach**–RUL analysis should be performed in order to select/reject/adjust "comparable" or "guideline" sale/license transactional data.

The customer relationships RUL analysis will typically have a direct and predictable influence on intangible asset value. The expected influence on value is summarized below.

- **Expected Influence on an Income Approach Valuation**–Normally, a longer RUL would indicate a higher value. The customer relationship value is particularly sensitive when the RUL is less than 10 years. The customer relationship value is not very sensitive when the RUL is greater than 20 years.
- **Expected Influence on a Cost Approach Valuation**–Normally, a longer RUL means a higher value. Normally, a shorter RUL means a lower value.
- **Expected Influence on a Market Approach Valuation**–The "market" should indicate an acceptance for the customer relationships RUL. If the subject RUL is different from guideline sale/license transactions, then adjustments to the transactional multiples may be required. If the subject RUL is substantially different from guideline sale/license transactions, then this may indicate a lack of marketability of the subject.

The following list presents the common determinants, or factors, that influence intangible asset RUL.

- Legal determinants
- Contractual determinants

- Functional determinants
- Technological determinants
- Economic determinants
- Analytical determinants

Each of these RUL determinants should be considered in the analysis of customer/client relationships. Typically, for customer/client relationships, the determinant that indicates the shortest RUL deserves primary consideration.

The Analytical RUL Method

With regard to customer/client relationships, the analytical method often provides the best indication of RUL. There are two procedures related to the application of the analytical method to customer/client relationships RUL estimation:

1. estimation of a historical customer/client attrition rate, and
2. development of survivor curves based on historical attrition rates.

In the analytical method, "survivor curves" are used to estimate the mortality or the decay rate of a group of similar assets (e.g., customer/client/subscriber relationships) as those assets age. The analytical method–and the survivor curve theory–is similar to the mortality theory used by insurance company actuaries in order to estimate the human life span. RUL analysis is the process of estimating the behavior of a group of assets (e.g., customers) by fitting a "test group" of the assets (e.g., customers) to various survivor curves. In that way, by selecting the survivor curve that best "describes" the historical decay patterns of the test group, the future mortality behavior of each customer in the group can be estimated.

Exhibit I illustrates a typical survivor curve. The x-axis represents the age of the customers, and the y-axis represents the percent of the original customers that are still surviving at any given age. For example, at age zero, 100 percent of the customer group is still surviving. As time passes, members of the customer group "retire" (i.e., are no longer customers of the company). Therefore, the percent of the customer group surviving decreases. This creates the downward sloping characteristic of the survivor curve. A survivor curve can be any mathematical function of age that can accurately depict the test group's mortality pattern.

The age at which 50 percent of the original customer group still survives is defined as the "average life." That is, a new customer relation-

ship would have an expected life of the average life of the customer group. In reality, customers are "live" (i.e., active) across a wide range of possible time units. However, the expected life (i.e., the mean life) for a new customer relationship is the average life for the customer group. There are three basic types of survivor curves in the analytical method:

(1) left mode,
(2) symmetric, and
(3) right mode.

A left mode survivor curve depicts a group that retires at a faster rate before the average life is reached and then at a slower rate after the average life is reached. In other words, if the left mode survivor curve accurately predicts a customer group's past behavior, it could be interpreted as the older customers being more loyal than the newer customers–and having a longer relative expected life. A symmetrical survivor curve predicts that a customer group will "retire" at a similar rate at any given relative age on either side of that customer group's average life. A right mode survivor curve is the opposite of the left mode survivor curve. The customers that have reached the customer group's average life tend to decay faster than a customer that has yet to reach the group's average life. Exhibit II illustrates the "curve structure" of a left mode, symmetrical, and right mode survivor curves plotted on the same graph.

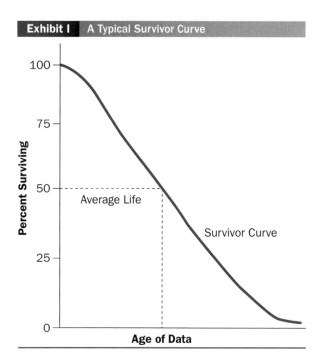

Exhibit I   A Typical Survivor Curve

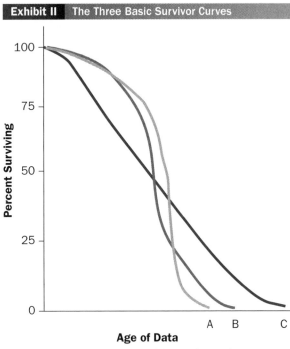

Exhibit II   The Three Basic Survivor Curves

Age of Data

Curve A illustrates a right mode survivor curve

Curve B illustrates a left mode survivor curve

Curve C illustrates a symmetrical survivor curve

The objective of RUL analysis is to estimate the specific RUL of each customer relationship. RUL is defined as the amount of time before a customer is expected to "retire" (and no further economic income can be expected from servicing that customer). An important procedure for estimating a customer's RUL is to calculate the "probable life" for each customer within the customer group. The probable life is the age at which a customer will "retire," given that it has already reached its current age. By subtracting the current age of a customer from its probable life, the RUL of the customer can be estimated. That is:

RUL = Probable Life minus Current Age.

The mathematical definition of the probable life of a customer relationship is the area under the survivor curve (i.e., using calculus, the integral) to the right of the current age of that customer. Every survivor curve has a corresponding probable life curve. For any customer relationship that is already "x" age units (e.g., months, years) old, this relationship can be summarized in the following form:

$$\text{Probable Life of the Customer Relationship} = \int_{\chi}^{\infty} \text{Survivor Curve}$$

Exhibit III illustrates the relationship between percent surviving and probable life. The probable life of a customer relationship at age "x" is described by the shaded area. By solving for the probable life in the equation above for all possible ages, a probable life curve can be constructed. A typical survivor curve and its corresponding probable life curve are illustrated in Exhibit IV.

To estimate the probable life of a customer relationship that is already "z" years old using Exhibit IV, first locate "z" years on the x-axis. Second, find the corresponding point on the survivor curve. Third, draw a ray parallel to the x-axis to the point of the intersection with the probable life curve. The probable life is obtained by moving down the y-axis to the number of years (or months) on the x-axis. Exhibit IV illustrates the probable life (i.e., point PL) of a customer relationship that is already "z" years old. The RUL of each customer relationship can be calculated by using the formula presented above.

There are several sets—or series—of survivor curve mathematical functions that may be used in the analytical method. These common survivor curve mathematical functions include:

- Iowa-type curves (the exponential function is a special case of this type of survivor curve);

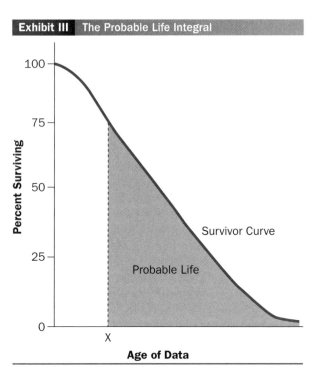

Exhibit III   The Probable Life Integral

Survivor Curve

Probable Life

X

Age of Data

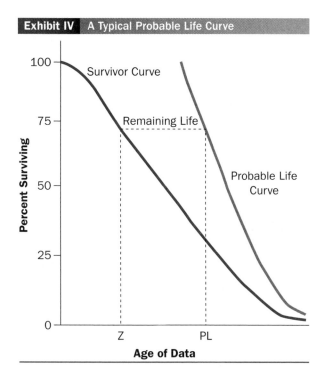

Exhibit IV A Typical Probable Life Curve

- Weibull distributions (Iowa-type curves themselves are a special case of this type of survivor curve);
- Gompertz-Makeham curves; and
- Polynomial equations.

All of these mathematical functions should be considered when selecting the best fitting survivor curve relative to a specific set of customer age characteristic data. In summary, by selecting a survivor curve that accurately depicts the past decay performance of a customer group, the future retirement pattern of the customer group can be estimated. From this retirement pattern, the RUL of each customer relationship can be calculated.

In the analytical method, the procedure used to select an appropriate survivor curve is called "curve fitting." The basic concept is to find the survivor curve that best depicts (i.e., fits) the customer group's prior retirement pattern. The following procedures are typically involved in selecting the best fit survivor curve:

1. Selection of a sample population of "retired" (inactive) customers: A statistically valid random selection of the most recent retired customers is generated. The key information needed for the retired customer sample is the start date and the retirement date of each retired customer relationship.

2. Selection of a sample population of "live" (active) customer relationships: A statistically valid random selection of active customer relationships is generated. The key information needed for the live customer sample is the start date of the customer relationship.

3. Creation of the survivor table: A survivor table is created by using the random samples of retired and live customer relationships described above. A survivor table indicates the percent surviving of the sample customer group at a given age. Exhibit V presents a typical survivor table. The percent surviving at a given age "x" is:

Percent Surviving
at Age x = [Percent Surviving at Age (x – 1)]
$\qquad$ × [1 – Retirement Rate at Age (x)]

The retirement rate at any given age is the ratio of the number of customers who retired at that age divided by the number of customers exposed to retirement at the beginning of the age interval. The number of customers exposed to retirement is simply the number of active customer relationships at the beginning of the age interval.

For example, with regard to Exhibit V, let's assume that:

1. at age interval 5, the percent surviving was 78.448%; and

2. at age interval 5, the retirement rate was 4.268%; then

3. the percent surviving at age interval 6 is (78.448%) times (1 – 4.268%) or 75.099%.

4. Plotting of the survivor table: By selecting the pairs of coordinates (x,y), where x is the age (i.e., the first column in Exhibit V) and y is the percent surviving (i.e., the last column in Exhibit V), an "actual" data curve is plotted. This is illustrated by the "P" markings on Exhibit VI.

5. Selection of best fit survivor curve: All predetermined survivor curves are plotted on the same graph as the "actual" (i.e., survivor table) data described above. These curves are called the "ideal" curves. The difference between the actual percent surviving (i.e., the survivor table) and the "ideal" percent surviving is the "fitting error" at the particular age being examined. By summing all the squares of the fitting errors for a given survivor curve, a ranking factor describing

the "fit" of the curve can be ascertained. The errors are squared both (1) to remove the "canceling" effect of negative fitting errors and (2) to put more emphasis on large errors. As a formula, the curve fitting procedure described above is:

$$\text{Ranking Factor} = \sum_{i=1}^{n} [\text{Survivor Table (age i)} - \text{Survivor Curve (age i)}]^2$$

where "n" is the number of entries in the survivor table selected for the fitting. The method described above is called the stub curve or stub period fitting process, and it is illustrated in Exhibit VI.

All potential survivor curves are fitted over a logical range of average lives, and a ranking factor is assigned to each fitting. The best fit curve is the survivor curve at the specified average life that has the smallest ranking factor. This procedure is typically called minimizing the sum of the squared errors. As each potential survivor curve is "fitted," a correlation coefficient is determined. The correlation coefficient is a ranking from -1 to +1 which describes how well the potential survivor curve fits the actual survivor table data. A correlation coefficient of

+1 suggests that the potential survivor curve–at the average life being fitted–accurately predicts the customer sample's past retirement pattern. A correlation coefficient of -1 suggests that the potential survivor curve being fitted is not a good estimator of the sample customer group's actual past retirement pattern.

Once a "best fit" survivor curve has been selected, the RUL for all active customer relationships can be calculated using the procedure described above. The RUL represents the remaining number of time periods that the company is expected to enjoy an economic benefit from the customer.

Customer Relationships Valuation

Numerous measures of economic income are relevant to the customer relationships valuation. Some of the common measures of economic income include the following:

- Gross or net revenues
- Gross income (or gross profit)
- Net operating income
- Net income before tax
- Net income after tax

Exhibit V	Percent Surviving Table				
Periodic Interval	Exposed to Retirement Beg. of Int.	New Starts	Retired During Interval	Retirement Rate (%)	Percent Surviving Beg. of Int.
1	305	61	27	8.852	100.00
2	244	37	12	4.918	91.143
3	207	28	12	5.797	86.665
4	179	15	7	3.910	81.641
5	164	15	7	4.268	78.448
6	149	14	5	3.355	75.099
7	135	13	5	3.703	72.579
8	122	8	3	2.459	68.891
9	114	8	3	2.631	68.172
10	106	11	1	0.943	66.378
11	95	4	0	0.000	65.752
12	91	15	10	10.989	65.752
13	76	4	1	1.315	58.526
14	72	4	2	2.777	57.756
15	68	6	0	0.000	56.152
16	62	8	1	1.612	56.152
17	54	47	2	3.703	55.246
18	7	1	1	14.285	53.200
19	6	0	0	0.000	45.600
20	6	2	2	33.333	45.600

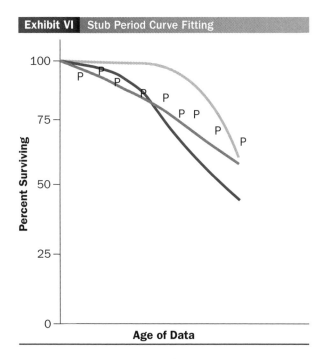

Exhibit VI   Stub Period Curve Fitting

Percent Surviving

Age of Data

- Operating cash flow
- Net cash flow

Given the different measures of economic income that may be used, an essential procedure in the customer relationships valuation is to ensure that the present value discount rate or the direct capitalization rate used in the analysis is derived on a consistent basis with the measure of economic income used. Although there are at least as many valuation methods as there are measures of economic income, all of the methods have similar conceptual underpinnings and similar practical applications. All of the customer relationships valuation methods may be grouped into two analytical categories:

1. Those that rely upon direct capitalization, and
2. Those that rely upon yield capitalization.

In a direct capitalization analysis, the analyst estimates the appropriate measure of economic income for one period (i.e., one period future to the valuation date) and divides that measure by an appropriate investment rate of return. The appropriate investment rate of return is called the direct capitalization rate. The capitalization rate is derived for a specified finite period of time, depending on the RUL of the customer relationships.

In a yield capitalization analysis, the analyst projects the appropriate measure of economic income for several discrete time periods into the future. This projection of prospective economic income is converted into a present value by the use of a present value discount rate. The present value discount rate is the investor's required rate of return, or yield capitalization rate, over the economic income projection period. The discrete projection period depends on the RUL of the customer relationships.

Illustrative Example: Customer Relationships Valuation

This illustrative example will present the valuation of customer/client relationships for property taxation purposes. Alpha Beta is a long-distance telephone services reseller, with both commercial and residential recurring customer/client relationships. Intangible personal property such as customer/client relationships are specifically exempt from property taxation in the local taxing jurisdiction. This example will estimate the value of the customer-related intangible asset of Alpha Beta, as of December 31, 2002 (the property tax assessment date).

Exhibit VII summarizes the valuation of the Alpha Beta recurring customer/client relationships. An income approach method is illustrated in Exhibit VII. Specifically, the yield capitalization method (using net cash flow as the appropriate measure of economic income) is illustrated. In this example, the average RUL of the Alpha Beta customer relationships is determined to be three years. This conclusion was based on an analysis of the historical "placements" and "retirements" of the company's customer relationships. In addition to the RUL of three years, the analysis indicated that the "survivor curve" and "retirement rate" of the customer relationships was estimated by an exponential function, as illustrated in Exhibit VII.

As presented in Exhibit VII, the indicated value of the Alpha Beta customer relationships intangible value is $800,000,000. This is the value of the discrete intangible asset that would be removed from the Alpha Beta overall unit value. This adjustment to the Alpha Beta enterprise unit value would appropriately recognize the property tax exemption for intangible personal property.

Summary and Conclusion

This article discussed the valuation of the customer/client relationships intangible asset as part of a property tax assessment or appeal. As

Exhibit VII — Alpha Beta Long Distance Resellers, Inc.
Valuation of Customer Relationships Intangible Asset
As of December 31, 2002 (in $000s)

Projections:

Years ending:	
Pre-tax operating profit margin (w/o depreciation):	28%
Effective income tax rate:	40%
Expected customer income growth rate:	4%
Present value discount rate:	15%
Starting number of customer relationships:	576,000
Starting annual revenue:	3,462,162
Average RUL:	3 years
Expected retirement rate:	Exponential function

Valuation variables	2002	2003	2004	2005	2006	2007	2008	2009	2010	2011
Percent of customer relationships surviving	100.00%	84.65%	60.85%	43.46%	31.14%	22.31%	15.98%	11.48%	8.21%	5.88%
Number of surviving customer relationships	576,000	488,000	348,000	250,000	179,000	129,000	92,000	68,000	47,000	34,000
Revenues from surviving customer relationships	3,462,162	3,065,574	2,284,278	1,702,320	1,268,538	945,187	704,531	525,133	391,256	291,426
Operating expenses		2,262,013	1,695,514	1,258,101	936,024	697,431	519,856	387,483	288,698	215,036
Depreciation and amortization expense		135,000	111,000	93,000	81,000	72,000	66,000	61,000	58,000	56,000
Total expenses		2,397,013	1,806,514	1,351,101	1,017,024	769,431	585,856	448,483	346,988	271,036
Pretax income		668,561	477,764	351,219	251,514	175,756	118,675	76,650	44,268	20,390
Income tax expense		267,424	191,106	140,488	100,606	70,302	47,470	30,660	17,707	8,156
After tax income		$401,137	$296,658	$210,731	$150,908	$105,454	$71,205	$45,990	$26,561	$12,234
Plus: Depreciation and amortization expense		135,000	111,000	93,000	81,000	72,000	66,000	61,000	58,000	56,000
Less: Capital charge on the tangible and other intangible assets used in the production of the customer income		(245,000)	(183,000)	(136,000)	(102,000)	(76,000)	(56,000)	(42,000)	(31,000)	(23,000)
Economic income cash flow		291,137	224,658	167,731	129,908	101,454	81,205	64,990	53,561	45,234
Present value factor @15% discount rate		.9302	.8089	.7034	.6116	.5319	.4625	.4022	.3497	.3041
Discounted net cash flow		270,816	181,681	117,982	79,452	53,963	37,557	26,139	18,730	13,756
Total discounted net cash flow		800,076								
Indicated value of the customer relationships intangible asset (rounded)		800,000								

in the appraisal of real estate, there are three approaches to the valuation of discrete intangible assets such as customer/client relationships: the cost approach, the market approach, and the income approach. The income approach is most often applicable to the valuation of customer/client relationships.

In the income approach, the value of customer relationships is based on the economic income earned by the company servicing the subject customers. Some of the common measures of economic income include operating income, net income, operating cash flow, and net cash flow. The selected measure of economic income is capitalized (through direct capitalization or yield capitalization) by an appropriate capitalization rate in order to estimate the customer/client relationship value. The RUL of the customer relationships will obviously impact the valuation results. For example, customer relationships with an RUL of three years will have a lower value than the same customer relationships with an RUL of 15 years, if all other factors are held equal. There are several methods to estimate the RUL of intangible assets. However, for customer/client relationships, the analytical method is the most common method.

Customer/client relationships are an important intangible asset of many service-oriented companies, such as transportation, utilities, and communications companies. Therefore, the valuation of this discrete intangible asset may be an important consideration in the ad valorem taxation of such companies.

A Critique of "Enhancement" and Other Theories for Taxing Intangibles: Part I

Richard G. Smith

This article originally appeared in the Summer 2002 issue of the *Journal of Property Valuation and Taxation,* © 2010 CCH, a Wolters Kluwer Law and Business. All rights reserved. Reprinted with permission from the *Journal of Property Valuation and Taxation.*

4

Editors' Note: This article is the first of two articles that address the topic of taxing intangible values in the appraisal of centrally assessed property.

The unit valuation of the property of transportation and telecommunications companies, energy-related companies, and other multistate businesses has been an accepted practice in ad valorem tax assessment since at least 1875.[1]

Unfortunately, a unitary value generally incorporates intangible values to the extent such values exist for a given business. The economic reality that a unitary or business enterprise value[2] includes elements of intangible value has caused problems, particularly in states where intangible property is exempt from taxation.[3] In those states, there is a direct conflict between the results of a unitary valuation and the requirement that intangible property be excluded from assessment and taxation. Even in states where intangible property is not specifically ex-

empt, there are uniformity problems where the property of centrally assessed taxpayers necessarily includes intangible values, while locally assessed taxpayers whose businesses also have intangible value are taxed in a way that does not include that value.[4]

In recent years, state taxing authorities have become increasingly sensitive to taxpayer claims concerning the taxation of intangible

This information was presented at the 31st Annual Wichita Program on Appraisal for Ad Valorem Taxation of Communications, Energy and Transportation Properties, Wichita State University, Wichita, Kansas.

Richard G. Smith *is a partner in the Boise, Idaho office of Hawley Troxell Ennis & Hawley LLP. His practice emphasizes the representation of clients in tax disputes in state and federal courts and before tax commissions and boards of tax appeals throughout the western United States.*

64501   Sig:

1. The unit method of valuation was approved by the United States Supreme Court in a very general way in *State Railroad Tax Cases,* 92 U.S. 575, 23 L.Ed. 663 (1875). The Court provided a more extensive analysis of the unitary approach in *Adams Express Co. v. Ohio,* 165 U.S. 194, 17 S. Ct. 305 (1897), in which the court held, with four dissenting votes, that the unitary approach did not violate the interstate commerce, due process, or equal protection clauses of the United States Constitution. Ever since, the unitary method has been accepted as a legitimate method of assessing the value of companies engaged in interstate commerce. *See Beaver County v. WilTel, Inc.,* 995 P.2d 602, 607 (Utah 2000) (citing *Adams Express* as authority for unitary assessment). It should be noted that the *Adams Express* case does not address whether unitary taxation is consistent with the uniformity requirements common to many state constitutions. (The lack of uniformity is an issue not expressly addressed in this article.) The *Adams Express* case is also distinguishable in this context because the Ohio statutes that were examined in that case appeared to allow the taxation of intangible elements of going concern value, and intangible property was not specifically exempt from taxation.

2. The terms "unit value," "unitary value," "business enterprise value," and "going concern value" are generally synonymous and are used interchangeably throughout this article.

3. A recent survey of the telecommunications industry showed that the intangible property of telecommunications companies was subject to tax in 17 states, while only three states imposed a tax on the intangibles of general business taxpayers. Thus, it appears that in most states intangible property is exempt from taxation. *See* Committee on State Taxation, *50-State Study and Report on Telecommunications Taxation* (Sept. 1999), *cited in* R. Cline, *Reducing Out-of-Line Telecommunications Taxes: State Responses to Increased Competition,* Presentation to the 30th Annual Wichita Program: Appraisal for Ad Valorem Taxation of Communications, Energy and Transportation Companies (Aug. 1, 2000).

4. *See Inter Island Telecommunications Co. v. San Juan County,* 125 Wash.2d 332, 883 P.2d 1380 (Wash. 1994). As noted in this case, state constitutions are sometimes interpreted in a way that imposes stricter requirements on uniformity than would be permitted under a federal constitutional analysis, which generally is liberal in allowing differences in the way interstate enterprises are taxed as long as there is a rational basis for the differences.

property, and many states have addressed the issue legislatively, by regulation, or in court decisions. However, even where the issue has been addressed, and even where intangibles are specifically exempt from taxation, issues still remain concerning how intangible values may be separated from the business enterprise value. The issues have arisen in at least three contexts in court decisions, appraisal literature and commentary, and administrative appraisal practice.

The most significant of these contexts concerns the practice of many states to include the intangible, going concern value of an enterprise as part of the "enhanced value" of the taxable property with which it is associated. This concept finds its roots in California case law, has been refined in California legislation and administrative practice, and has spread to other states.

A second area in which some variation of intangible enhancement value has been recognized involves the cost approach method of valuation. Normally, the "enhancement" component of business enterprise value is observed in the income approach because the capitalization of all of the earnings of a business inevitably captures the value contribution of the intangible assets to the production of those earnings. In the cost approach, however, there is also a concept discussed in appraisal literature known as "entrepreneurial profit" which, in some circumstances, is observed as an upward adjustment. This adjustment is based on the fact that an implicit cost of developing certain types of real property is the developer's profit expectation. Although this concept is primarily related to the valuation of such properties as hotels, shopping centers, office buildings, and industrial sites, some appraisers have recently advocated its use in the valuation of centrally assessed utilities and related properties.

Finally, a relatively recent mutation of the enhancement concept has been developed in the State of Wyoming, which, in this author's opinion, should be discouraged by the appraisal profession. Tax administrators in many states use an income-shortfall method to measure economic obsolescence in the cost approach. Although such an income-based calculation is subject to some criticism on a theoretical level because it tends to merge the cost approach with the income approach, it is a common method of making the difficult economic obsolescence adjustment. In Wyoming, however, tax administrators take this procedure a step further where

income levels exceed the investor's required rate of return. In these situations, Wyoming makes an upward adjustment in the cost approach similar to the downward obsolescence adjustment by increasing the book value of taxable assets by the percentage by which the actual returns exceed the investor's required returns. Although the resulting premium in the cost approach is almost certainly attributable to goodwill or the presence of other intangible assets that enable the business enterprise to achieve extraordinary returns, the adjustment is defended in Wyoming on the basis of consistency with the downward, economic obsolescence adjustment.

Although the economic enhancement adjustment in Wyoming appears to be an isolated phenomenon, it serves to illustrate the potential for confusion in the appraisal and legal treatment of enhanced value associated with the presence of intangibles in a business enterprise. This article will trace the history and review the current status of the conceptually and legally sound enhancement theory that has developed in analyzing the components of business enterprise value. It will study the development of this issue in California and will endorse the approach adopted in California, the leader in the formulation of tax policy in this discrete area of tax law. For intangibles that are not specifically excluded from the business enterprise value by the methods used in California or elsewhere in a manner consistent with appraisal principles, this article will recommend a method for allocating the residual "enhanced value" between tangible and intangible components. The article will then review the "entrepreneurial profit" and Wyoming obsolescence/enhancement theories and show, against the background of the proper application of enhancement theory, that these two variations have no appraisal foundation or substantial legal support for use in the valuation of utility or other centrally assessed business enterprises.

A Proper Model for Recognizing the Taxable Component of the Enhancement of Tangible Property

Summary of the Issues and a Recommended Model for Identifying the Taxable Component of Going Concern Enhancement

For ease of analysis and illustration, this article will discuss a hypothetical valuation and will arbitrarily divide business enterprise property values into four categories.

Before division, the unitary value of the business has been determined to be $100 million. The tangible real property and personal property assets within that going concern have been valued at $50 million, based upon a replacement cost new (RCN) methodology. These assets will be referred to as "Category 1 assets."

The second category of assets is represented by assets that give a company a special license or privilege, such as a public utility franchise, an FCC license, a patent, copyright, trademark, or similar asset of definable value. In some cases, such as with FCC licenses, that asset may actually have a traded market value that can be observed in auction sales of such licenses or in allocated values identified in purchase price allocations in a merger or acquisition. This hypothetical example assumes that "Category 2 assets" have a value of $20 million.

"Category 3 assets" are those which a company has developed as a result of years of building the operational systems, institutional practices, customer relationships, and the knowledge and skills of management and labor that allow it to use the tangible assets in order to generate a profit. Included within this category are such assets as a customer base, an assembled workforce, and favorable contracts. Category 3 assets have been valued at $20 million.

The fourth category of assets are those that may be referred to as "goodwill," going concern, synergistic value, or enhanced value. "Category 4 assets" allow the company to earn profits that may exceed the investor-required rate of return on the company's invested capital, or that could not be achieved without the combination of all of the assets working together as an operating unit.

Categories 1 through 3 yield a total "summation" value of $90 million–$50 million in tangible assets and $40 million in intangible assets. The residual $10 million of the $100 million business enterprise value may be assigned to the Category 4.[5]

This article will conclude that the law has increasingly recognized that Category 2 and Category 3 assets must be deducted from business enterprise value when they can be separately identified and valued as distinct assets. Depending upon how a given state defines the scope of its exemption for intangibles, Category 4 assets may not be specifically exempt and may be seen to "enhance" the value of both the tangible and intangible assets. In this example, this means that the $10 million residual value represents an enhancement pursuant to which the collection of assets operating as a going concern has produced additional value that can be attributed to both the tangible and intangible asset groups.

This article further concludes that it is unfair and inconsistent with both appraisal and legal principles to value the $10 million residual "enhanced" value exclusively as part of the tangible, taxable property base. Instead, the enhancement should be apportioned between the tangible and intangible asset groups. A rational method of apportionment is to use the relative fair market values of the taxable and exempt groups, so that five-ninths of the enhanced value component would be allocated to the taxable assets.[6] As will be demonstrated, such an approach is consistent with and follows naturally from the California cases that developed the enhancement concept, and the more recent cases that have addressed the issue.

The California Cases

A series of California cases has developed legal principles applicable to the enhancement theory that are consistent with appraisal methodology and that are fair and equitable in putting reasonable limits on the taxation of tangible asset value. Before proceeding with an analysis of these cases, it is necessary to have a basic understanding of the California law as it originally applied to the taxation of tangible and intangible property. The importance of these California cases will obviously vary to the extent a given state's laws are significantly different than California. However, it is submitted that this review is relevant to a reader in any state because California provides a useful model for how the enhancement theory should be applied.

Article XIII, Section 1 of California's constitution provides that "[u]nless otherwise provided

---

5. Intangible assets are separated into these categories for purposes of analysis only. Obviously, there may be more categories and more assets within a given category. Some assets, such as tradenames, trademarks, and going concern value, may be considered separate intangible assets or may be included within the overall goodwill of the business.

6. The fraction of 5/9 is derived by using in the numerator the $50 million for the tangible asset value, and in the denominator the total of this $50 million tangible asset value plus the $40 million for the two categories of intangible assets that are assumed to be exempt in this example. This fraction thus represents the proportion of taxable value to total identified value.

by this constitution or the laws of the United States ... all property is taxable and shall be assessed at the same percentage of fair market value." However, Article XIII, Section 14 of the constitution provides that the legislature has the power to provide for the assessment and levy of taxes upon all forms of tangible personal property and "all notes, debentures, shares of capital stock, bonds, solvent credits, deeds of trust, mortgages and any other legal or equitable interests therein." At one time, Section 111 of the Revenue and Taxation Code defined intangible personal property to include the same listing of property items identified in Article XIII, Section 14, and Section 212 provided that all of the listed items except "solvent credits" were exempt from taxation. At the time of the early California cases discussed herein, there was uncertainty concerning whether the combination of Section 14 of Article XIII and Sections 111 and 212 of the Revenue and Taxation Code limited the state's ability to assess intangible property to "solvent credits."

Roehm v. County of Orange

This issue was first addressed in 1948 in *Roehm v. County of Orange*.[7] This decision, authored by the famous jurist Roger Traynor, dealt with the question of whether a liquor license used in the operation of a going concern was subject to taxation under Article XIII, Section 1, or whether it was not subject to tax because it was *not* one of the listed intangibles that were specifically authorized to be taxed in Article XIII, Section 14, and Sections 111 and 212. In setting up the issue, Justice Traynor summarized the parties' positions, and noted the state's position that a liquor license has transferable value and has the characteristics of property, and that if the system of ad valorem taxation is to reach all property in the community, liquor licenses ought not be excluded. He observed, however, that the same reasoning could be applied to other forms of governmental permits, stock exchange seats, memberships, goodwill, and other assets "which have never been taxed as property in this state during its entire existence."[8]

Justice Traynor traced through the relevant constitutional and statutory provisions and reached the conclusion that only certain types of intangibles were subject to taxation, and that did not include liquor licenses. Having concluded that a liquor license is not subject to tax standing alone, the court then introduced the following important qualification to this conclusion:

> Intangible values, however, that cannot separately be taxed as property *may be reflected in the valuation of taxable property.* Thus, in determining the value of property, assessing authorities may take into consideration earnings derived therefrom, which may depend upon the possession of intangible rights and privileges that are not themselves regarded as a separate class of taxable property.[9]

Having introduced this qualification, the court never expanded upon it. Instead, it went on to discuss the policy reasons why the ad valorem taxation of intangibles has become practically impossible in our modern society. The court quoted commentators who had expressed the view that there were insurmountable problems in attempting to fairly value intangible property on a uniform basis, and also quoted from a California Tax Commission investigation that concluded that "[t]he taxation of such property at full valuation and at the full rate is an administrative impossibility and an ethical monstrosity."[10] The court noted that the legislative solution, which included only a certain limited class of intangibles as subject to taxation and even for those at a lower rate, reflected the view that intangibles are better taxed through the income tax system:

> All other types of intangible assets ... are exempted from taxation ... and are therefore not part of the taxable personal property in this state. This system of taxation is supplemented, however, by taxes imposed upon or measured by net income including income derived from all kinds of intangible rights and privileges. Such taxes were regarded by the legislature and the framers of the constitutional amendments to Article XIII of the California Constitution *as a sufficient burden on the benefits derived from the ownership of such rights and privileges.*[11]

Taken as a whole, *Roehm* is an endorsement of the principle that it is both appropriate and necessary for courts to give a broad and practical interpretation of the exemption of intangibles from taxation. Therefore, the court's qualifying language, concerning how intangible values can be "reflected in the valuation of taxable property," must be read with caution. The court simply and correctly observed that the

---

7. 32 Cal. 2d 280, 196 P.2d 550 (Cal. 1948).
8. *Id.* at 283.
9. *Id.* at 285 (emphasis added).
10. *Id.* at 288.
11. *Id.* at 289 (emphasis added).

value of tangible property "may depend upon the possession of intangible rights and privileges." This is, to a large extent, merely a restatement of the concept of "highest and best use." For a building designed as a tavern, for instance, to operate at its highest and best use as a tavern, it may require a liquor license, and without the license it may not be appropriately valued based on that highest and best use. In a certain sense, the intangible value is "reflected in the valuation of taxable property" because it enables the taxable property to achieve its highest and best use. This is not to say, however, that the intangible asset does not have a separate value, which may be appropriately excluded from a going concern, business enterprise value.

The easiest way to avoid the possibly conflicting interpretations of this "intangible values … reflected in the valuation of taxable property" language is to realize that this portion of the court's opinion is *dicta*.[12] It is left for later cases to determine how intangible values may be treated where the intangible is integrally linked with the operation of the tangible asset.[13]

ITT World Communications v. County of Santa Clara

The next significant California case was *ITT World Communications, Inc. v. County of Santa Clara*.[14] ITT had sought to restore a practice that had been used by the California Board of Equalization and then abandoned, whereby the appraiser was directed to use a cost approach method of valuation as a ceiling on value.[15] ITT

argued that any assessment in excess of the cost method must necessarily include part of its franchise value, which was exempt from taxation. The essential premise of the taxpayer's argument, as noted by the court, was that the value of a company's intangible property may be determined by deducting the value of tangible property from the total value of all of its property.

The court could have rested its decision upon a rejection of this simplistic argument by the taxpayer that a cost approach method of value would always represent a ceiling on the value of the tangible property. The court noted, for instance, that appraisal theory indicates that the cost approach should not represent a ceiling on value in a "thin market," or oligopolistic situation, because in such circumstances property would more likely be sold for the capitalized value of the earnings it would produce rather than its replacement cost.[16] However, the court went further than it needed to in suggesting that the entire difference between the cost approach value and the going-concern value may be attributed to the tangible, taxable property. Relying on the Supreme Court's *dicta* in *Roehm*, the court added further gloss on this enhancement concept by reasoning as follows:

> Although Appellant's franchise cannot be assessed and directly subjected to property taxation, the assessment of its taxable property may take into account earnings from *that property* that depend upon Appellant's possession of the franchise. Such an assessment would properly reflect the effect of the intangible value of possession of the franchise on the value of the tangible, taxable property.[17]

12. In addition, the court's specific language states that an assessor "may take into consideration earnings derived *therefrom*" in "determining the value of property" (Emphasis added). The term "therefrom" must mean the earnings derived from the property to be valued and subject to assessment and taxation, not the earnings derived from the entire business. See Colker, *The California Property Tax Exemption for Intangible Assets of Centrally Assessed Taxpayers: Illusion or Reality?"* State Tax Notes, April 24, 1995, at 1752.

13. A subsequent California case of marginal relevance to this issue was *Michael Todd Co. v. County of Los Angeles*, 37 Cal.2d 684, 21 Cal. Rptr. 604 (1962). The issue in *Michael Todd Co.* was how to tax motion picture film. The taxpayer contended that only the value of the physical negative itself should be subject to tax, while the assessor argued that the value of the copyright must be considered in determining the value of the overall property interest. The court declined to address directly the question of the extent to which the intangible property "adhered" to or was inseparable from the value of the tangible property, and instead focused on whether the assessment was discriminatory or constituted actual or a constructive fraud on the taxpayer. *Id.* at 695. It was important to the court's decision that the negatives in question would have no value without considering the benefit of the copyright that would be obtained by a purchaser of the negative. This fact alone makes the *Michael Todd* decision distinguishable from any case involving a centrally assessed taxpayer: The tangible property of any such taxpayer would still have substantial value without the influence of the intangible assets.

14. 101 Cal. App. 3d 246, 162 Cal. Rptr. 186 (1st Dist. 1980).

15. The variation of the cost approach that had been utilized by the State Board was the replacement cost new less depreciation method, or RCNLD.

16. *Id.* at 255.

17. *Id.* at 254 (emphasis added). The court also cited another case that was decided after *Roehm.* In *Western Title Guaranty Co. v. County of Stanislaus,* 41 Cal. App. 3d 733, 741, 116 Cal. Rptr. 351, the court stated as follows in language that was quoted in the ITT decision: "As we learned from *Roehm v. County of Orange, supra,* and *Michael Todd Co. v. County of Los Angeles, supra,* intangible values that cannot be separately taxed as property may be reflected in the valuation of taxable property . . . [T]he propriety of including nontaxable intangible values in the valuation of otherwise taxable property has been asserted by the courts in a variety of contexts, and market value for assessment purposes is the value of property when put to beneficial or productive use." See *ITT,* 101 Cal. App. 3d at 254.

Part of the confusion with this rather imprecise language, similar to the *dicta* in *Roehm*, is the statement that the assessment of taxable property may take into account earnings from "that property" that depend upon the taxpayer's possession of the intangible property.[18] By "that property," (i.e., the taxable tangible property), the court seemed to suggest that all of the earnings of the going concern might be attributable to the tangible property, because "possession of the franchise" has only an "effect" on the value of the tangible, taxable property. However, the court's decision failed to consider two economic principles.

First, although possession of intangibles such as a franchise issued by a public service commission or an FCC license issued to a telecommunications company may permit earnings to be derived from the tangible property with which it is associated, where no earnings would be possible without such an intangible asset, the converse is also true. Without the tangible property, the intangible assets also would have no economic function as part of the going-concern enterprise. Any argument from the *ITT* case that the entire earnings of the going concern can be assigned to the tangible assets proves too much: it essentially argues that the tangible assets dominate the going-concern value, that all value can be attributed to the tangible assets because without them the business could not function, and that the intangible assets merely permit those tangible assets to achieve their highest and best use. But using such a "with or without" analysis, the intangible assets would also be entitled to claim all of the going concern value. Clearly, a utility or telecommunications company, for instance, could not operate without the tangible assets, and yet no one argues that the tangible assets have no value because they are simply an appendage to or have an "effect" on the franchise or FCC license value. The argu-

ment that the tangible assets may be assigned all of the business enterprise value, and that the intangibles are only "along for the ride" because they are necessary to put the tangible assets into operation, displays a sort of arrogance on the part of the proponents of the assessment of tangible assets. In fact, tangible assets are in no sense "better than" or in any real sense different from intangible assets in the necessity of their contribution to the operation of a going concern.

Second, an expansive interpretation of *ITT* to include virtually all intangible value under the enhancement umbrella ignores the fact that the intangibles can be separately valued, and that the earnings of the going concern to which the court referred in *ITT* can be attributed in part and/or apportioned to those intangibles as an economic return upon those intangible assets. It is this principle in particular that distinguishes the latest and most important of the California court decisions.[19]

GTE Sprint Communications v. County of Alameda
In 1994, the First Appellate District of the California Court of Appeals decided *GTE Sprint Communications Corp. v. County of Alameda.*[20] In this case, the taxpayer's arguments were more sophisticated. The case involved a valuation of GTE Sprint's California property. The California Board of Equalization used variations on the three usual valuation methods, including variations of the cost approach producing a value of approximately $100 million, and a capitalized earnings approach (CEA) and a stock and debt method, each of which produced value indications of approximately $160 million.[21] Although there were not significant differences between the State Board and GTE Sprint concerning the going concern values, GTE Sprint appealed its assessment contending that the Board's values impermissibly included

---

18. See note 12, *supra.*

19. An intervening case of passing relevance on this issue was *ITT World Communications, Inc. v. City and County of San Francisco*, 27 Cal.3d 859, 210 Cal. Rptr. 226 (1985). In this case, the taxpayer argued that the assessment limitations and ceilings imposed by California's Proposition 13 should be applied to centrally assessed taxpayers. The court held that the Proposition 13 limits applied only to real and personal property, and essentially treated centrally assessed property as a separate type of property: "Unit taxation prevents real but intangible value from escaping assessment and taxation by treating public utility property as a whole, undifferentiated into separate assets (land, buildings, vehicles, etc.) or even separate kinds of assets (realty or personalty)."7 Cal. App. at 363.

    Much like *Roehm*, the court's broad description of the unit taxation method does not justify the interpretation that unit valuation allows the taxation of assets that are nontaxable under California law. The court was simply stating that unit valuation necessarily includes intangible value, without considering what types of intangibles should be *excluded* from the unit pursuant to applicable law.

20. 26 Cal. App. 4th 992, 32 Cal. Rptr. 2d 882 (1994).

21. *Id.* at 997. The stock and debt method was based in substantial part on the recent acquisition by GTE of the capital stock of Sprint.

the value of a broad range of intangible assets, including customer base, assembled workforce, favorable contracts, and goodwill. The presence of such intangibles was suggested by the $60 million difference between the cost approach value and the CEA and stock and debt values that would be expected to include substantial elements of intangible value.

The court acknowledged the holdings of the earlier California decisions to the effect that intangible values may be reflected in the valuation of taxable property. The court soundly rejected, however, the notion that the entire value of the intangibles could be included in computing the enhanced value of GTE Sprint's tangible property. The court quoted with approval the following testimony from GTE Sprint's appraiser:

> [T]he appraisal process involved first valuing the entire enterprise; then identifying the various components making up that operating enterprise. One category being tangible property; another large category being intangible assets. And that being comprised of several small items such as leasehold interests . . . . Then there is a process. . . wherein the appraiser looks at the total enterprise value and the value indications he has derived from various parts and, in consideration of all of the factors that come out of the investigation, he then draws the conclusion of value for each of the elements comprising the enterprise.[22]

Immediately after quoting this testimony, the court stated the following conclusion: "In our view the board and its appraisers erred in assuming that unit valuation, especially when calculated by the CEA method, necessarily taxes only the intangible values as they enhance the tangible property. This absolutest approach obscures the board's duty to exclude intangible assets from assessment."

In finding support for its decision, the court noted that the board's own appraisal manual endorsed the practice of separately valuing the income expectancy of intangibles. Further, in two recent board decisions affirmed by the California Court of Appeals, the board itself had deducted intangible asset values from the going concern value of one cable television company, and had rejected a unitary appraisal of another cable television operator for many of the same reasons.[23]

The key to the court's opinion was its recognition that where intangible assets have inde-

pendent value, it is error for the appraiser to fail to exclude intangible asset values from the unitary assessment. In its conclusion, however, the court left open the issue of whether there may be a "portion of the intangible values" that might represent enhancement of the tangible asset value. Specifically, the court stated that in further proceedings before the board, "both parties may present evidence as to the portion of the intangible values, *if any*, that can be deemed to enhance the value of the tangible property."[24] The court gave no guidance on how an intangible asset might have an "enhancement value" component that could be part of the taxable assessed value, while also retaining its identity and value as an exempt intangible. One clue for resolution of this ambiguity is in the court's use of the term "if any," suggesting that no portion of an intangible value might be deemed to enhance the value of tangible property where the intangible asset is specifically identified and valued. Another alternative, which is consistent with the court's holding and with appraisal theory, derives from the fact that it is common for a business enterprise value to exceed the total values of the specifically identifiable tangible and intangible assets of the business. That residual value would properly be the basis for an enhancement adjustment of the taxable property value if, as discussed in more detail below, it is recognized to be an enhancement of the value of both the tangible and intangible assets.

Subsequent California Legislation

In 1996, the California legislature amended Section 110 of the Revenue and Taxation Code to codify and clarify the *GTE Sprint* finding. This article will analyze this statutory amendment in some detail because it serves as a model that addresses many of the problems inherent in the improper inclusion of intangible values in the taxation of tangible, operating property. The 1996 legislation added the following subsections to Section 110:

> (d) Except as provided in subdivision (e), for purposes of determining the "full cash value" or "fair market value" of any taxable property, all of the following shall apply:
>
> (1) The value of the intangible assets and rights relating to the going concern value of a business using taxable property

---

22. *Id.* at 1005.

23. *Shubat v. Sutter County Assessment Appeals Board,* 13 Cal. App. 4th, 794, 17 Cal. Rptr. 2d 1 (Ct. App. 1993); *County of Orange v. Orange County Assessment Appeals Board,* 13 Cal. App. 4th, 524, 531-33, 16 Cal. Rptr. 2d 695 (Ct. App. 1993).

24. 21 Cal. App. 4th at 1008 (emphasis added).

shall not enhance or be reflected in the value of the taxable property.

(2) If the principle of unit valuation is used to value properties that are operated as a unit and the unit includes intangible assets and rights, then the fair market value of the taxable property contained within the unit shall be determined by removing from the value of the unit the fair market value of the intangible assets and rights contained within the unit.

(3) The exclusive nature of a concession, franchise, or similar agreement, whether de jure or de facto, is an intangible asset that shall not enhance the value of taxable property, including real property.

(e) Taxable property may be assessed and valued by assuming the presence of intangible assets or rights necessary to put the taxable property to beneficial or productive use.

(f) For purposes of determining the "full cash value" or "fair market value" of real property, intangible attributes of real property shall be reflected in the value of the real property. These intangible attributes of real property include zoning, location, and other such attributes that relate directly to the real property involved.

Section (d) (1) of this statute takes the holding of *GTE Sprint* one step further toward a full exclusion of intangible values. Where *GTE Sprint* suggested that intangible assets and rights may still be capable of enhancing the value of the taxable property, subject to proof, the statute unequivocally states that such enhancement shall not be allowed. Subsection (d) (3) clarifies that franchise value is one of the intangible assets that are deemed not to enhance the value of taxable property. Section (d) (2) specifies that where the unit approach is used to value an operating system, the fair market value of the intangible assets and rights shall be deducted from that unit value.

Subsections (e) and (f) preserve two principles of the valuation of tangible assets that are truly necessary as part of the "enhanced" value of tangible assets, and perhaps represent the true concept of enhancement for ad valorem tax purposes. Subsection (e) assures that taxable property may be valued by assuming the presence of the intangible assets necessary to put the taxable property to beneficial use. This statement essentially represents the more limited interpretation of *Roehm* and related cases—that for the tangible assets to achieve their highest and best use, one must assume the existence of intangible assets that are necessary to achieve this highest and best use. This is not to say, however, that the intangible assets, or the residual values above tangible asset value that are represented in a going concern valuation, are part of the value of the taxable property. Indeed, as noted above, the intangible values must be deducted from the unitary value. Subsection (e) recognizes only that the taxable property may be assessed under the highest and best use assumption.

Subsection (f) states a similar principle: that the "intangible attributes" of real property may be reflected in the value of that property. The term "intangible attributes" refers to "zoning, location, and other attributes that relate directly to the real property involved." Again, such a clarification is consistent with the total exemption of intangible values. No reasonable taxpayer would argue that real property values attributable to location or zoning are not part and parcel of the value of the property itself.

The approach of the California legislature arguably accounts for the entire difference between tangible asset value and going concern value, and classifies that difference as an exempt intangible. But in other states, even though the value differential can be explained by the presence of intangibles, a particular state's definition or treatment of specific intangibles may dictate a different result than California. In the hypothetical introduced earlier, going concern value was assumed to be $100 million and tangible asset values (Category 1) represented $50 million of that total. Two categories of intangibles that could be separately identified were each valued at $20 million, leaving a residual $10 million value. Once this residual value is identified, two issues arise. First, how should the residual amount be characterized? In other words, is the residual amount an element of goodwill, which itself might qualify as an intangible asset subject to exemption under the laws of a given state?[25] Or is the residual a type of synergistic effect that should not be considered goodwill but might be classified as a true enhancement of both the tangible and intangible assets?[26] Second, if the

---

25. Since 1993, goodwill has also been identified as an intangible asset eligible for amortization under section 197 of the Internal Revenue Code. 26 U.S.C. § 197.

26. *See Beaver County v. WilTel, Inc.,* 995 P.2d 602, 610-611 (Utah 2000), discussed in detail below, where the Utah Supreme Court treated the "physical and functional integration" of the taxpayer's tangible property, operating as a unit or a "network structure," as analogous to the location "attribute" of real property that is part of the value of the property itself.

residual does not represent an exempt intangible such as goodwill, and is thus properly a candidate for enhancing the value of the taxable property, should that enhancement component be allocated all to the tangible property or apportioned between the taxable and exempt property?

It is not clear from California's newly amended Section 110 whether goodwill would be included as an intangible asset. If it is, then under subsection (d)(2) it must be deducted from the value of the unit. If it is not, an analysis might be necessary to determine whether a portion of that residual value might be deemed to "enhance" the value of the taxable, tangible property. Although the California statute is not completely clear, the California Board of Equalization has taken the position that goodwill is an exempt intangible asset and should be deducted from the going concern value. This position is expressed in Chapter 5 of the *California Board's Appraisal Handbook*.[27] The chapter entitled "Advanced Appraisal" addresses the components of a going concern value and the methods available to an appraiser to properly exclude intangible values from the going concern.[28] The *California Appraisal Manual* specifically endorses the "residual" technique for excluding goodwill, and in doing so explicitly accepts the practice of assigning the $10 million residual value, in our example, to goodwill in the exempt class.[29]

As noted, the progressive approach of the California Board may not be the practice of other states,[30] and in those states where goodwill or perhaps other intangible assets are not recognized as being exempt, there is room for the enhancement theory and some method is needed to determine how much of the residual value of a business represents enhancement of the tangible assets and how much can be attributed to the intangible property.

A Practical Model for Determining Taxable, Enhanced Value[31]

As just noted, the necessity of determining an enhanced value and apportioning that value between tangible and intangible assets may depend upon the state law treatment of intangibles and the scope of the intangibles exemption. If the $10 million of Category 4 residual intangibles used in the hypothetical example represents goodwill and goodwill is not exempt under state law, then it is a possible candidate for enhancement to the tangible asset base. In addition, if the Category 4 is determined not to represent goodwill at all, but some other form of enhanced value, such as synergy or other amorphous going concern element of value, then this is another basis for considering the Category 4 residual as eligible for enhancement to the taxable asset base. Finally, it may be that intangibles in the Category 3 might be subject to an enhancement adjustment as well, because not all states recognize such assets as a customer base or an assembled workforce as intangibles eligible for exclusion from the unitary value.[32]

One must start with the realization, then, that the extent of the enhancement adjustment must depend upon the provisions of state law that define the scope of the intangibles exemption. The eligible enhancement adjustment may be zero, $10 million, $30 million, or even $50 million in our hypothetical example, depending upon how state law defines the exemption for intangibles. Whatever the amount of the

---

27. This Handbook represents an excellent expression of generally accepted appraisal principles, including citations not only to California case law but also to widely recognized appraisal literature.

28. The board's appraisal handbook is available on the Internet at the following address: boe.ca.gov/proptaxes. The current Appraisal Handbook section on advanced appraisal techniques has a December 1998 adoption date. The techniques recommended to exclude intangible values are to use approaches (such as the cost approach) to avoid the appraisal of the business enterprise activity, or to directly value the intangibles and deduct that intangible value from the unitary value.

29. Specifically, page 162 of the Appraisal Handbook states as follows:

    Goodwill, going-concern value, and similar intangible assets typically are valued using a residual technique. For an ongoing business enterprise, the appraiser will value all of the tangible assets and as many intangible assets and rights as possible using direct valuation methods. The difference between the sum of the values of the tangible and intangible assets and rights and the value of the entire business enterprise can be ascribed to goodwill, going concern, or similarly termed intangible assets.

30. *See Michigan Bell v. Treasury Department,* 445 Mich. 470, 518 N.W.2d 808 (Mich. 1994) (holding that under Michigan law, both tangible and intangible property are subject to assessment).

31. The author claims no credit for the recommended method for allocating enhanced value between taxable and exempt assets. The author is aware of several appraisers who have used or are aware of such a method for allocating enhancement value.

32. *See Merle Hay Mall v. Board of Review,* 564 N.W.2d 419, 424 (Iowa 1997) (distinguishing cable television cases and declining to exclude intangibles such as assembled workforce that are not specifically identified in tax exemption statute). *See also Ithaca Industries, Inc. v. Commissioners,* 17 F.3d 684 (4th Cir. 1994); *Burlington Northern R.R. Co. v. Bair,* 815 F. Supp. 1223 (S.D. Iowa 1993), *aff'd,* 60 F.3d 410 (8th Cir. 1995).

enhancement total, this article recommends that it be allocated between tangible and intangible values based on the relative values of the specifically identifiable assets that are taxable and exempt.

If the residual value of the business enterprise that is neither specifically taxable nor exempt is the $10 million Category 4 property, that amount should be apportioned between taxable and exempt assets based upon the proportion each bears to the total of taxable and exempt assets.[33] This would be the ratio of 5 to 9 resulting in an additional $5.5 million of taxable value for a total of $55.5 million.

If only Category 2 assets (i.e., franchises, licenses, copyrights, patents, and related assets) are exempt from taxation, valued at $20 million, and the additional Category 3 intangibles of $20 million are specifically taxable, the ratio of specifically taxable assets to the total of taxable and exempt assets would be $70 million (Category 1 plus Category 3) to $90 million, or 77.8 percent. This results in an additional $7.8 million of enhancement value and a total assessed value of $77.8 million.

Finally, if Category 3 assets are neither specifically taxable nor considered a "separable" asset that can be excluded from the unit value, they are arguably part of the residual enhancement, resulting in a total enhancement component of $30 million. The proper ratio to value the taxable component of this $30 million residual would be the ratio of the $50 million specifically taxable Category 1 assets to the $70 million total of taxable and specifically exempt assets, or 71 percent. The 71 percent applied to the $30 million residual would produce additional taxable value of about $21.4 million, for a total of $71.4 million of assessed value.

This recommended method of allocation based on relative fair market values of other property might be described as an unscientific or theoretically "naive" method. In similar contexts, there has been criticism of naive value allocation techniques that are based upon the income contribution of different assets or the book values of taxable assets compared with the unit as a whole. Such allocations are sometimes made, for instance, when a unit value must be segregated between operating and non-operating assets, an exercise that is similar in many respects to the parsing of enhancement value between tangible and intangible values. Problems with book value allocations focus on the fact that book value is often a poor surrogate for fair market value.[34] Complaints about income allocations center on the reality that a dollar of income from one investment may be worth more than a dollar of income from another, as evidenced by the widely varied price-earnings multiples by which the stock market compares the prices of securities to their current earnings.[35] A dollar of income from a company expected to achieve significant growth would be priced at a higher multiple than a security of a company with stable or declining past and projected earnings.

These difficulties are resolved in a method that begins with the fair market values of the other assets in the unitary asset group. The objection to the other naive techniques is that they do not use market value as a basis for allocation: If market value is being allocated, but the ratio by which it is allocated does not have market value in either the numerator or denominator, the result will represent market value only by coincidence. The method recommended here contains market value terms in both the numerator and denominator of the ratio used to allocate the enhanced value component.

This article's premise that some allocation of enhanced value must be made between tangible and intangible assets is permitted by the foregoing review of the case law and statutes of California, which has been the leader in this area, and is virtually compelled by economic and appraisal principles. The court in *GTE Sprint* flatly rejected the proposition that the entire residual value between identifiable, tangible property value and going-concern value can be characterized as enhanced value associated with the tangible assets. Nor is such a conclusion logical or reasonable from an economic

---

33. Determining the appropriate enhancement adjustment for taxable, tangible property may be more of an appraisal question than a legal one. However, the line between legal analysis and theoretical, appraisal justifications is imprecise, and there is a substantial overlap. Courts frequently refer to appraisal literature for guidance on rational and accepted methods of determining the "fair market value" objective generally established by statute. In turn, appraisal literature is frequently guided by principles set forth in court decisions.

34. *See Line Railroad Co. v. Department of Revenue,* 89 Wis.2d 331, 278 N.W.2d 487 (Wis. App. 1979).

35. *In re Southern Railway,* 313 N.C. 177, 328 S.E.2d 235 (N.C. 1985); *Southern Pacific Transportation Co. v. Department of Revenue,* 111 Or. Tax Rep. 138 (Or. Tax 1989).

or appraisal perspective. Thus, some allocation must be made. And where tangible and intangible assets are operating together as a unit, it is logical that the overall investment return associated with those assets can be shared equally among the assets. It is true, of course, that with an integrated set of assets, the loss of any one asset, tangible or intangible, might impair the earning capacity of the entire system, and so it could be argued that the incremental return on any single asset cannot be determined or is infinite. However, a rational view of the returns on individual assets or even groups of assets is that, for an integrated operating system, each asset should be assigned the average return for the integrated group as a whole.

From the perspective of tax policy and practical ease of tax administration, such an allocation methodology has substantial appeal. In the annual assessment process, it is often difficult for both the tax administrator and the taxpayer to complete sophisticated valuations of the components of a unitary value. To the extent easily applied appraisal methods can be used to determine the tangible asset values and identifiable intangible assets, the residual enhancement component can be allocated in a manner that is consistent with the time constraints and manpower limitations of both tax assessors and taxpayer representatives.

In summary, the enhancement component of unitary value is that portion of the unitary value that cannot be explained by the separate valuation of the tangible assets and the exempt, intangible assets. It is disingenuous at best to presume that this entire residual is an enhancement of the taxable property entirely, with no portion attributable to the exempt, intangible assets. Some reasonable method must be employed to allocate that residual between taxable and exempt assets. There is no good alternative to using a straight allocation based upon market values, and no principled reason why such an allocation is not proper.

A Critique of "Enhancement" and Other Theories for Taxing Intangibles: Part II

Richard G. Smith

This article originally appeared in the Fall 2002 issue of the *Journal of Property Valuation and Taxation*, © 2010 CCH, a Wolters Kluwer Law and Business. All rights reserved. Reprinted with permission from the *Journal of Property Valuation and Taxation*.

5

Editors' Note: This article is the second of two articles that address the topic of taxing intangible values in the appraisal of centrally assessed property.

Testing the Recommended Model by Comparison with Two Recent Court Decisions

The WilTel Case

In *Beaver County v. WilTel, Inc.*,[1] the Utah Supreme Court dealt with the telecommunications company's claim that an enhancement component was improperly included in the assessed value. Utah statutes at that time exempted a broad variety of intangibles from taxation, including goodwill.[2] The taxpayer attacked the Utah Tax Commission's valuation on a number of grounds, but its attack on the treatment of intangibles appeared to be unfocused and did not follow the "roadmap" provided by the *GTE Sprint* case from California. Specifically, the taxpayer adopted the argument used unsuccessfully in *ITT World Communications* to the effect that all value in excess of a cost measure of value for the tangible property must necessarily be associated with exempt, intangible values. The court rejected this argument and concluded that it was appropriate to apply the state appraiser's method, which "attempted to capture the fair market value of the company's property operating together as a single unit." The court stated the proposition that "fair market value reflects the benefit stream created by unitary operation

of *tangible property*," and then concluded that if the legislature had desired to limit the assessed value to the materials and installation costs of tangible assets, it could easily have done so.[3]

The court's analysis and conclusions are ambiguous, perhaps in part because of the disparate arguments presented to the court by the taxpayer, the Commission and its staff, and the intervening counties. The unnecessarily broad language of the court that it was appropriate to "capture the fair market value of the *company's property* operating together as a single unit" suggests a conclusion that the entire unitary value could be assessed notwithstanding the existence of intangibles. However, a contrary signal is given by the court's rejection of an argument by the county that the taxpayer's proposed values for "assembled workforce," "customer relations," and "goodwill and other intangibles" should be added to the taxpayer's cost approach value. The court noted that this approach is inconsistent with the specific exclu-

This information was presented at the 31st Annual Wichita Program on Appraisal for Ad Valorem Taxation of Communications, Energy and Transportation Properties, Wichita State University, Wichita, Kansas.

Richard G. Smith is a partner in the Boise office of Hawley Troxell Ennis & Hawley LLP. His practice emphasizes the representation of clients in tax disputes in state and federal courts and before tax commissions and boards of tax appeals throughout the western United States.

1. *Beaver County v. WilTel, Inc.*, 995 P.2d 602 (Utah 2000).
2. Utah Code Ann. §§ 59-2-1101(2)(g); 59-2-102(17). Subsequent to the *WilTel* decision, the Utah legislature amended the statutes to remove goodwill and "other intangibles" from the list of intangibles exempt from taxation, and also added the requirement that intangible property must be "capable of separate ownership." *See* Young, State High Court Rules on Non-tax Status, Value of Intangibles, *J. Multi-State Tax'n* (Oct. 2000).
3. 995 P.2d at 611 (emphasis added).

sion of "goodwill and other intangibles" from taxation under Utah law.[4] Another indication that the court was sensitive to the presence of intangibles and the necessity of excluding them is the following analysis, which set the stage for the court's rejection of a pure cost approach treatment of valuing the tangible assets as a means of excluding intangibles:

> However, *even excluding intangibles,* the *network structure* of WilTel's physical transmission facilities makes them worth far more on the open market than mere wires, trenches, and transformer stations could command. Unitary property cannot be regarded as merely land, buildings, and other assets. Rather, its value depends on the *interrelation and operation of the entire utility as a unit.* Many of the separate assets would be practically valueless without the rest of the system. Ten miles of telephone wire or one specially designed turbine would have a questionable value, other than as scrap, without the benefit of the rest of the system as a whole.[5]

The court then addressed the taxpayer's argument that this enhanced value that is created from the "network structure" of the taxpayer's facilities is a tax-exempt intangible. The court agreed with the counties and the commission that such enhancement is a taxable "attribute" of tangible property, much like location or a value-enhancing view of a hillside home. The court cited *The Appraisal of Real Estate* treatise for a description of the value characteristics of location as an attribute of property[6] and observed, "in other words, the augmentation in value results from property and market components, however incorporeal, that are not separately quantifiable as tax-exempt intangibles."[7]

The court's reliance on locational attributes of a telecommunications company as supporting an enhanced value of its property explains its decision in a way that recognizes the necessity of excluding intangible asset value, while also rejecting the argument that a cost valuation of the assets is an appropriate means of excluding intangible asset value. The court did not disagree with the concept that intangible asset values

could be excluded from the going concern, as long as the valuation attributes of the tangible property are still recognized. By rejecting the county's argument that specifically valued intangible assets should be added to a cost approach valuation, the court implicitly conceded that those same assets ought to be deducted from an income approach valuation that necessarily includes those intangibles, so long as the exclusion does not reduce the tangible asset value below a level which recognizes the enhanced value attributes of the "network structure."

Although the court described the "network structure" attribute of the tangible telecommunications property as a "location" influence, it is better described as an "assemblage" value attribute—the kind of synergy that is inherent in the efficient combination of property serving an economic purpose. "Assemblage" is defined in *The Appraisal of Real Estate* treatise as "incremental value that results when two or more sites are combined to produce greater utility."[8] Another appraisal authority describes assemblage and the related "plottage" concept as follows:

> Assemblage is the act of putting together separate typically adjacent parcels to create a single parcel of greater value than the cumulative value of the individual parcels; plottage is the incremental value that is created through the process of assemblage. For example, a developer may buy three out of the four parcels in a square city block for $1,000,000 each. If the entire assembled city block parcel is worth $10,000,000, then the remaining fourth parcel has the potential to experience assemblage and create plottage value.[9]

These commentators describe such features of real property as "intangible influences and non-intangible assets." This would support the Utah Supreme Court's approach in concluding that an assemblage of a "network" of utility, telecommunications, or related types of property may enhance the value of the tangible, taxable property.

The Utah Supreme Court's decision can thus be explained in a way that is wholly consistent with the methodology for excluding intangibles recommended in this article. Again, the court

---

4.   *Id.* at 611.

5.   *Id.* at 610 (emphasis added), citing Louis G. Bertane, *The Assessment of Public Utility Property in California,* 20 UCLA L. Rev. 419, 433 (1973).

6.   "Location is the time-distance relationships, or linkages, between a property or neighborhood and all possible origins and destinations of residents coming to or going from the property or neighborhood. *The Appraisal of Real Estate* 44 (Appraisal Institute, 10 ed., 1992)." *Id.* at 610.

7.   *Id.* at 610.

8.   *The Appraisal of Real Estate* 230 (Appraisal Institute, 11th Ed., 1996).

9.   Reilly & Schweihs, *Valuing Intangible Assets* 413 (1998).

would allow the exclusion of specific intangibles from the unitary value, because of its rejection of the counties' arguments that intangible values could be added to a cost approach estimate of value, and its statement that the taxable property might have a value exceeding its replacement costs, "even excluding intangibles," because of the "network structure" of the physical facilities. The court's endorsement of enhancement theory, therefore, can be seen more as a rejection of a simplistic cost approach method of valuing tangible property than as an acceptance of the erroneous proposition that all intangible value could be swept within the ambit of taxable property simply because it contributes to the "benefit stream created by the unitary operation of tangible property." By recognizing this "location" or assemblage value that adheres to the tangible property, the court simply recognized these types of enhancements as possible components of the residual difference between going-concern value and specifically identifiable tangible and exempt intangible assets.

Questions could arise, of course, concerning the specific amount by which a location or assemblage enhancement might explain the residual between going-concern value and specifically identified tangible and exempt intangible assets. For instance, in the example used in this article, where a $10 million residual is assumed to represent goodwill, some additional analysis may be necessary to determine whether that residual is, in fact, goodwill or is instead associated with some value-enhancing attribute of the tangible property. An appraiser could perform such an analysis by specifically valuing the goodwill component by some method other than the residual technique, which would assign the entire $10 million to goodwill.[10] There also may be methods of valuing the assemblage component separately. In states where goodwill is not exempt, the entire $10 million would fall within the enhancement component that would need to be allocated between tangible and exempt intangible assets. Finally, even in states where goodwill is exempt, the taxpayer may conclude that the difficulty of separating the goodwill component of this residual from the remaining tangible property attribute value is too great, and simply accept an allocation of the entire $10 million residual based on the relative values of the tangible property and specifically valued intangibles. The *WilTel* decision is consistent with any of these alternatives.

The RT Communications Case

In *RT Communications, Inc. v. State Board of Equalization*,[11] the Wyoming Supreme Court addressed the issue of the assessment and taxation of an "acquisition adjustment" premium the taxpayer paid over book value for the acquisition of three small telephone companies. The taxpayer claimed that the premium could be deducted from unitary value because it was "related to values associated with the business of the utilities such as goodwill, the certificate of convenience, and franchise rights." In a well-reasoned opinion, the court rejected this claim primarily on evidentiary grounds. The court's analysis is entirely consistent with the methodology recommended in this article, as well as the foregoing explanation of the *WilTel* case. At certain points, however, the court used imprecise and potentially overbroad language in describing the contours of the taxable enhancement component, which is certainly not surprising considering some of the confusing legal and economic analyses contained in the cases upon which it relied. However, on balance, the *RT Communications* case advances the development of the law related to the taxation of the enhancement component of unitary value.

The taxpayer in *RT Communications* acquired the telephone companies at prices that exceeded book value by a significant percentage. For accounting and regulatory purposes, the excess of the purchase price over book value is treated as an "acquisition adjustment." Typically, a utility is not permitted to earn a return on the acquisition adjustment component of the purchase price. The taxpayer argued that the acquisition adjustment represented intangible personal property that should be exempt from taxation under Wyoming law.[12] The taxpayer thus made

---

10. *See id.* at 388-91 (recognizing residual method, capitalized excess economic income method, and present value of future economic events method as alternatives in the valuation of goodwill in the income approach).

11. 11 P.3d 915 (Wyo. 2000).

12. The taxpayer also argued that the Wyoming Department of Revenue failed to make an adjustment for economic obsolescence in the cost approach, presumably on the theory that the acquisition adjustment was not earning an economic return. The court rejected this argument in part because the taxpayer did not provide information concerning the future income that could be expected from the property, and thus any deficiencies in income that might support an economic obsolescence adjustment.

the same argument that was rejected in *ITT* and *WilTel*–that the entire going concern value in excess of the book or replacement cost of tangible assets could be assigned to exempt intangibles and excluded from taxation. The Supreme Court rejected this argument for many of the same reasons as the California and Utah courts.

The court reviewed in some detail the legal and economic considerations involved in determining unitary or going concern value and in separating the intangible property value from the going concern with which it is associated. The court cited *WilTel, ITT,* and a number of commentators for two background principles supporting the consideration of intangible property as part of the enhancement of tangible property value. First, the court noted that "intangible value can affect the value of tangible property." The court quoted one commentator's analogy as follows:

> Trying to separate intangible rights from tangible value is comparable to trying to separate tangible value of the bricks and mortar of your house from the intangible rights found in your deed and building and occupancy permits to use and occupy the house. In other words, if you do not have the intangible right to live in your house and evict others from the premises, what possible value can the house have to you?[13]

This analogy is but a variation of the analysis used by the Utah court in *WilTel,* identifying *attributes* that are properly included within the consideration of tangible property values.

The court then identified a second argument for using intangible property to assess the value of tangible property: "the difficulty of separating intangible property from tangible property." The court quoted the following excerpt from another commentary which addressed this difficulty:

> The value of intangible assets is manifested in their ability to generate profits for the enterprise in excess of those necessary to provide a fair return on the value of the tangible assets and working capital of the business. Some intangible assets have value in their own right, such as franchises, patents, licenses, copyrights and the like. However, many of the intangible assets of a business enterprise derive their value from being a part

of the business and thus cannot be severed and sold separately. Some of these types of intangibles include a trained and assembled work force, management systems, customer base, and elements of "going-concern" value.[14]

This suggests that the court might draw a line between "franchises, patents, licenses, copyrights and the like," which can be severed and sold, and other types of intangibles, such as assembled workforce, customer base, and elements of going concern value, that cannot be severed and sold.[15] However, the court was never required to decide whether one or both of these categories were eligible for exclusion to the extent they could be separately valued. This is because "the telephone companies themselves made no attempt to allocate specific amounts to the values of the certificates of convenience and necessity, rights of way, or other intangible items of value that they contended were obtained when the property was purchased." Indeed, the taxpayers conceded "that some portion of the acquisition adjustments could represent enhanced value of the taxable property." But since they "could not, or would not, allocate separate values to these intangible assets, they cannot reasonably argue that the Department of Revenue could have or should have done so."[16]

There are three portions of the opinion that distill its holding and, although endorsing the underpinnings of the enhancement concept, recognize the important requirement of excluding intangible property. The court summarized its general agreement with the enhancement concept as follows:

> Although intangible personal property is exempt from taxation, it may add value to taxable, tangible property, and to that extent, it should be included in any assessment in order to properly reflect the true value of the property. Wy. Const. Art. 15, § 11.[17]

Though such a sweeping statement might otherwise be alarming to centrally assessed taxpayers, the court immediately followed that statement with the following limitation:

> In utilizing the unitary method, however, to the extent that intangible property has value beyond the

---

13. *Id.* at 924, quoting Lambert, *Cellular Telephone Companies: Property Tax Litigation in California,* J. Prop. Tax Mgmt. 15, 16 (1991).

14. *Id.,* quoting Michael E. Green & Terrence J. Benshoof, *Exclusion of Intangibles From The Unit Value,* 1 St. Tax Notes 547, 548-49 (1991).

15. Such a distinction would be similar to the distinction between Category 2 intangibles and Category 3 intangibles in the hypothetical used in this article.

16. *Id.* at 924.

17. *Id.* at 925. The provision of the Wyoming Constitution that is cited is entitled "Uniformity of Assessment Required," and provides, *inter alia,* that property "shall be uniformly valued at its full value as defined by the legislature," and that "all taxation shall be equal and uniform within each class of property."

enhancing effect on tangible property and is separable from those assets, it must be excluded. *GTE Sprint Communications Corporation v. County of Alameda*, 32 Cal. Rptr. 2d 882, 891 (Cal. Ct. App. 1994); § 39-1-201(a)(xxix).[18]

By citing *GTE Sprint* and paraphrasing its holding, the court adopted the requirement that intangibles must be removed from the going concern value. It also regrettably incorporated the ambiguities in that decision discussed earlier in this article. In the "conclusion" section of its opinion, however, the Wyoming court provided some additional clarification:

> The unitary method is a rational means of determining the fair market value of a public utility. Intangible personal property, although generally exempt from taxation, may be considered in valuing utility property to the extent that the property enhances the value of taxable, tangible property. This is an appropriate methodology to determine the fair market value of utility property. *However, the Department of Revenue shall, to the extent possible, remove the value of intangible personal property that is separable and identifiable.*[19]

These three quotations from the *RT Communications* decision can be synthesized and explained in much the same way as the *GTE Sprint* decision upon which it relies. First, to the extent intangible personal property is separable and identifiable, it should be deducted from the unitary value. This command is clear from the conclusion of the court's opinion (the Department "shall" remove intangible value), as well as its citation to *GTE Sprint*. What is not clear is what is meant by "separable." As noted throughout this article, intangibles such as Category 2 assets in the hypothetical used in this article–franchises, licenses, patents, and the like–may be both separately valued and capable of being severed from the unit and sold. Another category of intangibles, however, can be separately valued, but is less capable of being separately sold, similar to our Category 3 assets. The court also noted these types of intangibles in its reference to a tax article from which it quoted: "intangibles such as assembled workforce, customer base, and elements of going-concern

value that are 'intangible assets of a business enterprise [that] derive their value from being part of the business and thus cannot be severed and sold separately.'"

The court's quotation from this article suggests that it is a requirement of exclusion from the going concern value that the intangible be capable of being severed and sold separately from the business. According to the article it quoted, franchises, patents, licenses, copyrights, and related assets (i.e., Category 2) would satisfy the requirement, while assembled workforce, management systems, customer base, and elements of going-concern value (Category 3) would not. However, the distinction between these two categories of intangibles is not as clear as it may seem. A customer base, for instance, may very well qualify as an asset that can be severed and sold. As noted by one commentator:

> Customer intangibles of all types are frequently bought and sold in the commercial marketplace. In terms of how intangible asset analysts view these transactions, there are three ways in which customer intangibles are sold:
>
> 1. Separately from any other assets–that is, only the customer relationships are sold.
> 2. With certain other assets–for example, the customer relationships are sold with a non-competition agreement granted by the seller.
> 3. As part of the sale of a going-concern business or professional practice–that is, as one of the bundle of tangible and intangible assets.[20]

In any event, assuming one can identify the intangible assets that are "separable" and has excluded them from the going concern value, the court allowed for the taxation of any remaining "nonseparable" intangibles that may add value to the taxable, tangible property. This is the "enhancing effect on tangible property" to which the court must be referring that is not attributable to the "separable" intangible property. This would include the location or "assemblage" component to which the Utah court referred in *WilTel*, and which the court also recognized in *RT Communications*.[21]

---

18. *Id.* Section 39-1-201(xxix) was the statute that exempted "intangible personal property" from taxation.

19. *Id.* at 928 (emphasis added).

20. Reilly & Schweihs, *supra* note 9, at 341.

21. At one point in the court's opinion, it recognized this assemblage attribute when it quoted from another article, which observed as follows:

    To the extent that the total system value exceeds the aggregate physical value of the individual tangible assets, the appraisal includes the company's intangibles, principally "going concern value," which is the "value added by the property's assemblage into a going business" and the "franchise" which is the authority of the company to operate in a certain area. Amdur, *Property Taxation of Regulated Industries*, 40 Tax Law. 339 (1987).

This interpretation of *RT Communications* requires the recognition that the going-concern value may be fully allocated between tangible assets and specifically identifiable and "separable" intangible assets. In the hypothetical used here, for instance, the $100 million business enterprise value may be fully explained by the tangible asset value and the separate intangible value components, including goodwill. However, to the extent goodwill is not recognized as an exempt intangible, it may be included in this enhancing component of the tangible property. It is true, of course, that there may be substantial overlap between "assemblage" attributes of tangible property value and an intangible goodwill or going-concern component of value. The location or assemblage concept recognized in *WilTel* is better suited for the valuation of parcels of real property. An attempt to adapt the assemblage concept to the valuation of utilities, telecommunication companies, and related entities runs the risk of expanding the valuation "attribute" beyond its real meaning and intruding into the intangible property concepts of goodwill and going concern.[22] Notwithstanding the potential problems of distinguishing assemblage value from intangible going-concern or goodwill value, this author is confident that appraisers can make that distinction and determine whether there is any enhancing effect of intangible property beyond the identifiable value of that intangible. If there is, the identifiable value of the intangible must be excluded and any "enhancing effect" beyond that identifiable value may be part of the residual value that should be allocated between the taxable and exempt components of the going-concern value.

Before concluding the analysis of *RT Communications,* it is necessary to address an argument that has arisen since that opinion's publication. The Wyoming Department of Revenue now argues that for an intangible to qualify for exclusion from the business enterprise value, it is necessary not only that the intangible be "separable and identifiable," but that it does not contribute *in any way* to the operation of the business as a going concern and thus as part of its going-concern value. This argument apparently is based upon language in the opinion that the intangible asset may be excluded where it has value "beyond the enhancing effect on tangible property." If one were to argue that the "enhancing effect" of the intangible property consumes the entire difference between the tangible asset value and the going concern value, then the tax administrator has explained the entire residual difference and there is *no* intangible value beyond that enhancing effect.

This approach obviously overstates the holding in *RT Communications,* and would cause tangible enhancement to completely swallow all intangible property value. As noted throughout this article, any intangible property that is part of an integrated unit and is necessary to the operation of the unit will have an "enhancing effect" on the tangible property if the tangible property cannot operate without the intangible. Viewed in the extreme, all necessary intangibles would have an "enhancing effect on tangible property" that would explain the entire difference between tangible property value and business enterprise value. Such an argument, however, would mean that the only intangibles that would qualify for exclusion from the unit value would be those intangibles that are completely unnecessary to the operation of the unit—in essence, surplus property that could be sold without affecting the operation of the unit. Such an interpretation of *RT Communications* would stretch the enhancement concept beyond any reasonable shape, would represent no limit upon the inclusion of intangible value as part of unitary assessment, and would render meaningless the Wyoming court's citation to *GTE Sprint* and its conclusion that the assessor *shall* "remove the value of intangible personal property that is separable and identifiable."[23]

In summary, *RT Communications* supports the conclusion that intangible property value can and should be excluded from the business enterprise value where it can be separately identified and valued. If there is any residual value remaining, it may be that value created from the synergistic combination of both tangible and intangible components, and such a value increment from the combination of those assets could appropriately be considered as an enhancement element of value. The court did not address the

---

22. As noted earlier, many authorities, including the California Assessor's Handbook, recognize "going concern" as a separate intangible that is exempt from taxation. *See* Assessor's Handbook, "'going-concern value' is itself an intangible asset or right and is not assessable." *See also* I.R.C. § 197, 26 U.S.C. § 197. In that context, "going-concern value" is an increment of value in excess of the value of the identical tangible property and intangible assets and rights used in that business operation.

23. 11 P.3d at 928.

proposition presented here that this enhancement element should itself be divided between the tangible and intangible properties that are responsible for its existence. As reasoned throughout this article, however, such a conclusion would be a natural extension of the analysis that recognizes the contribution of intangible asset value to the going concern: If exempt intangible property is a recognized component of the going-concern value, then any value enhancement must be an enhancement to the intangible property as well as the taxable assets.

The Entrepreneurial Profit Adjustment Is Ill-Suited to the Appraisal of Utilities, Telecommunication Companies, and Related Entities

The concept of entrepreneurial profit arises in the cost approach of valuation. As will be observed, the concept has originated from, and has been applied almost exclusively to, the types of real estate development projects that truly have an "entrepreneurial" component. When an entrepreneur develops property, he or she expects to make a profit. When the project is completed and is ready for either occupancy or sale, this theory under the cost approach holds that the total "costs" of the property should include the contribution made by the entrepreneur– for which he expects to be compensated and which is thus an element of cost–of putting forth the effort and realizing the accomplishment of a finished project.

Some commentators have recently advocated the expansion of the entrepreneurial profit concept from its typical application in the real estate development context to an adaptation for the valuation of utilities, telecommunications companies, and related taxpayers that are centrally assessed.[24] However, *The Appraisal of Real Estate*, the "bible" of real estate appraisers, describes the basis for and shows the real estate development character of this concept, in the following passages:

> Because the entrepreneur provides the inspiration, drive, and coordination involved in the overall

project, the difference between the cost of development and the value of a property after completion is the *entrepreneurial profit* realized. The true measure of entrepreneurial profit is determined by surveying profit expectations in the market...

> . . . *Entrepreneurial profit is the difference between total cost of development and marketing and the market value of a property after completion and achievement of stabilized occupancy. . . .* The amount the entrepreneur actually receives by the end of the development and marketing periods is entrepreneurial profit. The frame of reference for entrepreneurial profit is backward-looking.

> . . . Entrepreneurial profit is that portion of cost that reflects the entrepreneur's contribution and reward for the risk and expertise associated with the development. The estimation of entrepreneurial profit is problematic, but the estimate is a necessary component of total cost. Several methods can be used to estimate entrepreneurial profit, but the estimate should reflect the market.[25]

It is obvious both from the specific language used in this treatise, and from the context, that the concept of entrepreneurial profit has several elements that are common to many real estate development projects, but which are not applicable to large business enterprises such as companies involved in the energy, telecommunications, or transportation industries. First, the concept involves the existence of an "entrepreneur." This would be a person (or entity) who brings the project together and who has the expertise and the willingness to undertake the risk necessary for its development. After development, the project can be sold, and the sale price reflects a reward for the risk undertaken and contribution made by that entrepreneur.

In many respects, the entrepreneur is similar to a typical residential homebuilder specializing in "spec" homes built for future sale but not for a particular buyer. The builder locates and purchases the land, obtains the building permits, hires the subcontractors, conducts and/or supervises the construction effort, and arranges for the marketing and sale of the property. When a buyer ultimately purchases the property, his or her total "costs" will naturally include a profit component for the builder, which will reward the builder for the use of his or her capital, expertise and actual time and effort devoted to completion of the project. There

---

24. *See,* e.g., Michael W. Goodwin, *Cost Approach Redux: Challenges and Pitfalls in Applying the Trended Investment Method* 3-5 (paper presented to the Northwest Property Tax Conference, Sep. 14, 1999); Michael W. Goodwin, *Costly Intangibles* 3 (paper presented to the Public Utilities Seminar, Mar. 25, 1999); Gaylord A. Wood, Jr., *Intangibles in Property Valuation* 9 (paper presented to the Northwest Property Tax Conference, Sep. 15, 1999).

25. *The Appraisal of Real Estate* at 347, 348, 361 (11th ed. 1996).

is an established market for new homes, and a means by which to estimate the element of the homebuyer's cost that is represented by entrepreneurial profit.

Implicit in this entrepreneurial concept is that this type of entrepreneur finishes one project and then moves on to another. Thus, *The Appraisal of Real Estate* describes an end point for measurement of the entrepreneurial profit–"completion and achievement of stabilized occupancy."[26] Although *The Appraisal of Real Estate* also indicates that "entrepreneurial profit can take the form of profit on a sale, additional return on an investment in operating property, or use value to the entrepreneur,"[27] clearly any additional value after completion of the project is not part of "entrepreneurial profit," and "use value" is not the equivalent of fair market value.[28]

Finally, the concept of entrepreneurial profit requires, in its application, a market for properties that are developed by entrepreneurs and then sold. It requires a thorough analysis of the many development projects in which the appraiser can evaluate the profit expectations and actual results of entrepreneurial efforts. *The Appraisal of Real Estate* observes as follows:

> Potential entrepreneurial profits should be derived through market analysis and interviews with developers to determine the expectations of profit required as motivation or incentive to undertake a particular development. Less emphasis should be given to historical profit margins. Historical profits are records of results and often differ from the anticipated profit that originally motivated the entrepreneur to proceed with a project. Profit is not as important as incentive.

> ...Estimating an appropriate amount of entrepreneurial profit is a continued challenge for appraisers because expectations of profit vary with different market conditions and property types. Typical relationships between profit and other costs are difficult to establish.[29]

The foregoing summary of the elements of the entrepreneurial profit concept demonstrates that it is limited in its application, and wholly inappropriate in the valuation of centrally as-

sessed taxpayers. There are no "entrepreneurs" who develop projects for companies in the energy, telecommunications, or transportation businesses, and there is no market in such properties from which any "entrepreneurial profit" could be estimated. Companies that invest in or construct facilities in these industries do not do so in order to earn a profit on discrete projects, by development and resale to the ultimate owner and user, but do so for complex reasons that are governed by macroeconomic considerations as well as the internal investment analysis conducted by every company.

Indeed, the addition of an entrepreneurial profit component to a replacement cost valuation approach would add an unnecessary, inappropriate, and duplicative component of cost to the valuation of the property of centrally assessed utilities and related taxpayers. This conclusion can best be demonstrated by examining the circumstances of a rate-regulated utility in the process of constructing a $100 million electric generation facility. The utility's cost of capital is 10 percent, which is also the rate of return allowed by the state public utilities commission. Accordingly, using simple principles of rate regulation and valuation, the $100 million investment will generate $10 million of income, and since the expected return is 10 percent, the fair market value of the investment is $100 million. Such a hypothetical example illustrates the intended effect of rate regulation–to enable a utility to make an investment in property that will allow it to achieve its cost of capital. In such cases, the cost of the property would ideally be equivalent to its market value.

If the entrepreneurial profit concept were adapted to this example, then perhaps an appraiser would add a 5 percent adjustment to the $100 million cost, resulting in a total value under the cost approach of $105 million. However, the regulatory commission would not allow the utility to earn a return on the additional $5 million of "entrepreneurial profit." Without an additional return, the fair market value of the property will

---

26. *Id.* at 341, 347.

27. *Id.* at 348.

28. See *id.* at 24-26 (differentiating investment value and use value from market value); *Joseph Hydro Associates, Ltd., v. Department of Revenue,* 10 Or. Tax Rep. 277, 283 (1986) considering specific income tax consequences to the seller is not appropriate; "This approach abandons the concept of market value or value in exchange and looks to the value to the owner. While there may be circumstances where this is appropriate, they must be extremely rare." See also *Bayridge Associates v. Department of Revenue,* 13 Or. Tax Rep. 24 (1994); *Boise Cascade Corp. v. Department of Revenue,* 12 Or. Tax Rep. 263 (1991); *Mathias v. Department of Revenue,* 11 Or. Tax Rep. 347 (1990) (quoting *Nichols on Eminent Domain,* Ch. 12, to the effect that "it is a well-accepted rule of valuation that the individual personalities and opportunities of particular owners must be ignored").

29. *The Appraisal of Real Estate, supra* note 25, at 350.

still be $100 million; the additional $5 million of "profit" is rendered meaningless in the valuation process, much like a "stranded" cost that has no remaining economic value to the company.

One reason for this conclusion is that the profit component of the investment is already considered in the 10 percent allowed rate of return. That 10 percent return reflects two features of the capital investment process for companies that are a large part of the entrepreneur's effort for which he expects a separate return. First, the 10 percent return is a *net* return, net of all expenses incurred. Thus, the utility's expenses incurred for engineering, development costs, and related expenses are either expenses that it may deduct in the ordinary course prior to calculating its 10 percent return, or are part of the capitalized costs of the investment upon which it is allowed the return. Second, the 10 percent return reflects the regulatory commission's (and perhaps the market's) assessment of the risk reward requirements of this particular type of investment. If that rate of return is fairly stated, it will fully compensate the developer (i.e., utility) for its "entrepreneurial efforts." Any additional compensation would be some type of extraordinary return that would not be allowed by regulators or which could not be expected in a competitive market place.

Although the foregoing example involves a regulated utility, the same analysis would apply to unregulated companies. Regulation is, after all, designed to be a substitute for competition, and where a public utilities commission puts a ceiling on allowed returns for regulated industries, the competitive marketplace performs the same function for unregulated companies. With either regulated or unregulated industries, the fundamental difference between such businesses and the real estate development "entrepreneur" is that the return the utility or related taxpayer expects will be a return earned from the operation of the assets, and it will obtain reimbursement of its expenses and a return on its capital from the operation of those assets over time. Neither the utility, its stockholders, or potential buyers in the marketplace expect there to be an element of entrepreneurial profit for which they will be separately compensated.

There is another issue involved in the adaptation of an entrepreneurial profit adjustment to the appraisal of centrally assessed property. *The Appraisal of Real Estate* notes the following concern about the practical measurement of entrepreneurial profit:

> . . . [S]ome practitioners observe that in owner built, owner occupied properties, entrepreneurial profit often represents an intangible. Entrepreneurial profit is realized only when the property is first sold, even if the sale takes place years after the property was built. Over time, entrepreneurial profit becomes obscured by the appreciation in property value.[30]

Even if the entrepreneurial profit concept had some theoretical merit for centrally assessed taxpayers, its relevance would be diminished if not completely lost by the realization that the "entrepreneurial profit" is, as suggested by *The Appraisal of Real Estate,* indistinguishable from the going concern intangibles that were addressed earlier in this article. The nature of the intangibles embedded in the going concern value is not as limited as *The Appraisal of Real Estate* suggests–to the "appreciation in property value"–but includes all of the intangibles that are necessary to the operation of the business enterprise.

A review of court cases involving the entrepreneurial profit adjustment shows that the concept has been applied almost exclusively to large real estate projects such as shopping centers, industrial facilities, office buildings, and special-use properties.[31] The only case found by this author that deals with an attempt to apply the entrepreneurial profit adjustment to utility type property is *Texas Eastern Transmission Corp. v. E. Amwell Township,* decided by the Tax Court of New Jersey in 1992.[32] In that case, Texas Eastern Transmission challenged the ad valorem property assessments of portions of its pipeline. Appraisers for both the taxpayer and the assessor used a replacement cost technique. The court framed the issue between these two appraisers as follows:

> The appraisers also differ over the necessity of an addition to replacement cost to account for entrepreneurial profit. Taxpayer's appraiser finds

---

30. *Id.* at 348-49.

31. A computer search of court cases and state administrative decisions produced 211 cases in which this appraisal concept was discussed. Except for the *Texas Eastern Transmission* case discussed in the text, none of these cases dealt with the valuation of a utility-type taxpayer, nor with a unitary operation comprising a wide variety of distinct assets functioning together as a going concern.

32. 13 N.J. Tax 24 (1992).

the concept inapplicable to this property, while the appraiser for the taxing districts adds an entrepreneurial profit factor of 10 percent of all replacement costs previously discussed. I conclude that the approach of taxpayer's appraiser is the correct one.[33]

The court quoted extensively from the Ninth Edition of *The Appraisal of Real Estate* for the appraisal justification for an entrepreneurial adjustment, and made particular note of the treatise's statement that the entrepreneurial profit adjustment should be made only "when appropriate."[34] The court reviewed New Jersey law applicable to the entrepreneurial adjustment issue and observed that "[a]n adjustment for entrepreneurial profit has not been allowed when the market provided no basis for it *or when the property was not of a kind whose development is undertaken to realize a real estate development profit.*"[35] The court then concluded that imputing entrepreneurial profit in the cost approach for an interstate natural gas transmission pipeline was inappropriate, for many of the reasons identified earlier in this article:

> There is simply no indication of any *market* against which to compare replacement cost. *Pipeline is not constructed by developers in the expectation of profit on its sale.* It is exclusively constructed by regulated operating companies for use in their business at *costs which are passed through to the ratepayers.* The absence of actual market transactions impelled Justice Handler to reject the pipeline sales offered to establish value under the market approach in *Transcontinental II.* The expert for the taxing districts has produced no market data in this case, and his reliance on the taxpayer's expectation of profit from the operation of the pipeline *confuses business profit with development reward.*[36]

With centrally assessed taxpayers, property is not constructed with the expectation of profit upon its sale. The costs of construction are passed through the ratepayers, or to custom-

ers in the competitive marketplace. There are no market transactions from which to measure an appropriate level of entrepreneurial profit that would be applicable to a centrally assessed taxpayer. The absence of market transactions in which entrepreneurial profit could be determined is, of course, a function of the fact that there are no such transactions in which this type of property is sold in a way in which entrepreneurial profit is realized. Finally, the court used reasoning similar to that applied earlier in this article regarding the valuation redundancy that would occur by confusing business profit with development reward: There is no development reward that is relevant in the construction of property in industries that are centrally assessed, and all returns from such property investments are captured in the expected returns from the operation of the integrated unit of which any particular facility might be only a part.[37]

In summary, the concept of entrepreneurial profit may be the proverbial square peg that some appraisers attempt to insert into a round hole. Neither legal principle nor appraisal methodology supports the calculation of an adjustment to the cost approach, in the appraisal of centrally assessed utility and related property, for the entrepreneur's expectation of profit in developing property for resale.

The Wyoming Variation of the Enhancement Adjustment: A Case Study of Enhancement Theory Running Wild

The enhancement adjustment that would result from adoption of the "entrepreneurial profit" concept, although objectionable on both legal

---

33. *Id.* at 40.

34. *Id.* at 42, quoting *The Appraisal of Real Estate* 350 (9th ed.) (emphasis added).

35. 13 N.J. Tax at 41, citing *Badische Corp. v. Kearny,* 11 N.J. Tax 385, 402 (1990) (improvements had suffered substantial economic obsolescence); *Litton Business Sys., Inc. v. Morris Plains Bor.,* 8 N.J. Tax 520, 533 (1986) (income and market approaches supported no increment in value for entrepreneurial profit); *Berkley Arms Apartment Corp. v. Hackensack,* 6 N.J. Tax 260, 272 73 (1983) (advanced age of improvements and limited extent of entrepreneurial effort required to convert rental apartment building to cooperatives rendered factor inappropriate).

36. 13 N.J. Tax at 42 (emphasis added), citing *Transcontinental Gas Pipeline Corp. v. Bernards Township,* 111 N.J. 507, 545 A.2d 746 (1988).

37. There are other cases that describe limitations on the entrepreneurial profit adjustment even for more limited-purpose, commercial properties. For instance, in *Vernon Woods of Edina v. County of Hennepin,* 1991 WL 95741 (Minn. Tax Ct. 1991), the court held that an adjustment for entrepreneurial profit is appropriate "only when a primary motive for the development was to turn a profit rather than to hold the property long term." In another case, the court held that while an entrepreneurial adjustment factor may be appropriate in the reproduction costs of a regional mall, it should not be applied to a highway overpass constructed by the same developer for access to the mall because the overpass "is not a commercial venture which an entrepreneur would be inclined to construct with the expectation of earning a profit separate from that derived from the mall itself." *Lawrence Associates v. Lawrence Township,* 5 N.J. Tax 481 (1983).

grounds and appraisal theory, would be relatively modest–perhaps 5 to 10 percent of the costs of the improvements to real property.[38] The current method used in Wyoming could vastly exceed that adjustment, and would have the tendency to consume the entire difference between tangible asset value and going concern value. Although the Wyoming methodology appears to be an isolated phenomenon, it represents an interesting case study for analysis of the extremes to which the enhancement principle can be extended.

The Wyoming method is best explained through a simple example. Assume that a taxpayer's net operating income (NOI) is projected to be $100 per year, and the relevant capitalization rate reflecting the appropriate level of risk for this investment is 10 percent. The value under the income approach would be $1,000. Assume further that the net book value of the company's assets is $1,200. The department's method of estimating economic obsolescence calculates the return on net investment–the $100 of NOI compared to $1,200 of net investment–for a return of 8.33 percent in this case. That return is then compared to the required return of 10 percent, which indicates a deficit in the required return of 1.67 percentage points, or 16.7 percent of the overall return. When this 16.7 percent shortfall is applied to the net investment of $1,200, an economic obsolescence adjustment is indicated in the amount of the $200 for a net value of $1,000–the same result achieved through the income approach.

This obvious circularity between the cost approach calculation and the income approach has led to criticism of the economic obsolescence adjustment in Wyoming.[39] As a result, the method was changed in 1996 to require that the appraiser consider a different net operating income figure for the economic obsolescence adjustment in the cost approach than the amount used in the income approach.[40] As a result, the appraiser in Wyoming now calculates an economic obsolescence adjustment by considering the historical economic performance of those assets, while in the income approach the appraiser projects the income expected from that same asset pool. Thus, the appraiser relies upon historical NOI results to a greater degree in the cost approach, and frequently will select a different NOI figure to be used in the cost approach obsolescence adjustment than the income projected for the income approach. For example, if the appraiser selects a $110 NOI amount for the cost approach as representative of the historical performance of the assets subject to appraisal, it would produce a rate of return of 9.17 percent (based on a $1,200 book value). Comparing this achieved return to the 10 percent required rate of return, there is an income deficiency of .83 percentage points, requiring an economic obsolescence adjustment of 8.3 percent, and a $99.60 reduction from net investment in the cost approach. This would produce a cost approach result of about $1,100, compared to the $1,000 value under the income approach.

The economic obsolescence adjustment will undoubtedly continue to be the subject of controversy in appraisal circles and in the courts.[41] However, the income-shortfall or income-deficiency method does have support in the ap-

---

38. *See American Cyanamide Co. v. Township of Wayne,* 19 N.J. Tax 46 (N.J. 2000), *affirming* 17 N.J. Tax 542 (1998). In this case, the court addressed the contentions of the appraisers for each party, one of which used a 5 percent factor for entrepreneurial profit, and the other a 10 percent factor. 17 N.J. Tax at 562. The court essentially used the 5 percent factor in allowing a combined adjustment of 10 percent to cover both overhead and entrepreneurial profit. *Id.*

39. The adjustment has been rejected by the Wyoming State Board of Equalization. See *Northwest Pipeline Corporation,* Doc. No. A-86-28; *Investigative Report in the Matter of the Review of the Property of Wyoming Rural Electric Cooperative Utilities,* Doc. No. 93-159, pp. 6-9, 25 (May 3, 1994).

40. This change came in part as a result of the recommendations of a special study on Department of Revenue valuation procedures that was commissioned by the Wyoming State Board of Equalization. The study, led by David Shank of Ad Valorem Services, Inc., covered a wide variety of appraisal practices in Wyoming, and made recommendations that were generally adopted to improve appraisal practices in the state.

41. In one recent case, the Oregon Supreme Court rejected the "income-deficiency method" of calculating obsolescence because, in that case, the appraiser's "cost indicator measured obsolescence by examining the projected income stream," and "therefore, Delta's income deficiency method is illogical, because it incorporates income figures that account for only owned assets, while it uses cost figures that account for both owned and leased assets. At worst, Delta's income-deficiency method strips the cost approach of its use as an independent determiner of value, because it will always track the result under the income approach." *Delta Airlines, Inc. v. Department of Revenue,* 328 Or. 596, 984 P.2d 836 (Or. 1999). *See also United Telephone of the Northwest, Inc. v. Department of Revenue,* 770 P.2d 43, 51 (Or. 1989) (The rate shortfall method "will always result in a value of exactly the same as the income approach because it shoves the cost out the back door. . . . Algebraically, the method cancels all cost in excess of the value indicated by the income approach as obsolescence.").

praisal literature, and it continues to be used in many states.[42] The specific issue addressed here concerns the extension of this income-shortfall method into an "income-enhancement" adjustment. In cases where the net operating income results of the taxpayer produce a rate of return that exceeds the capitalization rate, the Wyoming Department of Revenue adds a premium through the same calculation by which it calculated a discount for economic obsolescence. Unfortunately, the theoretical rationale for the economic obsolescence downward adjustment is not present for a similar but opposite upward adjustment.

The downward obsolescence adjustment is appropriate because of the inference that below-normal income levels are attributable to under-performing assets or external influences that systemically affect the income-producing power of a given set of assets. Indeed, unless deficient income levels can be explained by temporary fluctuations in the economy or the industry in which the taxpayer operates, or by particular factors specific to the company, it is reasonable to conclude that the reason is that the company's assets are, for whatever reason, impaired in their ability to produce an acceptable rate of return.

On the other hand, super-adequate rates of return are frequently the product of the intangibles that are part of the going concern unit of assets. It is logical that if the calculated rate of return on the net book value of tangible assets is 15 percent, while the cost of capital is 10 percent, then part of the actual return may be a return upon intangible assets that are not recorded on the company's books. In other words, a $150 income on booked tangible asset value of $1,000 produces the 15 percent return, but leaves out part of the asset base that produces that return. If there were intangible assets that were worth $500, they would fully explain the difference between the achieved return and the cost of capital, because tangible and intangible

assets would then be $1,500, producing the 10 percent return that was achieved at the $150 net operating income level.

The use of $500 as the "plugged" value for intangibles in the preceding example is not simply a coincidence. Extraordinary returns in a tangible asset rate of return analysis are not only an indication that intangible assets exist, but they are also a means by which to measure the value of those assets that may be explained as part of "goodwill" value. One recent treatise describes one of the components of goodwill as follows:

> The second component of goodwill is the existence of excess economic income. . . . Briefly, excess income is that level of income generated by a business that is greater than the amount that would be considered a fair return on all of the other tangible and intangible assets that are used in the business. The excess economic income component relates directly to the concept of goodwill as the value of a business (or other economic unit) that cannot be assigned to any other tangible assets or identified intangible assets of the business.[43]

The authors observe that goodwill is sometimes valued using a "general residual method," where it is assumed to be "the unidentified residual after the values of the total identified tangible assets are subtracted from the total value of the subject business."[44] However, it is also common for analysts to value goodwill in the way suggested earlier:

> Intangible value in the nature of goodwill is that value that is not assigned to: working capital assets (e.g., receivables and inventory), tangible personal property (e.g., machinery and equipment), real estate (e.g., land and buildings), intangible personal property (e.g., trademarks and patents), and intangible real property (e.g., leases and easements).[45]

It cannot be seriously questioned in today's economy that there are substantial intangible values associated with the operation of a going concern. It is disingenuous for a tax administrator to make an arbitrary "enhancement adjustment" to a cost approach value and assume

---

42. *The Appraisal of Real Estate* endorses a similar method for calculating "external obsolescence" by capitalizing the rent loss suffered by the property subject to appraisal. If normal market net operating income will be $8 per square foot, for instance, and income for the subject property has fallen to $6.25 per square foot, the $1.75 differential, multiplied by 4,000 square feet in the text's example, would produce a total rent loss of $7,000, which, capitalized by a capitalization rate of 10 percent, would show external obsolescence of $70,000. *See The Appraisal of Real Estate* at 393-94 (Appraisal Institute, 11th ed. 1996). This method is little different from the economic obsolescence adjustment used in many states. *See also* Western States Association of Tax Administrators, *Appraisal Handbook* 32 (1989) (although criticizing the income shortfall method, the handbook concedes that "capitalizing income losses identified with and attributable to antiquated assets or negative external influences is a sound method for estimating obsolescence provided deficiencies are measured against industry-wide norms rather than one company's performance").

43. Reilly & Schweihs, *supra* note 9, at 382.

44. *Id.*

45. *Id.*

indiscriminately that the enhanced value is somehow attributable to tangible, taxable assets. It is, first of all, inconsistent with appraisal theory, which recognizes the intangible character of the asset that is created by the ability of a firm to enjoy extraordinary returns on investment. More important, particularly in Wyoming, such practice is inconsistent with the recent *RT Communications* case, in which the court indicated that it is appropriate to deduct the value of exempt intangibles from a going concern valuation. In the face of this recent authority, Wyoming tax administrators not only fail to deduct an appropriate amount for intangible value that is present in an income approach, but compound the problem by *adding* intangible value components to the cost approach through the mathematical complement of the economic obsolescence adjustment. Such a practice is inconsistent with appraisal theory, both in general and as applied in the law to the valuation of centrally assessed property.

Conclusion

The influence of intangible assets has increased dramatically in our economy, as recognized as early as 1776 by Adam Smith in his treatise *The Wealth of Nations* and as confirmed since then by such economists as John Meynard Keynes, James Bonbright, and even Alan Greenspan.[46] In recognition of the growing contribution of intangibles to business enterprise value, some states have become more sensitive to the unfairness of taxing centrally assessed taxpayers based on values that are significantly dependent upon intangible value contributions, while locally assessed taxpayers escape such taxation.

State legislatures, tax administrators, and courts are to be applauded for their efforts in seeking a rational balance between the legitimate valuation of utilities and related taxpayers on a going concern basis, while also recognizing an appropriate amount of value for the exempt intangibles that contribute to that business enterprise value. The state of California, in particular, has been progressive in finding the right solution for a problem that inevitably leads to over-assessment and over-taxation of a specific group of taxpayers. Other states would be well-advised to follow California's example.

---

46. *See generally* Reilly & Schweihs, *supra* note 44, pp. 25-26. The reference to Alan Greenspan derives from speeches he has made in recent years expressing concern about levels of stock prices that far exceed the underlying asset values, prompting worries about an overvalued stock market and the risk of a stock market collapse considering the inadequacy of underlying asset value. Although Mr. Greenspan's comments relate to the overvaluation of stock prices compared to the underlying values of both tangible and intangible assets, they illustrate the point that all forms of the intangible value now play an increasingly significant if not dominant role in our economy.

Separating Business Enterprise Value from Real Estate Value

William D. Siegel, as published by New York Law Journal, *November 2005*

The holy grail of property tax attorneys is to exclude business enterprise value from the valuation for real estate. Unfortunately, efforts by the property tax bar have had limited success. Consider these four scenarios that clearly involve entrepreneurial effort beyond simply developing a building.

Joe Enterprise developed a 500,000 square-foot outlet center in Nowheresville, N.Y., located near a thruway exit and in the midst of farmland near a relatively depressed, aging city. The land was inexpensively acquired. Cheap cinderblock store buildings were erected and given an attractive "Olde Towne" motif. Total costs are only $80 per square foot.

Joe Enterprise has developed outlet malls across the nation. Because of his reputation and relationships, he has enticed 60 companies into signing leases averaging $25 per square foot, net rent.

Bill Megamall determined that a community is slightly understored and served by a 37-year-old regional mall barely keeping up with the times. He decides to go head to head, building a new mall diagonally across the Thruway exit from the existing mall.

The new mall is state of the art, and maybe more. The tenant mix is superb. Bill Megamall managed to entice two of the biggest drawing anchors (Nordstrom/Bloomingdale quality) to his mall. Several of the newest, most exciting theme restaurants and a 12-plex cinema signed up. Advertising and promotion are excellent. The crowds come and shop 'til they drop.

Jane Hospitality acquired a landmarked, architecturally renowned downtown 80-year-old office building with architectural highlights. She gutted the building and created a charming, efficient hotel with the latest in staffing innovations and operating systems, bearing the flag of the nation's most profitable franchise. The restaurants and bistros of France and Hong Kong were scoured for key kitchen and dining staff.

Jane's hotel was soon written up in travel magazines, receiving five stars for lodging and food, and put on the list of "10 most in" places to go. Its average daily rate and occupancy factors exceed the city's norm by 15 percent–even when compared to newer hotels of its five-star class.

Dennis Dogood grew up in the family nursing home business. Licenses for new homes are hard to get, but he managed to obtain one and constructs a 150-bed facility in a slightly out of the way suburban area. Medicare is soon paying $325 a day for skilled nursing services.

Dennis' staff includes nurses, physical therapists, occupational therapists, recreational therapists, dieticians and social workers, requiring extensive management. The nursing home operation also includes a great deal of personal property–including beds, recreational equipment, and kitchen equipment. His costs are slightly more than the $100 per square foot to build a hotel or office building. But, Dennis earns a considerable profit on the entire nursing home.

There is little doubt that business enterprise value exists. *The Appraisal of Real Estate,* 11th ed., states:

> Business enterprise value is a value enhancement that results from items of intangible personal property such as marketing and management skill, an assembled work force, working capital, trade names, franchises, patents, trademarks, non-realty related contracts or leases, and some operating agreements. Going-concern value is the value created by a proven

William D. Siegel *is a senior partner in the Oyster Bay law firm of Siegel Fenchel & Peddy, P.C. and the New York State member of the American Property Tax Counsel.*

property operation with income sufficient to pay a fair return to all the agents of production. It consists of the total value of the real property; personal property such as furniture, fixtures and equipment; and intangible personal property, or the business enterprise. Properties with a business value component include hotels and motels, restaurants, bowling alleys, nursing homes, and other labor-intensive operations. (Emphasis in original)

The authoritative treatise further states:

> The reporting requirements of [Uniform Standards of Professional Appraisal Practice] as well as certain assignments, such as appraisals for tax appeals or eminent domain, require that value be allocated among its various components, i.e., real estate, FF&E, business enterprise, and other intangibles. There are divergent methods of estimating business enterprise value and no single technique is universally accepted.

The Internal Revenue Code allows the segregation of non-real estate items and provides a shorter amortization period than the 38-year period for real estate. Section 197 allows taxpayers to amortize certain intangibles over a 15-year recovery period, including:

- Goodwill and going concern value;
- Work force in place, information base, customer and supplied based intangibles;
- Licenses, permits and other rights;
- Franchises, trademarks and trade names.

Amortizable items also include hotel and mall management teams, customer lists, tenant mixes, operating agreements with anchor stores and distinctive trade names, such as Fockerfeller Center, Mall of America or Roosevelt Field.

Despite extensive efforts property tax attorneys have so far only succeeded in separating business enterprise value for hotels and nursing homes.

The New York Court of Appeals long ago recognized the existence of business enterprise value for hotels. People ex rel Hotel Paramount Corp. v. Chambers, 298 N.Y> 372, 83 N.E.2d 839 (1949), involved the sale of the hotel and business of the old Hotel Paramount on Times Square in 1945 for $3 million. A year later, the stock sold for $3.6 million.

The Court held:

> Concededly, the sales prices of the hotel enterprise, as well as the hotel income, reflected not only the value of the real estate, the only proper subject of the real property tax–but the worth of such additional elements as management, good will, hotel furniture and furnishings, inventory of food and beverages and the usual hotel services. ... In these circumstances, the valuation of a transient hotel property is in essence the valuation of a 'specialty,' a term including real estate, which, unlike an apartment house or office building, produces income only in combination with a business conducted upon it.

The then-limited appraisal methodology allowed the Court to exclude business value only by treating the Hotel Paramount as "in essence" a "specialty."

New York is the only state using reproduction cost as the ceiling of value. The importance of this concept in separating business value from real estate value was made clear by the Iowa Supreme Court in Merle Hay Mall v. City of Des Moines Board of Review, 564 N.W.2d 419 (1977), which rejected the concept that business value should be omitted from the valuation of a regional mall because Iowa statutes did not provide for use of the cost approach as the sole method of value or the ceiling of value.

The most significant development in the valuation of hotels for assessment purposes was the publication of "The Valuation of Hotels & Motels for Assessment Purposes" by Stephen Rushmore and Karen E. Rubin in *The Appraisal Journal*, April 1984.

Among the points made in this seminal article were:

> Appraisers soon learn that lodging facilities are more than land, bricks, and mortar; they are retail-oriented, labor-intensive businesses necessitating a high level of managerial expertise. In addition hostelries require a significant investment in personal property (furniture, fixtures, and equipment) that has a relatively short useful life and is subject to rapid depreciation and obsolescence. All these unusual characteristics must be handled in a proper manner during the hotel valuation process in order to derive a supportable estimate of market value.

The article set forth a method to accomplish this which is too complicated to explain in this article. Newer methodologies, particularly those proffered by David C. Lennhoff, have more recently been developed. See, e.g., Lennhoff, *A Business Enterprise Value Anthology*, Appraisal Institute, 2001.

More recent cases have held business enterprise value to be excludable for hotels. See *Hilton Inns, Inc. v. Board of Assessors, Village of Tarrytown*, 39 Misc2d 792, 242 N.Y.S.2d 433, 436 (Sup. Ct. 1963), where the court held:

> Thus, the petitioner's hotel income is relevant and material herein. The village can employ its own experts to segregate that portion of the business income which is attributable to the real estate.

The first case to actually use an income method to value a hotel excluding business value was *Dann's Motel Corp./Lodge on the Green v. Board of Assessors, Town of Erwin Real Property Tax Administration Reporter*, No.1, p.5 (Sup. Ct. 1992):

> The court finds therefore that neither the market approach nor the reproduction cost–less depreciation methods–are appropriate. The method of income capitalization was utilized by both of the parties. ...
>
> The petitioner's expert appraiser... capitalized the net income after making adjustments to the income stream for management of the business and personal property. ...
>
> The court adopts the appraisal of the petitioner's expert.

See also *Blue Hill Plaza Inn, Inc. v. Assessor, Town of Orangetown*, 3 Real Property Tax Administration Report, No. 4, p. 4 (Sup Ct. 1995). This is probably the most relevant case on the methodology of the income approach since it is the only case in which both appraisers expertly used this method. The court largely adopted appraisals following the Rushmore methodology, disallowing a management fee, but allowing a 3 percent franchise fee.

A notable success in excluding business value was the nursing home case of *Tarrytown Hall Care Center v. Assessor, Town of Green-burgh*, Westchester County Sup. Ct. 2004, 12 Real Property Tax Administration Reporter, No. 2, p. 140, where the court described the appraisal method adopted as follows:

> Sterling [the appraiser for the taxpayer] stated that the profit and loss statements for the subject could not be used as a starting point because it

was impossible to estimate the revenues attributable to the real estate Medicaid patients on public assistance, and within those reimbursements are specific payments of use of the real estate.

The court further held that:

> The Court finds persuasive, however, Sterling's contention that the lion's share of net income should be attributed to the non-real estate aspects of the subject. It is clear that the great majority of the subjects' patients are on Medicaid (public assistance), and there is logic in Sterling's method of capitalizing Medicaid reimbursements [for the real property portion of the nursing home], with adjustments for Medicare reimbursements and private pay income.

Case law, especially in New York, has not yet advanced to the adoption of appraisal methodologies that separate business enterprise value for shopping center or mall properties. As noted earlier, the cost method may sometimes accomplish this, to some degree.

Even the leading proponents of separating the values in retail properties readily admit that, while appraisal literature defines going concern value and business enterprise value quite well, such literature "does not, however, provide adequate exposition on the variables that enter into the estimate of going concern value, thus affecting business enterprise value or intangible value." (Rabianski, "Going Concern Value, Market Value and Intangible Value," *The Appraisal Journal*, April 1996.)

In other words, we know it's there, but we cannot calculate it. Maybe someday it can be accomplished.

Valuation of Commercial Intangible Assets for Ad Valorem Tax Purposes

Robert F. Reilly

This article originally appeared in Volume 6, Issue 1 of the *Journal of Property Tax Assessment and Administration*, © 2010 CCH, a Wolters Kluwer Law and Business. All rights reserved. Reprinted with permission from the *Journal of Property Tax Assessment and Administration*.

The value of intangible assets used by industrial or commercial taxpayer corporations can be a controversial issue in ad valorem taxation. Some states tax certain intangible personal property for property tax purposes, while many states exempt it. In either circumstance, taxpayer corporation management needs to know the value of the corporation's intangible assets.

The value of intangible assets is particularly important in taxpayer corporation properties that are assessed by the unit valuation method. This method is often applied by taxing authorities to assess utility-type businesses, such as electric companies, natural gas utilities, water and wastewater companies, pipelines, railroads, airlines, and telecommunications companies. For ad valorem tax purposes, such taxpayers are often centrally assessed by state taxing authorities. In addition, the unit valuation method is sometimes applied to taxpayers that operate special purpose and integrated processing facilities, such as cable TV systems, race tracks, sports and entertainment facilities, mining operations, and petroleum refineries. For ad valorem tax purposes, such taxpayers are often assessed by taxing authorities at the local level. Nonetheless, local taxing authorities may still use the unit valuation method to assess these special purpose or integrated processing facilities.

The generally accepted unit valuation approaches and methods typically determine the value of the entire unit of taxpayer corporation operating assets. Such operating assets can include both (1) tangible operating assets (i.e., real estate and tangible personal property) and (2) intangible operating assets (i.e., intangible assets). Therefore, any unit valuation exercise typically concludes the value of all of the taxpayer corporation operating assets, both tangible and intangible. In jurisdictions that tax only real estate and tangible personal property, the taxpayer should adjust the unit value for the value of any commercial intangible assets because they are not subject to ad valorem taxation in the subject taxing jurisdiction.

To do so, taxpayer corporation management should first (1) identify and (2) value its commercial intangible assets. The taxpayer corporation will then subtract these intangible asset values from the overall unit value conclusion. The resulting residual amount represents the value of the taxpayer corporation's taxable real estate and tangible personal property.

Accordingly, taxpayer corporation management should be generally familiar with intangible asset valuation practices and procedures. Taxpayer corporation management (and/or the taxpayer's legal counsel) may (1) retain an intangible asset valuation analyst, (2) communicate the valuation assignment to the valuation analyst, and (3) rely on the valuation analyst's value opinion and valuation report. Further, the taxpayer's legal counsel may present the valuation analyst's report and expert testimony during the ad valorem tax assessment negotiation, appeal, or litigation. Those valuation analysts who practice in the ad valorem tax discipline should already be very familiar with the generally accepted intangible asset valuation ap-

Robert F. Reilly *is a managing director of Willamette Management Associates in Chicago, Illinois. He has been the principal analyst on more than 2,500 valuations of businesses, business interests, and intellectual properties in virtually every industry and business sector. He is a certified public accountant accredited in business valuation and a chartered financial analyst. Robert holds a master of business administration (MBA) in finance and a bachelor's degree in economics, both from Columbia University in New York.*

proaches, methods, and procedures. Taxpayer corporation managements, taxing authorities, the legal counsel for both parties, judges and other finders of fact, and other interested parties would be well served with a general familiarity of the intangible asset valuation process.

The following discussion first outlines the process that a valuation analyst typically follows in the identification of taxpayer corporation commercial intangible assets. It then summarizes the generally accepted approaches, methods, and procedures that a valuation analyst may use to quantify the value of a taxpayer corporation's intangible assets.

Business Enterprise Assets

From a valuation perspective, an asset is anything that (1) can be owned and (2) has value. If the taxpayer corporation owner or operator cannot own a subject economic phenomenon, then it is not an asset. If the subject economic phenomenon exists and can be owned–but it has no value, then it is not an asset. For an intangible asset to meet this first threshold test of existence (that is, for an intangible to be an asset), it should (1) be subject to private ownership and (2) have value.

For a variety of reasons, the valuation analyst will often group all business enterprise assets into the following four asset categories:

1. tangible real estate
2. intangible real property
3. tangible personal property
4. intangible personal property.

Therefore, one way to identify any type of taxpayer corporation asset (tangible or intangible) is to locate that asset in one of the four categories presented in table 1.

Real Estate Assets

Most taxpayer managements are familiar with the real estate category of assets. Real estate is tangible. It is considered tangible because its value comes from its physical elements. The fact that real estate is realty means that it is not moveable.

Real estate is either physically part of the earth (e.g., land) or it is physically attached to the earth (e.g., buildings). Therefore, real estate is (practically) immobile and the value of real estate comes from the owner's ability to occupy, traverse, build on, drill into, or otherwise physically interact with this tangible asset. Examples of real estate are easy to identify: land, land improvements, buildings and permanently affixed structures, building improvements, and the like.

Tangible Personal Property Assets

Most taxpayer managements are similarly familiar with the tangible personal property category of assets. Like real estate, tangible personal property is tangible. Again, that means that the value of tangible personal property comes from its physical elements.

The fact that tangible personal property is personal means that it is moveable. Personal property can be moved from one location (i.e., from one piece of real estate) to another. The value of tangible personal property comes from the owner's ability to physically interact with the asset. Examples of tangible personal property are also easy to identify: industrial machinery and equipment, trucks and transportation equipment, office furniture, computer and laboratory equipment, and so on.

Intangible Real Property Assets

Most taxpayer managements have at least a general familiarity with the intangible real property category of assets. This is because legal interests in real estate are often subdivided and transferred. Real property assets are the transferable legal interests in tangible real estate.

The value of a real property asset does not come from the ownership of the real estate itself. The ownership of the tangible real estate is vested in a separate party–the landlord, the lessor, or the licensor. What the real property asset owner possesses is the right to occupy, cross over, extract from, and otherwise use the subject real estate.

A real property asset is an intangible asset. The value of intangible real property comes from the legal rights it grants to a physical asset–not from the ownership of the physical asset itself. Examples of real property assets include leases, occupancy permits, building permits, surface rights, air rights, mining rights, water extraction rights, drilling rights, and so forth.

Table 1	The Four Categories of Business Enterprise Assets	
	Realty Assets	**Personalty Assets**
Tangible Assets	Tangible Real Estate	Tangible Personal Property
Intangible Assets	Intangible Real Property	Intangible Personal Property

These intangible assets are often documented in a license, lease, easement, or other contract. The tangible evidence of the intangible real property right is the document (e.g., the contract). The contract is an asset; it can be owned. The contract has a tangible element; it is a written document. The value of the contract, however, does not depend on the physical aspects of the contract document (i.e., the piece of paper). Rather, the value of the intangible real property contract depends on the legal rights (and economic expectations) associated with the contract document.

Intangible Personal Property Assets

Highly sophisticated taxpayer managements also are familiar with intangible personal property. Some less experienced observers automatically think of intangible personal property when they encounter the term intangible assets. That definition of intangible assets is actually too limited from a valuation perspective. Real property interests, as discussed earlier, are, in fact, intangible assets. However, it would not invalidate this explanation of commercial intangible assets if the discussion were limited to intangible personal property.

The value of intangible personal property comes from the legal rights, the intellectual property content, and/or the expected economic benefits that are associated with that intangible asset. Like all assets (both tangible and intangible), intangible personal property (1) can be owned and (2) has value.

Business Enterprise Intangible Assets

Valuation analysts often group all intangible personal property assets into four categories. Sometimes, this intangible personal property categorization process has accounting, taxation, regulatory, or legal significance. This categorization process is particularly relevant from an ad valorem tax valuation perspective. The reason is that the four different categories of intangible personal property assets (although fundamentally similar) have slightly different economic attributes. The four categories of intangible personal property assets are: (1) financial assets, (2) general intangible assets, (3) intellectual property, and (4) intangible value in the nature of goodwill.

Financial Assets

All taxpayer managements should be familiar with the first category of intangible personal

property assets–financial assets. Common examples of financial assets include cash, accounts and notes receivable, stocks and bonds, and other negotiable investment securities. When the financial assets owner is a taxpayer corporation, these intangible assets are recorded as "current assets" for financial statement purposes.

Although the inexperienced observer may not think of this type of property as an intangible asset, it may offer the most conceptually clear example of an intangible personal property asset. Consider the example of cash–in the form of a $100 bill. If the $100 bill is owned by a taxpayer corporation, it is recorded as cash (i.e., a current asset) on the corporation's balance sheet. Even if the $100 bill is owned by an individual, it is still recorded as cash (i.e., a current asset) if the individual prepares a personal financial statement.

There would likely be no question that the $100 bill (1) is an asset and (2) has value. However, the value of the $100 bill does not derive from the physical paper note. Rather, the value of the $100 bill results from the legal right of its owner to exchange the paper instrument for goods and services. This $100 bill is considered an intangible asset because its value comes from the expected economic benefits it can provide to the intangible asset owner.

General Intangible Assets

The second category of intangible personal property assets includes most other intangible assets. The economic attributes and common subcategorizations of this type of discrete (or individual) intangible asset will be presented during the valuation discussion. Because this category is quite broad, most intangible personal property assets can be classified as general intangible assets.

Intellectual Property

The third category of intangible personal property assets is called intellectual property. Intellectual property intangible assets are distinguished by their special legal recognition and, therefore, their specific legal rights. Four types of intellectual property are found within this category:

1. trademarks and trade names
2. patents
3. copyrights
4. trade secrets.

Intangible Value in the Nature of Goodwill

The fourth category of intangible personal property assets covers the intangible value of goodwill.

The experienced valuation analyst typically places the intangible value in the nature of goodwill into a separate category for various accounting, taxation, and other financial reporting purposes.

Intangible value in the nature of goodwill is often considered to be a residual intangible asset. That is, for valuation purposes, goodwill is often considered to be the intangible value component of a business enterprise (of whatever legal form) that cannot be specifically assigned to (or identified with) any of the three before-mentioned types of intangible assets. This is true for both (1) an individual's professional or celebrity goodwill and (2) a taxpayer corporation's institutional or business enterprise goodwill.

Nonetheless, like each of the other three categories of intangible personal property, goodwill (1) can be owned and (2) can have value. However, goodwill is not as easy to identify or to analyze as the other three categories of intangible personal property.

Figure 1 presents a list of some common intangible assets, both realty and personalty, that can be subject to valuation. It is not intended to provide an exhaustive list of intangible assets.

Types of Business Enterprise Assets

Business enterprise assets, whether in an industrial or a commercial taxpayer corporation,

Figure 1	Illustrative List of Intangible Assets

Intangible Personal Property Assets

Financial Assets

Options, warrants, grants, rights—related to securities

General Intangible Assets

Advertising campaigns and programs	Customer lists	Historical documents	Prizes and awards (related to professional recognition)
Agreements	Customer relationships	HMO enrollment lists	
Airport gates and landing slots	Designs, patterns, diagrams, schematics, technical drawings	Insurance expirations	Production backlogs
		Insurance in force	Proposals outstanding, related to contracts, customers, and so on
Appraisal plants (files and records)	Development rights	Joint ventures	
		Laboratory notebooks	Regulatory approvals (or exemptions from regulatory requirements)
Awards and judgments (legal)	Distribution networks	Landing rights (for airlines)	
Bank customers— deposit, loan, trust, credit card, and such	Distribution rights	Licenses—professional, business, and so forth	
	Employment contracts		Retail shelf space
	Engineering drawings and related documentation	Literary works	Royalty agreements
Blueprints and drawings	Environmental rights (and exemptions)	Litigation awards and damage claims	Shareholder agreements
Book and other publication libraries	FCC licenses for radio bands (cellular telephone, paging, and the like)	Loan portfolios	Solicitation rights
Broadcast licenses (e.g., radio, television)		Management contracts	Subscription lists (for magazines, services, and such)
		Marketing and promotional materials	
Buy-sell agreements	Favorable financing	Masks and masters (for integrated circuits)	Supplier contracts
Certificates of need for health¬care institutions	Film libraries		Technical and specialty libraries (books, records, drawings, and the like)
	Food flavorings and food product recipes	Medical (and other professional) charts and records	
Chemical formulations	Franchise agreements (commercial)		Technical documentation
Claims (against insurers and similar parties)		Newspaper morgue files	Technology-sharing agreements
Computer software (both internally developed and externally purchased)	Franchise ordinances (governmental)	Noncompete covenants	
		Nondiversion agreements	Title plants
	Manual (versus automated) databases	Open-to-ship customer orders	Trained and assembled workforce
Computerized databases	Government contracts		
Contracts	Government programs	Permits	Training manuals and related educational materials, courses, and programs
Cooperative agreements	Governmental registrations (and exemptions)	Prescription drug files	
Credit information files			
Customer contracts			

Figure 1 Illustrative List of Intangible Assets *(continued)*

Intangible Personal Property Assets *(continued)*

Intellectual Property

Brand names and logos	Musical compositions	Product designs	Proprietary technology—
Copyrights	Patent applications	Proprietary processes—	and related technical documentation
Development rights— intellectual property	Patents—both product and process	and related technical documentation	Trade secrets
Know-how and associated procedural documentation	Procedure ("how we do things here") manuals and related documentation	Proprietary products— and related technical documentation	Trademarks and trade names
Manuscripts			

Goodwill Intangible Assets

Going-concern value (and immediate use value)	Goodwill—professional
Goodwill—institutional	Personalty contracts
Goodwill—personal	

Real Property Assets

Development rights—land and other real estate	Mineral extraction rights
Easements	Natural resources
Favorable leases	Ore and mineral deposit database
Leasehold estates	Possessory interest
Leasehold interests	Real property use rights
Location value	Use rights—air, water, land

typically comprise the four principal categories of tangible and intangible assets discussed previously. Each of these four categories of business enterprise assets can be further divided into several subcategories. Table 2 expands the listing and relationships of the four categories of taxpayer corporation assets that were introduced in table 1.

Reasons to Analyze Commercial Intangible Assets

There are numerous reasons why a valuation analyst would be asked to value commercial intangible assets. These reasons can be aggregated into the following categories:

1. Transaction pricing and structuring
2. Intercompany use and ownership transfers
3. Financial accounting and fair value reporting
4. State and local ad valorem property taxation planning and compliance
5. Financing collateralization and securitization
6. Litigation claims and dispute resolution
7. Management information and strategic planning
8. Corporate governance and regulatory and/ or contractual compliance
9. Bankruptcy and reorganization analysis
10. License, joint venture, and other development or commercialization opportunities.

Figure 2 presents a list of specific uses within each category for an intangible asset valuation. The list is illustrative and not meant to be exhaustive.

When conducting an intangible asset analysis, such as those detailed in figure 2, the valuation analyst may consider one or more

Table 2 The Four Categories of Business Enterprise Assets with Illustrative Examples

	Realty Assets	Personalty Assets
Tangible Assets	land, building components, building structures	machinery and equipment, trucks and autos, computers, office equipment
Intangible Assets	leaseholds, easements and rights of way, mining and mineral rights	financial assets, general intangible assets, intellectual property, goodwill intangible value

1. Transaction pricing and structuring
- Pricing the sale of an individual intangible asset or a bundle of two or more intangible assets
- Pricing the license of an individual intangible asset or a bundle of two or more intangible assets
- Equity allocations in a de novo business enterprise or joint venture when different investors contribute different tangible assets and intangible assets
- Asset allocations in the liquidation of a seasoned business enterprise or joint venture when different investors receive tangible assets or intangible assets in exchange for their equity ownership

2. Intercompany use and ownership transfers
- Transfers of intangible assets between wholly-owned subsidiaries (or other business units) of a consolidated business enterprise
- Transfers of intangible assets between less than wholly-owned subsidiaries (i.e., those with different minority shareholders) of a consolidated business enterprise
- Cost accounting allocations and inventory pricing when in-process goods are transferred between entities with varying intangible asset ownerships in a consolidated business enterprise

3. Financial accounting and fair value reporting
- Business-acquisition purchase-price allocations among all required assets
- Goodwill and other intangible asset impairment testing
- Post-bankruptcy fresh-start accounting for all tangible and intangible assets

4. Taxation planning and compliance
- Business-acquisition purchase-price allocations among all acquired assets
- Depreciation and amortization accounting for purchased tangible and intangible assets
- Charitable contribution deductions of donated intangible assets
- Intercompany transfer pricing of intangible assets owned by cross-border subsidiaries of a multinational corporation
- State and local ad valorem property tax appeals related to exempt intangible assets

5. Financing collateralization and securitization
- Use of cash-flow-based intangible assets as collateral on corporate debt or financings
- Sale/leaseback or sale/licenseback financing of corporate intangible assets

6. Litigation claims and dispute resolution
- Intellectual property royalty rate analysis in infringement claims
- Breach-of-contract or noncompete-agreement damages claims
- Condemnation, expropriation, eminent domain, dissipation of corporate assets claims

7. Management information and strategic planning
- Formation of intellectual property joint venture, joint development, joint commercialization agreements
- Negotiation of inbound or outbound intellectual property (or other intangible asset) use, development, commercialization, or exploitation agreements

8. Corporate governance and regulatory compliance
- Custodial inventory of owned and licensed intangible assets
- Evaluation of insurance coverage of intangible assets
- Defense against infringement, torts, breach of contract, and other wrongful acts

9. Bankruptcy and reorganization analysis
- Use of intangible assets as secured creditor debt collateral
- Use of intangible assets as debtor in possession (DIP) secured debt collateral
- Sale or license of intangible assets as spin-off opportunity
- Use of corporate intangible assets in determination of solvency or insolvency

10. Development and commercialization opportunities
- Identification of license, spin-off, joint venture, and other commercialization opportunities
- Negotiation of license, spin-off, joint venture, and other commercialization opportunities

of the following related (but subtly different) quantitative objectives:

1. Estimation of a defined value associated with the specified ownership interest in the intangible asset

2. Measurement of the appropriate royalty rate or intercompany transfer price associated with the use of the taxpayer intangible asset

3. Quantification of the expected remaining useful life (RUL) of the ownership or operation (or associated rate of change in the value) of the taxpayer intangible asset

4. Determination of the amount of lost profits or other economic losses associated with a damages event suffered by the taxpayer intangible asset.

Taxpayer corporation management is usually most interested in the first type of commercial intangible asset analysis–i.e., estimation of a defined value for the subject intangible asset. There are, however, numerous similarities among the generally accepted approaches, methods, and procedures that the experienced valuation analyst employs in the performance of all four categories of commercial intangible asset analyses.

The Intangible Asset Categorization Process

When performing a valuation for ad valorem tax purposes, the valuation analyst will often group individual intangible assets into distinct categories. The commercial intangible assets included in each category are generally similar in nature and in function. In addition, the commercial intangible assets within each category often possess similar economic characteristics. Also, intangible assets are typically placed in the same category when similar valuation methods apply to that intangible asset type.

Valuation analysts commonly group commercial intangible assets into the following 12 categories:

1. technology-related (e.g., proprietary technology, patents, technical know-how)

2. customer-related (e.g., customer lists, customer contracts)

3. contract-related (e.g., exclusive rights agreements, favorable supplier contracts, technology-sharing agreements, franchise agreements)

4. data-processing-related (e.g., computer software, automated databases)

5. human-capital-related (e.g., trained and assembled workforce, noncompete covenants, employment agreements)

6. marketing-related (e.g., advertising materials, marketing brochures and materials)

7. location-related (e.g., leasehold interests, mineral or mining exploration rights)

8. license-related (e.g., operational or environmental licenses or permits, pollution-control permits)

9. artistic-related (e.g., literary works and other compositions)

10. engineering-related (e.g., engineering drawings and schematics, blueprints, proprietary documentation)

11. intellectual-property-related (e.g., patents, trademarks, copyrights, and trade secrets)

12. goodwill-related (e.g., goodwill and going concern value).

This intangible asset categorization is presented for illustrative purposes only. It does not represent any particular financial accounting, income tax, legal, or other authority. Further, assigning an asset to a particular intangible asset category does not affect the value conclusion. In other words, the economic attributes of an intangible asset do not change based on how that intangible asset is categorized.

There are also intangible asset categorizations common to financial accounting and income tax accounting. For example, the Financial Accounting Standards Board (FASB) *Statement of Financial Accounting Standards (SFAS) No. 141R* (FASB 2007) identifies the five intangible asset categories that are recognized under generally accepted accounting principles (GAAP) for purchase accounting purposes.

1. marketing-related (e.g., trademarks, trade dress, newspaper mastheads, internet domain names, noncompetition agreements)

2. customer-related (e.g., customer lists, order or production backlog, customer contracts and related customer relationships, noncontractual customer relationships)

3. artistic-related (e.g., plays, operas, ballets; books, magazines, newspapers, other literary works; musical works, such as compositions, song lyrics, advertising jingles; pictures, photographs; video and audiovisual

material, including motion pictures or films, music videos, televisions programs)

4. contract-related (e.g., licensing, royalty, stand-still agreements; advertising, construction, management, service or supply contracts; lease agreements (whether the acquiree is the lessee or the lessor); construction permits; franchise agreements; operating and broadcast rights; servicing contracts, such as mortgage servicing contracts; employment contracts; use rights, such as drilling, water, air, timber-cutting, and route authorities)

5. technology-based (e.g., patented technology; computer software and mask works; unpatented technology; databases, including title plants; trade secrets, such as secret formulas, processes, recipes)

This SFAS 141R list of intangible assets can also be applied for various GAAP fair value accounting valuation purposes. However, the SFAS 141R categorization of intangible assets is different from the categorization recognized by the Internal Revenue Service for business-acquisition purchase-accounting purposes. The income-tax-related intangible asset categorization that follows is presented in Internal Revenue Code Section 197 (26 U.S.C. 197 (d)(1)).

1. goodwill

2. going concern value

3. any of the following items:
   - workforce in place including its composition and terms and conditions (contractual or otherwise) of its employment,
   - business books and records, operating systems, or any other information base (including lists or other information with respect to current or prospective customers),
   - any patent, copyright, formula, process, design, pattern, know-how, format, or other similar item,
   - any customer-based intangible,
   - any supplier-based intangible, and
   - any other similar item.

As these lists illustrate, there are several alternative ways to categorize intangible assets. Each of these different categorizations reflects the priorities and objectives of the accounting, tax, or other organization making the categorization.

The important point is that both the valuation profession and various governmental and regulatory authorities recognize the existence of commercial intangible assets. And, each of these parties has developed an intangible asset categorization process to help it organize and analyze these commercial intangible assets.

Commercial Intangible Asset Economic Attributes

A valuation analyst may consider various economic attributes in the process of determining the existence of intangible assets. Naturally, before an intangible asset can be valued, it must be (1) identified and (2) analyzed. This discussion describes some of the economic attributes that help the valuation analyst determine that an intangible asset does in fact exist.

For an intangible asset to exist, (1) it must be an asset and (2) it must be intangible. An asset is anything that (1) can be owned and (2) has value. For an intangible asset, value comes from its intangible characteristics (i.e., its bundle of legal rights). By contrast, the value of a tangible asset comes from its physical or corporeal characteristics.

For an item to qualify as an intangible asset, it must exhibit some of the following economic characteristics or attributes:

1. The intangible asset should be subject to a specific identification and a recognizable description.

2. The intangible asset should be subject to legal existence, recognition, and protection.

3. The intangible asset should be subject to the right of private ownership, and that private ownership should be legally transferable.

4. There should be some tangible evidence or manifestation of the existence of the intangible asset (e.g., a contract, a license, a registration document, a listing of customers, a set of financial statements, and so on).

5. The intangible asset should be created or come into existence at an identifiable time or as the result of an identifiable event.

6. The intangible asset should be subject to being destroyed or to a termination of existence at an identifiable time or as the result of an identifiable event.

An asset that possesses many, or all, of these economic characteristics or attributes will typically qualify as an intangible asset. There should be a specific bundle of property rights associated with the existence of any intangible asset.

The inexperienced valuation analyst may assume that these attributes require that an intangible asset must be able to be sold separately–i.e., without any other asset. That assumption, however, is a fundamental mistake.

The intangible asset ownership interest should be able to be sold or otherwise transferred. However, the subject intangible asset may be sold (1) as part of a bundle of intangible assets or (2) as part of a bundle of both tangible and intangible assets. There is no valuation principle, recognized literature, or professional standard that indicates that the intangible asset must be able to be sold separately from any other asset.

Other economic characteristics or attributes can affect the value of an intangible asset. They include:

1. high market share
2. high profitability
3. lack of regulation
4. regulated (or protected) market position
5. monopoly position (or barriers to entry)
6. market potential
7. breadth of customer/consumer appeal
8. heritage or longevity
9. competitive edge
10. life-cycle status
11. uniqueness
12. ability to influence market prices
13. assemblage
14. liquidity (or illiquidity)
15. operational control (or lack of control).

These economic phenomena do not meet the economic-attribute or characteristics tests required to qualify as commercial intangible assets. A high market share, for example, may affect the value of an intangible asset, such as a trademark, but the economic attribute of a high market share is not itself a commercial intangible asset.

Generally Accepted Valuation Approaches and Methods for Commercial Intangible Assets

There are many methods and procedures that are appropriate for the valuation of taxpayer corporation commercial intangible assets. Because these valuation methods and procedures have many fundamental similarities and differences, they are typically categorized into three generally accepted valuation approaches. These three valuation approaches are based on fundamental economic principles. The three generally accepted intangible asset valuation approaches are: (1) the cost approach, (2) the market approach, and (3) the income approach.

These intangible asset valuation approaches encompass a broad spectrum of microeconomic principles and property investment dynamics. Each of the three generally accepted valuation approaches has the same objective: to arrive at a reasonable indication of a defined value for the commercial intangible asset. Accordingly, analytical methods and procedures based on the same economic principles are grouped into the same valuation approach.

The valuation analyst typically attempts to value the intangible asset using all three generally accepted valuation approaches so that a multi-dimensional perspective of the asset's value is obtained. However, individual methods and procedures associated with one of the three valuation approaches may or may not be applicable to the valuation of a particular intangible asset. Consequently, the selection of valuation methods and procedures used to value a particular intangible asset will depend on:

1. The unique characteristics of the subject intangible asset
2. The quantity and quality of available data
3. The purpose and objective of the analysis
4. The experience and judgment of the valuation analyst.

The objective of using more than one valuation approach for an intangible asset is to obtain mutually supporting evidence for the value conclusion. The valuation analyst's value conclusion is typically based on a synthesis of the value indications derived from each applicable valuation approach and method.

Market Approach Valuation Methods
The market approach is based on the economic principles of competition and equilibrium. These economic principles indicate that, in a free and unrestricted market, supply and demand factors will drive the price of an intangible asset to a point of equilibrium. The principle of substitution also influences the market approach because the identification and analysis of equilibrium prices for substitute intangible assets will provide pricing evidence for an intangible asset.

Market Approach Valuation Principles

The valuation analyst will often attempt to apply market approach methods first in the valuation process. This is because "the market"–that is, the economic environment where arm's-length transactions between unrelated parties occur–is often the best indicator of value.

However, the market approach may not be appropriate for the valuation of certain taxpayer corporation intangible assets. This is especially true if the condition of the intangible asset is not sufficiently similar to the intangible assets that are transacting in the marketplace. In that case, the transactional prices may not indicate the expected price for the subject intangible asset.

The price of a commercial intangible asset is not necessarily equal to its value. Value is often defined as an expected price, that is, the price that an intangible asset is expected to fetch in its appropriate marketplace. In contrast, price represents what one particular buyer paid to one particular seller for one particular intangible asset.

In any intangible asset sale transaction, either participant may have been influenced by nonmarket, participant-specific factors. If such influences did occur, and if they are not general to the marketplace, then the transactional price for that particular intangible asset may not be indicative of the expected price of the subject intangible asset.

Even if the subject intangible asset was itself bought or licensed, that subject transactional price should not be naively relied upon to indicate an expected future price. The reason is that the transactional price may have been affected by nonmarket, participant-specific influences.

The Market Approach Valuation Process

Within the market approach, there are somewhat fewer valuation methods available to the valuation analyst than either the cost approach or the income approach. Nonetheless, the practical application of the market approach involves a complex and rigorous analytical process. There is a general systematic process–or framework–to the application of market approach methods in intangible asset valuation. The principal procedures of this systematic process are summarized as follows:

1. Research the appropriate exchange market to obtain information about sale or license transactions involving guideline (i.e., generally similar) or comparable (i.e., almost identical) intangible assets that may be compared to the subject commercial intangible asset in terms of characteristics such as intangible asset type, intangible asset use, industry in which the intangible asset operates, date of sale, and so on.

2. Verify the information by confirming (a) that the data obtained are factually accurate and (b) that the sale or license exchange transactions reflect arm's-length market considerations. If the guideline sale or license transaction does not reflect arm's-length market conditions, then adjustments to the transactional data may be necessary. This verification procedure can also elicit additional information about the current market conditions for the sale or license of the subject intangible asset.

3. Select relevant units of comparison such as income multipliers or dollars per unit (that is, units such as "per drawing," "per customer," or "per location") and develop a comparative analysis for each selected unit of comparison.

4. Compare guideline intangible asset sale or license transactions with the subject intangible asset using the selected elements of comparison and adjust the sale or license price of each guideline transaction appropriately to the taxpayer corporation intangible asset. If such adjustments cannot be measured, then eliminate the sale or license transaction from consideration as a guideline for future valuation analyses.

5. Reconcile the various value indications produced from the analysis of guideline sale and/or license transactions into either (a) a single value indication or (b) a range of values. In an imprecise market–subject to varying economics–a range of values can provide a better conclusion for the commercial intangible asset than a single value estimate.

The reconciliation procedure is the last step in any market approach valuation analysis in which two or more value indications are derived from guideline market data. In the reconciliation procedure, the valuation analyst summarizes and reviews the data as well as the analyses that resulted in each value indication. The valuation analyst then resolves these value indications into either a range of values or into a single value indication for the subject intangible asset.

It is important that the valuation analyst consider the strengths and weaknesses of each value indication derived by examining the reliability and appropriateness of (1) the market data compiled and (2) the analytical procedures applied.

Cost Approach Valuation Methods

The cost approach is based on the economic principles of substitution and price equilibrium. These principles indicate that a willing buyer will pay no more for a fungible intangible asset than the cost to obtain (i.e., to . purchase or construct) an intangible asset of equal utility.

In other words, a willing buyer will pay no more for a fungible intangible asset than the price of an intangible asset of comparable utility. This utility can be measured in many ways, including functionality, desirability, and so on. Accordingly, an efficient market will adjust the price of all properties (including intangible assets) in equilibrium so that the price paid in the market is a function of the comparative utility of each property.

Within the cost approach, the cost of a fungible intangible asset is influenced by the marketplace. That is, the relevant cost is often the greatest amount that the marketplace is willing to pay for the fungible intangible asset. This value is not necessarily the actual historical cost of creating the intangible asset, and it is not necessarily the sum of the historical costs for which the willing seller would like to be compensated. This situation exists because value is not equal to cost–at least not to cost as measured in the historical accounting sense.

The conceptual foundation of all cost approach valuation methods is grounded in the following economic principles:

- The substitution principle. No prudent buyer would pay more for a fungible intangible asset than the total cost to create a new intangible asset of equal desirability and utility.

- The supply and demand principle. Shifts in supply and demand (1) cause costs to increase and decrease and (2) cause changes in the supply of different types of intangible assets.

- The externalities principle. Gains or losses resulting from external factors may affect the value of an intangible asset. For this reason, external conditions may cause a newly constructed intangible asset to be worth more or less than its cost.

Definition of Intangible Asset Cost

There are several generally accepted cost approach valuation methods. Each of these methods uses a particular definition of cost. The two most common definitions are:

1. reproduction cost new
2. replacement cost new.

There are subtle, but important, differences between these two definitions of cost. Reproduction cost new is the total cost, at current prices, to create an exact duplicate or replica of the subject intangible asset. This duplicate intangible asset would be created using the same materials, standards, design, layout, and quality of workmanship used to create the original intangible asset.

Replacement cost new is the total cost to create, at current prices, an asset with equal functionality or utility as the subject intangible asset. Functionality is an engineering concept that means the ability of the intangible asset to perform the task for which it was designed. Utility is an economic concept that means the ability of the intangible asset to provide an equivalent amount of satisfaction.

The replacement intangible asset would be (1) created with modern methods and (2) constructed according to current standards using state-of-the-art design and layout and the highest available quality of workmanship. Thus, the replacement intangible asset may have greater utility than the subject intangible asset. In this circumstance, the valuation analyst should adjust for this factor in the obsolescence analysis of the replacement cost new less depreciation method. Moreover, even though the replacement intangible asset performs the same task as the subject intangible asset, the replacement asset is often better (in some way) than the subject intangible asset. For example, the replacement intangible asset may yield more satisfaction than the subject intangible asset. In this case, the valuation analyst should adjust for this factor during the obsolescence estimation of the replacement cost analysis.

Several other definitions of cost can be applied in a cost approach analysis. For example, some valuation analysts consider measurement of cost avoidance to be a cost approach method. This method quantifies either historical or prospective costs that are avoided (i.e., not incurred) by the intangible asset owner due to the intangible asset ownership. In addition, some valuation analysts consider trended historical costs as an indication of value. In this method, actual historical asset development costs are identified and quantified and then trended to the valuation date by an appropriate inflation-based index factor. Regardless of the specific definition of cost used in the analysis, all cost approach valuation methods typically include a comprehensive and all-inclusive definition of cost.

Intangible Asset Cost Components

The intangible asset cost measurement (whether replacement cost, reproduction cost, or some other measure of cost) should include not only direct costs (e.g., materials) but also indirect costs (e.g., engineering and design labor). The intangible asset cost measurement also should take into consideration the intangible asset developer's profit (on the direct cost and indirect cost investment) and an opportunity cost/entrepreneurial incentive (to economically motivate the intangible asset development process). Furthermore, the intangible asset cost measurement should be reduced by all relevant forms of obsolescence–including economic obsolescence.

The developer's profit is a cost component that is sometimes overlooked in cost approach analyses. When creating an intangible asset, the developer first expects a return of all costs of material, labor, and overhead related to the development process. In addition, the developer expects a return *on* all the material, labor, and overhead costs related to the development process. For example, just as a building contractor expects to earn a reasonable profit on the construction of any residential, commercial, or industrial building, an intangible asset developer expects to earn a reasonable profit on the development of the intangible asset.

The developer's profit can be estimated using several procedures. One calculates a percentage return on the developer's investment in material, labor, and overhead. Another estimates a percentage markup–or a fixed-dollar markup–on the amount of time involved in the development process.

The valuation analyst sometimes disaggregates a developer's investment into two subcomponents: (1) the amount financed by external financing sources (e.g., banks and other financial institutions) and (2) the amount financed by the intangible asset owner directly. The developer's profit associated with the costs financed by external sources is analogous to construction-period interest accrued during the construction of a tangible asset.

Some valuation analysts add this construction-period interest to the developer's profit cost category, while other analysts include it in the overhead cost category. Usually, a higher rate of return is assigned to the cost amount financed by the intangible asset owner directly, as compared to that financed by external financing sources. The reason is that owner-financed costs are funded by equity while externally financed costs are funded by debt.

Opportunity cost is another cost component that is sometimes overlooked. Nonetheless, it should be considered an integral component of a cost approach analysis. The opportunity cost represents the amount of economic benefit required to motivate an intangible asset creator to enter into the development process.

For the purposes of cost approach analyses, intangible asset developers can be compared to real estate developers of shopping malls or residential apartment complexes. Both incur an opportunity cost associated with the development process in that the time (and resources) they devote to a particular project is time (and resources) they are diverting from another development project. Likewise, both the intangible asset developer and the real estate developer expect to be compensated for the conceptual, planning, and administrative effort associated with putting a project together. They both expect to be compensated for the period of time between when they initially begin production of the project and when they realize the project's full commercial potential.

The concept of opportunity cost is perhaps easier to understand in the context of the real estate developer. For example, from the time a real estate developer first begins to construct a shopping mall to the time when all of the retail stores are leased and occupied, the developer is likely to experience negative cash flow. The assumption–for the purposes of this example–is that this process has taken two years.

A real estate developer who instead purchased a fully leased shopping mall would likely have experienced a positive cash flow during that same two-year period. The opportunity cost of the foregone cash flow during the two-year development period is one indicator of the amount required to motivate the real estate developer to build a new shopping mall (instead of buying an existing one).

The same type of opportunity cost is necessary to motivate an intangible asset developer to produce a new patent, trademark, computer program, chemical formulation, food recipe, or other intangible asset. The intangible asset creator should be compensated for the risk of undertaking a new development process compared to the relatively low risk of using the last generation of technology, consumer brands, computer software, and so on.

All five subcomponents of cost–material, labor, overhead, developer's profit, and opportunity cost–should be considered as part of a comprehensive intangible asset cost approach analysis. So, while the cost approach utilizes a fundamentally different set of valuation analyses than the income approach, certain economic analyses are necessarily involved. These economic analyses (which can include some analysis of intangible asset income) provide indications of both (1) the appropriate levels of opportunity cost (if any) and (2) economic obsolescence (if any).

Obsolescence Adjustments

The replacement cost new of an intangible asset is the total cost to create, at current prices, an intangible asset having equal utility to the subject intangible asset. However, the replacement asset would be (1) created with modern methods and (2) constructed according to current standards, state-of-the-art design and layout, and the highest available quality of workmanship. Accordingly, the replacement intangible asset may have greater utility than the subject intangible asset.

Reproduction cost new is the total cost, at current prices, to construct an exact duplicate or replica of the subject intangible asset. This duplicate intangible asset would be created using the same materials, standards, design, layout, and quality of workmanship used to create the original intangible asset.

Whether the valuation analyst uses the replacement cost new method or the reproduction cost new method to value an intangible asset, the intangible asset's cost (however measured) should be adjusted for losses in value from:

1. physical deterioration
2. functional obsolescence
3. technological obsolescence (a specific form of functional obsolescence)
4. economic obsolescence (a specific form of external obsolescence).

Physical deterioration is the reduction in the value of an intangible asset due to physical wear and tear resulting from continued use. It is unlikely that a taxpayer corporation commercial intangible asset will experience physical deterioration. Nevertheless, the valuation analyst should consider this concept in a cost approach analysis.

Functional obsolescence is the reduction in value of an intangible asset caused by its inability to perform the function (or yield the periodic utility) for which it was originally designed. Technological obsolescence is a decrease in the value of an intangible asset when improvements in technology have made an asset less than the ideal replacement for itself. Technological obsolescence occurs when improvements in design or engineering technology enable a replacement intangible asset to produce a greater standardized measure of utility and production than the original intangible asset. Technological obsolescence is typically considered a specific form of functional obsolescence. Accordingly, the valuation analyst will capture all of the value influences due to both design flaws and changing technology in one category–under the heading of functional obsolescence.

Economic obsolescence is a specific form of external obsolescence. It measures the reduction in value of a commercial intangible asset from the effects, events, or conditions that are external to–and not controlled by–the intangible asset's current use or condition. The impact of economic obsolescence is usually beyond the control of the asset's owner or operator. For that reason, economic obsolescence is typically considered incurable.

In any cost approach analysis, the valuation analyst will estimate the amounts (if any) of physical deterioration, functional obsolescence, technological obsolescence, and economic obsolescence occurring in the taxpayer corporation intangible asset. As part of this estimation, the valuation analyst will consider the intangible asset's actual age–and its expected remaining useful life (RUL). This age/RUL consideration is an important component of the cost approach.

In the cost approach, the typical formula for quantifying the replacement cost new of a commercial intangible asset is:

> Reproduction Cost New
> – Curable Functional and Technological Obsolescence
> = Replacement Cost New.

Then, the following formula is often used to estimate the value of the commercial intangible asset:

Replacement Cost New
- Physical Deterioration
- Economic Obsolescence
- Incurable Functional and Technological Obsolescence
= Value.

Income Approach Valuation Methods

The income approach is based on the economic principle of anticipation (also called the principle of expectation). In this approach, the value of the intangible asset is the present value of the expected economic income to be earned from the ownership and/or operation of the intangible asset. As the name of this economic principle implies, the willing buyer "anticipates" the "expected" economic income to be earned from the commercial intangible asset.

This expectation of prospective economic income is converted to a present worth—that is, the indicated value of the taxpayer corporation commercial intangible asset. This conversion requires the valuation analyst to estimate the investor's required rate of return on the intangible asset generating the prospective economic income. This required rate of return will be a function of many economic variables, including the risk—or the uncertainty—of the expected economic income.

Measures of Intangible Asset Income

There are numerous alternatives for measuring economic income that may be relevant in the valuation of a taxpayer corporation commercial intangible asset. If properly applied, many different measures of economic income can be used in the income approach to provide a reasonable indication of value. Some common measures include:

1. gross or net revenues
2. gross income (or gross profit)
3. net operating income
4. net income before tax
5. net income after tax
6. operating cash flow
7. net cash flow
8. other types of income (such as incremental income).

Since many different measures of economic income can be used in this valuation approach, it is important that the valuation analyst ensure that the discount rate or the direct capitalization rate used is derived on a basis consistent with the measure of economic income chosen.

Types of Income Approach Valuation Methods

There are at least as many income approach valuation methods as there are alternative measures of commercial intangible asset economic income. All of these different income approach valuation methods can be classified into two groups: (1) direct capitalization methods and (2) yield capitalization methods. In addition, most of these income approach valuation methods can be grouped into five categories based on similar practical and conceptual considerations. These five categories of intangible asset income approach valuation methods can be summarized as follows:

1. Valuation methods that quantify the incremental level of intangible asset economic income—that is, the intangible asset owner or operator will expect a greater level of economic income (however measured) by owning or operating the subject commercial intangible asset as compared to not owning or operating the subject commercial intangible asset.

2. Valuation methods that quantify a decremental level of intangible asset economic costs—that is, the intangible asset owner or operator will expect a lower level of economic costs (such as required levels of capital costs or operating costs) by owning or operating the subject commercial intangible asset as compared to not owning or operating the subject commercial intangible asset.

3. Valuation methods that estimate a relief from a hypothetical royalty payment—that is, the amount of a royalty payment that a hypothetical third-party intangible asset licensee would be willing to pay to a hypothetical third-party intangible asset licensor to obtain the use of—and the rights to—the subject commercial intangible asset.

4. Valuation methods that quantify the difference in the value of the owner's or operator's overall business enterprise—or similar economic unit—as a result of owning the subject commercial intangible asset (and using it in the owner's or operator's business enterprise) as compared to not owning the subject intangible asset (and not using it in the owner's or operator's business enterprise).

5. Valuation methods that estimate the value of the subject intangible asset as a residual

from the value of the owner's or operator's overall business enterprise (or a similar economic unit), or as a residual from the value of the total intangible value of the owner's or operator's business enterprise (or a similar economic unit).

Direct Capitalization Methods

In a direct capitalization analysis, the valuation analyst (1) estimates a normalized measure of economic income for one period (i.e., a period future to the valuation date) and (2) divides that measure by an appropriate investment rate of return. The appropriate investment rate of return is called the direct capitalization rate.

The direct capitalization rate may be derived for a time period that is in perpetuity or for a specified finite period of time. The time period chosen will depend on the valuation analyst's expectation of the duration of the economic income stream.

Yield Capitalization Methods

In a yield capitalization analysis, the valuation analyst projects the appropriate measure of economic income for several discrete time periods into the future. This projection of prospective economic income is converted into a present value by the use of a present value discount rate.

The present value discount rate is the investor's required rate of return—or yield capitalization rate—over the expected term of the economic income projection. The duration of the discrete projection period—and whether or not a residual or terminal value should be considered at its conclusion—will depend upon the valuation analyst's expectation of the duration of the economic income stream.

The result of either a direct capitalization analysis or a yield capitalization analysis is the income approach value indication of the taxpayer commercial intangible asset.

Income Tax Amortization Adjustment

Regardless of whether the yield capitalization method or the direct capitalization method is used, there is one additional income approach procedure that the valuation analyst should consider. This procedure accounts for the cash flow effect of the income tax amortization deduction on an intangible asset that is purchased as part of a taxable business combination.

More often than not, the valuation analyst does not need to make this income tax amortization adjustment to the pre-adjusted income

approach value indication. However, the valuation analyst should consider whether such an adjustment is appropriate in each intangible asset income approach valuation analysis.

When an intangible asset is purchased as part of a taxable acquisition of a going concern business, the price of that purchased asset may be amortizable to the acquirer for federal income tax purposes. This amortization deduction is allowed under Section 197 (26 U.S.C. 197). That is why such intangible assets are referred to as Section 197 intangible assets. However, the valuation analyst should realize that:

1. Not all commercial intangible assets qualify as Section 197 intangible assets.
2. Section 197 intangible assets must be purchased as part of a business acquisition (and not on a stand-alone basis).
3. The business acquisition must be a taxable transaction, such as a cash for assets transaction under Section 1060 (26 U.S.C. 1060 (c)), and not, for example, a stock-for-stock merger under Section 368 (26 U.S.C. 368 (a) (1) (C–D)).
4. The intangible asset owner or operator contemplated in the defined standard of value should be a taxpayer that can use the amortization-related income tax deduction.

Therefore, before applying an income tax amortization adjustment, the valuation analyst should consider (1) if the subject intangible asset is a Section 197 intangible asset and (2) whether the subject intangible asset would normally sell as a Section 197 intangible asset. If the answer to either question is yes, then the valuation analyst can consider applying an income tax amortization adjustment.

Section 197 allows the business acquirer to amortize the fair market value (presumably, the price paid) of the purchased intangible asset over a statutory 15-year amortization period. This annual amortization is a deduction that reduces the acquirer's taxable income and, therefore, income tax expense. The value of this amortization deduction is the present value of the income tax savings over 15 years, valued at the present value discount rate used in the income approach valuation analysis. When applicable, this present value of the income tax savings is added to the pre-adjusted income approach value indication to arrive at the final income approach value indication for the subject intangible asset.

Alternatively, some valuation analysts use an income tax amortization factor as a shortcut to the 15-period tax expense savings calculation. The common income tax amortization factor formula is:

$$\text{amortization factor} = \frac{1}{1 - \left(\dfrac{\text{income tax rate} * \text{present value annuity factor}}{\text{amortization period}}\right)}$$

In this formula, the income tax rate should be the same tax rate that was used in the unadjusted income approach analysis. The present value annuity factor is the present value of an annuity of $1 for 15 years at the same present value discount rate that was used in the unadjusted income approach analysis. The amortization period is always 15 years for Section 197 intangible assets.

As an example, a business acquirer has a 40% effective income tax rate and a 20% present value discount rate. Using the amortization factor formula, the value adjustment to the intangible asset would be calculated as follows:

$$\text{amortization value adjustment} = \frac{1}{1 - \left(\dfrac{40\% * 4.6755}{15 \text{ years}}\right)}$$

amortization value adjustment = 14%

Assuming that the unadjusted income approach value indication for the subject intangible asset is $100, the amount of the amortization value adjustment is $14 after rounding (i.e., $100 * 14%). Thus, the total income approach value indication for the subject intangible asset is $114 (i.e., $100 unadjusted value + $14 income tax amortization adjustment).

This income tax amortization adjustment (however calculated) is intended to reflect the increment in net cash flow provided by the amortization-related income tax savings. This net cash flow increment is not contained in the unadjusted income approach value indication. This adjustment, then, properly reflects the amount of income tax expense that should be included in the income approach valuation analysis.

Since this adjustment relates only to income tax expense in the income approach, it is not applicable to either the cost approach or the market approach. In other words, an income tax amortization adjustment should not be considered in intangible asset valuation analyses based on either the cost approach or the market approach.

Summary and Conclusion

This discussion focused on the identification and valuation of taxpayer corporation commercial intangible assets—in particular, what taxpayer corporation managements (and other interested parties) need to know about the valuation of commercial intangible assets. First, this discussion summarized the procedures a valuation analyst may use (and the factors a valuation analyst may consider) to identify the existence of a taxpayer corporation intangible asset. Second, it summarized the generally accepted valuation approaches, methods, and procedures that a valuation analyst may use to estimate the value of a taxpayer corporation intangible asset.

There are numerous economic and legal attributes that a valuation analyst may consider in the identification of a taxpayer corporation's commercial intangible assets. For the valuation of commercial intangible assets, there are three generally accepted approaches—the cost approach, the market approach, and the income approach—that a valuation analyst may consider. Each of these valuation approaches has the same objective: to arrive at a reasonable value indication for the intangible asset. Within each of the three valuation approaches, there are numerous methods and procedures that may be appropriate for intangible asset valuation.

The selection of the appropriate valuation methods and procedures for a subject commercial intangible asset is based on (1) the characteristics of the taxpayer intangible asset, (2) the quantity and quality of available data, (3) the purpose and objective of the analysis, and (4) the experience and judgment of the valuation analyst. The final value conclusion for a commercial intangible asset is typically based on a synthesis of the value indications derived from each applicable valuation approach and method.

These generally accepted valuation approaches and methods are relevant whether (1) taxpayer commercial intangible assets are subject to ad valorem taxation or (2) taxpayer commercial intangible assets are exempt from ad valorem taxation. When intangible assets are exempt from ad valorem taxation, many taxpayer corporations may still be required to (1) identify and (2) value their commercial intangible assets. Taxpayers that are assessed based on unit valuation methods often must complete this analysis because the unit valuation conclusion typically includes both (1) taxpayer tangible assets and (2) taxpayer intangible assets. In such instances, taxpayer corporation managements have to adjust (i.e., reduce) the overall unit value conclusion by the value of their commercial intangible assets. The result of this adjustment (i.e., the residual amount) represents the value of the taxpayer corporation's taxable real estate and tangible personal property.

Reference

FASB. 2007. *Statement of Financial Accounting Standards No. 141R: Business Combinations.* http://www.fasb.org/pdf/fas141r.pdf.

Sharpening the Intangibles Edge

Baruch Lev

Neither markets nor managers accurately value investments in intangibles like R&D, studies show. The result: misallocated resources. The solution: read on.

Intangible assets—a skilled workforce, patents and know-how, software, strong customer relationships, brands, unique organizational designs and processes, and the like—generate most of corporate growth and shareholder value. They account for well over half the market capitalization of public companies. They absorb a trillion dollars of corporate investment funds every year. In fact, these "soft" assets are what give today's companies their hard competitive edge.

Yet extensive research indicates that investors systematically misprice the shares of intangibles-intensive enterprises. Sometimes the market overvalues intangibles—wildly, for some dot-coms—and wastes capital. For companies in established sectors, the reverse is more often the case: Investors undervalue intangibles. This burdens firms with an excessively high cost of capital, which in turn leads them to underinvest in intangibles, thereby squandering opportunities for the earnings and growth investors seek.

Managers, meanwhile, often fly blind when deciding how much they should invest in intangibles or which ones offer the best rewards. In the case of investment in research and development, for instance, companies not only spend too little but also shift resources from risky next-generation innovations that could be potentially lucrative to safer modifications of current products and technologies. What ought to be the cutting edge of corporate progress is as a result blunted, to the detriment of both companies and the economy.

How do you break this vicious cycle? How do you hone rather than dull the intangibles edge? Research that I and others have done into intangible assets, particularly those related to R&D, indicate that companies need to gener-ate better information about their investments in intangibles and the benefits that flow from them—and then disclose at least some of that information to the capital markets. Doing so will both improve managerial decisions and give investors a sharper picture of the company and its performance, which will lead to more accurate valuations and lower the cost of capital.

The Problem of Undervaluation

Most managers are quick to acknowledge that intangible assets are crucial to their company's success. The trillion dollars that—according to research by Federal Reserve economist Leonard Nakamura—U.S. companies spend annually on intangibles is on par with the total corporate investment in physical assets. Such investments are pervasive throughout the manufacturing and service sectors of all developed economies. Financial service firms, for example, invest substantial resources in product and service innovation, even if not through the centralized R&D units found in manufacturing companies. Moreover, the share prices of intangibles-intensive companies command a large premium over book value, reflecting an apparent recognition by investors of intangibles' value.

But look carefully beneath the shiny veneer of intangibles and you will find a knotty and unattractive reality, one in which information deficiencies both at companies and in the capital markets feed negatively on one another. Take the findings of the research I conducted with colleagues Doron Nissim of Columbia Univer-

Baruch Lev is the Philip Bardes Professor of Accounting and Finance and the director of the Vincent C. Ross Institute for Accounting Research at New York University's Leonard N. Stern School of Business. He is the author of Intangibles: Management, Measurement, and Reporting *(Brookings Institution Press, 2001).*

sity and Jacob Thomas of Yale on the market valuation of companies that invest in R&D.

We focused on U.S. industries between 1983 and 2000 with substantial R&D: drugs, biotech and chemicals, fabricated metals, machinery and computer hardware, electrical and electronics, transportation vehicles, scientific instruments, and software. (That was roughly 750 to 1,000 companies a year.) For each company in each year, we derived a figure for "R&D capital" by treating reported R&D expenditure as if it were a capital expense and amortizing it using industry-specific rates that we computed. We then ranked the companies in each year according to the "intensity" of their R&D capital (relative to total assets), grouping them into three portfolios: those of high, medium, and low R&D intensity. Finally, we calculated, for each portfolio and year, the average risk-adjusted stock returns in the ensuing three years. Thus, for the three portfolios of companies in, for example, 1983, the actual risk-adjusted returns were computed for 1984, 1985, and 1986. (Adjusting the portfolio returns for risk—a common methodology in finance research and practice—is essential, given the above average risk, and presumably above average returns, of R&D-intensive companies.) This procedure was repeated for each year from 1983 to 2000.

And here comes the crux of the exercise. If investors value fairly—that is, if they do not systematically under- or overvalue—the stocks of R&D-intensive companies, fully reflecting in stock prices the potential of R&D, then risk-adjusted portfolio returns in subsequent years should average to zero. But if investors consistently undervalue those stocks, subsequent portfolio returns should be significantly positive. Investors will bid up the prices of the erstwhile undervalued shares as they realize their valuation mistake when R&D-generated revenues and earnings turn out to be higher than expected. Our findings indicate just so: R&D-intensive companies were systematically underpriced by the market, as evidenced by the protracted large and positive returns over several years following portfolio formation. (For a depiction of this phenomenon, see the exhibit "Delayed Reaction.") A variety of studies— using different samples, time periods, and statistical tools—by myself and others have reached similar conclusions. Together, they demonstrate that investors are slow to recognize the full value of investments in R&D.

Investors don't undervalue these investments on a whim. They know that many R&D projects are iffy propositions, subject to both technological risk (Will it work?) and commercial uncertainty (Will it sell?). They've seen highly touted technologies turn into massive flops. But research clearly shows that their perceptions of the risk surrounding R&D investments are, on the whole, exaggerated.

Researchers can empirically demonstrate the unduly high uncertainty discount that investors apply to R&D-intensive companies because R&D expenditures are reported in corporate financial statements. Most other types of investments in intangibles—employee training, brand enhancement, the development of new organizational processes—are usually not fleshed out publicly or even systematically tracked within a company. But it stands to reason—reason supported by preliminary research—that such investments are also subject to the undervaluation syndrome, particularly because they are even less visible and less conspicuously linked to positive outcomes than R&D spending.

A Misallocation of Resources

What are the consequences of this syndrome? The high capital costs with which investors burden R&D-intensive companies when they persistently undervalue them can be very harmful. At the extreme, high cost of capital prevents such companies from raising funds in capital markets—a situation familiar to managers of science-based and high-tech companies during the postbubble years. While undervaluation might not hamper the Microsofts or the Pfizers of the world—companies with a proven record of turning intangibles into tangible results—it is a serious impediment to the multitude of smaller, younger, and far less profitable enterprises that are in dire need of affordable financing.

Just as worrisome is managers' reaction when markets offer a cold shoulder to R&D. For the most part, companies clamp down on R&D investment and move resources from basic research, aimed at creating next-generation technologies and products, to safer but far less rewarding incremental improvements in current technologies. This shift from "R" to "D" shows up clearly in recent annual surveys of the R&D investment plans for members of the Industrial Research Institute. The allocation of R&D funds to directed basic research declined every year from 1993 to 2003 in favor of modification and extension of current products.

This is a troubling development for business and the economy. Researchers consistently have found that the returns from basic research are, on average, substantially higher than those from product line extensions. More broadly, there are signs that companies have long been underinvesting in R&D. Annual rates of return on R&D have in recent decades hovered in the range of 25% to 30%, according to various studies I and others have done. This is substantially above the returns on physical assets and, just as telling, above firms' cost of capital, even after accounting for the relatively high risk of R&D. Investment returns exceeding cost of capital imply that the amount of funds firms have invested in these assets is less than optimal. Indeed, economists Charles Jones of Stanford and John Williams of the San Francisco Federal Reserve Bank have concluded that the level of R&D spending in the United States is roughly one-third of what it should be.

What's Going On Here?

Underpricing securities and misallocating corporate resources mean that both companies and investors are leaving substantial value on the table. Why would rational people give up large potential gains from optimal investments in intangibles? Simply put: The information they need to make better decisions is hard to get at.

Investors learn about an enterprise not only from its own public disclosures but also from observing its competitors. Thus, when a retailer, a financial service provider, or an oil and gas company publishes its financial reports, investors draw inferences from those reports about the performance and economic conditions of other firms in the industry. Indeed, a positive

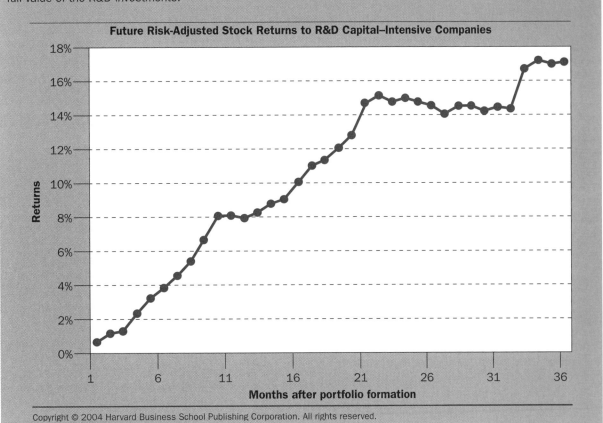

Delayed Reaction

An analysis of the stock price of companies that invest heavily in R&D demonstrates how investors frequently underprice the shares of intangibles-intensive enterprises. The return on a portfolio of such companies increasingly outperforms the market (on a risk-adjusted basis) as time passes, suggesting that investors are slow to realize the full value of the R&D investments.

Future Risk-Adjusted Stock Returns to R&D Capital–Intensive Companies

Returns (y-axis): 0% to 18%
Months after portfolio formation (x-axis): 1 to 36

earnings surprise at a given company will often trigger simultaneous share price increases throughout the industry. Investors can generalize in this way because, in many industries, economic conditions and the state of technology affect all companies more-or-less equally. Interest rate changes affect, to varying degrees, all financial service firms; oil prices and the threat of terrorism affect all airlines, resorts, and theme parks.

Generalizations about intangibles-intensive companies, on the other hand, are hard to come by, for two reasons. First, for intangibles such as brands and patents to be productive, they have to be unique. So, for instance, a successful clinical trial at Pfizer does not furnish any information about what's going on inside Merck or Novartis. Second, intangible assets, unlike many physical and financial assets, are not traded in active and transparent markets. Prices are aggregators of information: Oil prices enable investors to predict the performance of energy companies; commodities futures tell investors about the performance of agribusinesses. But there are no markets generating visible prices for intellectual capital, brands, or human capital to assist investors in correctly valuing intangibles-intensive companies.

Such an uninformative environment naturally calls for enhanced public disclosure about the amounts of and, insofar as possible, outcomes produced by investments in intangibles. But generally accepted accounting principles perpetuate the information deficiency. GAAP treats practically all internally generated intangibles not as investments but as costs that must be immediately expensed, thereby seriously distorting enterprise profitability and asset values. Furthermore, GAAP does not require firms to disclose any meaningful information about intangibles investments, except for aggregate R&D expenditures, lumping the rest of them in with general expenses. This keeps investors in the dark about, for example, how companies allocate R&D budgets to basic research, product development, and process improvements–not to mention the amounts being invested in a host of other intangibles, including software development and acquisition, brand enhancement, and employee training. The financial reports likewise provide no information on revenue generated by these investments, such as patent-licensing fees or the share of revenues coming specifically from new products. No wonder,

then, that investors, trapped in their forced ignorance about intangibles, apply an excessive uncertainty discount to the shares of intangibles-intensive enterprises. In capital markets, no news is bad news.

So why don't managers allay investors' concerns by voluntarily disclosing information about intangibles? The answer will surprise some: With few exceptions (primarily in the pharmaceutical industry), managers don't have the information because GAAP doesn't oblige companies to report it. For instance, few companies have the data needed to decide questions as basic as "Should we increase or decrease R&D spending?" or "Should we acquire technology rather than develop it in-house?" Answering these questions requires reliable information about the returns on R&D expenditures (realized and projected), classified by type of R&D (for new products, for improving processes) and evaluated against the cost of outsourcing. I have yet to encounter an organization that systematically develops this information.

The information brownout leaves companies only dimly aware of the relevant facts when making an array of important decisions, from whether they should outsource employee-training programs to whether they should increase their advertising budget or market products in collaboration with other enterprises. Granted, information about returns on intangibles that are not related to R&D, such as brands or employee training, is often difficult to determine. But most companies don't even have at hand reliable data on the investments themselves.

The Solution and Its Challenges

Much of the squandered value that intangible assets could generate can be recovered by both companies and investors if firms made more formal efforts to compile and report the information relating to intangibles that currently falls through the cracks of conventional accounting. Specifically, such efforts need to be aimed at producing two vital streams of information, one involving productivity, the other asset values.

The first information stream focuses on identifying the return on a company's investment in intangibles. The simplest case is probably R&D: Because benefits can be frequently attributed to investments in research and development, returns can be determined with some confidence and evaluated against alternatives. (For a description of how I did this at DuPont's textiles and interiors division, see the sidebar "Calculating the ROI of R&D at DuPont.") But even informally relating expenditures on product R&D to the subsequent share of revenues emanating from new products would highlight the company's ability to innovate and bring products expeditiously to market.

Calculating ROI is trickier in other areas, where the relationship between intangibles investments and their outcomes is more complex. For example, while there are a number of increasingly accepted methodologies for computing the returns on brand-building investments, there is less consensus about how to determine returns on investment in human capital. Even where there is an apparent link between, say, employee training and productivity, it isn't always possible to confirm a causal relationship between the investment and the positive result, given the variety of factors—information technology and so on—that affect employee productivity.

But some information is better than none, both for managers, as they make resource allocation decisions, and for investors, as they evaluate a company. Even where returns on investments in intangibles can't be calculated with precision, companies can at least track and disclose the investments themselves. Breaking out a company's expenditures in training, brand enhancement, information technology, and the like from general cost figures would let managers and investors see how those investments change over time and how they compare with those made at related companies.

And in some cases, computing ROI of intangibles may simply involve analyzing previously unexamined investments—for example, determining the additional costs and revenues generated by new business capabilities, such as an Internet-based distribution channel or online banking activity.

The second dimension of information that companies can quantify and disclose involves their "intangible capital." (A methodology for calculating intangible capital is summarized in the sidebar "Valuing a Company's Intangible Capital.") Developing this second stream of information requires a change in mind-set. Unlike

---

Calculating the ROI of R&D at DuPont

With $12 billion in annual sales, DuPont's textiles and interiors division has long spent considerable resources on R&D, aimed at both creating new products and enhancing the efficiency of chemical production processes. The latter is divided into efforts to decrease variable operating costs, such as raw materials and labor, and efforts to reduce fixed production costs, particularly through the design of more efficient production facilities. Although certain R&D investments are obviously warranted, it isn't clear how much to spend on each of these three R&D categories: product R&D, variable-cost process R&D, and fixed-cost process R&D.

To guide its resource allocation, DuPont asked me to come up with reliable estimates of the return on investment for each type of R&D. I focused first on data concerning inputs (the costs): primarily annual R&D spending in each category for the years 1985 to 2000. These data had to be carefully sanitized of various general cost allocations and other accounting artifacts in order to focus on real cash flows. Then I identified the outputs (the benefits) that flowed from the investments. The outputs of product R&D are, of course, revenues from the new products and improvements to existing products that emerge from the various R&D programs. I converted these revenue streams to free cash flows by subtracting all associated costs and capital expenditures. The outputs of the two types of process R&D were identified from detailed data on decreases in variable and fixed production costs attributed to R&D. Having thus obtained the cost and benefit streams for each type of R&D—and having purged the data and analysis of double counting, noncash items, and other "noise" factors— I was able to work out the ROI for each type of investment. That led to a number of fruitful insights.

I found, for example, that two-thirds of the value that new and improved products created for the division throughout the period could be attributed to product R&D—value amounting to hundreds of millions of dollars. The other third stemmed from brand enhancement activities. (Calculating this latter portion enabled me to estimate, as a byproduct, the ROI of the division's brand-building activities.) I also found that given the relatively large expenditures on product R&D, its ROI was only marginally above the cost of capital, indicating that its funding level was roughly adequate.

The big opportunities from R&D expenditures came from cost savings. The total value created by process R&D during the decade (in net present value) was roughly twice that of product R&D, and the ROIs were substantially higher. Most illuminating, the estimated return on the total R&D effort of the division was roughly three times the cost of capital, suggesting that DuPont's investment in the division's R&D fell short of the optimum. Being able to estimate returns for each type of R&D improved the division's resource allocation decisions and, in the words of the senior R&D executive, "brought real credibility to the value of R&D."

Valuing a Company's Intangible Capital

If investors don't fully recognize the value of your company's intangible assets, they may be undervaluing your stock. But how can you tell? By estimating the aggregate value of your company's intangible capital, you can determine if your company suffers from an intangibles-related undervaluation— or, perhaps, an overvaluation.

We start from an assumption that the enterprise's performance, as reflected by operating earnings, is generated by its physical and financial assets, enabled by intangibles: Well-trained employees enhance department store sales, for example, and process R&D cuts a plant's production costs. Since most tangible and financial assets are commodities, it is unlikely that by themselves they can contribute to above average earnings performance. So the value of intangible capital is derived by subtracting from earnings the average contribution of physical and financial assets in the company's industry. What remains is a figure that indicates the contribution of intangible assets to the company's performance and provides the basis for the valuation of intangible capital.

Thus, for example, if the annual operating earnings of the enterprise total $1,000, its physical assets are valued at $7,500, and the average return, or yield, on physical assets in the industry is 10%, then the normal contribution of physical assets to earnings is $750 (10% of 7,500). Assuming no financial assets, the residual earnings of $250 reflect the contribution of the enabling intangibles—what I call intangibles-driven earnings. Intangible capital is then calculated by computing the present value of the forecasted stream of intangibles-driven earnings. The detailed estimates and procedures underlying the computation of intangible capital are, of course, more involved than the simple process described in this stylized example. Among other things, enterprise performance is estimated from past and forecasted earnings to fully reflect the future contribution of intangibles, and historical asset values are converted to current values.

Using the chart "Undervalued or Overvalued?" which lists data for ten leading companies operating in diverse sectors, we may see how powerful the intangible capital measure can be. Although the estimated value of GE's intangible capital, a whopping $324 billion, comes as no surprise, the hefty intangible capital figures for two "old economy" companies—Exxon and Altria (Philip Morris)—are noteworthy. Clearly, intangible capital is an indicator of any well-run competitive enterprise, not just those in so intangibles-intensive a field as high tech.

More telling, however, is how the market perceives a company's intangibles and your ability to measure the gap between the company's market value and its true value, which takes into account those intangibles. With an estimate of a company's intangible capital, you can calculate what I call a company's comprehensive value: the net value of its physical and financial assets (derived from the balance sheet) plus the missing piece—the value of its intangible capital. Then you can compare this comprehensive value with the company's market value. In GE's case, the ratio of market-to-comprehensive value at the beginning of 2003 was 0.79, meaning that GE, according to my methodology, was undervalued by 21%. Pfizer, by contrast, was overvalued by 29%, Exxon fairly valued, and Altria undervalued by 45%. For investors, this market-to-comprehensive-value indicator is a more reliable measure of investment value than the widely used but flawed market-to-book ratio.

If my valuation of intangible capital is valid, then the shares of undervalued companies (those with comprehensive ratios below 1) should over time outperform the shares of overvalued companies (those with ratios above 1), as investors gradually realize their pricing error and adjust stock prices. Research I have done with Feng Gu, an accounting professor at Boston University, shows that this is indeed the case: During the 1980s and 1990s, low market-to-comprehensive-value stocks outperformed high market-to-comprehensive-value stocks by an average of 8.6% annually.

Undervalued or Overvalued?

By calculating a company's "comprehensive value," which takes into account its intangible assets as well as its physical and financial assets, you can assess whether the enterprise is undervalued or overvalued by investors. By our calculations, for instance, GE shares were undervalued by 21%, whereas Pfizer was overvalued by 29% in the same period.

Company	Estimated intangible capital (in $ billions)	Ratio of market value to comprehensive value
General Electric	324	0.79
Pfizer	200	1.29
Exxon Mobil	164	1.04
Altria Group	143	0.55
IBM	134	0.93
Merck	124	0.99
Microsoft	123	1.59
Verizon	105	0.80
Intel	95	1.09
SBC Communications	62	0.90

Value and ratios calculated as of January 2003.

capital or plant and equipment, intangibles are rarely considered assets whose performance must be continually monitored. But the expense mentality toward intangibles (derived, no doubt, from the fact that accountants universally expense all internally generated intangibles) should be replaced by an asset mentality.

Characterizing intangibles as assets that create future benefits can radically change how managers and investors see a business and make key decisions about it. Because a brand-building outlay, for instance, is thought of as a cost and is immediately expensed under GAAP, managers rarely ask the kinds of questions about it they would if it were considered an investment. They rarely monitor its effectiveness or ask what the proper amortization pattern should be. Must outlays in brand-building efforts be made every year (100% amortization), or is the promotion campaign sufficiently effective to last three years (33% amortization)? In the case of spending on information technology, an important question is whether an IT investment is a response to an immediate and temporary problem such as Y2K concerns. If so, it is a true expense. But if it represents a platform for long-term improvement, it really is an asset that should be amortized over the extent of its useful life. Similarly, managers need to determine when the revenue generated by "in-process R&D," an acquired company's

ongoing R&D projects, will start to accrue, how much it will be, and how long it is likely to flow, and then compare those expectations to subsequent realizations.

The primary benefit of having an asset mentality is that it drives management to structure the intangibles-related investments for maximum productivity and longevity. It may be advisable, for example, to spend somewhat more on an IT system so that it can, after a while, be used by several divisions, rather than just one. Viewing intangibles as assets also helps ensure that adequate property rights (such as patents and trademarks) have been secured for them; that they are sufficient for the task at hand (that the sales force, for instance, is adequately trained to meet the organization's growth plans); and that the company extracts maximal benefits from them (by, say, preventing competitors from infringing on intellectual property).

Investors, too, will benefit from this asset-based information. Comprehensive data on a company's intangible investments give investors a more complete picture of the company's capital than the one GAAP provides. These data, reflecting both tangible and intangible assets, will yield better metrics than such widely used measures of investment value as the market-to-book ratio. GAAP already requires that certain identifiable intangibles acquired from other

Prudent and Credible Disclosure

Disclosure of information to capital markets is a sensitive issue, fraught with hazards but also with opportunities. It raises important questions for executives: Should we engage at all in nonrequired disclosure? How should we balance investors' insatiable demand for information with the risk of aiding competitors? What sort of litigation exposure is created by voluntary disclosure? And, at the heart of the matter, will disclosure boost our stock prices and decrease our cost of capital?

To address some of these questions, I and colleagues Re-Jin Guo of the University of Illinois at Chicago and Nan Zhou of SUNY Binghamton examined in considerable detail the voluntary disclosure of intellectual property and product-related information made by 49 biotech companies at the time of their initial public offerings. We then looked at the capital market consequences of these disclosures. The focus on product development data, which GAAP does not require, was aimed at examining information that is both highly relevant to investors and very sensitive competitively. We chose the biotech industry because of its low barriers to entry and fierce competition.

For each of the 265 products under development at the 49 companies, we computed a disclosure score, reflecting the extent of information provided in five key categories: therapeutic specifications of the product, details of the target disease, results of clinical trials, future development plans, and market projections for the product. The degree of disclosure varied from product to product: More information, for instance, was released about products protected by patents, those at an advanced development stage, and those backed by venture capitalists. Still, our first observation was that practically all companies made extensive product-related information publicly available, despite the competitive hazards.

But more important, the extent of product-related disclosure was strongly and positively associated with important capital market variables. Fuller disclosure was related to narrower bid-ask spread of stocks (implying lower cost of capital), as well as to lower volatility in the company's stock price. Even in a fiercely competitive industry like biotech, the benefits of disclosure were considerable.

entities be reported as assets but not those developed in-house. There is no difference, in principle, between acquired intangibles and the internally generated intangibles we've been discussing here.

Will the proposed disclosures result in immediate benefits? Highly likely. Various research projects demonstrate that improved disclosure– particularly about innovation-related intangibles–is associated with reduced stock price volatility, narrower bid-ask spreads, and higher stock prices. (For a description of research showing that improved disclosure of intellectual property benefited companies in the biotech industry, see the sidebar "Prudent and Credible Disclosure.")

I am aware that such a call for enhanced disclosure is likely to trigger in the minds of managers two concerns: that competitors will benefit from access to proprietary information and that companies' exposure to litigation will increase. The first is obviously a valid concern, although one that is often exaggerated to thwart new SEC or FASB reporting requirements. Consider that pharmaceutical and biotech companies, operating in an intensely competitive environment, have for years disclosed certain elements of the information suggested by my proposal–the products in their pipeline, the prospective launch dates of new drugs, the life remaining on patents, and the like–without apparent competitive harm. Certainly, care and judgment should be exercised when communicating competitively sensitive information, but rarely is it optimal to keep mum.

It is easier to counter concerns about litigation exposure. The threat of lawsuits charging that a company has misled investors with overly optimistic statements exists mainly in the context of forward-looking information. But the disclosures I have proposed do not involve forecasts. Rather, they report factual information about investments that have already been made and the benefits that have flowed from them, such as revenues from recently introduced products. I don't propose that managers value individual intangible assets (just as individual physical assets aren't valued in financial reports), nor do I suggest indulging in speculation about future outcomes. Investors can make their own forecasts based on the facts the company

reports. Short of fraud, disclosure of facts does not increase exposure to litigation.

Work Still to Be Done

In an era when physical assets have essentially become commodities, the benefits intangible investments yield–increased productivity, improved margins, and, most important, innovative products and processes–are the only means companies can use to escape intensifying competitive pressures. Yet the information deficiencies surrounding intangibles cause serious share price distortions and misallocations of corporate resources that hinder performance and growth.

The proposals I have outlined for overcoming those problems are only a beginning. Corporations and accounting bodies should make systematic efforts to develop information and valuation templates that are capable of reliably reflecting the unique characteristics of intangible assets. These attributes include

- the enormous potential benefits intangibles can produce, which are typically realized only after extended periods of investment and development;
- the uncertainty surrounding the outcome of investing in intangibles;
- the exposure to infringement by competitors, due to the limited scope of property rights protection afforded to intangibles;
- the absence of active markets to guide valuation of intangibles and provide investors with exit strategies.

Capturing these attributes in an accounting system is a tall order, but some important steps have already been taken. For example, the FASB has recently stipulated that acquired intangibles be presented in financial reports at fair market value. The international accounting standards, which will become mandatory in Europe next year, call for the capitalization of certain internally generated intangibles. In Denmark, the Ministry of Trade, in conjunction with academics and a large number of companies, has developed innovative blueprints for disclosing information about intangible assets. The serious resource misallocations I have identified and discussed here should provide businesses with sufficient incentives to join–and even lead–such efforts.

Contemplating the Future of Business Enterprise Valuation

Robert W. Owens, PhD

This article originally appeared in the Spring 2006 issue of *The Appraisal Journal.*

Business enterprise value continues to be a perplexing issue. On the positive side, its conceptual validity is generally accepted, and it has attracted a number of advocates over the years within the appraisal discipline. On the negative side, it is not easily estimated, and it has caused considerable doubt among many appraisers concerning when and how to best deal with it. This article addresses major problem areas with the estimation of business enterprise value and offers three possible scenarios for the future. Of the scenarios presented, one is recommended as the best approach for addressing BEV issues.

Business enterprise value (BEV) can be defined as the portion of a property's sale price that captures the enterprise or business aspect of a sale, as opposed to the real estate and identifiable items of personal property used in conjunction with the real estate.[1] For approximately 25 years, BEV has been a regularly discussed topic among many commercial appraisers. It has garnered considerable interest at appraisal meetings; it has been addressed in a variety of ways and with a variety of property types in *The Appraisal Journal* and other real estate journals; it has been and is still covered in brief form in the Appraisal Institute's *The Appraisal*

of Real Estate; and most recently, it has been the subject of an anthology of published articles.[2]

In one respect, the past quarter century might be viewed as a trial period for the concept of BEV. The appraisal profession has given BEV considerable exposure, with the ultimate goal of deciding issues related to incorporating–or not incorporating–BEV into daily practice. Those who have followed the development of the BEV literature know that BEV has been, and continues to be, one of the most controversial topics within the appraisal community. A wide range of opinion exists regarding how best to deal with BEV. Especially significant, however, is the fact that very little progress has been made in establishing protocols for resolving areas of dispute.

Robert W. Owens, PhD, *is a professor of finance at Missouri State University, where he currently teaches courses on real estate principles, appraisal, and financial analysis. Owens received a BBA and an MBA from Texas Tech University, and a PhD from the University of Washington. He worked as a commercial appraiser for five years during the 1980s, and he has written articles published in a number of real estate and financial journals, including* The Appraisal Journal.

1. There are various definitions of *business enterprise value,* and the definition of the term has evolved over time. For example, *The Appraisal of Real Estate* 11th edition describes *business enterprise value* as "a value enhancement that results from items of intangible personal property such as marketing and management skills, an assembled work force, working capital, trade names, franchises, patents, trademarks, non-realty related contracts/leases, and some operating agreements." Appraisal Institute, *The Appraisal of Real Estate,* 11th ed. (Chicago: Appraisal Institute, 2001), 578. *The Appraisal of Real Estate* 12th edition describes *business enterprise value* as "the existence of a residual intangible personal property component in certain properties." Appraisal Institute, *The Appraisal of Real Estate,* 12th ed. (Chicago: Appraisal Institute, 2001), 641. The definition used here appears in Robert W. Owens, "Business Enterprise Value for Real Estate—Fact or Fiction?" *Real Estate Review* 31, no. 3 (Fall 2001): 3–9, 3.

2. Appraisal Institute, *The Appraisal of Real Estate,* 12th ed., 641–644; David C. Lennhoff, ed., *A Business Enterprise Value Anthology* (Chicago: Appraisal Institute, 2001). *The Appraisal of Real Estate* 12th edition uses the term "capitalized economic profit" as a preferred choice for BEV and the term "market value of the total assets of the business" as a preferred choice for the "going-concern value" of a business enterprise (641–642). Support for these and other new terms used in BEV discussions can also be found in Marvin L. Wolverton et al., "Allocation of Business Assets Into Tangible and Intangible Components: A New Lexicon," *The Appraisal Journal* (January 2002): 46–52.

The purpose of this article is to make the case for a particular plan regarding BEV that might bring some closure to the topic. The discussion that follows is not directed toward or against a particular person or group of persons or toward or against a particular BEV strategy, but rather represents the author's attempt to address various BEV issues and to move the general discussion forward. In particular, the goal of the article is to seek a better position for the appraisal community than the one currently staked out and to do so in a manner that is agreeable to the majority of interested parties. The article that follows examines some of the problem areas associated with BEV in general and with the various strategies proposed for estimating BEV. The article then presents three possible BEV scenarios for the future, with one of these representing the author's strong preference.

Problem Areas in General

Virtually every business enterprise has an element of real estate in it. It is difficult to envision how any business can exist without at least some form of leased or owned real estate. However, the degree of importance of the real estate to the success of a business can vary tremendously. This particular perspective might be envisioned in the form of a continuum moving from "little importance" for real estate on one end to "great importance" on the other. For example, a specialty software writer who replicates proprietary software for sale has little need for real estate relative to the revenue generated from the business. In this case, the real estate might be an almost negligible consideration in the overall business plan. On the other end of the continuum might be an owner of an apartment complex. In this case, the owner's business is the real estate, and the real estate is the business.[3]

This latter statement is important because the typical role of a real estate appraiser is to estimate the value of the real estate and not the value of the business enterprise. However, as most appraisers are aware, the line between the business and the real estate is not always a clear one. An appraiser asked to appraise the real estate associated with a restaurant knows that this is a much different exercise than appraising the business value of the same restaurant. Similarly, an appraiser asked to appraise the warehouse associated with a carpet supplier knows that this is not the same as appraising the value of the carpet business using the warehouse. What about a hotel or other property where the business enterprise is inextricably tied to the real estate? What exactly is the appraiser being asked to appraise? More specifically, is BEV, as a distinct value component over and beyond the value of the real estate and personal property, a valid part of a sale transaction? And if so, can BEV be meaningfully estimated?

An inherent characteristic of real estate and realty-based businesses is that once a purchase is made, the real estate must be managed well in order to ensure optimal results. This would imply that all forms of real estate possess at least the potential for creating BEV, described earlier as the enterprise or business aspect of a sale. Thus, the potential for BEV would exist with ownership of a collection of small-sized, residential rental properties; with ownership of a high-rise, multitenant office building; with ownership of a resort hospitality property; and with ownership of anything in between. In other words, it is not particularly difficult to accept the general premise associated with BEV, i.e., that good management can create value beyond the value of the physical assets. However, even when general agreement exists regarding the conceptual validity of BEV, estimating the portion of total sale price that might be identified as BEV is not an easy proposition, especially for those enterprises where the business is essentially the real estate and the real estate is essentially the business.

If BEV does exist, the main problem in estimating BEV associated with a particular property or business transaction is that BEV is not typically negotiated as a separate line item

---

3. Some of the ideas presented in this section of the article have been previously discussed by the author in "Business Enterprise Value for Real Estate— Fact or Fiction?" Many individuals have contributed to the BEV discussion over the years. Among the more insightful articles are the following: Jeffery D. Fisher and William N. Kinnard, Jr., "The Business Enterprise Component of Operating Properties," *Journal of Property Tax Management* (Spring 1990): 19–27; Norman G. Miller, Steven T. Jones, and Stephen E. Roulac, "In Defense of the Land Residual Theory and the Absence of a Business Value Component for Retail Property," *The Journal of Real Estate Research* 10, no. 2 (1995): 203–215; Kerry D. Vandell, "Business vs. Real Estate Value in Shopping Mall Valuation: A Critical Evaluation," paper presented at the 1999 Summer Appraisal Institute Conference, Orlando, Florida, June 26, 1999, published in *A Business Enterprise Value Anthology*, 211–225; and David C. Lennhoff, "Business Enterprise Value Debate: Still a Long Way to Reconciliation," *The Appraisal Journal* (October 1999): 422–428.

in a sale transaction. This means that no paper trail exists to help an independent observer identify the portion of total sale price that might be appropriately classified as BEV. This in turn presents a problem for those persons who wish to segregate the BEV portion of a transaction price, because they are forced to develop various strategies for indirectly estimating the value of BEV. The main problem with the estimates developed from these strategies is that they cannot be validated directly in the marketplace.

If BEV seems plausible as a conceptual construct but the estimates of BEV are judged suspect, then it is reasonable to ask if estimates of BEV are truly needed and if so, by whom. The response to this requires an investigation of the needs of those parties who might be impacted by BEV estimates. For example, sellers and buyers do not need BEV estimates at the time of a sale transaction since BEV is not typically segregated in their negotiations as a separate line item in the sale contract. In other words, any BEV that may transfer at time of sale is embedded in the overall sale price and is not highlighted as a matter of particular concern.

An estimate of BEV is also not needed by bankers or other professional financiers involved with properties being newly financed, because bankers are trained to identify the sources of possible loan repayment (including various forms of collateral) and to underwrite their loans accordingly. A banker is free to loan against land value, against the total of land and improvements value, or against some higher dollar amount that might incorporate BEV or other aspects of the business such as inventories, other personal property, and especially expectations regarding future cash flow. Personal collateral and guarantees that exist outside the business enterprise might be a major consideration as well. A competent banker is skilled at gathering all appropriate information for underwriting a loan.

A commercial real estate appraiser can provide an estimate of both current land value and the full value of the real estate assuming continued use of existing improvements as currently utilized. In some cases, it also may be valuable for the appraiser to estimate the full value of the real estate assuming the next best alternative use of existing improvements. The latter estimate would assist a banker in the event that the current business enterprise fails and is replaced by an alternative and less productive use. With these three estimates in hand, the banker can then tie the dollar amount and terms of the loan to the desired level of real estate collateral. The banker also can loan at a level above the highest of these three estimates if the banker chooses to loan against some form of business value as opposed to the real estate value alone. In short, it is the banker's primary job to assess value for lending purposes, wherever that value may be found and after fully considering all sources of collateral, including real estate. This is not the appraiser's job, and an appraiser's estimate of BEV is simply not needed or expected for this purpose.

This leads to the principal reason generally offered for appraisers to estimate BEV, which is to confine the value estimate for property tax purposes to only the market value of the real estate. Stated differently, a goal often suggested for BEV is to lower an overall property value estimate that might otherwise be used for property tax purposes, by subtracting an estimate of BEV, which should in turn reduce the property tax paid by a property owner. The property owner is thus the beneficiary, and, at a superficial level at least, this goal seems entirely legitimate. Why should a property owner pay property taxes on anything but the real estate if real estate is the basis for the tax? Similarly, if BEV can meaningfully be separated from the real estate and personal property, and the law requires that the tax be based on real estate value only, what obligation does a property owner have to pay more than his or her fair share? Why should a property owner not use all available cost-effective means to make sure that he or she does not pay more than a fair share?[4]

The key here is whether BEV can be meaningfully estimated. This is the main consideration in the following section of this article. However, there are other issues regarding

---

4. Without question, for property tax purposes, a property owner can and should use any legal means to properly reflect only the value of the real estate in a property's assessment. This may include a deduction for BEV. At the current time, use of BEV for property tax reduction purposes has received a mixed response from the nation's courts, see Marsha Kleffman, "Multi-State Survey: Update on 'Business Enterprise Value'" in *A Business Enterprise Value Anthology*, 369–379. For a discussion of the five major hurdles that must be addressed by tax authorities when attempting to use estimated market value of real estate for property tax purposes see Robert W. Owens, "Valuation and the Property Tax," *The Appraisal Journal* (July 2000): 340–350. One finding from that article is that these hurdles may be significant enough to warrant consideration of alternative strategies for taxing land and improvements.

property taxes and BEV that should be mentioned as well. For instance, widespread use of BEV for tax reduction purposes could produce a significant additional cost for property owners who make use of it and a significant extra cost for taxing authorities who can be expected to challenge its use. Additionally, widespread use of BEV for reducing property taxes could cause significant shifts in these taxes from one type of property to another or from one class within a property type to a different class. Over time, large-scale adoption of BEV for property tax reduction purposes might even play a major role in shifting property taxes from commercial properties to residential properties. None of this is necessarily good or bad, and current property tax policy is not beyond improvement. Still, if BEV adjustments were to become common, the impact on overall tax policy, especially property tax policy, could be tremendous.

Other aspects of using BEV for property tax reduction are worth noting as well. For instance, suppose some real estate participants discover that negotiating a specified portion of the sale price as BEV is desirable in order to support the property tax reduction process for a new owner. In this case, the BEV identified would not necessarily be driven by the underlying value of the real estate, but rather by a utilitarian motive to minimize property taxes. Disregarding any negative income tax consequences for one party or the other, a seller might be motivated to assist the buyer in claiming as much BEV as possible and might even expect a higher sale price for doing so. This may or may not be viewed as an ethical dilemma, but it definitely has the potential to greatly impact the negotiation process.

Further assume that a property owner does succeed in lowering a property tax assessment by claiming BEV relief, whether through cooperation of the seller or otherwise. This would raise additional, potentially noteworthy issues. For example, would a property owner with a reduced real estate estimate for property tax purposes be required to use the lower figure when calculating depreciation for state and federal income tax purposes, or would these two tax calculations continue to be treated separately as under current practice? Alternatively, what would happen if the county where this piece of property is located tries to acquire the property through eminent domain proceedings, and the

owner is on record through the tax appeals process as arguing that the real estate is not worth the overall amount paid for the property due to a BEV deduction? Similarly, how successful would a new owner be in convincing a banker that the full property sale price is the appropriate figure for loan collateral purposes, but that the real estate value reflecting the reduction for BEV is the appropriate figure for property tax purposes? Perhaps the banker would never discover the discrepancy or would be indifferent about it, but the point is that appraisers who actively support widespread use of BEV for tax reduction purposes may be exposing their clients to a host of potential problems down the road.

Problem Areas with Various Proposed Strategies

Several hundred articles have been written on various aspects of BEV during the past 25 years, many of them devoted to various strategies for estimating BEV. Since BEV indications are not generally available directly through the marketplace, the need for these strategies is obvious. Thus, different types of strategies have been proposed over the years, mostly directed toward a special class of property within a general property type. Some of these strategies are fairly simple and straightforward while some are quite complex; all are designed in one manner or another to separate BEV from other value components embedded in a real estate property, including real estate value and personal property value.[5]

From the author's perspective, most, if not all, of the BEV strategies that have been developed thus far suffer from at least one of three major problems; many suffer from more than one. These three major problems are (1) unsupported assumptions in developing BEV estimates, (2) internal inconsistency within the proposed approach, and (3) a questionable dependence on what might be referred to as "relative advantage" in estimating BEV.

Assumptions
The first of the three major problems is the use of unsupported assumptions in developing estimates of BEV. Assumptions in and of themselves are not bad. In fact, as most appraisers are well aware, an appraisal of any unit of real estate, residential or commercial, requires that assumptions be made based on the appraiser's

---

5. A good bibliography listing many of these articles is provided in *A Business Enterprise Value Anthology*, 359–368.

interpretation of market evidence. However, with a typical appraisal assignment, it is the market that ultimately keeps the assumption process within bounds. For example, when appraisers estimate individual items of revenue and expenses for an income property based on a variety of assumptions, they ordinarily will have operating expense ratios derived from the marketplace to test the total of operating expenses for the appraised property relative to its projected effective gross income. If the appraised property's operating expense ratio is too high or too low relative to market indications, this provides a signal for additional verification of the assumptions that underlie the individual revenue and expense estimates. Similarly, if one of the three major approaches to valuing the property, say the income capitalization approach, varies significantly from the other two approaches, this signal from the market suggests further investigation of underlying assumptions used with that approach. The key here is that the market is the ultimate barometer for the assumptions made by an appraiser.

With many of the BEV strategies that have been proposed, market support for the assumptions is either weak or nonexistent. Although a discussion of the strength of assumptions is essentially a matter of opinion, it is particularly unsettling to see a BEV proponent create a preferred BEV strategy by weaving together a series of weakly supported assumptions. The greater the number of poorly supported assumptions, the greater the potential for error. Since there is no independent market indication of BEV, all assumptions that underlie BEV estimating should be held to a very high standard, higher than the standard for assumptions underlying typical real estate appraisal assignments that are much easier to tie to market research.

Consider one example. Over the years, some BEV advocates in the hospitality property area have suggested (either implicitly or explicitly) that a reasonable ratio of value, appropriate for extracting a capitalization rate for BEV from an overall property sale price capitalization rate, is 70-20-10. That is, 70% of an overall property's value should be identified as real estate, 20% should be identified as BEV, and 10% should be identified as personal property. However, in this author's view, the empirical evidence provided by those who employ this assumption is extremely weak. No authoritative research study has ever been offered to support this position.

Even designing a research study to substantiate a 70-20-10 split is difficult to envision since there is no way to validate these percentages with arm's-length market indications. Why should hospitality properties, either a defined subset or in general, possess this particular breakdown of value components? Stated simply, very little theoretical or empirical support exists for the 70-20-10 assumption, and this support is not likely to be forthcoming.

Consistency

The second major problem with many of the BEV strategies is an internal inconsistency that is often easily identified. In the context of BEV strategy, internal inconsistency refers to BEV estimates derived from using a recommended strategy that are inconsistent with one or more of the assumptions used to develop that strategy. It is not unusual for the results of BEV estimation found in a proponent's own example to refute one or more of the assumptions integral to the strategy offered by the proponent. This internal inconsistency obviously suggests a flawed approach. How can assumptions that are promoted as derived in some manner from market evidence be inconsistent with a resulting BEV estimate that is dependent on these very assumptions for its calculation?

The reason for these inconsistencies is that BEV estimation is more concerned with allocation than valuation. Once the decision is made to allocate something, the door is open to literally thousands of possibilities, none of which is necessarily correct or incorrect because there is no external standard for validation. A counterpart to the distinction between allocation and valuation can be found in the accounting area and specifically in a branch of accounting called cost accounting. Although a college course in cost accounting can contain some useful information, a sizable portion of the course is devoted to the costing of products, which is often problematic. Product costing has very little to do with what a product might actually sell for in the marketplace, but has much to do with various allocation approaches that are used to allocate common costs to individual products. Common costs refer to any costs that are not unique to one unit of product or even to one type of product, but are spread internally within a company over many units and many different types of products in calculating inventory costs for financial statement presentation.

Two accountants operating with the same set of underlying financial information on common costs can reach widely varying results for inventory costing on a balance sheet or an income statement, depending on the various allocation strategies chosen for this purpose.

The similarity between cost accounting and BEV estimation is that neither has an underlying general theory that can guide the process toward a uniquely defensible solution. Just as there are thousands of possibilities for inventory costing, there are thousands of possibilities for BEV estimation, and internal inconsistencies are a product of a lack of underlying theory. In the inventory area, allocation of common costs explains why a defense contractor might sell to the federal government a replacement part at a mark-up over a fully allocated cost that would be well above what the part could be purchased for in the general marketplace. The defense contractor is not necessarily doing anything illegal because the formula used to allocate common costs is generally determined via a previously negotiated contract. But it is important to recognize that there is no definitive figure that the government should pay for the replacement part that can be established apart from the contract, and the dollar amount that the government pays may or may not be fair in the eyes of external parties. The allocated cost figure is a creation of the allocation assumptions used to create it, and nothing more, just as an estimate of BEV is a creation of the allocation assumptions used to create it, and nothing more.

Relative Advantage

The third problem with BEV strategies is that virtually all of them depend on what might be called "relative advantage" in order to progress toward a solution. As stated earlier, some of the BEV strategies can be quite complex, but regardless of complexity, once the full strategy is disclosed and understood, at the heart is often an attempt to value the real estate portion of the property based on the real estate of less sophisticated properties. Thus, the real estate for a trophy resort hotel would be valued as if it were part of a non-trophy hotel in the same market, or the real estate for a regional mall would be valued as if it were part of a shopping center located near the mall, or the real estate for a full-service retirement home would be valued as if it were a similar quality apartment complex located in the same general area.

Disregarding the proportion of overall value that might be viewed as personal property, the presumption for the relative advantage approach for estimating BEV with realty properties can be succinctly summarized. That is, any spread between overall property value and a lower real estate value suggested by less sophisticated properties is the result of greater managerial expertise and hence should be classified as BEV. This particular perspective is difficult for some to accept, especially since it implies that only the most sophisticated properties in a market can have BEV.

Several questions arise when using the relative advantage approach for BEV estimation. How exactly is an appraiser estimating BEV supposed to select the group of less sophisticated properties needed for comparison? For that matter, how is an appraiser who estimates BEV supposed to determine which properties are in an elite category such that they are candidates for BEV determined in this manner? Alternatively, should every property be considered a BEV candidate, which implies that part of an appraiser's work with any assignment should be to identify less sophisticated properties for BEV estimation? Along this same line, how is BEV determined for the very least sophisticated properties in a market, or are they precluded from the possibility of having BEV?

If the relative advantage philosophy were to be used extensively for property tax purposes, it would seem that all properties of a particular class would want to be taxed at the level of the least-sophisticated property that can be identified within the class. If Class A is the highest classification by quality, status, competitiveness, or other characteristics, with Class B and Class C the next lower classifications, then Class B properties would strive to be taxed at the Class C level, but Class A properties would strive to be taxed at the Class B level (which might include properties that had already argued to be taxed at the Class C level). The net result would suggest that all properties would be making an argument to be taxed at the Class C level for property tax purposes. Does this make any sense, and what happens in this case to the supposed legal tie between property taxes and market value?

Building on the preceding thought, an appraiser should not need to estimate BEV if the relative advantage approach is used for estimating BEV and its only use is to argue for a property tax reduction. In this case, an appraiser can save the energy expended to estimate BEV and an appeal simply can be made directly to the taxation authorities arguing that the real estate portion of the subject property should be taxed in the same manner as the targeted group of less sophisticated properties. This may or may not be a difficult case to make, but it is essentially what an appraiser is attempting to do (albeit indirectly) when BEV is estimated using relative advantage.

Scenarios for the Future

Given the previous thoughts and observations, three scenarios for the future of BEV seem most likely. These include (1) continuation of the status quo, (2) development of a quasi-legal structure, and (3) adoption of a proactive position.

Continuation of Status Quo

In the author's view, of the three scenarios for the future, continuation of the status quo is the least desirable. This is because there is no mechanism for determining if any progress is being made in resolving the various issues that surround BEV. More importantly, there is little guidance for today's practicing appraisers in how and where to proceed.

Since the *Uniform Standards of Professional Practice* (USPAP), as currently written, requires that appraisers identify and consider the effect on value of intangible items, including BEV, legitimate questions can be raised.[6] A partial list might include the following questions:

- Which particular properties and property types are subject to USPAP?
- What are the consequences for an appraiser who ignores this requirement because of the overall subjectivity involved?
- What strategies for BEV estimation are acceptable and what are the criteria for acceptability?
- Should there be a preferred strategy for estimating BEV for each major type of property, and who should make this decision?
- What theoretical basis should an appraiser use in deciding between competing strategies that might be used for a particular assignment, especially when weighing newer strategies that are recently published?
- Does a new strategy that is published in a major journal mean that previous strate-

gies suggested for similar types of property should no longer be used?
- What is the associated liability for choosing the wrong strategy?
- What are acceptable and unacceptable uses of BEV?

It is appropriate for appraisers to ask these and similar questions. If the status quo scenario is maintained, however, it will be difficult to make progress toward resolving these issues.

Development of Quasi-Legal Structure

A second possible scenario is the development of a quasi-legal structure within the Appraisal Institute or other national appraisal group to address BEV issues. It would be the responsibility of a duly appointed tribunal to address questions regarding BEV such as those previously mentioned. In particular, the tribunal would be charged with responsibility of determining which properties might qualify for BEV treatment and which strategies might be acceptable for BEV estimation. This would not be an easy assignment because it is not clear how various property types and subcategories within these property types would be selected for BEV treatment. Likewise, since BEV estimation is not supported with established theory, choosing one competing strategy over another would be difficult as well.

The accounting profession can provide additional guidance in this area. Both financial accounting used to prepare financial statements and tax accounting used to prepare state and federal income tax calculations are based on thousands of pages of rules and regulations. The reason for the many rules and regulations can largely be traced to an inability to define income in a uniquely defensible manner. Income (also called earnings) is clear in terms of what it is supposed to represent—essentially the change in a wealth position between two points in time. But actually calculating an income figure is difficult because all wealth is ultimately a function of future expectations, which cannot be known with precision. Thus, income cannot be uniquely defined and under current policy is a function of choices regarding revenue and expense estimates. The multitude of rules and regulations used to develop both financial accounting income and taxable income are thus largely

---

6. Appraisal Standards Board, Standards Rule 1-4(g), *Uniform Standards of Professional Appraisal Practice,* 2005 ed., Lines 667–673 (Washington, DC: The Appraisal Foundation, 2005).

devoted to defining what are allowable revenue and expenses and what are not.

The accounting discipline is currently embroiled in a major controversy that highlights the dangers of developing rules and regulations on less than solid theoretical grounds. Financial accounting regulators in the United States are being asked to approve changes that would more closely align U.S. accounting standards with international standards. This change would require U.S. companies to convert property, plant, and equipment financial records from historical costs to market value estimates for financial reporting purposes. Significant issues must be addressed prior to this change, including how to handle the logistics of such a massive change and the considerable associated costs. However, just as significant for the regulators in abandoning historical-cost records for property, plant, and equipment is that all previous depreciation estimates based on historical costs, spanning some 75 years or more, are suddenly deemed incorrect or at least incorrect relative to the new standard. This implies that all reported income figures over the same time period are incorrect as well, since depreciation is a major expense estimate used in income calculation. Such a sweeping change in the rules would give fairly clear evidence that accounting income has never been an accurate indication of financial performance, and that its long-time, premier status as a performance measure has been undeserved. In all, this is an unfortunate situation since millions of financial decisions are made every year based on reported accounting income figures.

If BEV were to be switched to a quasi-legal format similar to accounting, the expectation for the appraisal rules makers would be to operate like the accounting rules makers, attempting to promulgate rules and regulations to cover all potential situations. Since there is no proven theoretical underpinning to resolve the many problem areas that are likely to surface, the process would prove disappointing to many. On the other hand, if a quasi-legal structure were in place, appraisers would at least have some guidance in how to proceed in their attempts to deal with BEV on a daily basis.

Adoption of Proactive Position

A third possible scenario is to adopt a proactive position. This means to acknowledge that appraisers are in an awkward position in how best to deal with BEV, and that something needs to be done about it. As things currently stand, USPAP requires that appraisers pay at least some attention to BEV issues. While there is some limited guidance on this issue in *The Appraisal of Real Estate* and other appraisal texts, there still is uncertainty regarding exactly what appraisers should do to be fully in compliance with USPAP.

The proactive scenario that would seem appropriate at the current time can be divided into a series of action steps. A first step would be to separate future articles written by BEV proponents into a separate professional journal, perhaps underwritten by the Appraisal Institute or other major appraisal organizations. This step would be taken not to disparage those persons who seek answers in this area, but rather to acknowledge that the study of BEV is a relatively minor specialty area within the appraisal field today, one that will gain more acceptance only as significant unanswered questions are satisfactorily addressed. The new journal, which might be called *Allocation Strategies*, would represent a peer-reviewed outlet for those authors who wish to suggest various BEV strategies and for reporting of various successes that might have been achieved in property tax cases or of other aspects of BEV as deemed appropriate. It could be a quarterly or semi-annual publication, depending on the amount of interest shown. Alternatively, if publication of another journal is not considered cost-effective, a separate and clearly labeled section within *The Appraisal Journal* or another appraisal journal might be designated for future BEV articles.

The second action step would be to rewrite the materials on BEV in *The Appraisal of Real Estate* and other appraisal texts at the earliest opportunity to better address the realities currently faced by appraisers. Based on the preceding discussion, the points that might be stressed include the following items:

- Any real estate property may theoretically have an intangible component referred to as BEV, which represents the enterprise or business aspect of the property.

- Acknowledging the existence of BEV and actually estimating BEV in a defensible manner are two different things.

- No general underlying theory exists to differentiate one strategy for BEV estimation as better than another.

- BEV is more closely related to allocation than to valuation, which suggests that BEV is a unique specialty area within the appraisal field that should generally be viewed as an out-of-the-ordinary appraisal assignment.

- Most appraisal work to date involving BEV has been directed toward property tax reduction. While there is nothing necessarily wrong with this, the appraiser and property owner need to recognize that a reduced real estate value for property tax purposes may have negative implications for the owner in other areas such as the amount of income taxes due or the amount of a future condemnation award.

- Many of the BEV strategies proposed to date use a relative advantage approach, which essentially negates the need for a BEV estimate in property tax deliberations since a direct argument can be made for valuing real estate as if it were a less sophisticated property.

- An appraiser should be under no obligation to estimate BEV, unless requested by a client and mutually contracted.

- When an appraiser provides BEV services, some form of an appropriate disclaimer should be attached to the appraisal report to help control for unknown risks that might accompany BEV estimation. Similarly, an appropriate disclaimer needs to be made when an appraiser chooses to not provide a BEV estimate.[7]

A third action step is to lobby the Appraisal Standards Board to change the wording in US-PAP to better reflect the uncertain nature of BEV and the associated realities that appraisers must face in dealing with it. In fact, this might be considered the first order of business if a proactive scenario were to be adopted.

Conclusion

It is hoped that if all the items advocated for the proactive scenario were to occur, a majority of the interested parties would be satisfied with the result. Proponents of BEV would still be able to publish articles on the latest strategies and other significant BEV issues. Under this scenario, appraisers would be better equipped to address various aspects of BEV as they arise, including the decision to accept a BEV assign-

ment or not. As appraisers would become better equipped to address BEV, clients would become better informed regarding the implications and effects of BEV. In total, the appraisal community would be moving toward a BEV scenario that appears to be both manageable and compatible with current practice and away from two future scenarios that are much less satisfying in the author's view.

Comments on "Contemplating the Future of Business Enterprise Valuation"

Robert W. Owens's article, "Contemplating the Future of Business Enterprise Valuation" (Spring 2006), was a masterly job of concisely and understandably tracing in a moderate tone the dilemma faced by attorneys and appraisers in dealing with the business enterprise valuation (BEV) controversy. It would certainly be helpful if the industry could arrive at a consensus on how or if we should deal with BEV. However, as the BEV theory is a results-oriented approach whose sole purpose and usefulness is to reduce property taxes, it is doubtful that any industry-wide consensus will be reached. Instead, the likelihood is that the courts in each jurisdiction will tell appraisers how to deal with this theory, and the future holds more uncertainty.

Thomas J. Scheve, JD
Cincinnati, OH

Response to Comments on "Contemplating the Future of Business Enterprise Valuation"

I very much appreciate Mr. Scheve's commentary regarding my article. As I believe he is aware, my primary intent in writing the article was to contemplate the future of business enterprise valuation (BEV) as opposed to actually predicting it. Mr. Scheve may well be correct that an industry-wide consensus is unlikely and that jurisdictional courts will continue to decide matters of BEV on a case-by-case basis. In my article, I suggested this scenario as the least desirable of the scenarios presented. I have much difficulty envisioning how the significant questions surrounding BEV can be adequately addressed in a piecemeal manner

---

7. One example of such a disclaimer can be found in Robert W. Owens, "How Business Enterprise Value Applies in Nearly All Appraisals," *The Appraisal Journal* (April 1998): 125.

through multiple courtrooms in scattered jurisdictions. This might be described as a state or condition of perpetual disorder. If this is indeed the future for BEV, some day perhaps my article can serve as a point of reference to help explain how we got there.

Robert W. Owens, PhD
Springfield, MO

Part II
Hotels and Motels

Why the "Rushmore Approach" is a Better Method for Valuing the Real Property Component of a Hotel

Stephen Rushmore, MAI, CHA

This article originally appeared in Volume 1, Issue 4 of the *Journal of Property Tax Assessment and Administration*, © 2004 by International Association of Assessing Officers (IAAO). Reproduced with permission. All rights reserved by IAAO.

Does it sound reasonable that the real property component for a hotel accounts for only 36% of its total property value?

This was the result quoted for a hotel property valued for a recent court case (Chesapeake Hotel v. Saddle Brook Township 1999) using the "business enterprise approach." Calculating the same hotel's value using the Rushmore approach, the figure was closer to 60% of total property value.

How can two appraisal methods obtain such disparate results? The difference can be attributed to how each approach separates the real property component from a hotel's total property value. The business enterprise approach moves much of a hotel's total property value into the areas of business value and personal property, thus deflating the value of the real property component. While this significantly reduces a hotel's ad valorem tax assessment, it also has the potential of reducing its mortgage asset security value, which could severely restrict hotel owners from leveraging their acquisitions.

This article describes how the Rushmore approach is better suited to the valuation of hotel properties, first by offering background information on the business practices in the hotel industry and how they differ from other business enterprises and then by using as an example a step-by-step valuation of the hotel that was the subject of the litigation.

Business Practices in the Hotel Industry

The business enterprise approach may be applicable to the valuation of shopping centers and office complexes, but its theories break down when applied to the specialized business practices of hotel operations. The value of a hotel is made up of four components: land, improvements, personal property, and the going business. The land creates revenue based on its locational attributes. The improvements house the guest rooms. The guests sleep on the FF&E, and the business manages the entire operation.

When valuing hotels and motels for real property assessment purposes, where only the market value of the land and improvements is at issue, the appraiser must address the allocation of value among the four components in a manner that reflects actual hotel operating structures, customs, and economics.

Lodging facilities are more than land, bricks, and mortar; they are retail-oriented, labor-intensive businesses operating on daily

Stephen Rushmore, MAI, CHA, *is president and founder of HVS International, a global hotel consulting organization. He has provided consultation services for more than 10,000 hotels during his 35-year career specializing in complex issues involving hotel feasibility, valuations, and financing.*

Mr. Rushmore has written all five textbooks and the two seminars on hotel market analysis and valuation for the Appraisal Institute as well as three reference books on hotel investing. He is on the faculty of the Cornell Hotel School's professional development program.

Mr. Rushmore has a BS degree from the Cornell Hotel School and an MBA from the University of Buffalo. He holds an MAI designation from the Appraisal Institute and a CHA (Certified Hotel Administrator) from the American Hotel and Lodging Association.

He is one hotel consultant who actually invests in and owns hotels.

leases and requiring a high level of managerial expertise. In addition, hotels contain a significant investment in personal property (furniture, fixtures, and equipment or FF&E) that has a relatively short useful life and is subject to rapid depreciation and obsolescence.

The basis for valuing a hotel's real property component is the income approach, which takes a property's stabilized net income and capitalizes it into an estimate of value. The stabilized net income is intended to reflect the anticipated operating results of the hotel over its remaining economic life, given any or all applicable life-cycle stages of buildup, plateau, and decline. Therefore, such stabilized net income contains all of the revenue generated and expenses incurred by a hotel in carrying out its ongoing day-to-day functions of taking reservations; selling rooms; hiring, training, and directing staff; performing maintenance; purchasing equipment; and the myriad other activities needed to keep a hotel operating. In many instances, when a hotel has been open for several years, the appraiser may utilize the hotel's most recent actual net income as the stabilized net income if it conforms to the definition cited above.

The capitalization rate is the weighted cost of invested capital that takes the form of mortgage debt and equity. For property tax appraisals, the capitalization rate will also include the local tax rate expressed as a percentage of market value. This allows the appraiser to capitalize the net income before real estate taxes by assuming that the ultimate tax burden will equate to the municipally mandated relationship to market value.

Analyzing the "Going Business" Component

The business component of a hotel's income stream accounts for the labor-intensive, retail nature of its business activity, which depends upon continual customer acceptance and highly specialized management skills. In contrast to shopping centers or office buildings where tenants sign leases that can extend for ten to fifteen years, most hotels experience a complete turnover of tenants every one to four days. A hotel must therefore constantly market and sell itself in order to maintain a profitable level of occupancy. In addition, finding and retaining qualified labor has been an ongoing problem in the hotel industry because of the generally undesirable prevailing wage rates and working conditions. All of these challenges demonstrate the need for and the value of qualified hotel management to handle the complex business of operating a lodging facility.

Start-Up Costs

One of the main drivers the business enterprise approach uses for allocating additional income stream to the business component is a deduction it calls "business start-up costs." Proponents say that business start-up costs benefit any going concern over the long term. These costs include: assembled and trained work force, management and administration team, regulatory compliance, accounting and other business systems, pre-opening marketing, initial operating losses, working capital, and so forth. For a hotel, start-up costs are determined by utilizing typical pre-opening costs for similar lodging facilities as outlined in franchise offering circulars and calculating an amortization amount that would spread these costs over a 25-year period. The Rushmore approach makes no such deduction. Here's why.

All types of real estate incur a certain amount of business start-up costs. Before opening a new regional shopping mall, for example, the developer must spend a considerable amount of time and money searching for the desired mix of tenants, negotiating suitable leases, and preparing the space for occupancy. This effort requires targeted marketing and sales materials, professional leasing agents, attorneys, accountants, and the like. The mall itself needs to be heavily marketed to the local community through all types of media in order to build awareness and traffic. The mall's administration team needs to be recruited, and suitable accounting and management systems need to be implemented. And finally, as opening day approaches, the mall's operating and security staffs need to be hired and trained.

A similar business start-up process is followed during the development and opening of a hotel. However, the primary difference between the start-up process for a retail mall or office building and the one for a hotel is that the process essentially ends when the mall or office building opens and the space becomes fully leased. Aside from some minimal ongoing re-leasing activity and marketing, the large initial start-up cost becomes a one-time, non-recurring event because the tenants of retail and office space are obligated to stay typically five to fifteen years.

A hotel, on the other hand, is constantly seeking new tenants because hotel guests typically stay for only one to four days, and they usually do not make their reservations many weeks in advance. Therefore, a hotel's sales, marketing, and leasing efforts must be perpetual. Because start-up activities are such an integral part of a hotel's business operations, these expenses are included in the income statement. Recognizing this fact, the Rushmore approach does not make a separate deduction for initial start-up costs.

Work Force Assembly

The same thinking applies to the appropriateness of taking a special deduction for the start-up cost associated with assembling a work force. During a hotel's pre-opening phase, management personnel are recruited, staff and line employees hired, and everyone is trained–much like any other business. This process generally occurs over a two- to three-month period prior to opening. However, in the hotel industry, because of extremely high employee turnover, the process does not stop with the hotel's grand opening.

Timothy Hinkin and Tony Simons (2001) performed a study that showed that the mean level of turnover for a 98-hotel sample (ranging from 72 to 652 rooms) was 47% over a six-month period. This result indicates that the level of turnover is so high in the industry that hotels are constantly going through a hiring process. The authors further stated that these costs are directly reflected in the net operating income of the hotel.

Hinkin and J. Bruce Tracey (2000) of the Cornell University Hotel School co-authored an article based on their study which sought to capture the true costs of turnover in hotels. These included recruiting and attracting costs, selection costs, hiring costs, lost productivity costs, and separation costs. In one example, the authors compared the turnover costs for a front desk employee at four hotels–two in New York City and two in Miami. They found that the cost of turnover for a front desk associate averaged $5,827 for the two Miami hotels and $12,245 for the two New York City hotels. This example shows that the total cost of replacing a line-level employee can be significant.

Because the cost of assembling a work force is a continual expense for the hotel industry and because it is accounted for as part of net operat-

ing income, the Rushmore approach, unlike the business enterprise approach, does not deduct this expense as a start-up cost item.

Other Start-Up Costs

Other business start-up costs cited by the business enterprise approach and included in its start-up cost deduction are feasibility studies and appraisals, telephone systems, upgrading property management software, paying for licenses, complying with government regulations, purchasing inventories, and so forth. However, the Rushmore approach believes that none of these expenses are unique to the pre-opening phase of a hotel start-up. They are all recurring expenses that take place throughout the life of a hotel and are already accounted for in either the income and expense statement or the reserve for replacement. Therefore, under the Rushmore approach, no separate deduction is warranted.

Working Capital Deduction

A deduction for a return on a hotel's working capital is another device the business enterprise approach uses to decrease the income attributed to the real property component. Working capital is defined as current assets less current liabilities. For manufacturing businesses that carry large inventories and work-in-progress as current assets, a deduction for positive working capital may be appropriate. However, in a well-operated hotel, no working capital should exist because the hotel should be financing its accounts receivables with its accounts payables, thus keeping the ratio of current assets to current liabilities one to one. For this reason, the Rushmore approach does not include a deduction for working capital.

Benefits of Brand Affiliation

Another facet of the going business component that shows the divergence between the business enterprise approach and the Rushmore approach is how to account for the benefits that accrue from an association with a recognized hotel company brand through either a franchise or management contract affiliation. Chain hotels generally out-perform independents, and the added value created by this increased income is considered part of the business component.

Ninety years ago, an inexperienced hotel property owner was able to obtain qualified hotel management and a brand affiliation through a lease structure where the property owner leased the land and the building to a hotel company (tenant) that operated the property and paid rent. The rent paid to the owner represented the portion of the income attributed to the land and building.

Today, the hotel lease structure has been replaced by the management contract and franchise. Under this structure, when an inexperienced hotel property owner wants qualified hotel management, he or she enters into a management contract with a hotel company to take over the hotel's day-to-day operation. This allows the owner to assume a totally passive role with respect to the various business activities involved in running the hotel. The hotel company is paid a management fee for these services, which can be recognized as compensation for running the business, or as in the Rushmore approach, a portion of the income stream attributed to the business component.

When a hotel owner wants a hotel chain affiliation and the benefits associated with a brand and reservation system, there are two options. The first is to engage a hotel management company that brings both management expertise and a brand. These are called first-tier management companies and include chains such as Hyatt, Marriott, and Hilton. The second option is to use a hotel management company without a brand and contract separately with a hotel franchise company that will provide the affiliation and reservation system. Although some of the first-tier management companies will provide franchises (without management), most of these arrangements are made with pure hotel franchise companies such as Comfort Inn, Days Inn, Ramada, and Microtel. The franchise fee and other associated costs including reservation expenses, frequent traveler programs, training, information technology, and so forth which are paid to the franchiser also represent a portion of the income stream attributed to the business component.

Fees for hotel companies providing both management services and a brand are typically structured using a base fee and an incentive fee. The base fee is calculated as a percentage of total revenue and generally ranges from 2% to 4%. The incentive fee is usually structured as a percentage of profit, which when compared to the total revenue, could add another one or two percentage points.

Fees for hotel companies providing just management services (no brand) are typically structured using just a base fee ranging from 2% to 4% of total revenue. Under this scenario, when a brand affiliation is desired, the franchise fee paid to the franchisor ranges from 3% to 5% of rooms revenue (HVS International 2003a). When all of the other costs such as reservation expense, advertising assessment, frequent traveler program, training, and so forth are added to the franchise fee, the total cost of a franchise affiliation typically ranges from 6% to 10% of rooms revenue. Furthermore, these other costs are not typically allocated to the franchise fee expense line item; rather they are allocated to the rooms expense in the case of the reservation expense and frequent traveler program, or the marketing expense in the case of the advertising assessment, thereby removing additional income attributed to the business.

Impact of Management Quality

While both the Rushmore approach and the business enterprise approach consider management and franchise fees as income attributed to the business component, the business enterprise approach goes further and allocates additional income to what it calls "residual intangibles." The business enterprise approach defines residual intangibles as the contribution to or impact upon the operating performance of properties with superior brand affiliations and everything these brands embody, as evidenced by marketplace preference relative to competing brands. In the Rushmore approach, this deduction is called the "superior management adjustment" and is included in the income and expense statement. When valuing a hotel for property tax purposes, it is appropriate to adjust revenues down and/or expenses up if the financial performance reflects superior management. Conversely, it is appropriate to adjust revenues up and/or expenses down if the financial performance reflects inferior management. The goal in making these adjustments is for the stabilized income and expense statement to reflect competent management.

Examining the Personal Property Component

The personal property within a hotel consists of its furniture, fixtures, and equipment. Although some jurisdictions assess and tax personal property separately, it must be isolated and excluded from the real property components. Two calculations are needed to remove the personal property value from the income flow—a return of personal property and a return on personal property.

The return of personal property is necessary because FF&E has a relatively short useful life and must periodically be replaced. The Internal Revenue Service depreciation guidelines state that the life expectancy of hotel furnishings averages six to ten years. Although the replacement of the FF&E is a capital expenditure and is not included on an accountant's income and expense statement, it does represent a reduction in cash flow and equity return and has a negative effect on a property's market value. Hotel companies and appraisers account for the frequent replacement of FF&E by establishing an expense deduction known as a reserve for replacement. This fund, which reduces the hotel's cash flow in annual installments, is set at the amount necessary to replace all existing FF&E with new FF&E over an assumed useful life.

The return on personal property is the second calculation required to estimate the income attributed to the personal property so that it can be removed from the income stream. This calculation is based on the premise that a property component is entitled to an annual return equal to the cost of the capital that comprises that component.

The Rushmore approach considers the "Return on FF&E" to be the calculation in Table 3. Either formula can be used; both return the same results. The business enterprise approach considers the "return on" as procedure 1 in the same table and its "return of" to be procedure 2 in table 3. It then takes a reserve for replacement separately. The Rushmore approach considers the reserve for replacement to be the "return of FF&E." In essence, the reserve for replacement is the replacement of FF&E.

Side-by-Side Comparison

Now, to illustrate how the business enterprise approach and the Rushmore approach differ in their estimation of value, let's use as a real-life example the hotel that was the subject of a property tax dispute. This case was recently tried in the New Jersey Tax Court. The business enterprise approach had been used to prepare the original appraisal on behalf of the property owner. While an appraisal using the Rushmore approach was not performed for the case, testimony was presented that established the differences between the principles of the Rushmore approach and the tenets of the business enterprise approach.

The facts and figures used in this example are from the actual case and are part of the public record.

The subject property is the Saddle Brook Marriott Hotel in Saddle Brook, New Jersey. The hotel has a highly visible location adjacent to both Interstate 80 and the Garden State Parkway. Drive time to New York City is less than 30 minutes. The property is a 221-room, full-service, first-class hotel with restaurant, lounge, meeting facilities, and indoor pool. On the date of value, which was January 1, 1999, the hotel was operated by Marriott International under a management contract.

The owner's appraiser developed a stabilized income and expense statement using the hotel's actual operating results for 1998, making some slight adjustments and projecting them to 1999. His capitalization rate loaded with the equalized local tax rate was 12.4122%. Both the stabilized income and expense statement and the loaded capitalization rate seemed reasonable and were thus utilized by the Rushmore approach in its valuation. (See table 1.)

The result is what the Rushmore approach calls Net Income Before Business and Personal Property Deductions for 1999. In calculating this Net Income, all items of revenue and expense normally contained in a hotel's income and expense statement have been deducted with the exception of the following items: Management Fees, Reserve for Replacement, and Property Taxes. Management Fees and Reserve for Replacement will be deducted in a subsequent calculation, and Property Taxes are loaded into the capitalization rate. Both methods, up to this point, are in agreement.

Computing the Business Component

Table 2 shows the calculation of the Income Attributed to the Business. Both approaches agree on deducting a Base Management Fee equal to 3% of total revenue plus an Incentive Fee of 1.9% of total revenue. Management fees for hotel companies providing just management services (no brand) are typically structured using just a base fee ranging from 2% to 4% of total revenue.

Table 1　Net Income Before Business and Personal Property Deductions

	Business Enterprise Approach		Rushmore Approach	
Number of Rooms	221		221	
Occupancy	81%		81%	
Average Room Rate	$128.10		$128.10	
Revenue				
Rooms	$8,369,881	68.5%	$8,369,881	68.5%
Food and Beverage	$3,347,952	27.4%	$3,347,952	27.4%
Telecommunications	$259,466	2.1%	$259,466	2.1%
Other	$234,357	1.9%	$234,357	1.9%
Total Revenue	$12,211,656	100.0%	$12,211,656	100.0%
Departmental Expenses				
Rooms	$2,176,169	26.0%	$2,176,169	26.0%
Food and Beverage	$2,678,362	80.0%	$2,678,362	80.0%
Telecommunications	$168,653	65.0%	$168,653	65.0%
Other	$199,203	85.0%	$199,203	85.0%
Total Deparmental Expenses	$5,222,387	42.8%	$5,222,387	42.8%
Departmental Profit	$6,989,269	57.2%	$6,989,269	57.2%
Undistributed Expenses				
General and Administrative	$1,221,166	10.0%	$1,221,166	10.0%
Operations and Maintenance	$793,758	6.5%	$793,758	6.5%
Utilities	$488,466	4.0%	$488,466	4.0%
Marketing	$781,546	6.4%	$781,546	6.4%
Total Undistributed Expenses	$3,284,936	26.9%	$3,284,936	26.9%
Gross House Profit	$3,704,333	30.3%	$3,704,333	30.3%
Fixed Expenses				
Insurance	$175,000	1.4%	$175,000	1.4%
Equipment Rental	$65,000	0.5%	$65,000	0.5%
Total Fixed Expenses	$240,000	2.0%	$240,000	2.0%
Net Income Before Business and Personal Property Deductions	$3,464,333	28.4%	$3,464,333	28.4%

Table 2　Total Income Attributed to the Business

	Business Enterprise Approach		Rushmore Approach	
Base Management Fee	$366,350	3.0%	$366,350	3.0%
Incentive Management Fee	$235,480	1.9%	$235,480	1.9%
Business Start-up Costs	$337,919	2.8%	$0	0.0%
Residual Intangibles	$337,788	2.8%	$0	0.0%
Total Income Attributed to the Business	$1,277,537		$601,830	

Now, the two approaches start to diverge. Under the business enterprise approach, $337,919 is then deducted for Business Start-up Costs. The rationale is that hotels, like shopping malls or office buildings, incur costs before they open that benefit the business over its lifetime, but that are not reflected in its yearly operating budget. The Rushmore approach, on the other hand, takes no such deduction. Because of the high turnover inherent in hotel operations, both in terms of guest stays and staff retention, a property could be considered to be in continuous start-up mode. Therefore, these expenses have already been accounted for in the income and expense statement.

Another difference is that the business enterprise example makes an additional deduction of $337,788 for Residual Intangibles. This deduction is explained as necessary because the Marriott's Revenue per Available Room (RevPAR) is approximately 15% above the RevPAR of the other hotels in its competitive set. He then takes 15% of what he defines as Net Operating Income to Going Concern ($2,251,920) or $337,788.

While the concept of adjusting for superior results is consistent with the Rushmore approach, it is open to question whether its application in this case is appropriate. The Saddle Brook Marriott did indeed perform 15% above its "competitive" set, but the competitive set is not at all "comparable" to the Marriott. It consisted of a Howard Johnson, a Crowne Plaza, and a Holiday Inn. A Marriott hotel is classified by Smith Travel Research (n.d.) as an Upper Upscale chain based on the quality of its facilities and the room rates it is able to achieve. Howard Johnson and Holiday Inn are classified by Smith Travel as Midscale Chains (two categories below a Marriott) and Crowne Plaza is classified as an Upscale Chain (one category below a Marriott). While these three hotels might compete with the Marriott, they are certainly not comparable based on the quality of facilities and their ability to achieve similar room rates. Consequently, it should follow that they have lower RevPARs and overall values.

A more useful comparison would be to the RevPARs of other Upper Upscale hotels in Northern New Jersey. A specially commissioned Smith Travel Research trend report for all the Hilton Hotels, Hyatt Hotels, Sheraton Hotels, and Marriott Hotels in the Northern New Jersey area found that in 1999 the 25 hotels in this group achieved an occupancy of 76%, an average rate of $135.61, and a RevPAR of $103.65. The owner's appraiser projected that in 1999 the hotel would achieve an 81% occupancy, at an average rate of $128.10, which produces a RevPAR of $103.76–almost identical to its "comparable" set. This leads us to conclude that there is no residual intangible value for the subject property.

Therefore, the total Income Attributed to the Business is $1,277,537 under the business enterprise approach compared to $601,830 for the Rushmore approach– more than two times higher.

Computing the Personal Property Component

The next step is to account for the personal property component of the value. In the Rushmore approach, the calculation for deducting the per-

sonal property in place can be accomplished utilizing one of two procedures. (See table 3.) The first procedure removes from the income stream any income attributed to the FF&E in place by taking the value of the FF&E and multiplying it by the capitalization rate. When the reduced income stream is capitalized, it excludes the value of the FF&E in place. The Rushmore approach terms this deduction a return "on" FF&E or the income that was earned on the FF&E in place. The second procedure simply deducts the value of the FF&E in place from the capitalized value of the overall net income. Both procedures produce identical results, which is to isolate the value of the FF&E currently in the hotel.

These calculations can best be illustrated by using a hypothetical example. Assume a hotel's net income, including the income attributed to the FF&E currently in the hotel, is $1,000,000. The value of the FF&E in place is $750,000. An appropriate capitalization rate would be 12.5%. The value of the hotel, including the FF&E in place, is $1,000,000 divided by the 12.5% capitalization rate, which equals $8,000,000.

Under the first procedure, the income attributed to the FF&E in place is calculated by multiplying the value of the FF&E in place ($750,000) by the 12.5% capitalization rate, producing an income attributed to the FF&E in place of $93,750. Deducting this amount from

Table 3	Two Procedures for Computing the Personal Property in Place
Assumptions	
Net Income	$1,000,000
Capitalization Rate	12.5%
Total Property Value	$8,000,000
Value of FF&E in Place	$750,000
Procedure 1	
Value of FF&E in Place	$750,000
Capitalization Rate	12.5%
Income Attributed to FF&E in Place	$93,750
Net Income	$1,000,000
Less: Income Attributed to FF&E in Place	– $93,750
Net Income Without FF&E in Place	$906,250
Capitalization Rate	12.5%
Property Value Without FF&E in Place	$7,250,000
Procedure 2	
Total Property Value	$8,000,000
Less: Value of FF&E in Place	– $750,000
Property Value Without FF&E in Place	$7,250,000

the $1,000,000 Net Income produces a Net Income without FF&E in place of $906,250. When this amount is capitalized at 12.5%, the resulting property value of $7,250,000 excludes the $750,000 of FF&E in place.

Under the second procedure, the Net Income of $1,000,000 is capitalized at the 12.5% rate, producing a value of $8,000,000, which includes the value of the FF&E in place. To obtain the value of the property without the FF&E in place, the $750,000 value of the FF&E is deducted from the $8,000,000 property value, leaving a property value without the FF&E in place of $7,250,000.

Although both procedures produce the same results, Procedure 2 is simpler to explain to a jury than Procedure 1. Procedure 1 is typically utilized when the jurisdiction assesses personal property taxes and the tax rate needs to be loaded into the capitalization rate.

Table 4 shows the calculation of the Income Attributed to the Personal Property for the subject property along with the Value of the Real Property Only. Both the business enterprise approach and the Rushmore approach deduct a Reserve for Replacement equal to 5% of total revenue, which is at the high end of industry standards. The business enterprise approach then deducts a Return on FF&E of $143,606, which is designed to remove the value of the FF&E in place. The Rushmore approach opts for deducting the value of the FF&E in place after the value of the property is determined. This calculation produces a Total Income Attributed to the Personal Property of $754,189 for the business enterprise approach and $610,583

for the Rushmore approach. The next calculation takes the Net Income Before Business and Personal Property Deductions from table 1 and deducts Total Income Attributed to the Business and Total Income Attributed to the Personal Property, resulting in Income Attributed to Real Property and FF&E in Place. This amounts to $1,432,607 for the business enterprise approach and $2,251,920 for the Rushmore approach. Using a capitalization rate loaded with real estate taxes of 0.124122, the value with FF&E in place is $11,541,926 for the business enterprise approach and $18,142,795 for the Rushmore approach. Both approaches then deduct $1,511,640, representing the value of the FF&E in place, producing a Value of the Real Property Only of $10,030,286 for the business enterprise approach and $16,631,155 for the Rushmore approach. Table 5 shows the effect on value for each approach from the business and personal property deductions. The total business deductions for the business enterprise approach of $1,277,537 are capitalized by the Cap Rate Loaded with Real Estate Taxes, resulting in an Effect on Value for Business Deductions of $10,292,591. The same calculation applied to the Rushmore approach results in an effect of $4,848,697, or a difference of $5,443,894 between the two approaches.

A similar calculation for quantifying the Effect on Value for Personal Property Deductions takes the deductions for the Reserve for Replacement and Return on FF&E and capitalizes them with the loaded capitalization rate and adds back the FF&E in Place. The total effect on value is $7,587,831 for the business enterprise approach and $6,430,857 for the Rushmore

Table 4	Value of the Real Property Only			
		Business Enterprise Approach		Rushmore Approach
Reserves for Replacement		$610,583	5.0%	$610,583
Return on FF&E		$143,606		$0
Total Income Attributed to the Personal Property		$754,189		$610,583
Net Income Before Business and Personal Property Deductions		$3,464,333		$3,464,333
Less: Total Income Attributed to the Business		– $1,277,537		– $601,830
Less: Total Income Attributed to the Personal Property		– $754,189		– $610,583
Income Attributed to Real Property and FF&E in Place		$1,423,607		$2,251,920
Cap Rate Loaded with Real Estate Taxes		0.124122		0.124122
Value with FF&E in Place		$11,541,926		$18,142,795
Less: FF&E in Place		$1,511,640		$1,511,640
Value of the Real Property Only		$10,030,286		$16,631,155

Table 5	Difference in Value Between the Two Approaches		
	Business Enterprise Approach	Rushmore Approach	Difference
Effect on Value for Business Deductions			
Base Management Fee	$366,350	$366,350	
Incentive Management Fee	$235,480	$235,480	
Business Start-up Costs	$337,919	$0	
Residual Intangibles	$337,788	$0	
Total	$1,277,537	$601,830	
Cap Rate Loaded with Real Estate Taxes	0.124122	0.124122	
Effect on Value for Business Deductions	$10,292,591	$4,848,697	$5,443,894
Effect on Value – Property Value Deductions			
Reserve for Replacement	$610,583	$610,583	
Return on FF&E	$143,606	$0	
Total	$754,189	$610,583	
Cap Rate Loaded with Real Estate Taxes	0.124122	0.124122	
Value	$6,076,191	$4,919,217	
Plus FF&E in Place	$1,511,640	$1,511,640	
Effect on Value for Personal Property Deductions	$7,587,831	$6,430,857	$1,156,975
Total Difference in Value			$6,600,869

approach. The difference between the two approaches for this calculation is $1,156,975.

The total difference in value resulting from the application of the business enterprise approach and the Rushmore approach is more than $6,600,000.

Does It Pass the Reasonableness Test?

Based on the final outcomes, which approach seems to produce the most reasonable results? Because there is no hard data pertaining to sales of just hotel business components, conclusive proof to support either approach is not available. Therefore, a next-best solution would be to benchmark the results against other measures of value.

Table 6 starts with an estimate of Total Property Value. The Net Income Before Business and Personal Property Deduction of $3,464,333 is capitalized with the Cap Rate Loaded with Real Estate Taxes of 0.124122, resulting in a Total Property Value of $27,910,709, or about $126,000 per available room for both approaches. My rule of thumb is that a hotel should be worth 1,000 times its average room rate on a per-available-room basis. Based on a $128.00 average rate, this would equate to $128,000 per available room.

The next part of the table takes the value of the three components (personal property, busi-

ness, and real property) determined in tables 4 and 5 and demonstrates that when added together they total the previously calculated Total Property Value.

Lastly, table 6 shows the percentage relationship and the per-room value relationship of each component to the total value. It is these numbers that should prove useful in determining which approach produces the most logical conclusions.

Now the question is: Does it seem credible that the value of the real property component of a full-service, first-class hotel in a highly visible location just outside New York City is worth only $45,000 per room? That is the per room value when the real property accounts for just 36% of the Total Property Value. As a further benchmark, the HVS Hotel Development Cost Survey (2003b) shows the average construction cost for the real property component (land and improvements) for a first-class, full-service hotel is $123,000 per room. Therefore, would it seem reasonable that a hotel whose real property components are worth only $45,000 per room would still be capable of generating an 81% occupancy and a $128.10 average room rate? Or does a property with a per room value of $75,000 (based on a 17% business component and a 60% real property component) derived by the Rushmore approach seem more capable of producing these results?

Table 6	Proof of Value						
	Business Enterprise Approach				Rushmore Approach		
Net Income Before Business and Personal Property Deduction	$3,464,33				$3,464,333		
Cap Rate Loaded with Real Estate Taxes	0.124122				0.124122		
Total Property Value	$27,910,709				$27,910,709		
Proof of Value	Business Enterprise Approach	% of Total	Per Room		Rushmore Approach	% of Total	Per Room
Value – Personal Property Component	$7,587,831	27%	$34,334		$6,430,857	23%	$29,099
Value – Business Component	$10,292,591	37%	$46,573		$4,848,697	17%	$21,940
Value – Real Property Component	$10,030,266	36%	$45,386		$16,631,155	60%	$75,254
Total Property Value	$27,910,709	100%	$126,293		$27,910,709	100%	$126,293

Another test for the reasonableness of the conclusions derived from the business enterprise and Rushmore approaches is to look at the results if the cost approach were applied. The theory behind the cost approach is that the value of the real property component of a new hotel is the cost to acquire the land and construct the improvements. The value of the business component would therefore be the difference in the value derived by capitalizing net income using the income approach and the value derived by the cost approach.

If one were to utilize the cost approach for the Saddle Brook Marriott assuming the cost to buy the land and construct the improvements was the $123,000 per room cited from the HVS Hotel Development Cost Survey (2003b), an appraiser would have to estimate the depreciation on the improvements. Let's assume the land component of the $123,000 per room is worth $15,000 per room, leaving an improvement cost new of $108,000 per room. The business enterprise approach estimated the value of the real property component to be $45,000 per room, which equates to an improvement value of $30,000 per room after deducting the $15,000 per room land value. The Rushmore approach estimated the value of the real property component at $75,000 per room, which equates to an improvement value of $60,000 per room. The business enterprise approach therefore imputes a total depreciation of 72%, while the imputed depreciation under the Rushmore approach is 44%. While quantifying depreciation may not be the definitive test, does it nonetheless seem reasonable that an exceptionally well-located hotel–operating under the high standards required by the Marriott brand and achieving an occupancy of 81% and a competitive average room rate of

$128.10–would ever allow its improvements to depreciate 72%?

Finally, if the property owner were to apply for a real estate secured mortgage using the values generated by both approaches (assuming a 70% loan/value), he or she would qualify for $11,642,000 under the Rushmore approach compared to $7,021,000 under the business enterprise approach, a $4,621,000 difference.

Summary

While the business enterprise approach significantly reduces a hotel's ad valorem tax assessment, it also has the potential of reducing the mortgage asset security value that lenders rely upon when making hotel loans. This would appear to have a significant impact on hotel financings, transactions, and values. If the business enterprise approach is universally mandated for all hotel appraisals, it could severely restrict hotel owners from leveraging their acquisitions, which could lead to a significant decline in hotel values.

Thomas Dolan assisted in the preparation of this article.

References

Chesapeake Hotel v. Saddlebrook Township, Tax Court of New Jersey, Case nos. 1960- 1999, 2047-1999.

Hinkin, T., and Simons, T. 2001.The effect of employee turnover on hotel profits. *Cornell Hotel and Restaurant Quarterly,* 42 (4): 65-69.

Hinkin, T., and Tracey, J.B. 2000. The cost of turnover: putting a price on the learning curve. *Cornell Hotel and Restaurant Quarterly,* 41 (3): 14-21.

HVS International. 2003a. *Franchise fee analysis guide.* Mineola, NY: HVS International.

HVS International. 2003b. Hotel development cost survey. Mineola, NY: HVS International.

Smith Travel Research. n.d. *Smith Travel Research Chain Scales.* Hendersonville, TN: Smith Travel Research.

Letter from David C. Lennhoff, MAI, SRA, CRE

I am compelled to respond to this article due to the legitimacy readers less informed on this specialized topic may assign it as a published work. As the appraiser who valued the Saddle Brook hotel for the owner, I need to point out a couple of serious issues this article presents.

The first item that I wish to point out is the presentation relating to the "total property value." While it appears to be a valuation made by what the author terms the "BEV" appraisers, it is not. I made no valuation of the total assets of the business. I valued only the real property component, as required by law in the jurisdiction at issue. What is shown on page 26 of this article is the author's own erroneous calculation, using my income to the total assets with his real property capitalization rate. It is analogous to capping the income to an overall property with an equity dividend rate. It is wrong, misleading, and uninformed. It concludes my real property valuation was only 36% of the total asset value, when, in fact, it calculates to be more than 53% when done correctly. Equally glaring here is the misapplication of the load for real estate taxes, which results in taxing both the tangible and intangible personalty. The whole object of the assignment, after all, was to avoid just that.

The second point is the calculation of depreciation shown on page 27of the article. Here the author states, "the business enterprise approach therefore imputes a total depreciation of 72%, while the imputed depreciation under the Rushmore approach is 44%." No mention is made of the fact that the subject hotel was built circa 1966, and at the date of value, "overall condi-

tion was below-average with evident deferred maintenance" and significant functional obsolescence issues. Furthermore, recognizing that a typical hotel probably has a total economic life of no more than 40 years, the 72% depreciation suggests an effective age of about 29 years. The Rushmore depreciation suggests an effective age of less than 18 years. Which seems more reasonable for a hotel in only fair condition with an actual age of 33 years?

The most revealing and troubling undercurrent of this article is the author's concern that the method advanced in my appraisal "has the potential of reducing the mortgage asset security value that lenders rely upon when making hotel loans," which would "appear to have a significant impact on hotel financings, transactions, and values. If the business enterprise approach is universally mandated for all hotels appraisals, it could severely restrict hotel owners from leveraging their acquisitions..." I can appreciate the author's concern, as he professes to be an owner of hotels and is probably wearing his owner's hat; however, since when does a client's need for a number serve as the basis for proper appraisal methodology?

Based on my background as an instructor and writer on this topic, there are several excellent books I would recommend on the topic, in particular, the one by Gordon V. Smith and Russell L. Parr, *Valuation of Intellectual Property and Intangible Assets,* 3d ed. (John Wiley & Sons, Inc., 2000).

Letter from James Vernor, PhD, MAI

The recent article entitled "Why the 'Rushmore Approach' is a Better Method for Valuing the Real Property Component of a Hotel," by Stephen Rushmore, MAI, CHA, purports to explain and then criticize a new methodology for separating the value of intangibles from the value of a going concern to isolate the value of the real estate only. While Mr. Rushmore has made great contributions to hotel appraisal over the years, the article makes several serious errors and misstates the information in the newer approach.

The older approach to making this separation, described in this paper as the "Rushmore Approach," allocates a percentage such as 5% of the total gross revenues to an operating hotel property, leaving the other 95% to be capitalized as the Net Operating Income (NOI) of the hotel real estate. A number of thinkers have written articles, published in *The Appraisal Journal,* explaining that if this fee actually is paid for human services, then there is no return on or return of a business, and its very existence is denied.

The paper begins with problems of terminology. Recent thinking about the appraisal of operating property recognizes that a hotel, like many other types of operating properties, is really a going concern or a package of assets, and the real estate is only one of those assets. In order to perform direct capitalization, Mr. Rushmore needs to estimate the *stabilized* net operating income for the entire enterprise. That means that it is not enough that the contractor has turned an empty property over to the operator. To get to *stabilization,* it is necessary to have a trained workforce, permits and licenses, and some cash and receivables and, in many cases, a chain affiliation. Before the enterprise achieves the level of stabilized operations, there will have been some start-up costs and some initial losses. A successful hotel is likely to contain some business profit centers such as restaurants, retail stores, travel service tenants, and possibly other businesses. Many outstanding hotels owe some of their success to having a franchise or "flag."

All of these complementary assets comprise the Total Assets of the Business (TAB) and all have to be examined for having a component of the value of the TAB. When the total net income to the TAB is capitalized, the resulting value is of the TAB. Allocations are necessary in some uses of the appraisal such as ad valorem taxation, transfer taxes, condemnations, and establishing basis for depreciation. In other cases, the buyers and sellers may not care about the allocations and the appraiser does not need to make them. The Rushmore management-fee method fails to identify and evaluate the various components of the intangibles; rather the payment creates value for the hotel management company instead of the owner of the hotel business.

On page 19 he writes, "While both the Rushmore Approach and the business enterprise approach consider management and franchise fees as income attributed to the business component..." Actually the TAB approach treats these management and franchise fees as operating expenses of the hotel and not a determinant of the value of the intangibles in the hotel TAB.

The Rushmore paper does not distinguish between the real estate of the hotel and the concept of going concern or TAB. When he writes

that it is double counting to subtract the value of an item of personal property, he needs to distinguish what it is being subtracted from: is it the value of the going concern or the value of the real estate only? The former is proper. Similarly, it is proper to subtract the income associated with each personal property asset from the income to the going concern if one wants to capitalize income into real-estate-only value. That principle holds whether the income is a contractual, negotiated rent payment such as for furniture, fixtures, and equipment (FF&E) or is an imputed opportunity-cost-based return on an asset.

Recent literature explains the new terminology (Appraisal Institute 2002). While the concept of a going concern is not new, the term going concern *value* is imprecise and means something different to accountants and business appraisers. TAB explains exactly what is being appraised. Likewise, the term, "business enterprise value" has different meanings. In real estate appraisal literature, it has meant either the entirety of all the intangible components of a going concern, or sometimes only one of the intangibles associated with successful entrepreneurship. To some business appraisers, the term business enterprise value means the value of the entire enterprise. Because of this confusion over terms, modern thinking avoids the term business enterprise value. Nonetheless, the Rushmore article misidentifies it as the "business enterprise approach" instead of a more accurate name such as the total assets of the business approach or intangible assets.

While the paper recognizes pre-opening expenses, it misunderstands how to count them for valuation purposes. It says hotels are like malls and office buildings in that they incur start-up costs, but different in that the investment in this asset lasts longer for a mall or an office building. The paper argues that since there is a constant waning and replenishing of the start-up assets, they should be handled only by expensing in the profit and loss statement. This position confuses the initial creation of an asset with its periodic maintenance, and can be thought of by analogy to the original construction of any structure. If a property operates at *stabilized* levels, some construction outlays were completed in an earlier period. The asset takes on value because they have already been made. The fact that lower-skilled workers need to be replaced and retrained at a high rate doesn't mean that the entire management structure has to be replaced.

A recent article in *Journal of Property Economics* by Remsha (2004) provides an insight into how much time, effort, and expense goes into advertising for, interviewing, and paying headhunter fees for the top talent. Operating expenses that follow after the as-of date of stabilization do not double count the investment that allows the hotel to operate at stabilized levels.

Another asset that is required prior to achieving stabilized income is cash and its associated receivables. If the appraiser has capitalized the total income to the TAB, he has captured the value of all the assets that contribute to generating that income, and the non-realty assets need to be removed from the value of the TAB to get the value of the real estate only. Mr. Rushmore argues that working capital as defined by accountants is the net difference between current assets and current liabilities. But the property tax process requires asset values, not the equity in them. If this were not the case, appraisers would offset mortgage balances against the market values of the properties they are appraising for tax purposes. In any event, the work of appraisers is notoriously unhelpful in valuations of assets. Just compare the market capitalization of a publicly held company (plus its debt) to the statement of asset values in its balance sheet and one can appreciate how the depreciated book value of fixed assets misses the real values–for both fixed and intangible assets.

The paper seems to equate a superior brand affiliation (or flag) with superior management, and says that the Rushmore technique is to adjust revenues down or expenses up as needed to reflect normal management. His explanation of how much of an adjustment is appropriate is not offered here, but I find the differential RevPAR analysis of the TAB approach to be rational and reasonable. I do not think brand/flag is the same as management performance, but can result from many forces including historical significance; past notoriety; associations with famous traditions, persons or events; and the like.

The value of the going concern as estimated by Mr. Rushmore is based on a going concern capitalization rate, which I think is appropriate, but he loads it for 100% of the effective property tax rate. This is not consistent with the TAB or intangible assets approach as I know it and as I teach it in a course on the subject. In his valuing of the intangible or business assets, he applies the same cap rate as for the going concern, and it is also loaded for the real property taxes. Ap-

praisers who have studied the intangible assets or TAB approach see examples where the cap rates for business or intangible assets are substantially higher than either real estate cap rates or going concern cap rates. This is why Mr. Rushmore's values for these assets are so high and why they leave so little value for the real estate out of the value of the going concern.

The management fee method has been around for decades and many appraisers have used it over the years when separations have been mandated. But in the last 20 years there have been numerous articles finding fault with it (Dowell 1997; Hennessey 1993; Reynolds 1986). The author needs to address these arguments and show why his method works. I am persuaded that the management fee is a routine expense for these properties and removes none of the intangible business assets.

Adherents to the management fee approach argue that the buyers and sellers of hotel properties do not use the TAB approach to make these separations. That is a poor test. Appraisers frequently are required to think about property and its productivity in ways foreign to owners. For example, we impute a management fee for owner-managed properties in order to separate returns to labor from those to realty; and we infer an allowance for replacements when owners may not. It is doubtful that owners think about the difference between business and realty in any manner when not required to. One hotel appraiser has written, "Integra, Lorms & Belfrage has interviewed several hotel owners, brokers, and management companies who unanimously disagree with the philosophy that deduction of management and franchise fees remove all the business value component." (Belfrage 2001, 280)

Finally, it is deplorable that the correctness of an appraisal methodology should be determined by how one's client base will be impacted. Rushmore writes that the alternative approach "…could severely restrict hotel owners from leveraging their acquisitions, which could lead to a significant decline in hotel values." And in the conclusion he writes, "Anyone who owns and operates hotels will confirm that this difference would have a devastating impact on hotel financings, transactions and values." My view is that sophisticated owners and lenders have long understood the importance of intangible components in the businesses they trade and finance. The need to separate intangible assets from real property faces not only property taxpayers and assessors, but also those involved in the eminent domain and banking and accounting (Collins and Breckinridge 2005).

References

Belfrage, E.E. 2001. Business value allocation in lodging valuation. *The Appraisal Journal* (July).

Collins, K.W., and Breckinridge, Z. 2005. Business real estate appraisal problem. *American Banker* (February).

Dowell, B. 1997. Hotel investment analysis: in search of business value. *Assessment Journal* (March/April).

Hennessey, S. 1993. Myths about hotel business and personalty values. *The Appraisal Journal* (October).

Remsha, M.J. 2004. Intangible assets: What makes a business a going concern. *Journal of Property Economics* 1(1): 23-29.

Reynolds, A. 1986. Attributing hotel income to real estate and to personalty. *The Appraisal Journal* (October).

Wolverton, M., Lennhoff, D.C., Vernor, J.D., and Marchitelli, R. 2002. Allocation of business assets into tangible and intangible components: A new lexicon, *The Appraisal Journal* 70 (1).

The Other Side of the Marriott v. Saddle Brook Decision

John Garippa

This article originally appeared in the April 2006 issue of *Fair & Equitable*, © 2006 by International Association of Assessing Officers (IAAO). Reproduced with permission. All rights reserved by IAAO.

There are several thousand tax appeals filed each year to the New Jersey Tax Court. Of that number, more than 95 percent are settled prior to trial. In the end, the seven judges of the Tax Court decide and issue opinions for a few hundred cases. The tax court is the lowest trial-level court for an assessment case over $750,000 and its decisions are always subject to review by the appellate courts in New Jersey. While the decisions are interesting and fact sensitive, they are rarely, if ever, considered precedent setting.

More than three years ago, the Marriott v. Saddle Brook trial took place before the New Jersey Tax Court. At that time, the taxing jurisdiction and the taxpayer each presented valuation testimony. As part of the proofs of the taxpayer, testimony was presented that indicated the Appraisal Institute had introduced new theories and concepts of valuation as to hotel properties. A part of these proofs included evidence of the Course 800 materials offered by the Appraisal Institute. [The 800 course is no longer offered by the Appraisal Institute.]

At the conclusion of the trial, the Tax Court judge indicated that he would like to give the taxing jurisdiction the opportunity to bring before the court as a rebuttal witness, Mr. Stephen Rushmore, the architect of the pre-existing methodology utilized by the tax court. As such, Mr. Rushmore appeared solely as a rebuttal witness. Mr. Rushmore did not prepare an appraisal report, but rather confined his analysis to rebutting the valuation approach of the taxpayer.

Three years after the trial concluded, the tax court judge issued his opinion and affirmed the assessment of the taxpayer without any reduction in value. Moreover, the tax court indicated quite clearly that the decision did not categorically conclude that any one valuation analysis was preferable to another. Sadly, after three years time, there was no discussion of any of the trial testimony other than the conclusion that the assessment was reasonable. In fact, the trial court did not conclude to a discrete value.

In view of this set of facts, it became rather surprising to see the volume of materials published by Mr. Rushmore indicating that the Marriott v. Saddle Brook decision was "important precedent" finally setting to rest the superiority of his approach to valuation of hotel properties. The following discussion has been written so that objective readers can review the actual evidence of the case and decide this issue for themselves.

The Marriott Saddle Brook hotel is an older facility built more than 30 years ago. At the time of the trial, the evidence presented by both parties indicated that the hotel needed to be renovated and refurnished. In fact, several years after the valuation date before the court, the hotel would undergo such a major refurbishment. However, during valuation dates before the court, no such project was underway.

The hotel was valued for assessment purposes at $16 million. The taxpayer's expert valued

John Garippa was trial counsel for Marriott in the Saddle Brook case. He is the senior partner of Garippa, Lotz and Giannuario, with offices in Montclair, New Jersey; New York City; and Philadelphia. He is also President of the American Property Tax Counsel, the national affiliation of property tax attorneys.

the hotel at $9 million while the taxing jurisdiction's expert valued the property at $21 million.

The taxpayer's appraisal report relied significantly upon the Course 800 concepts in concluding to a value for only the real property. The taxpayer's appraiser, Mr. David Lennhoff, was one of the development team members of the course and displayed an encyclopedic knowledge of the evolution of appraisal theory as it related to income-producing property through the ever-evolving editions of the appraisal text.

Mr. Lennhoff removed from the income stream those elements of income that he believed were not related to the real property. In New Jersey, only real property can be assessed for tax assessment purposes.

Since the property was a 30-year-old hotel, significantly in need of refurbishment, Mr. Lennhoff examined whether the hotel was producing a greater percentage of income than its competing properties would expect. His analysis indicated that the subject property's greater drawing power was reflective of the power of the Marriott brand name. This brand name power allowed the property to draw on all of the reservation systems and all of the marketing expertise of the Marriott chain. This power and resultant increase in occupancy and income were due to the "business" and required a deduction from the value of the real property.

Mr. Lennhoff also deducted for start-up costs maintaining that a hotel requires significant investment in time and capital in order to become a business that produces income. Merely constructing the facility does nothing to make it a successful hotel operation. Because the starting point of the valuation was necessarily the revenue from the business operation, these start-up costs had to be removed.

The appraisal expert utilized by the township opined that the Marriott was worth $21 million for assessment purposes. However, during cross-examination, the expert admitted to the court that due to a mathematical error, the value was grossly overestimated and should be reduced to $16.5 million. It is important to note, that this admission of error does not appear in the decision of the court. However, at the time of the admission, the court was clearly aware of the magnitude of the error:

> The Court: "So that—it is a big difference. That's a difference of more than $5 million."
>
> The witness: "Correct, your Honor."
>
> The Court: "in ultimate final value conclusion."

It is also significant to note that this appraisal formed the very foundation of the evidence that the court relied upon to conclude that the hotel was fairly assessed.

Mr. Rushmore's testimony was rebuttal in nature, concluding that the approach relied upon by the taxpayer was inappropriate and not supported by the evidence. Mr. Rushmore derided the Course 800 concepts claiming they could not be relied upon by any credible appraisal experts. It is interesting to note that Mr. Rushmore admitted he had never attended the course or reviewed its materials. However, under critical cross-examination of Mr. Rushmore, evidence was produced that Mr. Rushmore's managing director in charge of the West Coast operation of his company, HVS International, utilized the very concepts adopted by the subject taxpayer, in her valuation in another tax appeal case. In that appraisal report of another Marriott hotel, Mr. Rushmore's partner removed much of the intangible value from the tax assessment of the property, including name-brand value and start-up costs. In fact, that other appraisal report was accepted by this tax court as evidence rebutting Mr. Rushmore's testimony. Sadly, after a three-year period of time, the sitting trial judge made no mention of this important evidence in his final decision.

Mr. Rushmore also opined that there was no need to deduct a value from the subject older hotel because of the Marriott "flag" or brand name. To buttress this testimony, Mr. Rushmore relied upon 16 luxury hotels throughout New Jersey to demonstrate that the income stream in Saddle Brook was no different from these other quality name-brand facilities. However, the testimony by Mr. Rushmore was sadly deficient in that regard. He was completely unable to:

1) identify where the hotels were located
2) identify how distant they were from Saddle Brook, New Jersey
3) describe how a customer would travel from those hotels to Saddle Brook.

Finally, in a startling admission to the court, he admitted that he had never even inspected these relied-upon facilities. In fact, Mr. Rushmore admitted that the only time he had ever inspected the subject Saddle Brook hotel was the night before his testimony before the court. This evidence was the cornerstone of Mr. Rushmore's opinion that there was no justification for a reduction in value for the Marriott "flag."

Perhaps the most telling part of the case, and an insight into the mind of the court, is revealed by the court's question to counsel as follows:

"Ultimately are we going, if we accept in a case like this, the contention that the Marriott name increases business value by a certain extent? Or are we going to have Donald Trump come in here and say, 'oh, this property is not worth the capitalization, it's worth less than the capitalization of the income because I, Donald Trump, have given my name to it and you should give me 20 percent off the otherwise demonstrable value of the property because it's a Trump property.' What the–where does this go?"

This question clearly displays a mindset relating to tax policy and not valuation theory. In fact, the concluding paragraph of the decision demonstrates the fact that after three years, the trial judge himself saw fit to say that the decision was only limited to the facts before him and was not a comment on the validity of any methodology.

"It bears emphasis that this decision is based upon the consideration of the reasoning and supporting data addressed in the record of this case for the particular adjustments proposed. It should not be understood as a definitive pronouncement on appraisal practices designed to extract real estate value from the assets of a business or as binding precedent with respect to adjustments of the kind proposed here, should they be offered in other cases with different records." *Cheasapeake Hotel v. Saddle Brook Tp.* 22 N.J. Tax 525, 536 (Tax 2005)

We appreciate Mr. Rushmore's tenacity in defending his theory. However, during cross-examination, he indicated that he presently owned more than 18 hotels. We are also aware of the fact that a most significant part of his appraisal practice is devoted to producing appraisals devoted to financing. However, for appraisal purposes in New Jersey, only the value of real property can be taxed for assessment purposes.

In the months subsequent to the decision, Mr. Rushmore has written extensively and spoken at length on the precedent-setting nature of the case and the primacy of his methodology over the Course 800 concepts. Objective readers can evaluate the decision as well as the testimony. In the end, appraisal theories evolve over many years. It is critical to note that the courts did not accept Mr. Rushmore's technique when it was first introduced. Only after a number of years and critical review was it properly accepted.

Hotel Valuation Myths and Misconceptions Revisited

David C. Lennhoff, MAI, SRA, and Heather J. Reichardt

Reprinted with permission from Willamette Management Associates *Insights* (Winter 2011).

This discussion summarizes the "whats and whys" of hotel intangible property allocations. And, this discussion reviews some of the recent judicial precedent related to the topic. This discussion will also clarify some of the misunderstandings that have developed about the withdrawal of the Appraisal Institute continuing professional education course, Separating Real and Personal Property from Intangible Business Assets (Course 800). Additionally, this discussion describes the importance of understanding the relationship between real estate and personal property (both tangible and intangible personal property) for a valuation engagement that concludes the market value of the hotel real estate only. Such a valuation engagement typically starts with the income (or the value) of the total operating assets of the hotel going concern business.

Introduction

Although the topic of separating hotel intangible assets and tangible assets has been around for much longer, this topic has received considerable intense attention in the past 10 to 15 years. This attention was aided by the introduction and presentation of the Appraisal Institute continuing professional education (CPE) course, Separating Real and Personal Property from Intangible Business Assets (course 800). That CPE course premiered around 2001.

With the Appraisal Institute withdrawal of course 800 in 2005, some observers may conclude that the issue has diminished in importance and has somehow lost its relevance. However, that conclusion could not be further from the truth.

If anything, there is now a greater awareness on the part of hotel valuation clients of the need to allocate the hotel total operating assets in situations where only the value of the real

estate is sought. This client awareness extends to valuation engagements related to secured lending, property tax assessment, and eminent domain and condemnation. Now more than ever, hotel owners, taxing jurisdictions, secured lenders, and valuation analysts should understand the composition of these business operating assets. This way, these interested parties can assure themselves that the hotel total assets have been properly parsed when that allocation is necessary in the valuation engagement. The evidence of this continued interest in the operating assets allocation process is ample. For example, in 2009, the Appraisal Foundation released an exposure draft related to the best practices for valuing intangible assets.[1] In addition, some of the federal banking agencies

David C. Lennhoff, MAI, SRA, is president of PGH Consulting, LLC, which has its office in Rockville, Maryland. He has been closely involved with the topic of this book since serving as a member of the Appraisal Institute's Study Group on Business Enterprise Value in 1997-1998. He was a development team member, chief reviewer, and frequent instructor of the original Appraisal Institute Course 800, Separating Real and Personal Property from Intangible Business Assets, and editor of the first edition of A Business Enterprise Value Anthology. Mr. Lennhoff continues to teach regularly for the Appraisal Institute, both nationally and internationally, and has been a frequent contributor to The Appraisal Journal since 1982.

Heather J. Reichardt is a Director of Property Tax for Marriott International, Inc., and she has been with the company since 1990. She is currently responsible for real estate tax management for various Marriott hotels in seven states, Canada, and the UK. Heather's professional memberships include the Institute for Professionals in Taxation (IPT) and the Royal Institution of Chartered Surveyors (RICS).

1. See *Identification of Contributory Assets and the Calculation of Economic Rents,* Exposure Draft (Washington, DC: The Appraisal Foundation, 2009).

appear to be moving toward a formal position regarding the valuation of intangible assets.[2]

This discussion considers the "whats and whys" of these tangible asset versus intangible asset allocations. And, this discussion will review some of the recent judicial precedent regarding the allocation of total operating assets. This discussion also clarifies some of the misunderstandings regarding the Appraisal Institute decision to withdraw CPE course 800.

Renting a Hotel Room

While this may be all too familiar to frequent travelers, it is worth taking a moment to describe the various services that are provided to a guest at a full service hotel. Due to "amenity creep," many of these services are also provided in limited service hotels. If a guest is entering a luxury or resort hotel, there are even more services. As these hotel services are listed below, let's contrast these services to the "services" (or lack thereof) that are provided when someone walks into an office building or a warehouse.

- Bellman helps carry luggage to the front desk.
- Valet parks the car.
- Front desk associate checks in the guest and provides keys to the guest room.
- Housekeeping staff has made a clean room available for the guest even if there was someone occupying the room hours before.
- Security personnel are doing their jobs, often unnoticed.
- Comfortable furniture and linens have been provided to sit/sleep on.
- Television and radio are provided for use while the guest is in the room.
- Possibly a mini-refrigerator is provided in the room (could be stocked with grocery items available for purchase).
- Lounge area is provided to watch television and meet with the other guests.
- Fitness room with equipment may be available for use.
- Swimming pool may be available (could be indoors in an area with inhospitable climate) for relaxation and recreation.

The daily room charge typically covers all the services listed above. True, there may be separate charges for some services provided in the hotel, such as phone and internet service, food and beverage service, resort/spa activities, and so on. But, there remains an inherent cost in establishing and managing these services in the hotel for the immediate and ongoing availability to the hotel guests.

There are few, if any, "services" provided to the office or warehouse tenant (other than building maintenance and possibly cleaning) when he/she rents this sort of space. The tenant gains the right to occupy an otherwise vacant office or warehouse bay. If the daily hotel room rate was simply conveying the right to occupy a vacant room, the experience would be akin to indoor camping. In that case, the hotel guest would need to provide all of the furniture, fixtures, equipment, and other services.

Operating the Hotel Business

The five unique elements of a stabilized hotel business operation are described in Table 1.

Valuation analysts should understand that any viable, operating, profitable hotel creates intangible asset value by providing some level of service above and beyond that of renting a vacant guest room. It is an error for valuation analysts to conclude that only nationally or internationally recognized hotel brands can create intangible asset value by providing services or allowing the use of their brand name(s).

Hotel developers invest in a certain number of nonrealty items that are considered standard for a viable hotel to operate. Figure 1 demonstrates the breakdown of the "total assets of the operating business" between tangible assets and intangible assets. This list of intangible assets is not intended to be all-inclusive.

Return "On" Intangible Personal Property

One component of the issue of the appropriate value allocation to intangible assets is the procedure of a return "on" this investment—that is, on any/all of the intangible assets listed above under the Intangible Property listing. In order to thoroughly explore this issue, it may be helpful to provide a definition and explanation of just what this return "on" calculation represents.

---

2. Kathleen W. Collins and Zonnie Breckinridge, "A Business Real Estate Appraisal Problem," *American Banker* 24, no. 170 (2005), p. 10.

Table 1	Unique Hotel Characteristics
1. Hotels are operating businesses	Aside from the component of leasing real estate, hotels conduct many other businesses such as restaurants, equipment rentals, business services, and so on.
2. Hotel leases are only 24 hours in duration	Hotel room nights are perishable, and countless transactions are involved in leasing hotel rooms during the course of a year.
3. Hotels are labor intensive	In order to accomplish the goals of (1) executing 24-hour leases and (2) operating other related businesses, hotels are very labor intensive.
4. Hotels are capital intensive	The excessive wear and tear on hotel real estate due to the public nature of the facilities requires annual expenditures for property renovation and improvements *that other real estate types do not require.* (emphasis added)
5. Hotels are typically "branded" with a chain affiliation	In essence, the chain affiliation partially replaces the real estate broker as a leasing agent.

Source: Pagliari, Joseph L., ed., *The Handbook of Real Estate Portfolio Management,* pg. 490.

Figure 1	Components of Total Assets of the Business

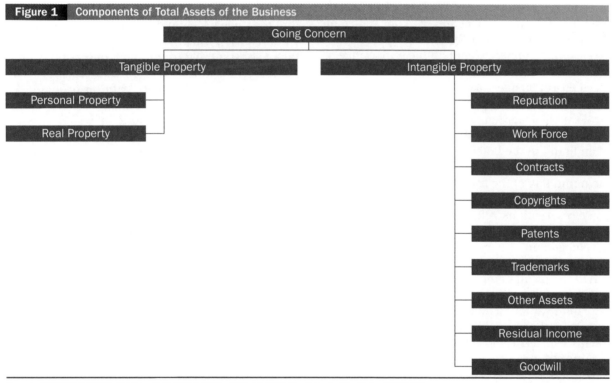

Source: Appraisal Institute, *The Appraisal of Real Estate,* 13th ed. (Chicago: Appraisal Institute, 2008), 30.

The Appraisal of Real Estate (13th edition) defines and explains the return "on" and return "of" calculations as follows:

> The notion that an investor anticipates a complete recovery of invested capital–plus a payment for the use of capital–prevails in the real estate market just as it does in other markets. The term "return of capital" refers to the recovery of invested capital. The term "return on capital" refers to the additional amount received as compensation for use of the investor's capital until it is recaptured.[3]

A more practical explanation of the concept of "return on" an investment is provided by Smith and Parr, in the Preface section of their 2000 textbook, *Valuation of Intellectual Property and Intangible Assets.*

> . . . the structure around which we value intangible assets and intellectual property is not without firm foundation. That rock is one of the immutable laws of business–"return on investment." Yes, large business transactions are sometimes made

---

3.   Appraisal Institute, *The Appraisal of Real Estate,* 13th ed. (Chicago: Appraisal Institute, 2008), p. 461.

to feed egos, thwart competition, and in haste. But, in the main and in the long run, businesspeople base those decisions on a careful (and correct) evaluation of the potential for earning a return on investment. Dollars are not committed for idle amusement. They are planted in order to grow—businesspeople are simply farmers with their own unique seeds and implements, trying to employ the classic agents of production in their own way.[4]

In the context of the hotel valuation and total asset allocation—in the situation where the value of just the real property is sought—this issue manifests itself in the appropriate value allocations to such assets as franchise agreements, working capital balance, business start-up costs, and potentially, unidentified intangible assets (as those represented in Figure 1). These intangible assets, as well as other intangible assets not mentioned here, are invested in the expectation of (1) a return of the investment and (2) a fair return on the investment. To quote Smith and Parr again, "We cannot emphasize enough the importance of the relationship of value and earnings. The raison d'être of business assets is to provide a return on the investment required to obtain them."[5]

Franchise agreements and related franchise rights are a good example of an intangible asset often found in the hotel valuation. With a franchise, the franchisee receives the right to use the name/flag of the franchisor. Accordingly, the franchisee will enjoy the instant image, the in-place reservations/referral system, the rewards program, the advertising and sales benefits, well developed and proven operating procedures, and the like. In exchange, the franchisor receives the payment of an initial fee plus regular royalty payments.

Some valuation analysts contend that, by deducting the annual royalty fee, the value of the franchise is removed from the subject hotel income stream. This procedure, however, fails to address the issue of an appropriate return on this intangible asset investment. Why, for example, would a hotel owner enter into a franchise agreement if the sum total of its franchise value is represented by the periodic license fee that the hotel owner pays to the franchisor?

A royalty rate rule of thumb, often called the 25 percent rule, illustrates this point.[6] This rule

of thumb suggests that the licensee will pay a royalty rate equivalent to 25 percent of its expected profits for the product/service that uses the subject intellectual property. Stated differently, the royalty rate represents only a fraction of the value of the intellectual property (e.g., franchise agreement) license.

The licensee enters into such a franchise arrangement expecting (1) to recover the royalty rate that he/she pays to the licensor and (2) to earn a suitable return on the payment of that royalty fee. If the licensee only expected to recover the franchise license fee, then he/she would never enter into the franchise agreement. "The theory underlying this rule of thumb is that the licensor and licensee should share in the profitability of products embodying the patented technology. The a priori assumption is that the licensee should retain a majority (e.g., 75 percent) of the profits because it has undertaken substantial development, operational, and commercialization risks, contributed other technology/intellectual property, and/or brought to bear its own development, operational, and commercialization contributions."[7]

This procedure is analogous to the hotel franchisor/franchisee relationship. And, this procedure illustrates that there should be a profit incentive for a licensee to pay royalties for the franchise license. This is not to suggest that this procedure is an appropriate method to value a franchise agreement. Rather, this discussion is presented simply to illustrate (1) the concept of the fair return "on and of" components of any intangible asset investment, and (2) the fact that, one way or another, if the value sought is just the real estate, then both the return of and the return on intangible assets should be accounted for.

Specific Intangible Asset Investments—Hotel Development

To develop a hotel with a nationally recognized franchise (Marriott, Sheraton, Hilton, Westin, etc.), the hotel developer invests in a number of non-realty items that are clearly described in the typical Uniform Franchise Offering Circular

---

4. Gordon V. Smith and Russell L. Parr, *Valuation of Intellectual Property and Intangible Assets,* 3rd ed. (New York: John Wiley & Sons, 2000), p. x.

5. Ibid., p. 66.

6. Gordon V. Smith and Russell L. Parr, *Intellectual Property: Valuation, Exploitation, and Infringement Damages* (Hoboken, NJ: John Wiley & Sons, 2005): pp. 410-426.

7. Ibid., p. 412.

(UFOC). The UFOC, also commonly known as a Franchise Disclosure Document, is a legally registered document provided to prospective franchisees setting out in detail all of the requirements necessary to qualify for a franchise from that particular franchisor. Including the addenda, a UFOC can be well over 400 pages long.

As mentioned above, each franchisor has spent significant resources to develop its proprietary operating systems and its current level of brand recognition. The franchisor is not going to license a franchise to a hotel operator who does not agree to use all of the franchisor processes, procedures, and systems. Such processes, procedures, and systems presumably have been proven to make franchises profitable and to preserve the brand standard. And, a new franchisee would not expect to pay a franchise fee for only the right to use the franchisor's name with no access to the appropriate resources, systems, etc., that will, presumably, ensure a profitable hotel project.

Table 2 presents a list of the representative items that a hotel franchisor will typically require the franchisee to procure, either directly from the franchisor or indirectly from another approved source. Additionally, Table 2 includes several requirements for hiring, training, and the like. These expenditures may not represent physical items to be procured, per se. However, these expenditures are investments that are made as part of the overall hotel development project.

Table 2 does not include the cost of every single item or fee that a new hotel franchisee,

developing a new full service, chain-affiliated hotel, would incur in the process of completing the project. However, the Table 2 items are unique in their inclusion in the overall investment for a hotel project versus an office or warehouse project.

Obviously, an office or a warehouse developer may or may not incur some of these expenses, such as advertising or working capital. However, most of these items are absolutely necessary for the final hotel product, that is, for the hotel business to start out on a successful footing. Therefore, if the valuation analyst is estimating the business enterprise value of an operating hotel property, then these items should be included in the valuation. However, if the valuation analyst is estimating the value of just the hotel real estate, then these items should be excluded from the valuation.

Intangible Asset Valuation Issues

The business start-up costs component of going concern value is a commonly misunderstood intangible asset. This is especially true when the subject property is an older hotel.

This misunderstanding has two facets. The first misunderstanding is that these start-up costs are simply ongoing costs in a hotel operation, expenses that are incurred repeatedly. The second misunderstanding is that these start-up costs were incurred initially at the time of opening—many years ago. Therefore, such start-up costs were amortized long ago and are no longer an appropriate deduction.

Table 2	Selected Nonrealty Franchise Development Costs	
Required Franchise Item	**Approximate Cost**	**Provider**
Initial franchise fee	$200/rm or $60,000; whichever is greater	Franchisor
Property management and reservations systems & in-person training	$163,000-$168,000	Franchisor/Equipment Suppliers
Other systems/training	$215,500 - $233,500	Franchisor/Equipment Suppliers
Pre-opening training & services	$82,500 - $102,000	Franchisor
Feasibility study	Up to $50,000	3rd Party Supplier
Kitchen/laundry equipment	Up to $4,700/room	3rd Party Supplier
Start-up costs (wages, prepaid expenses, licenses, deposits, etc.)	Up to $4,200/room	Suppliers; Franchisee
Pre-opening local advertising	Up to $170,000	Suppliers
3 months operating funds (working capital)	Up to $4,200/room	Suppliers; Franchisee
Furniture & fixtures	Up to $22,000/room	3rd Party Supplier
Professional interior design services	Up to $9,300/rm	3rd Party Supplier

Source: 2010 Renaissance Hotels Franchise Disclosure Document, 46-47.

With respect to the former misunderstanding, it is true that these costs occur repeatedly. For instance, a portion of the hotel assembled workforce is periodically turned over and personnel costs are incurred annually. However, this does not diminish the requirement of assembling the hotel workforce in the first place (e.g., preopening interviews, hiring and training). This misunderstanding is much like confusing the initial installation of a hotel roof with the requirement to continually maintain the hotel roof. Both sets of costs are necessary.

With respect to the second misunderstanding, it is true that the original hotel owner incurred the initial costs. With each transfer (or hypothetical transfer) of the subject hotel, the costs are passed along to the new hotel buyer. Accordingly, these costs are never "amortized."

An easy way to keep this concept straight is to consider how the valuation analyst would value the subject total assets—that is, (1) real property and (2) tangible and intangible personal property—using the cost approach. If the valuation analyst wants to conclude the value of a stabilized hotel operation, the analyst would have to add both tangible personal property (FF&E and inventory) and intangible personal property (business start-up costs, for example) to the cost new of the real property. This is true even if the subject hotel was 50 years old.

Figure 2 illustrates the flow of the start-up costs from hotel development through a subsequent hotel purchase. Unless the building is dark at the time of the transaction, the ini-

tial investment in the start-up costs would be recaptured by the hotel seller. And, the hotel buyer does not have to re-invest in all the start-up costs initially incurred. These going concern value start-up costs remain with the property.

Let's assume that the valuation analyst is estimating the value of the hotel real property only but doing so using sales or income for the hotel total operating assets. In that case, the start-up costs that are necessarily added in the cost approach valuation analysis would have to be removed from the operating sales and income streams used in the income approach valuation analysis.

Tangible Personal Property Allocation Issues

The most common source of confusion regarding tangible personal property is handling the allocation to FF&E in order to remove the FF&E from the overall hotel going concern value. Most valuation analysts recognize that, in order to accomplish this, both a return "on" and a return "of" this FF&E asset must be deducted from the hotel income stream. The misunderstanding comes from the relationship of (1) the deduction for the return "of" the FF&E and (2) the deduction of a replacement allowance as a standard, expected, and necessary operating expense.[8] If the hotel total operating assets are being valued, then a deduction for an FF&E replacement allowance is made. Few valuation analysts would argue with this procedure. Somehow, however,

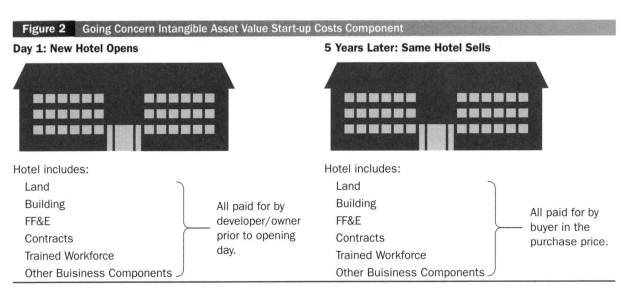

Figure 2   Going Concern Intangible Asset Value Start-up Costs Component

Day 1: New Hotel Opens

Hotel includes:
- Land
- Building
- FF&E
- Contracts
- Trained Workforce
- Other Buisiness Components

All paid for by developer/owner prior to opening day.

5 Years Later: Same Hotel Sells

Hotel includes:
- Land
- Building
- FF&E
- Contracts
- Trained Workforce
- Other Buisiness Components

All paid for by buyer in the purchase price.

8. *The Appraisal of Real Estate,* 13th ed., p. 459.

when just the hotel real property component is being valued, then the deduction of the FF&E represents the removal or separation of the FF&E from the real property. How is this allocation possible? If this procedure doesn't allocate FF&E value when the analyst is valuing the hotel total operating assets, then why would this procedure become an FF&E allocation when just the real property is being valued? The answer is, of course, it wouldn't.

In the case of the hotel real estate only valuation, the tangible personal property deduction has to be made twice. First, the FF&E replacement allowance operating expense deduction has to be made. Second, a deduction–representing both a return on and a return of this FF&E asset–is needed to remove the FF&E value from the hotel total operating assets value.[9]

Survey of Recent Judicial Precedent

Probably the best known recent decision relating to this topic involved the Saddle Brook Marriott Hotel in Saddle Brook, New Jersey. This property tax assessment appeal case was tried in 2002. However, the decision wasn't handed down until 2005. The concepts taught in Appraisal Institute course 800 were prominent in this judicial decision.[10]

Despite the fact that the assessor's valuation expert made a material mathematical error with which the court was clearly aware (to quote the judge from the transcript, "So that–it is a big difference. That's a difference of more than $5 million in ultimate final value conclusion."), the court ruled to uphold the property tax assessment.

It is important to note, however, that the trial judge qualified the significance of the decision by emphasizing, "This decision is based upon the consideration of the reasoning and supporting data addressed in the record of this case for the particular adjustments proposed. It should not be understood as a definitive pronouncement on appraisal practices designed to extract real estate value from the assets of a business or as binding precedent with respect to adjust-

ments of the kind proposed here, should they be offered in other cases with different records."

A similar result was reached in the Maryland Tax Court in 2006 in a case involving a Red Roof Inn.[11] In that case, similar arguments were advanced. Ultimately, the court could not bring itself to appreciate that intangible assets could exist in a limited service hotel, and the court ruled to uphold the property tax assessment.

Several other cases, however, resulted in conflicting judicial opinions. For example, in the 2004 WXII/Oxford-DTC Real Estate case,[12] the Loudoun County Circuit Court's decision in Virginia was diametrically opposite to the Saddle Brook decision. And, the Loudoun County Circuit Court decision centered on the Appraisal Institute course 800 concepts. In this matter, the judge found the Appraisal Institute course 800 concepts to be more accepted in valuing the real estate connected with, or part of, a going concern business.

Similar conclusions were found in three Marriott hotel cases in 2003 and 2004 by the Tennessee State Board of Equalization. The same Tennessee administrative law judge presided in all three decisions. However, in a subsequent case in 2005, in a matter involving a regional shopping mall, that judge reversed himself. The Tennessee administrative law judge appeared to be uncomfortable about whether there was broad acceptance of the Appraisal Institute course 800 concepts.

Several other judicial decisions were also relevant. In Canada, a 2005 decision involving the Fairmont Empress Hotel in Victoria ruled in favor of the valuation concepts with respect to the allocation of tangible personal property (FF&E), but against the valuation concepts with respect to business intangible assets.[13] And, in the Superior Court of California, County of Los Angeles, the judge in a 2009 case involving the Glendale Hilton granted a motion for summary judgment. The judge concluded that "the assessor's methodology necessarily failed to exclude from his valuation certain intangible

---

9. Heather J. Reichardt and David C. Lennhoff, "Hotel Asset Allocation: Separating the Tangible Personalty," *Assessment Journal* (Winter 2003), pp. 25-31.

10. *Chesapeake Hotel LP v. Saddle Brook Township,* 22 N.J. Tax 525 (N.J. Tax 2005).

11. *RRI Acquisition Company, Inc. v. Supervisor of Assessments of Howard County,* No. 03-RP-HO-0055, 2006 WL 925212 (Md. Tax Feb. 10, 2006).

12. *WXII/Oxford-DTC Real Estate, LLC v. Loudoun Cty. Bd. of Sup'rs.,* No. 29368, 2004 WL 2848543 (Va. Cir. Ct. Apr. 5, 2004).

13. *Fairmont Hotels v. Assessor of Area 01,* App. Nos. 2001-01-0028; 2002-01-00021, Property Assessment Appeal Board (Victoria, Canada 2003).

assets, such as a return on the franchise and management expenses, from his going concern valuation methodology. The Los Angeles County Assessment Appeals Board's subsequent adoption of the assessor's income approach valuation method is contrary to California law."

There are two noteworthy California Assessment Appeals Board decisions–one involving the Coronado Marriott Hotel (2009) and the second involving the La Jolla Marriott (2006), both in San Diego, California. The Board found that deductions for a RevPAR premium due to flag/franchise and for business start-up costs were appropriate and necessary above and beyond a deduction for just the hotel franchise fees and management costs. These fees and costs were recognized to be simply operating expenses. (One of the two Board decisions recognized all intangible assets except the RevPAR premium; the other Board decision accepted all intangible assets except for the business start-up costs.)

This discussion does not represent an exhaustive presentation of court cases involving intangible asset allocation issues. It is obvious from the decisions mentioned, however, that the courts have not reached consensus on this topic. As awareness of all sides of the intangible asset allocation issues intensifies, progress will undoubtedly be seen in the courts.

Course 800 Misconceptions

Some valuation analysts have inferred that course 800 was removed from the Appraisal Institute curriculum because of the Institute recognition that the concepts were not valid. Other valuation analysts inferred that the course 800 concepts were counter to the *Uniform Standards of Professional Appraisal Practice*. In fact, these assertions are nothing more than "old husbands' tales."

A 2008 "Fact Sheet" authored by the Appraisal Institute noted, "The Business Enterprise Value seminar was offered under the title 'Course 800' for approximately three years and then was withdrawn in 2005 for review and evaluation. The Appraisal Institute frequently does this with many courses and seminars, especially one that is a cutting edge and advanced educational offering."

This 2008 Fact Sheet continues, "The AI did not receive any communications, threats or otherwise . . . related to this advanced educational offering. The Appraisal Institute did not receive any such complaints about the seminar from such entities or persons. There were some complaints and some praise about the course from appraisers, as would be expected for any cutting edge educational offering." In 2005, a motion was passed unanimously by the Appraisal Institute Board of Directors adopting, among other positive course-related initiatives, "that the educational offering be revised and updated as soon as practical."[14]

Summary and Conclusion

Many valuation analysts do not give sufficient consideration to defining what it is that they are appraising. These valuation analysts don't carefully define the appraisal problem before they go about trying to solve it. The result is a value estimate that does not properly respond to the appraisal problem. In other words, best case, these valuation analysts end up providing the right answer to the wrong question.

Hotel valuations are particularly susceptible to this. This is because the valuation conclusion will be significantly different depending on whether the valuation analyst is estimating the value of the hotel total operating assets or of just the hotel real property. Many valuation analysts simply begin the valuation report by stating, "the market value of the hotel is. . . ." This statement is clearly not definitive enough to reveal exactly what bundle of assets it is that is really being valued. Neither the valuation analyst nor the valuation report reader seems to know the answer to this question.

When the valuation engagement calls for the value of just the hotel real property–such as in eminent domain/condemnation, secured lending, and property tax assessment–then the valuation analyst should carefully remove the value of the tangible personal property and the intangible personal property. This is where the valuation misunderstandings manifest themselves.

First, with the removal of the tangible personal property–for example, the FF&E and the inventory–the confusion centers on a perceived double counting. The valuation analyst inexperienced with hotel valuations may confuse the deduction of a replacement allowance with the removal of the tangible personal property.

This error is analogous to suggesting that when an analyst values an apartment build-

14. Memo from the Appraisal Institute to Chapter Presidents and Members, February 2008.

ing and deducts a replacement allowance for a roof, then the conclusion indicates the value of the apartment building without a roof. Clearly the tangible personal property adjustment still remains to be made even after the replacement allowance expense has been deducted. Not to perform this procedure would result in a hotel total assets valuation that still includes the value of the hotel FF&E.

The allocation to the hotel intangible assets is even a more misunderstood valuation procedure. Some valuation analysts incorrectly suggest that the deduction of a management fee and a franchise fee removes the operating business element from the hotel valuation. Actually, this procedure removes none of the operating business element (or the business-related intangible assets) from the hotel valuation.

Management fees and franchise fees are simply operating expenses. They do not create an intangible asset. Such operating expenses would necessarily be deducted even if the intended valuation subject was of the value of the total assets of the hotel business enterprise.

Often, the valuation analyst's problem relates to a lack of education. The very first Standard in the *Uniform Standards of Professional Appraisal Practice* includes the statement, "In developing a real property appraisal, an appraiser must be aware of, understand, and correctly employ those recognized methods and techniques that are necessary to produce a credible appraisal."

The comment to that Standard continues, "It is not sufficient for appraisers to simply maintain the skills and the knowledge they possess when they become appraisers. Each appraiser must continuously improve his or her skills to remain proficient in real property appraisal."

Sometimes, the resistance to accepting methodological advances relates to an entrenched position on the topic. Maybe not even a premeditated consideration, the valuation analyst simply fails to consider methodology different from what he/she has been practicing for years. Regardless, the issue of allocating value between tangible personal property and intangible personal property is a real one. And, as more and more attention is given to this value allocation issue, it will become more important for hotel valuation analysts and their hotel clients (and other interested parties) to have an adequate understanding of the related value allocation concepts and methodologies.

Intangibles Are the Real Thing

David C. Lennhoff, MAI, SRA

Reprinted with permission from *Probate & Property*, September/October 2004, published by the American Bar Association, Chicago.

Usually when a hotel or nursing home is sold, the total assets of the business are transferred. In such cases, the real property rarely is sold separate from the other assets unless distress is involved. Often, however, appraisers are asked to value just the real property component of the total assets of a business, particularly if lenders will lend or condemning authorities will compensate only on the real property component, or if the real property is subject only to real estate assessment. In these situations–and others– appraisers may be asked to allocate the total assets among the various component parts. This determination involves separating the tangible real and personal property from the intangible assets. This allocation, indeed the very existence of intangibles, remains one of the liveliest theoretical controversies in the appraisal profession.

Intangibles are getting a bum rap. The non-realty element of a going concern encompasses such valuable assets as relationships (name/flag, for example) and rights (above-market contract rent, among others). But intangibles are often portrayed as a figment of the imagination of the unscrupulous appraiser. See Richard Marchitelli, "Letters to the Editor: How Should Appraisers View Business Enterprise Value?"[1] Although areas of disagreement persist regarding how they are valued or separated from the total assets of a business, the theoretical underpinnings for the existence of intangibles are irrefutable. In fact, according to leading business appraiser, Gordon V. Smith, abundant authority exists, and it emanates from practice here in the United States as well as from the international community.[2] He cites as examples of this authority, the IRS, the Securities and Exchange Commission, the International Accounting Standards Committee, the Organization for Economic Co-operation and Development, and the Financial Accounting Standards Board/American Institute of Certified Public Accountants.

What is it that has created the controversy? Aside from the obvious financial stakes, two items represent the primary cause for the problem: inconsistent terminology and lack of a single method for performing the allocation. The problem is the result of a lack of direction on the topic from the Appraisal Institute, the leading provider of valuation education and publications. It was not until 2001 that an Institute course devoted to the topic appeared. This course, "Course 800: Separating Real and Personal Property from Intangible Business Assets," goes a long way toward closing the disagreement gap on the issue. This article will clear up the terminology, and then, using a hotel example, it will illustrate the primary stumbling blocks that cause the controversy relating to how the allocation is to be handled.

Terms of Art

Problems with terminology stem from the abundance of different meanings for the same terms. Consider, for example, "going concern value" and "business enterprise value." Notwithstanding the poor construction (market value of the going concern or business enterprise is much more precise), these two terms are used by dif-

David C. Lennhoff, MAI, SRA, is president of PGH Consulting, LLC, which has its office in Rockville, Maryland. He has been closely involved with the topic of this book since serving as a member of the Appraisal Institute's Study Group on Business Enterprise Value in 1997-1998. He was a development team member, chief reviewer, and frequent instructor of the original Appraisal Institute Course 800, Separating Real and Personal Property from Intangible Business Assets, and editor of the first edition of A Business Enterprise Value Anthology. Mr. Lennhoff continues to teach regularly for the Appraisal Institute, both nationally and internationally, and has been a frequent contributor to The Appraisal Journal since 1982.

1. *The Appraisal Journal* (July 1996): 336.
2. Gordon V. Smith, "What's in a Name? (or the Valuation of Intangibles)," unpublished manuscript, December 1998.

ferent groups to mean the same thing.[3] The same can be said for "goodwill."[4] Course 800 introduces several new terms to eliminate the problem.

- *Market Value of the Total Assets of the Business:* The market value of all of the tangible and intangible assets of a business as if sold in aggregate as a going concern.

- *Total Intangible Assets:* All of the intangible assets owned by a business (going concern), which can be further divided into two categories for valuation purposes–identified intangible assets and residual intangible assets.

- *Identified Intangible Assets:* Those intangible assets of a business (going concern) that have been separately identified and valued in an appraisal.

- *Residual Intangible Assets:* Those intangible assets of a business (going concern) that have not been separately identified and valued in an appraisal. The value of residual intangible assets equals the value of total intangible assets minus the value of identified intangible assets. Note that in most instances CEP (see below) will be an element of residual tangible assets.

- *Capitalized Economic Profit (CEP):* The value of a residual claim, which is subordinate to the opportunity cost claims of all agents of production employed by the business. It is the present worth of an entrepreneur's economic profit expectation from being engaged in the activity of acquiring an asset, or collection of assets, at a known price and then selling, or being able to sell, the same asset or collection of assets at a future uncertain price. The amount of the entrepreneur's expected profit, and consequent CEP, is determined by the nature of the risks taken and/or the expected return to the entrepreneur's innovation.

Once confusion created by unclear terminology is eliminated, the focus moves to the methods for allocation.

Methods for Allocation of Total Assets of a Business

Appraisers are often required to allocate the total assets of an operating property among its component parts: real property, tangible personal property, and intangible personal property. Condemnation, for example, frequently involves allocation when just compensation excludes tangible and intangible assets. Similarly, lenders often collateralize only the real property component and thus require an allocation. Real property assessments usually apply only to the real property, and therefore necessitate either direct valuation of this component–which is often not possible–or allocation of the total assets.

For a hotel property, tangible personal property would include the furniture, fixtures, and equipment (FF&E) and inventory. The intangibles might include an assembled workforce, cash and equivalents, business name, nonrealty contracts, nonrealty leases, business organization, and innovations (see Course 800). This allocation is necessary in situations in which only the market value of the real property is sought, despite the fact that market participants may rarely allocate in this manner. Regional mall buyers and sellers, for example, sell or buy the total assets of the business and are not concerned with allocating the value among the components. Some appraisers have used this as an argument for not separating the intangibles. That argument, however, is specious. Often appraisers are required to estimate or analyze a component value that by itself is not of particular interest to the buyers and sellers. This disinterest does not at all diminish the validity of the analysis. It is similar to the assignment to estimate the market value of a property that is not for sale. Take, for example, a special purpose, owner-occupied industrial property. Even though the owner may have no intention of moving, the concept of market value requires the appraiser to assume that the property has been on the market for a normal exposure period and that a transaction takes place. Furthermore, it is not appropriate in that situation to assume that the owner would be the buyer or tenant.

Hotel asset allocation has been addressed since at least 1983 in the textbook of the Appraisal Institute (or its predecessor) on hotel appraisal. The method advanced, however, was challenged almost from the day it was introduced.[5] In fact in the most recent edition of the

---

3. Marvin L. Wolverton, David C. Lennhoff, James D. Vernor, and Richard Marchitelli, "Allocation of Business Assets into Tangible and Intangible Components: A New Lexicon," *The Appraisal Journal* (January 2002): 46-48.

4. Ibid., 48–49.

5. Anthony Reynolds, "Attributing Hotel Income to Real Estate and to Personalty," *The Appraisal Journal* (October 1986): 615.

text, no model for allocation is discussed. Instead, the reader is directed to "recent Appraisal Institute publications."

The earlier model suggested that the separation of "business value" and tangible personal property (FF&E and inventory) could be accomplished by two simple calculations: for "business value," deducting the expense of management and franchise fees from the stabilized net income; for tangible personalty, subtracting a return "on" and a return "of" it from the income stream. The return "on" is calculated as a percentage of the value of the tangibles, while the return "of" can be measured either as a percentage of the total revenue or on a straight-line basis.

Deducting management and franchise fees from the income stream is necessary but removes no intangibles from it. These are simply operating expenses. If they represented the "business value" of a hotel, then nobody would ever own one. After all, a property owner enters into a franchise agreement in anticipation of recovering both the cost of the franchise and a return on that cost through increases in the property's performance. In fact, a fundamental concept of business assets valuation involves the anticipation of a return on the investment required to obtain them.[6]

The method to remove the tangible personalty advanced in the early texts is legitimate. The only area of concern relating to it is that some appraisers mistakenly confuse the return "of" deduction with a replacement allowance. Although the two calculations are the same, one does not replace the other. They are both necessary. A replacement allowance is simply a category of operating expense and is necessary regardless of whether the appraiser's assignment calls for an allocation of the tangible personal property. When an allocation is required, the deduction is made twice: first to represent the normal annual operating expense and then to provide the return "of" allowance.

Course 800 introduces methodology for estimating the value of the total assets of a business. Included are the three broad categories used by business appraisers: the comparable companies approach, the income approach, and the (sum of the) asset approach. The first is often used to estimate the value of a firm that is not publicly traded. It is most similar to the real property appraisers' direct capitalization model because it uses capitalization rates and multipliers. The second method approaches the value of the company as the present value of an expected revenue stream. It is most like the real property appraisers' discounted cash flow analysis. The asset approach adjusts assets and liabilities on a balance sheet to their respective market values. It has similarities to the cost approach.

Once the market value of the total assets of the business has been established, the value of the real estate component is then estimated as a residual. Using the hotel example, the model can be summarized as follows:

+ Value of Total Assets of the Business
− Market Value of the tangible personal property
− Market Value of the cash and equivalents
− Market Value of the skilled and assembled workforce
− Market Value of the name/flag/reputation
− Market Value of any residual intangible assets
= Market Value of the Real Property as a Residual

This same model can be applied using incomes rather than values. In other words, instead of deducting the market value of each component, the income for each is deducted from the income to the total assets of the business, leaving the residual income to the real property. This is then capitalized into the market value of the real property by dividing it by an appropriate overall capitalization rate.

Conclusion

Appraisers must adhere to the Uniform Standards of Professional Appraisal Practice (USPAP). These guidelines, which were promulgated by The Appraisal Foundation, represent the required minimum level of performance for appraisers across the country. The very first Standards Rule recognizes that the profession is constantly reviewing and revising appraisal methods and devising new ones and admonishes appraisers to continuously improve their skills to remain proficient. Methods for allocating or separating the assets of a going concern with a real property component are an excellent example of the application of this rule. Most appraisers welcome new ideas and methods that will assist them in performing their work competently. Some, however, are reluctant to hear of

---

6.   Gordon V. Smith and Russell L. Parr, "Valuation of Intellectual Property and Intangible Assets," 3d ed. (New York: John Wiley & Sons, Inc., 2000), 66.

change. Their reaction is to suggest that the new ideas and methods are simply more arguments to assist the unscrupulous in getting taxes reduced. This is unfortunate and untrue. The concepts presented in Course 800 are, for the most part, uncontroversial. Only a few are still being debated. Although the methods for allocation are new, they are thoroughly grounded in basic economic principles, principles that have been accepted by the mainstream for years. The good news is that those who are balking appear to be a minority.

Intangibles are real. An assembled and trained workforce, and flag and reputation, among others, are valuable components of a going concern. There can be no controversy about this fact. When an appraiser is asked to determine the value of just the real property, then these assets, and any tangible personal property, must be identified, quantified, and removed.

Hotel Investment Analysis II: What's the Real Deal?

Bernice T. Dowell

More than 15 years ago, I studied the impact of a trade name on the business of an operating hotel and how it should be looked at from an ownership perspective. Today there is still no definitive resolution by any recognized appraisal or court authority on how appraisers should treat the issue of separating the value of the real estate from the value of the going concern.

The Appraisal Institute released Course 800, Separating Real and Personal Property from Intangible Business Assets, which was developed by a team that included real estate appraisers and a business appraiser, to begin the process of identifying the issues, weeding out the problems, and developing a foundation upon which appraisers of any type could base their opinions of value. This course was met with much skepticism on the part of many old-school, tried-and-true real estate appraisers, especially those from the hospitality industry. Unfortunately, the Appraisal Institute's practice of releasing new courses for a specific period of time and then removing them from the educational offerings in order to conduct a formal review was deemed a victory by those who opposed it and a signal that the organization was reversing itself on the concept of business enterprise value.

During this period of review for Course 800, there have been several healthy debates regarding this issue, primarily concerning hotel assets. As a participant in many of these debates, it has become increasingly clear that some of the issues stem from a total disconnect in perspectives or, as most disagreements come about, a failure to communicate. Not everyone is speaking the same language, and some are not willing to change or try to advance the overall understanding of exactly what hotel assets are. In this article I would like to address a few of these key misunderstandings and try to provide more information than has previously been offered so that we may possibly gain greater clarity on the issues.

The Misunderstood Issues

1. Traditional hotel appraisers assume that the security for a hotel loan is the real estate; therefore, if business enterprise value allocates intangible value away from real estate, owners will not be able to get loans.
This first common assumption could not be further from the truth. Lenders are lending against the total assets of an operating hotel. This is the value that is supported by typical hotel appraisals relying primarily on an income capitalization approach to value and supported loosely by recent sales of operating hotels. Lenders understand that the assets securing the loan consist of real estate, tangible personal property, and intangible personal property. In fact, the title of the document that secures the loan is "Deed of Trust, Security Agreement, Financing Statement, Fixture Filing and Assignment of Leases, Rents, Security Deposits and Hotel Revenue."

The market value of the going concern produced in these lender-required appraisals is a value derived after a deduction for a base management fee (typically 3%), a franchise fee (typically 5%), and a reserve for replacement (typically 4%). It is worth noting here that the

Bernice T. Dowell *is a Senior Managing Consultant for Paradigm Tax Group in Washington, D.C. A former Senior Manager of KPMG and President of Cynsur, LLC, for the past 20 years she has focused her career on real estate transfer and property taxes on hospitality assets and the concept of removing the value of intangibles from a going concern. She developed interest in the issue as an employee in Marriott's tax department in 1991. While at Marriott she was a member of the inaugural class at George Washington University in the master of science in finance program, and she wrote her senior thesis on the topic of hotel investment analysis and the contributory value of a trade name to a going concern. That paper was included in the first edition of* A Business Enterprise Value Anthology.

14

reserve for replacement is also a lender requirement. The loan documents set forth that the owner must reserve 4% of gross revenue for replacements.

Lenders understand that this is the value of the total assets of the business. As proof for this statement, the following is an excerpt from the document that secures the loan:

> NOW, THEREFORE, THIS DEED OF TRUST WITNESSETH: that Borrower, in consideration of the premises, the Indebtedness evidenced by the Note, and other good and valuable consideration …. does hereby GRANT A SECURITY INTEREST IN AND PLEDGE TO TRUSTEE, IN TRUST, WITH THE POWER OF SALE AND RIGHT ON ENTRY, IN TRUST AND POSSESSION, for the benefit and use of Lender and its successors and assigns forever, all its estate, right, title and interest now owned or hereafter acquired in, to and under any and all property (collectively, the "Trust Estate") described in the following Granting Clauses:
>
> (A) The Real Property;
> (B) All additional lands, estates and development rights hereafter acquired by Borrower for use in connection with the Real Property …;
> (C) The buildings, foundations, structures, improvements and fixtures now or hereafter located or erected on the Real Property ("Improvements") …;
> (D) (i) all streets, avenues, roads, alleys …(collectively, the "Appurtenances");
> (E) The machinery, appliances, apparatus, equipment, fittings, fixtures, articles of personal property and goods of every kind and nature whatsoever …(hereinafter collectively called "Building Equipment");
> (F) Without limiting the generality of the provisions of any other Granting Clause, all of Borrower's rights, title, interest, privileges and franchises in and to the following…(collectively, "the Operating Assets"); …

Then the document explicitly lists the operating assets over six and half pages to include such items as bookings for guest rooms, all contracts for utility services, maintenance, operations including guarantees and warranties, the hotel management agreement, operating permits, contractual rights, leases and subleases, tangible personal property, and–last but not least–the "intangibles." Therefore, if the owner defaults on the loan, the lender can foreclose and take *all assets*–not just the real estate.

As shown here, the real estate is not the only security for the loan. The entire business is the security, and all assets must be properly satisfied under the terms of the loan documents. In fact, the current recession has left many operating hotels struggling to make debt service. Many owners have had to make choices regarding which expenses to cut, and some have even decided to stop paying their franchise fees. In many loan documents, failure to maintain the franchise is grounds for default and possible foreclosure. Lenders would probably advise owners to pay the franchise fees before debt service because *if* they had to foreclose, they would prefer to sell a property with a major brand.

2. Traditional real estate appraisers like to use the deduction of management fees and franchise fees to remove business value because it has been offered by a leading hotel appraiser and because it is easy.

The deduction of management fees and franchise fees is the most hotly debated old-school theory. Proponents of the business enterprise theory argue that these fees are nothing more than expenses for ownership, and deducting them from the income stream has no effect on "removing" the value of the business from the going concern valuation. While this makes perfect sense from an investor's perspective, many real estate appraisers are still not convinced that the management fee technique is incorrect.

To provoke deeper thought on this matter, perhaps a review of the history of operating hotels can shed some light on the genesis of this technique and reveal the fallacy in it. In the 1960s, hotels were built by developers (real estate market participants) and leased to operators (hotel management companies). Developers were real estate market participants and truly wanted a passive investment, meaning that they left the management of the business solely to the professionals. They were paid rent under the terms of a long-term lease agreement. The rent was usually determined as a percentage of the various income-producing categories: rooms, food and beverage, and other. The common rental formula was 25% of rooms revenue, 10% of food, 5% of beverage, and 5% of other. All monies left over after paying all the expenses of the operation and rent to the landlord went to the operators as payment for their business acumen.

This model clearly indicates who the owner of the real estate and the owner of the business are and clearly defines how to allocate the income from this symbiotic relationship. This model changed over time for one of two reasons: either hotel management companies realized that they could grow their business (management) substantially by operating properties under the terms of a management agreement, or developers realized that they could possibly increase their returns by assuming more of the risk of the business. Over time, the management agreement model has become the norm.

This model creates a situation in which the management company has no ownership interest in the hotel business. The management company is compensated primarily from gross revenue, so even in recessionary times when business is struggling and ownership is often left with nothing on the bottom line, management is still getting paid.

In the original model, in which the business manager is truly receiving all bottom-line profits as payment for his business acumen and the real estate owner is protected by a long-term lease, the payment to the management company truly was all of the business value. The switch to the management agreement model shifted most of the business risk to ownership such that the owner of the tangible property (real estate and personal property) was now participating in the risk and return of the business. The management company owns nothing but its contract with ownership; this contract is bilateral, meaning that both parties expect to gain from the relationship.

The traditional hospitality appraisers looked at this change from a lease to a management agreement as simply a "paper change." They offered that the management agreement fee was now the payment for the business (analogous to the residual position the management company originally had) and the bottom-line profits inuring to ownership were payment for the real estate (analogous to the lease payment they used to get). In fact, one major management company used to call their reports to ownership that showed the monies they received "rent letters," indicating that they still viewed their payments to ownership as rent. Although the mentality that nothing really changed from a business perspective existed, in actuality everything changed dramatically and the biggest change was that ownership now assumed most of the business risk in exchange for the expectation of gaining greater returns for this investment vis-à-vis what they could gain with a safer lease investment.

Owners, managers, and lenders are generally comfortable with the current model and understand it. Appraisers are comfortable with the model as long as the going concern is the

appraisal assignment. The debate and general lack of understanding stems from the few times when the value of the going concern needs to be allocated among the three general asset classes that make up the hotel investment: real estate, tangible personal property, and intangible personal property.

There are generally three distinct situations when the value of the going concern needs to be allocated:

- At the time of purchase (usually for income tax and transfer tax purposes)
- For real estate taxation purposes
- In condemnation situations

Most buyers and sellers in the marketplace do allocate the prices at the time of purchase primarily for all of the previously mentioned tax purposes. The purchase and sale agreement typically includes specific language that addresses the price allocation. In these situations, the price is recorded properly in the land records such that the transfer taxes are paid only on the value of the real estate and the deed is recorded to reflect the portion of the "price" paid for the real estate.

This leads to the discussion of the next argument purported by untrained real estate appraisers who resist allocating value to intangibles: "It's not done that way in the marketplace."

3. Real estate appraisers resist allocating any value to intangibles in a going concern appraisal of an operating hotel because they (a) embrace the management/franchise fee technique and (b) accept one support of that technique: that allocating value to intangibles is not done in the marketplace.
Appraisers do not make the market but rather measure the market after the fact with as much information as they can gather about recent sales. One battle cry against allocating the value of the going concern to all three major classes of assets that transact in a purchase of an operating hotel is that it is not done that way in the marketplace.

It is true that buyers and sellers in the marketplace do not price the real estate, the tangible personal property, and the intangibles to determine the ultimate price paid for the operating hotel. Buyers and sellers in the marketplace typically use a discounted cash flow analysis to price the entire transaction, but once the total price is agreed upon between buyer and seller, they then negotiate and agree to an allocation of that price for the real estate and personal property, both tangible and intangible.

In many deals, the parties to the transaction file Form 8594: Asset Acquisition Statement Under Section 1060 (used when buying or selling a business) with the IRS, reporting how the purchase price is allocated and agreed to between the parties for income tax treatment.

In disclosure states that tax the value of the real estate that is transferring title, the transfer tax is usually split between buyer and seller; therefore, both parties have an incentive to allocate the price to pay the proper amount of transfer tax.

Additionally, the buyer has the opportunity to record the deed with the proper amount for the real estate so that the real estate tax assessor gets better information to reassess based on the purchase price. While reporting agencies such as CoStar may report the total price of the transaction, real estate appraisers researching sales information should check the price recorded on the deed to determine the value of the real estate agreed upon between buyer and seller.

Allocating a Going Concern Price Paid for an Operating Hotel

While every deal is different, it is interesting to note when reviewing allocations agreed upon between buyers and sellers that the allocated values for each asset generally seem very reasonable when intuitively considering the investment. For example, the data set in Exhibit 1 shows how prices were allocated in some hotel sales that occurred over the past few years.

As shown in Exhibit 1, each individual transaction is unique, and the value of the real estate could range from a low of 60% to as much as 90%, but averaged approximately 73%. From an owner's or even a lender's perspective, these allocations seem reasonable. The data set also shows that both brands are adding value for the owners, although on average the Residence Inn brand outperforms the Homewood Suites brand.

This data set is the result of analyses I performed representing buyers in the transactions using a proprietary model based on the investor's investment criteria for the deal. This model has survived scrutiny by the IRS and financial auditors. The following is a limited discussion of the model to demonstrate how allocations can be made based on the actions of the buyers and sellers in the marketplace.

Deal Pricing Analysis

To understand how to make a reasonable allocation of a price that has been established in the marketplace, one only needs to look to the model used to develop the price. Investors usually make their pricing decisions based on a discounted cash flow (DCF) model. After thorough due diligence, buyers make projections of future operating cash flows and assume a sale at the end of the holding period.

The deal makers' projections of cash flows during the holding period represent the "return on" the investment, and the assumed sale at the end of the holding period provides the "return of" the investment. The investment in this case is an operating hotel that consists of real estate, tangible personal property, and various intangible assets (most notably a management agreement and franchise agreement). Implied within each cash flow is a return on investment in real estate, a return on investment in tangible personal property, and a return on investment in the business.

Returns on investment in real estate are usually represented by the expected rent from a lease. While hotels today are usually not leased, the original lease model is a valid proxy. And because there was a "common rental formula" for hotels that was based on percentages of the revenue streams, it is reasonable to use it to support an estimate of a probable rent stream for the hotel real estate. Appraisers attempting to measure the market find it difficult to support this model because of the lack of data in the marketplace; however, when allocating the price it makes perfect sense to use a well-accepted model with reasonably estimated data. In other words, the premise for this model assumes that *if* the real estate were leased, this is the amount of rent it would take. The rent estimate represents the return on investment in real estate.

The tangible personal property is a wasting asset that has to be continuously replaced. There is no expectation on the part of the investor for appreciation in value; however, there is an expectation of both a return on the investment and return of it. To estimate the part of the operating cash flow that represents the return on investment in tangible personal property, one merely applies an appropriate return rate to the depreciated value of the initial investment.

Because we are allocating a price that has been determined in the marketplace, the residu-

Exhibit 1 Hotel Price Allocation Data Set by Brand

	Real Estate	%	Tang. Pers. Prop.	%	Intang. Pers. Prop.	%	Total Price
Homewood Suites							
Georgia	$7,052,600	81.87%	$368,000	4.27%	$1,193,400	13.86%	$8,614,000
Georgia	5,254,500	79.90%	496,000	7.54%	825,500	12.56%	6,576,000
Georgia	3,043,200	71.42%	368,000	8.64%	849,800	19.94%	4,261,000
Maryland	12,423,500	62.39%	588,000	2.95%	6,901,500	34.66%	19,913,000
Colorado	10,530,900	68.91%	448,000	2.93%	4,303,100	28.16%	15,282,000
Florida	8,419,800	73.91%	448,000	3.93%	2,524,200	22.16%	11,392,000
Texas	7,460,500	81.36%	480,000	5.24%	1,228,500	13.40%	9,169,000
Texas	9,458,200	82.35%	544,000	4.74%	1,482,200	12.91%	11,484,400
Texas	5,994,400	84.05%	396,000	5.55%	741,600	10.40%	7,132,000
Virginia	16,259,600	61.60%	436,000	1.65%	9,701,400	36.75%	26,397,000
Pennsylvania	6,116,300	90.46%	364,000	5.38%	280,700	4.16%	6,761,000
Pennsylvania	10,554,500	68.65%	492,000	3.20%	4,328,500	28.15%	15,375,000
Oregon	9,059,700	70.88%	492,000	3.85%	3,230,300	25.27%	12,782,000
Virginia	9,204,100	69.01%	492,000	3.69%	3,690,900	27.30%	13,387,000
Utah	6,119,200	81.57%	392,000	5.23%	990,800	13.21%	7,502,000
Missouri	7,158,300	81.35%	580,000	6.59%	1,060,700	12.06%	8,799,000
Averages	$8,381,831	75.61%	$461,500	4.71%	$2,708,319	19.68%	
Residence Inn							
California	$10,746,500	75.83%	$840,000	5.93%	$2,584,500	18.24%	$14,171,000
California	19,127,800	62.58%	900,000	2.94%	10,537,200	34.48%	30,565,000
Georgia	9,164,700	69.19%	680,000	5.13%	3,400,300	25.68%	13,245,000
Georgia	7,107,000	74.50%	650,000	6.81%	1,783,000	18.69%	9,540,000
Georgia	4,246,200	79.04%	576,000	10.72%	549,800	10.24%	5,372,000
Georgia	10,645,400	68.82%	630,000	4.07%	4,192,600	27.11%	15,468,000
California	11,249,200	69.01%	855,000	5.25%	4,196,800	25.74%	16,301,000
Alabama	8,226,700	83.01%	640,000	6.46%	1,043,300	10.53%	9,910,000
Florida	8,141,900	77.79%	600,000	5.73%	1,724,100	16.48%	10,466,000
Massachusetts	6,161,500	81.13%	480,000	6.32%	953,500	12.55%	7,595,000
Colorado	9,836,500	62.84%	640,000	4.09%	5,176,500	33.07%	15,653,000
Illinois	9,950,200	64.33%	640,000	4.14%	4,877,800	31.53%	15,468,000
Illinois	9,263,500	78.14%	720,000	6.07%	1,871,500	15.79%	11,855,000
Ohio	6,822,900	86.66%	590,000	7.49%	460,100	5.85%	7,873,000
Ohio	9,935,300	80.66%	720,000	5.85%	1,662,700	13.49%	12,318,000
California	14,935,900	61.55%	945,000	3.89%	8,385,100	34.56%	24,266,000
California	21,397,300	60.64%	1,080,000	3.06%	12,810,700	36.30%	35,288,000
Texas	8,098,800	71.09%	600,000	5.27%	2,693,200	23.64%	11,392,000
Texas	9,651,200	65.95%	550,000	3.76%	4,432,800	30.29%	14,634,000
California	16,564,200	60.01%	840,000	3.04%	10,196,800	36.95%	27,601,000
Florida	7,744,300	65.84%	560,000	4.76%	3,458,700	29.40%	11,763,000
California	45,915,000	61.43%	2,160,000	2.89%	26,669,000	35.68%	74,744,000
California	24,934,400	62.61%	1,620,000	4.07%	13,272,600	33.32%	39,827,000
Tennessee	4,446,400	76.20%	420,000	7.20%	968,600	16.60%	5,835,000
Alabama	6,560,400	75.36%	470,000	5.40%	1,675,600	19.24%	8,706,000
Pennsylvania	5,870,100	75.45%	352,000	4.52%	1,557,900	20.03%	7,780,000
California	12,576,600	60.62%	795,000	3.83%	7,375,400	35.55%	20,747,000
New Mexico	10,215,100	70.70%	480,000	3.32%	3,753,900	25.98%	14,449,000
Washington	29,752,500	64.25%	1,350,000	2.92%	15,207,500	32.83%	46,310,000
Missouri	6,398,900	81.28%	416,000	5.28%	1,058,100	13.44%	7,873,000
Missouri	12,618,500	70.96%	608,000	3.42%	4,556,500	25.62%	17,783,000
Florida	6,989,200	68.60%	352,000	3.46%	2,846,800	27.94%	10,188,000
Averages	$12,040,441	70.81%	$742,469	4.91%	$5,185,403	24.28%	
Total Averages	$10,211,136	73.21%	$601,984	4.81%	$3,946,861	21.98%	

al cash flows–after estimating what is needed to satisfy the real estate and the tangible personal property–represent the cash flows for all of the intangible "business" assets. Exhibit 2, which corresponds to the first sale in the data set in Exhibit 1, illustrates how the buyer's DCF model breaks down for the three major asset classes.

The deal pricing analysis model examines the discounted cash flow analysis relied upon in pricing the transaction. As a result, the analyst can break down the buyer's analysis to explicitly state how the cash flows during the holding period cover the major asset classes (return on investment); and, upon sale at the end of the holding period, how the proceeds cover the return of investment in each asset class. In Exhibit 2, one can see upon sale in Year 5 the return of the initial investment in tangible personal property ($368,000) and the return of appreciated real estate value (7,934,044), as the initial investment was $7,052,600.

A further check on the validity of the model looks at the weighted average returns for the three asset classes versus the discount rate on the deal. For the first sale in the previous data set, the discount rate for the operating hotel was 12.55%. The weighted average of the asset classes shown in Exhibit 3, after employing the allocation model, closely approximates the deal.

The deal pricing analysis model used to allocate a price paid for an operating hotel starts with the buyer's expectations for the deal and explicitly models the implications of the discounted cash flow analysis with all of the buyer's investment criteria. This type of allocation is based on generally accepted valuation models and very reasonable estimates of data within the models supported by industry norms and survey data.

Conclusion

Hotel investment in today's environment of using a management agreement contract with a professional hotel operator should make it abundantly clear that the owner of the hotel is a very active participant in the hotel business. In fact, in addition to hiring management companies for the day-to-day operations, many owners also hire asset managers to actively manage their assets and assist them in negotiating with the managers to make business decisions that make sense for both the owner and the manager. As a result, owners very much have expectations that the management company and franchise operation they choose to invest in will provide benefits beyond their cost.

Lenders are very much aware that the money they are lending for an operating hotel

Exhibit 2	Discounted Cash Flow for Three Asset Classes				
	Year 1	Year 2	Year 3	Year 4	Year 5
Going concern cash flow	$758,000	$810,000	$835,000	$859,000	$883,000
Return on investment—tangible personal property	44,160	44,160	44,160	44,160	44,160
Real estate rental income	615,200	646,600	666,600	686,600	707,000
Residual Cash Flow	**$98,640**	**$119,240**	**$124,240**	**$128,240**	**$131,840**
Residual cap rate/reversion	9.00%				$10,203,556
Closing costs	2.00%				(204,071)
Less: return of investment—tangible personal property					(368,000)
Less: return of investment—real estate					(7,934,044)
Reversion of business value					1,697,440
Total Residual Cash Flows	**$98,640**	**$119,240**	**$124,240**	**$128,240**	**$1,829,280**
Discount rate	19.88%				
Net Present Value of Intangibles	**$1,038,404**				

Exhibit 3	Weighted Average of Asset Classes		
Asset Class	**Rate of Return**	**% of Value**	**Weighted Return**
Real estate	11.00%	83.37%	9.17%
Tangible personal property	12.00%	4.35%	0.52%
Intangible personal property	19.88%	12.28%	2.44%
Totals		100.00%	12.13%

is secured by a business, and an integral part of that business is the management agreement and/or franchise agreement. The documents securing the loan clearly and expressly delineate the assets pledged for security to include all tangible and intangible personal property.

Buyers and sellers in the marketplace routinely allocate the prices for closing to determine a proper amount of transfer taxes and for income tax reporting purposes. Allocating the prices does not make any statement about the lender's right to the income stream, which comes before the allocation. As a result, a good supportable allocation can be determined in various ways. The key to the allocation is that it is supported with recognized valuation models for each asset type.

Business Value Allocation in Lodging Valuation

Eric E. Belfrage, MAI, SRA

This article originally appeared in the July 2001 issue of *The Appraisal Journal*.

The business value component of hotel real estate is elusive to quantify, but is generally assumed to exist. Through consistent tracking of two physically similar hotel chains, we have conducted a matched pairs analysis. Using the industry performance unit of comparison revenue per available room (Rev Par) for six locations containing both chains, we were able to measure the contributory revenue associated with affiliation, management, and service–all primary components of business value.

This article incorporates two separate concepts dealing with the business value of hotels. The presentation of a matched pairs case study will prove the existence of business value in hotels. This is a controversial topic, and a clear consensus does not currently exist on its presence or measurement among lodging consultants. A methodology is also presented in this article to provide a "common sense" approach and a starting point or platform of agreement for this issue.

Business value in a hotel is inherent in the ongoing operation. It is created and maintained by three factors:

- Chain affiliation
- Management expertise
- Service (labor)

All components are labor intensive and require time and reputation to cultivate. Hotel chains create value by consistency, market perception, product support, reservation systems, traveler programs, advertising, etc. Once a critical mass is reached and a chain has an excellent reputation in these areas (i.e., Hampton Inns, Residence Inns, etc.), maximum business value is achieved.

Business rights are "lent" to hotel owners for a "maintenance charge," commonly known as franchise and management fees. Business value however, still resides in the capitalized value of net income after deduction of these fees. This is much like the reserve expense. The deduction of a reserve for the replacement of furniture, fixtures & equipment (FF&E) accounts is for the replacement of furnishings when they wear out. This represents the return of the personal property component. The actual value of existing FF&E still resides in the value of capitalized net income.

This theory is contrary to the conclusions of Stephen Rushmore's book, *Hotels and Motels.*[1] This text suggests that total property value is the capitalized net income before deduction of management and franchise fees. However, in practice, appraisers do deduct both franchise and management fees to determine market value. It is generally considered that going concern value is inherent in the resulting conclusion. Business contribution exists despite deduction of management and franchise fees.

When an operating hotel sells, the acquisition reperesents the ongoing business operation, which includes:

- Real estate
- FF&E
- Business

Eric E. Belfrage, MAI, SRA, ISHC, is the managing director for Integra Lorms & Belfrage of Columbus, Ohio. His background includes twenty-five years of independent fee appraisal and consulting experience. Mr. Belfrage has largely focused on consulting, evaluating, and appraising lodging property. He holds a bachelor's degree in Business Administration from Franklin University, Columbus, Ohio.

---

1. Stephen Rushmore, *Hotels and Motels: A Guide to Market Analysis, Investment Anaylsis, and Valuations.* (Chicago: Appraisal Institute, 1992): 247.

The FF&E portion is easily allocated based on its depreciated cost. Business value is more elusive and generally perceived to be "in there somewhere." However, in ad valorem tax cases, a real estate only allocation should be determined. A methodology for allocation is crucial to ensure hotel owners are not paying real estate tax on non-realty items. One of the challenges for an appropriate application is to present a straightforward and understandable methodology that can be easily communicated and grasped in litigation cases.

In *Hotels and Motels*, Rushmore states "Chain hotels generally out perform independents, the additional value created by increased profits is exclusively business related."[2]

Obviously, anyone with or without hotel experience could locate a site and construct a hotel. The creation of going concern value, however, includes selecting the appropriate affiliation, management team, marketing plan services, and even employee attitudes. How often has a patron selected an alternative property because of disorganization, uncleanliness, or an unfriendly employee attitude? These situations can be detrimental to property value (i.e., occupancy and rate) despite payment by the ownership of franchise and management fees.

Matched Pairs Analysis

An appropriate verification of the existence of business value can be quantified by comparing a hotel lacking management, franchise, and service components to a similar property possessing these components. An analysis of the two competitors' performance will reveal the difference in revenue. The value difference between these two facilities is the business contribution. Consider the following case study.

Case Study

Business value in a hotel can be determined by a matched pairs analysis. If two groups of hotels can be identified that possess similar physical characteristics–where the first hotel chain has little business value and the second hotel chain has a definite business value component–the contribution of business value can be isolated. Three components create business value: chain affiliation, management expertise, and service. Comparing the lack of these components to the presence of these components will isolate busi-

ness value in hotel property. While no operating hotel could be completely lacking in management or service components, we did locate a chain of properties (Chain A) that were not affiliated with a franchise nor had traditional hotel management expertise. They did, however, offer good service in the area of room cleanliness and physical plant maintenance. A direct competitor (Chain B) was then located at identical interchange locations that possessed national chain recognition and hotel management expertise.

A comparison of Chain A's performance to Chain B was made. Business value, of course, was created by revenue differences attributable to Chain B's name recognition and management abilities. The unit of comparison utilized by hotel companies includes both average daily rate and occupancy. Both were combined in a single category known as "revenue per available room" (Rev Par). A Rev Par comparison of the two chains was made.

For the Rev Par analysis to be accurate, both properties or groups of properties need to be nearly identical physically, and in location, in order to isolate the contributory value to franchise and management expertise. Specific physical data is shown in Table 1 for comparison purposes.

The physical considerations for these two chains are nearly identical. Chain A possesses six locations in common with Chain B in a major metropolitan area. These are suburban interchange locations and are in many cases literally next door to each other. In all cases, these two properties have the identical competitors. A performance comparison that isolated business components was therefore accomplished. We have cited the 1997–2000 Rev Par for each property. In Table 2 the change column reflects Chain B's relative increase in Rev Par in the same market.

For Chain A the average Rev Par was $26.41 in 1997, $26.42 in 1998, $24.66 in 1999, and $24.18 in 2000, compared to $33.54 in 1997, $35.20 in 1998, $35.01 in 1999, and $34.19 in 2000 for Chain B. This indicates a 27% to 42% increase in revenue directly attributable to chain affiliation and management expertise. Increased Rev Par can directly be translated into value contribution in Table 3.

The comparative analysis indicates that the 35% increase in sales (assuming comparable

---

2.   Ibid.

Table 1 — Physical Comparison Chart: Identical Locations in the Same Major Midwest Metropolitan City

Characteristics	Local Chain A*	National Chain B*
No. of properties	24	300+
Age	1984 to 1987	1973 to 1986
No. of stories	2–3	2–3
Entry type	Exterior corridor	Exterior corridor
Pool	Yes	Some
Locations	Suburban	Suburban
Price	Economy-limited service	Economy-limited service
Ownership structure	Company owned	Company owned/franchised
Amenities	Cable TV, local calls, & coffee	Cable TV, local calls, & coffee

* Cannot divulge identity due to confidentiality of performance statistics.

Table 2 — Rev Par Comparison

Location	Chain A 1997	1998	1999	2000	Chain B 1997	1998	1999	2000	Change 1997	1998	1999	2000
A) West	$24.14	$24.79	$23.45	$22.15	$36.53	$36.68	$38.39	$34.01	51%	48%	64%	54%
B) East	$27.48	$27.02	$23.23	$20.15	$33.62	$36.71	$37.87	$37.61	22%	36%	63%	87%
C) Northwest	$27.22	$28.03	$22.65	$21.09	$36.53	$37.59	$34.41	$32.56	34%	34%	52%	54%
D) North	$21.88	$22.41	$20.73	$21.24	$29.81	$30.93	$31.87	$31.88	36%	38%	54%	50%
E) University	$28.54	$29.66	$31.36	$35.53	$34.41	$35.74	$35.22	$38.44	21%	20%	12%	8%
F) South	$27.79	$26.60	$26.59	$25.11	$30.32	$33.54	$32.29	$30.19	9%	26%	22%	20%
Average	$26.41	$26.42	$24.66	$24.18	$33.54	$35.20	$35.01	$34.19	27%	33%	42%	41%

Note: Location within same Midwest City.

Table 3 — Comparative Value Analysis

Characteristics	Chain A	Chain B	Change
Property size	100 Rooms	100 Rooms	
Revenue per available room (Rev Par)[1]	$25.50	$34.50	
Sales per year	$930,750	$1,259,250	35%
Net income (35%)	$325,763	$440,738	
Value (OAR 12%)	$2,714,688	$3,672,813	
Rounded	$2,700,000	$3,700,000	37%
Value difference[2]		$1,000,000	
% of total value[3]			27%

1. Rounded average years 1997–2000.
2. Attributable to business.
3. Business contribution.

net income ratios and overall capitalization rates) results in a value difference of about $1 million or approximately 27% of property value. Stated another way, about 25% of the value of a Chain B hotel is attributed to the business component. This estimate is considered to be conservative as the service component of business value– i.e., guest care, cleanliness, etc.–exists in Chain A and therefore is not included in the above number. Obviously, refined capitalization could consider differing net income ratio and

overall for the two income streams. These, however, would likely be canceling. In our opinion, the allocation of business value for a successful well-run chain type limited-service hotel is quantified up to 25%. This case study compares a very successful well-known chain to a physically comparable, but localized chain, where maximum business value is measured. Under the theoretical "competent or typical management" scenario, a range in business value allocation of 15% to 20% appears reasonable.

Application of Methodology

The case study quantifies that a reasonable range of business value between 15% and 20% generally exists in hotel properties. Obviously the business value contribution can be more or less, depending on the quality of franchise affiliation, management, or service level. Integra Lorms & Belfrage has interviewed several hotel owners, brokers, and management companies who unanimously disagree with the philosophy that deduction of management and franchise fees removes all the business value component. In fact, we have completed consulting assignments for owners who have changed their affiliation, as the original franchise was not generating revenues in excess of fees. In other words, if total franchise fees approximate 9%, operators believe that a franchise relationship ought to contribute in excess of 9% of revenue. Successful chain affiliations generate between 15% and 25% of room nights sold to their franchisee. Interviewees indicated that for a franchise affiliation to be considered successful it ought to generate approximately *double* its cost. In fact, it is a common practice for hoteliers to track the percentage of room nights sold or revenue generated by the reservation system. If the reservation system generates, for instance, 18% and the total franchise costs are 9%, the annual revenue contribution to the business would be 18% (minus 9%) or 9%, assuming the room rate is consistent.

A similar quantification to the above is applicable for management fees. Most owners or employers would expect a contribution to income in excess of management fees. In marketing his firm for management services, one of our respondents specifically stated that their management company will provide additional net income equal to the annual management fee.

In order to determine an appropriate methodology to allocate the business value contribution to a specific hotel property, *it appears reasonable to utilize the capitalized value of the annual net income contribution made by affiliation and management expertise.* It does not appear possible to quantify the contribution of the service component. However, management and franchise fees are more "leadership" related and can be identified by the contribution discussed previously. These revenues clearly relate to business income as opposed to income associated with the real estate only. In the comparative value analysis of Chain B (shown in Table 3), the successful hotel generated room revenue of $1,259,250. This chain charges 9% total franchise fees. The average contribution to room sales for this chain is 18%. Therefore the revenue contribution is the difference, or 9%. Of course the chain affiliation may have an impact on the rate a hotel can charge. If the successful going concern became an independent, the rate may fall and would have an even greater impact on revenue. Conversely, if quality and condition is maintained, this impact may be minimized. An average management fee of 4%, contributing double its cost, indicates a total business revenue contribution (including affiliation) of 13% (9% franchise contribution plus 4% management).

The business revenue remaining in the cash flow after the deduction of franchise and management fees is demonstrated in Table 4.

Table 4	Affiliated Hotel Business Revenue Allocation
Revenue	$1,259,250
Generated by affiliation	
Total revenue from affiliation at 18%	$226,665
Previously deducted in cash flow at 9%	(113,333)
Balance of revenue remaining in gross income	$113,333
Generated by management	
Total (double 4% fee) attributed to management	$100,740
Previously deducted in cash flow 4%	(50,370)
Balance of revenue remaining in gross income	$ 50,370
Total business revenue remaining in gross income	$163,703

The total remaining business revenue of $163,703 is indicated. Value contribution can be determined by capitalizing the net business revenue. We have utilized the 35% net income ratio as in Table 3 (NOI ratio may vary by property). This indicates net revenue of $57,296. By utilizing the overall capitalization rate of 12% from Table 3, the value contribution is processed as follows:

Net revenue to business	$57,296
Overall rate	12%
Value	$477,467
Rounded	$500,000

Certainly an argument could be made that the net income could be higher due to some fixed expenses already considered in the NOI ratio. Conversely, the argument could also be made that a capitalization rate that is slightly higher than the overall rate should be used, given the business revenue risk. This is considered canceling.

Comparing the business indication to the overall value offers a percentage of going concern attributed to business value as shown in Table 5.

The contribution of business value at $500,000 indicates a percentage business value allocation of 13.5%. This is lower than the comparative value analysis in the case study (Table 3), indicating a value contribution by Chain B of $1 million over Chain A or 27% of Chain B's value. This is due largely to the difference in the rate that Chain B is able to charge for a room when compared to Chain A.

In the case study, an 11% lower occupancy was noted by Chain A when compared to Chain B, but a 26% downward impact on total sales occurred (see Table 6).

This is a 1 to 2.4 relationship. In other words, for every percent of occupancy impact, a 2.4% impact is felt in the Rev Par. The Rev Par impact based on the 9% occupancy contribution from affiliation (above fees) is 22%.

For this reason, the application methodology may be somewhat understated. However, clearly a business component of between 15% and 25% is reasonable in this case. Extraction of every dollar of contribution is obviously difficult as business value is so intermingled with real estate. Perhaps, as improved tracking of hotel statistics continues, additional development of this concept can evolve. For instance, the area of service contribution involves cleanliness and guest treatment, as well as employee attitudes, etc. The quantification of this component is not currently possible. The management and affiliation components provide "leadership" and, if not present, they could possibly negate good service. Continued study in this area is needed.

Conclusion

The above methodology inherently considers variables including the quality of franchise affiliation and management. This is because higher quality affiliation and management costs are generally charged at a higher percentage of revenue. The franchise revenue contribution is the difference between revenue generated by the specific affiliation and franchise costs. This method will therefore measure varying levels of value contribution, depending upon the success of the individual hotel.

At this time, there is no clear consensus on the issue of measuring the business value component for lodging property. The previous methodology serves as an easily quantifiable starting point to a platform of agreement in lodging valuation as to the contribution of the business component. This "common sense" and simple approach can be expressed and comprehended easily in litigation situations to those not involved daily with such concerns. This method is especially helpful in ad valorem tax situations where the real estate component must be isolated.

References

Appraisal Institute. *The Appraisal of Real Estate*, 11th ed., 414.

Egan, Patrick J. "Mixed Business and Real Estate Components in Hotel Valuation," *The Appraisal Journal* (July 1996): 246-251.

Hennessey, Sean F. "Myths About Hotel Business and Personalty Values," *The Appraisal Journal* (October 1993): 608-611.

Lennhoff, David C. "Business Enterprise Value Debate: Still a Long Way to Reconciliation," *The Appraisal Journal* (October 1999): 422-428.

Table 5	Affiliated Hotel
Going Concern Value	
Revenue	$1,259,250
Net income ratio	35%
Net income	440,738
Overall rate	12%
Value indication	$3,672,813
Rounded	$3,700,000
Business value allocation	$500,000
% Business contribution	13.5%

Table 6	Sales Impact Ratio		
	Chain A	**Chain B**	**Difference**
Average occupancy*	70%	62%	-11%
Average Rev Par	$34.50	$25.50	-26%
Occupancy to Rev Par impact			1 to 2.4

* Average for each chain for 1997–2000.

Lesser, Daniel H. and Karen E. Ruben. "Understanding the Unique Aspects of Hotel Property Tax Valuation," *The Appraisal Journal* (January 1993): 9-27.

Matonis, Stephen J. and Daniel R. DeRango. "The Determination of Hotel Value Components for Ad Valorem Tax Assessment," *The Appraisal Journal* (July 1993): 342-347.

Rushmore, Stephen. "Hotel Business Value and Working Capital: A Clarification," *The Appraisal Journal* (January 1987): 144-147.

The Effects of Hotel Brands on Market Values

John W. O'Neill, PhD, MAI

This study expands on existing research regarding the relationships between hotel brands and customer satisfaction by exploring the effect of hotel brands on market values. Drawn from a data set consisting of over 1,000 actual hotel sales transactions, the results of this study provide evidence that hotel market values, and particularly the values of midscale and upscale hotels, are significantly affected by their brands. Further discussions regarding the specific effects of a number of brands are provided. Findings suggest that hotel appraisers, owners, and corporate brand management could better understand the market value of hotel brands.

Introduction

In the hotel industry, the proliferation of new brands has drastically altered the lodging landscape in recent years. According to "The Largest Hotel Brands," a report that appeared in the July 2005 issue of *Hotels* magazine, there are 285 lodging brands worldwide. Depending on how a "new brand" is defined, six to eight new hotel brand names are introduced to the market per year. As stated in *Managing Brand Equity: Capitalizing on the Value of a Brand Name* by D. Aaker, it is generally recognized that brands create value for both consumers and companies. Consumers use brands as cues to infer certain product attributes, such as quality. Because loyal customers are less sensitive to price, generate positive word of mouth, and are willing to purchase more, corporate management has realized that brand names are among the most important assets of a company.[1]

Previous research, such as J. P. Walsh's article "Brands Add Value to Gain Advantage" from the September 2003 issue of *Hotel and Motel Management*, has also suggested that brand affiliation is an important contributor to hotel value. Although different valuation methods are applied to assess hotel market value, it has been widely regarded that the process of estimating hotel market value is an "art" as well as a "science." A number of financial indicators, such as net operating income (*NOI*), average daily rate (ADR), occupancy rate, and number of rooms, have proven to be among the most significant predictors of hotel market value.[2] Also, it is vital for hotel appraisers, owners, and operators to understand the effects of hotel brands on the market value of hotels.

Although branding has been increasingly studied by hospitality industry researchers, many aspects of branding remain to be explored.[3] Particularly, no research has been done examining the relationship between hotel brand names and hotel market values. To expand on previous research, this study examines the brand effect on hotel market value. The fundamental question this research project set out to answer is: What is the role of a brand in determining a hotel's market value? That is, are there value premiums for hotel properties affiliated with certain brands over those affiliated with

John W. O'Neill, PhD, MAI, is Associate Professor at the School of Hospitality Management at The Pennsylvania State University.

16

---

1. E. Anderson and V. Mittal, "Strengthening the Satisfaction-Profit Chain," *Journal of Service Research* 3 (2000): 107-120; J. Kapferer, *Strategic Brand Management: Creating and Sustaining Brand Equity Long Term* (Dover, NH: Kogan Page, 1997).

2. J.W. O'Neill, "An Automated Valuation Model for Hotels," *Cornell Hotel and Restaurant Administration Quarterly* 45, no. 3 (2004): 260-268; O'Neill and A. Lloyd-Jones, "One Year after 9/11: Hotel Values and Strategic Implications," *Cornell Hotel and Restaurant Administration Quarterly* 43, no. 5 (2002): 53-64.

3. W. G. Kim and H. B. Kim, "Measuring Customer-Based Restaurant Brand Equity," *Cornell Hotel and Restaurant Administration Quarterly* 45, no. 2 (2004): 115-130.

other brands? Based on a data set consisting of 1,067 actual hotel sales transactions, this study explores whether various hotel brands contribute differently to the values of hotels, while controlling for the most recognized value predictors such as *NOI,* ADR, occupancy rate, and number of guest rooms. By revealing different brand effects on different types of hotels, the results of this study are expected to assist current and potential hotel appraisers, owners, investors, and lenders, as well as corporate brand management, with their assessment of the power of brands in terms of hotel market values.

Hotel Branding and Market Value

Branding and brand equity have been popular topics in the marketing literature for years. *Brand equity* can be defined as the added value endowed by the brand to the product. According to *Managing Brand Equity,* the value of a brand is in what resides in the minds of customers and is primarily based on brand awareness, perceived quality, and brand loyalty. A model of brand value creation proposed by Keller and Lehmann indicates that brands first create value for customers by helping to assure them of a uniform level of quality. After customers become loyal to a brand, the brand owner can capitalize on the brand value through price premiums, decreased price elasticity, increased market share, and more rapid brand expansion. Finally, companies with successful brands benefit in the financial marketplace by improving shareholders' value, including stock price, price-earnings ratio, and overall market capitalization.[4]

Researchers have posited that branding is particularly critical in service industries such as the hotel business. The goal of hotel branding is clearly recognized as providing added value to both guests and hotel companies by building brand loyalty. According to P.C. Yesawich's article "So Many Brands, So Little Time," which appeared in the September 1996 issue of *Lodging*

Hospitality, 85% of business travelers and 76% of leisure travelers prefer to stay in branded hotels over independent properties. In experience-dominant industries such as hotels, the intangible nature of services causes guests to have a difficult time evaluating the content and quality of a service prior to, and even during and after, the consumption of the service. Consequently, hotel guests rely heavily on brand names to reduce the risks associated with the purchase and consumption of services. Therefore, strong brands enable hotel chains to quickly identify and differentiate themselves in the mind-set of customers. Moreover, from the company's point of view, previous research has suggested that the level of brand equity is positively related to a hotel company's financial performance (e.g., rooms revenue per available room, or RevPAR).[5] Realizing that brand ultimately drives stock price and shareholder value, the lodging industry has been recognized as a "brand-equity business" by Morgan Stanley in their 1997 report "Globalization: The Next Phase in Lodging."

Hotel investors apply different valuation methods to assess the market value of a hotel; market value is essentially an estimate of the likely sale price of real estate in a free and open market. In addition to the sophisticated appraisal approaches (i.e., cost approach, sales comparison approach, and income capitalization approach) that are most commonly used by commercial real estate appraisers, hotel investors also adopt simpler and more expeditious methods such as the ADR rule of thumb, which suggests that hotels should generate $1 in ADR per $1,000 in value per room. (Note that in the research cited, the ADR rule of thumb has been updated from $1 in ADR per every $600 to $1 in ADP per every $1,000 in value per room depending on the hotel type.) Moreover, hotel automated valuation models (AVMs) are also commonly used for this purpose. Among a number of factors that have been suggested to be related to hotel market values, AVMs

---

4. P. H. Farquhar, "Managing Brand Equity," *Marketing Research* 1 (September 1989): 47; K. L. Keller and D. R. Lehmann, "How Do Brands Create Value?" *Marketing Management* 12, no. 3 (2003): 26-40; T. Ambler, C. B. Bhattacharya, J. Edell, K. L. Keller, K. N. Lemon, and V. Mittal, "Relating Brand and Customer Perspectives on Marketing Management," *Journal of Service Research* 5, no. 1 (2002): 13-25.

5. S. Onkvisit and J.J. Shaw, "Service Marketing: Image, Branding, and Competition," *Business Horizons* 32 (January-February 1989): 13-18; L. A. Cai and J. S. P. Hobson, "Making Hotel Brands Work in a Competitive Environment," *Journal of Vacation Marketing* 10, no. 3 (2004): 197-208; K. Prasad and C. S. Dev, "Managing Hotel Brand Equity: A Customer-Centric Framework for Assessing Performance," *Cornell Hotel and Restaurant Administration Quarterly* 41, no. 3 (2000): 22-31; S. G. Bharadwaj, R. P. Varadarajan, and J. Fahy, "Sustainable Competitive Advantage in Service Industries: A Conceptual Model and Research Propositions," *Journal of Marketing* 57 (October 1993): 83-99; H. B. Kim, W. G. Kim, and J. A. An, "The Effect of Consumer-Based Brand Equity on Firms' Financial Performance," *Journal of Consumer Marketing* 20, no. 4 (2003): 335-351.

have revealed that *NOI* per room, ADR, occupancy rate, and number of rooms are the four most significant factors in predicting hotel values, while the effects of other important indicators such as capitalization rate, location, and property age are effectively captured by these four key factors.[6]

It has also been suggested that brand affiliation is linked to hotel value. In particular, it is believed that branded hotels have a financing edge. Since chain affiliation is incorporated in lenders' tight formulas from which to underwrite loans, obtaining financing for an independent hotel is generally more difficult than for a branded one. It has been suggested that more stringent underwriting criteria, such as lower loan-to-value ratios and higher interest rates, are common in the financing of unflagged (independent) hotel properties.[7] However, while the power of hotel branding on hotel value has been frequently cited in trade magazines, it has not been subjected to rigorous academic research. Exactly how brand contributes or diminishes hotel market value remains unstudied.

Methodology

To examine the role of brand names on hotel market values, this study uses a database drawn from over 2,500 hotel sale transactions from 1990 through 2005, made up of 1,233 transactions with complete hotel operating and descriptive information. For the 12-month period prior to each transaction, the database includes ADR (mean = $92.91), occupancy rate (mean = 65.8%), *NOI* (mean = $8,044 per room), sale price (mean = $84,868 per room), capitalization rate (mean = 9.55%), and room revenue multiplier or RRM (mean = 3.46). Other information in the database includes the number of guest rooms (mean = 210); property age (mean = 20 years old); location (city, state, and region); hotel type (economy, midscale without food and beverage (F&B), midscale with F&B, upscale, upper upscale, and luxury); and brand affiliation. Each hotel brand was categorized into the respective hotel type as defined by Smith Travel Research. This study applied Smith Travel Research's definitions of hotel

types both because they are independent of the subject research study and because they are well accepted and regarded in the hotel industry.

For the purposes of this research, brands with fewer than three sales transactions were excluded because those transactions are not able to fully represent their corresponding brands. Furthermore, transactions representing independent properties were excluded due to the difficulty and potential inaccuracy of coding them appropriately into the hotel types defined by Smith Travel Research. Such selection resulted in 1,067 hotel sales transactions, representing 47 of the top 100 brands listed in the previously mentioned 2005 report in *Hotels* magazine. A description of the sample is shown in Table 1. All brand names are provided in Table 3, which appears later in this study.

Analysis of covariance (ANCOVA) was conducted to examine the effects of brand on hotel sale price—i.e., market value measured as sale price per room. Because *NOI* per room, ADR, occupancy rate, and number of rooms have been revealed in AVMs as significant predictors of hotel market values, their effects are regarded as pre-existing and consequently should be controlled to precisely assess the effects of brand. Therefore, ANCOVA is an appropriate approach because it allows us to test the brand as the predictor (a categorical variable) while simultaneously controlling for the effects of *NOI* per room, ADR, occupancy rate, and number of rooms by

Table 1	Sample Characteristics		
Hotel Type	Number of Brands	Number of Hotels	Percentage of Total
Economy	5	68	6.37%
Midscale without food & beverage	9	219	20.52%
Midscale with food & beverage	7	188	17.62%
Upscale	14	302	28.31%
Upper upscale	8	266	24.93%
Luxury	4	24	2.25%
Total	47	1,067	100.00%

---

6. J. deRoos and S. Rushmore, "Hotel Valuation Techniques," in *Hotel Investments: Issues and Perspectives,* 3rd ed. (Lansing, MI: Educational Institute of the American Hotel & Lodging Association, 2003); J. W. O'Neill, "ADR Rule of Thumb: Validity and Suggestions for Its Application," *Cornell Hotel and Restaurant Administration Quarterly* 44, no. 3 (2003): 1-10; O'Neill, "An Automated Valuation Model for Hotels," *Cornell Hotel and Restaurant Administration Quarterly* 45, no. 3 (2004): 260-268.

7. J. M. Keeling, "Brands Have the Financing Edge," *Hotel and Motel Management* 216, no. 8 (May 7, 2001): 26; J. W. O'Neill and E. E. Belfrage, "A Strategy for Estimating Identified Intangible Asset Value: Hotel Affiliation Contribution," *The Appraisal Journal* (Winter 2005): 78-86.

treating these variables as covariates. Moreover, because the values of the response variable (sale price per room) are highly skewed, this variable was transformed by taking the natural log of the price per room to satisfy the statistical assumption of normality. As shown in the following section, ANCOVA was conducted in three steps: the entire data set, the entire data set with brands nested inside the six different hotel types defined by Smith Travel Research, and each of the six hotel types. In the last step, Tukey's multiple comparison tests were conducted to examine the pairwise difference between brands. Tukey's tests are "post hoc" statistical procedures that allow for the determination of which brands within each of the six hotel types significantly affect hotel market values.

Results

First, the overall brand effects on hotel market values were tested by conducting ANCOVA on the entire data set. Sale price per room of each transaction was the response variable in the model, where brand was the predictor and *NOI* per room, ADR, occupancy rate, and number of rooms were covariates. The results clearly show that, while all four control variables are statistically significant (which is consistent with previous research), brand also has a significant effect on price per room and accounts for a considerable increase in R-square (change in R-square = 0.075, $F = 39.10$, $p < 0.001$).

Previous research has also suggested that hotel market values differ significantly by hotel types.[8] To examine whether the previously revealed significant effects of brand are indeed due to variances among different hotel types, ANCOVA was reconducted with brands nested inside the six hotel types defined by Smith Travel Research to test the effects of brands within hotel types (i.e., economy, midscale without F&B, midscale with F&B, upscale, upper upscale, and luxury). The results again support the significant effects of the brands within hotel types on a price-per-room basis while taking into consideration the effects of the previously mentioned four key predictors ($F = 9.70$, $p < 0.001$).

Moreover, to gain further insight into how brands influence price per room in different hotel types, separate ANCOVA tests were applied for each of the six hotel types. In the meantime, to scrutinize which brands are particularly different from the other brands within the same type, Tukey's multiple comparison tests were conducted to examine the pairwise difference between brands. Again the four financial predictors (*NOI* per room, ADR, occupancy rate, and number of rooms) were controlled as covariates in each ANCOVA test. As shown in Table 2, the results of the six ANCOVA tests reveal that the mean value of price per room does vary significantly across brands among the midscale (with and without F&B), upscale, and upper-upscale hotels. However, there are no significant brand effects on either economy hotels or luxury hotels. That is, the midscale and upscale brands do significantly affect the hotel market values in their respective segments, while hotel market values are not significantly influenced by the brands in either the economy or luxury segments. The mean sale price per room of each specific brand is provided in Table 3.

Table 2	Brand Effect on Mean Price per Room by Hotel Type					
	Economy	Midscale w/o Food & Beverage	Midscale with Food & Beverage	Upscale	Upper Upscale	Luxury
N	5	9	7	14	8	4
Mean	$28,148	$53,112	$42,085	$83,141	$109,916	$322,305
Median	$29,998	$49,480	$46,875	$78,790	$109,363	$326,797
Standard Deviation	$9,104	$16,413	$12,762	$16,267	$24,936	$65,545
Minimum	$13,080	$31,136	$25,975	$60,728	$74,955	$241,262
Maximum	$35,504	$86,511	$53,126	$108,885	$150,320	$394,366
F Value	0.21	2.30*	2.38*	3.15†	4.41†	0.43

* $p < 0.05$.

† $p < 0.01$.

8. A. Singh and R. Schmidgall, "Financing Lodging Properties," *Cornell Hotel & Restaurant Administration Quarterly* 41, no. 4 (2000): 39-47.

Table 3   Mean Price per Room by Brand

Brand	Mean Price per Room	Brand	Mean Price per Room
Economy		**Midscale without Food & Beverage**	
Cross Country Inn	$13,080	AmeriHost	$52,905
Days Inn	$34,940	Comfort Inn	$43,212
Microtel	$29,998	Country Inn & Suites	$70,735
Super 8	$27,221	Fairfield Inn	$31,136
Travelodge	$35,504	Hampton Inn	$54,169
Segment Mean	**$28,148**	Holiday Inn Express	$49,480
Midscale with Food & Beverage		Sleep Inn	$44,649
Best Western	$53,126	TownePlace Suites	$86,511
Clarion	$50,585	Wellesley Inn	$45,219
Holiday Inn	$46,875	**Segment Mean**	**$53,112**
Howard Johnson	$25,975	**Upper Upscale**	
Ramada	$28,670	Doubletree	$74,955
Red Lion	$57,074	Embassy Suites	$108,812
Quality Inn	$32,288	Hilton	$106,489
Segment Mean	**$42,085**	Hyatt	$130,373
Upscale		Marriott	$109,915
Adam's Mark	$70,070	Renaissance	$119,710
AmeriSuites	$80,680	Sheraton	$78,761
Courtyard	$94,890	Westin	$150,320
Crowne Plaza	$62,365	**Segment Mean**	**$109,916**
Four Points	$75,352	**Luxury**	
Hawthorn Suites	$60,805	Fairmont	$394,366
Hilton Garden Inn	$92,890	Four Seasons	$350,115
Homewood Suites	$102,122	InterContinental	$241,262
Radisson	$60,728	Ritz-Carlton	$303,480
Residence Inn	$108,885	**Segment Mean**	**$322,305**
SpringHill Suites	$85,343		
Staybridge Suites	$76,901		
Summerfield Suites	$103,769		
Wyndham	$89,617		
Segment Mean	**$83,141**		

Discussion and Implications

The findings of this study indicate the existence of brand effects on hotel market values. In addition to the value predictors well recognized in hotel AVMs (*NOI* per room, ADR, occupancy rate, and number of rooms), brand affiliations contribute significantly to the variances in hotel values. The findings support the notion that the brand matters in assessing a hotel's value. However, how much the brand matters and affects value varies across hotel types.

It is interesting to find that brands influence hotel values more in midscale and upscale hotels than in the most inexpensive (economy) and expensive (luxury) hotels. One possible explanation based on further scrutiny of the data is that perhaps the most and least active, innovative, and well-positioned brands are in the midscale and upscale segments (i.e., there is a great deal of variance in the brands in the middle of the price range, but much less variance in the brands at the top and bottom of the price range). The following section will discuss specific brands that have significantly higher or lower prices per room compared to other brands in their respective segments, based on the results of Tukey's multiple comparison tests.

Among all "midscale without F&B" brands, TownePlace Suites and Country Inn & Suites significantly outperformed the other brands in market values, while Fairfield Inn values were lower compared to the rest of the group. It is not surprising to see that TownePlace Suites enjoys the highest average market value ($86,511 per room) because it is one of the newest extended-stay brands backed by Marriott and outfitted with spacious rooms and ample features and amenities not found in most non-suite brands in this category. Country Inn & Suites also stands out with a mean sale price per room at $70,735, and this achievement was at least partially attributed to its hotels' new physical plants, relatively consistent performance in guest satisfaction, and ADR increases.[9] On the other hand, it is important to point out that mean brand values are based on the types of hotels actually transacting within each brand during the period of time studied. For example, Fairfield Inns may have sold for a relatively low average price of $31,136 per room because the Fairfield brand management team is eliminating from its system older, first-generation properties constructed in the 1980s; therefore, many of these properties have sold during the past several years.

In the "midscale with F&B" segment, the Tukey's tests reveal that the variances in the sale prices among the brands studied are mainly caused by two underperforming brands: Howard Johnson ($25,975 per room) and Ramada ($28,670 per room). It may not be surprising that both brands have encountered difficulties in appropriately positioning themselves in the market. As hotel guests have been losing interest in the brands, it is reasonable that hotel investors are following this trend. Both brands have been working towards rebuilding their brand images through a "Project Restore" program, in which higher quality standards have been introduced, lower-quality properties have been "cleaned up," and stronger marketing initiatives have been launched. For example, it has been reported that nearly 20% of Howard Johnson franchisees received warnings to either comply with the newest franchise standards or reflag (change to a different brand affiliation), and over 15,000 substandard rooms were removed

from the Ramada chain in 2004 and 2005.[10] Additional time may be needed for the effects of such "rebranding" efforts to be shown on the market values of these branded properties.

It is also notable that, in follow-up ANCOVA tests, the mean sale price per room of the "midscale without F&B" segment ($53,112) is significantly more than the mean price per room of the "midscale with F&B" segment ($42,085), indicating that the latter segment, which is largely composed of older properties constructed in the 1970s and 1980s, is less attractive to hotel investors ($F = 6.12$, $p < 0.05$). Research in 2002 predicted that the average market value per room of these two hotel segments would "flip" in 2003 from the previous situation when midscale hotels with F&B were worth more per room than midscale hotels without F&B, and it now appears that flip has occurred.[11]

In the upscale segment, the statistical analyses indicate that the value leaders are industry innovators Residence Inn ($108,885 per room), Summerfield Suites ($103,769 per room), Homewood Suites ($102,122 per room), Courtyard by Marriott ($94,890 per room), and Hilton Garden Inn ($92,890 per room). The market value per room of each of these brands is statistically significantly greater than the mean prices per room of Radisson ($60,728), Crowne Plaza ($62,365), and Hawthorn Suites ($60,805). In the upper-upscale segment, Westin and Hyatt stand out with mean prices per room at $150,320 and $130,373, respectively, compared to Doubletree ($74,955 per room) and Sheraton ($78,761 per room). Based on the results of the Tukey's tests, the other brands in the upscale and upper-upscale segments did not vary significantly.

Considering the results of the four hotel types in which brands significantly influence hotel values, it appears that some of the most innovative and well-positioned brands, such as Residence Inn, Courtyard, and Westin, have established competitive advantages over their less well-positioned competitors in their respective market segments. Specifically, it may be that Radisson and Doubletree, similar to Howard

---

9. "Suite Dreams," *Consumer Reports* (July 2001); "Hotels: 50 Chains, 10 Ways to Save," *Consumer Reports* (July 2004); J. P. Walsh, "Hoteliers Convert Properties to Find Better Brand Partners," *Hotel and Motel Management* 218, no. 3 (February 2003): 23.

10. "Hotels: 50 Chains, 10 Ways to Save," *Consumer Reports;* J. Higley, "New Leader, Same Vision Drive Howard Johnson," *Hotel and Motel Management* 218, no. 7 (April 2003): 1; J. P. Walsh, "Group President Hired to Aid Cendant Brands," *Hotel and Motel Management* 218, no. 14 (August 2003): 6; Ramada, "Ramada Charts a Global Course to a Brand New World," *Hotel and Motel Management* 220, no.19 (November 2005).

11. J. W. O'Neill and A. Lloyd-Jones, "One Year after 9/11: Hotel Values and Strategic Implications," *Cornell Hotel and Restaurant Administration Quarterly* 43, no. 5 (2002): 53-64.

Johnson and Ramada in the midscale category, have confused guest perceptions of their brand images and consequently have been continuously ranked among the lowest in terms of brand awareness. The findings of this study suggest that such brand awareness disadvantages may be reflected in the hotel market values of the respective brands as well.

On the other hand, while Sheraton remains strong in terms of brand awareness among hotel guests, the system's "upgrading" efforts, similar to Fairfield Inn's, may partially contribute to the relatively lower market value shown in this study. Recent trends suggest that Sheraton has successfully implemented several key strategies, including upgrading quality standards, improving guest satisfaction, introducing an attractive prototype to expand into smaller markets, and joining Westin's bedding innovation with its Sweet Sleeper bedding product, all of which have led to strengthen the brand's market position and create more value for hotel investors. Consequently, Sheraton has been able to resume its growth speed, has become one of the top ten new development leaders in 2005, and may serve as an interesting model for brands such as Ramada, Howard Johnson, Doubletree, and Radisson.[12]

There are fewer variations among the luxury brands and economy brands studied. In the luxury segment, Four Seasons, Ritz-Carlton, Fairmont, and InterContinental are all long-renowned brands with relatively steady performance; therefore, it is not surprising that the market values do not vary significantly among these brands. Similarly, the brands studied in the economy segment do not show significant variance in terms of price per room. However, it should be noted that several active market players, such as Studio 6 and Extended Stay America, were not in the sample because there have been relatively few sales transactions of hotels of these brands; therefore, the results regarding this segment could be revised if more economy brands were to be included.

Furthermore, while the findings of this study are believed to add to the understanding of the relationship between hotel brands and market values, how to appropriately assess the effects of a brand is a complex task for hotel appraisers and owners. In the lodging industry, hotel brands are clearly linked to multi-dimensions, such as physical facilities, amenities, and service qualities and styles. This research project aims to contribute to the knowledge regarding the factors determining the market value of hotels; however, it does not simply mean that a brand's relationship with hotel market value is the only benefit a brand brings to hotel owners. Although it is important for hotel owners to be able to recognize the effects of a brand on hotel market value, other benefits associated with a brand should be considered to fully assess the total value of the brand.

Conclusions

This study is the first to empirically examine the relationship between hotel brands and market values. As expected, brands do significantly affect hotel values, particularly the values of midscale and upscale hotels. As brand switching has become increasingly common in today's hotel market, the findings of this study are expected to assist both hotel owners and corporate brand management teams to better understand the value of effective brands. For the hotel owners whose ultimate goal is to maximize hotel market value, recognizing the role of brand name in hotel market value is beneficial for their repositioning and reflagging decisions. For hotel companies' brand management, effectively assessing brand effects on hotel values can not only strengthen the overall value of brands and possibly improve the franchise sales for the brand but also signal weaknesses and assist with the development of reimaging, retrenchment, or remedial strategies when necessary.

Some limitations should be considered in the interpretation of these findings and, in the meantime, suggest directions for future research. First, as previously mentioned, the data selection criteria excluded a few brands with limited sales transaction volume, particularly in the economy segment. Specifically, the limited sample size in both the economy and luxury segments may affect the statistical results. Future research incorporating a database with an even more complete portfolio of brands may

---

12. Y. Morrison, "Lodging Segmentation Study Overview" (unpublished presentation at 2004 International Hotel/Motel & Restaurant Show Hospitality Leadership Forum, New York, NY, November 13, 2004); E. Watkins, "Growth Leaders," *Lodging Hospitality* 61, no. 7 (May 2005): 68; E. Watkins, "Brand Bonanza," *Lodging Hospitality* 61, no. 15 (November 2005): 56-63; S. Webb, "Starwood Cranks Up Development Engine," *National Real Estate Investor* 46, no. 4 (2004): 120-122; S. Paterik, "Sheraton Plans to Pay Guests for Bad Service," *Wall Street Journal* (September 6, 2002): B1.

shed more light on this topic. Second, this study does not analyze the effects of brand cost on hotel market value. It is reasonable to expect that more prestigious brands would require higher fees to be paid by the hotel owners. HVS International's Annual Hotel Development Cost Survey may be of assistance to hotel owners and investors in this regard. An interesting question for future research is whether the value premiums associated with strong brands are more or less than the accumulated costs of the brands. Previous research has suggested that such future research should be conducted at the hotel unit level.[13] Third, it should be noted that Smith Travel Research's brand classifications are primarily based on each brand's system-wide ADR. While this segmentation method is objective, it is arguable that a few brands could be categorized into different segments based on the facilities and services offered. For instance, one could argue that Hawthorn Suites might be classified as a "midscale without F&B" brand instead of an upscale one, thus eliminating the statistically significant differences between Hawthorn Suites and the leading upscale brands such as Residence Inn. There are always advantages and disadvantages in applying different brand classification methods, but applying the Smith Travel Research categorizations used herein is arguably the most objective categorization method for this type of research.

Finally, literature on brand extension suggests that parent companies may influence their respective brands. That is, differences among parent companies' branding strategies may account for the different effects among the brands. Although brand extension is out of the scope of the present research, how the branding strategies of parent companies influence the relationships between brands and hotel market values is worthy of further research.

Although it is not always simple for hotel owners to switch brands because of market reasons as well as because of financial reasons such as liquidated damages, they remain free to do so. Well-informed owners should be aware of the relative market values of the various brand options before them. Hotel brand management teams should be similarly aware. Previous research has discovered strong links between hotel brand quality level and hotel brand performance, which in turn has strong links with hotel market value. As a result, hotel brand management teams who wish to maximize hotel market value should seek to maximize brand quality through not only addressing brand reimaging, but through more remedial quality management as well.

13. J. W. O'Neill and E. E. Belfrage, "A Strategy for Estimating Identified Intangible Asset Value: Hotel Affiliation Contribution," *The Appraisal Journal* (Winter 2005): 78-86.

A Strategy for Estimating Identified Intangible Asset Value: Hotel Affiliation Contribution

John W. O'Neill, PhD, MAI, and Eric E. Belfrage, MAI, SRA
This article originally appeared in the Winter 2005 issue of *The Appraisal Journal*.

Although researchers and practitioners generally agree that intangible value exists in hotels, methodologies for estimating it continue to evolve. This article presents a strategy for estimating identified intangible asset (IIA) value and applies it to a paired comparison of two franchise-affiliated hotels in the same central business district. The analysis focuses on the benefits versus costs of affiliation. This research concludes that IIA value for affiliation exists to the extent that revenues attributable to affiliation exceed the cost of that affiliation. When costs of affiliation approach or exceed revenues from the franchise relationship, the IIA value for affiliation is limited or nonexistent.

Researchers and practitioners generally agree that intangible value exists in hotels.[1] Although the need to distinguish between tangible and intangible hotel value has been well documented, there is no general agreement regarding how to do so.

The lion's share of a hotel's intangible value is usually based on its brand name.[2] While there appears to be general agreement that a large portion of a hotel's total intangible asset (TIA) value is derived from its brand or franchise affiliation, the value contribution from franchise affiliation can vary widely despite relative uniformity in hotel franchise fees among similar brands. Therefore, using a hotel's franchise fees as the sole basis for estimating a hotel's intangible value may not always be the most appropriate technique for estimating intangible value.

This article presents a strategy for estimating a hotel's intangible value by comparing the market value of the total assets of the business (MVTAB) and value allocated to identified intangible assets due to the affiliation (IIA$_a$) of two affiliated hotels in the same central business district, valued as of the same date. Both properties are affiliated with internationally known hotel

John W. O'Neill, PhD, MAI, CHE, is a professor of lodging strategy and real estate at The Pennsylvania State University School of Hospitality Management. Previously, O'Neill was senior associate in the Hospitality Industry Consulting Group at the international accounting and consulting firm of Coopers & Lybrand in New York. O'Neill has also been a consultant to Marriott International, Hilton Hotels, Holiday Inn, Ritz-Carlton, and several financial institutions, and has served as an expert witness. He has previously published articles in numerous business and lodging publications, including The Appraisal Journal. He holds a BS in hotel adminstration from Cornell University, an MS in real estate from New York University, and a PhD in business adminstration from the University of Rhode Island.

Eric E. Belfrage, MAI, SRA, CRE, ISHC, is the managing director of Integra Realty Resources of Columbus, Ohio. His background includes twenty-five years of independent fee appraisal and consulting; his practice has largely focused on evaluating and appraising lodging properties. He has previously published in The Appraisal Journal. Belfrage holds a bachelor's degree in business administration from Franklin University, Columbus, Ohio.

1. See Heather J. Reichardt and David C. Lennhoff, "Hotel Asset Allocation: Separating the Tangible Personalty," *Assessment Journal* 10, no.1 (Winter 2003): 25–31; Eric E. Belfrage, "Business Value Allocation in Lodging Valuation," *The Appraisal Journal* (July 2001): 277–282; and William N. Kinnard, Jr., Elaine M. Worzala, and Dan L. Swango, "Intangible Assets in an Operating First-Class Downtown Hotel," *The Appraisal Journal* (January 2001): 68–83.
2. John W. O'Neill, "An Automated Valuation Model for Hotels," *Cornell Hotel & Restaurant Administration Quarterly,* 45, no. 3 (August 2004): 260-268.

A Strategy for Estimating Identified Intangible Asset Value: Hotel Affiliation Contribution
189
A Business Enterprise Value Anthology

companies, and they are direct competitors with one another. Having isolated the analysis for time differences, location, and market dissimilarities, comparison can be made of IIA_a, which, as previously noted, are largely attributable to brand affiliation for hotel properties. It should also be noted, however, that other identified intangible assets (IIA) value can be attributed to items such as workforce, contracts, cash, etc. This comparison does not attempt to allocate value to a specific chain, but rather to present a case study demonstrating the flexibility, robustness, and reliability of the methodology used for isolating IIA_a–a methodology intended to assist real estate appraisers and other real estate analysts undertaking hotel valuation assignments. Previous research has found that the analysis of hotel pairs is a valid approach for the estimation of the value of TIA.[3]

The methodology presented in this article concludes that when room-night sales (demand) attributable to the franchise/brand distribution channels exceed the relative ongoing cost of affiliation, intangible asset value (IAV) is generated. Conversely, when sales attributable to the franchisor approximate or are less than the cost of affiliation, IAV may be minimal or nonexistent. It should be noted, the methodology measures identified intangible assets attributed to affiliation only (IIA_a), and although IIA_a represents the majority of IIA for hotels, as previously stated, it excludes other IIA value attributed to items such as workforce, contracts, cash, etc.

To a very large degree, hotel chain affiliation creates IIA value; other components include service and management,[4] both of which are usually highly controlled and mandated by the hotel franchisor. Chain standards allow a hotel chain to achieve brand consistency, and therefore, loyal guests.[5] This relationship is best evidenced in the success of brand loyalty programs, such as Marriott's "Rewards" program or Hilton's "HHonors" program, at generating repeat business. Therefore, to some degree the resulting room nights delivered to a hotel through its distribution channels (e.g., 1-800 #, corporate Internet bookings, and travel agent relationships) are inclusive of the service and management components expected by the guest of a specific brand.

Franchise-controlled distribution channels are meticulously tracked for individual hotels by every franchisor and monitored closely by most hotel operators. Delivery of room nights is the currency of the franchise companies; i.e., it is what they have to sell. Virtually every hotel management professional knows down to the room night the number of rooms (and therefore room revenue) that has been provided by the franchise company. If the revenue for the given period does not exceed the cost of affiliation, the franchisee may be dissatisfied with the franchisee/ franchisor relationship. As actual empirical evidence, this quantification may be a reliable tool for the valuations professional appraisers perform in complying with the mandate of the *Uniform Standards of Professional Appraisal Practice* (USPAP) Standards Rule 1-4(g), which states: "An appraiser must analyze the effect on value of any personal property, trade fixtures, or intangible items that are not real property, but are included in the appraisal."[6]

The case study that follows will show the valuation of the total assets of the business (TAB) and identified intangible assets attributed to the hotel affiliation (IIA_a). A step-by-step analysis of the TAB and IIA_a quantification are included, resulting in a demonstration of two quite different indications of contribution. Both the net income incremental flowthrough methodology and the calculation of the appropriate intangible capitalization rates are discussed in a later section of this article.

Background

Table 1 outlines the valuation of two central business district (CBD) hotels in a major metropolitan city.[7] Although "Hotel A" has only an approximate 19% greater value on a per-guest unit basis, its IIA_a value is approximately five times that calculated for "Hotel B." One of the

3. Belfrage.
4. Ibid.
5. John W. O'Neill and Anna S. Mattila, "Hotel Branding Strategy: Its Relationship to Guest Satisfaction and Room Revenue," *Journal of Hospitality & Tourism Research* 28, no. 2 (2004): 156–165.
6. Appraisal Standards Board, Standards Rule 1-4(g), Lines 681–682, *Uniform Standards of Professional Appraisal Practice and Advisory Opinions 2004 Edition* (Washington, DC: The Appraisal Foundation, 2004), 120.
7. The case study properties were the subject of tax appeals and the information presented here is part of the public record of those tax appeals.

Table 1 Hotel Valuations

	Hotel A	Hotel B[1]
Physical		
Hotel affiliation	Hyatt	Crowne Plaza
Number of rooms	400	421
Location	CBD	CBD
Date of value estimate[2]	1/1/02	1/1/02
Year built	1983	1987[3]
Number of stories	22	5–12
Function space (sq. ft.)	17,000	10,000
Rack rate	$139	$159
Most recent renovation	1995[4]	1995[5]
Economics		
Average daily rate projection	$122[6]	$105
Occupancy projection	65%[6]	68%
RevPAR projection	$79.30	$71.40
Projected 2002 market RevPAR	$62.19	$62.19
Subject RevPAR yield	128%	115%
Projected room revenue	$11,577,800[6]	$10,971,660
Projected total revenue	$19,378,050	$16,300,816
Projected net income ratio	18.7%	19.7%
Projected NOI	$3,614,777	$3,208,147
Overall rate	11%	11%
Market value of total assets of business	$32,900,000[6]	$29,200,000
Value per unit	$82,250	$69,358
Furniture, fixtures & equipment[7]	$3,360,000	$2,300,000
Affiliation Statistics		
Brand identification, source of business report[8]	"Spirit" Distribution Report	Net Room Night Channel Report
Percent of room nights attributed to affiliation[9]	34%	15%
Revenues attributed to franchise[10]	$3,936,452	$1,645,749
Amounts included in expenses for affiliation costs	$1,937,805[11]	$1,206,883
IIA$_a$ revenue residing in cash flow (before operating expenses)[12]	$1,998,647	$438,866
Net income to IIA$_a$[13]	$999,324	$219,433
Intangible capitalization rate[14]	18%	18%
IIA$_a$ value indication[15]	$5,551,800	$1,219,072
Rounded	$5,600,000	$1,200,000
IIA$_a$/MVTAB	17%	4%

Notes:

1. Property consists of a 377-room Crowne Plaza and a 44-room boutique hotel, jointly operated.

2. Retrospective tax lien date.

3. Original construction of 278 rooms was in 1987; a 99-room addition was completed in 1997, along with the renovation of an adjacent, circa-1910 loft operated as a boutique hotel that also houses the property's food service division.

4. Complete renovation in 1995; some soft goods and TVs were replaced in 2000–2001; a $6,000,000 renovation was postponed due to 9/11 and planned for 2004.

5. Complete renovation in 1995; guest-room renovations totaling $3.2 million completed in 2000.

6. Assumes completion of renovations required by Hyatt.

7. Allocated based on personal property tax return. Also referred to as tangible personal property (TPP).

8. Distribution reports provided for analysis of room nights attributed to franchisor channels (1-800 #, corporate Internet, and global distribution channels, i.e., travel agents).

9. Reservations driven by various channels adjusted for walk-in business. Also adjusted for nonaffiliated revenue from the "Lofts" of Hotel B.

10. Annual rooms revenue multiplied by percentage attributed to affiliation.

11. Equivalent to 10% of total revenue (17% of rooms revenue); incorporates all-inclusive management/franchise agreement.

12. Based on total revenue attributed to affiliation, less costs of affiliation paid in various expense line items.

13. Based on application of net income flow through ratio to gross IIA$_a$ revenue.

14. Intangible capitalization rate quantified in subsequent section.

15. NOI attributable to IIA$_a$/intangible capitalization rate.

recently developed methods of measuring IIA_a is to consider in part excess market share.

> One measure of value attributable to these sort of intangible assets of an operating hotel is any indicated continuing excess of total annual room revenues per available room (RevPAR) over the competitive market norm that can be associated with the name, reputation, and flag affiliation of the hotel being appraised.[8]

The use of the revenue per available room (RevPAR) comparison attributing excess RevPAR over the natural market share does indeed partially quantify intangible value. However, the competitive set used to measure the fair share will likely contain similarly affiliated hotels. Each of these hotels will bring service, affiliation, and management components together to compete for its fair share. Earning RevPAR equal to the submarket average can be a positive accomplishment for an operator, and it does not necessarily represent a baseline below which no intangible value exists. The RevPAR analysis appears effective, but requires additional consideration to build up the total contribution of identified intangibles. Further, a hotel does not necessarily possess intangible value merely because of occupancy and average daily rate (i.e., RevPAR) premiums; its RevPAR premiums may be due to its physical location. This is the case for Hotel B. Recent research has concluded that such premiums are in fact often attributable to a hotel's location in its market, i.e., realty.[9]

The conclusions depicted in Table 1 under Affiliation Statistics show the total benefit of affiliation in both percentage of rooms sold and dollars of room revenue. The costs paid for that affiliation are deducted, resulting in the net benefit of the franchise. This methodology shows the cost versus benefit of the actual affiliation to the specific hotel. It employs the chains' own accounting of actual rooms attributed to their distribution channels. These channels provide guests through the toll-free reservation telephone lines, corporate Internet sites, and travel agent relationships, as opposed to reasons relating to real estate such as location, physical

characteristics, access, exposure, etc. Lesser and Rubin have indicated that

> The use of a recognized brand name generally increases a hotel's revenue-generating ability and thus adds to the hotel's bottom line, enhancing its value. Yet this portion of the property's value is clearly attributable to the brand name rather than the property's real estate component...[10]

In the literature, similar statements are made by both Dowell and Rushmore.[11] The Rushmore valuation method of determining TIA asserts that if management and franchise fees are removed from the cash flow, the residual value is real estate. This approach may be counter to market expectations that the affiliation component should generate revenues in excess of cost.

It is interesting to note that Hotel B actually maintains a higher stabilized-occupancy rate than Hotel A, yet attributes fewer occupied rooms to its affiliation. This difference is due in part to its location across the street from a convention center and heavy reliance on direct group sales that are generated by the city's convention facilities authority, as well as the property's own sales effort. These room sales are not directly attributable to the InterContinental Hotel Group (parent company of Crowne Plaza) affiliation, and are therefore property specific. In other words, the guests are staying at Hotel B in large part because of its convenient location relative to the convention center. This factor is not directly related to any of the components of intangible assets (service, affiliation, or management) and should therefore be attributed to real estate, as indicated by the previously discussed logic. Of course, it is possible that someone might choose to stay at an affiliated hotel in part because of its brand recognition, but not use the brand distribution channels to reserve a room. Room nights generated in this manner would not be specifically included in the methodology here. These room nights are not "identified," and therefore not considered as IIA revenue.

During the research process, the management company of Hotel B expressed dissatisfac-

---

8. Appraisal Institute, Course 800, "Separating Real and Personal Property from Intangible Business Assets," (Chicago: Appraisal Institute, 2001), 9–17; RevPAR is calculated as occupancy percentage multiplied by average daily rate.

9. O'Neill.

10. Daniel H. Lesser and Karen E. Rubin, "Understanding the Unique Aspects of Hotel Property Tax Valuation," *The Appraisal Journal* (January 1993): 9–27.

11. Bernice T. Dowell, "Hotel Investment Analysis: In Search of Business Value," *Journal of Property Tax Management* 4, no. 2 (Mar/Apr 1997): 46–53; Stephen Rushmore, *Hotels and Motels: A Guide to Market Analysis, Investment Analysis, and Valuations* (Chicago: Appraisal Institute, 1992), 247.

tion with the amount of business derived from the affiliation; it has considered alternate or independent operation, i.e., disaffiliating. This potential strategic shift is supported and demonstrated by the data shown in Table 1, which indicates minimal IIA_a contribution. In short, it is market-based proof that little IIA_a value exists for Hotel B, despite its quality brand affiliation and relatively high RevPAR yield. The converse is true for Hotel A. Its management is pleased with the maximization of value attributable to affiliation; approximately 34% of the rooms sold can be attributed to the hotel's affiliation with Hyatt Hotels Corporation. These are rooms sold as a result of being managed and franchised by the Hyatt corporate entity. Although approximately 17% of room revenue (10% of total revenue) is charged by the franchisor in an "all inclusive agreement," a significant amount of intangible revenue continues to reside in the cash flow. The capitalized net income attributed to IIA_a indicates the value attributed to affiliation for Hotel A.

Consider the pro forma revenue and expense summaries for the two hotels as presented in Tables 2 and 3. The Hyatt affiliation accounts for approximately 34% of room revenues, or about $3.9 million in revenue, based on its "Spirit" distribution report (the "Spirit" system is Hyatt's proprietary central reservation system). Management and franchise fees are combined under the all-inclusive agreement at 6% of total revenue (including food and beverage). Other fees paid to the franchisor include a 2% allocation to the room department expense, accounting for reservation expenses, and travel agent commissions paid as a result of the global distribution system (GDS) relationships held by the franchise company. Additional costs of affiliation are included in the marketing expense line item. This category includes chain advertising and guest loyalty program costs. These costs, as with those allocated to "rooms," are determined through a study of historic statements, and a review of the franchise agreement. The combined costs of affiliation paid by the hotel entity approximate 10% of total revenue (17% of room revenue) annually. Typically, franchise costs are based on room revenue; however, in some full-service upscale and upper high-end properties, a portion of costs of affiliation can be based on a ratio to total revenues. Generally, hotel operators assume the benefit of franchise relationships resides in the franchisor's ability

to produce guest room sales. This assumption exists because rooms are the most profitable hotel department/division, and usually represent the majority of revenue in a hotel operation. While it is possible that in full-service hotels, other departmental revenues, such as food and beverage revenue, could benefit from the affiliation, these revenues are not identified, and not included as IIA revenue in this methodology.

In the case of Hotel A, the subject receives a revenue enhancement of $3,936,452 (see Table 2) that was delivered to the property through the franchise relationship, not due to physical or real estate reasons. The cost (fees paid to Hyatt) associated with the receipt of this revenue totals $1,937,805, resulting in a positive gross benefit to the hotel of $1,998,647 annually, on a stabilized basis. Of course, this revenue is still subject to operating expenses. These calculations are detailed in Table 2. The net income incremental flow through (discussed later) at 50% is used to process the gross revenue, indicating net IIA_a for Hotel A at $999,324.

For Hotel B, about 15% of room revenue can be attributed to the InterContinental affiliation. This amount reflects the net contribution after having isolated and removed the rooms sold at the small boutique hotel operated in conjunction with this asset. Typically, an InterContinental affiliation will contribute a greater number of occupied rooms; however, in this case, group rooms attributed to the convention center are sold directly by the hotel and convention center staff. This situation understandably minimizes IIA_a because the rooms are sold due to location, i.e., real estate–related factors. Removal of the costs associated with affiliation, which total 11% of room revenue, leaves only $438,866 in gross IIA_a revenue (the net benefit of affiliation). Application of the 50% flow-through ratio offers $219,433 in net IIA_a revenue for Hotel B. These calculations are detailed in Table 3.

Incremental Flow Through of Net Operating Income

The incremental flow through of gross IIA_a revenue to net is reflected at a higher ratio than the overall net operating income (NOI) ratio. Comparison of matched-pair revenue streams was conducted to determine the flow through of gross IIA_a revenue to net. Samples of 14 comparable, full-service, U.S. hotel operating statements were selected that reflected multiple year operations

Table 2	Hotel A 2002 Pro Forma			
Description	**Total**	**Revenue from/to Franchise**		**Percent of Room Revenue**
Income:				
Rooms (400)	$11,577,800	$3,936,452		34.00%
Food & beverage	$6,453,200			
Telephone	$427,050			
Other	$920,000			
Total Revenue	$19,378,050			
Expenses:				**Percent of Total Revenue**
Operated Dept.				
Rooms	$2,952,339	$387,561		2.00%
Food & beverage	$5,033,496			
Telephone	$320,288			
Other operated dept.	$506,000			
Total Oper. Dept. Expenses	$8,812,123			
Undistributed Expenses				
Energy	$678,232			
Marketing	$1,162,683	$387,561		2.00%
Franchise fees	$0			
Repair & maintenance	$775,122			
Admin. & general	$1,550,244			
Total Undistributed Expenses	$4,166,281			
Management/ franchise (all inclusive)	$1,162,683	$1,162,683		6.00%
Fixed Expenses				
Insurance	$290,671			
Taxes	$556,394			
Other	$0			
Reserves	$775,122			
Total Fixed Expenses	$1,622,187			
Total Expenses	$15,763,273	$1,937,805		10.00%
		$1,998,647		*gross IIA$_a$ revenue before expenses*
Net Operating Income	$3,614,777	$999,324		*net IIA$_a$ revenue at 50% flow through*
Rooms Sold	94,900			
Occupancy	65.00%			
Average Daily Rate	$122.00			
Average F&B Per Occupied Room	$68.00			

with significant revenue (volume) changes. The data showed that on average, the top incremental 20.2% of total revenue resulted in a mean 55.7% rate of flow through to NOI. The data further showed that the range of top 13% to 38% of revenue experienced a rate of flow through to NOI of 35% to 67%. While additional research could be conducted to refine these conclusions, the analysis has relied on a 50% flow-through rate to NOI, which falls near the middle of the 35% to 67% range for comparable properties.

Capitalization Rate Determination

A major issue with processing net IIA$_a$ revenue is the lack of market support for an applicable matching intangible asset capitalization rate. Since the hotel intangible revenue does not sell separately from the real estate revenue, there is no market-based return criteria.

A reasonable method to determine the intangible capitalization rate is to prepare a band-of-investment table allocating value components to their appropriate real estate and nonrealty

| Table 3 | Hotel B 2002 Pro Forma |

Description	Total	Revenue from/to Franchise	Percent of Room Revenue
Income			
Rooms (421)	$10,971,660	$1,645,749	15.00%
Food & Beverage	$4,493,156		
Telephone	$209,000		
Other	$627,000		
Total Revenue	$16,300,816		
Expenses:			
Operated Dept.			
Rooms	$2,907,490	$219,433	2.00%
Food & beverage	$3,369,867		
Telephone	$146,300		
Other operated dept.	$501,600		
Total Oper. Dept. Expenses	$6,925,257		
Undistributed Expenses			
Energy	$489,024		
Marketing	$1,385,569	$493,725	4.50%
Franchise fees	$489,024	$493,725	4.50%
Repair & maintenance	$611,281		
Admin. & general	$1,467,073		
Total Undistributed Expenses	$4,441,972		
Management	$407,520		
Fixed Expenses			
Insurance	$163,008		
Taxes	$502,879		
Other	$0		
Reserves	$652,033		
Total Fixed Expenses	$1,317,920		
Total Expenses	$13,092,669	$1,206,883	11.00%
		$438,866	gross IIA_a revenue before expenses
Net Operating Income	$3,208,147	$219,433	net IIA_a revenue
Rooms Sold	104,492		
Occupancy	68.00%		
Average Daily Rate	$105.00		
Average F&B Per Occupied Room	$43.00		

items. To solve for the intangible capitalization rate, the following are necessary:

- An appropriate indication of the overall capitalization rate for hotel investments
- An appropriate indication of the overall capitalization rate for a comparable "real estate only" asset
- An appropriate indication of overall capitalization rate for the tangible personal property (TPP)

- An estimate of the percentage of the total assets of the business attributable to real estate, tangible personal property, and intangible assets

An algebraic equation can be used to solve for the return applicable to intangibles if the other variables can be approximated. Table 4 demonstrates the extraction of the intangible capitalization rate. Of course, refinements can tailor the variables in Table 4 to a specific set of property criteria; however, in this case, a more generic set of variables applicable to both Hotels A and B is employed.

Overall capitalization rates for hotel investments have been well documented by numerous national studies, including the nationally known, quarterly Korpacz Real Estate Investor Survey. The hotels that are the subject of this article are both institutional-grade, full-service properties that substantially conform to the capitalization rates reported by the Korpacz survey. The average overall rate for a full-service hotel investment is 10.77% according to the first quarter 2002 Korpacz report. For purposes of this analysis, and to conform to the overall rate used in the valuation of Hotels A and B, this indication has been rounded to 11%. This rate is applicable to the total assets of the business.

A good indicator of an overall capitalization rate for the real estate alone would be a property type that possesses minimal or no intangible value. Apartments, while requiring some management intensity, are generally not considered to have a large intangible component. The same Korpacz survey is used to estimate the overall capitalization rate applicable to a similar, investment-grade apartment property. This rate averaged 8.56% for the first quarter in 2002, rounded to 8.5% in Table 4.

Tangible personal property would understandably have a higher capitalization rate than either of the two returns cited previously, primarily because these assets are a depreciating class of property. Typically, hotel personalty such as furniture, mattresses, case goods, etc., is replaced as frequently as every 6 to 10 years. Generally, these items have little value at the end of the life cycle. A 15% capitalization rate for TPP is used in this analysis; this rate is based on typical furnishing finance rates and amortization periods incorporating both returns on and of value.

The percentage of the total assets of a business (TAB) that are allocated to the three components (realty, personalty, and intangibles) can be based on an iteration of the revenue percentages adjusted for various rates of return, or known values in the case of the depreciated value of personal property. Alternatively, this analysis applies percentage estimates cited in other published discussions on intangible value. The Appraisal Institute's Course 800 states: "Several recent studies have shown quite clearly that name recognition and good reputation for high-quality service ('name brand'), plus affiliation ('flag'), can add as much as 20% to 25% to the value of a successfully operating hotel."[12] Belfrage in his article indicates that "...a business component of between 15% to 25% is reasonable in this case."[13] For illustration purposes, the following allocation of value components are used: 70% real estate, 10% TPP, and 20% IAV. The calculation appears in Table 4.

In the above example, the difference between the hotel capitalization rate (R_O) and the real estate and TPP "products" (3.55%) can be divided by the intangible asset percentage (20%) to determine the required return to intangibles. Solving for X results in the following:

$$X = (R_O - (R_{RE} \times \%RE) - (R_{TPP} \times \%TPP))/\%TIA$$
$$X = (11.0 - (8.5 \times .7) - (15 \times .1))/.2$$
$$X = (11.0 - (5.95) - (1.5))/.2$$
$$X = (11.0 - 7.45)/.2$$
$$X = 3.55/.2$$
$$X = 17.75$$
$$X = 18\% \text{ (rounded)}$$

This calculation indicates the market would require an approximate 18% capitalization rate on this level of intangible revenue for comparable hotels of institutional grade. Of course, hotel assets that are not institutional grade would require a matching data set of return

Table 4	Extraction of Intangible Asset Capitalization Rate		
Position	Percent of Value	Capitalization Rate	Product
Real estate	70%	8.5%[1]	5.95
Personal property (TPP)	10%	15.0%	1.50
Intangibles (TIA)	20%	(x)	3.55
Total Rate (TAB)	100%		11.0[2]

1. Real estate R_o (based on first quarter 2002 Korpacz Real Estate Investor Survey—Apartments, average 8.56%, rounded 8.5%).

2. Hotel R_o (TAB) (based on first quarter 2002 Korpacz Real Estate Investor Survey—Full-Service Hotels, average 10.77%, rounded 11.0%).

12. Appraisal Institute, Course 800, 9-17.

13. Belfrage, 281.

requirements for both hotel and apartment (or alternate real estate vehicle) investments. Adjustments to the ratios of various components of value also may be required.

Value Calculations

Net operating income attributable to the intangible affiliation revenue capitalized at the appropriate capitalization rate (calculated in this case at 18%) offers the following value indications attributed to the affiliation for each property:

Net IIA$_a$ Revenue:
R(IIAa) = IIA$_a$ value attributed to franchise affiliation

Hotel A:
$999,324/18% = $5,551,800, rounded $5,600,000

Hotel B:
$219,433/18% = $1,219,072, rounded $1,200,000

Conclusion

Having controlled for time, location, and market characteristics, this case study demonstrates a method of allocation of IIA value attributable to affiliation (IIA$_a$). Other intangibles that are not readily quantifiable may exist. This method incorporates a cost-benefit analysis capitalizing the actual net revenues attributed to the specific franchise relationship, after deducting the associated costs. The methodology is market-based because it employs the properties' own empirical tracking reports generated by the franchise companies to estimate revenue attributed to affiliation.

Flexibility is demonstrated by comparison of the property fundamentals. Hotel A offers an understandably higher IIA$_a$ value in this case because the net IIA$_a$ revenue is substantially greater than with Hotel B; greater reliance is placed on the franchise relationship to generate room sales for Hotel A. The process automatically accounts for the lower level of reliance on affiliation of Hotel B, placing more value on the real estate due to locational attributes, a large portion of which relates to the adjacent convention center (an attribute credited to real estate only).

The reliability of this process is supported by its market-related conclusions as evidenced by the operator of Hotel B indicating dissatisfaction with the franchise affiliation. The application of this methodology indicated a substantially lower contribution to value, consistent with management's assertion. As was determined in the research process, minimal IIA$_a$ value is not necessarily related to the specific affiliation; in this case it is due to the group destination of the adjacent convention center, allowing/ requiring greater than typical direct sales. These direct sales are attributed to real estate attributes, not intangibles. The methodology presented herein inherently accounts for this factor and consistently measures the contribution to the intangibles attributable to franchise affiliation.

The specific conclusion of this study is that identified intangible assets related to affiliation (IIA$_a$) exist to the extent that revenues attributable to affiliation exceed the cost of that affiliation. The reverse is also true; when costs of affiliation approach or exceed revenues from the franchise relationship, the IIA$_a$ is limited or nonexistent. In these cases, hoteliers often inherently realize the lack of contribution by repositioning through alternate franchise affiliation or independent operations.

The following letters to the editor originally appeared in the Summer 2005 issue of *The Appraisal Journal*.

Comments on "A Strategy for Estimating Identified Intangible Asset Value: Hotel Affiliation Contribution"

I commend John W. O'Neill, PhD, MAI, and Eric E. Belfrage, MAI, for the deliberate approach that they employed in arguing their position in "A Strategy for Estimating Identified Intangible Asset Value: Hotel Affiliation Contribution" (Winter 2005). However, I find the quantity of assumptions and the subjectivity regarding these assumptions troublesome.

At least five major assumptions are used by the authors to estimate the value of the hotel intangibles. These include: (1) the proper items in the intangibles category to measure (in this case, only "identified intangible assets due to affiliation"); (2) the revenue stream generated by brand affiliation; (3) the proper flow-through rate to establish the proportion of brand affiliation revenue that flows through to net operating income; (4) the proper percentage to assign to each major asset category within the band-of-investment capitalization methodology; and (5) the proper capitalization rate to assign to real estate and to personal property in solving for the intangibles capitalization rate as extrapolated from the total rate estimated for the overall business enterprise.

In the article, the authors suggest that franchise-controlled distribution channels are meticulously tracked by franchisors to establish the delivery of room nights to hotels and that this information can be used to establish the net benefit of brand affiliation to a hotel. They admit that this calculation excludes intangible components other than brand affiliation, which is presumably too subjective to estimate. No attempt is made to augment the brand affiliation estimate with value attributable to patrons who stay because of brand recognition but do not book through brand affiliation channels or with value attributable to food and beverage purchases made by brand patrons. These are clearly additional benefits that are associated with brand affiliation that would add credibility to the result.

My particular concern is that using the percentage of rooms sold through the affiliation as a measure of intangibles contribution misses the main point regarding brand contribution. In essence, the value associated with brand affiliation can be truly estimated only when the brand is removed. In order to make this type of projection, an appraiser must estimate how many of the current patrons using the brand affiliation reservation system or otherwise staying at the property because of the brand would no longer do so if the brand were to be removed. Stated more simply: what amount of total business revenue, including food and beverage revenue, would be lost without the brand affiliation? I have seen no research on this but would guess that it would vary greatly from property to property depending on how aggressive management becomes when a brand is removed.

The need to use a rate of flow-through is understandable since gross income needs to be converted to net operating income (NOI). However, the range of possibilities offered in the article is discomforting. The amount of incremental revenue associated with brand affiliation must first be estimated, and from this estimate the proper flow-through percentage must be estimated. The authors sampled 14 full-service properties and found with these properties that the top 13% to 38% of revenue experienced a rate of flow-through to NOI of 35% to 67%. This is quite a range and can account for a sizable difference in the valuation results.

An unavoidable requirement in the authors'

methodology involves a capitalization rate for intangible assets. They acknowledge that there is no market-based return criteria for intangibles. Hence, this rate is estimated based on component weighting in a band-of-investment calculation. In particular, they need a percentage weighting the total assets of the business attributable to real estate, tangible personal property, and intangible assets in order to solve for the capitalization rate for intangibles. This raises concerns; for example, how was 10% chosen as the percentage weighting for personal property? For many hotel properties, the value of existing personal property is extremely low due to a limited market for large quantities of the same furniture. By contrast, high-quality or unique furniture in top-of-the-market properties is notoriously difficult to value.

An additional problem is the percentage estimate for intangibles in the band-of-investment calculation. The authors suggest that this percentage can be based on an iteration of revenue percentages adjusted for various rates of return. I am not sure how this would work, especially given the problem of identifying income from intangibles. Alternatively, they suggest use of a percentage cited in published sources that does not appear to be backed by comprehensive empirical studies.

The authors' examples are at odds with their use of a 20% weighting for intangibles. For Hotel A, they estimate an intangibles value of $5,600,000, or 17% of the estimated market value of the total assets of $32,900,000; for Hotel B, they estimate an intangibles value of $1,200,000, or 4% of the estimated market value of $29,200,000. If all assumptions used by the authors in the band-of-investment calculation for Hotel B remain unchanged except that intangibles are weighted at 4% and real estate at 86%, the resulting capitalization rate for the intangibles is no longer 18% but rather 55%. At a minimum, this is very confusing. How can a 20% weighting in calculation of an intangibles capitalization rate be used to estimate the intangibles value for Hotel B when the results suggest a 4% weighting is the more appropriate percentage for the same property?

I am uncomfortable with economic policy or economic decision making based on such a subjective process. This leads to the more basic issue of the motivation for estimating intangibles value in the first place. If the only reason is to satisfy a particular rule of the *Uniform Standards* of *Professional Appraisal Practice*, then perhaps it is time to rethink the intent of the rule. Perhaps a statement should be inserted to the effect that many types of real estate enterprises use personal property or possess intangible components of some variety, but efforts to separately identify the market value of these property features are extremely subjective, and the results of the exercise serve little economic purpose.

On the other hand, if the primary reason for estimating intangibles is to lower property tax assessments by assigning a portion of overall property value to intangibles, there is a better way. Specifically, rather than indirectly estimating real estate value by subtracting out personal property value and intangibles value, with all associated vagaries, a direct calculation can be substituted. For example, the authors argue that the real estate component in the band-of-investment calculation should be estimated using the capitalization rate for apartments. In other words, they make the assumption that the real estate portion of the property is equivalent to comparable-quality apartments. I do not personally agree with this due to basic construction differences; however, others are free to go before a taxing authority and make this argument (perhaps using the cost approach as their main valuation technique) and they may indeed prevail. If they were to succeed in reducing the value of total assets for a particular hotel to comparable-apartment value of the real estate alone, they would do so arguing their position directly instead of through the more complicated indirect approach presented in the article. Either way, the authors are fundamentally arguing that the real estate component for the hotel is equivalent to apartment construction, but the direct approach avoids the necessity of estimating values for tangible personal property and intangibles.

The main reason that valuing intangibles is unique among appraisal assignments is that there is no direct market validation and there never will be. Thus, any particular methodology for estimating this type of value cannot be judged superior because there is no market-based benchmark for comparison. In particular, introducing adjustments for intangibles into property tax assessments is problematic, but is one of several major issues that appraisers may need to address when making the case for tax adjustments. (For interested readers, I suggest my article on property tax published in the July 2000 issue of *The Appraisal Journal*.)

I recognize that the authors have shared a sincere effort to address what is, under current standards, a very real concern when appraising hotels and other real properties with a possible intangibles component. However, I am unconvinced regarding the methodology, primarily due to interpretation issues regarding the various assumptions. In my view, the appraisal profession needs to be extremely careful in offering solutions to problems that cannot be supported at some level with solid market evidence.

Robert W. Owens, PhD
Springfield, MO

Response to Comments on "A Strategy for Estimating Identified Intangible Asset Value: Hotel Affiliation Contribution"

We appreciate Robert W. Owens, PhD, commending us for the deliberate approach we employed in our article, "A Strategy for Estimating Identified Intangible Asset Value: Hotel Affiliation Contribution" (Winter 2005). The estimation of the value of intangible assets in hotels is something about which we are greatly interested and concerned, both from the standpoint of our research and because we have been asked to testify in court on such matters.

In our latest article, we address what we perceive to be limitations of the currently most-used approaches for estimating hotel intangible asset value. As we discuss in the article, one current approach posits that hotel intangible asset value is based on the cost of management and franchise fees. We believe this approach may be contrary to hotel owner expectations that the management and franchise affiliation should generate greater revenues than costs.

Another current approach for estimating hotel intangible asset value asserts that intangible asset value is based on hotel premiums over market occupancy and average daily rate. We believe this approach may have a shortcoming in its assumption that hotel performance premiums are strictly due to the intangible assets of the business. In fact, our research uncovered evidence suggesting that such premiums may be largely attributable to location, i.e., realty.

In a practical sense, our research may indicate that, in many instances, actual hotel intangible asset value is probably greater than that estimated by the cost of management and franchise fees, but less than that estimated by hotel premiums over market occupancy and average daily rate. Thus, we believe that the existing methodologies serve the benefit of framing an important topic of discussion and analysis. We hope that our research more precisely pinpoints a market-based methodology that is useful to appraisers and other analysts. As Dr. Owens points out, such a methodology must be "supported at some level with solid market evidence."

We hope that our research also serves the purpose of bringing a broader perspective to this topic. Specifically, we bring both an academic and professional perspective to this issue.

Having appraised hundreds of hotels, we always appreciate discourse on this topic; however, we disagree with many of Dr. Owens's points. For example, he suggests that the percentage of guest rooms sold through a hotel brand affiliation may not accurately reflect intangible asset value because a hotel's loss of its affiliation could be minimized by aggressive management that replaces displaced business. We concur that a loss of affiliation could be minimized by aggressive management replacing displaced business, but would argue that such aggressive management would in fact represent intangible value. Thus, our methodology for estimating intangible value subsumes any such remaining intangible value, post affiliation.

Dr. Owens suggests that an easier approach to estimate intangibles is indirectly through the cost approach. While we agree that applying the cost approach would be easier, we disagree that it is the most appropriate technique to apply for hotel valuation. In fact, in our discussions with hotel investors, we consistently find that grantees do not establish an acceptable purchase price based on the cost approach. Rather, employing the income approach, supported by the sales comparison approach, more accurately reflects the hotel marketplace.

An interesting point raised by Dr. Owens is the basic issue regarding the motivation for estimating intangibles in the first place. He suggests that the primary reason for doing so may be to satisfy the *Uniform Standards of Professional Appraisal Practice* and that perhaps it is time to rethink the intent of the rule. That point may be a legitimate one. While we do not necessarily intend to support the Uniform Standards of Professional Appraisal Practice in its current form, we also do not necessarily anticipate dramatic changes to it in the near future, and therefore, we have suggested a practical methodology practitioners may implement that is reliable, valid, and satisfies current professional requirements.

Ultimately, we agree with Dr. Owens that the primary reason that valuing intangibles is unique in appraisal assignments is that there is no direct market validation and there never will be. Based on our research, we believe that our methodology represents the state-of-the-art, market-supported approach with respect to such intangible asset value estimation for hotels.

John W. O'Neill, PhD, MAI, CHE
University Park, PA

Eric E. Belfrage, MAI, CRE, ISHC
Columbus, OH

Hotel Asset Allocation: Separating the Tangible Personalty

Heather J. Reichardt and David C. Lennhoff, MAI, SRA

This article originally appeared in the Winter 2003 issue of *Assessment Journal*, © 2003 by International Association of Assessing Officers (IAAO). Reproduced with permission. All rights reserved by IAAO.

Operating hotels are labor-intensive businesses that comprise much more than just real property. Typically they contain three major components: real property, tangible personal property, and intangible personal property. Furthermore, the latter two–the personalty–can represent a significant part of the market value of the total assets. Stephen Rushmore, for example, says a hotel's FF&E "can account for up to 25 percent of the total property value" (Rushmore and Baum 2001). Figure 1 illustrates the components that frequently make up the total assets of a hotel going concern. (Business valuers show monetary assets, including inventory, as a separate category. The Appraisal Institute lumps those assets in with the personal property: cash as an intangible and inventory as tangible personalty.)

For various reasons–not the least of which is the *Uniform Standards of Professional Appraisal Practice* (USPAP)–the total value must be allocated among the components. (The USPAP mandate is to "analyze the effect on value of any personal property, trade fixtures, or intangible items that are not real property but are included in the appraisal. A separate valuation, developed in compliance with the Standard pertinent to the type of property involved, is required when the value of a nonrealty item or combination of such items is significant to the overall value.") If a cost approach is used and the purpose is to estimate the market value of the total assets of the business (MVTAB), then the tangible and intangible personal property would be separately valued and added in to the value of the real property. In the case of the income and sales comparison approaches, if the purpose is to estimate just the market value of the real property, the contributions of the tangible and intangible personal property would have to be deducted or allocated.

Reynolds observed some time ago that each of these items "requires a fair return on its respec-tive investment worth" (Reynolds 1986). That there is at least an expectation of such a return is self evident: Why else would an investor make the investment? A return of investment, of course, is also expected. This concept is no different than a mortgage loan: The lender gives the loan amount in expectation of receiving the full amount back, plus an acceptable return on that amount. It is also consistent with basic business value principles, which state that "the value of the enterprise is dependent on the ability of all the assets to earn a reasonable return. The raison d'être of business assets is to provide a return on the investment required to obtain them" (Smith and Parr 1994).

Judging from the number of professional journal articles, lots of thought has gone into the topic of allocating the assets. Examples have been proffered. Still, areas of gray persist. This article will limit itself to the tangible personalty;

Heather J. Reichardt *is a director of lodging property tax for Marriott International, Inc.*

David C. Lennhoff, MAI, SRA, *is president of PGH Consulting, LLC, which has its office in Rockville, Maryland. He has been closely involved with the topic of this book since serving as a member of the Appraisal Institute's Study Group on Business Enterprise Value in 1997-1998. He was a development team member, chief reviewer, and frequent instructor of the original Appraisal Institute Course 800, Separating Real and Personal Property from Intangible Business Assets, and editor of the first edition of* A Business Enterprise Value Anthology, *and has been a frequent contributor to* The Appraisal Journal *since 1982.*

The statements made or views expressed by authors in Assessment Journal *do not necessarily represent a policy position of the International Association of Assessing Officers.*

18

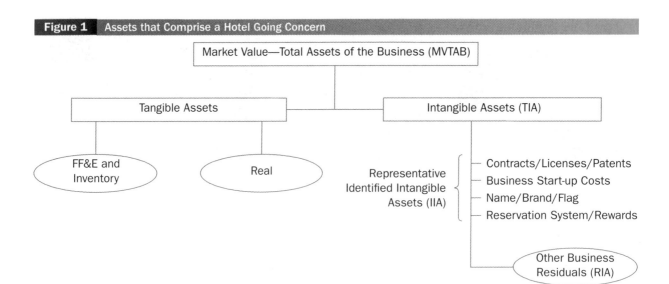

Figure 1 Assets that Comprise a Hotel Going Concern

for a hotel, this primarily comprises the furniture, fixtures, and equipment. It will review the various issues relating to allocation–principal among them being the basis for the return "of" amount; what role, if any, the assessed value of the personalty plays; and methods for capturing the return "on" amount–then describe a straightforward, theoretically sound way to do it.

Current Thinking: Tracing the Evolution

Recognition of the need to allocate components of an operating enterprise has existed for some time. Examples of ways to do it are harder to find. Probably the first widely accepted method for separating the tangible personalty from the total assets for hotel properties was presented by Stephen Rushmore in his monograph for the American Institute of Real Estate Appraisers, *The Valuation of Hotels and Motels* (Rushmore 1978). The same model, with minor variations, appeared in subsequent versions of the book and numerous articles by him. Challenges to it appeared quickly (Hennessey 1993). Most, unfortunately, did not include an alternative method.

The most significant issue with respect to Rushmore's model is the intermingling of a return "of" personal property and a replacement allowance for it. The need to deduct both a return "of" and a return "on" is not disputed (Rushmore and Baum 2001). Rushmore claims that the replacement allowance accounts for the return "of" the investment in the personalty. This concept is quickly dismissed by a simple

example. A replacement allowance is almost always deducted in a conventional apartment appraisal, to allow for replacement of such things as the roof. By doing so, however, no one would suggest that you end up with the value of an apartment without a roof. Why then would it be reasonable to suggest that the deduction of a replacement allowance for the hotel tangible personal property results in the value of the real property without it? Similarly, when a hotel sells, the price for the going concern–that is, the price for the total assets of the business–is typically negotiated using income and expense assumptions that include a replacement allowance for both the furniture, fixtures, and equipment (FF&E) and other short-lived items. The purchaser understands, however, that he or she will be acquiring the land, building, and FF&E. The investor certainly does not believe the deduction for a replacement allowance results in a price exclusive of the personalty. Clearly, both a return "of" and a replacement allowance are necessary.

Return "of" Tangible Personal Property

Return of capital is defined in the *Dictionary of Real Estate Appraisal* as "the recovery of invested capital, usually through income and/or reversion" (Appraisal Institute 2002). An investor in a hotel contributes the value of the personal property–mostly FF&E–in the expectation of recapturing that investment in much the same way the investment in the land and buildings is recaptured. Figure 2 illustrates this concept.

Figure 2   Return "of" and "on" FF&E

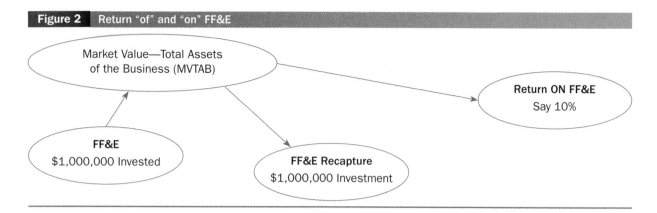

A valuation of the real property component of a hotel going concern must properly exclude the personal property. In a cost approach, it is simply not added in. If this method is applicable, it is often the most compelling. Older hotels, however, usually involve substantial depreciation, and frequently the cost approach cannot be applied reliably. As an alternative, the appraiser can work with an income approach and sales comparison approach. Both of these, however, have as their starting point either the income or value of the total assets of the business. Therefore, both require a deduction that represents the market value, as of the date of appraisal, of the personalty in place. Often a good starting point for the appropriate amount is cost new, from which depreciation must be deducted. Benchmarks for the cost are amply available in various hotel company franchise offering circulars (FOCs). Another source of FF&E costs across various product lines is the 1998 survey conducted by US Realty Consultants, Inc. (Hathaway and Iaannucci 1998). Cost is not value, however, and care must be exercised when considering it as a measure.

Pitfalls

Often, the assessed value of the tangible personal property is used as a surrogate for its market value. Usually, however, these amounts cannot be relied on as a reasonable indicator. There are several reasons for this.

First, most assessments of the tangible personal property component are based on voluntary reporting of original costs by the owner/manager of the property. Every owner has a different view of what is reportable and taxable. Also, the amount paid is frequently not a legitimate basis for value. Large hotel owners and operators are able to purchase in bulk, at prices that would not be available to an individual owner in the hypothetical market of the value estimate. It is not the price to the current owner that is important. Rather, it is the amount a single, typical buyer would pay, as of the date of appraisal.

Second, most jurisdictions set the value of the tangible personal property reported based on "percent good" tables that in many cases do not accurately reflect the tangible personal property market. Also, the actual experience or practice of hotel operators often does not support the useful lives used by the jurisdictions for hotel FF&E.

Table 1 illustrates the variety of actual 2001 "fair market values" indicated by tangible personal property assessments for comparable hotels outfitted with similar FF&E located in different jurisdictions across the United States.

Replacement Allowance *Is* an Expense

The idea that a replacement allowance removes the tangible personal property from the income and results in income to the real property reveals a fundamental misunderstanding of the concept.

Table 1	FF&E Assessment Comparison			
State	**# Rooms**	**Year Built**	**Business Personal Property Fair Market Value**	**Fair Market Value/Room**
CA	344	1991	$1,946,354	$5,658
GA	372	1990	1,009,983	2,715
MD	275	1990	1,638,340	5,958
VA	254	1990	683,621	2,691

Source: Marriott International, Inc.

The definition in the *Dictionary of Real Estate Appraisal* (Appraisal Institute 2002) is as follows:

> An allowance that provides for the periodic replacement of building components that wear out more readily than the building itself and must be replaced during the building's economic life.

It is one of three categories of operating expenses recognized by the Appraisal Institute as "the periodic expenditures necessary to maintain the real property and continue the production of revenue" (Appraisal Institute 2001). The other two categories are fixed expenses and variable expenses. Although the definition refers to building components, an investment in a hotel property requires a replacement allowance expense for the tangible personalty as well. This is because the revenue production at issue with a hotel is that related to the total assets rather than just the real property.

Sophisticated hotel investors and managers are aware of the necessity of maintaining not only the condition of the hotel real estate but also the FF&E. Most management contracts with nationally recognized hotel managers include language that requires the establishment of an FF&E reserve account. These funds are used on an ongoing basis to maintain the marketable condition of the property. They are not used for routine repairs and maintenance. In fact, the two are frequently separately referenced in the management agreement.

The following is the definition of an "FF&E Reserve" from an actual hotel management contract between a large hotel real estate investment trust (REIT) ownership entity and a nationally known hotel management company.

> Management company shall establish a reserve account (the "FF&E Reserve") in a bank designated by Management Company (and approved by Owner, such approval not to be unreasonably withheld) to cover the cost of:
>
> i.   Replacements and renewals to the Hotel's FF&E and
>
> ii.   Certain routine Capital Expenditures such as exterior and interior painting, resurfacing building walls, floors, roofs and parking areas, and replacing folding walls and the like....

The fact that the contract specifies the reserve fund be used for both tangible personal property replacement and short-lived building components is a strong indication that a hotel replacement allowance is simply intended to serve the function of expense rather than as a vehicle for allocating, recapturing, or deducting the personalty.

In addition to the requirement to set up the reserve account, each contract typically states the exact amount to be set aside, usually expressed as a percentage of gross revenues. Other sources for an appropriate amount to allow for this expense category include Smith Travel Research publications such as the *HOST Report*, and any of the several good investment criteria surveys that track hotels. Another excellent reference detailing the true cost of necessary replacement allowances is *CapEx 2000–A Study of Capital Expenditures in the U.S. Hotel Industry*, published by the International Society of Hospitality Consultants. Note, as with all real property valuations, the amount used in income capitalization must be consistent with the relationship expressed by the overall capitalization rate.

Return "on" FF&E Investment

When a company considers adding a new employee, it does so expecting to recoup in one way or another the cost of the employee—salary, benefits, etc.—and earn a return on that cost. In a similar way, when an investor decides to invest tangible personal property in an operating business, he anticipates receiving both the value of the personalty back plus a return on it. If all he expected to get back were the value of the personalty, why would he invest? This return "on" is most easily handled by a deduction from the income to the total assets of the business and is usually calculated by multiplying the value of the tangible personalty by the appropriate yield rate. See figure 2 for an illustration of this concept.

The rate of return would be higher than that for the real estate and lower than that for the intangibles, considering the relative risks represented by each. Rushmore suggested a rate equal to a chattel mortgage as indicative of the cost of capital for this item—or, in the absence of direct evidence of a chattel mortgage, a rate two to five points above real estate mortgages (Rushmore and Rubin 1984). There are some precautions that must be considered in making these adjustments/deductions. First, care must be exercised in selecting an appropriate rate, as all investments cannot be expected to provide equal returns. For example, the addition of a four-car garage on a $150,000 house would undoubtedly result in less of a return than the same garage added to an $800,000 house. The same concept would apply to the FF&E investment. Also, it would be incorrect to deduct unrealizable returns on the personalty if the entire investment is performing so poorly that the real estate appears to be worthless (this plight can occur). Obviously, in such a situation, the income cannot provide adequate return to any of the components, or at least not at the level that might have been anticipated going in.

Summary

Most appraisers recognize that a hotel going concern is comprised of real property and tangible and intangible personal property. Properly recognizing the intangibles causes the bulk of the controversy. Methods for allocation of the tangible personalty, however, are often deficient, too, usually for one of the following reasons: First, the replacement allowance is confused with providing a return "of" deduction. As a result, an expense for "reserves" is made, but the return "of" is not captured. In this instance, even if a return "on" is deducted, the result is a value estimate that is purportedly only real property, but actually includes tangible personal property too. The situation is exacerbated by assuming only FF&E is included in the allowance, thereby failing to provide sufficient monies even to cover just the replacement allowance expense for the short-lived items. Replacement allowances for realty-related components, such as the roof or paving, are not addressed. Second, the value of the tangible personal property is deducted from the bottom line, but no other deduction is made. This results in an overstatement of the real property, as the return "on" the personalty has not been captured.

The concept is really quite simple: All elements of a going concern require expectation of a return "of" the investment and a return "on" it. Therefore, if you are valuing just the real property component of a hotel going concern and you are using income or sales prices (comparables) that represent the total assets of the business, both a return "of" and "on" the tan-

gible personal property must be accounted for by deductions from either the income or value. In addition, as with all real property valuations, a replacement allowance is a necessary expense and must be provided, either as a line item deduction or through the use of a higher overall capitalization rate.

References

Appraisal Foundation. 2002. *Uniform Standards of Professional Appraisal Practice.* Washington, DC: Appraisal Foundation.

Appraisal Institute. 2001. *The Appraisal of Real Estate,* 12th ed. Chicago: Appraisal Institute.

Appraisal Institute. 2002. *The Dictionary of Real Estate Appraisal,* 4th ed. Chicago: Appraisal Institute.

Hathaway, Peter, and John Iaannucci. (Fall) 1998. Survey shows FF&E cost disparity between limited and full-service hotels. See jwalker@usrc.com.

Hennessey, Sean F. (October) 1993. Myths about hotel business and personalty values. *The Appraisal Journal.*

Reynolds, Anthony. (October) 1986. Attributing hotel income to real estate and personalty. *The Appraisal Journal:* 616.

Rushmore, Stephen. 1978. *The Valuation of Hotels and Motels.* Chicago: American Institute of Real Estate Appraisers.

Rushmore, Stephen, and Erich Baum. 2001. *Hotels and Motels–Valuations and Market Studies.* Chicago: Appraisal Institute.

Rushmore, Stephen, and Karen E. Rubin. (April) 1984. The valuation of hotels and motels for assessment purposes. *The Appraisal Journal,* 270–88.

Smith, Gordon V., and Russell L. Parr. 1994. *Valuation of Intellectual Property and Intangible Assets.* New York: John Wiley & Sons.

Part III
Miscellaneous Property Types

Use of the Income Approach in Valuing a Sand and Gravel Property in a Condemnation Proceeding

Thomas W. Hamilton, PhD, CRE, FRICS, and Jan A. Sell, MAI, SRA, FRICS, SR/WA, CCIM

Reprinted with permission from *Real Estate Issues*® (Vol. 34, No. 2, 2009), published by The Counselors of Real Estate® . CRE® is a nonprofit professional organization for leading real estate advisors around the world. Visit www.cre.org for more information.

Introduction

The legal concept of "market value" is applied by courts to determine the amount of just compensation for takings. "Market value" has been defined as "what a willing buyer would pay in cash to a willing seller," but "just compensation" has no clear definition or valuation methodology. This article finds that valuing sand and gravel property using the income approach is the most appropriate method of valuation, and that valuation experts should use the same valuation process that is used by owner/operators when buying or leasing land.

Valuing Special Use Properties

The essential problem in the valuation of special use properties is the lack of availability of adequate data from the sales of comparable properties. In some cases, there may be a lack of sales within a reasonably defined market area or a lack of specific information about the existing sales to make essential adjustments and draw a reasonable value conclusion.

In recent years, the Supreme Court has stated, "when market value has been too difficult to find, or when its application would result in manifest injustice to an owner or the public, courts have fashioned and applied other standards."[1] This situation is usually considered to exist when the property involved in the taking is a special use property. Sand and gravel properties, by their nature, are special use properties.

Comparable sand and gravel sales are relatively few and infrequent compared to other types of properties, such as office buildings or retail commercial buildings. In instances where some local sales of sand and gravel properties

have occurred, it is often difficult, if not impossible, to analyze these sales because the price paid depends on the remaining reserves (or degree of depletion) as of the date of sale, and this information is usually unavailable. According to the Uniform Appraisal Standards for Federal Land Acquisitions:

> In order to properly develop a sales comparison approach to value for a mineral bearing property, the appraiser needs to understand the level of information available concerning the mineralization found on the subject property. It is then important to identify comparable sales that had similar levels of information concerning mineralization available at the time of sale. The verification of data concerning the comparable sales is a critical

Thomas W. Hamilton, PhD, CRE, FRICS, *is associate professor of real estate at the University of St. Thomas in St. Paul, Minnesota. He earned a bachelor's, master's and doctorate degree in urban land economics from the University of Wisconsin-Madison. Hamilton also earned a master's degree in finance from the University of Wyoming. He has published several articles on property tax assessment issues and real estate valuation, and regularly consults with energy and telecommunication companies.*

Jan A. Sell, MAI, SRA, FRICS, SR/WA, CCIM, *is a real estate appraiser and consultant and president of Sell & Associates, Inc. in Tempe, Arizona. He earned a bachelor's degree in business administration from Arizona State University in Tempe, Arizona, and a master's degree in real estate appraisal from the University of St. Thomas in St. Paul, Minnesota. Sell holds a real estate broker's license in Arizona and manages numerous investment groups. He has been involved in valuation of real estate property interests since 1972 and has been recognized as an expert witness in numerous state and federal courts.*

component of this analysis, and the assistance of experts in identifying all necessary areas of inquiry during the verification process may be required.[2]

Sand and gravel operators mine minerals (aggregate) for use in almost all types of construction. Demand for the materials is based upon the need for new construction materials for both private and public projects. Owners of sand and gravel businesses either purchase or lease land for their operations. When leasing land, they negotiate a rate per ton, or a percentage of gross sales for all extracted materials. This rate is referred to as a royalty rate. When all of the materials are mined, the landowner or operator can then use the property for an inert landfill. Materials deposited for use in reclaiming the land are charged at a rate per ton, and property owners are paid a royalty rate on a per-ton basis.

The income approach is generally reliable for sand and gravel properties because it is based upon estimating the net rental income derived from royalty rates or the sale of material over a period of time. The value is then estimated using a discounted cash flow analysis.

Understanding Market Value and Condemnation Proceedings

In a condemnation proceeding, the legal concept of "market value" is applied by the courts to determine the amount of just compensation for takings. Market value has been defined as "what a willing buyer would pay in cash to a willing seller,"[3] and "just compensation"[4] has never been reduced to a single formula. "Rather than a general formula, various ways of valuing property are appropriate depending on the circumstances."[5] The market value concept implies a prospective or hypothetical sale of the subject property and is generally viewed by courts to correspond most closely to the direct sales comparison (or market data) approach to value. Although in most cases this approach is preferred, in the case of "special purpose" or "special use" properties, other methods may be considered by courts to be more appropriate.

"Properties treated by courts as special use properties include church properties, cemeteries, schools, historic properties, commercial enterprises such as a warehouse, a scrap-metal yard, a sand and gravel production business, a horseradish factory... ."[6] The concepts of special use properties and special purpose properties are similar in that they imply peculiar or unique characteristics inherent to the property that would not normally be found in other, recently sold properties. A special purpose property is defined as one that:

- "has physical design features peculiar to a specific use;
- has no apparent market other than to an owner-user;
- has no feasible economic alternative use."[7]

In most jurisdictions, where a property is determined by the courts to be a special use property, three alternative methods of valuation may be considered: the cost approach, the income approach and/or a modified market data approach. The valuation expert's role becomes magnified in the condemnation of a special use property; as such, the selection of methods or techniques must be soundly demonstrated to the jury. The valuation of a special use property is a prime example of where an expert's opinion could be excluded at trial if the expert uses a legally improper valuation method. Additionally, the expert's opinion must meet the Daubert Standard[8] to ensure relevancy and reliability. Applicable questions regarding the admissibility of an approach, method or technique include:

- have you used this approach before when appraising this type of property;
- are there treatises that support use of this approach;
- do other valuation experts use this technique or approach;
- is this technique recognized and used by market participants; and
- are there published articles regarding the valuation approach?

Because of these issues, an expert witness must be careful that his or her opinions and/or approaches to value are not excluded from court testimony. In order to accomplish this task, certain groundwork must be employed.

The Valuation Rubric

The valuation expert must be knowledgeable on the property type and have experience in appraising such a property in the geographical area. The valuation expert also must be able to cite treatises or publications that support the methodology, including:

- *The Appraisal of Real Estate*, 13th Ed.;

- *Real Estate Valuation in Litigation,* 2nd Ed., by J. D. Eaton, MAI, SRA;
- Various publications by the International Right of Way Association;
- Local publications that address valuation issues within the particular jurisdiction;
- Case law;
- Numerous articles, guides and references that describe the proper valuation methods and procedures.

A valuation expert must decide upon the methodology that will be employed in a valuation assignment for a special use property that is not atypical to other valuation assignments. It is also the valuation expert's responsibility to use the approaches that are supported by the market. Therefore, even with a multitude of good comparable sales, the valuation expert can also use the income approach.

Case Analysis

In a study conducted to determine the process for buying or leasing property, eight sand and gravel property owners and/or operators in the Phoenix metropolitan area were surveyed. The survey findings revealed consistent criteria used by the owner/operators in the decision-making process when purchasing or leasing a sand and gravel property. All eight participants stated that their decisions were based upon the quantity and quality of the material beneath the overburden (surface or top soil). To estimate the mineable reserves, owners need reasonably reliable information, and in some cases owners engage an engineer to perform test borings at certain locations and depths across the property. The owner/operator would then develop a mining plan based upon the mineable reserves, which would result in a residual amount that they could pay for the property. All eight participants said that they did not use the price per acre in their decision-making process. The conclusion drawn from these interviews is that the actions of knowledgeable parties in this market segment rely on a cash flow analysis (income approach) in their decision-making process. Under these conditions, it is typical that such special use properties cannot be valued reliably using only the sales comparison approach. "The income capitalization approach can be especially applicable when the property under appraisal is already being mined, and thus the historical in-

come stream flow from the property is available for analysis."[9] For properties that produce a predictable income stream, the income approach may be considered by the courts. Stated simply, the method involves estimating the annual net income likely to be produced by the property and the number of years over which the owner could reasonably expect this level of income. "The present value of this income stream is calculated by applying a (discount) rate, which is intended to approximate the net rate of return on investment reasonably expected by the owner."[10]

Profit Considerations

In most condemnation cases, the profit from a business operation carried on at the property is not considered a valid basis for estimating just compensation. This is due to the speculative nature of profit estimates, and to depending more on the nature of the business operation and/or the skill of the business owner (value of the enterprise) than on the intrinsic characteristics of the property itself (value of the real property). "In applying the income capitalization approach, appraisers must take care to consider only the income that the property itself will produce—not income produced from the business enterprise conducted on the property (i.e., the business of mining)."[11] In specific relation to a sand and gravel property, this situation is unique because operators both purchase and lease properties specifically for the mining of materials. In both scenarios, the cost of operations is taken into consideration. When property is leased, the operator pays rent to the landowner in the form of a royalty. The royalty is a dollar amount per ton of extracted material. The royalty rate is typically based upon the quality of the material, the location of the source relative to the market, the supply and demand for the product, the cost associated with the extraction and the price that the market would bear for the product. "The royalty is the amount that a buyer would pay the landowner for the right to remove the materials, with the buyer bearing the expense of extraction."[12]

Court Precedence

"In United States v. 103.38 Acres of Land (1984), the Sixth Circuit Court of Appeals held that the royalty capitalization method would be competent evidence of mineral value if:

- an active market for the minerals in place is established;
- transactions in the market commonly take the form of royalty payments;
- the valuation witness possesses the requisite industry experience to give an opinion."[13, 14]

"The income approach to value, using a royalty rate in a sand and gravel property, was determined to be the appropriate method in Maricopa County v. Robert Barkley, (1990)."[15]

The Supreme Court of Missouri in St. Louis v. Union Quarry accepted the income method based on the income stream being both stable and directly attributable to the property itself rather than to an activity conducted on the property that relies on the talent or skills of the owner. As was explained in Union Quarry: "The general rule (that lost profits are inadmissible), however, must be given an exception *ex necessitate* where the business is inextricably related to and connected with the land where it is located, so that an appropriation of the land means an appropriation of the business; where the evidence of net profits apparently is clear, certain and easily calculable, based upon complete records; where past income figures are relatively stable, average and representative, and future projections are based upon reasonable probability of permanence or persistence in the future, so that conjecture is minimized as far as possible, and where the body fixing the damages would be at a loss to make an intelligent valuation without primary reference to the earning power of the business."[16]

Condemning agencies often argue that an income approach cannot be used in the valuation of a sand and gravel operation because it is a business enterprise. Consequently, the property owner will argue that real property rights are being acquired and an income approach is warranted since "minerals are an integral part of real estate, and mineral rights are real property under U.S. law."[17] In the case of a sand and gravel operation, the business value (business enterprise) is not part of the equation because royalty rates are used as the "rental income" to the real property only. As noted previously, royalty income is what a landowner would charge an operator to mine materials situated on the property. "In developing an estimate of value by the income capitalization approach for a mineral property, it is generally recognized that the most appropriate method of capitalization is yield capitalization, most notably discounted cash flow (DCF) analysis. The income that may be capitalized is the royalty income, and not the income or profit generated by the business of mining and selling the mineral. For this reason, the income capitalization approach, when applied to mineral properties, is sometimes referred to as the royalty income approach. DCF analysis has been recognized by the courts as an appropriate method of valuation to be employed in the valuation of mineral properties."[18]

According to the survey conducted of sand and gravel operators in the Phoenix metropolitan area, it is common practice to pay landowners a royalty rate on a per-ton basis for extracting aggregate materials. Therefore, the market supports the use of an income approach in the valuation of sand and gravel properties. "In developing an estimated income stream, the property royalty rate can be derived from comparable mineral lease transactions, and the mineral unit price to which the royalty rate is applied may be derived from appropriate market transactions."[19]

The U.S. Securities and Exchange Commission (SEC) requirements regarding the reporting of mineable materials focus on investor protection. The basis of this protection is mineable reserves, and these reserves must be proven and probable. The SEC rules similarly restrict the reporting of valuation estimates of reserves. The SEC's definition of a reserve is: "That part of a mineral deposit which could be economically and legally extracted or produced at the time of the reserve."

This SEC policy is intended to reduce speculative value estimates based upon non-quantitative mineral reserves. Therefore, it is imperative for an appraiser to develop his or her opinion of market value based upon the quantity and quality of the mineral reserves. Again, referencing interviews of operators, their purchase or lease decision is based upon mineable aggregate. Everyone surveyed stated that, as part of their "due diligence," they would want information concerning the quantity and quality of the materials. Some indicated that, at times, this may include performing core drillings.

Another recent specific example of special use properties being valued using the income approach for condemnation is that of a privately owned airport parking lot. This case faced the courts in North Carolina in Charlotte v. Huriahe, et. al., (2006). "The matter at stake was substantial–the city's sales comparison approach would award $842,000, while the landowner's income approach totaled $2,000,000. In the end, both the trial court and the Court of Appeals sided with the landowner, finding that a well-constructed income approach provided the more accurate indication of land value of an airport parking lot."[20]

Clearly, this process is also directly applicable to quarry operations, landfill sites, sand and gravel operations and various other extractive industries where the income to the owner is predictable and is directly derived from the land itself. In most of these cases, the property includes a resource or some intrinsic element that is subject to depletion. Based on its rate of extraction, the level and duration of future income may be readily projected. In addition, its value (if any) once depleted may be estimated and taken to be a reversionary value. Therefore, such properties are ideally suited to discounted cash flow analysis and may be valued on the basis of their net present value.

Summary

The income approach may be used in estimating market value in condemnation proceedings for certain property types, including special use properties. Based on the above findings, the most appropriate method of valuing sand and gravel property is the income approach. For this property type, valuation experts should use the same valuation process that is used by owner/operators when buying or leasing land, if only to reflect the marketplace and these market transactions. In such cases, the royalty income stream is both stable and directly attributable to the property itself, rather than to the business activity conducted on the property or one that relies primarily on the talent or skill of the owner. Furthermore, the future royalty income may be reliably forecasted, analyzed and valued based on a conventional discounted cash flow analysis.

Endnotes

1. Duvall, Richard O. and Black, David S., JD, "Methods of Valuating Properties Without Compare," *Appraisal Journal,* (January 2000) p. 2.
2. Uniform Appraisal Standards for Federal Land Acquisitions, Chicago, IL, Section D-11, p. 97.
3. United States v. Commodities Trading Corp., 339 U.S. 121, (1950).
4. United States v. Cors, 337 U.S. 325, 69 S. ct. 1086, 93 L. Ed. 1392, (1949).
5. United States v. Miller, 317 U.S. 369, 63 S. ct. 276, 87 L. Ed. 336, (1943).
6. Duvall, op. cit p. 3.
7. Schumtz, George I., *Condemnation Appraisal Handbook,* (Englewood Cliffs, NJ: Prentice Hall, 1963), p. 163.
8. Daubert v. Merrell Dow Pharmaceuticals 509 US 579 (1993).
9. Uniform Appraisal Standards, op.cit. p. 97.
10. Duvall, op. cit. p. 6.
11. Uniform Appraisal Standards, op.cit. p. 97.
12. Maricopa County v. Robert Barkley, 168 Ariz. 234; 812 P.2d 1052; 1990 Ariz. App. LEXIS 398; 75 Ariz. Adv. Rep. 48, (1990).
13. Nichols on Eminent Domain, 3d, 14F21.
14. United States v. 103.38 Acres of Land, 660 F.2d 208, (6th Cir. 1984).
15. Maricopa County op. cit.
16. Duvall, op. cit. p. 7.
17. Ellis, Trevor R., & Abbot, David M., Jr., *Regulatory Trends in Mineral Property Valuation – An International Perspective,* (ASA, AI and ASFMRA), 31.
18. Uniform Appraisal Standards, op. cit. p. 98.
19. Ibid.
20. *The Greenfield Advisor,* Seattle, Washington. Issue 2-3, June 2006, p. 1.

Quantifying Net Income Attributable to Business Intangibles for a Hotel-Operated Full-Service Day Spa

Peter A. Wolman

This article originally appeared in the Fall 2005 issue of *The Appraisal Journal.*

For competitive reasons, upper-upscale and luxury hotels are increasingly adding full-service day spas. Because spas present the opportunity for a separate profit center, appraisal analysis is necessary to determine the existence of business intangibles and their magnitude. The Uniform Standards of Professional Appraisal Practice (USPAP) requires, depending on the circumstances, that appraisers identify non-realty (tangible and intangible personal property) included in an appraisal and, if appropriate, the effect on value of such non-realty. Based on an actual assignment, this article provides a straightforward methodology for such identification and quantification, followed by a test of reasonableness.

Spa resort hotels, where spa services are integral to the hotel operation itself, have existed for many years as a specialized subset of the hospitality industry. Now, the full-service day spa,[1] or some variation of it, is becoming an increasingly common ancillary feature at upper-upscale and luxury hotels.[2]

In an intensely competitive hotel business environment, a day spa offers another point of differentiation, although certain upper-tier hotels are adding a spa simply to remain competitive. At some hotels, a spa may only amount to high-cost, uneconomic "amenity creep," whereas at others it presents a new potential profit center as an operated department. That notwithstanding, a spa may also incrementally increase hotel revenue per available room (RevPAR) by virtue of being a desirable feature/amenity and by conferring (or enhancing) a prestige factor. Although all business-oriented real estate, including hotels, requires analysis for business intangibles, this article focuses on a day spa because (1) it is one of the newer hotel-operated departments of significance that an appraiser may confront (others include specialized recreational facilities such as a water park), and (2) in many circumstances it is a hotel's highest revenue generating "other operated department."

In many hotel assignments, appraisers value total assets of the business (TAB), which includes real property, and tangible and intangible personal property,[3] because that is typically sold or financed. However, certain situations–such as acquisition accounting, *ad valorem* tax assessments, and recordation/transfer fees–require valuation (or allocation) of only the real and tangible property components of TAB. In this type of

Peter A. Wolman *is vice president of Delta Associates, a Transwestern Company in Vienna, Virginia. He earned a BS in business administration from the Real Estate Center in the Kogod College of Business Administration at American University in Washington, DC.*

---

1. A day spa may be defined as "A clean, safe, and nurturing environment offering an array of spa treatments administered by highly trained and licensed technicians. It is usually a self-contained facility, but may also be combined with a salon. Clients frequent this spa for a few hours or a day. Overnight accommodations are not required." Day Spa Association.

2. In 2003, there were an estimated 12,100 spas in the United States that generated approximately 136 million spa visits. The largest segment was day spas, which accounted for 60% of spa visits and 49% of industry revenue. Comparatively, although the resort/hotel segment captured 27% of spa visits, it garnered 41% of industry revenue. International Spa Association, *ISPA 2004 Spa Industry Study;* http://www.experienceispa.com/ISPA.

3. See Appraisal Institute, Course 800 Handbook: *Separating Real and Personal Property from Intangible Business Assets* (Chicago: Appraisal Institute, 2001), 4–11, 5–3 to 5–11; and Appraisal Institute, *The Appraisal of Real Estate,* 12th ed. (Chicago: Appraisal Institute, 2001), 641–644. Also see David C. Lennhoff, ed., *A Business Enterprise Value Anthology* (Chicago: Appraisal Institute, 2001).

appraisal, USPAP requires a two-phase analysis. First, relevant to the type and definition of value, and intended use of the appraisal, Standards Rule 1-2(e)(iii) requires identification of "any personal property, trade fixtures, or intangible items that are not real property but are included in the appraisal."[4] Second, given the scope of work, USPAP Standards Rule 1-4(g) requires analysis of "the effect on value of any personal property, trade fixtures, or intangible items that are not real property but are included in the appraisal."[5] This article presents analysis techniques applicable to identifying the existence or absence of business intangibles for a hotel-operated spa, and if present, a methodology to quantify such intangibles.

Spas are a logical extension for upper-tier hotels because of the steady stream of prospective clients in a relaxed atmosphere. Spas and such hotels tend to enjoy a symbiotic relationship, because a day spa is quite complementary to a luxury hotel, as evidenced by the acquisition of Bliss Spas by Starwood Hotels & Resorts Worldwide, Inc., in January 2004. Marketing appeal of a spa as a stress eliminator and luxurious indulgence is well received by clientele already attracted to luxury-oriented hotels. Yet, despite their glamorous image, many day spas do not require especially high-end real estate in which to successfully conduct their business. Although a few spas in hotels are elaborate structures, a recently inspected example was below-grade, windowless, converted space that nonetheless was quite suitable for operation of a rather successful spa business.

Valuation Issues

Similar to other operated departments in a hotel (e.g., conference/convention services, and food and beverages), a successful spa will generate net operating income (I_o) above market rent for the real estate. That excess net income (that is, I_o exceeding market rent that a spa operator would pay for use and occupancy of the real estate) is an intangible because it reflects a return to the spa business, not to the real property. As spas represent primarily a personal service with comparatively minimal real estate (as evidenced by relatively high gross sales per square foot), it is rather obvious that a successful operation involves a considerable amount of business intangibles.

The question of market rent for the real estate is directly answered when a hotel owner/operator decides to lease space at market rate and terms to a spa operator. These arrangements are similar to hotels that lease space to restaurant operators such as Ruth's Chris, Fleming's, Shula's or other popular, branded national chains. Of course, by doing so, hotel owners cede all potential for department business profit to the independent operators. Some hotel owners/operators prefer not to incur the initial capital expenditures of space fit-up (tenant improvements) and furnishing (FF&E), as well as the additional business risk (including start-up costs) of operating the spa, a specialized business that they may not be specifically trained for or experienced in. Some hotels may engage recognized brand-name spa operators such as Canyon Ranch and Golden Door to manage a facility.

Hotels with a profitable full-service spa may find that spa revenue is generated primarily by local residents, rather than by overnight guests. Because in such situations the spa is essentially generating its own business, instead of relying on room-nights sold (although, as noted earlier, a spa may contribute to hotel RevPAR), business intangibles are more readily isolated because spa net income is not a direct function of the hotel business itself. In a recent assignment of an upscale conference/resort-type hotel in an affluent northeast United States suburb, approximately 95% of spa revenue was attributable to non-hotel guests. The alternative to a hotel for a day spa operator is to lease space in a shopping center or in a stand-alone building. Retail-oriented real estate, such as a day spa, is typically leased on a net basis, and is composed of minimum base rent–usually calculated as a percentage of [or at least bearing a close relationship to] gross sales–plus operating expense reimbursements. Although some retail centers, particularly larger malls, may also impose an administrative charge typically equal to about 15% of expense reimbursements (essentially a landlord-added "load"), such a fee is excluded here, because it would not be appropriate to a hotel leasing space to a spa operator.

Methodology

The practical problem facing appraisers is a lack of meaningful, comparable leasing to spa

---

4. Appraisal Standards Board, *Uniform Standards of Professional Appraisal Practice,* 2005 ed. (Washington, DC: The Appraisal Foundation, 2005), 17.

5. USPAP, Lines 667–668.

4. Appraisal Standards Board, *Uniform Standards of Professional Appraisal Practice,* 2005 ed. (Washington, DC: The Appraisal Foundation, 2005), 17.

5. USPAP, Lines 667–668.

216 Quantifying Net Income Attributable to Business Intangibles for a Hotel-Operated Full-Service Day Spa

A Business Enterprise Value Anthology

operators by hotels. Therefore, the economics of such a lease must be modeled by alternative means. A straightforward procedure for estimating market rent for the real estate involves a residual technique that eliminates the intangible (business) portion of spa net operating income.[6] The result is then validated by a test of reasonableness. The following presents this methodology as applied to an actual assignment, although it has been modified for illustrative purposes.

1. **Develop a minimum base rent.** As shown in *Dollars & Cents of Shopping Centers: 2004,* the median percentage rent for day spas is equal to about 5.5% of gross sales (6.0% in a super-regional mall and 5.0% in a community center, upscale versions of which are both high-amenity retail venues).[7] Gross sales can be developed from the subject's historical data; competing or other actual day spa data; published benchmark data; or best, a combination of all.[8] Relying on the subject's established operating history for this example, gross sales are projected at $1,500,000, which includes all revenue from spa and salon (if applicable) services, as well as retail sales of complementary products. At 5.5%, as per *Dollars & Cents of Shopping Centers,* minimum base rent would be $19.64 per square foot.[9] Note that the space is leased "as is," with the tenant responsible for all tenant improvements.

2. **Add operating expense pass-throughs.** Similar to common area maintenance (CAM) and other costs allocated to tenants in a retail center, add operating expense pass-throughs (converted to a pro rata, square-foot basis) including total undistributed expense, management fees, and fixed expenses (real estate tax and insurance). These expenses do not include a replacement allowance for furniture, fixtures, and equipment (FF&E) and short-lived items, which would be separately analyzed in aggregate for an appraisal of the real property component of a hotel. (FF&E specific to a spa is in most cases comparatively small relative to a hotel's total FF&E.) In this example, the subject's established operating expense history is analyzed in conjunction with competing hotel- expense comparables and published benchmark data.[10] Based on this analysis, operating expense pass-throughs are projected at $22,600 per hotel guestroom in aggregate, which converts to $25.58 per square foot. The minimum base rent of $19.64 per square foot is added to operating expense pass-throughs of $25.58 per square foot resulting in total rent for the spa real estate of $45.22 per square foot.

3. **Conduct a test of reasonableness.** A direct test of reasonableness of the estimate of total rent is comparables of local retail-type leasing activity. As an alternative test of reasonableness, the total rent equates to tenant cost-of-occupancy, i.e., total occupancy costs (base rent plus expense passthroughs divided by gross sales) of about 12.7%, which compares to *Dollars & Cents of Shopping Centers: 2004* at about 14% to 16.5%.[11] Note, however, that market rent and tenant affordability are distinct concepts, and are often misapplied as if they were synonymous.[12]

---

6. *The Appraisal of Real Estate,* 643. Note that such business income would be included for valuation of TAB.

7. Urban Land Institute, *Dollars & Cents of Shopping Centers: 2004* (Washington, DC, 2004). For a discussion of the application of percentage of gross sales in minimum base rent, see Richard C. Sorenson, *Appraising the Appraisal: The Art of Appraisal Review* (Chicago: Appraisal Institute, 1998), 107.

8. See Day *Spa Benchmarks and Day Spa Business Report,* Day Spa Association; *Benchmarker-Health Club/Spa Report,* Hospitality Research Group of PKF Consulting; and International Spa Association, *ISPA 2004 Spa Industry Study.*

9. Note that in promotional materials, many hotels tend to overstate spa size by including their pools and fitness centers, because non-hotel guest spa patrons may also have use of these hotel facilities that are usually located adjacent to the spa. However, a lease for the spa would typically include only the gross leasable area (GLA) where spa business would be conducted. No adjustment to the rent is necessary for the typical hotel recreational facilities because the hotel would provide them for guests with or without a spa.

10. *Annual Trends in the Hotel Industry,* Hospitality Asset Advisors International, Inc., http://www.hotel-online.com/Trends/PKF/Trends/index.html; and *The HOST Study,* Smith Travel Research, http://www.smithtravelresearch.com.

11. Based on *Dollars & Cents of Shopping Centers: 2004* data, computed median cost-of-occupancy (aggregate of all tenants) for super-regional malls is 13.7% for national, and 16.5% for East Region, where the subject is located. *Dollars & Cents* lists median gross sales (national) at $272 per square foot for day spas compared to $305 per square foot for overall aggregate (non-anchor tenants) in East Region super-regional malls, and at $310 per square foot for spas compared to $268 per square foot overall in East Region community centers. Urban Land Institute, *Dollars & Cents of Shopping Centers: 2004* (Washington, DC, 2004).

12. Richard Marchitelli and John Melaniphy, "Counseling for Retail Properties and Performance Measures," in *Shopping Centers and Other Retail Properties: Investment, Development, Financing, and Management,* ed. John R. White and Kevin D. Gray, 493 (New York: John Wiley & Sons, 1996).

Cost-of-occupancy analysis only provides guidance to maximum economically sustainable rents, which may well exceed market rent (sometimes significantly).

4. **Results.** The resulting difference between spa department profit and market rent (base plus pass-throughs) for the spa real estate is tangible and intangible personal property attributable to the spa business. Applying these parameters indicates total rent for the real estate in this example of $189,924 ($45.22 per square foot). Subtracting this amount from spa department profit of $450,000 (developed from the established operating history) equals $260,076, which is the portion of the spa's net income attributable to tangible and intangible personal property (inclusive of spa FF&E), a rather significant amount after capitalization. Ta-

ble 1 shows the computation of the subject spa business's intangibles.

Note that a lease could contain an overage rent clause specifying payment of a percentage of gross sales over a certain breakpoint (above minimum base rent), but such overage rent is strictly a function of the business performance of a tenant, not necessarily market rent for the real property, and therefore is itself an intangible. As such, collection of overage rent is usually speculative,[13] and thus applicable only to TAB, but not to the real property component.

Conclusion

This methodology clearly delineates I_O for the spa real property asset based on market rent, from I_O of a hotel-operated spa department as a separate profit center. The indicated market rent

Table 1	Spa Business Intangibles in a Hotel		
Guest Rooms	300		
Hotel GBA	265,000 sq. ft.		
Spa Revenue (Gross Sales)	$1,500,000		
Spa GLA	4,200 sq. ft.		
Gross Sales/sq. ft.	$357/sq. ft.		
Percentage Rent*	5.5% of gross sales		
Minimum Base Rent	$19.64/sq. ft.		
Operating Expense Pass-Throughs			
Total Undistributed Expenses	$16.98/sq. ft.		$15,000/room
Management Fees (Base + Incentive)	$3.96/sq. ft.		$3,500/room
Insurance	$0.68/sq. ft.		$600/room
Real Estate Tax	$3.96/sq. ft.		$3,500/room
Total Expense Pass-Throughs	$25.58/sq. ft.[†]		$22,600/room
Total Tenant Cost (Base Rent + Pass-Throughs)	$45.22/sq. ft.		
Annual Total Real Estate Rent	$189,924		
Spa Revenue	$1,500,000		
Minus Spa Department Expense	$1,050,000	70.0% of department revenue	
Spa Department Profit	$450,000		
Minus Annual Total Real Estate Rent	$189,924		
Spa Business Intangibles	**$260,076**		
Test of Reasonableness			
Cost-of-Occupancy			
Annual Total Real Estate Rent	$189,924		
Divided by Spa Revenue	$1,500,000		
Cost-of-Occupancy	**12.7%**		

* *Dollars & Cents of Shopping Centers: 2004*

† Excludes replacement allowance

13. James D. Vernor and Joseph Rabianski, *Shopping Center Appraisal and Analysis* (Chicago: Appraisal Institute, 1993), 209; and *The Appraisal of Real Estate,* 483.

for the spa is validated by a cost-of-occupancy test of reasonableness. In this example, net income generated by a successful spa business creates intangibles evidenced by profits that considerably exceed market rent for the real estate. For situations where only the income to the real property component of hotel TAB is sought, that portion of spa income can be reliably segregated.

Nursing Facilities: Assets, Interests, and Ownership Structures

James K. Tellatin, MAI

This article originally appeared in the Summer 2009 issue of *The Appraisal Journal*.

This article discusses the assets, interests, and ownership structures of nursing facilities. The appraisal of a nursing facility typically involves the valuation of the total assets of the business, including the real estate interest and the tangible and intangible personal property assets. The assets may be held by a single entity or the ownership may be fragmented for economic and legal reasons. In performing an appraisal, it is important to identify, understand, and properly treat the assets being appraised. For consistency purposes, the appraiser should verify the assets and liabilities that are included in the transactions that are used to develop comparable sale and lease data.

Most appraisal assignments relate to the sale or financing of nursing facilities. Typically, a combination of the fee simple interest in the real estate, tangible personal property or furniture, fixtures, and equipment, and intangible assets are included in the purchase price or as security for the mortgage or loan agreement. However, there are many instances in which the appraiser will be requested to estimate only the value of a specific interest in the real estate or intangible personal property assets. For instance, property tax assessments should exclude the value of the intangible assets. FHA-insured mortgages obtained through HUD are underwritten on the value of the tangible assets (real estate and major movable equipment), but this agency also requires the appraiser to estimate the value of the total assets of the business. The valuation of nursing facilities with a leased fee or leasehold interest may or may not include the tangible or intangible personal property.

A nursing facility's assets include:

- Real estate—fee simple, leased fee, or leasehold
- Tangible personal property—furniture, fixtures, and equipment
- Intangible personal property—including assembled work forces, licenses, certifications, approvals such as certificates of need (CON), patient records, goodwill, and management

Note that most appraisal engagements and sales transactions exclude current assets (working capital, cash, accounts receivable, etc.) from the purchase price consideration. Similarly, seller liabilities stay with the seller, and the buyer or successor in the business typically gains indemnity for the seller's liabilities. It is impor-

James K. Tellatin, MAI, has appraised several thousand nursing facilities and various types of senior housing and hospital properties in nearly every state in the United States. Tellatin has contributed two articles to The Appraisal Journal on nursing facility valuation topics and developed the "Appraisal of Nursing Facilities" seminar for the Appraisal Institute. He has also lectured and instructed governmental, financial, and professional association groups on healthcare valuation issues throughout the nation. He has spoken at national conferences for the National Investment Center for the Seniors Housing & Care Industry (NIC), Robert Morris Associates (RMA-The Risk Management Association), the International Association of Assessing Officers (IAAO), and the World Research Group. Tellatin has also been instrumental in the development of appraisal guidelines for healthcare properties for the U.S. Department of Housing and Urban Development (HUD). He is the founding partner in Tellatin, Short & Hansen, Inc.*

The material in this article originally was published as chapter 4 in James K. Tellatin, *The Appraisal of Nursing Facilities* (Chicago: Appraisal Institute, 2009).

tant to confirm what current assets and liabilities, if any, were included in the consideration.

Definitions of *going-concern* and *total assets of a business* follow:

> *Going-concern.* A going concern is an established and operating business with an indefinite future life.[1]

> *Total assets of a business.* The tangible property (real property and personal property, including inventory and furniture, fixtures and equipment) and intangible property (cash, work force, contracts, name, patents, copyrights, and other residual intangible assets, to include capitalized economic profit) of a business.[2]

Several terms are used to describe this value and will be used interchangeably in this discussion.

Business enterprise value is defined as:

> *Business enterprise value (BEV).* A term applied to the concept of the value contribution of the total intangible assets of the continuing business enterprise such as marketing and management skill, an assembled work force, working capital, trade names, franchises, patents, trademarks, contracts, leases, and operating agreements.[3]

Real Estate Assets

Real estate interests may include fee simple, leased fee, and leasehold interests.

A fee simple interest is found when the ownership of the real estate and the operating rights for the facility are controlled by the same party or closely related parties, whereby agreements between related parties can or will collapse into a single entity for purposes of conveyance to a new party. *Fee simple estate* is defined as:

> Absolute ownership unencumbered by any other interest or estate, subject only to the limitations imposed by the governmental powers of taxation, eminent domain, police power, and escheat.[4]

The leased fee interest is the interest held by the lessor or landlord. The interests of the landlord include the right to receive rent during the term of the lease plus the right to receive the leased assets back at the lease termination. Typically, nursing facilities are leased on an absolute net basis, whereby the tenant is responsible for expenses associated with the leased premises and the landlord has little or no

responsibilities. The assets leased may include the real estate, tangible personal property, and intangible assets. Note that many nursing facility leases are vague or silent regarding successor rights to licenses, certifications, and other necessary intangible assets for the continuation of the business. In leases in which the tenant is required to cooperate with the landlord in transitioning the facility to the next operator, the landlord may be required to compensate the tenant for the tangible personal property. *Leased fee interest* is defined as:

> An ownership interest held by a landlord with the rights of use and occupancy conveyed by lease to others. The rights of the lessor (the leased fee owner) and the lessee are specified by contract terms contained within the lease.[5]

The leasehold interest provides the tenant with the rights to use the property to operate the facility, hopefully for a profit. The tenant may have the right to sublease the facility, changing this interest to a "sandwich" leasehold. The tenant, acting as the operator, will be the licensed entity and will possess the certifications, provider agreements, and other formal responsibilities in operating the nursing facility. Since most facilities are leased on an absolute net basis, the tenant is typically responsible for all maintenance and capital expenses during the lease term. The tenant will typically invest fairly substantial capital (working capital, replacement funds, and additions of building and equipment assets) in the enterprise over the lease term, so the lease should be long enough to fully recover the capital investment. Most leases include renewal or extension options, and some grant the tenant purchase options and first rights of refusal. *Leasehold interest* is defined as:

> The interest held by the lessee (the tenant or renter) through a lease transferring the rights of use and occupancy for a stated term under certain conditions.[6]

Tangible Personal Property—Furniture, Fixtures, and Equipment

Personal property is defined as:

> Identifiable tangible objects that are considered by the general public as being "personal," e.g., furnishings, artwork, antiques, gems and jewelry, col-

---

1. *The Appraisal of Real Estate,* 13th ed. (Chicago: Appraisal Institute, 2008), 29.
2. *The Dictionary of Real Estate Appraisal,* 4th ed. (Chicago: Appraisal Institute, 2002), 293.
3. Ibid., 37–38.
4. Ibid., 113.
5. Ibid.
6. Ibid.

lectibles, machinery and equipment; all tangible property that is not classified as real estate... movable without damage to itself or the real estate.[7]

Nursing facilities require furniture and equipment in nearly every area of the building(s). Patients typically bring only some of their personal items with them; beds and room furniture is typically provided by the facility. The operator may lease some equipment and fixtures such as vehicles, computer systems, dishwashers, and perishable décor items (plants and aquariums) that require frequent, specialized servicing. Outside providers, such as therapy companies and pharmacies, may provide their own exercise equipment and medicine carts.

Intangible Personal Property

Several definitions are fundamental to any discussion of intangible personal property.

> *Business enterprise* is defined by the Uniform Standards of Professional Appraisal Practice (USPAP) of The Appraisal Foundation as "an entity pursuing an economic activity."

> *Business assets* are "tangible and intangible resources other than personal property and real estate that are employed by a business enterprise in its operations."

The intangible assets of a nursing facility typically include:

- Licenses, certifications, and approvals (such as certificates of need) from government agencies and regulators
- Assembled workforces, including licensed, certified, and trained employees
- Patient records
- Goodwill
- Management
- Vendor contracts
- Trade names

Nursing facility operators enter into a series of agreements with government authorities. These agreements include a licensure agreement with the state agency responsible for licensure (typically within the state department of health) and provider agreements with the state agency that administers the Medicaid program (often contained within the state department of social services) and with Medicare. Other licensing and certifications are required at the facility level.

Staff and consultants may need certifications issued at local, state, and federal levels. Local licensing and other regulations may be required for fire and safety, food services, and zoning compliance. Verification that the facility remains in compliance with various licenses, certifications, and other regulations is essential for the operator, investors, major creditors (mortgagee or landlord), and those underwriting and evaluating the assets of the business. The appraiser typically does not confirm or verify that all necessary licenses and certifications to operate the facility are current, but the appraisal report should include a stated assumption that those items are current and complete.

While licensed or certified staff and outside consultants (administrators, nurses, nurse aides, therapists, physician consultants, social workers, dieticians, etc.) are directly or indirectly employed by the operator of the facility, they also must adhere to the licensing laws and standards of their respective professional licensing agencies and professional organizations. Violations of laws and standards can result in disciplinary action against the facility and/or individuals, which will often have an adverse impact on the value of the assets of the going concern.

Allocation of the Assets of the Business or Going Concern

USPAP does not specifically require that an allocation of assets be made, but it does require the appraiser to analyze the effect on value of non-real property items.[8] As required by Title XI of the Financial Institutions Reform, Recovery and Enforcement Act of 1989 (FIRREA), the market value of the real estate must be identified and valued separately. Methods for allocating the going-concern value of a nursing facility or any other real estate-intensive business continue to be debated. Under typical circumstances, the going-concern value for a highly profitable nursing facility will exceed the depreciated cost of the tangible assets, which suggests that there is intangible value.

In most cases, the whole is greater than the sum of its parts. The business could not operate if any one of its major assets were absent. If a facility loses its license because of inadequate care or a tenant terminates a lease taking the license (sometimes referred to as the *certificate of need*)

---

7. Ibid.

8. *Uniform Standards of Professional Appraisal Practice, 2008-2009 Edition,* Appraisal Standards Board, The Appraisal Foundation, Standards Rule 1-4(g).

and/or the patients and staff to a replacement facility, the value of the whole and the individual assets are suddenly and severely diminished. In fact, the value is often reduced to a small fraction of the physically depreciated cost if a new license for the building cannot be obtained.

Ownership Structure Issues

The ownership of a nursing facility enterprise is often fragmented, with an operating entity in possession of the license(s), certifications, and business operations, while the ownership of the tangible assets (real estate and personal property) and the management are controlled by other related or unrelated parties.

In 2005, 66.0% of Medicare- and/or Medicaid-certified nursing facilities were owned by for-profit concerns; 27.9% were owned by private non-profits; and the other 6.1% were government-owned.[9]

In this legally complex and litigious business, the division of control and ownership can minimize some types of liability. The appraiser must properly identify the interest being appraised and identify the entity or entities that control that interest.

Figure 1 illustrates a basic ownership structure for a nursing facility. Note that ownership structures will vary considerably and are often restricted by state laws.

The typical structure for a multi-facility nursing home company will place each facility "owned" or leased from a third-party landlord into a separate real estate company and operating company. Each operating company will then contract for services with related or third-party management, therapy, pharmacy, and other service providers. The flow chart in Figure 2 illustrates a typical structure.

The operator is the licensed entity responsible for conducting all necessary and required activities of the nursing facility. These functions are managed at the facility level by a licensed administrator, who oversees the overall operations of the facility, and a licensed registered nurse, designated as the Director of Nursing (DON), who supervises the nursing staff. The licensed operator will be the entity certified for Medicaid and Medicare and will enter "provider agreements" with Medicare, Medicaid, private insurance companies, and other government agencies. Agreements are also reached with each patient directly. The staff is employed by the licensed operator although the operator may rely on third-party services to satisfy certain functions.

The operating entity may contract to lease the property from a related or unrelated owner. Likewise, it may contract with related or unrelated parties for management and ancillary (therapy and pharmacy) services. Note that leases and management and ancillary service agreements may or may not contain rates, escalator clauses, terms, or other conditions

Figure 1	Nursing Home Ownership Diagram

Real Estate Ownership

Related-Party Ancillaries (Therapy, Pharmacy, etc.)

Nursing Facilities

Operating Entity License

Management Company

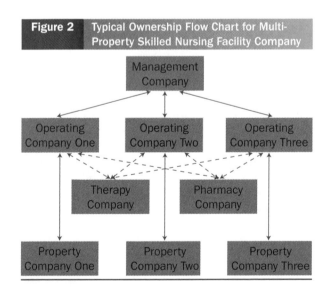

Figure 2	Typical Ownership Flow Chart for Multi-Property Skilled Nursing Facility Company

Management Company

Operating Company One Operating Company Two Operating Company Three

Therapy Company Pharmacy Company

Property Company One Property Company Two Property Company Three

---

9. Centers for Medicare & Medicaid Services, CMS, NHCompare database, available at http://www.medicare.gov/NHCompare.gov.

consistent with prevailing levels and terms in the market.

If the operating entity differs from the owner of the real estate, a lease probably exists. Related-party leases typically collapse into the operating entity when these interests are being conveyed to a third party through a sale and lease. Loans secured by property mortgages should somehow bind together the ownership interests in the tangible assets (real estate and furniture, fixtures, and equipment, or FF&E) and the operating rights that are associated with licenses, provider agreements, Medicare and Medicaid certification, certificates of need, and other valuable agreements. Also, landlords should have the ability to regain the operating rights at the termination of the lease. Foreclosure on the real estate interest is of limited value to the owner of the mortgage if the operator discontinues or transfers the business to a different location, rendering the existing building hollow and empty or without a license, staff, or patients.

The management of a nursing facility is often conducted off site through a management agreement with a related or third-party company.

Therapy services and prescription drugs are significant expenses for most skilled nursing facilities that provide for the dispensing of these services and products through licensed professionals. Since economics often prohibits full-time employment of these professionals at any given facility, operators typically contract with outside concerns to provide these services on an as-needed basis. The ownership of these providers may or may not be related to the operator. Many nursing home companies with many beds within a concentrated geographic area find it feasible to establish and operate therapy companies that not only provide therapy to patients in their facilities, but also to other nursing facilities on an inpatient basis or through outpatient programs at various venues. Some companies view their ancillary businesses as profit centers and will divert earnings from the facility's operating level by charging amounts that exceed the market rates. When analyzing the operations of a nursing facility, the appraiser should carefully compare third-party ancillary expenses with market levels. Excessive payments for ancillary services to related parties can misrepresent the financial condition of a facility; this practice can also reduce the debt service and rent coverage ratios required by operating covenants

in mortgages and leases. Moreover, failure to adjust excessive charges from related parties will result in the underestimation of the market value of various property interests and rental value. Further discussion of ancillary expenses is presented later.

In a typical appraisal of the fee simple interest, the combined entities will be appraised as one. If the analyst is not careful, lenders, third-party landlords, and other creditors who have based their investment decisions on the "whole" will have an investment that is actually secured by something less than the whole and be exposed to elevated, and maybe unknown, risks.

Most sale transactions and financing structures will incorporate the assets of all the entities that control portions of the business enterprise into a single transaction. Considerable care should be taken by appraisers, analysts, and others who apply transaction prices to evaluate nursing facilities (and other going concerns) for investment decisions.

When examining related party, or even third-party, relationships, care should be exercised to determine if the party contracts are set at market levels. Some operators will shift profits from the facility level to real estate, management, or ancillary businesses. Accepting the operating statements without measuring the expenses reported against market levels may result in an inaccurate valuation.

For example, if a rent reset agreed to by an unrelated landlord and tenant requires the new rent to be based on a calculation using a market level of earnings, adjusting the tenant's related-party management fees and ancillary services contract to market levels is critical. A clever tenant may attempt to divert some of the earnings at the facility level to related parties to have a lower rent calculation.

In many instances, a landlord and tenant will dispute the ownership of the certificate of need or the right to the operating rights (license) at the termination of a lease or when exercising a purchase option. The value of a profitable facility without a license or certificate of need is often dramatically less than the value of that same facility with the license intact.

Landlords, lenders, and other creditors should carefully write their lease and loan agreements so that, in the event of lease termination or a creditor's action against the debtor, the operating entity will cooperate to facilitate a seamless transition that transfers the facility's license(s), certification(s), workforce, patient records, and other intangible assets to a succeeding operator.

Well-operated facilities with significant service revenue (income from therapies, the sale of medical supplies, etc.) can produce value that substantially exceeds the replacement costs of real and tangible personal property and the expense of obtaining licenses, approvals, a workforce, and management.

Valuing For-Profit and Non-Profit Nursing Facilities

As Tables 1, 2, and 3 show, 66.0% of all Medicare- and/or Medicaid-certified nursing facilities in the United States are controlled by for-profit concerns. For-profit entities control 68.0% of all certified beds and 67.1% of all occupied beds, based on survey data collected by the Centers for Medicare & Medicaid Services (CMS) in 2005.

Many studies suggest that non-profit nursing facilities experience fewer survey deficiencies and have higher nursing staff ratios and operating expenses. As Table 4 shows, government-controlled facilities have the highest percentage of Medicaid-only certified facilities. Non profits have the greatest percentage of Medicare-only certified facilities. There is a net migration of patients from non-profit to for-profit nursing facilities.

Non-profit facilities tend to operate at higher expense levels, are less aggressive in their private-pay rate structures, and are often less profitable than otherwise similar for-profit facilities. Non-profit facilities have several operating advantages in that they are often exempt from local property tax, pay no income tax, and have access to lower-cost debt available through tax-exempt bond financing.

In appraising non-profit facilities, one of the first questions to resolve is how to treat the ownership. It may be necessary to appraise the facility under two assumptions. First, it can be appraised assuming it remains a non profit and will have certain tax and financing advantages, offset to some degree with higher operating expenses. Second, an assumption can be made

| Table 1 | Percentage of Nursing Facilities Certified for Medicare and/or Medicaid in the U.S. by Type of Control in 2005 |

Percentages of Total Certified Facilities

Ownership Type	Facilities	Licensed Beds	Occupied Beds	Occupancy
For profit	66.0%	68.0%	67.1%	84.4%
Government	6.1%	6.7%	6.6%	84.7%
Non profit	27.9%	25.3%	26.3%	88.8%
Totals	100.0%	100.0%	100.0%	85.5%

Source: Centers for Medicare & Medicaid Services, CMS, NHCompare database, available at http://www.medicare.gov/NHCompare.gov.

| Table 2 | Total Nursing Facilities Certified for Medicare and/or Medicaid in the U.S. by Type of Ownership Control in 2005 |

Ownership Type	No. of Facilities	Licensed Beds	Occupied Beds
For profit	10,563	1,141,635	963,699
Government	971	112,257	95,096
Non profit	4,469	425,086	377,359
Totals	16,003	1,678,978	1,436,154

Source: Centers for Medicare & Medicaid Services.

| Table 3 | Hospital-Based and Chain-Owned Nursing Facilities by Type of Control in the U.S. in 2005 |

Ownership Type	No. of Facilities	Facilities Within Hospital	Total NFs by Control Type in Hospitals	Part of a Chain	Total NFs by Control Type That Are Part of a Chain
For profit	10,563	176	1.7%	6,468	61.2%
Government	971	343	35.3%	78	8.0%
Non profit	4,469	888	19.9%	1,825	40.8%
Totals	16,003	1,407	8.8%	8,371	52.3%

Source: Centers for Medicare & Medicaid Services.

Table 4	Breakdown of Medicare- and Medicaid-Certified Facilities by Type of Ownership			
By Facility	**For profit**	**Government**	**Non profit**	**Total**
Medicaid-only	458	226	306	990
Medicare-only	293	57	507	857
Dual certification	9,812	688	3,656	14,156
Totals	10,563	971	4,469	16,003
Percentage of totals				
Medicaid-only	4.3%	23.3%	6.8%	6.2%
Medicare-only	2.8%	5.9%	11.3%	5.4%
Dual certification	92.9%	70.9%	81.8%	88.5%
Totals	100.0%	100.0%	100.0%	100.0%

Source: Centers for Medicare & Medicaid Services.

that the facility is converted to for-profit ownership. In this case, the valuer will need to adjust the operating forecast to include taxes, higher interest rates, and lower operating costs, consistent with expense levels for comparable for-profit facilities in the same or similar market areas. Adjustments for occupancy characteristics and rates will also be needed. Converting from a non-profit to a for-profit facility, or vice versa, will impact a facility's Medicaid reimbursement in most states that apply facility-specific, cost-based reimbursement schemes. The valuation approach for a non-profit ownership should be discussed and agreed on by the appraiser and the client when the appraiser is engaged.

Exposure and Marketing Time

News of an impending change in ownership often causes fear among nursing home staff and patients. For this reason, nursing facilities are often marketed quietly. Broadcasting the sale may cause some staff and patients to leave, thus impacting value. States must approve all changes of ownership (ChOWs) for licensed nursing facilities. The process varies by state, and in some states it can be quite lengthy. States must assure the public that the new ownership (licensed operator) is morally, ethically, and financially capable of meeting the obligations required. Because of the secrecy that surrounds the marketing of nursing care facilities, exposure and marketing time are difficult to measure objectively. In addition to actual sales data, interviews with operators who are active in the market or brokers who specialize in selling long-term care facilities can provide sufficient information to address these subjects in the appraisal report.

Summary

The appraisal of a nursing facility typically involves the valuation of the total assets of the business, including the real estate interest and the tangible and intangible personal property assets. Real estate interests may include fee simple, leased fee, and/or leasehold rights. Tangible personal property includes furniture, fixtures, and equipment. Intangible personal property usually includes assembled workforces, various local and state licenses, certifications, approvals, patient records, goodwill, and management know-how. These assets may be held by a single entity or the ownership may be fragmented between various related and unrelated parties.

The assets are generally divided for economic and legal reasons. In performing an appraisal or, for that matter, underwriting a financial transaction, it is important to identify, understand, and properly treat the assets being appraised. While the assets may be controlled by separate entities, the combining of these interests may be necessary for valuation purposes. Lenders often secure their loans by binding the assets of related parties to a single loan; real estate tax assessments are typically based on the fee simple interest, despite the presence of existing leased fee and leasehold interests. The reversion rights to personal property assets at the expiration of a lease are often disputed by the parties when the lease agreement is unclear as to the ownership rights. Current assets (working capital, cash, accounts receivable, etc.) and all liabilities are typically excluded from an appraisal assignment. For consistency purposes, the appraiser should verify the assets and liabilities that are included in the transactions that are used to develop comparable sale and lease data.

Proprietary Earnings of Assisted Living and Nursing Facilities under HUD Valuation Guidelines

James K. Tellatin, MAI; Sterling E. Short, MAI; and C. Mark Hansen
This article originally appeared in the Winter 2005 issue of *The Appraisal Journal.*

This article examines treatment of proprietary earnings and management expenses under HUD's lending program for assisted living and skilled nursing facilities. HUD valuation guidelines require allocation of a portion of NOI to proprietary earnings with the remainder of NOI corresponding to real estate and major movable equipment. Misapplications of valuation techniques for proprietary earnings and management expenses often lead to overstated value conclusions. The best approach includes management expenses and applies a capitalization rate derived from sales after netting out proprietary value and earnings.

The Federal Housing Administration (FHA), as part of the U.S. Department of Housing and Urban Development (HUD), is a significant lender to the nursing and assisted living sectors of the senior-care and housing industry. Each year, HUD insures billions of dollars in health care loans originated through its Multifamily Accelerated Processing (MAP) program. MAP was implemented in 2000. MAP was considered revolutionary at that time because unlike the previous HUD lending program, it allowed approved commercial lenders to perform much of the loan processing and underwriting, including contracting and reviewing third-party appraisals, market studies, project capital needs assessments, engineering, and environmental reports. Prior to MAP, HUD personnel conducted the underwriting and performed many of these functions, including oversight of third-party professionals.

Proprietary Earnings

Statutory law governs the FHA insurance program to insure mortgage-backed loans on tangible assets, i.e., real estate and major movable

equipment (MME). For health care facilities, which are referred to as Section 232 projects, HUD recognizes that assisted living and skilled nursing facilities include tangible as well as intangible assets. According to HUD's *MAP Guide*, "the appraiser must first identify the overall

James K. Tellatin, MAI, *is an appraiser and principal with Tellatin, Short & Hansen, Inc. in St. Louis, where his focus has been on appraising health care facilities for the past 20 years. He has been involved in the appraisal of more than 3,500 nursing facilities, 400 senior housing properties, and 100 hospitals. Tellatin is a previous contributor to The Appraisal Journal and is the developer and instructor for the Appraisal Institute's seminar "Appraisal of Nursing Facilities." He has lectured and written about health care facility valuation issues for Robert Morris Associates, National Investment Center for the Senior Housing and Care Industries, World Research Group, International Association of Assessing Officers, and other organizations. Tellatin has also testified on numerous nursing home valuation issues in courts throughout the United States.*

Sterling E. Short, MAI, *is an appraiser and principal with Tellatin, Short & Hansen, Inc. in St. Louis, where his focus has been on appraising nursing facilities for the past 15 years. He is coauthor of an award-winning article for the National Investment Center for the Senior Housing and Care Industries on nursing home profit source modeling. Short has also coauthored an extensive book for a private, major lending institution concerning Medicaid reimbursement principles, regulatory policies, and financial conditions as they relate to lending to nursing facilities for 35 states.*

C. Mark Hansen *is an appraiser and manager of the western division of Tellatin, Short & Hansen, Inc. in Salem, Oregon. He has been appraising and preparing market studies for nursing and assisted living facilities for more than 10 years. This is his first contribution to The Appraisal Journal.*

22

'Business Value' a.k.a. 'Going Concern Value' prior to establishing a proprietary income adjustment and 'Real Estate Only' value."[1] As such, HUD policy requires the appraiser to provide a market value estimate for the tangible assets (real estate and MME) in addition to a separate market value estimate of the total assets of the business (TAB). The *MAP Guide* does not require the appraiser to separate the value of the realty and tangible personal property (MME). In the income capitalization approach section of the HUD appraisal form (HUD-92264-HCF), the appraiser must first estimate the net operating income (NOI) attributable to the going concern and then deduct a portion of the NOI for proprietary earnings correlating to the value for the intangible assets. HUD requires a minimum proprietary earnings deduction of 10% for assisted living facilities and 15% for skilled nursing facilities. The remaining NOI is presumably attributable to real estate and MME assets.

Scope of Article

This article addresses issues that involve misapplications and/or inconsistencies in policy that effectively substitute a lesser proprietary earnings amount for management expenses, and the failure to assure that the same considerations are addressed in derivation of overall capital rates from comparable sales and other market data. This article is not intended to judge the appropriateness of HUD's proprietary earnings deduction method for allocating the value of the total assets of a business. Moreover, the scope of the article does not include methods for developing and supporting the proprietary earnings deduction (the *MAP Guide* provides limited direction on this subject). Conventionally applied proprietary earnings percentages, operating expense margins, and capitalization rates will be applied throughout this article for illustration purposes. These conventional figures are not supported in order to limit distractions from the primary topics of this article.

Even prior to the MAP program, the underwriting and lending practices associated with Section 232 projects evolved into a situation in which incorrect valuation techniques became widely accepted. The proprietary income adjustment has always been confusing for underwriters and appraisers. The authors of this article have assisted in the development of some methods adopted by HUD as part of the *MAP Guide* (revised March 15, 2002). Specifically, HUD appraisals traditionally only concluded the values for the tangible assets. Recent policy and guideline changes require the appraiser to provide an opinion of the market value of the going concern or total assets of the business as well as HUD's traditional nonproprietary (realty and major movable equipment) value. The inclusion of a "going-concern" value provides HUD with a reality check against actual comparable sales (sales comparison approach) and the cost approach. The cost approach was once used to set the upper value limit for HUD health care mortgages. However, confusion over proprietary earnings persists as a valuation problem such that concluded values for only the tangible assets often exceed amounts that are reasonable for the total assets of the business.

The concept of proprietary earnings is confusing because HUD guidelines suggest that management expenses are captured within the proprietary earnings deduction. As a result, HUD guidelines indicate that management expenses should be excluded from operating expenses. However, the appraiser should not simply eliminate management expenses without considering whether the real expense of management is covered within the proprietary earnings estimate and if there remain earnings to provide an adequate return on the intangible assets. If the category of management or central office expense is excluded from the operating expenses, then are these expenses covered elsewhere, such as within general and administration cost centers? Is the proprietary earnings deduction actually intended to be a substitute for management and central office expense, plus satiating a market return on intangible assets?

This article will

- Establish the generally recognized valuation method used by underwriters and appraisers for commercial lenders;
- Present the fundamental problem with excluding management expenses and theorizing that the deduction of proprietary income can be substituted for the management expenses in developing the value of the tangible assets;
- Show the exacerbating effect of incorrectly extracting and applying capitalization rates

---

1. U.S. Department of Housing and Urban Development, "Valuation Analysis," in *MAP Guide,* Chap. 7, 22. See the HUD Web site for PDF file, http://www.hud.gov/offices/hsg/mfh/map/mapguide/chap07.pdf.

via the inappropriate treatment of management and proprietary earnings for the tangible and intangible asset components; and

- Present the best solution for valuing the tangible and intangible assets in the scope of HUD appraisal engagements.

Distinction Between Management Expenses and Proprietary Earnings

Management expenses are real and necessary costs. They include a wide array of off-site functions required to effectively and efficiently operate a long-term care facility, including, but not limited to, centralized accounting; developing, modifying, and enforcing operating policies; staff recruitment; payroll services; legal services; group purchasing; maximizing Medicaid and Medicare reimbursement; financial management; and overall supervision.

Most operators and buyers of assisted living and nursing facilities are entities that operate multiple facilities; other than a limited and diminishing number of mom-and-pop operators, these management functions are almost always conducted in central office settings where greater cost and operating efficiencies are achieved, or contracted to third-party vendors. In addition, lenders usually incur outside management expenses in a foreclosure situation with little or no corresponding reduction in staffing levels at the facility level.

Proprietary earnings are intended to compensate the ownership for its intangible assets, which according to the *MAP Guide* include management fees. The definition of proprietary earnings or income does not appear in *The Appraisal of Real Estate, The Dictionary of Real Estate Appraisal,* the *Uniform Standards of Professional Appraisal Practice and Advisory Opinions,* or the *MAP Guide.*[2] However, the term *proprietary* is defined in Merriam-Webster's *Dictionary of Law* as "something that is used, produced, or marketed under exclusive legal right of the inventor or maker."[3]

The proprietary earnings adjustment is intended to separate the nonrealty and non–major

movable equipment earnings and value from the whole business in order to satisfy federal law that prohibits the FHA program from insuring loans on intangible personal property. The *MAP Guide* implies that the entire amount of proprietary earnings represents NOI, since the entire earnings are capitalized in an example found in Chapter 7.[4] Thus, by this example, management expenses are not included in the proprietary earnings deduction.

HUD states that "when deriving the final 'Real Estate Only' value (HUD's insurable value determination), and when preparing the HUD 92264 and HUD 92264a, a management fee should not be included as an operating expense under Section 232. Management fees are viewed as a portion of the proprietary income deduction, so that applying a management fee in the 'Real Estate Only' analysis and in preparation of the HUD 92264 and HUD 92264a would be a duplication of expenses, thus unfairly penalizing the property."[5] This article will show that the deduction for proprietary earnings is often less than typical management expenses and will not be sufficient to cover real management or central office expenses and still provide a return to intangible property assets.

Comparing Valuations With and Without Management Expenses

Using typical operating margins for a nursing facility, the following two tables contrast the differences in the typical commercial valuation and the current, generally accepted HUD method for the valuation of the tangible assets only, in which management expenses are simply eliminated without making other adjustments. The example shown in Table 1 could be a subject property or an analysis of a comparable sale.

Table 2 uses the same property and estimated revenues and operating expenses, but substitutes proprietary earnings for management expenses, resulting in an overstated valuation for the tangible assets under HUD guidelines.

In the commercial valuation shown in Table 1, a deduction of $320,000 is taken for manage-

2. Appraisal Institute, *The Appraisal of Real Estate,* 12th ed. (Chicago: Appraisal Institute, 2001); Appraisal Institute, *The Dictionary of Real Estate Appraisal,* 4th ed. (Chicago: Appraisal Institute, 2002); Appraisal Standards Board, *Uniform Standards of Professional Appraisal Practice and Advisory Opinions* (Washington, DC: The Appraisal Foundation, 2004); and HUD Web site, *MAP Guide.*

3. *Merriam-Webster's Dictionary of Law* (Springfield, MA: Merriam-Webster, Inc., 1996).

4. HUD Web site, *MAP Guide,* Chap. 7, 22–23.

5. HUD Web site, *MAP Guide,* Chap. 7, 23.

Table 1 — Typical Commercial Valuation, With Management Expenses

Total Potential Gross Revenue		$8,888,889
Occupancy Rate		90.0%
Effective Net Revenue (ENR)	$162.35 PPD	8,000,000
Operating Expenses, Before Management/Proprietary Earnings	$135.57 PPD	6,680,000
Unadjusted NOI	$26.79 PPD	1,320,000
Less Management Expense (4.0% of ENR)	$(6.49) PPD	(320,000)
NOI to TAB		$1,000,000
Capitalized Value of TAB (13.33%)	$50,000 $/Bed	**$7,500,000**
	1.07 ENR Multiplier	
Maximum Loan Offered at Typical Loan-to-Value Ratio, Commercial Financing (75%)		$5,625,000

Note: Calculations may be rounded

PPD = per patient day

Table 2 — HUD Valuation Method for Tangible Assets—No Management Expenses

Total Potential Gross Revenue		$8,888,889
Occupancy Rate		90.0%
Effective Net Revenue (ENR)	$162.33 PPD	8,000,000
Operating Expenses, Before Managevment/Proprietary Earnings	$135.57 PPD	6,680,000
Unadjusted NOI	$26.79 PPD	1,320,000
Less Proprietary Income (15% of NOI)	$(4.02) PPD	(198,000)
NOI With Deduction for Proprietary Revenue, No Management Expense		$1,122,000
Capitalized Value of the Tangible Assets—HUD "Real Estate Only" Value (13.33%)	$56,100 $/Bed	**$8,415,000**
	0.95 ENR Multiplier	
Maximum HUD Loan Offered at Loan-to-value Ratio (85%)		$7,150,000

Note: Calculations may be rounded

ment expenses, while in the HUD example in Table 2, the management expenses are erroneously included with $198,000 for proprietary earnings. As a result, the NOI for the real estate and MME (tangible) assets is $122,000 greater than the NOI for the entire business. It is irrational for the NOI allocated only to the tangible assets to exceed the NOI of the total assets of the business when the highest and best use is clearly the continuation of the nursing or assisted living facility use. Furthermore, profit and loss statements for nursing and assisted living facilities typically have line items for management or central office expense allocations, but do not have an account for proprietary earnings.

Table 2 shows that the proprietary earnings represent 2.5% of the net revenue. No known management company or chain operator could manage a health care facility at this expense level without experiencing losses. In this example, proprietary earnings must nearly double before reaching a minimally acceptable management fee of 4.0% of net revenue.

States are obligated to reimburse nursing home operators for "reasonable" management expenses; proprietary earnings are not reimbursable. If the amount of proprietary earnings is less than the management and/or central office expense allowed by a state's Medicaid reimbursement rate settlement and reported in the Medicaid cost report of the facility, then the Medicaid revenues may be overstated; hence, the estimated NOI is overstated as well.

Only by coincidence will the substitution technique make some sense, since management expenses are typically calculated as a percentage of effective net revenue while proprietary earnings are calculated as a percentage of NOI. The example in Table 3 demonstrates the expense margin required in order for proprietary income to equal management expenses.

As shown, the operating expense margin would always need to be 73.3% for the 15.0% proprietary income calculation to equal management expense at 4.0% of effective net revenue. Higher expense margins will necessitate higher proprietary earnings deductions in order to maintain the same management or central office expense offset. Nursing facilities typically operate at a higher expense margin than applied in Table 3, and a higher expense margin will result in a lower NOI and a proprietary income that is less than the management expenses. Even if management expenses and proprietary income coincidentally resulted in equal amounts, the unintended result is the same NOI for the tangible assets as for the entire business. If the same capitalization rate is applied to the same income, the value is of course the same. The intent of HUD in requiring a deduction for proprietary earnings is to produce a tangible asset value that is less than the market value of the total assets of the business or going-concern value. The lower valuation allows HUD to finance 85% of the "appraised" tangible-asset value, or 90% if the loan involves new construction for a for-profit entity. Nonprofits may borrow up to 90% on existing property and 95% on new construction. At this point, it should be recognized that it is problematic to substitute the proprietary income for the management expenses.

The previous examples demonstrate another misstep made by lenders and appraisers that exacerbates the valuation error for the HUD tangible asset valuation. In the examples, the same capitalization rate is applied to arrive at the market value of the total assets of the business enterprise value and the HUD tangible asset value. It is applied under the premise that if proprietary earnings are a substitute for management expenses, then the capitalization rates should also be equal. To be clear, management is an operating expense, while proprietary earnings are something other than an operating expense—more akin to a return to intangible personal property assets.

Most overall capitalization rates derived from comparable sales as presented in valuations, as well as those quoted in market surveys, represent the relationship of NOI to TAB, and the operating expenses include management expenses, but not proprietary earnings.[6] If the NOI attributable to the tangible assets is actually greater than that for the TAB, as shown in the HUD example (Table 2), then the capitalization rate for the HUD example should actually be higher than in the conventional method (Table 1). As will be shown, the NOI and the tangible assets should correlate.

Table 4 shows the impact of capitalizing these incomes into value and applying HUD's loan-tovalue parameters. In both cases, the overall capitalization rate is 13.33%, which is the same overall capitalization rate applied in the commercial valuation for the TAB.

Based on substituting proprietary earnings for management expenses, the HUD value (tangible asset value) exceeds the market value of the total assets of the business. Using HUD's maximum loan-to-value for a for-profit owner, an FHA-insured, nonrecourse loan would be 95.4% of the market value for the total assets of the business. Also in Table 4, the proprietary earnings represent 2.5% of total revenue, an amount less than typical management expenses.

As previously stated, the newest version of the HUD *MAP Guide* requires appraisers to develop an estimate of the market value of the going concern (essentially TAB) as well as an opinion of the value of the real estate and major movable equipment or tangible assets. Where the substitution method for developing the tangible assets components has been applied, many appraisers have elected to forgo this requirement or apply a sum-of-the-parts approach,

Table 3	Minimum Expense Margin Necessary for Proprietary Earnings to Equal a Four Percent Management Expense
Effective Net Revenue	$8,000,000
Management Expense Percentage	4.0%
Management Expense	$320,000
Effective Net Revenue	$8,000,000
Operating Expense Margin (Excluding Mgmt.)	73.3%
Operating Expenses	$5,866,667
NOI	$2,133,333
Proprietary Earnings Percentage	15.0%
Proprietary Earnings	$320,000

6. Average capitalization rates for skilled nursing facilities from three frequently quoted sources are as follows: National Investment Center for the Seniors Housing & Care Industries (December 31, 2003)—13.6%; *Senior Care Investor*, Levin & Associates—13.5%; and *Senior Housing Investment Survey*, Spring 2004, Senior Living Services, Inc.—13.1%.

	Conventional TAB Valuation with Management Expenses, No Proprietary Earnings	Valuation of Realty and MME, Proprietary Earnings Substituted for Management Expenses
NOI Used in Capitalization	$1,000,000	$1,122,000
Management or Proprietary Earnings Deduction	($320,000)	($198,000)
Value of TAB	$7,500,000	
HUD Non-Proprietary Value (Rounded)		$8,415,000
Loan-to-Value Ratio	75.0%	85.0%
Loan Amount (Rounded)	$5,625,000	$7,150,000
Maximum Loan Amount Per Bed/Unit (150 beds or units)	$37,500	$47,667
Proprietary Earnings as Percent of Effective Net Revenue (ENR)		2.5%

whereby an estimated, separate value for the proprietary (intangible) assets is added to the tangible assets estimate. This valuation methodology is certainly not employed by companies buying assisted living and skilled nursing facilities or other property types that are real estate-intensive businesses, such as hotels or hospitals. This approach may have evolved because HUD changed the appraisal guidelines from simply seeking an opinion of value for the tangible assets to also requiring an opinion of the market value for the total assets of the business. Rather than reinvent the wheel, these appraisers have simply added the intangible value to the HUD tangible asset value—as they have traditionally and incorrectly developed it. Table 5 shows the incorrectly applied sum-of-the-parts technique.

If accepted by HUD, the erroneous value conclusion of the tangible assets shown in Table 5 will result in a nonrecourse loan that exceeds 95.0% of the market value (MV) of the total assets of the business (FHA-insured loan $7,150,000/$7,500,000 MVTAB).

Table 6 compares the sum-of-the-parts technique to the conventional approach for the valuation of the total assets of the business, in which whole value is estimated first.

The sum-of-the-parts methodology results in an erroneous value conclusion for the total assets of the business. Using this approach, total assets of the business are $1,707,000 more or 22.8% greater than when derived through the generally applied valuation methodology. The HUD tangible asset value also exceeds the value of the TAB under the typical commercial valuation method by $915,000 or 12.0%. As shown, if accepted by HUD, this erroneous valuation technique will result in a nonrecourse loan that ap-

proximates the market value of the total assets of the business. Congress certainly did not intend for this type of value relationship to occur when it required that FHA-insured loans be made only on realty and major movable equipment.

Correct Valuation Approach when Excluding Management Expenses

The rationale and illustrations presented thus far have demonstrated that substituting proprietary income for management expenses can be and often is misapplied, resulting in an overstated capitalized value that significantly exceeds reasonable value relative to the cost and sales comparison approach indications for the tangible assets. Table 6 shows the magnitude of the problem. Using this example, if a facility actually sold for $7,500,000 under normal market conditions, the HUD going-concern value would be $9,207,000. This price/value relationship makes no sense. HUD's *MAP Guide* suggests that the proprietary earnings may be capitalized into a value indication;[7] thus, the earnings are viewed as NOI to the nonrealty and MME assets. Therefore, there is no management or other operating expense associated with the proprietary earnings and corresponding capitalized intangible asset value. However, still to be addressed are the MAP guidelines that direct management expenses to be excluded from the operating expenses.

The appraiser should incorporate the expense of performing the management functions somewhere else in the operating expense estimate. These expenses could be included in one or more categories, including proprietary expense (different from proprietary earnings),

---

7.   HUD Web site, *MAP Guide,* Chap. 7, 22.

a Total Potential Gross Revenue	$8,888,889
b Occupancy Rate	90.0%
c Effective Net Revenue (ENR)	8,000,000
d Operating Expenses, Before Management/Proprietary Earning	6,680,000
e Unadjusted NOI	1,320,000
f Proprietary Income Deduction (15% of NOI of TAB)	198,000
g **Capitalized Value of the Intangible Assets of the Business or Nonrealty and Non-MME Assets (25%)** (f ÷ 0.25)	**$792,000**
h NOI Attributable to Realty and Major Movable Equipment (e – f)	1,122,000
i HUD Realty and MME Value, Capitalized at Tangible Asset Capitalization Rate of 13.33%, Rounded	**$8,415,000**
j **Incorrect Market Value of the Total Assets of the Business (g + i)**	**$9,207,000**
Maximum HUD Loan Offered at 85% Loan-to-value Ratio, Rounded	$7,150,000

Note: *MAP Guide* (Chapter 7, page 22) shows an example whereby a 25% capitalization rate is applied to the proprietary earnings to produce an estimate of intangible value.

Table 6 Comparison of Conventional TAB Valuation to HUD Sum–of–the–Parts Valuation

	Conventional TAB Valuation with Management Expenses, No Proprietary Earnings	Valuation of Realty and MME, Proprietary Earnings Substituted for Management Expenses
NOI Before Management or Proprietary Earnings Deduction	$1,320,000	$1,320,000
Management or Proprietary Earnings Deduction	($320,000)	($198,000)
NOI Used in Capitalization	$1,000,000	$1,122,000
Value of TAB ($1.0 MM NOI/13.33% cap. rate)	$7,500,000	
HUD Value - Tangible Assets ($1,122,000/13.33% —as incorrectly applied)		$8,415,000
Value of Proprietary Earnings ($198,000/25.0%)		792,000
HUD Going-Concern Value or Total Value of the Realty, MME, and Proprietary Assets—Sum of the Parts		$9,207,000
Loan-to-Value Ratio	75.0%	85.0%
Maximum Loan Amount	$5,625,000	$7,150,000
Maximum HUD Loan-to-Conventional Value or TAB		95.3%

administrative, and/or central office/management. The appraiser's treatment of management expenses should be supported by expense comparables that clearly distinguish management from administrative expenses. Proprietary earnings should also compensate the ownership for the factors of production: land, labor, and capital. Capital includes major movable equipment (personal property), working capital, and all other nonlabor intangibles. The intangibles that are compensated by the proprietary earnings might include the certificate of need, which in some states is transferable and often sold for substantial consideration.

The correct application of valuation theory is simple. The principle of consistency is paramount in any valuation analysis. In dealing with the proprietary income and management ex-penses, the identical process used to determine the subject NOI should be applied to the sales in order to extract accurate market capitalization rate data. Consistency may be applied in several ways, as shown in the following techniques.

Since management expenses are real and necessary, the capitalization rate should be extracted in a manner that maintains the consistent exclusion of management expenses from the operating expenses. If appraisers exclude management or central office costs from operating expenses, they should add back the expenses for those management and central office functions to the NOI of each sale to arrive at a consistent, market-derived overall capitalization rate. To be consistent with the NOI derivation of the subject, the following steps must be taken to extract the capitalization rate of a sale.

The example in Table 7 is a continuation of an earlier illustration that produced an overall capitalization rate of 13.33% for the total assets of the business, reflecting the inclusion of management expenses. If each comparable sale used in the development and support of the overall capitalization rate applied in the HUD valuation is developed in the manner just shown, then the exclusion of the management expenses is consistent with the procedures used in the development of the NOI of the subject. As a result, a higher overall capitalization rate would be applicable for both the total assets of the business and the real estate and major movable equipment.

Continuing with the previous example, but considering the subject as a comparable sale, the price can be allocated between the tangible and intangible assets for extracting a capitalization rate for the tangible assets.

In the example in Table 8, a market-derived capitalization rate for the nonproprietary HUD value has been extracted from this sale information through use of a residual technique, whereby the proprietary earnings and intangible value are removed from the NOI and sale price. Logically, the $150,000 attributable to proprietary earnings warrants a higher capitalization rate than the $850,000 allocated to the realty and major movable assets. Most skilled nursing facilities derive a substantial amount of profit from therapy and other ancillary revenue, particularly related to Medicare funding. These services are closely tethered to human endeavors; while tangible assets are necessary to deliver the services, the major ingredients employed in generating profit from ancillaries are labor and management, and have less to do with real estate assets. Medicare is very specific

Table 7	Analysis of a Comparable Sale, with Deductions for Proprietary Earnings and Intangible Value, Excluding Management Expenses		
a Sale Price – Total Assets of Business			$7,500,000
b Effective Net Revenue		$8,000,000	
c Operating Expenses, Excluding Management Expenses		6,680,000	
d NOI		$1,320,000	
e Indicated Overall Cap. Rate for TAB, without Management Expenses (d ÷ a)			17.6%
f Proprietary Earnings @ 15% of NOI (d × 0.15)		$198,000	
g Proprietary Earnings Capitalization Rate, per MAP Guide		25.0%	
h Proprietary Earnings Value (f ÷ g)			($792,000)
i Indicated Value of Tangible Assets (a – h)			$6,708,000
j NOI with Deduction for Proprietary Revenue, No Management Expense (d – f)			$1,122,000
k Indicated Overall Cap. Rate for Realty and MME, without Management Expenses (j ÷ i)			16.7%

Table 8	Correct Method for Extracting Capitalization Rate for Tangible Assets*		
Sale Price			$7,500,000
Effective Gross Revenue		$8,000,000	
Total Operating Expenses, Including 4.0% ($320,000) for Management		(7,000,000)	
NOI of TAB or Going Concern		1,000,00	
Implied Overall Capitalization Rate for TAB	13.33%		
Proprietary Earnings Percentage	15.00%		
Proprietary Earnings Deduction		(150,000)	
NOI Allocated to Real Estate and MME		850,000	
NOI Allocated to Proprietary Earnings or Intangible Assets		(150,000)	
Capitalization Rate for Intangible Assets**	25.00%		
Estimated Value of the Proprietary Earnings or Intangible Assets			(600,000)
NOI Allocated to Tangible Assets		$850,000	
Sale Price Allocated to Tangible Assets			$6,900,000
Implied Capitalization Rate for Tangible Assets	12.32%		

* Realty & MME
**(See *MAP Guide* Example, Chapter 7, Page 22)

in its formulation of therapy and capital reimbursement. In most cases, the NOI or earnings derived from capital reimbursement (interest, depreciation, and rent), are significantly less than those derived from the therapy component through Medicare. Rather than focus on the specifics of how the capital reimbursements and earnings from therapy and ancillary services can be allocated between tangible and intangible assets, this analysis addresses HUD valuation guidelines as related to proprietary earnings and management expenses. Sales of small, profitable therapy or pharmacy businesses often trade at earnings multipliers of 3.0 to 5.0, or capitalization rates of 20.0% to 33.3%. Using a 25.0% capitalization rate for the proprietary earnings, the portion of the sale price allocated to the intangible assets in Table 8 is $600,000 ($150,000/25.0%). Thus, the remaining NOI and price for just the tangible assets produce a market-derived capitalization rate of 12.3% for the tangible assets.

By applying this rate extraction technique to a set of comparable sales, the appraiser formulates a reliable set of tangible asset capitalization rates that can be employed in the HUD valuation. The need to analyze revenue and operating expenses for the subject and comparable sales in a consistent manner is of utmost importance.

Other adjustments to the NOI calculations of the comparable sales for a HUD MAP appraisal assignment may include inflation trending and capital reserves. According to MAP guidelines, revenues and expenses must exclude inflationary trending to future dates. Also, HUD replacement reserve requirements are typically greater than industry norms for conventional appraisal assignments. Average replacement reserves for nursing and assisted living facilities range from $350 to $500 per bed/unit. HUD reserves, determined by a third-party professional contractor, are usually greater; the appraiser might consider adjusting the operating expenses of the comparable sales to reflect higher reserves required by HUD.

The real solution for appraising the market value of the tangible assets of a nursing or assisted living facility for HUD assignments is to include management expenses for the subject and comparables, and to make proprietary earnings deductions from the NOI for the subject and the comparable sales used to extract capitalization rates. Including management as an operating expense is consistent with the standard accounting classification and procedures used by the industry, and it avoids inconsistencies with Medicaid cost-based, reimbursement rate setting. The elimination of management expenses for the subject but not the sales used to extract overall rates will produce erroneous value indications that are unreasonable when measured against other valuation techniques (mainly the sales comparison approach). While HUD does not yet require management to be included as an expense, this policy does not relieve the appraiser from performing consistent valuation analyses. If management expenses are eliminated from the subject, then they must also be eliminated from the sales data used to derive the capitalization rate. Moreover, the appraiser should clearly state and demonstrate that management expenses have been eliminated from the expenses of the sales; better yet, the sales should be shown and analyzed both ways. The appraiser should also demonstrate that the proprietary earnings will adequately cover the management expenses that have been eliminated as an operating expense and will provide a reasonable return to the intangible assets.

If appraisers rely on national survey capitalization rate data, they should explain and show adjustments to the capitalization rates for the management-expense add back. No known national survey data would allow a management fee add back since operating expense margins are not included in these surveys and would need to be assumed. The steps to extract national, average capitalization rates without management expenses for a nursing facility are presented in Table 9.

Table 9 shows that the national, average capitalization rate for nursing facilities increases 180 basis points after excluding management as an expense and adjusting for HUD proprietary earnings. As expense margins and proprietary earnings percentages decline, the HUD proprietary earnings capitalization rate premium without management expenses declines. This relationship could be the case with assisted living facilities; however, by increasing the expense margin and proprietary earnings percentage, the capitalization rate premium increases.

Conclusion

In HUD's *MAP Guide*, proprietary earnings are treated as net operating income since the entire amount is capitalized into an intangible value in-

National Average Skilled Nursing Capitalization Rate	13.50%	
Average NOI Margin, Including Management Expenses	20.00%	
Typical Management Expense (percent of revenue)	4.00%	
Effective Net Revenue	$8,000,000	
National Average NOI Margin, Including Management Expenses	20.00%	
NOI Including Management as an Expense	$1,600,000	
National Average Skilled Nursing Capitalization Rate		13.50%
Indicated Market Value of the Total Assets of the Business		$11,851,852
Add Back Management Expenses (4.0% of Revenue)	320,000	
Adjusted NOI	$1,920,000	
Indicated National Average Overall Rate, Adding Management Expenses to NOI		16.2%
HUD Nonproprietary Capitalization Rate w/o Management Expenses		
Adjusted NOI	$1,920,000	
Less Proprietary Earnings (15%)	(288,000)	
NOI Attributable to Tangible Assets	$1,632,000	
Indicated Market Value of the TAB		$11,851,852
Capitalized Value of Proprietary Earnings ($288,000/25.0%)		(1,152,000)
Implied Price for Tangible Assets		$10,699,852
NOI Attributable to Tangible Assets	$1,632,000	
National Average Cap. Rate for Tangible Assets, w/o Management Expenses		15.3%

dication; therefore, management expenses are not a part of the proprietary earnings. Moreover, even if management expenses were part of the proprietary earnings, the proprietary earnings deduction would need to substantially exceed the minimum prescribed amounts to adequately cover normal management expenses and provide some return to intangibles. Table 10 shows a typical nursing facility situation, where combining real and necessary management expenses with the minimum proprietary earnings deduction of 15% results in a 39.2% total adjustment to the NOI.

Table 11 summarizes the often misapplied HUD appraisal method (column 2) and compares it with conventional commercial appraisal methods (column 1), neither of which results in an accurate allocation of value between the tangible and intangible assets. Columns 3 and 4 show modifications to the HUD methodology that provide a more accurate allocation of value, and one that does not overstate the value of the tangible assets.

Given HUD's existing MAP appraisal guidelines and the decision to include or exclude management expenses from the HUD valuation, it is the responsibility of appraisers to apply consistent appraisal principles to their work rather than to allow the formulation of unrea-

sonable conclusions. The traditional practice of rationalizing that the proprietary income deduction is a substitute for management expenses is an ill-conceived method.

The *MAP Guide* suggests that management is not an expense within the proprietary earnings deduction since the entire proprietary earnings deduction is capitalized into an indication of the proprietary or intangible value. As shown, using typical proprietary earnings percentages and operating expense margins produces amounts for proprietary earnings that are significantly less than the hard costs for management, and it leaves little room for profit to the management. The sum-of-the parts method is problematic when the tangible value is overstated. If the management expenses are excluded from operating expenses, then the principle of consistency requires the same treatment to the comparable sales, resulting in higher capitalization rates. However, this method results in abnormally high capitalization rates in comparison to industry or standard market data due to the exclusion of the management expenses. Remember that HUD needs two values: a TAB and a tangible asset (realty and MME) value. The best valuation method is to include management expenses when developing an opinion of the

Table 10	Combining Management Expenses and Proprietary Earnings for "Correct Proprietary Earnings Deduction"	
Effective Net Revenue (ENR)	$8,000,000	
Operating Expenses, w/o Management Expenses	(6,680,000)	
Unadjusted NOI	$1,320,000	
Less Management Expense (4.0% of ENR)		$(320,000)
Less Proprietary Income (15% of NOI)		(198,000)
Management Expense and Proprietary Earnings		$(518,000)
Management Expense and Proprietary Earnings as % of Unadjusted NOI		-39.2%

market value of the total assets of business. The best approach for the HUD realty and MME or nonproprietary value is to simply deduct the estimated proprietary earnings, and capitalize the adjusted NOI by a market-derived capitalization rate developed from sales by adjusting the price for proprietary value and NOI for proprietary earnings. This approach provides the clearest analysis and substantially reduces the potential for misleading value conclusions. The percentage difference between the TAB and the nonproprietary value could be used as an adjustment to the TAB value indication developed in the sales comparison approach since the sale prices for nursing and assisted living facilities typically include the tangible and intangible assets.

	Conventional Value of TAB with Management Included Proprietary Earnings Excluded	Sum-of-the-Parts Valuation, Proprietary Earnings Substituted for Management with Real Estate Capitalization Rate	Exclusion of Management but Inclusion of Proprietary Earnings without Substitution	HUD Valuation Including Management and Proprietary Earnings as Deductions
a Total Potential Gross Revenue	$8,888,889	$8,888,889	$8,888,889	$8,888,889
b Occupancy Rate	90.0%	90.0%	90.0%	90.0%
c Effective Net Revenue (ENR)	8,000,000	8,000,000	8,000,000	8,000,000
d Operating Expenses, Excluding Management Exp.	6,680,000	6,680,000	6,680,000	6,680,000
e Unadjusted NOI	$1,320,000	$1,320,000	$1,320,000	$1,320,000
f Less Management Expenses (4.0%)	(320,000)	N/A	N/A	(320,000)
g NOI Attributable to TAB	$1,000,000	Not Provided	$1,320,000	$1,000,000
h Proprietary Earnings (15.0% of NOI before Management Exp.)	N/A	(198,000)	(198,000)	(198,000)
i HUD-Defined NOI to Tangible Assets	N/A	$1,122,000	$1,122,000	$802,000
j Capitalization Rate for TAB	13.3%	Not Provided	17.6%	13.3%
k Capitalization Rate for HUD Tangible Assets	N/A	13.3%	16.7%	12.3%
l Cap. Rate for Proprietary Earnings or Intangible Assets	N/A	25.0%	25.0%	25.0%
m Capitalized Value of HUD-Defined Tangible Assets	N/A	$8,415,000 (i ÷ k)	$6,380,000(i ÷ k)	$6,510,353 (i ÷ k)
n Capitalized Value of Intangible Assets or Prop. Assets	N/A	792,000 (h ÷ l)	1,120,000 (o − m)	989,647(o − m)
o Indicated Market Value of TAB	$7,500,000 (g ÷ j)	$9,207,000 (m + n)	$7,500,000 (g ÷ j)	$7,500,000 (g ÷ j)
p Loan Amount	$5,625,000(o × 0.75)	$7,152,750(m × 0.85)	$5,423,000(m × 0.85)	$5,533,800 (m × 0.85)
q Loan Amount as % of Conventional Value of TAB	75.0%	95.4%	72.3%	73.8%
r Proprietary Earnings as % of Net Revenue	N/A	2.5%	2.5%	2.5%
s Amount Overleveraged, HUD Guidelines	None	$1,618,950	None	None
t Correct Method(s) for HUD Valuation	Not Applicable to HUD	Wrong	Good	Best

Business Enterprise Value in Special Purpose Properties

Stephen R. Clark, MAI, ASA, and John R. Knight, PhD

This article originally appeared in the January 2002 issue of *The Appraisal Journal.*

Measuring business enterprise value (BEV) is an important part of many appraisal assignments, but debate continues over the appropriate techniques for extracting this component of going concern value. In this article, we propose a new method for estimating BEV in certain special purpose properties. This technique could be used to supplement value estimates obtained from other approaches, especially for properties that depend on a stabilized occupancy for achieving going concern value. We illustrate our proposed methodology with a hypothetical example.

There has been considerable interest over the past decade on the part of the appraisal industry in identifying and measuring the business enterprise component of value in a variety of real estate property types. Evidence of this attention is the recent debate over the existence and pervasiveness of business enterprise value (BEV) at the summer 1998 meeting of the Appraisal Institute in Orlando, Florida, and the recent publication by the Appraisal Institute of a book on the topic entitled, not surprisingly, *A Business Enterprise Value Anthology.*[1]

Appraisal literature features an abundance of articles addressing the valuation of various properties with a focus on the segregation of intangible components from the tangible assets. Most state laws hold only real property and other tangible assets subject to taxation so the importance of separating these components of value is most apparent in property tax assessment. Intangible assets, though they may enhance the value of the total operating enterprise, are not subject to *ad valorem* taxes. Property tax assessment appeals have become a multibillion dollar industry, so the importance of measuring the BEV compo-

nent of a property has become critical. Providers of debt and equity capital are also interested in the proportionate contribution of the real property and the business enterprise to value, inasmuch as the allocation affects the appropriate discount rate for future expected cash flows.

While BEV applies in nearly all appraisals, special purpose properties deserve special consideration because of the pervasiveness of the BEV component for this property type.[2] Since the special-use nature of such properties makes separating the real estate and the business enterprise components especially difficult. In this article we develop a conceptual framework for making such a separation in the case of special purpose properties that derive value by achieving a stabilized occupancy. We demonstrate our method using an assisted living facility as an example, although many other businesses (e.g., skilled nursing, congregate care, and health club facilities; marinas;

Stephen R. Clark, MAI, ASA, *is an independent fee appraiser in Stockton, California. His practice involves both business and real estate valuations including eminent domain assignments, senior housing projects, special purpose properties, property tax appeals, consulting and litigation support. He is also a real estate broker specializing in business brokerage and development land brokerage.*

John R. Knight, PhD, *is associate professor of finance and real estate and director of the Real Estate Institute in the Eberhardt School of Business at University of the Pacific in Stockton, California. He has published articles in several real estate and economics journals, including* The Appraisal Journal, Real Estate Economics, Journal of Real Estate Finance and Economics, *and* Journal of Real Estate Research.

23

---

1. David Lennhoff, *A Business Enterprise Value Anthology* (Chicago: Appraisal Institute, 2001). An excerpt of the book appears in the July 2001 edition of *The Appraisal Journal.*
2. Robert W. Owens, "How Business Enterprise Value Applies in Nearly All Appraisals," *The Appraisal Journal* (April 1998): 117–125.

mobile home parks) fall into the category of special purpose properties. Before proceeding with our example, we provide the rationale for our approach by discussing it in the context of existing methods of allocating the sources of value.

Business Enterprise Value Defined

As defined in *The Appraisal of Real Estate*, 11th ed.,[3] business enterprise value is "a value enhancement that results from items of intangible personal property, such as marketing and management skill, an assembled work force, working capital, trade names, franchises, patents, trademarks, non realty-related contracts/leases, and some operating agreements." The difficulty in estimating BEV stems from the fact that the business enterprise is not traded separately in the market. Rather, it is traded as one component of a going concern that includes the real estate and tangible personal property as well. Martin Benson[4] expresses the summation relationship of what constitutes going concern value as:

$$GC = RE + FF\&E + BEV$$

In this equation, FF&E (furniture, fixtures, and equipment) includes all tangible personal property, which, depending on the circumstances, might include net working capital and inventory.

Valuing the going concern is fairly straightforward using discounted cash flow techniques or an income capitalization approach. The difficulty arises when there is a need to decompose the going concern value into the various elements as required for assessment and condemnation assignments. Also, the Uniform Standards of Professional Appraisal Practice (USPAP) require that the components be appraised separately when the contribution of nonrealty items to overall value is significant. This is clear from Standard 1-4(g), which states, "an appraiser must analyze the effect on value of any personal property, trade fixtures, or intangible items that are not real property but are included in the appraisal." The USPAP comment further clarifies this requirement:

> Competency in personal property appraisal (see Standard 7) or business valuation (see Standard 9) may be required when it is necessary to allocate the overall value to the property components. A separate valuation, developed in compliance with

Standards pertinent to the type of property involved, is required when the value of a non-realty item or combination of such items is significant to the overall value.

There is no dispute that BEV exists; rather, the debate centers around its pervasiveness. Where should the line be drawn? In distinguishing between BEV and real estate value, it is fundamental to recognize that income generated from a business conducted within the real estate is not the appropriate measure of real estate value. Instead, that income is the value of the going concern. For many special purpose properties, the business enterprise component is substantial, so the potential for error is large if going concern value and real estate value are confused.

The Three Approaches to Value

Extracting the components of value poses problems regardless of whether the cost, income capitalization, or sales comparison approach is used. The cost approach may be applied to the real estate and FF&E components of the going concern, but obtaining an estimate of vacant land value may be difficult and estimating the functional and external obsolescence, especially with older properties, may introduce substantial error. Of course there is always a fundamental issue when using cost as a proxy for value. The issue is that there may be little relationship between cost and market value unless one subscribes to the "greater fool" theory. Finally, applying the cost approach to estimate the business enterprise component of a going concern is difficult even to conceptualize, much less to operationalize.

Applying the income capitalization approach is fairly straightforward when valuing the going concern, but allocating the income stream to the various components of value is quite difficult, as is determining the capitalization rates to use for each of the components. In a recent article, David Lennhoff and Peter Wolman[5] provide an excellent discussion of the difficulties associated with four variations of the income capitalization approach. The four variations are estimating the rental portion of the income stream using conventional apartment rents, capitalizing residual income to real estate,

---

3. Appraisal Institute, *The Appraisal of Real Estate,* 11th ed. (Chicago: Appraisal Institute, 1996). New terminology introduced in *The Appraisal of Real Estate,* 12th ed. clarifies some of the confusion about terminology related to business enterprise value.

4. Martin Benson, "Real Estate and Business Value: A New Perspective," *The Appraisal Journal* (April 1999): 205–212.

5. David C. Lennhoff and Peter A. Wolman, "Valuation of Continuing Care Retirement Communities: Worth Another Look," *The Appraisal Journal* (January 2000): 57–63.

capitalizing residual income to the business enterprise, and using the relationship between the capitalization rate for the real estate and the going concern to apportion the income streams. In addition to the problems the authors identified regarding these methods, it should be noted that none addresses the strict interpretation of the USPAP requirement for *separate* value estimates of the going concern components.

The sales comparison approach is especially problematic. Comparable sales of special purpose properties are typically quite sparse, and even when comparables can be found, the value implied by the transactions is that of the going concern, not of the individual components. The real estate, tangible personal property, and business enterprise are not sold separately, so the separate values are not identified by market transactions. Valuation of the individual components of value is especially difficult for special purpose properties where the business enterprise component is substantial. As Lennhoff and Wolman note, "Many simply conclude (not incorrectly) that techniques are currently in development, as debate on methodology continues."

A Method for Estimating BEV

Our purpose here is to propose a new method of estimating BEV to supplement the appraiser's existing arsenal of techniques. The method is specifically directed at special purpose properties (e.g., assisted living, skilled nursing, and congregate care retirement facilities; health clubs; marinas; mobile home parks) wherein going concern value depends on attaining stabilized occupancy. The insight driving our approach is that the value added to a project during absorption is the business enterprise value of the going concern, and that this value can be measured as the present value of the income forgone by the developer during the rent-up period. The technique provides the separate valuation of BEV required by USPAP. In addition, it provides a means of reconciling the value estimate attained by the cost approach (real estate and FF&E) with the value estimate reached by the income capitalization approach (going concern).

There is a continuous scale that reflects varying degrees of business enterprise value in going concerns that depend on stabilized occupancy. We do not argue that income from washers and dryers or soft drink machines in an apartment building may constitute a BEV

meriting separate valuation. The accounting principle of materiality supports the inclusion of such income as miscellaneous or ancillary to the rents received from apartment units. Consider, however, an apartment complex rented exclusively to senior citizens. The rental income of the complex includes fees for services such as meals, social activities, monitoring of health conditions, and dispensing medications, as well as transportation to doctors and shopping. In this case, it is apparent that much more than the mere rental of real estate is involved in generating the income. In some fashion, the income streams must be segregated so that the real property value and the BEV can be segregated.

One way to segregate these income streams is to examine the potential income lost between the completion date of the facility and the date on which stabilized occupancy was achieved. The present value of that lost income represents the difference between the cost of the land, improvements, and FF&E and the market value of the property as a going concern once stabilized occupancy is achieved. The application of our proposed methodology is illustrated below with a hypothetical example.

BEV in Special Purpose Properties— An Example

Walker Woods is a hypothetical assisted-living facility appraised as proposed construction. The 80-unit facility is licensed for 110 residents, but has an expected occupancy of 100. The four-story, 65,000- square-foot structure is proposed on a three-acre parcel in an "in fill" area of a city with a population of 500,000. In California, an assisted-living facility is licensed by the State Department of Social Services and provides that caretakers assist residents in dressing, bathing, grooming, and the dispensing of medications. These facilities also offer meals and transportation services for shopping and medical appointments for residents. Many of these facilities offer other "in-house" services such as beauty salons. In addition, space within the facility is provided for regular visits from chiropractors, podiatrists, physical therapists, and other health care professionals.

The affluent neighborhood surrounding the site offers easy access to shopping and medical facilities including an acute care hospital within one mile of the facility. A market study indicates that all the subject units can be rented to paying residents without the need for government-subsidized residents. In this market, double occupancy is common in about 10% to 12% of the private studio, one-bedroom units. The second person is usually a spouse, sister, or other related party.

The expenses for Walker Woods are divided into fixed and variable categories. The fixed expenses include those expenses that do not vary with occupancy as well as a minimal threshold level of some variable expenses. For example, some utilities are not variable, such as outside yard lighting and the utilities of the building's common areas. Individual rooms, however, would not be heated or cooled until they are occupied. Another example of a minimum threshold is meal service, where a minimal level of staffing is required to serve, whether facility occupancy is 20 or 50 residents.

Table 1 shows the estimates of value based on applying the three traditional appraisal approaches. Note that the cost approach reflects the market value of the subject at the time of completion (certificate of occupancy obtained from the local building department), whereas the income and direct sales comparison approaches reflect market value at stabilized occupancy. The cost approach value is identical to the old R-41(b) type valuations required in the late 1980s by banking regulators. The cost approach renders a value approximately $1.3 million less than the reconciled market value based on stabilized occupancy. This difference is an indication of the intangible business enterprise value associated with achieving stabilized occupancy. Note also that the 5% entrepreneurial profit reflects that building the facility (i.e., the cost approach) is not a tremendous risk factor. Unlike conventional apartments, a senior citizen complex is not likely to invoke protests from neighbors. In fact, most communities will readily give the zoning and other entitlements necessary to build this type of facility. For these

Table 1	Estimates of Value for Walker Woods Assisted Living Facility

Income Capitalization Approach

40 private one-bedroom units rented at $2,500/month	$1,200,000
20 private studio units rented at $1,900/month	$456,000
20 semi-private, one-bedroom units rented to 40 residents at $1,400/month per person	$672,000
Additional income collected for rental of beauty salon space at $400/month	$4,800
Additional income from leases of medical space to health care professionals $600/month	$7,200
Seven double-occupancy, one-bedroom units—added rental income $350 each per month	$29,400
Additional care Level II* for 20 residents at $200/month	$48,000
Additional care Level III* for 20 residents at $400/month	$96,000
Total annual potential gross income	$2,513,400
Vacancy and collection loss 5%	($125,670)
Effective gross income	$2,387,730
Fixed expenses (maintenance, property taxes, insurance, management, some utilities, and a threshold level of some variable costs) $12,750/unit	$1,020,000
Variable expenses (staff salaries, food, some utilities, miscellaneous) $6,510/unit	$520,800
Net operating income	$846,930
Overall capitalization rate—derived from comparable sales	11.5%
Indicated market value by direct capitalization	$7,364,609

Direct Sales Comparison Approach—$90,000/unit	$7,200,000

Cost Approach

Total direct and indirect costs of construction	$4,600,000
Total personal property	$350,000
Market value of land	$750,000
Entrepreneurial profit (5%)	$285,000
Total value indicated by cost approach	$5,985,000
Reconciled going concern market value—at stabilized occupancy	$7,300,000

* Level II and Level III refer to elderly residents that require extra care due to special needs and possible limited mobility.

reasons, the lion's share of entrepreneurial profit is attributed to achieving stabilized occupancy, not constructing the building.

The market value of the assisted living facility at the time of completion, but prior to occupancy, is an extremely risky point in time for the developer. Almost by definition the sale of the facility at this point in time would be distressed, since buyers would suspect that something was wrong with either the project or the market. Or, they may suspect some other issue is forcing the original developer to sell prior to realizing stabilized occupancy. From the buyer's perspective there would be little inclination to discount the future lost revenue. After all, from the buyer's perspective, a dollar of lost income one, two, or six months from now is almost as bad as a dollar lost today. From the seller's perspective, however, there would be very little inclination to sell the property and business opportunity at this critical point in time.

The market value concept is based on both buyer and seller being informed of relevant facts. In this instance, both buyer and seller have equally compelling reasons not to want to buy and sell, respectively. Therefore, we believe the appropriate way to deal with the income lost during absorption is to use a purely financial methodology that discounts the lost cash flow at the appropriate yield rate. The appropriate discount rate can be developed from the market derived capitalization rate[6] by adding the estimated growth rate of net operating income. In this example, the growth rate in net operating income is expected to be 3%. The discount rate, therefore, is 14.5% (capitalization rate plus expected growth rate). This discounted cash flow methodology is based on some simplifying assumptions, summarized as follows:

- Average effective gross income per resident per month is $1,990.

- Preleasing results in 20 residents by the end of the first month.

- After the first month, absorption is uniform at 4 residents per month.[7]

- It will take about 20 months to reach stabilized occupancy (96 residents—4% vacancy and 1% collection loss).

- Fixed expenses are $85,000 per month and will be incurred each month during the absorption period.

- The variable expenses are $434 per resident per month and will be incurred as a function of occupancy.

As seen in Table 1, once stabilized occupancy is attained, the stabilized monthly net operating income is $846,930/12 months = $70,578. However, the stabilized NOI occurs only after the absorption is complete (in the example, 20 months) and income is lost to the owner during the rent-up period. For example, in the first month after completion the lost income is the effective gross income ($1,990 × 80 = $159,200) less the variable expenses not incurred for the absent residents ($434 × 80 = $34,720).

Therefore, the lost income during the first month after completion is $159,200 – $34,720 = $124,480. Discounting the lost income back to the beginning of the month at 14.5% produces a present value for the first month's lost income of $122,999. Table 2 provides a schedule of the discounted cash flows for forgone income during the 20-month absorption period.

The indicated present value of the lost income from this methodology is about $1.2 million, which is consistent with the BEV suggested by the residual technique. That technique implied BEV of $1.3 million, the difference between the total going concern value and the cost of the real estate that includes a normal entrepreneurial profit margin for building the facility. The final conclusion would be based on thoughtful reconciliation of these two methodologies and others that might be brought to bear on the problem. It should be clear, however, that this approach and the residual approach are measuring the same thing, namely, the intangible BEV associated with stabilized occupancy.

We chose a proposed construction example for the purpose of clarity, but our technique is by no means limited to such assignments. The model provides a separate, as opposed to residual, valuation of the business enterprise component of going concern value and could be applied to any going concern where the occupancy is the primary determinant of the BEV. Even

---

6. A capitalization rate of 11.5% lies between the capitalization rates applied in the industry and the blended capitalization rates for assisted living facilities. See Anthony J. Mullen, "A Note on Underwriting and Investing in Senior Living and Long-Term Care Properties: Separating the Business from the Real Estate," *Journal of Real Estate Portfolio Management* (1999): 301.

7. For the quarter ended 3/31/01, the National Investment Center for the Seniors Housing and Care Industry (www.nic.org) reports a move-in rate of 3.9 units per month for properties not yet stabilized.

End of Month	Number of Residents	Lost Rent Less Variable Expenses Not Incurred	Lost Net Operating Income	14.5% Present Worth Factor	Discounted Net Income Lost
1	20	80 × ($1,990 − $434)	$124,480	0.9881	$122,999
2	24	76 × ($1,990 − $434)	$118,256	0.9763	$115,453
3	28	72 × ($1,990 − $434)	$112,032	0.9646	$108,066
4	32	68 × ($1,990 − $434)	$105,808	0.9531	$100,846
5	36	64 × ($1,990 − $434)	$99,584	0.9417	$93,778
6	40	60 × ($1,990 − $434)	$93,360	0.9305	$86,871
7	44	56 × ($1,990 − $434)	$87,136	0.9194	$80,109
8	48	52 × ($1,990 − $434)	$80,912	0.9084	$73,500
9	52	48 × ($1,990 − $434)	$74,688	0.8975	$67,032
10	56	44 × ($1,990 − $434)	$68,464	0.8868	$60,714
11	60	40 × ($1,990 − $434)	$62,240	0.8762	$54,535
12	64	36 × ($1,990 − $434)	$56,016	0.8658	$48,499
13	68	32 × ($1,990 − $434)	$49,792	0.8554	$42,592
14	72	28 × ($1,990 − $434)	$43,568	0.8452	$36,824
15	76	24 × ($1,990 − $434)	$37,344	0.8351	$31,186
16	80	20 × ($1,990 − $434)	$31,120	0.8252	$25,680
17	84	16 × ($1,990 − $434)	$24,896	0.8153	$20,298
18	88	12 × ($1,990 − $434)	$18,672	0.8056	$15,042
19	92	8 × ($1,990 − $434)	$12,448	0.7960	$9,909
20	96	4 × ($1,990 − $434)	$6,224	0.7865	$4,895
				TOTAL:	$1,198,828

in the case of a facility having already attained stabilized occupancy, the model could be used to quantify the value associated with achieving it.

BEV is more fluid than real estate value and will vary considerably depending on market conditions. A facility that goes from 95% to 75% occupancy because of a new competitive project in the community has had a serious loss in its BEV. The market value of the real estate may also be affected by economic obsolescence, but the primary impact will be on the BEV.

Some may argue that only the special services in an assisted living facility should be treated as BEV and that some core component of the income is simply the rental of an apartment unit. We disagree with this notion because the entire package of facility and services is what is available to the prospective resident; there is no opportunity to simply rent an apartment in these facilities.

Achieving Stabilized Occupancy as a Measure of BEV

There are some critical questions to be asked regarding the methodology. Does it fully reflect all the elements of intangible value in an assisted living facility? Such elements would include a knowledgeable and well-trained staff, a well-trained marketing team (well connected to the medical community, social workers, churches, and other referral sources in the community), and a long-standing reputation of quality care. All these intangible aspects of the business translate directly into the cash flow of the business and are captured by this new methodology.

This methodology also may be used to measure the intangible BEV of an existing facility. The appraiser can establish the appropriate absorption rate by examining the most recent facilities to absorb in a community or, better yet, facilities currently approaching maximum capacity. It is intuitive to think that intangible BEV will change based on market conditions. However, it may be less intuitive to recognize that when market conditions deteriorate and the time to fill a facility increases, the intangible BEV will actually increase. Although both the tangible and intangible values will change based on changing market conditions, the BEV is arguably more volatile than the real estate value. Achieving stabilized occupancy in an uncertain or weak market has greater risk and thus must be rewarded by greater intangible BEV.

There are actually several potential scenarios that could impact both the real estate value and the BEV. First, assume that the absorption rate decreased from 4 residents per month to 3. Clearly this would result in greater lost income during absorption, implying a larger intangible BEV. At the same time, however, there could actually be a change in what constitutes stabilized occupancy from 5% vacancy and collection loss to 6% or 7% vacancy and collection loss. This would have the effect of lowering the total going concern value. An overall weaker market demand for the units in the facility could also effect the capitalization and yield rates. The net effect of these factors would have to be evaluated specifically. We contend, though, that while the total going concern value would go down (because of lower net income and higher capitalization rate), and the underlying real estate value would also go down, the BEV in this scenario would increase. Moreover, the volatility of the BEV would be greater than that of the underlying real estate value.

Next, assume that the market improves and the facility could be absorbed at a rate of 5 residents per month instead of 4. The facility would absorb more quickly and less rent would be lost during absorption. To simplify, assume that there is no change in the level of stabilized occupancy and there is likewise no change in the capitalization and yield rates. In this instance, the total enterprise value is unchanged: the intangible BEV will go down (less risk) and the underlying real estate value, therefore, will increase. This makes sense intuitively because the profitability of simply building the facility should increase and the risk associated with filling the facility should decrease. The 5% entrepreneurial profit that we cited in the cost approach might increase to 6% or 7%.

Conclusion

In this article, we propose a new methodology for estimating the BEV component of special purpose properties that derive their value from achieving stabilized occupancy. While not intended as a replacement for the traditional approaches to value, the method supplements, supports, and validates the values of the going concern components estimated by other means.

One advantage of the method is that it provides a separate valuation for BEV, as required by USPAP for properties where intangibles comprise a substantial proportion of going concern value. By separately measuring BEV, this technique can be used to estimate the value of the real estate component of a property as a residual of the total going concern value. It also can be used for all special purpose properties achieving value through stabilized occupancy, even those properties that are already fully occupied.

References

Appraisal Institute. *The Appraisal of Real Estate*, 12th ed. (Chicago: Appraisal Institute, 2001).

Appraisal Institute. *A Business Enterprise Value Anthology* (Chicago: Appraisal Institute, 2001).

Benson, M. "Real Estate and Business Value: A New Perspective." *The Appraisal Journal* (April 1999): 205–212.

Key Financial Indicators, The National Investment Center for the Seniors Housing and Care Industry, www.nic.org.

Kinnard, W. N. Jr., E. M. Worzala, and D. L. Swango. "Intangible Assets in an Operating First-Class Downtown Hotel." *The Appraisal Journal* (January 2001): 68–83.

Lennhoff, D. C. "Business Enterprise Value: Introduction." *The Appraisal Journal* (July 2001): 341–342.

Lennhoff, D. C. and P. A. Wolman. "Valuation of Continuing Care Retirement Communities: Worth Another Look." *The Appraisal Journal* (January 2000): 57–63.

Lennhoff, D. C. "Business Enterprise Value Debate: Still a Long Way to Reconciliation." *The Appraisal Journal* (October 1999): 422–430.

Owens, R. W. "How Business Enterprise Value Applies in Nearly All Appraisals." *The Appraisal Journal* (April 1998): 117–125.

Mullen, A. J. "A Note on Underwriting and Investing in Senior Living and Long-Term Care Properties: Separating the Business from the Real Estate." *Journal of Real Estate Portfolio Management* (1999): 299–302.

Mullen, A. J. and R. C. Wetzler. "Assisted Living Properties: A Prudent Lender's Investment Analysis." *The RMA Journal* (December 2000): 56–60.

Billboard Valuation: Fundamental Asset Allocation Issues

Dwain R. Stoops, MAI
This article originally appeared in the April 2003 issue of *The Appraisal Journal*.

"A problem well defined is half solved" is an axiom worthy of consideration in the valuation of outdoor advertising assets. This article advances the concept of the money trail, or the observation of the direction and derivation of the income flow, as a key factor in the identification and allocation of the various assets of an outdoor advertising firm. The money trail is the essence of the principle of contribution, which is the basis of asset valuation.

In recent years a critical need to replace, reconstruct, or expand the aging highway transportation infrastructure has necessitated the acquisition of rights-of-way on which billboards are located. The determination of just compensation for outdoor advertising assets involves many complex and confusing legal and valuation problems. A complete discussion of the issues is beyond the scope of this article. Rather, this article focuses on fundamental asset allocation issues critical in billboard valuation. How can appraisers objectively identify the specific assets being taken by the acquiring authority? What is the nature of an outdoor advertising business? Are billboard structures real or personal property? Is an outdoor advertising firm a real estate-based business, analogous to a hotel, office building property, or an apartment complex or is it a service-based advertising business, analogous to other advertising media businesses such as television, radio stations, and newspapers?

Solutions to billboard valuation problems require an understanding of the relationships and interconnections between real estate assets and the total assets of a business enterprise as a going concern. It is imperative for appraisers to clearly and succinctly identify, define, and allocate the assets to be appraised in order to properly apply appraisal methods based on sound and generally accepted valuation principles. The primary emphasis throughout this article will be consideration of the money trail, i.e., the observation of the direction and derivation of the income flow in the production process. The money trail is a key factor in the proper identification and allocation of assets in any business enterprise.

Identification of assets is especially germane to controversial situations in the valuation of outdoor advertising assets, commonly called billboards. Improperly identified assets are the primary cause of the widely diverse opinions of value between professional appraisers. In this article, the term "outdoor advertising assets" will be used instead of "billboards." The term "outdoor advertising assets" is more descriptive of the various components that comprise the total assets of a business enterprise that provides advertising services within the ambit of the advertising industry. The term "billboard" in this article will refer to the tangible sign structure used as a business fixture to display advertising messages.

Much of the valuation controversy surrounds the issue of whether outdoor advertising business assets are real property or personal property. The outdoor advertising industry has taken the unique position in eminent domain situations that the total assets of an outdoor advertising business enterprise are real property assets and, therefore, should be compensated as other real property taken for public use. Based on this perspective the

Dwain R. Stoops, MAI, is president of MetroSouth Realty Services, Inc. of Nixa, Missouri, a real estate valuation research and consulting firm. Stoops is an independent fee appraiser/consultant engaged exclusively in valuation research and consulting for eminent domain situations involving outdoor advertising assets. He served as a panel member in the Crossfire Session on "Determining the Value of Billboards," at the 2002 IRWA International Education Seminar in Mobile, Alabama. He is a state-certified general real estate appraiser in the states of Missouri, Illinois, Mississippi, Virginia, South Carolina, and Kansas.

24

industry claims that the total revenue generated by the total assets of the business is real estate rental income, thereby circumventing the legal barrier prohibiting lost profits as a proper element of compensation for land taken in condemnation proceedings. However, in property tax situations the same industry argues very persuasively that billboards and other assets of the outdoor advertising business are personal property that should not be taxed as real property. In opposition, the acquiring entities generally contend that the only real property assets are the fee simple or leasehold interests in sign site locations.

With these opposing points of view, it is not uncommon for expert witnesses to offer opinions of value of outdoor advertising assets that differ by 2 to 5 times in valuation. This is not the typical variance due to an appraiser's interpretation and judgment of market data, but rather is an indication that different assets are being considered in the valuation process. The appraisers are in essence valuing different properties.

This article addresses the identification and allocation of outdoor advertising assets from the economic perspective of the business firm as a going concern,[1] with special emphasis on the money trail. It is especially important to understand the concept of the outdoor advertising firm as an entity that brings together various factors of production, including land, labor, and capital. The outdoor advertising firm produces a product for sale in the advertising market in exchange for a flow of revenue representing a return on and of the opportunity costs required to attract the factors of production. The return on the total business investment or the economic profit is the remainder of gross revenues after payment of all factor costs. Appraisers are well aware of the importance of the quantity, quality, and duration of cash flow in estimating value. Equally important is the direction and derivation of the income flow (money trail) in identifying and allocating the various assets or factors of production that are brought together and managed by the outdoor advertising firm.

Application of the Money Trail Concept

Several controversial questions and difficult valuation problems have developed regard-

ing the identity and value allocation of outdoor advertising assets in eminent domain situations. While the most discussed question is whether billboard structures are real or personal property, it is evident that the basic underlying question that needs to be addressed is the proper identification and allocation of the various assets of an outdoor advertising business enterprise as a going concern. Billboard structures are not the only assets generating revenue flow to the outdoor advertising business firm. A close observation of the direction and derivation of the money trail associated with each asset will assist in its identification and allocation in the overall production process. Assets contribute value to the entity that is the recipient of their money flow. Based on the money trail the typical billboard structure is not real property because it generates no income flow to the real estate. It cannot improve the real estate, as the industry claims, without providing some benefits to the land.

By the same concept the sign site upon which the billboard is located is a real property asset because it contributes a money flow (land rent) to the real estate; hence, it has real property value that can be estimated as a basis for just compensation. It can be very confusing at this point because outdoor advertising companies consider sign site locations as intangible business assets, which are distinct from real property sign sites.

The intent of this discussion of the outdoor advertising money trail is to provide a clearer understanding of the nature and identity of the billboard structure, the sign site, and the other assets as factors of production of an outdoor advertising business operation. An overview of a typical outdoor advertising business firm will provide a clearer understanding of the relationships and interconnections of the total assets of an outdoor advertising business operating as a going concern. Following the flow of money into and out of the firm provides a basis for defining and separating the tangible real and personal property from the intangible business assets of the firm.

"Appraisal problems are half solved when the property is well defined" is a valuation axiom worth consideration here. It also brings the

---

1. Many of the concepts and principles discussed and advanced in this article are based on Appraisal Institute, Course 800: "Separating Real and Personal Property from Intangible Business Assets," Course Handbook (Chicago: Appraisal Institute, 2002), developed by Marvin L. Wolverton, MAI, with the assistance of David C. Lennhoff, MAI, SRA, Richard Marchitelli, MAI, Maureen Mastroieni, MAI, James D. Vernor, MAI, James Budyak, ASA, and the late William M. Kinnard Jr., MAI, SRA.

appraiser into compliance with the USPAP[2] requirement to identify and consider the effect on value of any personal property, trade fixtures, or intangible items that are not real property but included in the appraisal.

Overview of a Typical Outdoor Advertising Firm

An overview of a typical outdoor advertising business firm will serve two purposes: (1) to familiarize the reader with the total assets of an outdoor advertising business and (2) to observe the nature of the assets based on the money trail concept. The following illustrates a typical outdoor advertising business enterprise based on industry data.

A typical outdoor advertising company is an advertising firm engaged in the production of outdoor advertising services to a wide range of customers on outdoor advertising display panels located along public highways and streets. Advertising services involve displaying customers' messages for exposure to a traveling audience or in the industries own words, "[Posters] are sold much like radio. They are sold in showings; they're packaged and sold with a signal that you distribute throughout the marketplace…."[3] This signal distribution service includes more than simply painting ads or posting vinyl printed sheets on sign display panels. Other services include planning, packaging, sales, and verification of showings or postings, periodic rotation and maintenance of ad copy, and in some instances the creative design and production of vinyl ad copy sheets. An outdoor advertising company recognizes revenue as advertising services are sold. Revenue is the result of a balanced combination of land, labor, and capital as factors in the production process.

Factors of Production

Land
Land factors are the natural resources required by the outdoor advertising business firm as locations for office and shop facilities and billboard structure sites. Legal sign sites for billboard locations are relatively scarce assets that are necessary in the production of outdoor advertising services. The typical outdoor advertising firm leases approximately 95% of all sign sites from landowners. The value of the land factors is reflected by the market price paid for fee land or easements, or the market rents paid to landlords. When leased fee sign sites are taken in eminent domain acquisitions, the landowner is due the fair market contributory value of the sign site to the fee simple land taken, based on the expected flow of market rent to the land. If the contract rent is below market rent, the outdoor advertising tenant may be due some bonus value compensation for recognizable rent savings over the lease contract period or until the landlord's first opportunity to increase the rent to market levels.

Labor
Labor factors are the human resources that provide necessary contributions in the production process, including office, production and maintenance workers, and management and sales personnel. The efforts and contributions of the owner/operator of the firm are assets regarded as a special class of labor. The value of the factors of labor is based on the opportunity costs payments in the form of training, salaries, and benefits.

Capital
Capital factors are the manufactured resources and financial assets required by the outdoor advertising business firm. These include bank credit facilities and notes, buildings for office and shop facilities, furniture, fixtures, and equipment. Fixtures include billboard structures designed for bulletin or poster panels used as advertising communication devices. Bulletins are larger panels (typically 14' x 48') used to display permanent or rotating messages at high traffic volume locations providing long-term directional or high impact and high circulation ads. Posters are smaller panels (typically 10.5' x 24') sold in showings tailored for specified market coverage, at lower traffic volume locations for product branding and other short-term awareness messages. The equipment assets include tools and machines used in production and rolling stock used by management, sales, and service/maintenance personnel. The value of the capital factors is based on the opportunity costs of borrowing, purchasing, leasing, developing, erecting, and maintaining each factor for use in the advertising service production process.

---

2. The Appraisal Foundation, *Uniform Standards of Professional Appraisal Practice,* 2003 ed. (Washington, D.C.: The Appraisal Foundation, 2003): SR 1-4(g).

3. Sean Reilly, Vice President of Lamar Media Corporation, in a presentation at the First Union Securities' Nantucket Conference, June 28, 2001.

Assets of an Outdoor Advertising Firm

As a business enterprise the outdoor advertising firm acquires and manages tangible and intangible assets as factors of production for maximum productivity and profitability of the firm. The market value of the total assets of the business depends on an optimal blend of assets.

Tangible real property assets include real estate owned or leased by a firm as locations for offices, shops, and signs. Tangible personal property includes office and shop equipment, rolling stock, and, arguably, the billboard structures, all used in production of advertising services.

Intangible assets of an outdoor advertising firm consist of business resources such as working capital, site locations, customer lists and contracts, noncompete agreements, permits, licenses, records, systems and procedures in place, assembled and trained workforce and management team, and goodwill. The going concern operation of an outdoor advertising business depends to a significant extent upon the continued services of the executive officers and other key management and sales personnel.[4] It is important to note that the intangible site location assets are not the same as the tangible real property interest. Site locations are going-concern business assets based on the capitalized value of the annual sign site rent over the term of the ground lease. Consideration of this intangible asset as real property in condemnation valuation will result in double compensation for the sign site to the landlord and the tenant.

All assets functioning profitably together as a going concern affect the market value of the total assets of an outdoor advertising firm. As a going concern the business enterprise is expected to continue operation indefinitely with sufficient income to pay a fair return to all the factors of production. It is anticipated that the firm will maximize the difference between revenue and cost, thereby realizing a fair return on the total assets of the firm.

Earnings before interest, taxes, depreciation, and amortization (EBITDA) of an outdoor advertising business typically range from 35%

to 50% of net revenue. An analysis of 192 annual financial statements of public and private outdoor advertising companies from 1991 to 2001 reflects an average EBITDA of 38.3%. The same study indicates an average sign site rent expense ratio of 15.4%, based on total net revenues (gross ad sales less agency fees). Currently, new sign site leases are renting in a typical range of 15% to 25% of net revenue. The increase in the sign site expense ratio is an indication that landowners are becoming more knowledgeable of the contributory value of legal sign sites.

Marketplace of the Outdoor Advertising Business

An outdoor advertising business operates within the media market of designated market areas (DMA).[5] It is in competition with other outdoor advertising businesses, as well as other media including radio, television, newspapers, and direct mail marketers. The production of revenue and the value of an outdoor advertising business are affected by changes in advertising market trends. Real estate market trends have little affect on the outdoor advertising business except in the land factors market of sign sites, which are generally subordinate land uses to the highest and best use of the larger parcel of land.

Outdoor Advertising Asset Acquisitions

Acquisitions of outdoor advertising assets may include the total assets of another business firm or selected fill-in assets to augment the buyer's inventory of display locations. There are several economic advantages in asset acquisition, including increased economies of scale in accounting and administrative functions and increased market penetration.

Another economic advantage in business expansion by acquisition is the tax-deductible, non–cash flow expense of amortization of goodwill[6] and certain other intangible assets. All acquisitions by outdoor advertising companies are generally accounted for under the purchase method of accounting, with each acquisition being allocated to assets acquired and liabili-

---

4. SEC Form 10-K, "2001 Annual Report of Lamar Media Corporation," (March 21, 2002): 11, 20.

5. A designated market area is a television or broadcast market area assigned by Nielsen Media Research for use in planning, buying, and evaluating television audiences.

6. The adoption of SFAS No. 142, "Goodwill and Other Intangible Assets," effective January 1, 2002, eliminates the full amortization expense for goodwill, except for impairment that may not be recoverable.

ties assumed based on fair market value at the date of acquisition. Allocation data from several hundred recent sales of outdoor advertising firms indicate that it is typical for acquisition prices to be allocated in ranges of 2% to 5% for current assets, 24% to 34% for property, plant, and equipment, and 64% to 74% for goodwill and other intangibles. The acquired other intangibles generally include sign site locations, customer lists and contracts, and noncompete agreements.

These tax advantages have a definite impact on the acquisition prices paid for outdoor advertising assets. Outdoor advertising companies that are aggressive in acquisition activities may be non–income tax paying businesses for several years through amortization expense tax deductions.

Internal Asset Growth Strategies

An outdoor advertising company can enhance its revenue and cash-flow growth by employing highly targeted, local marketing efforts to improve its display occupancy levels and by increasing advertising rates. Also, the business can upgrade its existing displays and construct new structures at new locations. New legal sign sites are becoming increasingly difficult to find, however. A recent study[7] of 191 cities in 45 states with year 2000 populations of 150,000 or more indicates that 80% of the cities allow new outdoor advertising signs to be constructed subject to local regulations.

As new legal sign sites become scarcer, their cost (land rent) as factors of production will increase commensurate with the demand for the production of advertising services. The two factors that are required in the development of new structures are land (a legal site) and an approved sign structure. Of these, the legal site is most scarce and limited. The structure is readily available at a typical cost of $40,000 to $60,000. For both site and structure to function as factors of production in the outdoor advertising operation, a sign permit is required. Sign permits are site-specific and nondiscretionary, i.e., they are readily obtainable at a relatively nominal cost contingent upon the erection of a code-approved structure at a legal location. Based upon the scarcity factor, the legal sign site is a critical asset to be considered in the allocation of outdoor advertising assets. The value of each factor (sign, site, and structure) is reflected in its rental and/or construction costs, including the cost of obtaining the required permit.

Consideration of Identification and Allocation Issues

Identification and allocation issues encountered in the valuation of outdoor advertising assets become clearer when examined using the fundamental economic principle that the flow of money brings assets together in the creation of value. The money trail is a compass providing guidance in the proper allocation of assets by pointing to the direction of money flowing into or out of an outdoor advertising business enterprise. These observations provide an objective basis for the identification of each asset that contributes to the production of the total business revenue. The allocation of asset value is not an easy task; especially the intangible business assets in an industry that is still very private with restricted disclosure of specific data and information regarding operations and asset sales. However, based on the predictable direction of money flow, the assets to be appraised can be properly identified, which is the first step in solving the complex problems in valuing outdoor advertising assets.

A review of real estate appraisal literature reveals two general premises regarding the identification and allocation of outdoor advertising assets as a basis for valuation. The first premise, termed the "business-related premise," is defined by Steven Cantwell, MAI, in his 1999 article: "The [outdoor advertising] asset that sells in the marketplace usually consists of: a sign structure, a site interest (usually a ground lease or a legal right to occupy a particular location), a permit, and the potential to generate advertising revenue (the advertising business component)."[8] The opposing premise, termed the "real estate-related premise," is succinctly defined by Rodolfo J. Aguilar, MAI, in his recent article: "All activities of a sign owner relate directly to [an outdoor advertising structure] being rented to a tenant/ advertiser, a purely real estate related function."[9]

---

7.   Alan C. Weinstein, "A Study of Local Regulation of Outdoor Advertising in the Major Cities of Each State," executive summary (Cleveland State University, 2001).

8.   Steven M. Cantwell, MAI, "Billboard Valuation Without Distortion: The Heathrow Decision," *The Appraisal Journal* (July 1999): 251.

9.   Rodolfo J. Aguilar, PhD, "The Appraisal of Off-Premise Outdoor Advertising Billboards," *Right of Way Magazine* (September/October 2000): 17.

Extensive research and analysis of the nature of the total assets of the outdoor advertising business based on the money trail concept supports the conclusion that the business-related premise is the proper basis for identifying the assets of an outdoor advertising business enterprise. The business-related premise recognizes the distinct separation of the tangible assets, real and personal property, and intangible business assets for proper allocation of value. The preceding overview of the typical outdoor advertising firm reveals that the intangible assets of the operating business represent a significant component of the total assets of an outdoor advertising firm and that assets must be properly identified and allocated in development of opinions of fair market value as a basis of just compensation.

It is very important that appraisers properly identify and allocate the assets that are dictated by law to be compensable in the jurisdiction of the taking. If state law requires compensation for the loss of tangible personal property, business income, or other intangibles, e.g., goodwill, then every effort must be made to identify and allocate those tangible or intangible assets to develop an opinion of their fair market value. However, in states that do not allow compensation for personal property, goodwill, or loss of business income, it is not proper to camouflage the total assets of the outdoor advertising business in a real estate package to be valued by capitalizing the total business revenue. Due to differing laws in many states, appraisers must consider the money trail concept in the identification and allocation of the assets that are taken in the various eminent domain situations.

Real Estate-Related Premise: Total Assets Considered Real Estate Assets

In his 1994 monograph Donald Sutte, MAI concluded that "...sign industry sales indicate that signs are real property and do not reflect significant business interests."[10] It is very important to note that the terms "signs," "signboards," "outdoor advertising signs," or "billboards" as

used in the real estate-related premise do not refer simply to the tangible sign structure as real property, but include the total assets of the outdoor advertising business as real estate assets. This necessary inference is clear in Sutte's conclusion to his discussion of business and real estate value:

> The author's investigation of numerous sales transactions involving thousands of displays indicated that the business interests were not significant and generally corresponded with the real estate interests. In fact, in most ways signboard sales are quite similar to transactions involving standard real estate....As applied to outdoor advertising signs, this term [business interests] is synonymous with the real estate interests.[11]

The real estate-related premise is based on the assumption that typical billboard structures are real estate improvements or leasehold improvements, that the advertising business revenue is real estate rent earned by leasing display space for occupancy by tenant-advertisers, and that the total business revenues can be capitalized into real property value. In effect, it is assumed that the total assets of an outdoor advertising business are real property. The development and application of this premise is the predominant feature of Sutte's book, as evidenced in the following remarks concerning the valuation process.

> Since we have concluded that sign interests represent real estate, the market value definition is extremely important to the final estimate of value.... Because the use of signboard space is conveyed as a leasehold interest, signs may be considered real estate and the income approach may be adopted to their valuation.[12]

This same real estate-related premise is espoused by Paul Wright and Jeffery Wright, ASA, in their recent book, wherein the authors conclude, "There are strong arguments supporting the idea that signs are real property; perhaps the most convincing point is that a billboard is site-specific."[13] They suggest in the appraisal process that billboards be valued the same as other real property assets,[14] considering the three traditional approaches to value. Ron Nations, MAI, and Donald Oehlrich, MAI, after applying the three-part fixture test con-

---

10. Donald T. Sutte, MAI, *The Appraisal of Outdoor Advertising Signs* (Chicago: The Appraisal Institute, 1994): 19.

11. Ibid., 14.

12. Ibid., 39–40.

13. Paul Wright and Jeffrey Wright, ASA, *Billboard Appraisal: The Valuation of Off-Premise Advertising Signs* (American Society of Appraisers, 2001): 54.

14. Ibid., 168.

clude, "It is the contention of this article that a billboard structure is a fixture and is real estate."[15] Likewise, Rodolfo Aguilar, MAI, agrees with this conclusion by stating, "…sign structures and the bundle of rights that attaches to them amply qualify under the definition of real estate…. Consequently, all three approaches to market value must be considered…."[16] Aguilar's comment in regard to the intention of the party who attached the sign structure–"Undoubtedly the owner's intention is to make the structure a permanent fixture at the chosen location for the duration of his estate in the property, i.e., his lease term"[17]–is more probative to the position that the tenant does not intend for the billboard structure to become a permanent fixture of the real property.

It is interesting to note in his 2001 article,[18] Charles F. Floyd points out that the same fixture test was used as persuasive evidence by the outdoor advertising industry in a tax court case, wherein the court held that billboard signs were personal property. In their 1998 article[19] Charles Floyd, Mark P. Hodgdon, and Steven R. Johnson, MAI, SRA, agreed that billboard structures are trade fixtures and therefore personal property assets of the outdoor advertising business operating upon the leased premises.

A quick glance at the money trail indicates that the money flowing from the typical billboard structure is a portion of the revenue stream generated by the sale of advertising services, which is flowing to the outdoor advertising business enterprise, not to the real estate. Therefore, the billboard as a factor of advertising production is a business improvement and not a real estate improvement. In order for a personal property trade fixture to become an item of real estate it must contribute value (money flow) to the land. The only outdoor advertising money flowing to the real estate is the site rent paid by the outdoor advertising tenant for the use of the land as a production

site in operation of the advertising business. The site rent is not generated by the sign structure, but by the right to occupy and use the site for a business operation. The typical sign structure, unrelated to the sign site, is a trade fixture used in the advertising business as a capital factor of production. The opportunity cost payment for its contribution to the firm is the capital expenditure of its development, or the rental payment, as a leased fixture. Either way, the factor cost is based on the reproduction cost of the sign structure. This is a very important concept to keep in mind when the law requires compensation of the sign structure.

Valuation Problems of the Real Estate-Related Premise

The scope of this article allows only a brief summary of some of the valuation problems associated with consideration of the total assets of an outdoor advertising business as a real estate-based property. If outdoor advertising assets qualify under the definition of real estate, then as Aguilar concluded, "all three approaches to market value must be considered."[20] However, the real estate-related premise rejects the cost approach as not reflecting the market thinking of the buyers and sellers of outdoor advertising.[21] This raises a red flag for the appraiser. Wright and Wright contend that:

> Cost, or tangible asset value, is seldom relevant to the final determination of the fair market value of a billboard today because effective gross income and earnings are far more important. Some of the best signs being built in 2001 may cost $50,000 or $60,000, but the market value once they are in place may be 10 or 15 times that amount.[22]

A recent statement by a prominent attorney that represents the outdoor advertising industry in condemnation cases illustrates the cost approach problem very succinctly. He said, "[The] cost approach makes no sense . . . depreciated replacement cost as compensation is totally

---

15. Ron L. Nations, MAI, SRA and Donald P. Oehlrich, MAI, "The Valuation of Billboard Structures," *The Appraisal Journal* (October 1999): 413.

16. Aguilar, 13.

17. Ibid., 14.

18. Charles F. Floyd, PhD, "Are Billboards Real Property or Personal Property?" *Right of Way Magazine* (March/April 2001): 6.

19. Charles F. Floyd, PhD, Mark P. Hodgdon, Esq., and Stephen R. Johnson, MAI, SRA, "Appraising Outdoor Advertising Signs: A Critical Analysis," *The Appraisal Journal* (July 1998): 305–315.

20. Aguilar, 13.

21. Sutte, 41.

22. Wright and Wright, 82.

inadequate."[23] The true sense of this statement is that it makes no dollars or cents for the outdoor advertising business to use the cost approach to value the total assets of a going concern business enterprise.

It is obvious based on common sense reasoning and the money trail, that the cost of developing an asset (sign structure) as a factor of production is not equal to the value of the total assets of a business enterprise. It is commonly recognized that when the cost approach value is well below the value indication of the sales comparison or income approaches that intangible business assets are involved. The appraiser has the responsibility to identify and allocate all assets that are not real estate.

In his 1994 monograph, Sutte holds that, "the sales comparison approach is the key to the valuation of outdoor advertising signs. . . . the relevant unit of comparison applied in the sales comparison approach is the gross income multiplier."[24] The first problem is that a gross income multiplier is not a unit of comparison to be adjusted to the subject property. Secondly, an income multiplier method is a form of income capitalization, which is properly applied in the income approach. But more importantly, wherever the gross income multiplier is used there are certain limitations in its use. *The Appraisal of Real Estate* chapter on direct capitalization gives the following warning:

> Appraisers who attempt to derive and apply gross income multipliers for valuation purposes must be careful for several reasons. First, the properties analyzed must be comparable to the subject property and to one another in terms of physical, locational, and investment characteristics. Properties with similar or even identical multipliers can have very different operating expense ratios and, therefore, may not be comparable for valuation purposes.[25]

The author recently analyzed approximately 100 sales of outdoor advertising assets with operating expense ratios ranging from 25% to 85%. A linear regression and correlation analysis indicated virtually no correlation ($r^2 = 0.011$) between gross income multipliers and operating expense ratios. In his 2000 article Aguilar argues,

> [I]t is also incorrect to assert that the income approach reflects the "business" value of a billboard.

The expense data, which include all operating and management cost, effectively eliminate the "business" component from the income figures. Thus, the computed net operating income (NOI) applies entirely to the real estate, in the same manner that the NOI of a hotel, office building, or an apartment complex exclusively reflects the value attributable to the realty.[26]

There are two problems with this position: (1) the assembled management team is not the only business resource, or intangible asset in the firm; and (2) the management operating expense reflects only the cost of the management labor factor and not its benefits to the business enterprise.

Business-Related Premise: Recognition of Real and Personal Property and Intangible Assets

The distinction between the real estate-related and business-related premises, as used in this paper, is solely intended to emphasize the differences in methods of identifying and allocating the assets of an outdoor advertising business. The business-related premise is an objective method of identifying and allocating assets by recognition of the classical economic principles that hold that the value of each factor of production (land, labor, and capital) is based on the opportunity cost payments that are necessary to attract and retain each productive agent.[27] This premise provides a basis for a proper understanding of the relationships and interconnections between the real estate assets and the total assets of a typical outdoor advertising firm as a going concern. It promotes the observation of the money trail in identifying the direction and derivation of income flows into and out of the business enterprise.

The overview of the typical outdoor advertising business identified the factors of production, indicating that the majority of the assets are not real estate based. This supports the conclusion that the outdoor advertising business entity is not comparable to office buildings and apartment complexes. Ironically, the industry's claim of similarity with an operating hotel business may be valid to a point, thereby providing

---

23. Joseph L. Lyle Jr., Esq., *Condemnation of Outdoor Advertising Signs;* presentation at the IRWA meeting in Norfolk, Virginia on April 25, 2002.

24. Sutte, 42, 43.

25. Appraisal Institute, *The Appraisal of Real Estate,* 12th ed. (Chicago: Appraisal Institute, 2001): 546–547.

26. Aguilar, 17.

27. Appraisal Institute, Course 800, 3–8, 3–9.

strong evidence that there are more than real estate assets involved in an outdoor advertising enterprise. In his 1998 article, Peter H. Gloodt, MAI, ISHC, concluded:

> Clearly, looking at the mix of business and real estate services that are commingled in the revenue generated by a hotel enterprise leads to the conclusion that the fundamental nature of a hotel is a hospitality business whose largest capital asset is an investment in real estate but whose most important operating asset is a collection of intangible business resources and relationships.[28]

Arguably, the similarity of hotels and billboards ends with the fact that an outdoor advertising business's largest capital asset is not in real estate. A review of the consolidated balance sheet for Lamar Advertising Company on December 31, 2001 indicates that intangible assets account for 59% of the firm's total assets.

Finally, the fact that a billboard costing $50,000 to $60,000 to build can have a value of $500,000 to $900,000 is a sure indication that there are considerably more business resources involved in a service-based outdoor advertising business than a real estate-based enterprise. It is unimaginable for a hotel, office building, or apartment complex to have value 10 to 15 times its developed cost.

Conclusion

As with all eminent domain valuation issues that must be addressed according to jurisdictional directives, there are many different situations in various states that pose difficult problems for appraisers. The purpose of this article is not to address all the problems and questions, but rather to stimulate serious debate on fundamental issues within the appraisal profession that will contribute to the enrichment of knowledge relating to the identification and allocation of assets of an outdoor advertising business operation. The money trail concept will work in identifying assets and allocating value because it is based on the principle of contribution, which is "The concept that the value of a particular component is measured in terms of its contribution to the value of the whole property, or as the amount that its absence would detract from the value of the whole."[29]

References

Aguilar, Rodolfo J. "The Appraisal of Off-Premise Outdoor Advertising Billboards." *Right of Way Magazine* (September/October 2000): 12–19.

Appraisal Institute. Course 800: "Separating Real and Personal Property from Intangible Business Assets." Course Handbook. Chicago: Appraisal Institute, 2002.

Appraisal Institute. *Dictionary of Real Estate Appraisal,* 4th ed. Chicago: Appraisal Institute, 2002.

Appraisal Institute. *Real Estate Valuation in Litigation,* 2d ed. Chicago: Appraisal Institute, 1995.

Appraisal Institute. *The Appraisal of Real Estate,* 12th ed. Chicago: Appraisal Institute, 2001.

Cantwell, Steven M. "Billboard Valuation Without Distortion: The *Heathrow* Decision." *The Appraisal Journal* (July 1999): 246–254.

Floyd, Charles F. "Are Billboards Real Property or Personal Property?" *Right of Way Magazine* (March/April 2001): 6.

Floyd, Charles F., Mark P. Hodgdon, and Stephen R. Johnson. "Appraising Outdoor Advertising Signs: A Critical Analysis." *The Appraisal Journal* (July 1998): 305–315.

Gloodt, Peter H. "Hotel Valuation: Splitting the Hospitality Business From the Real Estate Assets." *The Journal of Multistate Taxation and Incentives* (July/August 1998).

Kanner, Gideon. "Billboard Valuation." *The Appraisal Journal* (April 1979): 298–305.

Lennhoff, David C. *A Business Enterprise Value Anthology.* Chicago: Appraisal Institute, 2001.

Nations, Ron L. and Donald P. Oehlrich. "The Valuation of Billboard Structures." *The Appraisal Journal* (October 1999): 412–421.

Sutte, Donald T. *The Appraisal of Outdoor Advertising Signs.* Chicago: Appraisal Institute, 1994.

The Traffic Audit Bureau for Media Measurement & Outdoor Advertising Association of American. *Planning for Out-of-Home Media: How to Plan, Buy, and Create Out-of-Home Media,* 2001 ed. New York & Washington D.C.

---

28. Peter H. Gloodt, MAI, ISHC, "Hotel Valuation: Splitting the Hospitality Business From the Real Estate Assets," *The Journal of Multistate Taxation and Incentives* (July/August 1998).

29. Appraisal Institute, *The Dictionary of Real Estate Appraisal,* 4th ed. (Chicago: Appraisal Institute, 2002): 63.

Weinstein, Alan C. "A Study of Local Regulation of Outdoor Advertising in the Major Cities of Each State." Executive Summary. Cleveland State University, 2001.

Wright, Paul and Jeffrey Wright. *Billboard Appraisal: The Valuation of Off-Premise Advertising Signs.* American Society of Appraisers, 2001.

Detecting Intangible Asset Value (or Capitalized Economic Profit) in Sales to REITs: A Practical Framework for Analysis

David C. Wilkes and Steven A. Shapiro, CRE

Reprinted with permission from *Real Estate Issues®* (Winter 2004-2005) published by The Counselors of Real Estate®. CRE® is a nonprofit professional organization for leading real estate advisors around the world. Visit www.cre.org for more information.

"To begin with there is no such thing as 'value,' except in the eyes of the beholder. And one must understand where the beholder is coming from."[1]
–Bertram Lewis, *"Do Syndicators Overpay?"*
The Appraisal Journal, *April 1985*

Many contend that real estate investment trusts (REITs) overpay on an individual asset basis. Whether this is true can be significant for tax assessment purposes. Previous commentary posited that intangible value existed (or did not) in such sales as a general rule. The industry is variegated. Some purchases are non-market due to factors common to REITs, while others represent market value. A fuller understanding of the factors that might lead to overpayment, and an analysis of the sale at hand on a case-by-case basis is needed. This article should assist in determining whether a REIT purchase price may have been influenced by non-market factors.

Introduction: The Need for an Analytical Tool

The real estate investment trust (REIT) is a dominant player in today's real estate marketplace. Following exponential growth over the course of the last decade, REIT-owned properties and sometimes entire REIT portfolios can now be found in every major central business district (CBD). Most suburban markets and even many rural areas are home to REIT-owned shopping centers, apartments, industrial/warehouse properties, offices, and golf courses, among many other property types.

REIT investing increased from a market capitalization in 1991 of $8.78 billion held by 86 equity REITs to $151.2 billion held by 149

equity REITs in 2002.[2] Sales of properties and entire private real estate portfolios to real estate investment trusts soared through the mid- to late-1990s. Today, despite a slowing of sales ac-

David C. Wilkes *is a partner at the New York law firm of Huff Wilkes, LLP. He is the Senior Editor of* Real Estate Review *(West Group/NYU), the Editor-in-Chief of the New York State Bar Association's monthly magazine, the* Journal, *and Vice Chair of the American Bar Association's Property Tax Committee. He received a law degree from Boston University and a master's degree in real estate appraisal from New York University's Real Estate Institute, where he was awarded the Norman Weinberg Prize for Excellence, graduating first in his class. He is an adjunct professor of real estate at NYU, and a member of the Legal Committee of the International Association of Assessing Officers (IAAO). He is the recipient of the IAAO's 2003 Distinguished Research and Development Award for his work in the field of REIT valuation.*

Mr. Wilkes gratefully acknowledges the long-standing support and insight of D. Kenneth Patton, CRE, Dean of the NYU Real Estate Institute, and the late Professor Michael F.X. Waters, former Director of Academic Affairs at the Real Estate Institute, without whom this research would not have been feasible.

Steven A. Shapiro, CRE, *is Senior Director of Property Taxation for Mack-Cali Realty Corporation, a New Jersey-based real estate investment trust. He is a designated member of the Counselors of Real Estate (CRE), a charter member of the National Property Taxpayers Association, a member of the Institute for Professionals in Taxation and International Association of Assessing Officers. He holds multi-state appraisal certifications and serves on the editorial advisory board of* Real Estate Review. *He received his bachelor of arts from Richmond College in psychology.*

25

Detecting Intangible Asset Value (or Capitalized Economic Profit) in Sales to REITs: A Practical Framework for Analysis

259

A Business Enterprise Value Anthology

tivity among REITs and a general change in the motivations related to raising capital through public offerings, REITs remain a powerful force in today's national real estate market.

The flurry of REIT activity over the last 10 years leaves a trail of purchase prices that may or may not be significant in the appraisal process for property tax valuation. These purchase prices, like any others, are of primary interest to assessors, many of whom presume them to be a fair reflection of ordinary market value. There has been extensive research on REITs generally over the last 15 years.[3] Much of this research focused on issues of concern primarily to the investing public and REIT performance from a shareholder's point of view. Yet there remains only limited treatment of REITs at the asset level, which is the predominant concern of *ad valorem* professionals.

In most cases, a recent arm's length sale of real property provides high-quality evidence of value. Yet, many appraisers, investment analysts, and REIT property tax managers (and even some assessors) contend that REIT purchase prices are not indicators of market value because the prices REITs pay for property include value for items that are not "realty." In our experience, this contention is sometimes true, but not in every case.

Because of their ability to extract more value from a given parcel of real estate than conventional bidders while still obtaining the same or a better return on investment, the REIT will often be able to pay more and will pay more to get the property—or the portfolio—it wants. As Hardin and Wolverton observed in the context of apartment REITs,[4] just as data supported the notion that properties obtained via foreclosure sold at a discount to market value, so too can it be hypothesized that REITs have in many cases either chosen, or been "forced into acquisition strategies that made over payment for individual properties more probable." It is also often true that a REIT may be buying much more than just the real estate, although this is often not reflected in portfolio purchases in which a total purchase price is allocated among many individual properties.

In the end, just as most individual properties have their own unique characteristics, so do the transactions involving them. As a result, some generalizations may be made but each sale requires careful analysis to determine whether, in fact, the price paid is above market value for ad valorem taxation. The purpose of this article is to provide a practical guide to several of the areas that would require examination in order to determine whether the price paid includes so-called intangible value.

Distinguishing Between Market Value and Investment Value

Because a REIT's corporate objectives are not usually the same as those of ordinary real estate investors, we begin by considering the difference between investment and market value. Investment value has been defined as "the value of an investment to a particular investor, based on his or her investment requirements, as distinguished from market value, which is impersonal and detached."[5] The investment value of an asset is the amount a specific investor might pay for the asset, as opposed to the amount the unidentified, hypothetical market purchaser might pay. In determining investment value one must consider the unique motivations, opportunities, investment criteria, conditions of sale, risk tolerance, cost of capital, and other investment variables of an identifiable purchaser.

In determining market value, on the other hand, each such variable would be detached from specific investor identification, and would instead be determined by the general characteristics of the market as a whole, the characteristics of the reasonable, prudent investor.

In every purchase there is investment value, because it is equal to the amount the successful purchaser believed the asset was worth. In many cases, this amount is also reasonably within the range of, or coincides with, the market value of the asset. One may find, for example, that two-thirds of all office buildings within a given market are sold within a price range of just 20 percent of each other. With the accumulation of many purchases by "typical" investors of fairly similar assets, purchasing patterns begin to take shape (particularly in an active market) and values will fall within a normally distributed bell curve. Multiplied over many transactions, the investment value of a particular asset to one ordinary investor begins to also influence the investment value of a similar asset to another ordinary investor by shaping investment expectations. Then there are the outliers. The foreclosure sales, the bankruptcies, the sales between relatives, the business enterprise sales, the portfolio purchases. These all have an

260 *Detecting Intangible Asset Value (or Capitalized Economic Profit) in Sales to REITs: A Practical Framework for Analysis*

A Business Enterprise Value Anthology

associated investment value, but each is, almost by definition, not necessarily market value.

For assessment purposes in most jurisdictions, property is to be assessed at market value and not investment value where investment value is different from market value. In most jurisdictions, a recent arm's length sale is legally considered strong evidence, and the sale is therefore considered indicative of market value. The key, then, is determining when a particular sale is not equal to market value.

In dealing with a sale of property to a REIT, the first order of business is to compare the purchase price with current local sales data. If the local market price range for office properties is predominantly between $160 and $200 per square foot and the subject sale is at $180 per square foot, the investment value for the subject is fairly equivalent to the market value and a more probing analysis of the sale is not likely to reveal otherwise. In contrast, if the purchase is at $300 per square foot, the analyst would be irresponsible in summarily concluding this to be the market value of the subject property. Though it may well turn out to be market value (for a variety of reasons one might imagine), closer analysis is still required.

Frequently, such pricing anomalies occur in sales to REITs. This article is intended to provide a (nonexhaustive) overview of the specific factors one might consider in determining whether a seemingly above-market price was produced by investment variables unique to the REIT investor and unavailable to the ordinary market participant. Significant in this analysis is the identification of the characteristics of the investors in the local market. To an extent, a large CBD may not only have a great number of REIT participants who enjoy similar investing advantages, it will likely have other institutional market participants such as pension funds and insurance companies that mimic many of the REIT advantages such as a lower cost of capital and reduced risk through diversification of assets and tenancies. A suburban or rural market may see greater contrast among the players and their respective abilities to pay a premium. Here too, one must be cautious in making distinctions, for with larger CBD properties, a seemingly minor difference between the profiles of two institutional purchasers may be greatly magnified, such as through cost-savings based on one company's ability to self-manage its buildings.

The REIT Acquisition Mindset

The *ad valorem* standard that governs taxation of real property requires the assessment professional to stand in the shoes of the hypothetical purchaser, make the assumptions of that purchaser, seek the return on investment of that purchaser, and assume the concerns of that purchaser relative to risk. Presumably, then, one arrives at a value that should roughly equate to the amount a typical market participant would pay for the asset. To the extent that a REIT purchaser may make different assumptions, anticipate a different return from a given set of rents, and anticipate risk differently from other purchasers, a value may be produced that is correspondingly different from what an appraiser might consider the fair market value of the asset.

Therefore, in addition to acknowledging the definitional distinction between market value and investment value, one must begin the analysis with an understanding of the factors a REIT acquisition team would be concerned with and contrast those factors with the approach taken by an ordinary investor.

Like any investor, each REIT is somewhat different in its approach to buying and operating real estate, so generalizations about how REITs do business are limited. Nevertheless, common threads run through a great many REIT acquisition and holding strategies, particularly as a result of their obligations to shareholders. This can be said to characterize a common REIT approach, or mindset, and that will often differentiate the amount a REIT will offer for a given asset from those of other investors.

Non-REIT real estate investors tend to buy property primarily in the hope of substantial asset appreciation over the holding period, anticipating much of the return on investment will accrue through the residual value of the property at the time of disposition or refinancing. Cash flow is primarily a concern to the extent that rents must cover operating expenses, reserves, and debt service so that there is no negative outlay of cash beyond the initial equity. A common example is the so-called "taxpayer" property, in which the property owner accepts the prospect of doing little better than breaking even (paying the taxes) during the holding period, which is offset by the build-up of wealth in the asset's appreciation over time.

Detecting Intangible Asset Value (or Capitalized Economic Profit) in Sales to REITs: A Practical Framework for Analysis

261

A Business Enterprise Value Anthology

In contrast, REITs prioritize cash flow and its growth ahead of asset appreciation in their acquisition strategy. A building with a strong cash flow projection will ultimately be more desirable to shareholders in the company than a building that may operate on a razor-thin margin but hold out the possibility of significant appreciation in 15 years. Like virtually all public companies, a REIT's shareholders have little interest in the disposition value of the corporation's assets and are mainly focused on an assurance of positive and growing cash flow over a long period of time. In a REIT, the corporation's assets are its real estate holdings, which are a vehicle for the generation of income as opposed to the accumulation of personal wealth through net asset value. The same is true, for example, of the value of a railroad corporation, in which it is the ability of the railroad's assets—trains, rail lines, shipping contracts, and workforce—to generate income, and not in the physical assets themselves. As in any corporation, REIT shareholders would surely be outraged if the corporation in which they held stock decided one day that the company could generate more immediate and substantial cash by simply disposing of its assets.

In his examination of the reduction of unsystematic risk in lease portfolios through a so-called Monte Carlo Simulation, Colacino[6] suggested the concept of "baskets" of commercial office leases being pooled and traded in a secondary market. To a great extent, it can be said that the REIT model does exactly this: the corporation is merely the securitizing entity that gathers together a vast volume of cash flows from its leases and sells securitized ownership rights in those cash flows to those purchasing stock in the company.

As a result of this cash flow-oriented approach to real estate investing, REITs tend to have longer holding periods for their assets than non-REIT real estate investors. To dispose of assets that generate a reliable source of cash flow, even at an opportune time for sale, is often contrary to the corporate strategy of a REIT. As in most industries, the liquidation of a major revenue-generating asset is considered an "extraordinary" event under generally accepted accounting principles (GAAP) that could materially distort the depiction of a company's performance for forecasting purposes.

This approach is also aided by the REIT's lack of "below-the-line" expenses such as debt service (or at least less than typical) and income taxes. This means a REIT may produce a profit from the same cash flow that would have allowed the traditional investor to merely break even, and for which the traditional investor would probably have paid less for the asset.

So long as the REIT can predict that a property—or more often a portfolio as a whole—will produce the desired cash flow then it becomes irrelevant to the REIT what the market value of a particular property might be from the perspective of the ordinary investor. The following disclaimer from a REIT prospectus is typical of the industry approach to investing:

> The company did not obtain appraisals of the fair market value of any of the original properties or related assets that the company will own immediately after consummation of the Offering. The public offering price of the shares and the related underlying valuation of the company have been determined primarily by capitalizing estimated cash flow of the company available for distribution, the enterprise value of the company as a going concern and other factors, rather than through a property by property valuation based upon historical cost or current market value. This methodology has been used because management believes it is appropriate to value the company as an ongoing business, rather than with a view to values that could be obtained from a liquidation of the company or of individual properties owned by the company.[7]

As discussed in detail below, it is also true that a REIT acquisition team may employ different assumptions in modeling potential returns than ordinary investors will. It is this very belief on the part of REIT managers as buyers of property that they can obtain efficiencies in operation—regardless of whether they are correct in their belief—that may make it more likely that the REIT will acquire its properties at a premium.[8] Another major concern to the acquisition team, particularly when assembling a multibillion dollar portfolio purchase, is the passage of time. The acquisition team may often operate within a much larger corporation in which the concerns of other departments—such as the property tax director who must wrangle with the after-effects of a transaction—are of only moderate concern at the time of purchase. More significant is the goal of simply closing the deal—a mark of success or potential failure for the acquisition team, which is often characterized by a highly short-term outlook. The net asset value of the portfolio as a whole may be important, but haggling over individual proper-

262 Detecting Intangible Asset Value (or Capitalized Economic Profit) in Sales to REITs: A Practical Framework for Analysis

A Business Enterprise Value Anthology

ty values rarely occurs. If the deal can be closed while paying what some might say was more than market value for an individual asset, the overpayment is of little significance compared to the costs of a failure to close the whole portfolio because another player jumped in at the last minute while the first was haggling.

The cost of an overpayment relative to net asset value may also pale in contrast to the increased transaction costs, such as accruing interest on a billion-dollar loan, that would be incurred if the parties were to dicker over individual asset values. In perspective, so long as the overall price relative to the overall cash flow obtained makes sense, the deal should go forward as quickly as possible.

With these concepts in mind, it quickly becomes apparent that our goal of determining market value for ad valorem taxation purposes may be a very different objective from what the typical REIT is aiming for when it purchases property.

Operating Efficiencies, Self-Management, and Tenant Services May Increase REIT Investment Value

As noted, REITs may well purchase their properties in part on the belief that greater returns will be generated simply because of the REIT operation and the efficiencies the company brings as an owner and operator of a large portfolio of real estate.[9] When analyzing a particular transaction price to determine whether it contains some component of intangible value paid by the REIT, one must consider the operations of the particular REIT involved. Often, itemized income and expense statements generated for the property a year or more after purchase, particularly as compared to operating statements from the previous owner, can reveal operational changes due solely to REIT ownership.

Other items of information will be available to the appraiser through researching the particular REIT's business operations, such as the particular types of ancillary services the company may provide which may include management, security, cleaning services, and other potential profit centers. Research may also reveal any economies of scale that may be realized through centralized property management and suppliers, in-house designers and planners, and other portfolio-oriented cost advantages.

For example, in the context of office or warehouse properties, a portfolio of 50 build-ings in a single market may require no more than two or three on-staff managers to oversee operations. Because the REIT can be an owner-operator (unlike, say, a pension fund owner), the REIT saves money in the first instance by avoiding the costs and fees associated with third-party management. Because many properties are concentrated in one area, the REIT further saves money through the economy of scale of a handful of staff covering multiple buildings.

The total salary expense for this management staff will be a small fraction of the fees that any other investor would pay for a third-party management company to oversee 50 buildings, or sometimes just a single large property. Depending on the type of properties in which the particular REIT specializes, this concentration of properties will have a similar effect on all manner of supplies and costs related to the operations of the real estate, such as insurance, repair and maintenance items.

This added premium value for management services is quantifiable, and often generates a greater "investment value" for a given property to the REIT than the general market value of the property. The hypothetical pro forma comparison (Figure 1) demonstrates how the value of self-management can be isolated by adjusting only management fees to derive an estimate of a portion of the intangible value that may be attributed to REIT-ownership.

Additionally, the economy of scale principle lends itself to the operation of the ancillary businesses that can be operated by the REIT mentioned above, all of which can turn an ordinary property with a limited cash flow into one with multiple profit centers not available to the ordinary investor. Such services may include a wide variety of items such as security, trash collection, providing heat and light, and cleaning services. Distilling the value of such profit centers and the "intangible" value of a major sophisticated management operation is not much different in methodology from that which is often employed in the valuation of regional and superregional shopping centers. Rent differentials and operating expense ratios among comparable properties may be helpful indicators of the degree of additional value attributable to non-market factors. These profit centers are considered in the REIT's determination of its investment value in a given property or portfolio.

Detecting Intangible Asset Value (or Capitalized Economic Profit) in Sales to REITs: A Practical Framework for Analysis

263

A Business Enterprise Value Anthology

Figure 1

	Non-REIT Ownership		REIT Ownership	
		PSF		PSF
Income				
Total Base Collected Rents				
320,000 SF Avg. Occupancy	$7,840,000	$24.50	$7,840,000	$24.50
Escalations & Recoveries (Actual)	$396,800	$1.24	$396,800	$1.24
Parking & Other Income (Actual)	$35,200	$0.11	$35,200	$0.11
Total Recoveries	$432,000	$1.35	$432,000	$1.35
Potential Gross Income	$8,272,000	$25.85	$8,272,000	$25.85
Marketing Vacancy (Market - 97%)	$8,023,840	$25.07	$8,023,840	$25.07
Effective Gross Income	$8,023,840	$25.07	$8,023,840	$25.07
Operating Expenses				
Utilities (not recovered in base rent)	$1,020,800	$3.19	$1,020,800	$3.19
Operating Services	1,113,600	$3.48	1,113,600	$3.48
General & Administrative	12,800	$0.04	12,800	$0.04
Management	321,782	$1.01	22,000	$0.07
Reserves for Replacement (EGI)	0	$0.00	0	$0.00
Real Estate Taxes	1,024,000	$3.20	1,024,000	$3.20
Amortized Leasing Commissions	156,800	$0.49	156,800	$0.49
Amortized Tenant Improvements	326,400	$1.02	326,400	$1.02
Total Expenses	$3,976,182	$12.43	$3,676,400	$11.49
Net Operating Income	$4,047,658	$12.65	$4,347,440	$13.59
Valuation Analysis:				
Net Operating Income	$4,047,658		$4,437,440	
Capitalization Rate	0.09750		0.09750	
Fair Market Value	$41,514,441	$129.73	$44,589,128	$139.34

Difference:
$9.61 P SF

Capitalization of Management Savings:
Savings PSF: $9.61 PSF
× 320,000 SF:
$3,075,200
Total Value of REIT Self-Management:
$3,075,200

Diversity Effects on the Portfolio Value of Real Property

Generally a property valued in a portfolio is less risky than the same property valued alone.[10] By combining one property with others the risk of the single asset is reduced, and the portfolio effect is "the extent to which the variation in return on a combination of assets (a 'portfolio') is less than the sum of the variations of the individual assets."[11] REITs are a classic example of portfolio owners.

Even in a single property this principle can be achieved through lease term diversification: different termination dates would even out the cash flow of the portfolio compared with the cash flows of the individual properties. Viewed as a whole, the portfolio owner's properties contain a broad array of leases with differing terms.

We term this concept generally as "Diversity Effects," which may be further divided into two distinct types of Diversity Effects: (1) the Regional Diversity Effect (RDE), and (2) the Local Diversity Effect (LDE) (Figure 2).

264

Detecting Intangible Asset Value (or Capitalized Economic Profit) in Sales to REITs: A Practical Framework for Analysis

A Business Enterprise Value Anthology

Figure 2

Regional Diversity Effect (RDE)		**Local Diversity Effect (LDE)**
· diversify holdings		· economies of scale
· offset regional economic risks	**Diversity Effects**	· tenant transferability
· national tenant base		· moderation of risk

Regional Diversity Effect

Aside from overall growth of income from a portfolio, much of a REIT's core business strategy and objective is focused on the moderation of overall risk to the company and its total cash flow. A single-asset real estate investor faces a relatively greater level of risk, even in the ownership of a top-notch, fully-leased Class A building, when compared with the overall level of risk experienced by an investor who owns multiple properties, even if each of those properties are less than ideal.

By applying the RDE to their advantage, REITs typically own multiple properties in several distinct markets throughout the country, often owning properties thousands of miles apart, as opposed to owning multiple properties in only one area. Where an entire region may experience an economic downturn, perhaps due to a major local employer's decision to downsize, other portions of the REIT's portfolio may be situated in regions that continue to experience growth. The overall risk and performance level of the portfolio may remain virtually unchanged.

As a result of the RDE, the REIT may be able to employ a risk tolerance that is atypical of most other players in the particular real estate market. This is generally not a market factor but rather a question of investment value for the particular REIT, indicating that the purchase price is unnaturally skewed.

Local Diversity Effect

The Local Diversity Effect (LDE) has at least two major components, some of which has already been touched upon here:

Economies of Scale

As discussed above, in any one market a REIT may own many buildings of similar use within a relatively small radius. One office REIT that we examined owns over 50 properties with a radius of about four to five miles of each other. This high concentration of assets creates tremendous econo-

mies of scale in the operation and oversight of the real estate, as well as a significant impact on the local portfolio's risk level. The subsequent addition of a full office park or only one or two additional properties within the local market may not require any significant addition of staff to perform management functions. This local concentration of properties creates a variety of cost savings advantages for the REIT over other property owners and it also significantly reduces overall risk.

Tenant Transferability

The second major component of LDE is a reduction of local risk to the portfolio, which is a direct result of Tenant Transferability. In the example above in which an office REIT owns more than 50 properties within a small geographic area, the REIT holds leases with some 200 office and warehouse tenants renting space in blocks of anywhere from 500 square feet to 200,000 square feet. Buildings fall within a broad range of Class C to Class A space. Because of the close proximity of one building to another (many are adjacent to or across the street from others in the portfolio), the REIT has a major advantage over the single-building owner, because the REIT's tenants can be moved into other REIT-owned buildings as the tenants' space needs change over time. This reduces the overall vacancy rate of the portfolio, thereby reducing risk and maintaining cash flow, and is an attractive feature to incoming tenants who may be attracted by–and pay more for–the knowledge that they can be accommodated as their needs change. Furthermore, the costs of a leasing broker may often be omitted entirely or significantly reduced.

A Comparison of Discounted Cash Flow (DCF) Factors

It is important to consider and contrast the way in which REITs and non-REITs may formulate DCF models (in those cases in which appraisals are prepared). Discounted cash flow analysis is a useful tool in the income approach because it

Detecting Intangible Asset Value (or Capitalized Economic Profit) in Sales to REITs: A Practical Framework for Analysis **265**

A Business Enterprise Value Anthology

makes explicit the factors and assumptions that go into the investment decision, whereas direct capitalization only implies these factors. As a result, DCF can often provide a revealing look at what an investor was thinking when it determined that a particular property met its investment criteria, would produce a desired return, and was worth bidding a particular purchase price. We provide below just a few points in which, in our experience, it appears that a typical REIT DCF analysis might differ from that of the non-REIT investor (Figure 3).

Holding Period

REIT executives we interviewed indicate that REITs tend to project longer holding periods for particular properties than many other investors. The REIT is primarily interested in long-term cash flow rather than the return on sale. A longer holding period means that a REIT has a greater opportunity to meet its desired level of return while possibly accepting less-than-stellar performance in the early years of an investment. This type of approach would not be apparent if the appraiser were to look only at the sale price and first year's NOI. A long holding period also tends to smooth out overall risk caused by real estate cycles. For example, if an investor purchased a property in 1988 and held it for only five years, the investor would have sold it near the bottom of the market in 1993. In contrast, if an investor were to purchase the same property on the same date, and hold it for 10 years, the investor would have enjoyed the recovery of the market in the late 1990s, and owned a more valuable property in 1998 with higher rents.

Internal Rate of Return/ Discount Rate

Anecdotal evidence indicates that REITs typically accept an apparently lower internal rate of return on a given investment for a given set of projected cash flows than ordinary real estate investors. A lower discount rate for a given set of cash flows will produce a higher initial investment, or purchase price. This appears to be acceptable to the REIT again due to the REIT's ability to maximize the profit potential of each below-the-line dollar in a way most others cannot duplicate. There are at least two ways in which the REIT accomplishes this:

- The REIT as a tax-favored entity: the REIT is a taxfavored entity for federal tax purposes. The REIT's taxable income is only taxed at the shareholder level, in contrast to other corporations, and therefore a dollar of before tax NOI carries greater value for a REIT than it would for an ordinary owner. The REIT can meet or exceed returns obtained by other property owners who might pay substantially less for the investment.
- The REIT enjoys a lower level of risk and favorable position in the capital markets: as will be discussed below, the level of risk enables many REITs to maintain a concomitantly lower debt level and cost of capital than typical real estate investors, which means that more cash flow accrues directly to the benefit of the REIT and its shareholders.

Forecast Income and Expenses

As a result of the Local Diversity Effect that produces a variety of economies of scale, discussed above, a REIT's DCF for a given property will likely indicate lower costs for many expense items than would be projected by non-REIT investors, again allowing the REIT to offer a higher price and still produce the desired return. Additionally, with its typically dominant local market position, a given REIT may be able to negotiate better rentals with tenants and derive additional income from some of the potential profit centers noted above, thus generating

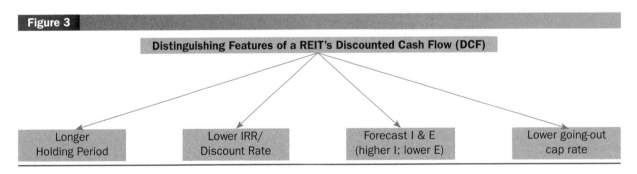

Figure 3

Distinguishing Features of a REIT's Discounted Cash Flow (DCF)

| Longer Holding Period | Lower IRR/ Discount Rate | Forecast I & E (higher I; lower E) | Lower going-out cap rate |

266

Detecting Intangible Asset Value (or Capitalized Economic Profit) in Sales to REITs: A Practical Framework for Analysis

A Business Enterprise Value Anthology

greater revenue out of a property than the ordinary investor would obtain. The average market participant will likely be more conservative in its forecasts of future income and expenses.

Going-Out or Terminal Capitalization Rate

The remaining DCF factor that is worthy of attention is the terminal capitalization rate used by the REIT. This is the capitalization rate the investor estimates for the sale of the property at the end of the holding period. Because the REIT will tend to hold its assets for a longer holding period, as discussed above, this is a more remote consideration than the other DCF factors, but it nevertheless will impact the REIT's return on investment and the price the REIT will pay. With higher rents, lower expenses, and reduced overall risk, to a certain extent the REIT will have set in place the factors necessary to raise the terminal value of the property.

Capital Structure and Capital Sources in REIT Transactions

In the 1990s, REITs had extreme flexibility in obtaining new equity for acquisitions through stock offerings. Today, REITs are often in stiff competition with other institutional purchasers and some of the ease with which REITs raised capital is gone. Foreign investors today enjoy significant advantages in their access to low-cost capital. However, REITs still enjoy significant advantages over many other real estate investors in cost of capital, access to capital markets, and capital structure. At least three issues related to the sources and use of capital are relevant to our discussion: (1) the cost of capital, (2) debt/equity level, and (3) effects on risk (Figure 4).

As a general investment principle, so long as an investor can access capital cheaper and on a less risky basis than other investors, that investor will be able to spend more while still achieving a desired return.

Like most publicly traded corporations, REITs access capital from a variety of sources not generally available to private real estate investors. Today's REITs may obtain capital from a combination of sources that may include commercial lenders, pension funds that are willing to lend money in a mortgage transaction, major lines of credit, and the issuance of debt in the public markets. A REIT may typically buy and sell multiple properties in a single transaction, perhaps accessing a billion or more dollars and, depending on the credit of the REIT, enjoying preferred terms in comparison to other investors. At times, when REITs also enjoy a favorable reputation among stockholders, many REITs readily issue stock to raise large sums of cash with few strings attached. The transaction costs that REITs incur tend to be significantly lower than those charged to non-REIT investors.

The cost of capital in such transactions is frequently measured against LIBOR, with preferred borrowers enjoying interest rates closer to LIBOR than other borrowers. As compared with other investors, large REITs will in many cases borrow capital at 150 to 200 basis points below more conventional real estate borrowers.

Another difference in the use of capital by many REITs is the debt-equity level in a REIT transaction. Most conventional real estate loans today are in the range of 70 percent of value. A REIT, in contrast, will tend to borrow at the entity level rather than at the property level. Consequently, debt is often kept well below ordinary loan-to-value ratios, and the capital market and credit rating agencies typically require most REITs to operate at relatively low loan-to-value ratios. In addition to lowering overall risk, the result is also lower debt service payments that would reduce the below the line cash flow.

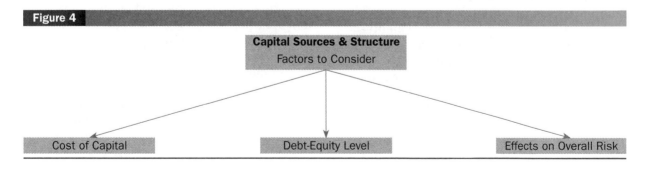

Figure 4

Capital Sources & Structure
Factors to Consider

Cost of Capital   Debt-Equity Level   Effects on Overall Risk

Detecting Intangible Asset Value (or Capitalized Economic Profit) in Sales to REITs: A Practical Framework for Analysis   **267**

A Business Enterprise Value Anthology

Purchases Often Involve More Than Just Real Estate

The foregoing concentrates on a variety of factors that may affect the investment value of specific properties or an entire portfolio to a REIT, primarily as that value relates to the cash flow characteristics of those properties. An entirely different factor that has historically been found in many REIT purchases is the value paid for items having virtually no direct relationship to the real estate at all.

Currently, mergers and acquisitions involving REITs seem to have diminished from the levels seen in the late 1990s, with the exception of several sectors. However, when these transactions do occur, the acquiring REIT typically pays a lump sum to obtain the entire business operations and assets of the acquired real estate company. In short, the REIT is buying the assets of another REIT, and along with those assets are many intangibles typically associated with any large corporation. The acquirer inherits many of the general and administrative expenses of the acquired company with the hope of a successful integration and resulting economies of scale. The amount paid often includes tens of millions of dollars relating to the immediate vesting of stock options, changing of control, payments under employment contracts, refinancing of debt, fees for investment bankers, auditors, attorneys, and a host of other major transaction costs that may be buried within a multi-billion dollar deal. If, as is frequently the case, the total purchase price of the transaction is simply allocated among the buildings comprising the acquired portfolio based upon square footage, it is apparent such an allocated purchase price will not be equivalent to the market value of the individual properties; the stated price is composed of a significant amount of non-realty value.

This is perhaps one of the most straightforward examples of capitalized economic profit forming a portion of the purchase price. In examining a particular sale for property tax assessment purposes, one must thoroughly investigate the circumstances of the sale before concluding that the sale is equivalent to market value. Where an acquisition of another company has occurred, the purchase is not necessarily viewed as simply the acquisition of real estate, but rather an ongoing business.

When reviewing a reported sale to a REIT, particularly where it is known that the sale involved a merger or acquisition, a good place to start–what may also be referred to as a "sanity check"–is to compute the direct capitalization rate of the transaction. While there are many genuine realty-related factors that might skew this rate (such as a large vacancy that is anticipated to be absorbed quickly), an extraordinarily low first-year capitalization rate is often the first indication that the purchase money went to more than just the real estate value.

While REITs may often pay institutional investor capitalization rates for many of the reasons discussed earlier in this article, there is a point at which the indicated rate becomes so extraordinarily low that it cannot be considered indicative of the real estate market, at least not an indication of what ordinary local investors are paying in a particular market.

Conclusion

Though the REIT industry has changed, adapted, and matured in recent years with general economic trends, REITs continue to attract attention among property tax practitioners and to play a dominant role in many real estate markets. In some jurisdictions in which property tax appeals may remain unresolved for many years at a time, such as New York, REIT purchases made in the late 1990s are still directly at issue. Moreover, REITs remain distinguished from many other, more traditional real estate investors in their approach to buying and operating real estate. As such, the investment value of a given property to a REIT may or may not be the same as for an ordinary investor and consequently may not always equate to market value. It should be apparent that these transactions often require far greater analysis and investigation than those involving more "ordinary" investors. The analyst must inspect and understand the pro forma in far greater depth than with other transactions, research the characteristics of the REIT purchaser as a company, including the size, scope, and geographical location of its portfolio, its capital sources, and its general risk characteristics, among many other factors. One must also investigate thoroughly the components of the transaction itself to determine whether the REIT has paid for intangible and other assets of another business that are incorporated into the purchase price but which may have nothing to do with the underlying real estate for tax assessment purposes.

268

Detecting Intangible Asset Value (or Capitalized Economic Profit) in Sales to REITs: A Practical Framework for Analysis

A Business Enterprise Value Anthology

Endnotes

1. Bertram Lewis, "Do Syndicators Overpay?" *The Appraisal Journal* (April 1985).

2. National Association of REITs Online, http://www.nareit.com/researchandstatistics/marketcap.cfm (Aug. 15, 2003).

3. John B. Corgel, W. McIntosh and S. H. Ott, "Real Estate Investment Trusts: A Review of the Financial Economics Literature," *Journal of Real Estate Literature* (1995): 3:1.

4. William G. Hardin, III and Marvin L. Wolverton, "Equity REIT Property Acquisitions: Do Apartment REITs Pay a Premium?" *Journal of Real Estate Research* (1999): 17:1/2.

5. American Institute of Real Estate Appraisers, *The Dictionary of Real Estate Appraisal* (Chicago: American Inst. of Real Estate Appraisers, 1984).

6. Michael D. Colacino, "Monte Carlo Simulation: Stochastic Contracting in Landlord and Tenant Lease Portfolios" *Real Estate Review* (Spring 2001): 31:1.

7. Quoted in William N. Kinnard, Jr. and Mary Beth Geckler, "There is REIT Value and Pension Fund Value, but Neither Is Market Value (Usually)" (Paper presented at 1995 ABA/IPT Advanced Property Tax Seminar, New Orleans, March 1995), 4-5.

8. See Note 4.

9. Id.

10. Brigham, Eugene F., *Fundamentals of Financial Management* (Chicago: The Dryden Press, 1983), 157.

11. Id. 805.

Detecting Intangible Asset Value (or Capitalized Economic Profit) in Sales to REITs: A Practical Framework for Analysis **269**

A Business Enterprise Value Anthology

Convenience Stores and Retail Fuel Properties: Essential Appraisal Issues

Robert E. Bainbridge, MAI, SRA

The following is an excerpt from Chapter 7 of *Convenience Stores and Retail Fuel Properties: Essential Appraisal Issues* by Robert E. Bainbridge, MAI, SRA, published in 2003 by the Appraisal Institute.

Real Property, Personal Property, and Business Value

Convenience stores are businesses. As such, their value is derived from several sources. The appraiser should explain to all parties involved in the appraisal how the value estimate is allocated to the various constituent parts. Standard Rule 1-2 (e)[1] requires the appraiser to distinguish real property from non-realty in developing a real property appraisal. A convenience store consists of tangible and intangible assets, as shown in the accompanying figure.

Tangible and Intangible Assets

Tangible assets can be classified as real property, personal property, or trade fixtures. *Intangible assets* are assets of the business that are not tangible real property nor tangible personal property. Components of tangible and intangible assets are shown in Table 7.1.

The property's site and building components are universally recognized as real property assets. Disagreement can arise as to how the fuel service is classified. Fuel service includes underground storage tanks, dispensers, and canopies. Convenience store appraisers usually classify the fuel service as part of the real property. However, whether the fuel service is classified as real property or personal property makes little difference in the valuation. The contributory value of the fuel service should be the same under either classification. The appraiser must be consistent in how the fuel service is classified for the subject property and the comparable sales.

Consider the two examples shown in Table 7.2. Assume that the building has 2,500 square feet. Which price per square foot should the appraiser apply to the subject property? It depends on how the appraiser classifies the subject's fuel service. If the subject's fuel service is not considered part of the real estate, it would be inappropriate to base the subject's value on the higher indication of $240 per square foot.

Twenty years ago, it was common for the petroleum supplier to own the fuel dispensers,

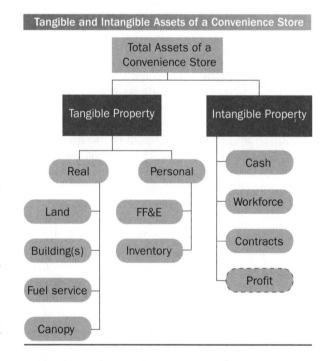

Tangible and Intangible Assets of a Convenience Store

Robert E. Bainbridge, MAI, SRA, is the recipient of the Appraisal Institute's George L. Schmutz Award for his 2003 book, Convenience Stores and Retail Fuel Properties: Essential Appraisal Issues. Mr. Bainbridge holds a master of science in real estate appraisal from the University of St. Thomas. His column on real estate–related issues appears in Convenience Store News magazine.

---

26

1. The Appraisal Foundation, *Uniform Standards of Professional Appraisal Practice,* 2003 ed. (Washington, DC: The Appraisal Foundation, 2003), 16.

Table 7.1	Components of Tangible and Intangible Assets	
Tangible Assets		**Classification**
Site		Real property
Building		Real property
Fuel service and canopy		Real property or trade fixtures
Furniture, fixtures, and equipment		Trade fixtures or personal property
Inventory		Personal property
Intangible Assets		**Classification**
Cash		Non-real property
Franchises and licenses		Non-real property
Goodwill		Non-real property
Skilled workforce		Non-real property
Other		Non-real property

Table 7.2	Classification of Fuel Service			
Sale with Fuel Service Included			**Sale with Fuel Service Not Included**	
Site	$100,000		Site	$100,000
Building	$250,000		Building	$250,000
Fuel service	$250,000			
Total	$600,000		Total	$350,000
Price/sq. ft.	$240		Price/sq. ft.	$140

canopy, and signage and lease them to the fuel retailer. Under those conditions, it was convenient and common to think of the fuel service as trade fixtures and not part of the real property. Although no physical change has taken place, today it is more common for the convenience store operator to own the dispensers, canopy, and signage and for the fuel service to be considered part of the real property. The classification does not affect the value opinion of these components. However, the appraiser and client should understand what is included in the appraisal assignment and how the assets are classified. The convenience store appraisal report should state the classifications clearly.

Many real estate appraisers are unfamiliar with business valuation, which is a separate appraisal discipline. However, it is critical for the convenience store appraiser to recognize that the value of a convenience store may include values other than that of the real property. Some fundamental concepts of business appraisal must be recognized. First, convenience stores operate as income-producing entities and are bought and sold as such. Convenience store income is gener-

ated by the tangible and intangible assets. Second, the economic return to the tangible assets, such as the site, building, fuel service, and equipment, is received first. Business value economic theory states that the income produced by a convenience store must first be applied to the investment requirements of tangible assets such as the site, building, fuel service, equipment, and inventory.[2]

Intangible assets such as goodwill only have value if excess earnings exist over and above the required investment return on the tangible assets. The appraiser should not assume that goodwill exists in every case. Frequently, small single-store operations will not have any excess earnings and, consequently, no goodwill value. If the appraisal assignment includes a chain or corporate ownership of several stores, the real estate appraiser is advised to obtain the services of a qualified business appraiser to assist in developing the appraisal. For example, a chain of several stores may realize operating cost savings because general and administrative expenses are spread over several stores. Economies of scale such as this may create a cost advantage that a single-store operation does not

2. This concept is the basis for Revenue Ruling 68-609, published by the Internal Revenue Service, which discusses the valuation of intangible assets. For an authoritative statement regarding the priority of the economic return to tangible assets, see Jay E. Fishman, MBA, ASA, CBA, and Shannon P. Pratt, DBA, FASA, CFA, *Guide to Business Valuations,* 12th ed. (Fort Worth: Practitioners Publishing Company, 2002), 7-28.

enjoy. A trained and assembled workforce is an intangible asset that has economic value.

Because convenience stores frequently sell as going concerns and often must be analyzed as going-concern entities that include tangible and intangible assets, it is highly recommended that convenience store appraisers attend the Appraisal Institute's Course 800, Separating Real and Personal Property from Intangible Business Assets. Much of the procedure and theory in the following valuation sections is based on this course.

Capitalizing EBIDTA

Capitalizing EBIDTA provides an indication of the market value of the convenience store operation's going concern. All of the convenience store's tangible and intangible assets are included in the value estimate because they all contribute to EBIDTA.

In addition to including the value of the tangible and intangible assets, capitalization of EBIDTA includes business profit. Together, the tangible assets, intangible assets, and capitalized economic profit (business profit) make up what the Separating Real and Personal Property from Intangible Business Assets course calls the *market value of the total assets of the business (MVTAB)*. MVTAB can be estimated by capitalizing EBIDTA. Capitalization rates can be extracted from the market just as they would be for any other property. However, capitalization of EBIDTA does not distinguish any of the tangible and intangible assets or provide a measure of the contributory value of any of the component parts. For example, capitalization of EBIDTA does not give the appraiser a measure of economic profit or indicate if economic profit even exists. The appraiser must remember that,

when capitalizing EBIDTA, any economic profit that exists is included in the value estimate.

The client may ask the appraiser to estimate the real estate's value when a loan will be secured by a real estate mortgage. When the appraiser is required to estimate the value of the real estate associated with a convenience store operation, further refinements to EBIDTA are necessary.[3] EBIDTA components should be separated into their respective economic returns as tangible and intangible assets. These returns (income) are shown in Table 7.3.

A residual income approach can be used to estimate the value of the real property. Once EBIDTA has been determined, the appraiser allocates the portion of the income stream that represents the return to the FF&E and any intangible assets, including capitalized economic profit. The remaining income is the portion of EBIDTA that represents the return to the real estate. This portion of the income stream can then be capitalized by the appraiser into a value estimate for the real estate.

This residual-income economic framework is the basis of the income capitalization approach as applied to convenience stores. It reflects the way the convenience store industry views the role of the real estate in the operation of the business enterprise and the purchase decisions of buyers and sellers of convenience store properties. The remainder of this article discusses refining EBIDTA into an income estimate for the real estate.

Calculating EBIDTA

Four steps are followed to calculate earnings before interest, depreciation, taxes, and amortization: estimate gross sales, deduct for shrink,

Table 7.3	Economic Returns for Tangible and Intangible Assets
Tangible Assets	**Classification**
Site	Real property
Building	Real property
Fuel service and canopy	Real property or trade fixtures
Furniture, fixtures, and equipment	Trade fixtures or personal property
Inventory	Personal property
Intangible Assets	**Classification**
Franchises and licenses	Non-real property
Skilled workforce	Non-real property
Goodwill	Non-real property
Other	Non-real property

---

3. *Uniform Standards of Professional Appraisal Practice,* Standard Rule 1-4g. As noted earlier, depending on the intended use and user, USPAP requires personal property and intangible items to be separated from real property when developing a real property appraisal.

estimate product margins, and deduct annual operating expenses. Calculating EBIDTA is the first step in developing the income capitalization approach for a convenience store.

Estimating Gross Sales

If the property is an existing convenience store, its historical sales levels should be examined. The current year's year-to-date income should be annualized and compared to the last three years' income levels to determine whether the subject store's trend in gross sales is flat, upward, or downward. The appraiser should be sure to remember that road construction, a building expansion, or other unusual circumstances can significantly affect sales in any period. The appraiser should compare the subject's trend to the industry trend using sources such as the State of the Industry Report published by the National Association of Convenience Stores.

As discussed previously, gross sales consist of fuel sales and in-stores sales. Generally the direction of fuel sales and in-store sales are the same. It is unusual for in-store sales to move upward while fuel sales are moving downward. It is generally not necessary to break out the different grades of gasoline. In-store sales include all sales other than fuel sales: merchandise, food service, and other, such as carwash income. Income categories have different margins and must be tracked separately. If the price of a particular product category, such as cigarettes or gasoline, jumps significantly in one year, the gross sales will appear much higher than the previous year's gross sales. However, the increase in gross sales will not usually affect gross profit. These volatile movements occur at the wholesale level and are in turn reflected in retail prices. If anything looks unusual in the subject's pattern of gross sales over the last few years, the appraiser should ask the owner-operator about it.

Deducting for Shrink

Shrink is product loss caused by damage or the expiration of the product's freshness date. A percentage allowance for shrink is deducted from gross sales. A 1% allowance is typical, but sometimes the percentage is higher than 1%. Shrink of more than 2% is unusual.

Estimating Product Margins

The *product margin* is how much income remains after paying the wholesale cost of the merchandise. The annual wholesale cost to the store is commonly called the *cost of goods sold* on the operating statement. Fuel margins for each grade of gasoline may be different, but they are aggregated into one average called the *pool margin.* Typically, pool margins are about 9% to 13%; they may be less in a highly competitive market with hypermarkets. In-store margins are usually higher than fuel margins and typically range from 28% to 34%.

The appraiser should ask the owner-operator about the subject's historical margins and compare the historical margins to industry standards. Margins can and do change from year to year, but historically category margins have stayed within a comparatively narrow range.

If the subject's historical margins are extraordinarily low, the retail prices at the subject store may be too low. In a highly competitive market, margins would be expected to be lower. For example, the industry reports that fuel margins at competing convenience stores commonly drop to 0% to 4% when a hypermarket such as Wal-Mart begins selling gasoline.

The national average product margins for nearly everything sold in a convenience store can be found in sources such as the State of the Industry Report published by the National Association of Convenience Stores. For proposed stores, the margins must be projected. Projected margins for new stores must be consistent with information reported in the earlier sections of the appraisal report that analyze market supply and demand. If the subject's market is oversupplied and has a location quotient of 0.75, projecting margins higher than the industry average would be inappropriate.

The margin's mathematical complement is the cost of goods sold. If the pool margin for fuel is 10%, the cost of goods sold for the fuel category is 90%. The appraiser should use the margin to compute the dollar amount of the cost of goods sold for each category. The appraiser then deducts shrink and the cost of goods sold from gross sales to arrive at gross profit.

Using the fuel margins identified above, assume that a store has $1,000,000 in fuel sales for the year. The computation of net sales is

Fuel sales	$1,000,000
Less: Cost of goods sold	$900,000
Less: Shrink (1%)	$10,000
Gross profit	$90,000

Notice that shrink is deducted from total sales rather than from gross profit. The cost of goods sold is figured from gross sales, not gross sales after the shrink allowance has been deducted. Completing the arithmetic in this order is important because the owner-operator absorbs all of the shrink loss and pays all of the wholesale costs.

Deducting Annual Operating Expenses

After deducting shrink and the cost of goods sold, the owner-operator pays the annual operating expenses, which include the items listed below. In figuring the percentage allowance for each of the following items, the industry makes the percentage calculation from total sales before shrink. The appraiser should compare the subject's operating performance to published convenience store industry averages. For example, the State of the Industry Report is published every year. The operating expense categories below reflect the way the industry categorizes stores' operating expenses. With the help of industry standards, the appraiser's task of establishing and common sizing operating expenses for the reconstructed statement is comparatively easy. *Common sizing* is the practice of analyzing the owner's operating statement by calculating the annual itemized expense as a percent of gross sales. It is a better way to track trends in operating expenses than simply looking at nominal dollar amounts.

With the exception of labor costs, the numbers in the labor expense category are relatively small. The total of all items in the labor expense category should be approximately 7% to 13% of total sales. Because labor costs are the largest component of operating expenses, the appraiser should carefully consider and verify them as much as possible. It may not be appropriate to use the actual historical wages on the owner's operating statement because they may not accurately reflect any wages the owner has taken out of the business.

Labor Costs

Labor is usually the largest category of annual operating expenses on the owner's operating statement. Labor expense includes all employee compensation. Wages, payroll taxes, workers' compensation, health insurance, and other employee benefits are grouped together.

The owner's profits are not expensed with labor costs but are considered later as part of the profit allowance. The appraiser will have to use good judgment if the store is a "mom and pop" operation and the owners are the only employees. In this instance, a fair wage should be deducted for what would normally be paid to employees. If the owner contributes personal labor to the store's operation, the allowance deducted from the labor costs should reflect the opportunity cost of that level of labor contribution, whether it is an entry level wage or the potentially high cost of hiring a store manager.

Later in the analysis of EBIDTA, an allowance is made for owner profit. Owner profit is separate and distinct from the owner's wages. The labor expense category can vary widely from one store to another depending on how labor-intensive the operation is. A full-size, co-branded restaurant requires more employees than a self-serve food operation does. Labor costs usually range from 4% to 9%.

Insurance

Insurance includes liability and business insurance, but not fire coverage for the real estate improvements. The insurance allowance is usually 0.1% to 0.5% of total sales.

Royalty Fees

The appraiser should not confuse royalty fees with franchise fees. A *franchise fee* is an upfront charge the operator pays to use the licensed concept. For example, Burger King usually charges $37,500 for a franchise. *Royalties* and *advertising fees* are ongoing payments to the franchisor to cover administrative and marketing costs. They are annual fees based on a percentage of gross or net sales. The appraiser must remember that for a quick service restaurant, or QSR, royalty will be based on food service sales, not on fuel sales. QSR royalty fees range from 4% to 8% of food service sales. Royalties for an operation are usually 0.1% to 0.2% of gross sales.

Advertising Fees

Some operations spend little on advertising; others have billboards, radio spots, and newspaper advertisements. Advertising expenses often reflect the operator's business philosophy. Advertising is one of the few items the operator may consider an optional expense. It can vary widely and be cut drastically in a year of poor revenue. Typically, an allowance of 0.1% to 0.2% of total sales is appropriate for operations that do not have nationally branded food service.

The advertising costs of nationally branded food service, such as McDonald's or Wendy's, are specified in the franchise agreement and figured as a percentage of either gross or net food service sales. Some companies combine royalties and advertising into a single payment.

Industry averages for advertising apart from the amounts included in royalty fees are about 0.3% of gross sales.

Supplies

Supplies include all purchases of items not for resale that are used in the management and operation of the business. Cleaning products and office supplies fall into the supply category. This category usually ranges from 0.5% to 0.7% of gross sales.

Utilities

Utilities include water, sewage, electricity, and natural gas. Appraisers should know that some heating requirements can be met using the heat emitted by refrigeration compressors. The heat emitted by refrigeration compressors is often recycled to heat a building in cold weather. BP Oil Company is experimenting with mounting PV solar panels on their canopies to generate electricity. The company asserts that 10% to 20% of a convenience store's electrical needs can be supplied by PV solar panels. Usually utilities constitute 1.0% of total sales.

Motor Fuel Drive-Offs

The convenience store industry tracks motor fuel drive-offs in a separate expense category. Motor fuel drive-offs increase when fuel prices are high. According to industry averages, motor fuel drive-offs accounted for 0.1% of gross sales in 2000.

Cash Short/Over

As with most retail sales businesses, cash balances for the year are usually reconciled in a separate account on the annual statement. Cash short means that less money came into the cash register than should have. The appraiser will usually find the operating statement lists a "cash short" amount, rather than a "cash over" amount. Cash short typically comprises 0.1% of gross sales, according to industry averages.

Other

Non-categorized, miscellaneous items can be figured at 1.2% of total sales. In addition to the items discussed above, the convenience store appraiser will frequently find deductions for depreciated book value, store rent, repairs, maintenance, and mortgage interest on the actual operating statement because these items are eligible for income tax deductions. Depreciated book value and mortgage interest should not be included as expense items. Although depreciated book value and mortgage interest are legitimate income tax deductions, they are not included on the appraiser's reconstructed statement as developed here. The appraiser cannot compare the overall percentage of operating expenses on the reconstructed statement to the published industry average because the published industry average will include items that the appraiser has not included in the reconstructed operating statement.

After deducting annual operating expenses for net sales, the convenience store appraiser arrives at net earnings, or the earnings before interest, depreciation, taxes, and amortization (EBIDTA). Capitalizing EBIDTA provides an indication of the market value of the total assets of the business (MVTAB) as if sold in aggregate or as a going concern.

The capitalization rate for developing MVTAB can be extracted from sales of convenience stores when EBIDTA is developed for the sale property. EBIDTA is divided by the sale price. Typically, the R_{TAB} (capitalization rate for the market value of the total assets of the business) will be higher than R_O, the overall capitalization rate of the real estate only. The theoretical reasons for the difference in capitalization rates include the shorter economic lives of FF&E and the higher investment risk associated with intangible assets such as capitalized economic profit (CEP).

Separating Real Estate Value from EBIDTA

Most business appraisers allocate the income to the real estate by presuming that the real estate's value is already known. Business appraisers commonly rely on real estate appraisers to estimate the value of the real estate. Once the value of the real estate is known, the business appraiser then allocates that portion of the business income that represents a return to the real estate. After also deducting the economic return to any other tangible assets, such as trade equipment, the amount of income remaining represents the economic return to the intangible assets of the business. But what if the value of the real estate is not known? Can the appraiser estimate the value of the real estate for a convenience store by examining the income stream to the overall business enterprise?

The answer is, yes. The appraiser quantifies the income that can reasonably be allocated to the other tangible assets and to the intangible assets. The income remaining after the allocation is that portion of EBIDTA that is generated by the real estate. Following the discussion in the Appraisal Institute's Separating Real and Personal Property from Intangible Assets course, the identification of tangible and intangible assets and the profit component for a convenience store operation may be thought of as follows:

1. Real property
   Land, site improvements (parking, forecourt paving, canopy) and building or buildings (store, fuel dispensers, USTs, QSR, carwash structure)

2. Tangible personal property or FF&E
   Freestanding coolers and freezers, shelving, gondolas, food service cookers, freestanding stainless steel sinks, hot dog rollers, tables, chairs, computers, office equipment, inventory, etc.

3. Intangible business assets
   Cash and equivalents, assembled workforce, business name, non-realty contracts, innovations.

Economic profit is all revenue not captured as a return on the value of the real property, tangible personal property, or any other intangible asset of the going concern. The authors of the Separating Real and Personal Property from Intangible Assets course state:

> ...economic profit is a residual claimed by entrepreneurial activity (risk taking and/or innovation). It is what remains after satisfying the opportunity cost claims of all agents of production embodied in the going concern.[4]

Residual Real Estate Income Allocation

The income allocation with real estate as the residual can be performed by making the following deductions to EBIDTA:

EBIDTA
– Tangible assets, non-realty such as FF&E income
= Residual income to real property, intangible assets, and economic profit

The intangible assets and economic profit are deducted from the remaining income to isolate the portion of the subject's income that provides an economic return to the real estate.

Deducting Return for Other Tangible Assets and FF&E

Part of the revenue that a convenience store generates originates from the personal property, non-realty equipment, and other tangible, non-real estate items used in the operation of the business. A deduction is made for the portion of the income stream attributable to non-realty items. When a full-size fast-food restaurant such as a 2-in-1 is present, the equipment value can be as much as 16% of the real estate's value. For smaller QSRs and stores with no branded food service, the value of equipment is considerably less. The deduction for income to furnishings, fixtures, and equipment represents the economic return required by the quantity and quality of FF&E that is present in the operation.

The economic return can be calculated in one of two ways. The value of the equipment can be estimated and an annual economic return allowance can be calculated, or an allowance for the annual return to equipment can be made based on a percentage of net earnings. An appropriate annual return for FF&E would be 15% to 20%, based on a 10% return on invested capital in FF&E and considering a life expectancy of 10 to 15 years. The net earnings allocation to FF&E would be between 1% and 5%. The process for calculating the economic return to the equipment is shown in Table 7.4.

Either of these methods can produce the same allocation to FF&E. Estimating the value of used equipment can be difficult for the real estate appraiser. The return on value method can more readily be applied to new equipment.

If the equipment's value cannot be determined, an allocation of net earnings may be used by the appraiser. Once the income allocation to the equipment has been made, the appraiser can check the results. The appraiser should simply capitalize the income to equipment at an appropriate rate to produce an estimate of value for the FF&E.

Although the convenience store appraiser estimates the equipment's value as part of the process of deriving the income to real estate, the appraiser must be cautious when applying these results to a professional opinion of equipment value. The real estate appraiser should not

---

4.   See the Appraisal Institute's Course 800, Separating Real and Personal Property from Intangible Assets, 5-8.

Table 7.4	Calculating the Economic Return to Equipment

Income to FF&E Based on Return of Value

$30,000 value of FF&E

18% economic rate of/on return

$5,400 annual economic return

The deduction from EBIDTA for FF&E is $5,400.

Income to FF&E Based on Allocation of EBIDTA

$225,546 net earnings

2.5% allocation

$5,638 annual economic return

The deduction from EBIDTA for FF&E is $5,600.

offer a conclusion about the equipment's value that the client regards as a professional opinion.

Deducting Intangible Asset Returns and Business Profit

The deduction for intangible asset returns and business profit is one of the most challenging and subjective judgments in convenience store appraisal. No simple formula or multiplier can be applied that is appropriate for every store. Moreover, the profit margins of the past may not reflect the current market. The appraiser should be aware that, in this residual allocation to real estate, what is not classified as intangible asset returns and business profit will flow to the real property and FF&E. In other words, the less income allowed for profit, the more income flows to the tangible assets. Consequently, when the income stream to the real estate is capitalized, it will indicate a lower or higher value to the real estate, depending on how much income was allocated to intangible asset returns and business profit.

All of the previous computations used to arrive at net earnings were fairly straightforward. They were achieved with simple arithmetic and can be easily corroborated. At this point the appraiser's task becomes more difficult. In estimating the economic return to the intangible assets and business profit, the appraiser must use skill, judgment, experience, and common sense. If up to this point the methodology of convenience store appraising could have been called science, at this point it becomes art.

The appraiser must ask, "Do the tangible assets receive the business's economic return first?" In other words, do the tangible assets have a priority economic claim over the intangible assets? This is largely an irrelevant question when the business operates at a profit. However, when the business does not earn a profit, this question can be vitally important. Business appraisers state that the tangible assets receive their economic return first, before any other assets of the business. A commonly used business appraisal method is the excess earnings method. In *Guide to Business Valuations*,[5] the authors state that intangible assets earn a return only after the economic return requirements for the tangible assets have been satisfied. In other words, the business's intangible assets have value only if there are excess earnings.

In allocating income, the investment requirements of the tangible assets are satisfied first, then the intangible assets. Finally, business profit remains. If the business does not have excess earnings but provides enough economic return to meet the requirements of the tangible assets, the intangible assets have no value and no business profit exists. Intangible assets and profit always have a secondary, or subordinate, claim on earnings to the tangible assets.

Some convenience store operations will have no profit. In the highly competitive and saturated markets that most stores operate in today, few stores will have excess earnings.

The profit allowed on the reconstructed statement should also be consistent with the appraiser's previous allocation of any labor contributed by the owner-operator. Frequently, the owner-operator contributes labor to the business's operation. If the appraiser made no wage allowance for the owner under labor costs, the allowance for owner's compensation must be made at this time. In many markets today, after allowing for working wages for the owner or owners, little or no business profit remains. In other words, the operation of the convenience store only allows the owner or owners to make wages and pay bills.

Indications that intangible value and business profits exist in a convenience store operation may include

- Gross profits significantly above industry norms
- Location quotients higher than one

---

5. Jay E. Fishman, Shannon Pratt, et al., *Guide to Business Valuations,* 12th ed. (Fort Worth: Practitioners Publishing Company, 2000), 7-28.

- Capitalized EBIDTA values that are higher than the replacement cost less depreciation of the tangible assets plus land value

Indications that no returns are available for intangible assets or business profit could include

- A pattern of declining gross profits over the past several years
- Location quotients substantially lower than one
- New competition since the time of the subject's original construction
- The opening of a Wal-Mart fuel center or other mass merchandiser selling motor fuel within the subject's market

These are only indications. The comments of the owner and other competitors in the area will also help the appraiser determine whether the local trade area is profitable for convenience store operators. During interviews with buyers and sellers, the appraiser will ask how much of the sale price is attributable to intangible business value. The answer to this question affects the allocation of the subject's income to intangible assets and business profit.

Estimating the subject store's profit is difficult, so it is important for the convenience store appraiser to closely follow the convenience store industry and the issues that convenience store operators confront. If the appraiser understands and recognizes these factors, he or she can exercise the skill and judgment required in allocating earnings to intangible assets and profit. For example, during the boom years of the 1980s and 1990s, the convenience store industry was experiencing rapid growth in sales and gross profits. As expected, new stores were constructed on almost every good corner. Nearly every store made a profit. The situation today is dramatically different. With market saturation of existing stores and mass merchandisers gaining market share in fuel sales, store profits are minimal and even nonexistent for many operations. The industry is struggling and it is rare to encounter a store with significant excess earnings.

The appraiser cannot make a mechanical allocation for profit simply because the estimate derived represents the business's total assets. For example, in one actual assignment a convenience store appraiser determined that a proposed convenience store and truck fueling facility in a small rural town was not financially feasible. The determination was based on the appraiser's calculation that the capitalized EBIDTA would be insufficient to cover the cost of the real property assets. The appraiser demonstrated this fact with a projection that the capitalized EBIDTA would approximate $500,000 and the cost new of the improvements plus land value was more than $1,200,000. Clearly, the proposed project was not feasible. However, the appraiser went on to allocate a substantial amount of projected income to "business profit." This was a mistake. No business profit can exist in a situation where the investment requirements of the tangible assets are not met. If the project is not feasible in the first place, how can it be making a profit? The appraiser was simply not thinking about these issues and made an artificial, unsupported allowance for profit when none was warranted.

Under the most favorable industry operating conditions, returns to intangible assets and business profit will constitute no more than 15% to 20% of gross profit, which is about 30% to 35% of EBIDTA. Some economic return is required for the real and personal property and it too must be allocated.

The convenience store appraiser can employ a sensitivity analysis to gauge the resulting effect of various profit allocations on the real estate's value. Table 7.5 shows three examples of an income allocation to intangible assets and business profit. The examples show how different allocations can affect the residual income to the real estate.

Note that the residual income to real estate gets smaller as the profit allowance increases. Consequently, the capitalized value of the residual income declines as more of the earnings are allocated to intangibles and business profit. The appraiser must recognize the inverse relationship between the allowance to intangible assets and business profit and real estate value.

The convenience store industry records annual profit margins in publications such as the State of the Industry Report. The published pre-tax profit can be used as an industry proxy for the allowance for intangibles and business profit. Although the pre-tax profit is computed differently by the industry, it can be a useful yardstick for illustrating industry trends. The appraiser is advised not to use the pre-tax profit in direct comparison to the return allowance for intangible assets and business profit. In 2000 the pre-tax profit was 14.3% of gross profit adjusted for interest expense.

Table 7.5	Allocation of Return on Intangible Assets and Business Profit		
	No Profit Allowance 0%*	Moderate Profit Allowance 10%*	High Profit Allowance 20%*
EBIDTA	$200,000	$200,000	$200,000
Return on intangible assets and business profit	$0	$20,000	$40,000
Residual return to real estate	$200,000	$180,000	$160,000
Real estate cap rate	12.0%	12.0%	12.0%
Real estate value	$1,666,666	$1,500,000	$1,333,333

* As a percent of EBIDTA

When the appraiser's analysis of the convenience store industry and the subject's trade area indicate that no excess profits exist, the appraiser can begin the income allocation analysis assuming no allowance for a return to intangible assets and no profit for the subject store. The resulting value estimate for the real estate can then be compared to the indications from the cost and sales comparison approaches. If the preliminary value indication for the store's real estate appears too high, incremental increases in the profit allowance can be made to reduce the economic return to the real estate. For example, if the first allocation resulted in a value to the real estate that was higher than the site's value and the replacement cost of the improvements, the allocation of income to the real estate is too high.

Capitalizing Remaining Income to Real Estate

After deducting allowances for a return to FF&E, intangible assets, and business profit, the remaining income accrues to the real estate. The industry considers the real estate to be the land, buildings, and fuel service. From the real estate income the appraiser makes further deductions for maintenance and repairs and for the reserve requirement of the real estate improvements. The deductions for real estate expenses are treated just as they are in appraisals of other types of real estate. At this point, the appraiser capitalizes the remaining income into a value estimate for the real estate.

The capitalization rate is best derived from the sales used in the sales comparison approach. As discussed earlier in this chapter, the appraiser should collect sales operating income data in addition to the sale price and physical description of the property. Now the operating information from the comparable sale properties can be used in developing overall capitalization rate estimates

for the subject property. To develop market-based capitalization rates, an operating income analysis should be performed for every sale that was used in the sales comparison approach. The use of electronic spreadsheets simplifies the calculations. Real estate capitalization rates for convenience stores are usually between 9% and 14%.

The appraiser should be cautious when applying someone else's capitalization rate to the income stream developed. To be consistent, capitalization rates must be developed and extracted from the comparables in the same way they were derived for the subject. A trade association's definition of net income may be different than the appraiser's. A proprietary database may calculate net income differently than the appraisal industry. Inaccurate value estimates may result from developing the income to real estate and then applying a capitalization rate that was supplied by a third party. Unless the appraiser knows exactly how the third party calculated the net income, third-party sources are not useful in supplying capitalization rates. For example, although the National Association of Convenience Stores does not provide capitalization rates, it does provide nationwide averages for pre-tax profit. The appraiser might be tempted to try to use the pre-tax profit in the profit allocation of net earnings. However, it is difficult to ascertain how the pre-tax profit was calculated. Similarly, the convenience store industry's definition of lease income cannot be directly applied to the appraisal of convenience stores.

An operating income analysis and capitalization are illustrated in Table 7.6 and Table 7.7. Three columns are shown so the appraiser can visually compare the industry standard and actual subject performance to the appraiser's projection of sales and operating expenses.

Because the operating expense section of this example closely parallels the industry standard expense categories as published by the National Association of Convenience Stores, it facilitates direct comparison of the subject's operating performance to published industry benchmarks. However, for appraisal purposes some modifications to the NACS operating expense model are necessary.

In creating the reconstructed operating statement, the appraiser should exclude the following expenses published by the NACS:

- Personal property taxes
- Depreciation/amortization
- Store rent
- Equipment rent
- Repair and maintenance

These expense items are excluded because the appraiser will make subsequent computations to the income stream that pertain to personal and real property. As a result, the appraiser must not deduct the above expense items at this point in the analysis. In the NACS expense benchmark, the items in the above list generally total 4% to 6% of gross sales. The appraiser should recognize that the typical NACS operating expense total published in the State of the Industry Report will be 400 to 600 basis points higher than the appraiser's reconstructed total annual operating expenses as a percent of gross sales.

Table 7.6	Reconstructed Operating Statement					
		Projection		**Actual Amount Stabilized**		**Industry Standard***
Estimated gallons per year		1,180,000		1,180,287		1,014,000
Average price/gallon		$1.50		$1.50		$1.50
Fuel dollars		$1,770,000		$1,770,431		$1,199,000
Merchandise (in-store) sales		$737,000		$737,000		$757,000
Food service		$0		$0		
Carwash		$0		$0		
Other		$0		$0		
Total sales		$2,507,000		$2,507,431		
Shrink	1.00%	$25,070	1.00%	$25,074		
Cost of goods sold:						
Fuel	88%	$1,542,024	88%	$1,542,399		89%
Merchandise	68%	$496,148	68%	$496,148		68%
Food service	35%	$0	35%	$0		
Carwash	20%	$0	20%	$0		
Other	0%	$0	0%	$0		
Margin	18%		18%			20%
Gross profit		$443,758		$443,809		
Less operating expenses:						
Labor costs	7.00%	$175,490	7.00%	$175,500		7.0%
Liability insurance	0.10%	$2,507	0.10%	$2,500		0.1%
Royalty fees	0.10%	$2,507	0.10%	$2,500		0.1%
Supplies	0.59%	$14,791	0.59%	$14,794		0.5%
Advertising	0.30%	$7,521	0.30%	$7,500		0.3%
Utilities	1.00%	$25,070	1.00%	$25,000		1.0%
Motor fuel drive-offs	0.10%	$2,507	0.10%	$2,500		0.1%
Cash short/over	0.10%	$2,507	0.10%	$2,500		0.1%
Other	1.20%	$30,084	1.20%	$30,000		1.2%
Subtotal	10.49%	$262,894	10.48%	$262,794		10.4%
EBIDTA**	7.21%	$180,773	7.22%	$181,015		

* Industry standard in NACS State of the Industry Report for 2000.

** EBIDTA is earnings before interest, depreciation, taxes, and amortization.

Table 7.7 Projected Operating Profile Summary

Gross sales	100%	$2,507,000
Cost of goods sold	81%	$2,038,172
Operating expenses/shrink	11%	$288,054
EBIDTA	7%	$180,773

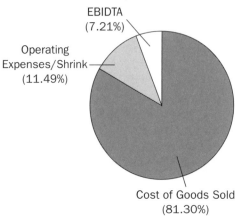

EBIDTA
(7.21%)

Operating
Expenses/Shrink
(11.49%)

Cost of Goods Sold
(81.30%)

Contribution to Gross Profit

Gross profit	$443,758
Add: shrink	$25,070
	$468,828

Contribution Categories		**Contribution Ratios**
Fuel	$227,976	49%
Merchandise	$240,852	51%
Food service	$0	0%
Carwash	$0	0%
Other	$0	0%
		100%

Intangible Assets in the Shopping Center: Identification and Valuation

David C. Lennhoff, MAI, SRA, and James D. Vernor, PhD, MAI

Problem Overview

Many appraisal assignments fail to sufficiently define the property being appraised. As a result, many valuations that are presented as real estate appraisals actually include value attributable to the efforts of people and personal property. For example, if an appraiser capitalized all the income from an assisted living center for retirees, he or she would capture the value of the total assets, including the real property, furniture, vehicles, and equipment. Also included would be the value resulting from the business of caring for seniors, including food service, medications supervision, organized activities, transportation to appointments, and some medical therapy services. This would be an example of an operating property, traditionally called a *going concern* by real estate appraisers, and more recently known as the *total assets of the business* (TAB). Another example would be a golf course in which value derives from course fees plus profit centers such as food and beverage sales, retail shop sales, and golf cart rentals. Many types of property involve the sale of goods and services in addition to real estate shelter. Examples include car washes, billboards, convenience stores, hotels, and shopping centers.

Sometimes investors don't care how the appraiser categorizes the asset, they just need a value as a total price to pay. Other times a seller might need to know how much to list an asset for in a disposition. However, for other purposes the client usually needs the value broken down between real and personal property in order to meet legal or policy requirements in lending, taxation, or condemnation. A value needs to be allocated at the time of purchase for both income tax depreciation and transfer tax purposes, during the operations for ad valorem property taxes, and at the time of condemnation.

This article will explore these issues relative to shopping centers. We will suggest some of the many components of a shopping center that could be recognized as intangible personal property and present some definitions for assets and intangibles. This discussion will explore the many reasons why these distinctions need to be made and the arguments raised in support of (or against) the existence of intangible assets. Selected court cases will be reviewed. Real estate appraisers have only recently become interested in this topic; but accountants, their regulators, and business appraisers have

David C. Lennhoff, MAI, SRA, CRE, FRICS, *is President of PGH Consulting, LLC, in Rockville, Maryland. He has appraised a wide variety of properties, including those having intangible components, and has testified in numerous jurisdictions regarding intangibles. He has served on many committees in leadership capacities for the Appraisal Institute and has taught nationally and internationally for the Appraisal Institute. He has been involved in the development and revision of many Appraisal Institute courses, including Course 800, Separating Real and Personal Property from Intangible Business Assets, and was a frequent instructor for that course. He has been awarded the James H. Pritchett Award, the Armstrong/Kahn Award, and the William N. Kinnard, Jr., PhD, Award from the Appraisal Institute as well as the International Association of Assessing Officers Donehoo Essay Award and the Martin S. Katz Memorial Award from the American Property Tax Counsel.*

James D. Vernor, PhD, MAI, *is chair emeritus of the real estate department at Georgia State University in Atlanta, Georgia, where he has specialized in real estate finance, valuation, and market research. He is active in consulting and appraising and teaches nationally and internationally for the Appraisal Institute. He has been awarded the Appraisal Institute's James H. Pritchett Award and William N. Kinnard, Jr., PhD, Award. He has been involved in the development and revision of many Appraisal Institute courses, including Course 800, and was a frequent instructor for that course. He is also one of the authors of* Shopping Center Appraisal and Analysis, *2nd ed., published by the Appraisal Institute.*

27

been thinking about intangible asset valuation for a longer time. Some of their ideas will be reviewed in this article as well.

Identifying Intangible Assets

Accounting literature and business valuation texts are full of examples of intangible assets, some of which are found in shopping centers. Possible sources of intangible assets in any type of property include the following:

- Customer lists and relationships
- Supplier relationships
- Permits, licenses, and copyrights
- Brand of product or firm
- Resales of utilities
- Stroller rental fees
- Marketing association fees
- Operating agreements
- Anchor inducements
- Favorable contracts
- Leases above market
- Trained and assembled workforce
- Monopoly and attractive site location
- Naming rights
- Cash and receivables or net working capital
- Trade secrets, franchises, and industry know-how
- Value of profit centers
- Image and reputation
- Markup on management fees or expense recoveries
- Return of and on start-up costs
- Percentage rent above market rent

As to what exactly an intangible asset is, the premiere American appraisal thought leader, the Appraisal Institute, offers the following definition of *intangible property,* which was taken from the *Uniform Standards of Professional Appraisal Practice* (2010-2011 edition): "Nonphysical assets, including but not limited to franchises, trademarks, patents, copyrights, goodwill, equities, securities, and contracts as distinguished from physical assets such as facilities and equipment."[1]

Standards Rule 1-2 of the *Uniform Standards of Professional Appraisal Practice*

(USPAP) states, "In developing a real property appraisal, an appraiser must ...identify the characteristics of the property that are relevant to the type and definition of value and intended use of the appraisal, including...any personal property, trade fixtures, or intangible items that are not real property but are included in the appraisal.[2]

At present there is no course, seminar, monograph, or text from the Appraisal Institute that treats intangible assets and how to recognize them, value them, or remove them from a going concern or the TAB in order to isolate real property value when it is necessary. Several prominent business appraisal writers have addressed the topic in depth, however. Two such experts are Robert Reilly and Gordon Smith.

According to Reilly, "In order for a taxpayer intangible asset to exist, (1) it should be an asset and (2) it should be intangible. An asset is anything that (1) can be owned and (2) has value. For an intangible asset, its value comes from its intangible characteristics (i.e., its bundle of legal rights). In contrast, for a tangible asset, its value comes from its physical or corporeal characteristics."[3]

Some of the economic characteristics or attributes that are necessary for qualification as an intangible asset include the following:

- The intangible asset should be subject to
  - A specific identification and recognizable description
  - Legal existence, recognition, and protection
  - The right of legally transferable private ownership
  - Being destroyed or terminated at an identifiable time or as the result of an identifiable event.
- There should be some tangible evidence or manifestation of the existence of the intangible asset (e.g., a contract, a license, a registration document, a listing of customers, a set of financial statements, etc).
- The intangible asset should be created or come into existence at an identifiable time or as the result of an identifiable event.

In other words, there should be a specific bundle of property rights associated with the existence of any intangible asset. An asset that

---

1. *The Dictionary of Real Estate Appraisal,* 5th ed. (Chicago: Appraisal Institute, 2010), 102.
2. *Uniform Standards of Professional Appraisal Practice,* 2010-2011 ed. (Washington, D.C.: The Appraisal Foundation, 2010), U-17.
3. Robert F. Reilly, "The Identification and Valuation of Taxpayer Commercial Intangible Assets for Gift and Estate Tax Purposes," *Insights* (Autumn 2008): 3-18.

possesses many, or all, of these economic characteristics or attributes typically qualifies as an intangible asset.

The inexperienced valuation analyst may assume that the previously mentioned attributes indicate that an intangible must be able to be sold separately–that is, without any other asset. However, this assumption would be a fundamental mistake. The intangible asset ownership interest should be able to be sold or otherwise transferred. However, the subject intangible asset may be sold as part of a bundle of intangible assets or as part of a bundle of both tangible assets and intangible assets. There is no valuation principle, literature, or course material that indicates that the intangible asset must be able to be sold *separately* from any other assets.

It should be noted that in the previously cited quote, Reilly is writing within the frame of reference of federal gift and estate taxes. It is likely that some of his criteria reflect thinking from court cases or law and regulation that has not been applied to assets within a real estate context.

Gordon Smith and Russell Parr have written in *Intellectual Property: Valuation, Exploitation, and Infringement Damages* that "Accounting theory defines intangibles as assets that do not have physical substance, that grant rights and privileges to a business owner, and that are inseparable from the enterprise. Accounting theory also defines them as assets for which the determination and timing of future benefits is very difficult." Finally, Reilly writes that intangible assets are subject to "identification, legal existence and protection, and the right of private ownership."[4]

The International Valuation Standards Council (IVSC) recognizes the topic of intangible assets under the label of trade-related properties (TRP) and prints a list of them in their *International Valuation Standards* (IVS). The IVS definition of *going-concern value* differs from that usually used by American appraisers. It states *going-concern value* to be "intangible elements of value in an operating business resulting from factors such as having a trained workforce, an operational plant, and the necessary licenses, systems, and procedures in place." The Appraisal Institute's definition of *going-concern value* (from *The Dictionary of Real Estate Appraisal*, 5th ed.) is "the market value of all the tangible and intangible assets of an established and operating business with an indefinite life, as if sold in aggregate; more accurately termed the *market value of the going concern*." Otherwise, it seems that Guidance Note (GN) 4 in the IVS follows USPAP as well as *Intellectual Property* closely.[5]

There have been several attempts to classify intangible assets. According to GN 4, an intangible asset can be either identifiable or unidentifiable in a valuation context. Any unidentifiable intangible asset associated with a business or group of assets is generally termed *goodwill*. The principal classes of identifiable intangible assets are as follows:

- Marketing-related
- Customer or supplier-related
- Artistic-related
- Technology-related

According to GN 4, assets may be either contractual or noncontractual. These categories are used for convenience in organizing and analyzing the assets but obviously are not mandatory.

Reasons for Appraising Intangible Assets

Skeptics of intangible asset theory and treatment demean it as a tactic just to reduce property taxes, but there are many reasons to identify and value these assets. As far as tax disputes are concerned, valuing intangibles is not a tax ploy; it is following the law, in which those taxes are to be levied on real property rather than personalty. Business writers have offered many reasons for the recognition of intangible assets, such as the following from GN 4:

- Acquisitions, mergers, and sales of businesses or parts of businesses
- Purchases and sales of intangible assets
- Reporting to tax authorities
- Litigation and insolvency proceedings
- Financial reporting

Reilly offers the following reasons for separating and valuing intangibles:

- Federal gift, estate, and income tax reasons
- Transaction pricing and structuring
- Intercompany use and ownership transfers

---

4. Gordon V. Smith and Russell L. Parr, *Intellectual Property: Valuation, Exploitation, and Infringement Damages* (New York: John Wiley and Sons, 2005), 13; Reilly, "The Identification and Valuation of Taxpayer Commercial Intangible Assets."

5. Revised International Valuation Guidance Note No. 4, *Valuation of Intangible Assets*, 2010.

- Financial accounting and reporting
- State and local ad valorem property taxation, planning, and compliance
- Financing collateralization and securitization
- Litigation claims and dispute resolution
- Management information and strategic planning
- Corporate governance and regulatory/contractual compliance
- Bankruptcy and reorganization analysis
- License, joint venture, and other development or commercialization opportunities
- Depreciation under Section 197 of the Internal Revenue Code[6]

The Economic Theory

The Last Decade: Total Assets of the Business, Going Concern, and Capitalized Economic Profit

Recent thinking on the concepts of total assets of the business, going concern, and capitalized economic profit has uncovered confusion in terms, led to some new replacement terms, and produced at least one industry course. The terms that have caused confusion are *business enterprise value* (BEV) and *going concern.*

To some in the field, *business enterprise value* has meant all of the intangibles in an operating firm; to others it has only meant the capitalized present value of the entrepreneur's contribution. To business appraisers it was likely to mean the entire value of all the assets of a business. In traditional appraisal language, the term *going concern* describes a business or operating property, such as a hotel or golf course that includes business profit centers. Business appraisers are more likely to think that going-concern value is the equity position in a business firm's balance sheet. The term *going-concern value* is confusing because it doesn't define what kind of value–market value, value in use, or investment value–has been contemplated for the going concern.

In response to these possible confusions, the authors of a 2002 *Appraisal Journal* article proposed a new lexicon.[7] The term *going concern* is still used, but *total assets of the business* (TAB) precisely describes the bundle of rights that includes real property; tangible personal prop-

erty such as furniture, fixtures, and equipment (FF&E); and intangibles associated with the business. The list of total intangible assets (TIA) can be expanded to include workforce, contracts, brand/name, and others, leaving perhaps some *residual intangible assets* (RIA) including *capitalized economic profit* (CEP), as shown in Exhibit 1. This list of intangible assets is only suggestive rather than exhaustive. The convergence of appraisal terms and methods with those of accounting will likely further change the terminology.

The Arguments Favoring the Existence of Intangibles

After reviewing research literature in business and economics and assessment case law, the late William Kinnard and Jeffrey Fisher have

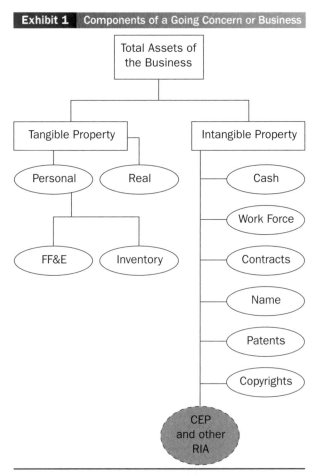

Exhibit 1 Components of a Going Concern or Business

Source: Marvin Wolverton, David C. Lennhoff, James D. Vernor, and Richard Marchitelli, "Allocation of Business Assets Into Tangible and Intangible Components: A New Lexicon," *The Appraisal Journal* (January 2002): 46-52, and Appraisal Institute Course 800, Separating Real and Personal Property from Intangible Business Assets.

---

6. Reilly, "The Identification and Valuation of Taxpayer Commercial Intangible Assets."

7. Marvin Wolverton, David C. Lennhoff, James D. Vernor, and Richard Marchitelli, "Allocation of Business Assets Into Tangible and Intangible Components: A New Lexicon," *The Appraisal Journal* (January 2002): 46-52.

both concluded that a *business value* component does indeed exist. They and others have cited many uses commonly thought to be combined with *business value,* including hotels, resorts, nursing homes, and private hospitals.[8] These properties are characterized by a high degree of business managerial ability and entrepreneurial effort, both of which contribute to the viability of the business and the value of the real estate.

The value of an asset derives from its productivity, with a fair market rate of return allocated to each of the agents of production. These agents have traditionally included land, labor, and capital, with land frequently presumed to represent the residual. Kinnard and Fisher rely on current microeconomic theory; they argue that a fourth agent, entrepreneurship, needs to be recognized and accorded a return (profit) and that entrepreneurship rather than the land is the residual agent.

Classical economics did not recognize the role of the entrepreneur as a risk taker or an agent of change and innovation. The idea of the entrepreneur arose around the year 1930. Today these functions are recognized and the entrepreneur is thought of as the factor of production that combines land, labor, and capital to meet an actual or potential demand for the good or service.

Following Kinnard, when all the traditional agents of production have been accorded a fair return at market rates (now called *contributing asset charges* or CAC), the residual may belong to an entrepreneur as a surplus or economic profit.[9] *Economic profit* is profit over and above the financial return that is sufficient to keep a factor of production in that activity; this level of financial return is referred to as *normal profit* for the entrepreneur. However, economic profits do not last long in competitive markets, as other producers bid up the prices of inputs and new production depresses the prices of the output. But when less-than-perfect competition exists, the economic profits may extend over time and can conceptually be converted into capitalized economic profit (CEP). It is this CEP that was formerly identified and less well understood as business enterprise value (BEV). Now it is but one of several types of intangible assets, and a residual asset at that.

According to this thinking, there are elements of entrepreneurship in the creation of a shopping center, throughout its construction, and subsequently in its operation. First, the labor is allocated a market return through the payment of salaries and wages. Second, the invested capital receives its mortgage interest or equity cash flows. Third, the land is afforded a fair market return (at market value for generic retail land) and, finally, any remaining income to the shopping center enterprise is considered to be a return for the entrepreneurship of the owner-operator in the form of a normal profit and possibly an economic profit in excess of the normal profit. Kinnard and Fisher stressed that entrepreneurship is especially significant in a center that has been successfully promoted and leased over several years. The capitalized present value of the residual income stream creates an intangible business value or business enterprise value that should not be imputed to the land.

The concept of entrepreneurship in operations has been developed by Maxwell Ramsland and William Kinnard. Special services provided by management include earning leasing fees from space rentals; maintaining an optimal tenant mix; coordinating janitorial, trash removal, and security operations; collecting and paying taxes and insurance premiums; overseeing grounds and improvements; arranging advertising and promotional activities to attract customers; providing utilities; and offering business counseling to tenants.[10] For all of these services, the owner/manager can develop sufficient expertise in creating economic profits.

Kinnard asserts, "It has long been held that any excess of contract rental over market rental is an intangible." This concept is presented in the 13th edition of the Appraisal Institute's textbook *The Appraisal of Real Estate* and in *Intellectual Property: Valuation, Exploitation, and Infringement Damages.* Jeffrey Fisher and George Lentz

---

8. William N. Kinnard, Jr., "Valuing the Real Estate of Regional Shopping Centers Independently of Operating Business Value Components: A Review of Recent Research" (paper prepared for AIREA annual meeting, Chicago, May 3, 1990); Jeffrey D. Fisher and William N. Kinnard, Jr., "The Business Value Component of Operating Properties: The Example of Shopping Malls" (paper presented at the 1989 National Conference of the International Association of Assessing Officers, Fort Worth, TX, September 20, 1989); Jeffrey D. Fisher, "Mall and Department Store Valuation" (working paper prepared for the Center for Real Estate Studies, Indiana University, March 1989).

9. *The Identification of Contributory Assets and Calculation of Economic Rents* (Washington, D.C.: The Appraisal Foundation, 2010).

10. Maxwell O. Ramsland, Jr., and William N. Kinnard, Jr., "Quantifying Business Enterprise Value for Malls," *The Appraisal Journal* (April 1999).

have observed that shopping center management is able to renew tenants at above-market rates because those tenants believe in the additional enterprise value of the center, its operation, and the synergistic image it presents to customers.[11]

William Townsley and Michael Kelly agree, writing that rents for mall tenants are set by landlords based on expectations of future business rather than real estate.[12] A percentage of sales revenues accrues to a business value and is not real estate. Only the base rents for new tenants are a reliable signal as to return *on* and *of* the real estate. The landlord collects percentage rent based on the tenant's business success, and, in his or her ability to audit the tenant's books, is effectively a partner in that business. Because the tenant does not have an equivalent insight into the landlord's business and profits, he or she is at a disadvantage in renewal negotiations, effectively making the landlord a monopolist. Real estate value is revealed by capitalizing the net operating income (essentially base rents), leaving the rest as return on business.

Two methods are suggested by Townsley and Kelly for estimating these base rents. In a cost-based approach, the feasibility rent rate on depreciated reproduction cost plus land value indicates the landlord's requirement for return *on* and *of* the invested capital. In the income capitalization approach, the base rents, calculated by size category and extended into a weighted average for the entire center, point to net operating income (*NOI*) per square foot.

Townsley and Kelly do not address issues such as:

• How to derive land value considering the position of the site on the development timescale

• Whether to pick a capitalization rate or discount rate for real estate only instead of inferring a rate from sales of going concerns

• Whether the base rents should be looked at as teaser rates or initial year concession rates to induce signing

• Details such as how to handle non-pass-through expenses for vacant space or items below the line, such as leasing commissions and tenant improvement allowances

On this same point, Robert Martin and Scott Nafe have written:

> The fact that similar-size tenants in similar locations in malls pay vastly different rents clearly illustrates how contract rental rates being charged for space in shopping malls bear little relevance to the value of the underlying real estate. Mall rents are more a function of the business success of each tenant and the sales volumes and profit margins earned by merchants selling different types of goods.[13]

Mark Eppli associates intangible value with department store image. His regression studies have shown that the primary reasons consumers shop at regional centers are location, comparison shopping, and department store fashion image. Eppli argues that while the portion of sales attributable to location should be associated with real estate value, the portion of sales associated with image produces intangible value. The value attributable to reducing search costs through enhancing the tenant mix and facilitating comparison shopping is indeterminable. Based on a study of over 4,500 nonanchor leases from 54 American shopping centers, he demonstrates how 21.5% of the value should be associated with nonrealty image factors of the anchor department stores.[14]

Richard Sorenson has addressed the issue as follows:

> The sales of shopping centers and malls often include intangibles in addition to real property. The analysis of selling prices must include the elimination of intangibles, fixtures, and business value. A sale price may be overstated unless the appraiser carefully considers what has been paid for the fixtures that will revert at the end of the lease, the value of the management team acquired, if any, and anything paid for retail operations independent of the business of renting space. These specific intangible items may be regarded as business value, but in aggregate they represent only a small portion of a shopping center's total value. As is the case with many income-producing properties, it is difficult to measure and separate tangible and intangible components in terms of their value contributions because the components are all integrated.

11. Kinnard, "Valuing the Real Estate of Regional Shopping Centers Independently of Operating Business Value Components"; Jeffrey D. Fisher and George H. Lentz, "Measuring Business Value in Shopping Malls" (paper published by the School of Business, Indiana University, Bloomington, September 1989).

12. William J. Townsley and Michael J. Kelly, "Quantifying Business Value at a Regional Mall," *Journal of Property Tax Management* 2, no. 3 (1991).

13. Robert S. Martin and Scott D. Nafe, "Segregating Real Estate Value from Nonrealty Value in Shopping Centers," *The Appraisal Journal* (January 1996) and reprinted in David C. Lennhoff, ed., *A Business Enterprise Value Anthology* (Chicago: Appraisal Institute, 2001).

14. Mark Eppli, "Value Allocation in Regional Shopping Centers," *The Appraisal Journal* (April 1988) and reprinted in the first edition of *A Business Enterprise Value Anthology*.

Supporting the notion that the rent payments include a business value, Sorenson writes:

> Mall rents are typically based not on the square footage occupied by a tenant but on the tenant's profit margins and projected sales volume. (In contrast, in-line stores with local retailers are charged rent per square foot.) Mall rents are closely tied to the business success of each tenant and the sales volumes and profit margins earned by merchants selling different types of goods. By charging a percentage of gross sales as rent, the mall owner is able to capture a portion of the business success of mall tenants. Increases in rents are typically based on increases in gross sales, so as the mall tenant's business increases, so does the rent.[15]

The Conundrum of Low Capitalization Rates for Intangibles

If intangible assets exist in a super-regional mall, why are the observed capitalization rates for this asset class among the lowest of real estate capitalization rates? One might normally expect that intangible assets are more fragile and less durable than most real estate, and hence the rates of capitalization should be higher. Indeed, most businesses probably sell at capitalization rates higher than most real estate. But an explanation can be found in the theory of capitalization rates as applied in the yield capitalization formulas. One formulation of this model is:

$$R = Y - CR$$

where:

- R represents an overall capitalization rate
- Y represents an investor target yield (discount rate) for that asset
- CR represents the market typical expectation for annual growth in net operating income and resale value

If yield rates are commensurate with the risk in regional centers, the capitalization rate will be depressed by large expectations for growth in future incomes and resale values. The explanation may be that investors expect higher rates of growth in the income (and value) of the regional center than they do from other classes of real estate alone, probably because of the opportunity for such an increase benefitting from the growth in the value of the business.

The Opposition Theorists and Theories

Some of the arguments against recognizing intangible business value have been summarized by Arthur Gimmy. He argues that mall land prices uniquely make up the difference between sale price and the depreciated replacement cost of the buildings and other improvements because the sites are monopolistic and unrelated to surrounding retail site prices. (However, monopoly value itself can be recognized as an intangible.) Other arguments from Gimmy, with our thoughts in parentheses, are as follows:

- Appraisers and investors have traditionally not recognized shopping malls as businesses. (Real estate appraisers are late to recognize intangibles in general. As malls receive more attention for taxing, financing, condemnation, and calculating depreciation deductions under the Internal Revenue Code, this will change.)

- Mall businesses have not been sold separately, exchanged, or valued outside of a tax appeal assignment. (Ample authority now says intangibles do not have to be separated from their associated assets to exist. See the previous discussion regarding accounting theory and business appraisal.)

- Mall management does not conduct itself in a manner separate from a specialized real estate management team, is unlicensed, and does not consider itself as a taxable revenue entity. (Separation is not required; nor is licensing. Income taxes are paid on intangible asset-generated income streams.)

- Malls really only comprise a large group of individual businesses and, as such, are only a means for these businesses to succeed and contribute to the economic health of the community.[16] (When the identity of the owner of a mall matters a great deal in assembling a tenant mix, it is investment value rather than real estate in the hands of a typical market participant. The group has a synergy created by the mall owner and manager.)

One of the most intellectual examinations of the business enterprise argument was undertaken by Kerry Vandell.[17] He examined the eco-

---

15. Richard C. Sorenson, *Appraising The Appraisal: The Art of Appraisal Review* (Chicago: Appraisal Institute, 2006), 107-8.

16. Arthur E. Gimmy, "Conflict at the Mall: The Tax Reduction Solution," *Appraisal Views* 3, no. 2 (second quarter 1990).

17. Kerry D. Vandell, "Business vs. Real Estate Value in Shopping Mall Valuation: A Critical Examination" (paper presented at the 1999 Summer Appraisal Institute Conference, Orlando, June 26, 1999, and reprinted in the first edition of *A Business Enterprise Value Anthology*.)

nomic rationale for nine arguments for business enterprise value and concluded the following (with our thoughts in parentheses):

1. Site values reflect the benefits of agglomeration economics, not business value. (Agglomeration results from good customer relationships cultivated by the owner and manager. Revenues resulting from a percentage of sales are more a function of human activities than land productivity.)

2. Store branding leads to lower rent paid to a landlord, but if mall branding were transportable, then it would lead to business value. (The naming for fee of, for example, Discovery Mills disproves this argument, but mall brand is not yet a major source of intangible value.)

3. Entrepreneurial returns are possible only if unique to the owner, and they dissipate upon sale of the mall. (They certainly can dissipate over time in a changing environment.)

4. Overage rent is just part of market leasing terms for the real estate. (It is indeed customary, but it is a function of who the tenant is and how well his/her business performs at the location created by the owner/manager.)

5. Utility resales do generate both return *on* and *of* conversion outlays and marketing expenditures, and are hence business value.

6. Non-real-estate service center incomes are non-real-estate value.

7. In valuing the going concern, one should remove the revenues and expenses of the business centers. (We agree with the preceding three points.)

8. In the face of rollover lease premiums, the initial rental concessions were operating expenses rather than evidence of business value. (Does this argument apply to the money given to anchors to induce their tenancy? Why not call them capital investments to create value–of an intangible nature?)

9. The excess of the value of a leased fee estate over the value of a fee simple estate is non-assessable per state law; methodologically it should be treated like a cash equivalency adjustment. (We can agree with this argument as it applies in most states.)

The Appraisal Institute sponsored a panel debate about the intangibles topic at their an-

nual meeting in 1999. A summary report for the arguments against business value listed the following points:

*   Allocating prices and operating incomes usually involves substantial judgment and is not based on verified market evidence.

*   Entrepreneurship is not a fourth factor of production but a specialized form of labor.

*   A component, in order to be an intangible and separate from the real estate, must be separable for transfer of ownership and survivable afterward.

*   Courts have regularly ruled against the existence of business value, stating that it is not the result of a generally accepted appraisal practice but used only for tax cases.[18]

The team arguing the case against intangibles produced a five-point test to determine whether a business value exists:

1. What is the business?

2. Is the owner of the business also the owner of the real estate?

3. Is the business separately transferable to another location?

4. Can the real estate be transferred without the business?

5. How does the income to the owner of the business differ from the market rent of the real estate?

As will be seen in the review of accounting discussions and the methods of business appraisers, separability and transferability of these assets is not universally required. However, the nature of the intangible asset and what causes the revenues can be explained.

Court Cases on Intangibles

As fervently as some appraisers hold to the existence of intangible value centers, the points remain to be proven consistently in courts. Court decisions have consistently ruled against an intangible business value in shopping centers. This section presents comments on some court cases that have dealt with these issues. Although most of these cases are somewhat dated, the discussion has merit because of their specific applicability to the topic at hand. While there are a few more recent decisions involving

---

18. David C. Lennhoff, "Business Enterprise Value Debate: Still a Long Way to Reconciliation," *The Appraisal Journal* (October 1999) and reprinted in the first edition of *A Business Enterprise Value Anthology*.

regional malls (Eden Prairie Center, for example), they will not be discussed here for various reasons, such as pending appeals.

In an early case, the Southridge Mall in Greendale, Wisconsin, was assessed shortly after it was sold. The owners failed in arguments that part of the sale price reflected a component of business value, that the mall was part of a group purchase and was not sufficiently exposed to the market prior to the sale, and that the assessor failed to consider the impact of an assumed mortgage.[19] The most important finding concerning a business value was that the tax assessment could include as a component of value the property's transferable income-producing capacity, as reflected in a recent sale. The decision quotes the Wisconsin law that assessable property "include(s) not only the land itself but all buildings and improvements thereon, and all fixtures and rights and privileges appertaining thereto." The decision went on to state that the key was whether the value is attached and passes with the property, stays with the seller, or dissipates. The taxpayer's case seems compromised by the filing of a Wisconsin Real Estate Transfer Return showing a value close to that of the assessor's.

Two interesting non-shopping-center parallels were presented in the Southridge case in which part of the value of a property derived from the business operated on the real estate for which that business was not transferable. Heritage Cablevision v. Board of Review involved an assessor's appraisal of a property using the income capitalization approach in which the court found that the income to be imputed to the real estate should not properly include the income generated by the cable franchise.[20] The real estate in Madonna v. County of San Luis Obispo was appraised by capitalizing the income to an inn with restaurant and shops, and the court found that capitalizing "enterprise income" was inappropriate and misleading.[21]

In another case the court considered whether the income arising from certain business relationships is the result of the operating agreement and to be considered intangible. They determined that the incomes in question were the result of management rather than the operating agreements per se and hence were transmissible with the real estate.[22] They observed that no operating agreements were ever transmitted without the real property, that operating agreements are covenants that run with the land and do not create recognizable intangible value, and that if there is an intangible customer base, it belongs to the anchor stores and not the mall owner.

In Lawrence Assoc. v. Lawrence Twp., the court held that a percentage lease effectively makes the landlord the business partner in the tenant's business, and the rents collected are more indicative of the value of the tenant's business than the value of the real estate. Because of the circumstances of the case, the court held that the income capitalization approach should be used for the in-line space and the cost approach should be used for the anchors.

In that same Lawrence case, the court rejected the argument that utility resale income is intangible business income since the lease established the arrangement as a condition of occupancy.[23] In the Barton Creek Square case, the shopping center owner hadn't reported certain intangibles to the US Securities and Exchange Commission (SEC) or to its shareholders as required under relevant statutes, so its argument in the property tax case failed.[24] The jury decided that the valuation should not include the value derived from the operating agreements and profit centers (such as utility resales and pushcarts), but the judge overruled. The case was settled later at the level of the appellate court.

Courts are notoriously reluctant to depart from precedent and have rejected arguments for intangible value components because "business enterprise value" is not a recognized method.[25] In 1997, the Iowa Supreme Court decided the property tax case of the Merle Hay Mall for the

---

19. Wisconsin, *ex rel.* N/S Associates v. Board of Review, 164 Wis.2d 31, 473 N.W.2d 554 (1991), noted in *The Appraisal Journal* (April 1992): 297.

20. 457 N.W.2d 594 (Iowa 1990).

21. 39 Cal.App3d at 59, 113 Cal.Rptr. 916.

22. Simon Property Group L.P. v. Robert Boley, Manager of assessment for Jackson County, Mo. State Tax comm. App. Nos. 95-30038 through 95-30041, 95-30043 and 95-30044.

23. Lawrence Assoc. v. Lawrence Twp., 5 N.J. Tax 481 (Tax 1983).

24. Simon Property Group Texas, L.P. v Travis Central Appraisal District, Austin #3-96-001 62-CV.

25. Merle Hay Mall v. City of Des Moines Board of Review, 564 N.W. 2nd 419 (Iowa 1997).

years 1993 and 1994.[26] At issue was whether certain intangibles such as the worth of the business organization, management, assembled work force, working capital, trade names, and franchises are properly excludable from assessment. Iowa law provides that assessed values not be based on certain named intangible assets, but the court ruled that the assessors were not required by law to disregard all other intangible assets and, therefore, some unnamed intangible assets could be considered. The court also ruled that despite below-market rental rates for one anchor, the assessed value was to be based on market rents and the interest in property being appraised was, effectively, the fee simple interest. Since the concept of business enterprise value is not a "generally accepted" appraisal theory, as was required by Iowa law, it was rejected.

In a 1995 Minnesota Supreme Court decision concerning the 1990 and 1991 property taxes for the Rosedale Shopping Center, the issue was whether $28 million in cash outlays by the mall owner to an anchor for capital improvements to induce that anchor to remain and improve its store at the Rosedale Mall instead of moving to the new Mall of America should be deducted in a discounted cash flow (DCF) analysis.[27] The Supreme Court affirmed the tax court decision that those outlays should be deducted.

In 1995, the Minnesota tax court issued an opinion on the market value of the Southdale Mall in Minneapolis for the years 1990, 1991, and 1992. Like the Rosedale Mall, Southdale is within the Minneapolis metropolitan area. Also like Rosedale, a key issue was whether costs of anchor inducements to extend the operating agreement and construct a new store should be deducted from income in a DCF income analysis. The tax court decided that they should be. The taxpayer's expert appraiser attributed approximately one-third of the value of the going concern to nonreal components, which were described as the unique drawing power of the Dayton's anchor store presence, radius restrictions on that anchor competing in the nearby Mall of America, and the aggregate drawing power of the three anchors in the mall. The tax court opined that these aspects were fully treated in the deductions of the cash

flows to induce Dayton's to remain, and further adjustments would be "double counting" the deduction for anchor inducements.[28]

In the Hanes Mall case, the taxpayer questioned whether the mall was assessed uniformly and argued for intangible business value in the mall's internal profit centers.[29] The taxpayer argued that the cost approach should have been considered to reveal an upper limit of value to the fee simple value of the real estate without the intangibles. The County's expert argued that because the market doesn't consider business value in the purchase of real estate, appraisers shouldn't either. This decision indicates that the income capitalization approach is the most reliable method and did not address the matter of intangibles. An observer noted that stroller income was recognized as nonrealty.

The decisions generally reveal a reluctance to accept the concept of intangible business value, even though the cases have frequently resulted in substantial dollar reductions in assessed value. Utility resales and other business activities have seldom been separated from the real estate incomes. When taxpayers have tried to offer a cost approach to reveal intangible values in contrast to value indications of the income capitalization approach, courts have found the cost indication unreliable.

Other property types have recognized business value. There seems to be little debate that properties such as hotels, motels, golf courses, and various kinds of congregate health care facilities have a business value component. In one court case, the appropriate base for imposition of a real property transfer tax in a bulk sale of power-generating plants was to exclude intangibles such as a work force in place, open purchase orders, existing obligations, contracts, a multi-plant premium, a rapid market entry premium, favorable financing, and emissions credits (i.e., pollution rights).[30]

The Latest Thinking from Accounting Authorities

The Financial Accounting Standards Board
For 30 years, the Financial Accounting Standards Board (FASB) in the United States and

---

26. Merle Hay Mall v. City of Des Moines.

27. Equitable Life Assur. Society of US v. County of Ramsey, 530 N.W.2d 544 (1995).

28. Equitable Life Assurance Society of the United States v. County of Hennepin, 1995 WL 702527 (Minn. Tax 1995).

29. *In re* Appeal of Winston-Salem Joint Venture, 144 N.C.App. 706, 551 S.E.2d 450 (2001).

30. County of Los Angeles, et al. v. Edison International et al.; Superior Court of the State of California, No BC238277, 2002.

the International Accounting Standards Board (IASB) have been moving from a system of depreciated historical cost accounting for valuing assets on balance sheets to a system of "mark-to-market (M2M)" or fair value accounting.[31] While "M2M" accounting is not mandatory for all real estate assets yet, it does seem to be in the future and is required in certain circumstances, such as mergers of companies. Because publicly held owners of real estate are not allowed to mark up their assets in financial reports, they will continue to be carried at less than value; as a result, investors cannot assure that management is achieving sufficient market returns in the management of those assets. (Marking *financial* assets to market values has been part of generally accepted accounting practices, or GAAP, for some time.) Other reasons for contracting appraisals are not affected by FASB, such as for tax purposes or to advise the purchase of a single piece of property. Of course, while reporting companies are not required to report appreciating real estate values in their financial statements, many choose to do so in footnotes.

According to the *Dictionary of Financial Terms*, the FASB

- Is an independent, self-regulatory board that establishes and interprets GAAP

- Operates under the principle that the economy and financial services industry work smoothly when credible, concise, and clear financial information is available

- Periodically revises its rules to make sure corporations are following its principles. The corporations are supposed to fully account for different kinds of income, avoid shifting income from one period to another, and properly categorize their income.[32]

Two of the most important Statements of Financial Accounting Standards by the FASB are Statements 141R and 142, which provide the accounting framework under GAAP for asset valuation and the allocation of the purchase price of a company by another to the various assets, both tangible and intangible. Property, plant, and equipment (PP&E) must be reevaluated for every merger transaction, and remaining lives must be assigned to component assets.[33]

While Statement 141R appears to apply to the valuation of assets for financial reporting purposes including intangibles during mergers, Kenneth Rogers reports that the SEC has applied it more broadly to real estate acquisitions. Based on this information, Rogers urges real estate investors to have their closing attorneys make the intangible asset allocations prior to and included in the closing statement, so that they will be considered in future property tax assessments and properly excluded.[34]

The FASB standards provide the term *fair value* instead of the more customary *market value*, but Rogers thinks they provide the same result except in a few rare situations. *Fair value* has been defined in FASB Statement 157.

Asset lives are determined by the appraiser and may be either "definite lived" or "indefinite lived." Definite lived assets are subject to depreciation expense each year according to their remaining lives; these assets lead to a charge against earnings per share. Indefinite lived assets are not depreciated but must be examined for impairment each year; accordingly, these assets do not reduce earnings per share (EPS) when no impairment exists. Corporate financial managers prefer asset categorization that does not lead to charges against EPS. For financial reporting purposes by publically held companies, the remaining lives for each asset are the result of some valuer's judgment, in contrast to the accounting for income taxes in which all intangible assets are written off over 15 years despite their remaining life.

Goodwill is defined by the FASB as the ultimate residual asset, when the sums of all other assets add up to more than the price paid for a target company (plus liabilities assumed); it is not amortized but rather examined for impairment. From the standpoint of an acquiring company, the way to minimize expenses that reduce EPS is to assign the maximum to goodwill. As a result, the SEC and auditing firms try to assure that the maximum amounts have been assigned to amortizable assets and the minimum to indefinite lived assets and goodwill.

---

31. This section draws from Alfred M. King, *Fair Value for Financial Reporting: Meeting the New FASB Requirements* (Hoboken, NJ: John Wiley and Sons, 2006). Mr. King holds an AB, MBA, CMA, and CFM, and is Vice Chairman of Marshall & Stevens and past Chairman of the Accounting Committee of the Institute of Management Accountants.

32. *Dictionary of Financial Terms* (Lightbulb Press, 2008), http://financial-dictionary.thefreedictionary.com/FASB.

33. King, *Fair Value for Financial Reporting,* Chapter 1.

34. Kenneth J. Rogers, "FAS 141 Implications for Transfer and Property Tax," *National Real Estate Investor* (May 2006).

What is interesting in a real estate context is that FASB lists 29 intangible assets that could be identified. Many have never been considered by real estate appraisers. Four common categories of intangible assets are:

1. Patents and technology
2. In-process research and development
3. Software
4. Customer relationships

The FASB identifies the three traditional techniques for making appraisals for all types of assets: the market approach (also commonly known as the sales comparison approach), the cost approach, and the income capitalization approach. It vastly prefers the market approach based on observable and verifiable transactions and assigns the cost and income capitalization approaches to a lower level of reliability. When applying the market approach, appraisers are expected to model the behavior of typical market participants and develop an opinion of what an asset will likely sell for as opposed to what a buyer would likely pay. Traditional distinctions are made between value in exchange versus value in use, and the former is required.

The use of fair value accounting is very controversial. Changes in the values of assets in the balance sheet are reported in the income statement and flow through as profits or losses. Volatility in asset values is magnified in the income statement because asset values are usually greater than incomes, and so a relatively slight change in a balance sheet asset value will result in a much greater *relative* change in the income. Financial managers know that stock holders and prospective investors do not like volatility in return and as a result require a higher rate of return to hold that stock. Under such circumstances, it becomes more expensive to issue new stock. King feels that traditional valuation methods can be applied to any asset. He writes that he has "never met an asset that could not be valued."[35]

One of the interesting techniques accepted in fair value estimating is the use of probability weighted present values in circumstances of uncertainty, such as the valuation of a likely liability arising from losing a lawsuit. This technique is covered in FASB Concept Statement 7, but is probably viewed today by most real estate appraisers as only an academic and experimental tool, notwithstanding the fact that such valuation methodology has been a regular part of the Appraisal Institute curriculum.[36] Such probabilistic valuation may be an answer to those who argue that intangible assets are too hard for real estate appraisers, and appraisers shouldn't even try to handle them.

Because the FASB has judged a cost approach to be less reliable than a market approach, the Board distrusts a cost-based valuation of a trained and assembled workforce and instructs that this asset may not be presented as an asset in a financial statement. However, in the authors' judgment, the workforce value must be estimated in the allocation of income to other assets such as in-process research and development (IPR&D).[37]

The International Valuation Standards Council

The International Valuation Standards Council (IVSC) has a membership that includes the major national valuation standard-setters and professional associations from 41 different countries.[38] Their headquarters are in London and the Council's American members are the Appraisal Institute and the American Society of Appraisers. The IVSC is a nongovernmental organization member of the United Nations.

The IVSC was founded in 1981 as a joint venture of the UK-based Royal Institution of Chartered Surveyors (RICS) and the United States–based Appraisal Institute with the purpose of developing a set of common international real estate valuation standards for financial reporting, in conjunction with the development of the International Accounting Standards (IAS, now known as the IFRS) by the International Accounting Standards Committee (IASC, now known as the IASB). The IVSC now pursues the "harmonization" of international real estate valuation practices in general and plans on introducing standards for all types of asset classes (such as real estate, business, and nontangible assets).

In the words of the IVSC,

> Revised Guidance Note No. 4 *Valuation of Intangible Assets* identifies and defines the principal

---

35. King, *Fair Value for Financial Reporting*, Chapter 3.
36. Ibid., 62.
37. Ibid., 68, 123.
38. For more information, visit www.ivsc.org.

approaches and methods used in intangible asset valuation, with the objective of reducing the diversity of terminology, and making valuation reports more comprehensible to users worldwide. The new Guidance Note No. 16 *Valuation of Intangible Assets for IFRS Reporting Purposes* draws the attention of valuers, and those commissioning valuations for use in financial statements, to the principal accounting requirements of the International Financial Reporting Standards (IFRS) under which the valuations are prepared and provides guidance on the appropriate valuation response.[39]

Methods of Intangible Asset Valuation

An exploration of methodology can start with governmental authorities and proceed to the texts of business value practitioners. The IVSC and their Guidance Note (GN) 4 will be considered first.

GN 4 proposes to "identify the principal approaches and methods used in intangible asset valuation and define them, with the objective of reducing the diversity of terminology and making valuation reports more comprehensible to users."[40] It offers the established three approaches commonly in use for real property: the sales comparison approach (also known as the market approach), the income capitalization approach, and the cost approach.

GN 4 is clear that the object of the analysis is market value as opposed to a value in use or investment value. The Note recognizes the limits of the market approach in practice due to the scarcity of relevant transactions or the lack of a clear valuation metric. The usual type of adjustments may have to be qualitative instead of quantitative. Consider the following examples:

- The brand being valued may be considered to command a more dominant position in the market than those involved in the transactions.

- A drug patent being valued may have greater efficacy and fewer side effects than those involved in the transactions.

As a result of these practical difficulties, the market or sales comparison approach is often used as a test of reasonableness for values derived by other methods.

The income capitalization approach for intangibles works as it does for real property. According to GN4, Paragraph 4.18, "Valuation methods under the income approach determine the value of an intangible asset, by reference to the present value of income, cash flows, or cost savings that could actually or hypothetically be achieved by a market participant owning the asset."

Paragraph 4.20 identifies three principal intangible asset valuation methods within the income capitalization approach:

1. The relief-from-royalty method, sometimes known as the royalty savings method

2. The excess earnings method

3. The premium profits method, sometimes known as the incremental income method

Relief-from-Royalty or Royalty Savings Method

Paragraph 4.25 of GN4 provides that "The relief-from-royalty method calculates the value of an intangible asset by reference to the value of the hypothetical royalty payments that would be saved through owning the asset, as compared with licensing the asset from a third party. It involves estimating the total royalty payments that would need to be made over the asset's life, by a hypothetical licensee to a hypothetical licensor. Where appropriate, the royalty payments over the life of the asset are adjusted for tax and discounted to present value."

Excess Earnings Method

According to GN4, Paragraph 4.33, "The excess earnings method determines the value of an intangible asset as the present value of the cash flows attributable to the subject intangible asset after excluding the proportion of the cash flows that are attributable to other assets."

Premium Profits or Incremental Income Method

Paragraph 4.29 of Guidance Note 4 states, "The premium profits method involves comparing the forecast profit stream or cash flows that would be earned by a business using the intangible asset with those that would be earned by a business that does not use the asset. The forecast incremental profits or cash flows achievable through use of the asset are then computed. Forecast periodic amounts are capitalized through use of either a suitable discount factor or suitable capitalization multiple."

---

39. Revised International Valuation Guidance Note No. 4, *Valuation of Intangible Assets*, 2010.

40. Ibid.

Techniques for developing discount rates under the IVSC may include built-up rates; these are quite out of favor in American real estate appraisal circles due to the difficulty of supporting the estimates for the various risk premiums.

Cost Approach

The cost approach for intangibles also works as it does with real estate. Paragraph 4.44 of GN 4 states that "The cost approach, often known as the depreciated replacement cost approach, determines the value of an intangible asset by calculating the cost of replacing it with an asset with similar or identical service capacity."

According to Paragraph 4.45, "This approach is mainly used for those intangible assets that have no identifiable income streams or other economic benefits." And, according to Paragraph 4.47, "In practice, there are only a few types of intangible assets that lend themselves to application of this method."

Traditional Business Appraisers' Approaches

Business appraisers generally stand in agreement with the suggestions of GN 4. Robert Reilly elaborates on the previously mentioned methods in his online newsletter and adds that because developers of intangible assets also expect an entrepreneurial incentive, one should be included in a cost approach to valuation.[41] He points out that intangible assets are subject to the same kind of depreciation as real property and that remaining useful lives (RUL) must usually be estimated.

Reilly explains that there are at least five methods to consider in an income capitalization approach:

- Valuation methods that quantify the incremental level of intangible asset economic income (the intangible asset owner/operator expects a greater level of economic income (however measured) by owning/operating the subject commercial intangible asset as compared to not owning/operating the subject commercial intangible asset)
- Valuation methods that quantify a decremental level of intangible asset economic

costs (the intangible asset owner/operator expects a lower level of economic costs– such as other required levels of capital costs or operating costs–by owning/operating the subject commercial intangible asset as compared to not owning/operating the subject commercial intangible asset)
- Valuation methods that estimate a relief from a hypothetical royalty payment (the amount of a royalty payment that a hypothetical third-party intangible asset licensee would be willing to pay to a hypothetical third-party intangible asset licensor in order to obtain the use of and rights to the subject commercial intangible asset
- Valuation methods that quantify the difference in the value of the owner/operator overall business enterprise or similar economic unit as a result of owning the subject commercial intangible asset (and using it in the taxpayer owner/operator business enterprise), as compared to not owning the subject intangible asset (and not using it in the taxpayer owner/operator business enterprise)
- Valuation methods that estimate the value of the subject intangible asset as a residual from the value of the taxpayer owner/operator overall business enterprise (or of a similar economic unit), or as a residual from the value of an overall estimation of the total intangible value of the taxpayer owner/operator business enterprise (or of a similar economic unit)[42]

Reilly concludes that the selection of the appropriate valuation methods and procedures to value a taxpayer commercial intangible asset is based on:

1. The characteristics of the taxpayer intangible asset
2. The quantity and quality of available data
3. The purpose and objective of the analysis
4. The experience and judgment of the valuation analyst

The final value conclusion for the taxpayer commercial intangible asset is typically based on a synthesis of the value indications derived from each applicable valuation approach and method.[43]

---

41. Reilly, "The Identification and Valuation of Taxpayer Commercial Intangible Assets," 15.
42. Ibid., 17.
43. Ibid., 18.

Reilly presents a lucid discussion of the relief-from-royalty method with examples and data sources—both hard copy and online.[44]

Gordon Smith and Russell Parr write about intellectual property (including know-how, trade secrets, contract rights, and customer relationships) and call it "the foundation of commercial power."[45]

Chapter 7 of Smith and Parr's *Intellectual Property: Valuation, Exploitation, and Infringement Damages* lays out the traditional three approaches to classical valuation and discusses their application to various intangible assets. Separate chapters are then devoted to a more detailed examination of each of the three approaches.

Chapter 22 discusses an old rule of thumb, which suggests that a licensee might commonly pay about 25% of his or her profits for the use of an intellectual product. Testing shows some reliability of this 40-year-old rough rule of thumb when no better data exists. Valuers would then forecast these results based on sales forecasts for the licensee, subtracting *all* expenses, including indirect expenses.

One of the more advanced treatments of these topics by Robert Reilly and Robert Schweihs is a collection of 24 essays by various authors, *The Handbook of Business Valuation and Intellectual Property Analysis.* Chapter 15 of this book treats discount rates and capitalization rates, and Chapter 18 presents an intellectual property ad valorem case study. Both discussions are consistent with mainline valuation theory for real and personal property assets.

More Arguments Against Intangibles

Now that the definition of intangible assets and the theory and methods for their valuation have been discussed, we can move on to some of the arguments raised in testimony opposing the recognition or valuation of these assets. These arguments have been raised in litigation concerning various property types and will likely arise in cases involving shopping centers. These arguments are presented as follows, with reasonable answers provided for each argument.

- **Argument:** Cash and working capital do not have to be treated in any valuation because an adjustment in the closing statement removes them from the transaction.
  Answer: That might work in the adjusting of sales comparables, but if the income

capitalization approach is used, the income is that to all of the assets, including working capital. The corresponding CAC needs to come out.

- **Argument:** Trained and assembled workforce is paid for by payroll deductions in the income statement.
  Answer: Any property operating at stabilized occupancy needs to have the full complement of contributing assets in place in order to command the market rate of rents. An assembled workforce has value because money does not have to be spent again to recruit and train the workers. It is a value that doesn't wane as long as the asset is in its highest and best use. By analogy, one cannot argue that a roof has no stock value because maintenance expenses are incurred to keep it up.

- **Argument:** Start up and marketing expenses should not be used because the concern/property is well established.
  Answer: Imagine one is appraising a business property using a replacement cost approach. All of the construction costs have been gathered, site improvement costs have been added, and a market-supported site value is combined with the other costs. Is the valuation finished? What we have at this point is the value of an empty building. If the objective is to value a stabilized property in operations, additional expenditures must be made for leasing fees, other marketing outlays, and some early losses. As with the workforce investment, the outlays give way to a valuable asset because they don't have to be made again.

- **Argument:** Appraisers shouldn't recognize or place values on intangible assets because the market doesn't do it.
  Answer: Sometimes market participants don't care about disaggregating a price they pay for a bundle of assets, and the appraiser may not have to either if he or she is appraising for the same purpose. However, many clients do in fact need the asset values separated as part of their intended use of the report. An earlier section listed many reasons why assets are appraised. For property taxes, for example, the removal of the intangible assets from an ad valorem real estate appraisal

---

44. Reilly, "The Relief from Royalty Method of Intellectual Property Valuation," *Insights* (Autumn 2008).

45. Smith and Parr, *Intellectual Property,* Chapter 2.

is done because it is required by the law in many jurisdictions, despite whether it would be done by a buyer and seller in evaluating a purchase/sale of an existing going concern.

- **Argument:** Store locations next to prestigious anchors enjoy better real estate. **Answer:** When "who the tenant is" really matters, the resulting value is value in use/investment value instead of market value. The IVSC recognizes this in GN 4. For example, a location adjacent to Nordstrom's for a chair retailer in a mall adds a value beyond market value.

On the Supportability of Intangibles

Identifying and measuring intangible assets has long been a challenging task for real estate–oriented appraisers, especially in adversarial situations, but as real estate appraisal converges on business valuation and international valuation standards, it will get easier. In the short run it will be important for owners of intangible assets to pick their battles carefully—with the right assets, in the right political jurisdictions, and in the right courts. It seems that some assets will be easier to support than others. In this sense we see supportability in two dimensions:

- The asset fits definitions that are already recognized by appraisers and accountants.
- The data needed for its valuation is presently clearly available or could be with some planning.

We have attempted our own very subjective judgment about which assets are more or less easily supported, starting with the list of assets which appeared early in this article. Our estimations appear in Exhibit 2.

Summary and Conclusions

Some argue that intangibles do not need to be separated from a going concern because buyers don't do it. But many clients have an intended use for the valuation that does, in fact, require separation.

Real estate appraisers as a group have little experience in the valuation of intangibles and frequently overlook them in many assignments. Court cases involving malls usually have not been decided in favor of the recognition of intangibles. Many of these decisions were driven by faulty arguments, poor evidence or preparation, and political concerns. Some cases were settled prior to decision.

Regulatory agencies, accountants, and business appraisers have much experience with intangibles and are accustomed to identifying them and assigning values based on the accepted three approaches, with primary emphasis on the income capitalization approach.

The discussion of FASB Statement 141R appears to apply to the valuation of assets for financial reporting purposes, including intangibles acquired during mergers, but Kenneth Rogers reports that the SEC has applied it more broadly to real estate acquisitions.[46] Based on this, Rogers urges real estate investors to have their closing attorneys make the intangible asset allocations prior to and included in the closing statement, so that they will be considered in future property tax assessments and properly excluded.

Much work remains to be done to get real property appraisers comfortable with recognizing and separating intangible personal property assets from the real property of a going concern. Regardless, there are legitimate situations in which this is needed and appropriate. Appraisers must either get up to speed on the principles, methodologies, and techniques, or be prepared to relinquish these assignments completely. Simply put, if you don't know why it needs to be done or how to do it, then you cannot be the one to do it. Related professions such as accounting and business valuation and their regulators will likely provide much of the needed impetus to real estate appraisers for this intellectual development.

---

46. Rogers, "FAS 141 Implications for Transfer and Property Tax."

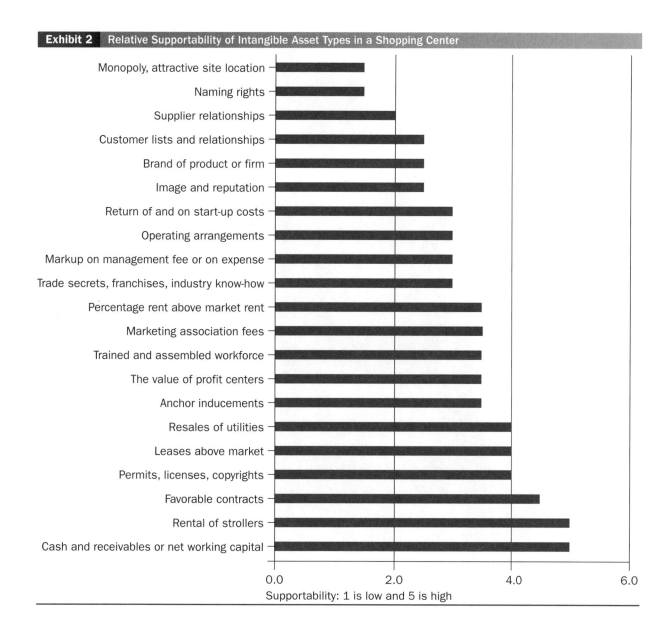

Supportability: 1 is low and 5 is high

Appendix

Business Enterprise Value Case Law Update: 2000-2010

James Popp, Esq., and Sarah Weldon, Esq.

I. Hotels

Arizona

Resort was valued under its current use, not under the use to which resort might be put if it were sold and redeveloped
Potomac Hotel Limited Partnership v. Maricopa County, 1 CA-TX 05-0004 (Arizona Ct. App. 2005)

Taxpayer asserted Marriott Mountain Shadows Resort had been excessively valued by the county. The property was a 337-room resort, and uncontested expert testimony established that the resort suffered from functional and physical obsolescence and lacked certain desirable features. Additionally, the resort failed to provide amenities generally available in other resorts in its class, including in-room mini bars, under-the-counter refrigerators and a spa.

The county attempted to introduce evidence related to sale negotiations regarding the potential sale of the property. The record indicated that if a sale did occur, any sale would be conditioned upon the contract purchaser obtaining specific redevelopment plans from the town at some future date. Thus, any sale of the resort would likely result in a change in its current use, rendering negotiations essentially irrelevant. The court noted that only valuation evidence related to the resort's current usage should be considered in determining the resort's taxable value. State statute defined "current usage" as "the use to which property is put at the time of valuation." The court further noted that neither current usage nor full cash value based thereon should be affected by the use to which the property might be put if it were purchased and redeveloped. The court ultimately ruled in favor of taxpayer and found that the county had excessively valued the resort.

California

Court deducts value of brand premium as intangible in the income approach; considers start-up costs as one-time expenses
In re the Assessment Appeal of Coronado Marriott Hotel, Marriott International, Inc., App. No. 06-02143, Assessment Appeals Board No. 3 (2009) (California)

Taxpayer appealed the assessed value of an upper-scale non-luxury hotel enterprise commonly known as the Coronado Marriott Hotel. The property included a full-service restaurant, 15 meeting rooms, a spa, fitness center and a heated swimming pool. The parties agreed that the income capitalization approach was appropriate for valuing the subject property, and they even agreed on the net operating income (NOI) of the subject. The difference between the assessed value and the value determined by taxpayer resulted from the parties' disparate treatment of intangibles and was also a function of the parties' differing methodologies regarding calculation of a capitalization rate.

The property derived its income from the collective product of "going concern," which was comprised of every component of the hotel—the land and improvements; the furniture, fixtures, and equipment; and all shops, restaurants, spas, business centers, and related amenities—and intangible personal property. Intangible personal property was defined here as the value enhancement resulting from marketing, management skill, the assembled work force, the brand name or "flag" of the hotel, working capital and franchise. The income approach used by taxpayer's appraiser removed all such intangible value from the income stream. The approach employed by assessor's appraiser deducted a management fee from the stabilized net income to remove a portion of the business component from the income stream and further deductions were made for chain affiliation. This valuation

28

method, sometimes known as the "Rushmore Approach," was ultimately rejected by the court.

Taxpayer asserted that there should be a deduction of the return on and of business start-up investment and a deduction for the brand-name "Marriott." The brand-name deduction was predicated on the subject property's Revenue Per Available Room (RevPar) compared to the RevPar of other properties within the subject property's "competitive set." Taxpayer argued, and the court agreed, that the difference in the subject's RevPar and the RevPar of the competitive set was attributable to the hotel brand name.

The court accepted taxpayer's contentions regarding the brand-name deductions but also, like assessor, found that no deduction of income attributable to start-up and transition costs was appropriate. The court noted that these costs were generally "one-time" expenses, and it stated that a deduction of such costs would only be appropriate if the hotel was still benefitting from them and if the costs could be specifically identified and limited to those that produced business value, as opposed to those that produced real estate value.

Inclusion of hotel franchise and assembled work force in "going concern" value of a hotel constituted impermissible assessment of intangible assets

EHP Glendale LLC and Eagle Hospitality Trust, Inc. v. County of Los Angeles, No. BC385925, Court's Ruling on Taxpayers' Motion for Summary Judgment (2009) (California)

Taxpayers, owners of a Hilton hotel, alleged that the county assessment appeals board ("the Board") improperly assessed its intangible assets and rights, including the Hilton franchise, the hotel restaurant and lounges, food services, retail businesses operating within the hotel, the hotel's parking concession, the health club operating within the hotel, the hotel's other operating service centers, and the hotel's assembled workforce. Taxpayers appealed the ruling of the Board to the Superior Court, which granted summary judgment in taxpayers' favor. The Board subsequently appealed this ruling to the Court of Appeals in the Second Appellate District. The appellate court held that the trial court erred in granting taxpayers' motion for summary judgment on an incomplete record and further, that even the incomplete record indicated that there were triable issues of material fact in dispute. The appellate court ultimately

reversed the ruling and remanded the case to the trial court.

Throughout the proceedings, taxpayers contended that the "going concern" value for the entire hotel impermissibly included the Hilton franchise or "flag" and the expertise and experience of managers and employees at the hotel, while the only deduction made by assessor from the "going concern" value of intangibles was equal to the expenses associated with the franchise and management agreements. The trial court agreed with taxpayers and determined that the assessor's valuation was improper, noting that if the assessor used all of the income from operating the hotel to obtain his initial valuation, he was then required to not only deduct the expenses relating to the intangible income, but also to include a return on the non-taxable assets.

The trial court rejected assessor's attempt to justify his failure to deduct the full value of the intangibles and rights by characterizing such assets as "intangible attributes of real property necessary to put the property to beneficial and productive use." Although assessor likened taxpayers' intangibles, such as a franchise and experienced management team, to zoning, location and other attributes that relate directly to the real property, the trial court noted that there was a stark difference between assuming the presence of intangible assets and rights for the purpose of determining the highest and best use of a property and directly assessing the value of such assets and rights. The trial court further noted that the intangibles at issue were not intangible assets of real property. As the assessor erred in his application of the "going concern" valuation method that he purported to apply and as a result impermissibly subjected intangible assets to taxation, the case was remanded by the trial court to the assessment appeals board for further proceedings.

The appellate court stated that the trial court effectively made a credibility determination in favor of taxpayer's expert and that such determination was an issue to be decided by the Board at the administrative level, not by the trial court. The appellate court further opined that "the role of the trial court and this court is to decide whether substantial evidence supports the Board's finding as to valuation." *EHP Glendale et al. v. County of Los Angeles,* 193 Cal.App.4th 262 (Cal.App. 2 Dist. 2011). Additionally, the appellate court noted that taxpayer was not entitled to a trial de novo in the trial court, and that "it is presumed that the Board has properly performed the duties entrusted to it and, absent a showing otherwise by the taxpayer, the presumption is that the assessment of the Board is both regularly and correctly made." *Id.*

Business start-up deductions considered intangibles in valuation of hotel

In re the Application of Massachusetts Mutual Life Insurance Company (La Jolla Marriott Appeal), App. No. 0401790, Assessment Appeals Board No. 4 (2006) (California)

Taxpayer appealed the valuation of a hotel commonly known as the La Jolla Marriott Hotel. The parties' dispute largely turned on the treatment of the intangible property, which included the going concern business operation of the hotel owner, the trained and assembled work force in place, working capital, and name-brand affiliation with Marriott International, which was comprised of the Marriott management, reservation system and frequent guest programs. Both parties agreed that the income approach to valuation was most appropriate for the subject property.

Taxpayer asserted that an income approach that capitalized all of the net operating income would indicate a value for all three categories of assets and would therefore erroneously include nontaxable value. In order to arrive at a value for only the taxable real property, it was necessary to use an imputed income approach. Taxpayer presented two alternative methods of establishing the value of the subject property under such approach. To impute sufficient income to the nontaxable intangible personal property under the "Rushmore Approach,"[1] the management fees paid by the owner of the property to the property manager to operate the property were treated as the amount that should be imputed to the intangible personal property (and thereby removed from the income to be imputed to the taxable real property). This approach was based on the rationale that such fees are paid to conduct the business enterprise and thus "remove" the business value. Assessor also relied on this approach in valuing the subject property.

Taxpayer also presented another approach to imputing sufficient income to the nontaxable intangible personal property. Under this approach, referred to here as the "business start-up approach," taxpayer deducted the management fees paid to the manager as before but also explicitly calculated and deducted a return on and

of the owner's investment in the owner's intangible personal property. This was accomplished by calculating a fair annual return on and of the typical business start-up costs required to put the business enterprise in place, such as the initial franchise fee, pre-opening advertising, pre-opening training and working capital.

The court ultimately rejected the Rushmore Approach and determined that the business start-up approach was the preferable means of imputing income to intangible personal property. The court noted that the business start-up methodology was supported by state law, as it resulted in the explicit identification and removal of the return on and of an owner's investment in intangibles and further noted that use of the Rushmore Approach, as assessor's sole valuation methodology, was tantamount to taxing the intangible assets of an enterprise.

Maryland

Management fee deducted from income; but no adjustment for brand or start-up costs

RRI Acquisition Company, Inc. v. Supervisor of Assessments of Howard County, No. 03-RP-HO-0055, 2006 WL 925212 (Md. Tax 2006)

Taxpayer appealed assessor's determination of the value of a Red Roof Inn and asserted that assessor's appraisal of the property impermissibly included tangible and intangible personal property. The property was a limited service hotel that contained 108 rooms and 117 parking spaces. The court was faced with determining how to distinguish the tangible and intangible personal property value from the real estate value of the subject hotel.

Taxpayer contended that a hotel is a business enterprise and is comprised of many assets, which in their totality equate to the total value of the business. Taxpayer further contended that the income approach should be utilized to separate the real estate from other assets, and that this could be accomplished by distinguishing the revenue derived from the tangible and intangible personal property attributable to the business enterprise from that attributable to the real estate.

Assessor asserted that all payments made to the entity that manages and operates the subject property constituted business income generated by the exercise of management and entrepreneurship, and these payments, along

---

1. The Rushmore Approach is a valuation methodology that is well-known in the appraisal industry and was created by Stephen Rushmore; it is both accepted and refuted in jurisdictions in the United States and Canada.

with a portion of the overall income realized by the employment of furniture, fixtures and equipment, were to be excluded from the computation of realty income subject to capitalization. Under the method relied upon by assessor, separate adjustments were made to provide for the periodic replacement of the personal property and also for the yield on the investment in personal property.

Taxpayer contended that, in addition to the adjustments made by assessor, several additional adjustments were required to be made to arrive at an accurate valuation of the real property used in a hotel operation. These additional adjustments were designed to deal with value attributable to personal property, the hotel franchise or "flag," various residual intangibles including goodwill and business and credit relationships, and developmental and start-up outlays associated with the initiation of the hotel business. The methodology of taxpayer's expert further evaluated brand-specific intangibles by measuring the extent to which the subject property outperformed other hotels within its "competitive set." Such competitive set was defined as a group of properties in the same geographical area whose real property is generally equivalent. Assessor countered such methodology with the assertion that the intangible value attributed by taxpayer's expert to brand affiliation, based upon data obtained from the competitive set, was flawed, as it did not give proper consideration to location, market segment or other differences between the subject property and the properties considered part of the allegedly competitive set.

The court ultimately rejected taxpayer's methodology and accepted the value derived by assessor's valuation expert, noting that it was better supported by market data. The court further noted that the methodology used by taxpayer's expert had some soundness but was largely academic and did not reflect the realities of the real estate market's treatment of intangibles.

Massachusetts

Board rejects assessors' claim for adjustment to reflect allegedly poor management
SLT Realty LP v. Board of Assessors of the Town of Barnstable, Docket Nos. F272349; F277463, Appellate Tax Board of Massachusetts (2009)

Taxpayer owned a 224-room, full-service resort hotel known as the Sheraton Hyannis Resort. The hotel was constructed in the 1960s and was an irregularly shaped building with multiple wings. It was surrounded by a golf course and contained a gift shop, meeting rooms, a health club and spa facility, a conference center, an indoor pool, executive offices, parking for 290 automobiles, and four separate food and beverage outlets. The board determined that the income capitalization approach was the appropriate valuation methodology to use in valuing a hotel.

Assessors contended that the fair cash values determined by taxpayer's expert did not take into account the allegedly poor management of the subject hotel. Assessors stated that valuation of a hotel required the assumption that the hotel was under competent management, noting that if a hotel was not being properly managed, an appraiser was "justified in projecting improved operating results based on competent management." The board found that, even if it accepted assessor's assertion regarding the competent management adjustment, there was no evidence on the record to support a finding that the subject hotel was poorly managed during the relevant time periods. The board ultimately rejected assessors' poor management argument. Further, it determined that the income capitalization approach under which appellant's expert valued the subject property was the most reasonable approach to valuation.

Michigan

Tax tribunal rejected property owner's claim that hotel value should be adjusted to reflect deductions for intangibles such as banquet hall contract, cost of a national hotel chain affiliation, pre-opening and marketing costs, and existing reservation contracts
Amway Grand Plaza Hotel v. City of Grand Rapids, MTT Docket No. 237807 (Mich. Tax Tribunal 2001)

Taxpayer owned the Amway Grand Plaza Hotel (the "subject property") in Grand Rapids, Michigan. The subject property was a 682-unit, full-service convention hotel made up of a 12-story hotel, a 29-story tower, a "lobby link" that connected the hotel with the tower, and a 10-story, 30,440-square-foot parking garage. Taxpayer appealed its assessed value; the appropriate methodology to be used in determining the property's value under the income approach became the central issue analyzed by the Michigan Tax Tribunal ("the Tribunal").

The Tribunal focused on the taxpayer's deductions for business value—described as an "intangible," the value of which could not be included in the valuation of the assessable real property–and set the standards for determining when, in the application of the income approach, items of intangible personal property must be broken out and must be accorded separate values that are not to be included in the assessable value of the real and/or personal property involved.

Upon thorough review of the evidence, the Tribunal stated that it found no support for taxpayer's claims of selectively deducting income-producing items ostensibly "of its choosing." The tribunal further stated that taxpayer's experts seemed to be extracting "at will" income rightfully attached to the intertwined functions of business and property (both real and personal). Such extractions included the catering/concession contract under which the hotel's banquet hall was operated; the cost of a national hotel chain affiliation, including related physical improvements and expenditures; pre-opening/marketing costs; and the existing advance reservation contracts. The Tribunal opined that it "found that not one piece of evidence existed" to support taxpayer's extractions among the 29 comparable sales entered into evidence by both parties.

The Tribunal ultimately pointed out that under Michigan law, valuation was required to equal market value (the "usual selling price"), and that the absence of market evidence regarding business indicated that there was no additional market value to be adjusted when determining the value of the subject property. Accordingly, the Tribunal found no merit to deducting from the going concern anything other than personal property and the liquor licenses in effect at the subject property.

New Jersey

Court limited business value adjustments in valuation of hotel under the income approach to management and operation fees
Chesapeake Hotel LP v. Saddle Brook Township, 22 N.J. Tax 525 (N.J. Tax 2005)

Taxpayer, owner of a hotel known as Saddle Brook Marriott (the "subject property") appealed its assessed value as determined by taxing district. The property was a 12-story, 221-room hotel. For a period, including the relevant tax year, taxpayer contracted with the Marriott Corporation to manage and operate the hotel. Taxpayer's income from the property consisted of the net operating income of the hotel after the payment of various fees to Marriott under the management and operating agreement.

Because the income was not income from the rental of the real estate but rather the net income of a business conducted at the facility, valuation of the fee simple interest in the real property by capitalization of income required that prior to the capitalization of the realty income, the income attributable to the use of the realty be separated from the total income generated by the operation of the business. The assessor and taxpayer's experts appraised the subject property under the income capitalization approach, although they employed different methodologies in doing so.

Under the assessor's income approach, all payments to the owner and operator of the hotel constituted business income generated by the exercise of management and entrepreneurship. Such payments were thus excluded from the computation of realty income subject to capitalization. Taxpayer's expert proposed additional adjustments designed to deal with the value attributable to personal property. These adjustments included the hotel franchise or "flag," various residual intangibles including goodwill and business and credit relationships, and developmental and start-up outlays associated with the initiation of the hotel business. After a detailed discussion regarding the methodology used by each party in calculating the subject property's value under the income approach, the court determined that the methodology employed by assessor was best supported by the record and upheld the assessed value of the property. The court noted that its decision should not be understood as a definitive pronouncement on appraisal practices designed to extract real estate value from the assets of a business, nor should it be understood as binding precedent with respect to the use of adjustments under the income approach in other cases.

Ohio

Value of a hotel and adjacent office building were properly determined by subtracting the business value and value of personal property from the property's value as a going concern
Fairlawn Associates, Ltd. v. Summit County Bd. of Revision and Fiscal Officer, No. 22238, 2005 WL 956989 (Ohio Ct. App. 2005)

Owner of a hotel and an adjacent office building successfully challenged the assessment of its property. The appraisal report submitted by the property owner's expert determined the value of the subject property as a going concern. The personal property and business value were subtracted from the total going concern, and the remaining value was attributed to land and buildings. The lower court determined that this valuation evidence was sufficient to support a reduction in value, noting the expertise of property owner's appraiser and his use of an empirically proven methodology. Upon the determination that property owner's evidence was sufficient, the burden shifted to the board to rebut such evidence. The board failed to do so, and the court ultimately upheld the value determination of property owner's appraiser, which established the property's assessable value by subtracting the business enterprise value component from the total going concern.

Oregon

Hotel's income approach removed business value by deducting the management and franchise fees
Hilton Hotels Corp. v. Jackson County Assessor, 2003 WL 21443402 (Or. T. C. Magistrate's Div. 2003)

Taxpayer appealed the valuation of its full-service hotel. Taxpayer's estimate of the hotel's value was derived using a composite of the sales comparison and income capitalization approaches to value. Assessor's appraisal placed primary reliance on the cost approach using data from Marshall & Swift.

Assessor's appraiser relied primarily upon the cost approach because of a belief that the food and beverage side of the operation were required to be separated from the room rental business. Assessor insisted that such distinction was necessary to separate "business" from "non-business" income and further contended that the cost approach eliminated the need for an adjustment to remove personal property value. In utilizing the income and comparable sales approaches, assessor valued the hotel itself using room revenues and added the estimated rent from leasing the restaurant and banquet facilities.

The court agreed with taxpayer's assertion that market participants and lenders considering the acquisition of a full-service hotel would consider the income and expenses anticipated from the overall operation. The evidence il-

lustrated that the property was, and had been, managed by prominent, experienced corporations. None of these corporations chose to lease the restaurant and banquet facilities to third parties and operate the property as a limited service hotel, a premise on which assessor's cost approach depended.

Although the court accepted taxpayer's income approach, it was mindful of assessor's concern that the business value inherent in the data, and the influence of a franchise agreement under which the property operated, would be impossible to remove. Taxpayer responded to such concern by contending that the subject was a full-service hotel, that the restaurants and meeting spaces were integral parts of its operation, and that as a result, the income and expenses arising from the restaurants and meeting spaces should be included with the other categories of income and expenses. Taxpayer supported its assertion by directing the court to an Appraisal Journal article[2] on hotel valuation which, in its discussion of the income approach, indicated that a hotel's business value could be removed by deducting the management fee and the franchise fee. The court accepted such rationale and ultimately accepted the value derived from taxpayer's reconciliation of the income and comparable sales approach as the property's real market value.

Valuation isolating business value associated with hotel food and beverage operation, leases, and franchise fees under its income approach was appropriate
Hilton Hotels v. Umatilla County Assessor, 2003 WL 22846400 (Or. T.C. Magistrate's Div. 2003)

Taxpayer owned a full-service hotel. Taxpayer valued the property using the sales comparison approach and the income approach. County's appraiser utilized the income, the sales comparison, and the cost approaches. The court determined that county's sales comparison approach included skewed data and that the age of the property indicated that little weight should be given to county's cost approach. The county's appraiser alleged that the property was owned by one party and leased and operated by another, and as the property was under lease, the operating statements were difficult to value. County's appraiser expressed concern that the income statements analyzed included lease pay-

---

2.   Lesser, Daniel H., MAI, and Karen E. Rubin, *Understanding the Unique Aspects of Hotel Property Tax Valuation,* The Appraisal Journal 9, 17-19 (January 1993).

ments and fees that should not be included in arriving at a net operating income, and county's appraiser additionally expressed doubt that the business value associated with the property's food and beverage operation, as well as the leases and franchise fees, could be properly isolated and removed from the income statement.

The court found county's arguments unwarranted, as taxpayer removed its business value from the net operating income by subtracting the management and franchise fees.[3] The court agreed with county's assertion that lease payments should not be included as an expense in deriving net operating income, but further found that taxpayer had already appropriately excluded lease payments from the expenses in its income approach. This analysis led the court to hold that taxpayer's methodology presented the most persuasive estimate of the property's real market value, and as such, the real market value should be reduced.

Tennessee

Court allowed adjustments under the income approach for intangibles such as an assembled and trained workforce, start-up costs, and brand-specific business assets
In re Essex House Condo Corporation a/k/a Marriott Courtyard Airport, Tenn. State Board of Equalization (2003)

Taxpayer owned a three-level, 145-room Courtyard Marriott hotel. The property was valued by the assessor using the income capitalization approach. Taxpayer's expert offered testimony which employed the income capitalization approach, the sales comparison approach and the cost approach. The court found that the testimony and appraisal report of taxpayer's expert constituted the best evidence because it considered all three approaches to value and because taxpayer's expert properly separated the value of the real property from the value of the tangible and intangible personal property.

The court noted that although taxpayer's expert gave greatest weight to the income approach, he addressed the need to consider all three approaches to value. Taxpayer's expert noted that hotel investor acquisition motivation is income-oriented and rarely relies on the cost approach. Further, he noted that the sales comparison approach was not a particularly

valid hotel valuation model because hotels were generally sold as a "going concern," and as such, it was difficult to isolate the real property component. Taxpayer's expert relied most heavily on the income capitalization approach, stating that an investment property's value is a function of its income and that the income approach allowed for market-supported deductions of non-realty items.

In deriving the hotel's value under the income approach, taxpayer's expert first calculated the net operating income (NOI) of the property as a going concern. Next, he removed the return on/of furniture, fixtures and equipment; return on/of startup costs including the assembled and trained workforce, management and administration team, regulatory compliance, accounting and other business systems, and pre-opening marketing; and the return on/of brand-specific intangibles. The calculations resulted in an NOI attributable to the real property. Taxpayer's expert then determined and applied the tax-rate loaded capitalization rate, which he applied to the real property NOI for each year. The court accepted this methodology and rejected that employed by county assessor's expert, who isolated the value of the subject property's realty component by merely allowing for a management fee, franchise fee, reserves and a deduction for the reported value of tangible personal property.

Canada

Hotel's intangible property should be deducted from the total assets of the business
Hilton Canada Inc. v. Municipal Property Assessment Corporation Region No. 09 and the City of Toronto, Complaint No. 1440556 and 1374713 (Toronto, Canada) (2006)

The subject property was the Toronto Hilton, a 601-room, full-service hotel with five restaurants and bars, banquet and conference room facilities, a fitness center and a pool. Taxpayer protested the assessed value of the subject property and the assessment review board was faced with determining if a deduction should be made from the total value of the business for intangible personalty, consisting of brand, cash and receivables, assembled work force, and pre-opening marketing and sales. Both taxpayer and taxing units agreed that the most appropriate

---

3. Taxpayer's rationale was supported by an article it presented as an exhibit: Lesser, Daniel H., MAI, and Karen E. Rubin, *Understanding the Unique Aspects of Hotel Property Tax Valuation,* The Appraisal Journal 9, 17-19 (January 1993).

valuation method for the subject property was the income approach, using the standard hotel *pro forma.*

Taxpayer's appraisal experts testified that a hotel is a package of numerous assets, deployed together and described in appraisal terminology as total assets of the business (TAB), and that it was necessary to recognize and remove tangible personal property assets and intangible personal property assets from the TAB to arrive at the value of the real estate. Taxpayer's expert asserted that there were numerous intangible assets contributing to the profitability of a hotel as a going concern, including the hotel's "brand" or "flag" (the name, reputation and goodwill from affiliation with a well-known hotel operating company such as Hilton), cash and receivables, assembled workforce, and pre-opening marketing and sales. Taxpayer's expert further asserted that such intangible assets had been identified and quantified in accordance with the methodologies discussed in the Appraisal Institute's Course 800.

The board found that the concept of the contribution of intangible personal property to the business value of a hotel was not a myth and stated that when such intangible property could be identified and quantified, it should be deducted from the total assets of a business. The board ultimately found that the hotel's brand value—which included income attributable to name recognition, reputation, identity, established marketing relationships, corporate data models, corporate programs and services, copyrights, trademarks, logos, permits and licenses, reservation and referral systems, proprietary distribution systems, and proprietary guest programs—had been removed by a royalty fee deduction and that no further deductions should be made. The board accepted the evidence presented by taxpayer and determined that an additional deduction should be made for an assembled and trained workforce, as such workforce was of considerable value. The board rejected taxpayer's contention that pre-opening sales and marketing expenses should be deducted from the TAB, as the subject property had been open since 1974 and the contribution of such pre-opening expenses was no longer part of the business value.

Court allows and rejects deductions of certain intangibles in valuation of a landmark hotel
Fairmont Hotels v. Assessor of Area 01, App. Nos. 2001-01-0028; 2002-01-00021, Property Assessment Appeal Board (Victoria, Canada) (2003)

Taxpayer appealed the assessed value of the Fairmont Empress Hotel. The hotel is a luxury full-service hotel located in the scenic inner harbor of Victoria, British Columbia; it opened in 1908 and is considered a landmark. Taxpayer contended that assessor had impermissibly included the value of non-assessable intangible assets in valuing the subject property and further, that deductions from the value of the property as a going concern, or from the Total Assets of the Business (TAB), should be made for brand/goodwill, working capital, assembled work force, pre-opening sales and marketing and initial start-up losses. Assessor countered with the argument that the only intangible asset to be deducted from the value of the going concern was brand/goodwill, and if other intangible assets were present, they could be accounted for in separate adjustments.

The court extensively discussed the various approaches to extracting the value of intangible assets from the value of property as a going concern. The court gave in-depth analysis of both the "Rushmore Approach" and the approach to valuation outlined in "Course 800," and it discussed the components of each before it made conclusions on the various assets that were alleged to be un-assessable intangibles.

The court determined that the value of an assembled workforce was "inextricably intertwined" with the hotel's real estate, as the business of the hotel was to generate income through the nightly rental of rooms and the provision of other guest services to support that basic function. Further, the high turnover rate of a hotel's workforce necessitated increased expenditures on recruiting, hiring and training new employees. Such expense was deductible from the income stream. The court noted that the equation of a deduction for workforce replacement to intangible value would, in effect, be "double counting." The court came to the same conclusion regarding pre-opening start-up costs and initial losses, stating that there was no evidence that such costs have market value that could be independently appraised, and to the extent that the pre-opening and startup costs could even be valued, such value was inextricably intertwined with the real estate and could not be separated. The court noted that although there was likely value in intangible factors such as location, architecture, history and prestige, such value was also inextricably intertwined with the realty.

II. Low-Income Rental Housing

Arizona

Low-income housing tax credits were intangible property and should not have been added to the value of property; the restricted income potential related to such credits did impact property's value
Cottonwood Affordable Housing v. Yavapai County, 72 P.3d 357, 402 (Ariz. Tax 2003)

Taxpayer owned a low-income housing project. Although the parties agreed that the income approach was the appropriate valuation method, taxpayer contended that the actual income and expenses should constitute the basis for such valuation. County asserted that because the property operated under the federal Low Income Housing Tax Credit (LIHTC) program, market rents generated by "regular" commercial apartment complexes should form the basis for valuation or alternatively, that the credits themselves should be added to the income stream. The court was required to determine if the LIHTCs constituted intangible property, whether such LIHTCs should be included in the value of taxpayer's property, and finally, whether the restrictions imposed by the LIHTC program should be considered in valuing taxpayer's property.

The court looked to the holdings of other states and gave deference to the Appraisal Institute's Uniform Standards of Professional Appraisal Practice (USPAP) and the related advisory opinions. One such advisory opinion recognized that "LIHTCs are an example of an incentive that results in intangible property rights," and the court accordingly held that the LIHTCs at issue constituted intangible property that should not be added to the value of taxpayer's property or considered as part of taxpayer's income stream. The court explained that because LIHTCs were sums of money being paid by the federal government as an investment incentive and were not "income flowing from the rental of the property," the credits did not significantly affect the project's marketability, were not an integral part of the real estate, and

any value the credits had were to the property's owner, not to the property itself.

The LIHTC program required substantial restrictions to be placed on the property for a minimum of 15 years, and as such, the value of the property was significantly impacted. The court reasoned that because a willing buyer who was aware of the relevant restrictions would pay less for a low-income housing project than for a regular commercial apartment complex, the property should not be valued as though a buyer would not consider the restrictions. The court ruled that the value of the subject property should be determined from its restricted income potential without regard to the LIHTCs themselves, which created a disincentive for a current owner to sell and little, if any, incentive for a new buyer to buy.

Connecticut

Subsidies built into the rental rates at a housing complex for elderly residents with low to moderate income were not considered to be intangible assets
Executive Square, Limited Partnership v. Town of Wethersfield, 2006 WL 240417 (Conn. Super. Ct. 2006)

Taxpayer owned a housing complex for elderly residents earning low or moderate income, which was operated under a regulatory agreement with the state housing finance authority. The agreement required all tenants to be elderly and have low or moderate income levels; eligible residents were permitted to apply for federally subsidized rents. At the time of suit, the rental rates at the subject property were approximately 140 percent of market rents. The income approach was used by the appraisers employed by both parties.

Taxpayer asserted that the property should have been assessed as a fee simple estate without regard to the leased fee value, and he further utilized in his income approach a "market rent" lower than the actual rental rates at the subject property. Taxpayer argued that the subsidies built into the subject property's rental rates were intangibles and as such, should not be used to determine the property's market value. The court rejected taxpayer's argument, noting that although individual tenants received subsidies, no part of the subject property's contract rent converted to an intangible asset. The court ultimately held that, contrary to taxpayer's contentions, the contract rent generated by the property could not be compared to so-called "market rent" developed from the unregulated conventional apartment market for purposes of determining the value of the property.

Florida

Inclusion of low-income housing tax credits in deriving a capitalization rate resulted in an impermissibly low capitalization rate and a market value that was significantly higher than fair market value
Holly Ridge Limited Partnership v. Pritchitt, as Putnam, etc. 936 So. 2d 694 (Fla. Dist. Ct. App. 2006)

Taxpayer owned apartments built with tax credit financing under a Low Income Housing Tax Credit (LIHTC) program. Under the LIHTC program, credit recipients were also required to comply with certain restrictions and requirements related to the subject property. Owners were required to set aside units for rental by low-income residents, were prohibited from changing rent rates during a resident's tenancy, and were required to provide on-site health care, food and clothing assistance, certain activities, and credit counseling. Appraisers were prohibited by statute from considering LIHTCs as "income" for purposes of property valuation and were required by statute to consider any land use regulations incumbent on property when determining such property's value.

The appraisers for both parties utilized the income capitalization approach in deriving the value of the subject property. Although assessor's appraiser did not include the LIHTCs as income under such approach, he impermissibly factored in the impact of the LIHTCs in deriving his capitalization rate. As such, his capitalization rate was unreasonably low and resulted in a market value that was significantly higher than the fair market value of the subject property. The court remanded the case for a new trial and further stated that it interpreted the statutory prohibition against the consideration of LIHTCs in appraisal of property for taxation purposes as a legislative attempt to define LIHTCs as "intangible personal property," which could not be taxed by local government entities.

Idaho

Low-income housing tax credits were not intangible contract rights and were required to be considered as income when determining the market value of subject apartment complexes
Brandon Bay, Ltd. Partnership v. Payette County, 132 P.3d 438 (Idaho 2006)

On appeal, the county disputed the determination of the trial court that the Low Income Housing Tax Credits (LIHTCs) claimed by owners of low-income apartment complexes were contract rights and were specifically excluded by statute from being considered in the assessment of such complexes. Taxpayers asserted that such contract rights were intangible personal property that could not be a factor in the valuation process. Under the definition promulgated by the Idaho Tax Commission, contracts and contract rights were "enforceable agreements, which establish mutual rights and responsibilities, and rights created under such agreements." After analysis of such statutory provisions, the court rejected taxpayer's assertion.

The court noted that the state had no power to create a LIHTC and that the LIHTCs were created by Congress in the Internal Revenue Code. As such, any agreement taxpayers entered regarding the allocation of the LIHTCs was simply a vehicle through which the credits could be claimed and was not a contract right exempt from consideration in the valuation of taxpayers' property. The court further opined that LIHTCs were better characterized as "rights and privileges belonging to the land," as they did not exist separately from the ownership right in the subject property, and that as the LIHTCs were part of the stream of benefits flowing from the property, they should be considered as income in determining the property's value.

Indiana

Low-income housing tax credits were required to be considered in the calculation of an obsolescence adjustment to the value of the subject property
Hometowne Associates, LP v. Maley, 839 NE 2d 269 (Ind. Tax Court 2005)

Taxpayer owned low-income housing that was developed under the federal Low Income Housing Tax Credit (LIHTC) program. Although the sole issue on appeal was the board's denial of an obsolescence adjustment requested by taxpayer, the court discussed the nature of LIHTCs and their effect on the taxable value of the subject property.

Although taxpayer maintained the LIHTCs were intangible property and should thus be excluded, the court rejected such contention. The court noted that it had previously aligned itself with jurisdictions holding that LIHTCs were required to be considered in determining the existence and amount of obsolescence affecting low-income housing complexes, particularly when such obsolescence largely resulted from the rental restrictions required under the LIHTC program. Consequently, the court rejected taxpayer's first calculation of the obsolescence adjustment made to the value of the property and accepted taxpayer's second calculation, which reflected the value of the LIHTCs and resulted in a lesser obsolescence adjustment.

Michigan

Low-income housing tax credits have a profound effect on apartment complex's fair market value and failure to include such credits in valuation results in an artificially depressed value
Huron Ridge, L.P. v. Ypsilanti Township, 737 N.W.2d 187 (Mich. Ct. App. 2007)

Taxpayer, owner of a low-income apartment complex, asserted that the tax tribunal erroneously included in its valuation of the property the Low Income Housing Tax Credits (LIHTCs) that taxpayer received in exchange for maintaining certain rent restrictions. Taxpayer asserted that such LIHTCs were intangible property and were exempt from taxation of real property. The court sought to determine whether or not the LIHTCs were intangible assets, and if they were, whether or not they related directly to the property.

The court ultimately held that although LIHTCs may be considered intangible assets, the effects of the LIHTCs on the property must be considered in the valuation process. Further, the court concluded that the purpose of LIHTCs was to stimulate demand for ownership interests in low-income housing projects by attaching a valuable tax credit to that interest, and it stated that "there would be no market for private investments in low-income housing development" without tax incentives. The court noted that development of the property would not have been financially feasible without financing predicated on the assignment of the LIHTCs to private investors, and it even went so far as to state that the fair market value of properties subject to LIHTCs was "not merely influenced by, but is primarily driven by" the tax credits. The court additionally stated that the appraised value of the property and properties similarly situated would be artificially depressed without inclusion of the value of the tax credits.

Missouri

Low-income housing tax credits are intangibles that essentially make no contribution to the market value of housing projects
Maryville Properties, LP v. Nelson, 83 S.W.3d 608 (Mo.App.2002)

Taxpayer owned a rent-restricted apartment complex that included Low Income Housing Tax Credits (LIHTCs). Taxpayer contended that the LIHTCs and accelerated depreciation constituted intangible property that could not be included in valuation.

The parties disputed the proper test for defining intangible personal property. Taxpayer asserted that the test for intangibility was whether or not property had "no intrinsic and marketable value, but is merely representative or evidence of value." Tax assessor argued that the test for intangibility was "whether the disputed value is appended to the property and thus transferable with the property or is it independent of the property so that it either stays with the seller or dissipates upon sale," and that because LIHTCs were transferable only with the land, they constituted "transmissible value." Assessor subsequently asserted that the LIHTCs were not intangibles and asserted a test for intangibility. Assessor suggested that the test was: (1) the intangible asset must be identifiable; (2) must be capable of private ownership; (3) must be marketable; and (4) must possess value and have the potential to earn income. The court eventually concluded that establishing a satisfactory definition of intangible property for real estate valuation purposes was "difficult."

The court recognized that although LIHTCs appeared to add value to a property, they actually were a deterrent to sale, as the original owner that received the credits likely achieved much of his return through the tax credits themselves. It further held that LIHTCs were not characteristics of the subject property but were rather assets having direct monetary value; the restricted transferability of LIHTCs did not destroy their "essential status as intangible property having value primarily to their owner." The court held that true value for ad valorem tax purposes was the "hypothetical price that could be agreed upon between a willing seller and buyer" and that, because LIHTCs made no direct contribution to the market value of the subject housing projects, the tax commission had erroneously applied the law in considering the LIHTCs in establishing the value of the subject property.

Ohio

Rent restrictions relating to property developed under low-income housing tax credit program were required to be considered in property's valuation, but the credits themselves were separable intangible assets
Woda Ivy Glen Ltd. Partnership v. Fayette Cty. Bd. Of Revision, 902 N.E.2d 984 (Ohio 2009)

Taxpayer owned single-family homes located on 60 parcels of land developed pursuant to the federal Low Income Housing Tax Credit (LIHTC) program. The board of tax appeals had rejected taxpayer's appraisal of the property, which valued the parcels as a single economic unit based on rent-income analysis and comparable sales of rental properties, and instead accepted the board's cost-based valuation of the property. The board questioned taxpayer's valuation of the property as a single economic unit and further criticized taxpayer's use of the income approach because it took into account the use restrictions placed upon the property as a result of the LIHTCs.

Taxpayer established that LIHTC property was subject to severe rent restrictions for at least 15 years under the federal program and for an additional 15 years under agreement with the state. The restrictions were binding on a property owner's successors, were required to be recorded in the property's chain of title, and resulted in a limitation on the property's gross potential income. The court ultimately held that in the context of appraising the property for tax purposes, the use restrictions imposed under the LIHTC program constituted "governmental restrictions for the general welfare" and were required to be taken into account when determining such property's value. The court further determined that the board of tax appeals erred in accepting the utilization of the cost approach in valuing the property, as such approach im-

properly reflected the affirmative benefit of the LIHTCs themselves, which were required to be categorized as separable intangible assets.

South Dakota

Both the restricted rental rates and low-income housing tax credits related to the subject apartment complexes should be considered in determining the properties' value
Town Square v. Clay County Board of Equalization, 704 N.W.2d 896 (S.D. 2005)

The owner of two apartment complexes subject to the federal Low Income Housing Tax Credit (LIHTC) program asserted that the county equalization board improperly appraised the properties without considering the impact of the LIHTCs on the properties' value. The central issue was whether the "true and full value" of the property must be calculated using market rent rates or whether the actual reduced rents should be used, and if so, whether the LIHTCs should also be included in the valuation.

Both parties agreed that the income capitalization approach should be used when valuing the properties. However, taxpayer asserted that the actual restricted rents, rather than hypothetical market rents, should be the measure used in the income capitalization approach but that the LIHTCs themselves should not be considered, as they were intangibles and thus were not taxable. Although the court agreed with taxpayer's contention that the actual restricted rents should be used in the valuation of the subject properties, it rejected taxpayer's assertion that the LIHTCs were not an appropriate factor in determining the properties' value.

The court determined that both the restricted rental rates and the LIHTCs themselves should be considered in valuing the subject properties. Whether or not the LIHTCs were intangible assets was irrelevant, as the state made no distinction between tangible and intangible property for purposes of taxation. As the court further pointed out, the LIHTCs were encompassed by the state's broad definition of real property as the "land and all rights and privileges thereto belonging." Additionally, the court determined that to ignore the LIHTCs would be tantamount to ignoring the realities of the market, as such LIHTCs served to counteract the restricted rental rates. To consider the restricted rental rates in isolation without consideration of the LIHTCs would yield an artificially depressed property value.

Tennessee

Low-income housing tax credits were appropriately considered in the valuation of apartment complexes and such consideration did not constitute direct taxation of the credits themselves
Spring Hill, L.P. v. Tennessee State Board of Equalization, 2003 WL 23099679 (Tenn. Ct. App. 2003)

Taxpayers, owners of three apartment complexes that qualified for and used Low Income Housing Tax Credits (LIHTCs), asserted that the county improperly considered the present value of the LIHTCs in valuing the properties.

Taxpayers asserted that because the LIHTCs were intangible property, they could not be taxed and were not allowed to be considered in the valuation of the property for tax purposes. The state board of equalization contended that the inclusion of the present value of the LIHTCs in the assessment of the properties did not constitute direct taxation of the credits themselves. The board further argued that under the relevant law, it was appropriate to include all property interests in assessing property value, both value-enhancing interests and value-reducing interests, and regardless of whether the LIHTCs were considered intangible property, they were properly included in the assessment of the subject property.

The court concluded that the trial court properly found that the LIHTCs related directly to the property and were not, as taxpayers contended, intangible benefits that were severable from the subject properties. As such, the board's balancing of the value-enhancing factors related to the LIHTCs with the factors that reduced value, such as the rent restrictions placed on the subject properties, yielded an appropriate result and reflected the "sound, intrinsic, and immediate" value of the properties.

Washington

Federal tax credits received by owners of low-income housing projects constituted intangible personal property and could not be considered in valuing the subject property, but rent restrictions associated with such tax credits were required to be considered
Cascade Court Limited Partnership v. Noble, 20 P.3d 997 (Wash. Ct. App. 2001)

Taxpayers, owners of low-income housing projects subject to rent restrictions, contended that

the board of tax appeals impermissibly refused to take rent restrictions into account when valuing the subject properties under the income capitalization approach. The rent restrictions were directly related to tax credits received by taxpayers under a federal program. The court rejected the reasoning of the board of tax appeals, which had held that, because the rent restrictions at issue were undertaken voluntarily, they should be disregarded when valuing the subject property. The voluntary nature of the rent restrictions was found to be irrelevant, as even a voluntary transaction burdening real property must be considered in such property's assessment. As taxpayers did not have the right to charge market rent under the rent restrictions, which sometimes were in effect for up to sixty years, such restrictions clearly affected the price for which a willing buyer would purchase the subject properties and were required to be considered in determining such properties' market value.

The court further determined that the board of tax appeals erred in holding that the federal tax credits at issue should be included in the assessed value of the subject properties. The court stated that because tax credits were intangible personal property, they were not subject to real property taxation under the relevant state statutes. As such, assessor's consideration of the tax credits in determining the value of the property was erroneous.

III. Industrial

California

Above-market power purchase agreement was appropriately considered in the valuation of cogeneration power facility
Watson Cogeneration Company v. County of Los Angeles, 98 Cal.App.4th 1066, 120 Cal.Rptr.2d 421 (Cal. Ct. App. 2002)

Taxpayer, an independent power producer that owned and operated a cogeneration power facility, asserted that the county improperly considered the actual income stream resulting from an above-market, government-facilitated power purchase agreement in its valuation of the property. Taxpayer contended that the agreement was an intangible asset and was exempt from property tax. The court rejected taxpayer's assertions and noted that California decisions have repeatedly held that the value of intangible property may be included in the valuation of otherwise taxable tangible property, even if such intangible property, standing alone, could not be directly subjected to assessment.

In determining the value of the property, the income approach was used. Taxpayer did not dispute the use of this approach but instead contended that it was improperly applied, as the assessor did not remove from the assessment the value of the power purchase agreement, an intangible asset. Taxpayer further contended that the issue was whether the county could tax the property based not upon its fair market value, but upon the income it received pursuant to an intangible above-market purchase agreement. The court stated that undisputed evidence established that the highest and best use of the property was as a power facility selling power pursuant to the above-market purchase agreement. As such, the value of the property could best be estimated in terms of its actual income. The court further noted that the purchase agreement at issue was the result of government incentives and regulations specifically intended to encourage the development of the property. Such a purchase agreement assured a long-term stable income stream and facilitated the financing for the property's development. The power purchase agreement was inextricably intertwined with the creation and operation of the property and should be considered in its valuation.

Connecticut

Deduction of business enterprise value approach in deriving the value of a nuclear power station was not appropriate
Dominion Nuclear et al. v. Town of Waterford, 2007 WL 4171584 (Ct. Super. Ct. 2007)

Taxpayers owned a nuclear power station. Taxpayers had purchased the subject property as a going business for $1,288,768,000. The sale price included the real property, personal property, nuclear fuel, workforce, materials and supplies, construction work in progress, and other intangible assets. Approximately 18 months after the subject property was purchased, taxpayers' appraiser concluded that the property's value was $1,000,000,000 and an appraiser employed by the town valued taxpayers' real and personal property at $1,343,600,000.

The court noted that the town's analysis of the property was problematic because the value was based on the business enterprise approach, under which an increase in value could

be attributed to intangible factors such as the business acumen of new management, market forces involved in setting the price of electricity, and new power plant purchase agreements. These factors were likely to increase the value of the total business but did not necessarily increase the value of the tangible real and personal property, which generally depreciated over time. From the business's total value as derived under the business enterprise value approach, the town's appraiser deducted the value of the business's workforce as an intangible asset, as well as the value of operating manuals, software assets, and the business's working capital. Taxpayers' appraiser employed the business enterprise approach as well, although his conclusion as to value was much lower than the town's.

The court emphasized the necessary allocation of real property value, tangible personal property value and intangible personal property value under the business enterprise approach, and it further noted with disapproval that because such approach, as used by both parties' appraisers, dealt with the value of the subject property to its investors, its use to measure the fair market value of the subject's real and tangible personal property was suspect. Additionally, the court noted that because the methodology of both appraisers included the depreciation of intangible assets, and as such intangible assets were not intrinsically valuable but were valued for what they represented, it was difficult to rationalize their depreciation. The court ultimately concluded that none of the methodologies employed by taxpayers' appraiser, the town's appraiser and the appraiser who performed the initial assessment of the subject property were particularly credible, but the subject property had been overvalued nonetheless. In accepting the evidence presented that it found most reliable and rejecting the evidence that it found most suspect, the court arrived at the fair market value of $1,122,000,000.

Maine

Above-market purchase agreement was an intangible asset "inextricably entwined" with a hydroelectric power generation plant and was properly considered in its valuation
Uah-Hydro Kennebec, L.P. v. Town of Winslow, 921 A.2d 146 (Me. 2007)

Taxpayer, owner of a megawatt hydroelectric power generating plant, contended that town's assessor impermissibly considered an above-market purchase agreement in determining the value of the property. Taxpayer asserted that, as it had the opportunity to sell its rights under the purchase agreement, such agreement should not be considered intangible property necessary to put the property to its highest and best use. In opposition to such assertion, assessor argued that taxpayer's physical facilities and the purchase agreement at issue were inextricably entwined. Assessor asserted that taxpayer's tangible assets could not be separated from the purchase agreement while maintaining the full value of both. It also stated that taxpayer's status as a "qualifying facility" under the purchase agreement was the product of regulatory approvals by federal and state agencies, and such approvals, like governmental licenses and permits, should be considered when determining the highest and best use of a commercial facility.

Taxpayer asserted that the appraisal of the property as a hydroelectric plant operating under the value-enhancing purchase agreement, rather than as a plant selling electricity in the deregulated open market, was discriminatory and resulted in physically identical properties having different values for tax assessment purposes. Taxpayer further asserted that because other power producers opted to sell or renegotiate their purchase agreements while it chose not to, inclusion of the value of the purchase agreement in town's assessment of the subject property was, in effect, a tax on taxpayer's business judgment. The court rejected such arguments, noting that town's assessment properly recognized taxpayer's benefits from its unique regulatory status and as such, did not violate the principle of uniformity and was not discriminatory.

The court likewise rejected taxpayer's argument that town's assessment of the subject property was illegal, as the purchase agreement was an intangible asset and should not have been considered in valuation for the purpose of ad valorem taxation. Taxpayer unsuccessfully argued that even if the court accepted town's contention that the purchase agreement was taxable so long as it was an intangible asset "inextricably entwined" with the power generation plant, a tangible asset, the purchase agreement was not inextricably entwined with the plant (and was thus not taxable) because it could be terminated or sold separately from the plant at any time. Because the subject property's qualifying-facility status under the governmental regulations that facilitated the purchase agreement continued to define the property's current use, the court held that the purchase agreement was inextricably entwined with the tangible property and was properly considered in town's assessment.

Michigan

Power purchase agreement was excluded from consideration in determining value of cogeneration plant

Midland Cogeneration Venture v. City of Midland, 2004 WL 212459 MTT Docket No. 242614 (Mich. Tax Tribunal 2004)

Taxpayer owned the largest cogeneration plant in the country. In a typical cogeneration facility, a fossil fuel is burned to provide heat energy that is converted into both electric power for sale to an electric utility and electric power and steam that is sold to an adjacent unrelated business for use in a manufacturing process. Among many other issues, the court was faced with determining whether a power purchase agreement (PPA) to which taxpayer was a party should be considered an intangible asset that was exempt from taxation. Taxpayer presented expert testimony asserting that the PPA was severable from the property and was thus exempt, while city's expert asserted that the influence of the PPA was to be considered in valuing the subject property.

The PPA in question was a contract between taxpayer and another entity in which the other entity agreed to pay the "avoided cost" for capacity and energy from taxpayer for a period of time. The PPA was above-market in both capacity and energy. Experts for taxpayer and city indicated that PPAs, in general, are and have been sold separately from a property's real estate. City's expert also asserted that the PPA at issue here was directly tied to the facility, was integrally intertwined with it, and thus had no value without the facility and the right to operate the facility. City's expert presented a business valuation that relied on the revenue from the PPA and included the value of the PPA in its value conclusion.

The court noted that neither party presented evidence that allowed the determination of what, if any, market value the PPA added to the subject property as an intangible "value influencer." The court further noted that courts in the state had specifically required that parties making an argument that intangible assets are value influencers must produce market evidence of the influence of such intangible asset on the value of real and tangible personal property. The city failed to do so, and the court found that any influence that the PPA might have had on the value of the taxable real and personal property should not be considered in the valuation of the subject property.

Pennsylvania

Income approach was rejected in the valuation of a nuclear-powered electric generation facility because of the difficulty separating the income stream attributable to realty from the income stream attributable to business enterprise
In re PP&L Inc., 838 A.2d 1 (Pa. Commw. Ct. 2003)

Taxpayer owned a nuclear-powered electric generation facility. Taxing entities asserted that the trial court erred in rejecting the implementation of the income approach in determining the value of the property. The trial court had determined that the income approach was not controlling and stated that under the income approach, there was no reasonable way to separate the portion of the income stream attributable solely to taxable realty from the income stream attributable to the business enterprise located on the subject property.

In contending that use of the income approach was appropriate, the taxing entities relied on cases which held that the income approach was the most appropriate approach for appraising property typically purchased as an investment, as such property was valued by the purchaser for its ability to produce income. Taxpayer countered the taxing entities' assertion by stating that the cases provided that the income approach was only appropriate if the income stream could be separated from the property itself and from the business on the property. Further, taxpayer argued that the trial court appropriately recognized the economic reality of business income and the problem of distinguishing it from income generated by the property itself. Taxpayer noted that even the valuation expert engaged by the taxing entities recognized that business income could not be used to value real property. The court concluded that the trial court's rejection of the income approach was proper and further concluded that the trial court did not err in selecting a valuation approach that focused on the property itself, as distinguished from the enterprise operating on

the property, the "value in use" of the property, and from the machinery, equipment and other intangible assets associated with the property.

IV. Nursing Homes/Care Facilities
Connecticut

Business value was removed in valuation of deteriorating nursing home facility
Cruess Realty Co. v. City of Waterbury, 2006 WL 2808257 (Ct. Super. Ct. 2006)

Taxpayer appealed the valuation of two structures that housed a chronic and convalescent nursing home and an adult day care facility. The occupancy rates of both facilities were in decline due to a lower number of private patients in comparison to Medicaid patients.

There were three separate appraisals of the property performed under the comparative sales approach and two appraisals performed under the income capitalization approach. Under the comparative sales approach, one appraiser analyzed the property using comparable sales of nursing homes with all licenses in place. Another used comparable sales of operating health care facilities, including sale of components related to the value of the business. The third appraiser, hired by defendant city for the foreclosure proceedings against taxpayer, analyzed the property as a "shuttered" or closed facility and did not use comparable sales that included movable property, bed rights or business licenses.

Under the income capitalization approach, one appraiser analyzed the property using market conditions and relied upon expenses developed from information supplied by other nursing homes in the area, based on actual reported occupancy rates, Medicaid reimbursement rates, and guidelines for an adjustment of the business value associated with the operation of a nursing home and an adult day care center. No adjustments were made for any of the functional problems with the building, the dwindling number of self-pay patients, or for the location of the facility in a high-crime area. The court found that this appraiser's failure to consider such adjustments rendered the appraisal unreliable. The second appraiser's income approach was based upon first establishing the overall business value of the property, then making a deduction to allow for the value of the personal property and the residual business assets to arrive at the real property value. He appraised the business as a "going concern" but considered the low level of occupancy and the resulting low level of operating income. The court ultimately determined that the property had been over assessed.

Twenty percent of a skilled nursing facility's value was allocated to its intangibles
Avon Realty, LLC v. Town of Avon, 2006 WL 932388 (Conn. Super. Ct. 2006)

Taxpayer owned a 120-bed skilled nursing facility. Appraisers for both parties valued the subject property for assessment purposes as a going concern because of the difficulty in separating the value of the business operating on the subject property from the value of the real estate portion that supports such business. The appraisers then subtracted furniture, fixtures and equipment (FF & E) and intangibles to arrive at what they considered to be the real estate portion of the subject's value. Both appraisers utilized the income capitalization and sales comparison approaches to value in analyzing the property.

Upon reviewing both appraisers' analyses under the going concern approach to value, the court noted that such approach was extremely subjective. Taxpayer's expert defined "going concern" value as being "composed of, but not limited to, the physical real estate, management and employees, intangibles such as a Certificate of Need (CON) and licenses, developed procedures, methods and systems; marketing, advertising, and promotion already implemented; start-up expenses and established financial relationships; sources of supplies already established and inventories."

The court recognized that the valuation process required the valuation of a total business enterprise, and that such enterprise included goodwill, business management skills, reputation, a trained workforce, CON, location and FF & E. Such elements were both tangible and intangible. The court ultimately found that the subject property's intangibles, not its real estate, were its major components of value. The court further observed that the real estate was worth little without the intangibles. Given the importance that intangibles added to the subject's valuation, the court deemed it appropriate to allocate 20 percent of the subject's $6,000,000 going concern value to intangibles and the remaining 80 percent to the real estate.

Michigan

One-time entry fee charged by senior retirement facility was business value and was properly excluded from the determination of the facility's true cash value
Freedom Village of Holland v. City of Holland, 2003 WL 21465330 (Mich. Ct. App. 2003)

Taxpayer owned a seven-story senior citizen apartment complex, which contained 347 rentable units, seven guest rooms, and common use areas including a theater, dining facilities, full-service bank, barber shop, laundry rooms, gift shop, medical clinic, delicatessen, convenience store, library, gymnasium, indoor pool and spa, auditorium, post office, billiards room, woodworking shop, and meditation chapel. The property generated revenue from four primary sources: entry fees, resident services fees, resident services and interest income. The entry fee was a lump sum, which was generally refunded to each resident's estate upon the resident's death. In exchange for such entry fees, the residents received health care and related services, insurance-type benefits, and occupancy at the subject property. The monthly service fees charged to residents covered operations and maintenance at the property and were based upon the size of the apartment unit, the location of the unit and the number of occupants residing therein.

The court stated that in determining the true cash value of the property, the income derived from the entry fees paid by the residents was business value that was properly excluded from the taxable property, but it stated that the monthly service fees were appropriately included as a relevant factor in determining the true cash value of the property.

New York

Not-for-profit home for adults had no inherent business value
Miriam Osborn Memorial Home Ass'n v. Assessor of City of Rye, 841 N.Y.S.2d 821 (N.Y. Sup. Ct. 2007)

Taxpayer owned a not-for-profit home for adults. The property had 381 dwelling units, and although taxpayer did not receive rent for the residential areas of the property, it did receive monthly resident fees for meals, personal care and various other goods and services.

In appraising the property, taxpayer's appraiser valued it as a not-for-profit home for adults and employed the income approach, calculating the property's potential gross income using comparable rental properties. After calculating the net operating income, effective tax rate and capitalization rate to obtain the market value of the subject property, taxpayer's appraiser did not make a deduction for business value, asserting that there was no inherent business value in the property. Assessor's appraiser incorrectly evaluated the property as a private for-profit facility and did not use the income directly attributable to the property—such as rental income or imputed rental income—in computing the property's income under the income approach. Instead, assessor's appraiser took the actual revenues from the resident fees, added the subject's business revenue, calculated business expenses for the enterprise, and capitalized this sum.

The court found that taxpayer's calculation of value under the income capitalization approach was more persuasive, noting that assessor improperly used revenues from resident fees paid to the subject in his calculations. Use of such revenues was inappropriate, as the fees at issue included payments for all of the services provided to residents by the subject, many of which were unrelated to the property. The court noted that statute required the property to be valued under its current use as a not-for-profit home for adults rather than as a private, for-profit facility. Further, the court determined that the property had no inherent business value in the years at issue, and as such, assessor's deduction of a portion of the property's gross income stream as income attributable to business enterprise was inappropriate.

V. Recreation/Entertainment

Connecticut

In golf course valuation, income derived from personal property and intangible property should be deducted from the total value of the course as a going concern
Whispering Pines Golf Club LLC v. Township of Hamburg, 2003 WL 22138010 (Ct. App. Mich. 2003)

Taxpayer owned property that consisted of an 18-hole golf course, a clubhouse, restaurant and banquet facilities, exercise area, and meeting rooms.

The tax tribunal concluded that the income approach was the most appropriate method by which to value the property, although it relied on the market or cost approaches for "correlation purposes." The tax tribunal concluded that the income earned from golf cart rentals was properly calculated under the income approach and that personal property should be deducted from the capitalized income.

Taxpayer argued that the tax tribunal erred by including golf cart rentals in its calculation of total revenues. Although taxpayer included the income generated by the personal property in the restaurant and banquet facilities, it argued that because golf carts were personal property, not real property, it was improper to include the income they produced for real property tax assessment purposes. The income produced by the golf carts, they asserted, should be isolated and deducted.

The court noted that according to the appraisal textbook *Golf Courses and Country Clubs: A Guide to Appraisal, Market Analysis, Development, and Financing,*[4] it was important to segregate the elements of real property, personal property and intangible property when valuing a golf course. However, the only component that was not subject to assessment or taxation was the business enterprise component. Such component was comprised of intangible property "such as marketing and management skill, an assembled work force, working capital, trade names," and similar items.[5] The court ultimately determined that although the tax tribunal properly included the income from the golf cart rentals in its calculations of the golf course's total value as a going concern, the tribunal erred in failing to make a deduction to account for the value of the golf carts.

New Jersey

Casino hotel was a "limited market" property, not "special purpose;" management fee considered business income and excluded in computation of realty income subject to capitalization
City of Atlantic City v. Ace Gaming LLC, 23 N.J. Tax 70 (N.J. Tax Ct. 2006)

Taxpayer owned the Sands Hotel and Casino in Atlantic City, New Jersey. The court noted that casino hotels were "limited-market" property, as there were relatively few potential buyers at any particular time, but that casinos were not special

---

4. See Arthur E. Gimmy, MAI, and Martin E. Benson, MAI, *Golf Courses and Country Clubs: A Guide to Appraisal, Market Analysis, Development, and Financing* (Chicago: Appraisal Institute, 1992), p. 113.

5. *The Appraisal of Real Estate* (Chicago: Appraisal Institute, 11th ed. 1996), p. 453.

purpose, use or design properties. The city asserted that the challenge of valuing a casino hotel lay in the extraction of the business enterprise value from the going concern value produced by capitalization of the casino hotel's income, and it cited prior case law regarding the extraction of business value from conventional hotels.

The casino was ultimately valued under the income approach alone, and the court was persuaded by the city's argument in favor of using the Rushmore Approach[6] to valuing the property. Under such approach, all payments made by a property owner to the entity that manages and operates the business on the property are considered business income and are thus excluded in the computation of realty income subject to capitalization. Adjustments are also made for the income realized by the employment of furniture, fixtures and equipment. The court noted that this approach had never before been applied to a casino hotel, as opposed to a conventional hotel.

South Carolina

Intangible value of a golf course was required to be deducted under the income capitalization approach

The Ocean Course Golf Club, Ltd., Osprey Point Golf Company, Turtle Point Golf Company, and Marsh Point Golf Company v. Charleston County Assessor (Consolidated), Administrative Law Court of South Carolina (2005)

Taxpayer protested the assessed value of four golf courses located on an island resort. The property was under common management with two tennis centers and a hotel located on the island. Management also operated a villa rental program that marketed and rented approximately 600 condominiums and houses to island visitors. The court emphasized that the marketing and sale of vacation golf packages that combined lodging and golf was a core business component of the resort on which the subject property was situated.

The court noted that the operation of a golf course was a business with many potential revenue streams and that the decisions of management were instrumental in the creation and maintenance of such revenue. The court further noted that the purchase and sale of a golf course business usually involved all of the assets incident to such various income operations. These

assets sometimes included improvements, intangible personal property (such as a well-recognized name, the right to use well-known course designers' names, goodwill, registered trademarks, logos, employment and management contracts, service agreements, and an existing trained work force capable of competently operating the business), and tangible personal property. These assets were often termed "total assets of business" (TAB).

The court determined that the income capitalization approach was the best method under which to value the property. The court noted that the golf course businesses from which income and expenses were derived under the income approach were comprised of tangible and intangible personal property that added positive value to the golf course operations. Such tangible and intangible personal property should not be included in the value of real estate for ad valorem tax purposes. The court stated that tangible and intangible personal property, in addition to business value, were required to be deducted after capitalization of the net income. Ultimately, the court remanded the case to the county assessor but specifically stated that the assessor's valuation should exclude tangible and intangible personal property, including business value, from the value of the real estate.

Assessor's deduction of management fee was insufficient to separate real property from business value in golf course valuation

Sea Pines Plantation Co., Inc. v. Beaufort County Assessor, Docket No. 01-ALJ-17-0018-CC, South Carolina Administrative Law Judge Division (2002)

Taxpayer owned three golf courses. The property could not be developed for other purposes because deed restrictions required the land to be used as golf courses or open space.

The court noted that when using the income capitalization approach to value the subject property, only the income of the real estate was to be considered when determining the property's net operating income and the value of personal property should be separated from the real estate. The personal property in this case included golf carts, food and beverages, restaurant equipment, and items sold in a pro shop. Revenues generated by the pro shop sales and the food and beverage operations were generated from personal property.

---

6. The Rushmore Approach is a valuation methodology developed by Stephen Rushmore; it has been both accepted and rejected by courts across the United States and Canada.

The assessor's expert performed an appraisal utilizing the income capitalization approach. The court noted that assessor's expert failed to separate the value of the real estate from the value of the subject property's going concern and included in his calculations all of the revenues derived from the pro shop operation, the food and beverage operation, the restaurant, and the golf cart rental operation. In other words, he included all of the revenues derived from the subject's personal property. Assessor's expert used a management fee in an attempt to back out, or separate, the personal property and business value from the value of the real property.

In his income approach, taxpayer's appraiser first calculated the income attributable to the real property of the golf courses by subtracting from the total revenues all revenues derived from the golf cart operations, the food and beverage operations, the pro shop, and the restaurant. He essentially left only revenues derived from memberships and greens fees. He then added in an imputed rent for the pro shop, food and beverage, restaurant, and golf cart rental operations. The expenses directly attributable to the real estate were calculated, and the expenses related to the golf cart, food and beverage, restaurant, and cart rental operations were specifically excluded. The unallocated corporate administrative expenses were calculated and subtracted from the restated revenue. The court determined that the imputed rent approach utilized by taxpayer's expert was a proper method of valuation but that the value obtained thereby was too low, largely due to taxpayer's improper allocation of corporate expenses to lower the course's net operating income. Taxpayer's expert re-computed such allocation and the court ultimately accepted the values derived under taxpayer's revised calculation.

VI. Communications/Telecom

Kentucky

Cable television company's franchises were considered "operating property;" non-operating intangible property included stocks, bonds, and copyrights that were not used in taxpayer's provision of cable television services
Revenue Cabinet, Commonwealth of Kentucky v. Comcast Cablevision of the South, 147 S.W.3d 743 (Ky. Ct. App. 2007)

Taxpayer owned a cable television company. Taxpayer was required to obtain a franchise agreement from the local government in each area in which it operated. The terms of such franchises were not exclusive, were for a limited number of years, and were not renewed automatically. At the lower court level, taxpayer asserted that the revenue cabinet was required to identify and separate non-operating intangible assets in valuing the property and further asserted that certain intangible value, including future values associated with future investments and property acquisitions, was non-operating intangible property that had been improperly classified as tangible operating property. The lower court ruled in favor of taxpayer, and the revenue cabinet contended on appeal that its classification of taxpayer's non-operating intangible value was erroneous.

The revenue cabinet argued that the non-operating intangible property identified by taxpayer's appraisal was actually taxable operating property because it comprised the franchise. The court determined that for purposes of taxation under the relevant state statutory scheme, "franchise" was the earning value ascribed to the capital of a domestic public service corporation by reason of its operation as a domestic public service corporation. As such, taxpayer's franchise was operating property. The court noted that the business enterprise value determined by taxpayer's appraiser was equal to taxpayer's total operating property, which was comprised of the tangible operating property and the franchise. The court determined that taxpayer's non-operating intangible property was the intangible property, such as certificates of stock, bonds or copyrights, that taxpayer did not use in the provision of its cable television services.

Utah

Valuation of telecommunications company as a single unit did not constitute the impermissible taxation of intangible property
Beaver County v. WilTel, Inc., 995 P.2d 602 (Utah 2000)

Telecommunications company sought review of a state tax commission decision and asserted, among other things, that the commission's assessment included nontaxable intangibles. The court rejected taxpayer's assertion that taxation of the subject property's unitary value constituted taxation of intangible property. The court recognized that even excluding intangibles, the network structure of taxpayer's physical transmission facilities made them worth far more on the open market than mere wires, trenches and transformer stations were worth individually. The court further noted that the physical and functional integration that allowed taxpayer's wires, cables and transmission facilities to operate as a unit was analogous to real property location as a time-distance relationship, or linkage, and that such location factor was part of the value of the property itself, as it could never exist nor be valued separately.

Although assessor agreed with this concept of enhanced value, it contended that taxpayer's proposed values for an assembled work force, customer relations, goodwill and other intangibles should be added thereto. The court rejected such contention and likewise rejected taxpayer's argument that the subject property should have been assessed solely on the basis of cost rather than under the income approach as a single unit. The court ultimately held that a combination of the yield capitalization value with a cost assessment value sufficiently captured the unitary value of the property while appropriately excluding intangibles.

Wyoming

Intangible assets that were not considered "necessary" or "integral" to cellular telephone companies were included in companies' property value because no credible evidence was offered during the valuation process regarding the deductible value of such intangible assets
Airtouch Communications, Inc. v. Department of Revenue, State of Wyoming, 76 P.3d 342 (Wyoming 2003)

Taxpayers, owners of cellular telephone companies contended that the values applied to their properties were improper because the value of intangible property was not deducted.

Taxpayers' property was assessed by department of revenue under the unitary method. This method determined the value of the property as a whole, without reference to individual parts, and is generally used in the valuation of properties which derive their value from interdependent assets working together. The value of taxpayers' property was thus determined as a unit under both the income capitalization approach and the cost approach.

Taxpayers' central contention was that the difference between the subject property's net

book value–or cost value indicator–and the value derived under the income approach reflected the value of taxpayers' intangible assets, and that such intangible value should have been deducted. The intangible assets at issue included taxpayers' federal communication commission (FCC) licenses and their customer bases. The department contended that the FCC licenses and customer bases at issue were "necessary" or "integral" to the operation of taxpayers' business and as such, were not exempt.

The court rejected the department's assertion that taxpayers' FCC licenses and customer bases were taxable because they were "necessary" or "integral" to taxpayers' business. However, the court upheld the department's valuation of taxpayers' property, noting that taxpayers could not criticize the failure to properly deduct the intangible value of their licenses and customer bases, as they failed to provide any information that would have allowed the department to determine such intangible value. The court emphasized that in accepting the department's valuation, it did not intend to infer that governmental licenses and customer lists were never to be considered exempt intangibles.

VII. Shopping Centers
Massachusetts

Business enterprise value of a super-regional mall relied upon six specific factors that supported intangible value
Northshore Mall Limited Partnership, et al. v. Board of Assessors of the City of Peabody, Appellate Tax Board of Massachusetts (2004)

Taxpayers owned a large "super-regional" shopping center and appealed its assessed value. A "super-regional" shopping center offers extensive variety in general merchandise, apparel, furniture and home furnishings, as well as a variety of services and recreational facilities. Taxpayers' expert estimated the value of the property using the cost approach, the sales comparison approach and the income capitalization approach. The cost approach was ultimately disregarded, and the sales comparison approach was not relied upon because the comparable sales analyzed invariably involved sales of leased fee, as opposed to fee simple, rights in the mall property.

Taxpayers' appraiser relied upon six different factors that allegedly supported a business or intangible value in shopping malls. Those factors were operating agreements, mall image, reputation and customer base, established trade name and reputation of anchor stores, "agglomeration economics" created by the assemblage of the anchor tenants and brand-name line tenants, trademarks, and advertising and promotional activities unique to the mall. Taxpayers' appraiser contended that such factors created an overall going concern of substantial complexity that included both real estate and business enterprise value. He isolated the business enterprise value by tagging percentage rent receipts and specialty leasing revenues as income generated from the mall business. He then capitalized that revenue by 15 percent to estimate business enterprise value. Taxpayers' appraiser also proposed an alternative methodology in which the 15 percent capitalization rate was applied to a management fee of five percent of total revenue.

The court ultimately found taxpayers' expert's income capitalization methodology to be unreliable, but it never specifically made any determination regarding the appropriateness of his business enterprise value deduction. The court determined that the property was not overvalued for the seven tax years in question.

North Carolina

Tax commission rejected the valuation methodology employed by owner of a "super regional" shopping mall, which segregated the $50 million intangible value from the value of the real property
In re Winston-Salem Joint Venture, 551 S.E.2d 450 (N.C. Ct. App. 2001)

Taxpayer owned a "super regional" shopping mall with an appraised value of $140,000,000. The commission had reduced the property's value from the original assessed value of $162,725,000, but it rejected taxpayer's assertion that the value of the real property was $80,000,000. The court affirmed the commission's decision, rejecting taxpayer's contention that the commission erred in failing to apply or properly consider the cost approach method in appraising the subject property and in adopting commission's assessment of the property's value.

The court's discussion centered on taxpayer's insistence that the cost approach was not properly applied in the valuation process. The commission had accepted the property value

determined by commission's expert witness, who had primarily used the income approach.

Taxpayer's expert had asserted that the value of the property was composed of three parts: the real estate, the mall's internal profit centers and the intangible personal property associated with the mall's business. Taxpayer's expert opined that in order to determine the fair market value of the property, an appraiser was required to identify and segregate the property's non-realty elements. Taxpayer's expert utilized a direct capitalization analysis and a discounted cash flow analysis and established that the value of the property as a going concern was $130,000,000 with a non-realty value of $50,000,000. He concluded that the value of the real property was $80,000,000. Although commission's expert considered the business value analysis when determining the value of the property, he rejected such concept because, based on his experience, regional mall investors did not recognize the concept of business value when investing in the particular market at issue. The court affirmed the commission's finding that the true value of the property was $140,000,000, the value that commission's expert determined using the income approach.

Ohio

External obsolescence deduction based on sales per square foot was improperly considered in valuation of a department store
Higbee Company v. Cuyahoga County Board of Revision, 839 N.E.2d 385 (Ohio 2006)

Taxing entities and taxpayer disputed the appraised value of a department store. The property was one of four anchor stores attached to a shopping mall and had been constructed in the preceding year. Assessor contended that the board of tax appeals erred by accepting a valuation based on the current business use of the property rather than a valuation based on value-in-exchange. The taxing entities asserted that by accepting the deduction for external obsolescence calculated by property owner's appraiser, the board of tax appeals accepted a valuation based on value-in-use rather than value-in-exchange. Further, the entities asserted that the board erred in accepting a business valuation based on sales per square foot, as opposed to a real estate valuation opinion.

The two methods used by property owner's appraisers to calculate the applicable external obsolescence deduction were the capitalization of income loss method and a sales shortfall method. Under the capitalization of income loss method, property owner's appraiser calculated his rental deficiency by first calculating the rental amount he estimated that an investor would require as a return on his property, then subtracting from that estimate the rental amount he thought the property would generate. To calculate the rental amount that he thought the property would generate, the appraiser used the rental amount determined under his income approach to value, which was based on sales per square foot. Under the sales shortfall method, property owner's appraiser calculated the shortfall in sales between the sales predicted by the department store versus the store's actual sales, and between department store's average sales, as determined under the income approach, and its actual sales. The court rejected both methods of calculating external obsolescence deductions.

In rejecting the methods used by property owner's appraisers to determine external obsolescence, the court noted that both methods depended on the success, or lack of success, of the department store business as measured by sales per square foot. The court further opined that if it is real property that is being valued, its valuation cannot be made to vary depending on the success or lack thereof of the business located on that property and further, that although the location of a property may influence the sales made by a merchant operating a business at such location, the merchant's business practices may also have a large influence on sales. The court finally stated that the business factors and the real-property factors must be separated during the valuation of the property for tax purposes.

VIII. Landfills/Waste Collection

Pennsylvania

Testimony relating to a landfill property's "value-in-use" was prohibited in determining the actual value of such property
F&L Realty v. Lackawanna County Bd. of Assessment & Revision of Taxes, 2005 WL 4875759 (C.P. Lackawanna, November 16, 2005) (Pennsylvania)

Taxpayers owned a sanitary landfill. The landfill property included an office, scale house, truck wash facility, tire shredder, maintenance

headquarters, a guardhouse, a quarry scale house and radiation monitoring facilities. Upon other parcels of the property were a gas transfer station, portions of a storm water management system, a leachate treatment facility and a powerhouse. The parties' central dispute was based upon their disagreement regarding the factors that could legally be considered by a valuation expert witness in determining the "actual value" of the subject property.

The court noted that consideration of fixtures, machinery and equipment go inherently to the present use by the present owner of property. The consideration of the value of such property in determining the value of real property could thus constitute an impermissible consideration of value-in-use.

The court's opinion further discussed the potential implications of using the income approach in valuing certain properties, including the difficulties that sometimes arose in separating the income stream solely attributable to taxable realty from the income stream that flowed from a business operated on such realty. Finally, the court discussed the precedent related to the treatment of certain fixtures, machinery and equipment, noting that even if such property is affixed to realty, they were not necessarily always included as taxable real estate. The court ultimately found in favor of taxpayers, holding that the appraisal reports relevant to the subject parcels of property should be prepared without consideration of any expert testimony related to value-in-use under the income, cost or comparable sales approaches to value. The court additionally extended such prohibition of value-in-use to "special purpose" properties.

Virginia

Assessment of landfill property under income approach did not constitute the assessment of the landfill permit itself, an intangible asset
Shoosmith Bros., Inc. v. County of Chesterfield, 601 S.E.2d 641 (Va. 2004)

Taxpayer owned a property containing a sanitary landfill. Taxpayer contended that the assessor committed error by using the income method in assessing the landfill property because the assessor factored in income generated by taxpayer's use of the land as a landfill, for which a permit was required, and such permit was a non-transferable use permit that did not run with the land. Taxpayer alleged that the landfill permit was an intangible asset and that the income approach was thus improper, as intangibles were not subject to taxation, and taxpayer essentially asserted that the consideration of the use of the property constituted assessment of the permit itself. The court rejected taxpayer's contentions and held that consideration of a property's highest and best use was required when performing an assessment, irrespective of whether such use was conducted pursuant to a transferable or non-transferable permit.

The court additionally rejected taxpayer's other arguments and held that because consideration of the use of taxpayer's land was required in assessing the fair market value of the property, the assessor did not commit error in assessing the landfill property as a landfill using the income method of assessment. The court further reiterated that assessment of the land in such a manner did not constitute assessment of an intangible asset. As such, the court found that the trial court did not err in rejecting the testimony offered by taxpayer's expert regarding the fair market value of the subject property.

IX. Other/Miscellaneous

Idaho

Value of business goodwill was appropriately excluded from valuation of senior citizen mobile home park
The Senator, Inc. v. Ada County, Bd. of Equalization, 67 P. 3d 45 (Idaho 2003)

Taxpayer owned the subject property, a mobile home/manufactured home park in which residents were required to be age 55 or over. Taxpayer contended that the county assessor improperly included business goodwill in valuing the real property.

Business goodwill is considered to be intangible personal property that is exempt from taxation. One of taxpayer's appraisal witnesses testified that the difference between the value of the property obtained under the cost approach and the value obtained using a gross rent multiplier was business goodwill. Taxpayer's other appraisal witness testified that the difference between the value of the business obtained under the income approach and the value of the tangible assets determined under the cost approach was goodwill. The court did not find such testimony reliable. The county's appraisal witnesses used all three approaches—the cost

approach, the sales comparison approach and the income approach—in valuing the subject property but gave greatest weight to the income approach. The county contended that goodwill was not included in their valuation under any of the three approaches. The court ultimately determined that taxpayer failed to prove that the assessments of the subject property included business goodwill.

Iowa

Consideration of franchise-to-franchise sales under the sales comparison approach did not constitute impermissible consideration of intangible business value
Soifer v. Floyd County Bd. Of Review, 734 N.W.2d 775 (Iowa 2009)

Taxpayer owned a franchise for a McDonald's restaurant. Taxpayer leased the subject property from the company and under the terms of their agreement, was responsible for payment of property taxes. Taxpayer protested and appealed the assessment of the property, and the court of appeals ultimately determined that the board had excessively appraised the subject property and discounted the testimony of the board's expert. The board appealed to the state supreme court.

Expert witnesses for both parties placed greatest weight on the sales comparison approach in determining the value of the subject property. The board's experts claimed that the only comparable sales were of properties being used for franchise restaurants that were going to continue to be used for the same purpose after sale, as a franchise property had "architectural appeal…that the general public recognizes," and that there was value in such architecture that was captured only when the sale was a franchise-to-franchise sale. Taxpayer's experts contended that a "similar" property, for the purpose of a comparable sale, was a property that was used for restaurant purposes in general and was not limited to a continuing fast-food franchise. They further contended that sales of franchise property for other uses were probative of the subject's market value and constituted a competent basis for expert opinion.

Taxpayer asserted that the board's expert's reliance on only franchise-to-franchise sales inappropriately included some kind of intangible business value. The court noted that under Section 441.21(2) of the Iowa Code, an assessor was specifically prohibited from considering "special value or use value of the property to its owner, and the good will or value of a business which uses the property as distinguished from the value of the property as property." The court also noted, however, that property must be valued based on its present use, including any functioning commercial enterprise on the property.

Taxpayer additionally challenged the use of franchise-to-franchise sales in valuation of the property because purchasers of McDonald's properties were bound by a non-compete clause, which prohibited the purchaser from using the property as a fast-food franchise restaurant for 20 years after purchase. Taxpayer argued that under such a restriction, the actual market value of the subject was more accurately reflected by sales of franchise properties to non-franchise purchasers. The court rejected this argument, stating that the valuation of the subject property as if it were not a viable McDonalds would be contrary to the principle that assessed property must be valued based on its present use. The court additionally noted that the use restriction required by McDonald's should not negatively impact the property's value because it was self-imposed.

The court ultimately vacated the decision of the court of appeals and determined that although taxpayer's sales comparison approach methodology constituted a competent basis for expert opinion, the board's experts' utilization of franchise-to-franchise sales in their analysis was more credible evidence of the property's value.

Ohio

Above-market rent charged under long-term drugstore lease did not constitute a separate "business value" component of property's purchase price
Rhodes, Aud. v. Hamilton County Board of Revision, 885 N.E.2d 236 (Ohio 2008)

Taxpayer asserted that Walgreens drugstore's long-term lease on the property should have been considered in determining the appropriate appraised value of the subject property. The property had been purchased by taxpayer in an arm's-length transaction in the year preceding the relevant tax year and its purchase price was utilized by the county auditor in determining the taxable value of the property.

The court rejected taxpayer's contention that a recent, arm's-length sale between a willing buyer and a willing seller did not establish a property's true value if the subject property was encumbered by a long-term lease to the above-referenced Walgreens drugstore.

Taxpayer also contended that the sale price did not establish the real property's value because it reflected the value of the underlying realty in addition to the value of the lessee's drugstore business. Although the testimony of taxpayer's expert witness indicated that the rent charged under the drugstore lease exceeded "market rent," as the property's rent was $26 per square foot under the lease and market rent was only $10 per square foot, such testimony did not establish the existence of a separate "business value" component of the sale price. The court was not persuaded by taxpayer's argument regarding the implications of the above-market rent and pointed out that although the lessee's business might have affected the value of the fee simple interest, taxpayer did not purchase any interest in the drugstore's business.

Price paid for "goodwill" under purchase contract was not necessarily dispositive of business value for property tax purposes
St. Bernard Self-Storage, L.L.C. v. Hamilton County Bd. of Revision, 875 N.E.2d 85 (Ohio 2007)

In the valuation of its self-storage facility, taxpayer asserted that the allocation in the purchase contract of approximately half the purchase price to the goodwill of the associated business should be subtracted to yield the value of the real estate, as it reflected a business value that must be separated from the realty. The storage facility had been purchased by taxpayer in an arm's-length transaction, and the purchase agreement reflected that taxpayer had paid $1,000,000 for the real estate and personal property (other than goodwill) and had paid $950,000 for goodwill. The price paid for goodwill had been negotiated and reflected what taxpayer understood to be the business's "good relationship with the community."

The court held that in the context of valuing property for tax purposes, such an allocation is not to be taken as indicative of the value of the real property at issue unless other indicia on the face of the contract, the circumstances attending the allocation, or some other independent evidence established the propriety of the allocation.

Because the business of taxpayer was to lease space, and because the definition of "real property" for tax purposes encompassed the "rights and privileges...appertaining to the land and improvements," the court determined that the rental revenue related to such rights and privileges and thus constituted part of the value of real property as opposed to a separate business value. Additionally, the court determined that the board was correct in finding no evidence in the record to support the existence of a business value that could actually be severed from the real estate and be transferred or retained separately. As such, taxpayer failed to prove the existence of any business value severable from the real property and the allocation of goodwill was thus properly disregarded, as it did not pertain to any separable value.

Virginia

Income attributable to intangible assets was required to be deducted from the income derived from the total assets of the business in the valuation of a training and conference center

WXII/Oxford-DTC Real Estate, LLC v. Loudoun Cty. Bd. Of Sup'rs, No. 29368, 2004 WL 2848543 (Va. Cir. Ct. 2004)

Taxpayer owned a training and conference center. The property was built by the Xerox Corporation for the training of its employees and included offices, guest rooms, training facilities, meeting space, eating facilities, a reception area and warehouse space. The property was historically used exclusively for the corporation's private training and was never marketed to the public. In the year preceding the first tax year at issue action, the property was sold to taxpayer. Taxpayer intended to do extensive renovations and to market the property as a national conference center available to groups from all over the world.

The court found that the board erred in failing to deduct from the property's income the income attributable to intangibles and a replacement allowance and that the income approach used by the county assessor included an income calculation impermissibly derived from the business being conducted on the property–specifically, the income derived from the "Complete Meeting Package" sold to groups using the center for conferences.

The court discussed the appraisal methodologies used by both parties' experts and found that the methodology employed by taxpayer's appraiser was more reasonable than the methodology employed by assessor's expert. Taxpayer's expert determined that the best way to value the property was under the income approach. He recognized that the use of the property was being changed, and as a result, the value of intangibles, such as start-up expenses and the cost of assembling a work force, had to be determined before the value of the real estate could be ascertained. Assessor's expert did not consider a value for the intangibles. Taxpayer's expert contended that the value of the property was due to the conference center business operated thereon and that the real estate was just a part of the center as a going concern. As such, the value of the real estate was required to be segregated out of the value of the going concern.

Taxpayer's expert asserted that a business's total assets were comprised of intangible personal property, which included assembling a work force, business start-up costs and any favorable contracts; tangible personal property, which included furniture, fixtures, equipment and inventory; and real property. After determining the net income derived from the total assets of the business operating on the property, taxpayer's expert deducted income attributable to the tangible and intangible personal property to establish the net income attributable to the real estate. The net income attributable to the real estate was then divided by the appropriate capitalization rate to ascertain the real estate's value. The court was persuaded by taxpayer's expert and the court ultimately held that because of the uniqueness of the property, its value was derived from its use and not from the land and buildings located thereon.